Praise for *The Origins of Political Order*

"Ambitious and highly readable."
—*The New Yorker*

"Political theorist Francis Fukuyama's new book is a major accomplishment, likely to find its place among the works of seminal thinkers like Jean-Jacques Rousseau and John Locke, and modern moral philosophers and economists such as John Rawls and Amartya Sen . . . It is a perspective and a voice that can supply a thinker's tonic for our current political maladies."
—Earl Pike, *The Plain Dealer* (Cleveland)

"In many respects, Fukuyama is an ideal guide for this enormous undertaking. He combines a deep expertise in political institutions with an impressive familiarity of world history, philosophy and social theory. An engaging writer, his prose crackles with sharp observations and illuminating comparisons, and the book marshals a breathtaking array of stimulating facts and provocative generalizations. Who knew, for instance, that the tsetse fly retarded the spread of Islam into sub-Saharan Africa? Simply as a compendium of fascinating minutiae and social science theory, the book offers a treasure trove to the casual student of political history . . . More important, Fukuyama's book can help us appreciate why so many countries fail to combine the strong institutions, rule of law and accountability that are the hallmark of peaceful and prosperous nations."
—Eric Oliver, *San Francisco Chronicle*

"Genuinely a masterpiece."
—Jordan Michael Smith, *The Christian Science Monitor*

"Fukuyama's intellectual instincts hard-wire him into the most geopolitically strategic—not to mention dangerous—corners of the world . . . [He] is arguably the world's bestselling contemporary political scientist . . . His new book, *The Origins of Political Order*, seeks to understand how human beings transcended tribal affiliations and organized themselves into political societies . . . His books have taken on not only politics and philosophy, but also biotechnology and that tinderbox of an idea: human nature. 'He's incredibly intellectually honest,' says Walter Russell Mead, a historian of American foreign policy. 'He goes where his head takes him. His first duty is to the truth as he sees it.'" —Andrew Bast, *Newsweek*

"*The Origins of Political Order* . . . begins in prehuman times and concludes on the eve of the American and French Revolutions. Along the way, Fukuyama mines the fields of anthropology, archaeology, biology, evolutionary psychology, economics, and, of course, political science and international relations to establish a framework for understanding the evolution of political institutions. And that's just Volume One . . . At the center of the project is a fundamental question: Why do some states succeed while others collapse?" —Evan R. Goldstein, *The Chronicle of Higher Education*

"The evolving tension between private and public animates this magisterial history of the state . . . Fukuyama writes a crystalline prose that balances engaging erudition with incisive analysis. As germane to the turmoil in Afghanistan as it is to today's congressional battles, this is that rare work of history with up-to-the-minute relevance." —*Publishers Weekly* (starred review)

"[An] exceptional book." —David Keymer, *Library Journal*

"Human social behavior has an evolutionary basis. This was the thesis in Edward O. Wilson's book *Sociobiology* that caused such a stir . . . [In] *The Origins of Political Order*, Francis Fukuyama of Stanford University presents a sweeping new overview of human social structures throughout history, taking over from where Dr. Wilson's ambitious synthesis left off . . . Previous attempts to write grand analyses of human development have tended to focus on a single causal explanation, like economics or warfare, or, as with Jared Diamond's *Guns, Germs, and Steel*, on geography. Dr. Fukuyama's is unusual in that he considers several factors, including warfare, religion, and in particular human social behaviors like favoring kin . . . 'You have to be bowled over by the extraordinary breadth of approach,' said Arthur Melzer, a political scientist at Michigan State University who invited Dr. Fukuyama to give lectures on the book. 'It's definitely a magnum opus.'" —Nicholas Wade, *The New York Times*

"Sweeping, provocative big-picture study of humankind's political impulses . . . Endlessly interesting—reminiscent in turns of Oswald Spengler, Stanislaw Andreski and Samuel Huntington, though less pessimistic and much better written." —*Kirkus Reviews*

"Political theorist Fukuyama presents nothing less than a unified theory of state formation, a comparative study of how tribally organized societies in various parts of the world and various moments in history have transformed into societies with political systems and institutions and, in some cases, political accountability . . . This wide-ranging and frequently provocative work also carries the mantle of the great nineteenth-century sociologists." —Brendan Driscoll, *Booklist*

David Fukuyama

FRANCIS FUKUYAMA

THE ORIGINS OF POLITICAL ORDER

Francis Fukuyama is the Olivier Nomellini Senior Fellow at Stanford University's Freeman Spogli Institute for International Studies and Resident at the Center for Democracy, Development, and the Rule of Law. He has taught at the Paul H. Nitze School of Advanced International Studies of The Johns Hopkins University and at the George Mason University School of Public Policy. He was a researcher at the RAND Corporation and served as the deputy director in the State Department's policy planning staff. He is the author of *The End of History and the Last Man*, *Trust: The Social Virtues and the Creation of Prosperity*, and *America at the Crossroads: Democracy, Power, and the Neoconservative Legacy*. He lives with his wife in Palo Alto, California.

ALSO BY FRANCIS FUKUYAMA

America at the Crossroads: Democracy, Power, and the Neoconservative Legacy

State-Building: Governance and World Order in the Twenty-first Century

Our Posthuman Future: Consequences of the Biotechnology Revolution

The Great Disruption: Human Nature and the Reconstitution of Social Order

Trust: The Social Virtues and the Creation of Prosperity

The End of History and the Last Man

THE ORIGINS OF POLITICAL ORDER

THE
ORIGINS OF
POLITICAL ORDER

From
Prehuman Times
to the
French Revolution

·

FRANCIS FUKUYAMA

FARRAR, STRAUS AND GIROUX

NEW YORK

FARRAR, STRAUS AND GIROUX
18 West 18th Street, New York 10011

Copyright © 2011 by Francis Fukuyama
Maps copyright © 2011 by Mark Nugent
All rights reserved
Printed in the United States of America
Published in 2011 by Farrar, Straus and Giroux
First paperback edition, 2012

Grateful acknowledgment is made for permission to reprint the following material: Excerpts from *Islam from the Prophet Muhammad to the Capture of Constantinople. I: Politics and Government*, edited and translated by Bernard Lewis, copyright © 1987 by Bernard Lewis. Reprinted by permission of Oxford University Press. Excerpts from *Sources of Chinese Tradition*, 2d ed., edited by William Theodore de Bary and Irene Bloom, copyright © 1999 by Columbia University Press. Reprinted with permission of the publisher.

The Library of Congress has cataloged the hardcover edition as follows:
Fukuyama, Francis.
    The origins of political order : from prehuman times to the French
Revolution / Francis Fukuyama.— 1st ed.
        p.   cm.
Includes bibliographical references and index.
ISBN 978-0-374-22734-0 (alk. paper)
    1. State, The—History.   2. Order—History.   3. Comparative government—
History.   4. Democracy—History.   I. Title.

JC11 .F85 2011
320.9—dc22

                                                              2010038534

Paperback ISBN: 978-0-374-53322-9

Designed by Abby Kagan

www.fsgbooks.com

17 19 20 18 16

Cover art: (*spine, from top*) The Great Wall, photograph from the collection of Beth Middleworth • Saber (detail on spine, full saber on back cover), sixteenth century. Steel, shagreen, gold. Bequest of George C. Stone, 1936, The Metropolitan Museum of Art, New York, NY. Image copyright © The Metropolitan Museum of Art / Art Resource, NY • India circa 1840, photograph from the collection of Beth Middleworth • Charles I, king of England, courtesy of the New York Public Library • Male figure (detail on spine, full figure on back cover): Inyai-Ewa people, Korewori River, Middle Sepik region, Papua New Guinea, sixteenth to nineteenth century. Wood. The Michael C. Rockefeller Memorial Collection, Purchase, Nelson A. Rockefeller Gift, 1965. The Metropolitan Museum of Art, New York, NY. Image copyright © The Metropolitan Museum of Art / Art Resource, NY.

IN MEMORY OF

Samuel Huntington

CONTENTS

PREFACE

This book has two origins. The first arose when my mentor, Samuel Huntington of Harvard University, asked me to write a foreword to a reprint edition of his 1968 classic, *Political Order in Changing Societies*.[1] Huntington's work represented one of the last efforts to write a broad study of political development and was one I assigned frequently in my own teaching. It established many key ideas in comparative politics, including a theory of political decay, the concept of authoritarian modernization, and the notion that political development was a phenomenon separate from other aspects of modernization.

As I proceeded with the foreword, it seemed to me that, illuminating as *Political Order* was, the book needed some serious updating. It was written only a decade or so after the start of the big wave of decolonization that swept the post–World War II world, and many of its conclusions reflected the extreme instability of that period with all of its coups and civil wars. In the years since its publication, many momentous changes have occurred, like the economic rise of East Asia, the collapse of global communism, the acceleration of globalization, and what Huntington himself labeled the "third wave" of democratization that started in the 1970s. Political order had yet to be achieved in many places, but it had emerged successfully in many parts of the developing world. It seemed appropriate to go back to the themes of that book and to try to apply them to the world as it existed now.

In contemplating how Huntington's ideas might be revised, it further struck me that there was still more fundamental work to be done in explicating the origins of political development and political decay. *Political Order in Changing Societies* took for granted the political world of a fairly late stage in human history, where such institutions as the state, political parties, law, military organizations, and the like all exist. It confronted the problem of developing countries trying to modernize their political systems but didn't give an account of where those systems came from in the first place in societies where they were long established. Countries are not trapped by their pasts. But in many cases, things that happened hundreds or even thousands of years ago continue to exert major influence on the nature of politics. If we are seeking to understand the functioning of contemporary institutions, it is necessary to look at their origins and the often accidental and contingent forces that brought them into being.

The concern over the origin of institutions dovetailed with a second preoccupation, which was the real-world problems of weak and failed states. For much of the period since September 11, 2001, I have been working on the problems of state and nation building in countries with collapsed or unstable governments; an early effort to think through this problem was a book I published in 2004 titled *State-Building: Governance and World Order in the Twenty-first Century.*[2] The United States, as well as the international donor community more broadly, has invested a great deal in nation-building projects around the world, including Afghanistan, Iraq, Somalia, Haiti, Timor-Leste, Sierra Leone, and Liberia. I myself consulted with the World Bank and the Australian aid agency AusAid in looking at the problems of state building in Melanesia, including Timor-Leste, Papua New Guinea, Indonesian Papua, and the Solomon Islands, all of which have encountered serious difficulties in trying to construct modern states.

Consider, for example, the problem of implanting modern institutions in Melanesian societies like Papua New Guinea and the Solomon Islands. Melanesian society is organized tribally, into what anthropologists call segmentary lineages, groups of people who trace their descent to a common ancestor. Numbering anywhere from a few dozen to a few thousand kinsmen, these tribes are locally known as *wantoks*, a pidgin corruption of the English words "one talk," or people who speak the same language. The social fragmentation that exists in Melanesia is extraordinary. Papua New Guinea hosts more than nine hundred mutually incomprehensible languages, nearly

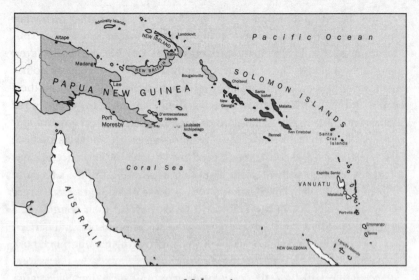

Melanesia

one-sixth of all of the world's extant tongues. The Solomon Islands, with a population of only five hundred thousand, nonetheless has over seventy distinct languages. Most residents of the PNG highlands have never left the small mountain valleys in which they were born; their lives are lived within the wantok and in competition with neighboring wantoks.

The wantoks are led by a Big Man. No one is born a Big Man, nor can a Big Man hand that title down to his son. Rather, the position has to be earned in each generation. It falls not necessarily to those who are physically dominant but to those who have earned the community's trust, usually on the basis of ability to distribute pigs, shell money, and other resources to members of the tribe. In traditional Melanesian society, the Big Man must constantly be looking over his shoulder, because a competitor for authority may be coming up behind him. Without resources to distribute, he loses his status as leader.[3]

When Australia granted independence to Papua New Guinea and Britain to the Solomons in the 1970s, they established modern "Westminster"-style governments, in which citizens vote for members of parliament in regular multiparty elections. In Australia and Britain, political choices revolve around a left-of-center Labour Party and a conservative party (the Liberal Party in Australia, the Tories in Britain). Voters by and large make decisions based on ideology and policy (for example, whether they want more government protections or more market-oriented policies).

When this political system was transplanted to Melanesia, however, the result was chaos. The reason was that most voters in Melanesia do not vote for political programs; rather, they support their Big Man and their wantok. If the Big Man (and an occasional Big Woman) can get elected to parliament, the new MP will use his or her influence to direct government resources back to the wantok, to help supporters with things like school fees, burial costs, and construction projects. Despite the existence of a national government with all of the trappings of sovereignty, like a flag and an army, few residents of Melanesia have a sense of belonging to a larger nation, or being part of a social world much beyond their wantok. The parliaments of PNG and the Solomons have no coherent political parties; they are full of individual leaders, each striving to bring back as much pork as possible to his or her narrow base of supporters.[4]

Melanesia's tribal social system limits economic development because it prevents the emergence of modern property rights. In both Papua New Guinea and the Solomon Islands, upward of 95 percent of all land is held in what is known as customary land tenure. Under customary rules, property is private but held informally (that is, with no legal documentation) by groups of kinfolk, who have both individual and collective rights to different strips of land. Property has not only an economic but also a spiritual significance, since dead relatives are buried in certain spots on the wantok's land, and their spirits continue to inhabit that place. No one in the wantok, including the Big Man, has the exclusive right to alienate title to the land to an outsider.[5] A mining or palm oil company seeking a concession has to negotiate with hundreds or sometimes thousands of landowners, and there is no statute of limitations on land claims under traditional rules.[6]

From the standpoint of many foreigners, the behavior of Melanesian politicians looks like political corruption. But from the standpoint of the islands' traditional tribal social system, the Big Men are simply doing what Big Men have always done, which is to redistribute resources to their kinsmen. Except that now they have access not just to pigs and shell money but also to revenues from mining and logging concessions.

It takes only a couple of hours to fly from Port Moresby, Papua New Guinea's capital, to Cairns or Brisbane in Australia, but in that flight one is in some sense traversing several thousand years of political development. In thinking about Melanesia's political development challenges, I began to wonder how any society had ever made the transition from a tribal- to a state-level society, how modern property rights had evolved out of customary ones, and how formal legal systems, dependent on a kind of third-party enforcement that does not exist in traditional Melanesia, first made their appearance. On further reflection, however, it seemed to me that it was perhaps a conceit to think that modern societies had progressed so far beyond Melanesia, since Big Men—that is, politicians who distribute resources to their relatives and supporters—are ubiquitous in the contemporary world, including the U.S. Congress. If political development implied movement beyond patrimonial relationships and personalistic politics, one also had to explain why these practices survived in many places and why seemingly modern systems often reverted to them.

The answers to many of these questions were not to be found in *Political Order in Changing Societies*; in revisiting Huntington's topic, this prehistory would require considerable clarification.

Hence the current book, which looks at the historical origins of political institutions as well as the process of political decay. This is the first of two volumes, and it deals with political development from prehuman times up to roughly the eve of the French and American revolutions. The present volume is about the past—indeed, it starts not with recorded human history but with mankind's primate ancestors. The first four parts deal with human prehistory, the origins of the state, the rule of law, and finally accountable government. The second volume will bring the story up to the present, paying special attention to the impact that Western institutions had on institutions in non-Western societies as they sought to modernize. It will then describe how political development occurs in the contemporary world.

It is extremely important to read this volume in anticipation of what is to come in the second. As I make clear in the final chapter of this book, political development in the modern world occurs under substantially different conditions from those in the period up until the late eighteenth century. Once the Industrial Revolution occurred and human societies exited the Malthusian conditions they had experienced up to then, a new dynamic was added to the process of social change that would have huge political consequences. Readers of this volume might get the impression that some of the long historical continuities described here mean that societies are trapped by their histories, but in fact we live today under very different and more dynamic conditions.

This book covers a large number of societies and historical periods; I also use material from disciplines outside my own, including anthropology, economics, and biology. Obviously in a work of this scope, I have had to rely almost exclusively on secondary sources for the research. I have tried to pass this material through as many expert filters as possible, but it is nonetheless likely that I have made both factual and interpretational mistakes along the way. While many of the individual chapters will not pass muster with people whose job it is to study particular societies and historical periods in depth, it does seem to me that there is a virtue in looking across time and space in a comparative fashion. Some of the broader patterns of political development are simply not visible to those who focus too narrowly on specific subjects.

PART ONE

Before the State

1

THE NECESSITY OF POLITICS

The third wave of democratization and contemporary anxieties about the future of liberal democracy; how both the Left and the Right entertain fantasies about the abolition of government; how contemporary developing countries represent the fulfillment of these fantasies; how we take institutions for granted but in fact have no idea where they come from

During the forty-year period from 1970 to 2010, there was an enormous upsurge in the number of democracies around the world. In 1973, only 45 of the world's 151 countries were counted as "free" by Freedom House, a nongovernmental organization that produces quantitative measures of civil and political rights for countries around the world.[1] That year, Spain, Portugal, and Greece were dictatorships; the Soviet Union and its Eastern European satellites looked like strong and cohesive societies; China was caught up in Mao Zedong's Cultural Revolution; Africa saw the consolidation of rule by a group of corrupt "presidents for life"; and most of Latin America had fallen under military dictatorship. The following generation saw momentous political change, with democracies and market-oriented economies spreading in virtually every part of the world except for the Arab Middle East. By the late 1990s, some 120 countries around the world—more than 60 percent of the world's independent states—had become electoral democracies.[2] This transformation was Samuel Huntington's third wave of democratization; liberal democracy as the default form of government became part of the accepted political landscape at the beginning of the twenty-first century.[3]

Underlying these changes in political systems was a massive social transformation as well. The shift to democracy was a result of millions of formerly passive individuals around the world organizing themselves and participating in the political life of their societies. This social mobilization was driven by a host of factors: greatly expanded access to education that made people more aware of themselves and the political world around them; information technology, which facilitated the rapid spread of ideas and knowledge; cheap travel and communications that allowed people to vote with their feet if they didn't like their government; and greater prosperity, which induced people to demand better protection of their rights.

The third wave crested after the late 1990s, however, and a "democratic recession" emerged in the first decade of the twenty-first century. Approximately one in five countries that had been part of the third wave either reverted to authoritarianism or saw a significant erosion of democratic institutions.[4] Freedom House noted that 2009 marked the fourth consecutive year in which freedom had declined around the world, the first time this had happened since it established its measures of freedom in 1973.[5]

POLITICAL ANXIETIES

At the beginning of the second decade of the twenty-first century, malaise in the democratic world took several distinct forms. The first was the outright reversal of democratic gains that had occurred in countries such as Russia, Venezuela, and Iran, where elected leaders were busy dismantling democratic institutions by manipulating elections, closing down or buying independent TV and newspaper outlets, and clamping down on opposition activities. Liberal democracy is more than majority voting in elections; it is a complex set of institutions that restrain and regularize the exercise of power through law and a system of checks and balances. In many countries, official acceptance of democratic legitimacy was accompanied by the systematic removal of checks on executive power and the erosion of the rule of law.

In other cases, countries that seemed to be making a transition from authoritarian government got stuck in what the analyst Thomas Carothers has labeled a "gray zone," where they were neither fully authoritarian nor meaningfully democratic.[6] Many successor states to the former Soviet Union, like Kazakhstan and Uzbekistan in Central Asia, found themselves in this situation. There had been a broad assumption in the years following the fall of the Berlin Wall in 1989 that virtually all countries were transitioning to democracy and that failures of democratic practice would be overcome with the simple passage of time. Carothers pointed out that this "transition paradigm" was an unwarranted assumption and that many authoritarian elites had no interest in implementing democratic institutions that would dilute their power.

A third category of concern has to do not with the failure of political systems to become or remain democratic but rather their failure to deliver the basic services that people demand from their governments. The mere fact that a country has democratic institutions tells us very little about whether it is well or badly governed. This failure to deliver on the promise of democracy poses what is perhaps the greatest challenge to the legitimacy of such political systems.

An example of this was Ukraine. Ukraine surprised the world in 2004 when tens of thousands of people turned up in Kiev's Maidan Square to protest manipulation of that country's presidential election. These protests, which came to be known as the Orange Revolution, triggered a new election and the rise of the reformer Viktor Yushchenko as president. Once in power, however, the Orange Coalition proved utterly feckless, and Yushchenko himself disappointed the hopes of those who supported him. The government quarreled internally, failed to deal with Ukraine's serious corruption problem, and presided over a meltdown of the economy during the 2008–2009 global financial crisis. The result was the election in early 2010 of Viktor Yanukovich, the very man accused of stealing the 2004 election that had triggered the Orange Revolution in the first place.

Many other species of governance failure plague democratic countries. It is well understood that Latin America has the highest level of economic inequality of any region in the world, in which class hierarchies often correspond to racial and ethnic ones. The rise of populist leaders like Hugo Chávez in Venezuela and Evo Morales in Bolivia is less a cause of instability than a symptom of that inequality and the feeling of social exclusion felt by many who are nominally citizens. Persistent poverty often breeds other kinds of social dysfunctions, like gangs, narcotrafficking, and a general feeling of insecurity on the part of ordinary people. In Colombia, Mexico, and El Salvador, organized criminality threatens the state itself and its basic institutions, and the failure to deal effectively with these problems has undermined the legitimacy of democracy.

India, to take another example, has been a remarkably successful democracy since its independence in 1947—an achievement all the more remarkable given its poverty, ethnic and religious diversity, and enormous size. (Why a longer historical view of Indian political development should lessen our surprise is the subject of chapters 10–12.) Nonetheless, Indian democracy, like sausage making, looks less appealing the closer one gets to the process. Nearly one-third of Indian legislators, for example, are under some form of criminal indictment, some for serious crimes like murder and rape. Indian politicians often practice an overt form of patronage politics, in which votes are traded for political favors. The fractiousness of Indian democracy makes it very hard for the government to make major decisions on issues like investments in major infrastructure projects. And in many Indian cities, glittering high-tech centers of excellence exist next to African-style poverty.

The apparent chaos and corruption of democratic politics in India has frequently been contrasted to the quick and efficient decision making of China. Chinese rulers are not constrained by either a rule of law or democratic accountability; if they want to build a huge dam, bulldoze neighborhoods to make way for highways or airports, or mount a rapid economic stimulus package, they can do so far more quickly than democratic India.

A fourth broad source of political anxiety concerns the economy. Modern global capitalism has proved to be productive and wealth-creating beyond the dreams of anyone living before the year 1800. In the period following the oil crises of the 1970s, the size of the world economy almost quadrupled,[7] and Asia, based on its openness to trade and investment, saw much of its population join the developed world. But global capitalism has not found a way to avoid high levels of volatility, particularly in the financial sector. Global economic growth has been plagued by periodic financial crises, striking Europe in the early 1990s, Asia in 1997–1998, Russia and Brazil in 1998–1999, and Argentina in 2001. This instability culminated, perhaps with poetic justice, in the great crisis that struck the United States, the home of global capitalism, in 2008–2009. Free markets are necessary to promote long-term growth, but they are not self-regulating, particularly when it comes to banks and other large financial institutions. The system's instability is a reflection of what is ultimately a political failure, that is, the failure to provide sufficient regulatory oversight both at a national and an international level.[8]

The cumulative effect of these economic crises has not necessarily been to undermine confidence in market-based economics and globalization as engines of economic growth. China, India, Brazil, and any number of other so-called emerging market countries continue to perform well economically based on their participation in global capitalism. But it is clear that the *political* job of finding the right regulatory mechanisms to tame capitalism's volatility have not yet been found.

POLITICAL DECAY

The latter point suggests an urgent but often overlooked area of concern about democracy's future. Political institutions develop, often slowly and painfully, over time, as human societies strive to organize themselves to master their environments. But political decay occurs when political systems fail to adjust to changing circumstances. There is something like a law of the conservation of institutions. Human beings are rule-following animals by nature; they are born to conform to the social norms they see around them, and they entrench those rules with often transcendent meaning and value. When the surrounding environment changes and new challenges arise, there is often a disjunction between existing institutions and present needs. Those institutions are supported by legions of entrenched stakeholders who oppose any fundamental change.

American political institutions may well be headed for a major test of their adaptability. The American system was built around a firm conviction that concentrated political power constituted an imminent danger to the lives and liberty of citizens. For this reason, the U.S. Constitution was designed with a broad range of checks and balances by which different parts of the government could prevent other parts from exercising tyrannical control. This system has served the country well, but only because at certain critical junctures in its history when strong government was necessary, it was possible to forge the consensus to bring it about through the exercise of political leadership.

There is unfortunately no institutional guarantee that the system as designed will always check tyrannical power yet allow exercises of state authority when the need arises. The latter depends in the first instance on the existence of a social consensus on political ends, and this has been lacking in American political life in recent years. The United States faces a series of large challenges, mostly related to fixing its long-term fiscal situation. Over the past generation, Americans have spent money on themselves without paying their own way through taxation, a situation that has been exacerbated by years of too-easy access to credit and overspending on both a household and governmental level. The long-term fiscal shortfall and foreign indebtedness threaten the very basis of American power around the world, as other countries like China gain in relative stature.[9]

None of these challenges is so enormous that it cannot be resolved through timely, if painful, action. But the American political system, which should facilitate the formation of consensus, is instead contributing to the problem. The Congress has become highly polarized, making the passage of legislation extremely difficult. For the first time in modern history, the most conservative Democrat in Congress is more liberal than the most liberal Republican. The number of seats in Congress won by a margin of 10 percent or less, meaning that they are up for grabs by either party, has fallen steadily from nearly two hundred in the late nineteenth century to only a little more than fifty in the early 2000s. Both political parties have become much more ideologically homogeneous, and deliberative debate between them has deteriorated.[10] These kinds of divisions are not historically unprecedented, but in the past they have been overcome by strong presidential leadership, which has not been forthcoming.

The future of American politics rests not just in politics but also in society. The polarization of Congress reflects a broad trend toward the growing homogenization of neighborhoods and regions, as Americans sort themselves out ideologically by where they choose to live.[11] The trend towards associating only with like-minded people is strongly amplified by the media, where the proliferation of communication channels ends up weakening the shared experience of citizenship.[12]

The American political system's ability to deal with its fiscal challenges is affected not just by the Left-Right polarization of Congress but also by the growth and power of entrenched interest groups. Trade unions, agribusinesses, drug companies, banks, and a host of other organized lobbies often exercise an effective veto on legislation that hurts their pocketbooks. It is perfectly legitimate and indeed expected that citizens should defend their interests in a democracy. But at a certain point this defense crosses over into the claiming of privileges, or a situation of gridlock where no one's interests may be challenged. This explains the rising levels of populist anger on both the Right and Left that contribute to polarization and reflect a social reality at odds with the country's own legitimating principles.

The complaint by Americans that the United States is dominated by elites and powerful interest groups reflects the reality of increasing income and wealth inequality in the period from the 1970s to the early 2000s.[13] Inequality per se has never been a big problem in American political culture, which emphasizes equality of opportunity rather than of outcomes. But the system remains legitimate only as long as people believe that by working hard and doing their best, they and their children have a fair shot at getting ahead, and that the wealthy got there playing by the rules.

The fact is, however, that rates of intergenerational social mobility are far lower in the United States than many Americans believe them to be, and lower than in many other developed countries that traditionally have been regarded as rigid and stratified.[14] Over time, elites are able to protect their positions by gaming the political system, moving their money offshore to avoid taxation, and transmitting these advantages to their children through favored access to elite institutions. Much of this was laid bare during the financial crisis of 2008–2009, when it became painfully clear that there was little relationship between compensation in the financial services sector and real contributions to the economy. The industry had used its considerable political muscle to dismantle regulation and oversight in the previous decade, and continued to fend off regulation in the crisis's aftermath. The economist Simon Johnson suggested that the power of the financial oligarchy in the United States was not too different from what exists in emerging market countries like Russia or Indonesia.[15]

There is no automatic mechanism by which political systems adjust themselves to changing circumstances. The story of the failure to adjust, and thus the phenomenon of political decay, is told in later pages of this volume. There was no necessary reason why the Mamluk Sultanate in Egypt couldn't have adopted firearms earlier to meet rising external threats, as the Ottomans who ultimately defeated them did; nor was it inevitable that emperors in the late Ming Dynasty in China would fail to tax their citizens adequately to support an army that could defend the country from the Manchus. The problem in both cases was the enormous institutional inertia existing behind the status quo.

Once a society fails to confront a major fiscal crisis through serious institutional reform, as the French monarchy did after the failure of the Grand Parti in 1557, it is tempted to resort to a host of short-term fixes that erode and eventually corrupt its own institutions. These fixes involved giving in to various entrenched stakeholders and interest groups, who invariably represented people with wealth and power in French society. The failure to balance the country's budget led to bankruptcy and the delegitimization of the state itself, a course that finally terminated in the French Revolution.

The United States is not in nearly as serious a moral and fiscal crisis as ancien régime France. The danger, however, is that its situation will continue to worsen over time in the absence of some powerful force that will knock the system off its current dysfunctional institutional equilibrium.

FANTASIES OF STATELESSNESS

A common thread links many of our contemporary anxieties about the future, from authoritarian backsliding in Russia to corruption in India, to failed states in the developing world, to entrenched interest groups in contemporary American politics. It concerns the difficulties of creating and maintaining effective political institutions, governments that are simultaneously powerful, rule bound, and accountable. This might seem like an obvious point that any fourth grader would acknowledge, and yet on further reflection it is a truth that many intelligent people fail to understand.

Let's begin with the question of the receding of the third wave and the democratic recession that has taken place around the world in the 2000s. The reasons for our disappointments in the failure of democracy to spread do not lie, I would argue, on the level of ideas at the present moment. Ideas are extremely important to political order; it is the perceived legitimacy of the government that binds populations together and makes them willing to accept its authority. The fall of the Berlin Wall marked the collapse of one of democracy's great competitors, communism, and the rapid spread of liberal democracy as the most widely accepted form of government.

This is true up to the present, where democracy, in Amartya Sen's words, remains the "default" political condition: "While democracy is not yet universally practiced, nor indeed universally accepted, in the general climate of world opinion democratic governance has achieved the status of being taken to be generally right."[16] Very few people around the world openly profess to admire Vladimir Putin's petronationalism, or Hugo Chávez's "twenty-first-century socialism," or Mahmoud Ahmadinejad's Islamic Republic. No important international institution endorses anything but democracy as the basis for just governance. China's rapid growth incites envy and interest, but its exact model of authoritarian capitalism is not one that is easily described, much less emulated, by other developing countries. Such is the prestige of modern liberal democracy that today's would-be authoritarians all have to stage elections and manipulate the media from behind the scenes to legitimate themselves. Not only has totalitarianism virtually disappeared from the world; authoritarians pay a compliment to democracy by pretending to be democrats.

Democracy's failure, then, lies less in concept than in execution: most people around the world would strongly prefer to live in a society in which their government was accountable *and* effective, where it delivered the sorts of services demanded by citizens in a timely and cost-effective way. But few governments are actually able to do both, because institutions are weak, corrupt, lacking capacity, or in some cases absent altogether. The passion of protesters and democracy advocates around the world, from South Africa to Korea to Romania to Ukraine, might be sufficient to bring about "regime change" from authoritarian to democratic government, but the latter will not succeed without a long, costly, laborious, and difficult process of institution building.

There is in fact a curious blindness to the importance of political institutions that has affected many people over the years, people who dream about a world in which we will somehow transcend politics. This particular fantasy is not the special province of either the Left or the Right; both have had their versions of it. The father of communism, Karl Marx, famously predicted the "withering away of the state" once the proletarian revolution had achieved power and abolished private property. Left-wing revolutionaries from the nineteenth-century anarchists on thought it sufficient to destroy old power structures without giving serious thought to what would take their place. This tradition continues up through the present, with the suggestion by antiglobalization authors like Michael Hardt and Antonio Negri that economic injustice could be abolished by undermining the sovereignty of states and replacing it with a networked "multitude."[17]

Real-world Communist regimes of course did exactly the opposite of what Marx predicted, building large and tyrannical state structures to force people to act collectively when they failed to do so spontaneously. This in turn led a generation of democracy activists in Eastern Europe to envision their own form of statelessness, where a mobilized civil society would take the place of traditional political parties and centralized governments.[18] These activists were subsequently disillusioned by the realization that their societies could not be governed without institutions, and when they encountered the messy compromises required to build them. In the decades since the fall of communism, Eastern Europe is democratic, but it is not thereby necessarily happy with its politics or politicians.[19]

The fantasy of statelessness most prevalent on the Right is that the market economy will somehow make government unnecessary and irrelevant. During the dot-com boom of the 1990s, many enthusiasts argued along the lines of the former Citibank CEO Walter Wriston that the world was experiencing a "twilight of sovereignty,"[20] in which the political powers traditionally exercised by states were being undermined by new information technologies that were making borders impossible to police and rules difficult to enforce. The rise of the Internet led activists like John Perry Barlow of the Electronic Frontier Foundation to issue a "Declaration of Independence of Cyberspace," where governments of the industrialized world were told, "You are not welcome among us. You have no sovereignty where we gather."[21] A global capitalist economy would replace the sovereignty of democratic governments with the sovereignty of the market: if a legislature voted for excessive regulation or restricted trade, it would be punished by the bond market and forced to adopt policies deemed rational by global capital markets.[22] Fantasies of a stateless world have always found a sympathetic audience in the United States, where hostility to the state is a staple of American political culture. Libertarians of various stripes have suggested not just rolling back an overgrown welfare state but also abolishing more basic institutions like the Federal Reserve Board and the Food and Drug Administration.[23]

It is quite legitimate to argue that modern governments have grown excessively large, and that they thereby limit economic growth and individual freedom. People are right to complain about unresponsive bureaucracy, corrupt politicians, and the unprincipled nature of politics. But in the developed world, we take the existence of government so much for granted that we sometimes forget how important it is, and how difficult it was to create, and what the world would look like without certain basic political institutions.

It is not only that we take democracy for granted; we also take for granted the fact that we have a state at all that can carry out certain basic functions. Fairfax County, Virginia, a suburb of Washington, D.C., where I lived for many years, is one of the richest counties in the United States. Every winter, potholes appear in the county's roads as a result of the seasonal freezing and thawing after winter storms. And yet by the end of the spring, all of those potholes get magically filled so no one has to worry about breaking an axle in one. If they don't get filled, the residents of Fairfax County get angry and complain about the incompetence of local government; no one (apart from a few specialists in public administration) ever stops to think about the complex, invisible social system that makes this possible, or why it takes longer to fill potholes in the neighboring District of Columbia, or why potholes *never* get filled in many developing countries.

Indeed, the kinds of minimal or no-government societies envisioned by dreamers of the Left and Right are not fantasies; they actually exist in the contemporary developing world. Many parts of sub-Saharan Africa are a libertarian's paradise. The region as a whole is a low-tax utopia, with governments often unable to collect more than about 10 percent of GDP in taxes, compared to more than 30 percent in the United States and 50 percent in parts of Europe. Rather than unleashing entrepreneurship, this low rate of taxation means that basic public services like health, education, and pothole filling are starved of funding. The physical infrastructure on which a modern economy rests, like roads, court systems, and police, are missing. In Somalia, where a strong central government has not existed since the late 1980s, ordinary individuals may own not just assault rifles but also rocket-propelled grenades, antiaircraft missiles, and tanks. People are free to protect their own families, and indeed are forced to do so. Nigeria has a film industry that produces as many titles as India's famed Bollywood, but films have to earn a quick return because the government is incapable of guaranteeing intellectual property rights and preventing products from being copied illegally.

The degree to which people in developed countries take political institutions for granted was very much evident in the way that the United States planned, or failed to plan, for the aftermath of its 2003 invasion of Iraq. The U.S. administration seemed to think that democracy and a market economy were default conditions to which the country would automatically revert once Saddam Hussein's dictatorship was removed, and seemed genuinely surprised when the Iraqi state itself collapsed in an orgy of looting and civil conflict. U.S. purposes have been similarly stymied in Afghanistan, where ten years of effort and the investment of hundreds of billions of dollars have not produced a stable, legitimate Afghan state.[24]

Political institutions are necessary and cannot be taken for granted. A market economy and high levels of wealth don't magically appear when you "get government out of the way"; they rest on a hidden institutional foundation of property rights, rule of law, and basic political order. A free market, a vigorous civil society, the spontaneous "wisdom of crowds" are all important components of a working democracy, but none can ultimately replace the functions of a strong, hierarchical government. There has been a broad recognition among economists in recent years that "institutions matter": poor countries are poor not because they lack resources, but because they lack effective political institutions. We need therefore to better understand where those institutions come from.

GETTING TO DENMARK

The problem of creating modern political institutions has been described as the problem of "getting to Denmark," after the title of a paper written by two social scientists at the World Bank, Lant Pritchett and Michael Woolcock.[25] For people in developed countries, "Denmark" is a mythical place that is known to have good political and economic institutions: it is stable, democratic, peaceful, prosperous, inclusive, and has extremely low levels of political corruption. Everyone would like to figure out how to transform Somalia, Haiti, Nigeria, Iraq, or Afghanistan into "Denmark," and the international development community has long lists of presumed Denmark-like attributes that they are trying to help failed states achieve.

There are any number of problems with this agenda. It does not seem very plausible that extremely poor and chaotic countries could expect to put into place complex institutions in short order, given how long such institutions took to evolve. Moreover, institutions reflect the cultural values of the societies in which they are established, and it is not clear that Denmark's democratic political order can take root in very different cultural contexts. Most people living in rich, stable developed countries have no idea how Denmark itself got to be Denmark—something that is true for many Danes as well. The struggle to create modern political institutions was so long and so painful that people living in industrialized countries now suffer from a historical amnesia regarding how their societies came to that point in the first place.

The Danes themselves are descended from the Vikings, a ferocious tribal people who conquered and pillaged much of Europe, from the Mediterranean all the way to Kiev in southern Ukraine. The Celtic peoples who first settled the British Isles, as well as the Romans who conquered them, and the Germanic barbarians who displaced the Romans, were all originally organized into tribes much like those that still exist in Afghanistan, central Iraq, and Papua New Guinea. So were the Chinese, Indians, Arabs, Africans, and virtually all other peoples on earth. They owed primary obligation not to a state but to kinfolk, they settled disputes not through courts but through a system of retributive justice, and they buried their dead on property held collectively by groups of kin.

Over the course of time, however, these tribal societies developed political institutions. First and foremost was the centralized source of authority that held an effective monopoly of military power over a defined piece of territory—what we call a state. Peace was kept not by a rough balance of power between groups of kin but by the state's army and police, now a standing force that could also defend the community against neighboring tribes and states. Property came to be owned not by groups of kinfolk but by individuals, who increasingly won the right to buy and sell it at will. Their rights to that property were enforced not by kin but by courts and legal systems that had the power to settle disputes and compensate wrongs.

In time, moreover, social rules were formalized as written laws rather than customs or informal traditions. These formal rules were used to organize the way that power was distributed in the system, regardless of the individuals who exercised power at any given time. Institutions, in other words, replaced individual leaders. Those legal systems were eventually accorded supreme authority over society, an authority that was seen to be superior to that of rulers who temporarily happened to command the state's armed forces and bureaucracy. This came to be known as the rule of law.

Finally, certain societies not only limited the power of their states by forcing rulers to comply with written law; they also held them accountable to parliaments, assemblies, and other bodies representing a broader proportion of the population. Some degree of accountability was present in many traditional monarchies, but it was usually the product of informal consultation with a small body of elite advisers. Modern democracy was born when rulers acceded to formal rules limiting their power and subordinating their sovereignty to the will of the larger population as expressed through elections.

The purpose of this book is to fill in some of the gaps of this historical amnesia, by giving an account of where basic political institutions came from in societies that now take them for granted. The three categories of institutions in question are the ones just described:

1. the state
2. the rule of law
3. accountable government

A successful modern liberal democracy combines all three sets of institutions in a stable balance. The fact that there are countries capable of achieving this balance constitutes the miracle of modern politics, since it is not obvious that they can be combined. The state, after all, concentrates and uses power, to bring about compliance with its laws on the part of its citizens and to defend itself against other states and threats. The rule of law and accountable government, on the other hand, limit the state's power, first by forcing it to use its power according to certain public and transparent rules, and then by ensuring that it is subordinate to the will of the people.

These institutions come into being in the first place because people find that they can protect their interests, and the interests of their families, through them. But what people regard as self-interest, and how they are willing to collaborate with others, depends critically on ideas that legitimate certain forms of political association. Self-interest and legitimacy thus form the cornerstones of political order.

The fact that one of these three types of institutions exists does not imply that the others do so as well. Afghanistan, for example, has held democratic elections since 2004 but has an extremely weak state and is unable to uphold laws in much of its territory. Russia, by contrast, has a strong state and holds democratic elections, but its rulers do not feel bound by a rule of law. The nation of Singapore has both a strong state and a rule of law bequeathed to it by its former British colonial masters but only an attenuated form of democratic accountability.

Where did these three sets of institutions originally come from? What were the forces that drove their creation and the conditions under which they developed? In what order were they created, and how did they relate to one another? If we could understand how these basic institutions came into being, we could then perhaps better understand the distance that separates Afghanistan or Somalia from contemporary Denmark.

The story of how political institutions developed cannot be told without understanding the complementary process of political decay. Human institutions are "sticky"; that is, they persist over time and are changed only with great difficulty. Institutions that are created to meet one set of conditions often survive even when those conditions change or disappear, and the failure to adapt appropriately entails political decay. This applies to modern liberal democracies encompassing the state, rule of law, and accountability as much as to older political systems. For there is no guarantee that any given democracy will continue to deliver what it promises to its citizens, and thus no guarantee that it will remain legitimate in their eyes.

Moreover, the natural human propensity to favor family and friends—something I refer to as patrimonialism—constantly reasserts itself in the absence of strong countervailing incentives. Organized groups—most often the rich and powerful—entrench themselves over time and begin demanding privileges from the state. Particularly when a prolonged period of peace and stability gives way to financial and/or military crisis, these entrenched patrimonial groups extend their sway, or else prevent the state from responding adequately.

A version of the story of political development and political decay has of course been told many times before. Most high schools offer a class on the "rise of civilization," which presents a broad overview of the evolution of social institutions. A century ago, the historical account presented to most American schoolchildren was highly Euro-, and indeed, Anglocentric. It might have begun in Greece and Rome, then progressed through the European Middle Ages, the Magna Carta, the English Civil War and Glorious Revolution, and thence perhaps on to 1776 and the writing of the U.S. Constitution. Today, such curricula are far more multicultural and incorporate the experiences of non-Western societies like China and India as well, or else dwell on history's marginalized groups like indigenous peoples, women, the poor, and so on.

There are several reasons to be dissatisfied with the existing literature on the development of political institutions. First, much of it is not comparative on a sufficiently broad scale. It is only by comparing the experience of different societies that we can begin to sort through complex causal factors that explain why certain institutions emerged in some places but not in others. A lot of theorizing about modernization, from the massive studies of Karl Marx to contemporary economic historians like Douglass North, has focused heavily on the experience of England as the first country to industrialize. The English experience was exceptional in many ways but is not necessarily a good guide to development in countries differently situated.

The multicultural approaches that have displaced this narrative in recent decades are not for the most part seriously comparative. They tend to select either positive stories of how non-Western civilizations have contributed to the overall progress of humankind, or else negative ones about how they were victimized. One seldom finds serious comparative analysis of why an institution developed in one society but not in another.

The great sociologist Seymour Martin Lipset used to say that an observer who knows only one country knows no countries. Without comparison, there is no way of knowing whether a particular practice or behavior is unique to the society in question or common to many. Only through comparative analysis is it possible to link causes, like geography, climate, technology, religion, or conflict, to the range of outcomes existing in the world today. In doing so, we might be able to answer questions like the following:

- Why are Afghanistan, the jungle regions of India, the island nations of Melanesia, and parts of the Middle East still tribally organized?
- Why is China's default condition to be ruled by a strong, centralized government, while India has never seen that degree of centralization except for very brief periods over the past three millennia of its history?
- Why is it that almost all of the cases of successful authoritarian modernization—countries like South Korea, Taiwan, Singapore, and China—are clustered in East Asia, rather than in Africa or the Middle East?
- Why have democracy and a strong rule of law taken root in Scandinavia, while Russia, subject to similar climactic and geographical conditions, experienced the growth of unconstrained absolutism?
- Why have countries in Latin America been subject to high inflation and economic crises repeatedly over the past century, while the United States and Canada have not?

The historical data presented in this book are interesting precisely because they shed light on the present and explain how different political orders came to be. But human societies are not trapped by their pasts. If modern states emerged in China or Europe as a result of certain factors like the constant need to prepare for and fight wars, this does not necessarily mean that weak states in Africa today must replicate this experience if they are to modernize. Indeed, I will argue in Volume 2 that the conditions for political development today are very different from what they were in the periods covered by Volume 1. The social deck is being constantly shuffled by economic growth, and international factors impinge to a much greater extent on individual societies than they did in the past. So while the historical material in this book may explain how different societies got to where they are now, their paths to the present do not determine their futures, or serve as models for other societies.

CHINA FIRST

The classic theories of modernization written by such towering figures as Karl Marx, Émile Durkheim, Henry Maine, Ferdinand Tönnies, and Max Weber tended to regard the experience of the West as paradigmatic of modernization as such because industrialization took place first in the West. This focus on the West is understandable since the explosion of productivity and sustained economic growth that occurred after about 1800 in Europe and North America was unprecedented and transformed the world into what it is today.

But development is not only about economics. Political institutions develop, as do social ones. Sometimes political and social development are closely related to economic change, but at other times they happen independently. This book focuses on the *political* dimension of development, the evolution of government institutions. Modern political institutions appeared far earlier in history than did the Industrial Revolution and the modern capitalist economy. Indeed, many of the elements of what we now understand to be a modern state were already in place in China in the third century B.C., some eighteen hundred years before they emerged in Europe.

It is for this reason that I begin my account of the emergence of the state in Part II with China. While classic modernization theory tended to take European development as the norm and ask why other societies diverged from it, I take China as a paradigm of state formation and ask why other civilizations didn't replicate the path it followed. This is not to say that China was better than other societies. As we will see, a modern state without rule of law or accountability is capable of enormous despotism. But China was the first to develop state institutions, and its pioneering experience is seldom referred to in Western accounts of political development.

In beginning with China, I skip over other important early societies like Mesopotamia, Egypt, Greece and Rome, and the civilizations of Meso- and South America. The decision not to cover Greece and Rome at greater length in this volume requires further explanation.

The ancient Mediterranean world set precedents that were extremely important to the subsequent development of European civilization, which from the time of Charlemagne on were self-consciously imitated by European rulers. The Greeks are commonly credited with having invented democracy, in which rulers were not hereditary but selected by ballot. Most tribal societies are also relatively egalitarian and elect their rulers (see chapter 4), but the Greeks went beyond this by introducing a concept of citizenship that was based on political criteria rather than kinship. The form of government practiced in fifth-century Athens or under the Roman Republic is probably better described as "classical republicanism" rather than "democracy," since the franchise was given to only a limited number of citizens, and there were sharp class distinctions that excluded large numbers of people (including the numerous slaves) from political participation. These were, moreover, not liberal states but highly communitarian ones that did not respect the privacy or autonomy of their citizens.

The classical republican precedent established by Greece and Rome was copied by many later societies, including the oligarchic republics of Genoa, Venice, Novgorod, and the Dutch United Provinces. But this form of government had one fatal defect that was widely recognized by later writers, including many of the American Founding Fathers who thought deeply about that tradition: classical republicanism did not scale well. It worked best in small, homogeneous societies like the city-states of fifth-century Greece, or Rome in its early years. But as these republics grew larger through conquest or economic growth, it became impossible to maintain the demanding communitarian values that bound them together. As the Roman Republic grew in size and diversity, it faced irresolvable conflicts over who should enjoy the privileges of citizenship and how to divide the spoils of empire. The Greek city-states were all eventually conquered by monarchies, and the Roman Republic, after a prolonged civil war, gave way to the Empire. Monarchy as a form of government proved superior in its ability to govern large empires and was the political system under which Rome achieved its greatest power and geographical extent.

I will return to the question of classical republicanism as a precedent for modern democracy in Volume 2. But there is good reason for paying closer attention to China than to Greece and Rome in studying the rise of the state, since China alone created a *modern* state in the terms defined by Max Weber. That is, China succeeded in developing a centralized, uniform system of bureaucratic administration that was capable of governing a huge population and territory when compared to Mediterranean Europe. China had already invented a system of impersonal, merit-based bureaucratic recruitment that was far more systematic than Roman public administration. While the total population of the Chinese empire in 1 A.D. was roughly comparable to that of the Roman empire, the Chinese put a far larger proportion of its people under a uniform set of rules than did the Romans. Rome had other important legacies, particularly in the domain of law (discussed at greater length in chapter 18). But although Greece and Rome were extremely important as precursors of modern accountable government, China was more important in the development of the state.

Among the societies to be compared with China is India. India graduated from a tribal to a state-level society at about the same time as China. But then, around twenty-five hundred years ago, it took a big detour due to the rise of a new Brahmanic religion, which limited the power that any Indian polity could achieve and in some sense paved the way for modern Indian democracy. The Middle East at the time of the Prophet Muhammad was also tribally organized; it took not just the advent of a new religion, Islam, but also a curious institution of slave-soldiers to enable certain polities in Egypt and Turkey to turn themselves into major political powers. Europe was very different from these other societies insofar as its exit from tribalism was not imposed by rulers from the top down but came about on a social level through rules mandated by the Catholic church. In Europe alone, state-level institutions did not have to be built on top of tribally organized ones.

Religion is also key to the origins of the rule of law, which is the subject of Part III. Religiously based law existed in ancient Israel, India, the Muslim Middle East, and also the Christian West. It was Western Europe, however, that saw the strongest development of independent legal institutions that managed to take on a secular form and survive into the present day.

The story of the rise of accountable governments in Part IV is also largely a European one. But Europe was hardly uniform in this respect: accountable governments arose in England and Denmark but not in France or Spain; Russia developed a form of absolutism comparable in its power to that of China. The ability of certain societies to force accountability on their sovereigns, then, depended on a host of specific historical conditions such as the survival of certain feudal institutions into modern times.

The sequencing of political development in Western Europe was highly unusual when compared to other parts of the world. Individualism on a social level appeared centuries before the rise of either modern states or capitalism; a rule of law existed before political power was concentrated in the hands of centralized governments; and institutions of accountability arose because modern, centralized states were unable to completely defeat or eliminate ancient feudal institutions like representative assemblies.

Once this combination of state, law, and accountability appeared, it proved to be a highly powerful and attractive form of government that subsequently spread to all corners of the world. But we need to remember how historically contingent this emergence was. China had a strong state, but without law and accountability; India had law and now has accountability, but has traditionally lacked a strong state; the Middle East had states and law, but in much of the Arab part it lost the latter tradition. Societies are not trapped by their pasts and freely borrow ideas and institutions from each other. But what they are in the present is also shaped by what they were in the past, and there is not one single path that links one to the other.

TURTLES ALL THE WAY DOWN

The purpose of this book is less to present a history of political development than to analyze some of the factors that led to the emergence of certain key political institutions. A lot of historical writing has been characterized as ODTAA—"one damn thing after another"—without an effort to extract general rules or causal theories that can be applied in other circumstances. The same can be said of the ethnographies written by anthropologists, which are highly detailed but deliberately shy away from broad generalization. That is definitely not my approach, which compares and generalizes across many civilizations and time periods.

The overall framework for understanding political development presented here bears many resemblances to biological evolution. Darwinian evolution is built around the two principles of variance and selection: organisms experience random genetic mutation, and those best adapted to their environments survive and multiply. So too in political development: there is variation in political institutions, and those best suited to the physical and social environment survive and proliferate. But there are also many important differences between biological and political evolution: human institutions are subject to deliberate design and choice, unlike genes; they are transmitted across time culturally rather than genetically; and they are invested with intrinsic value through a variety of psychological and social mechanisms, which makes them hard to change. The inherent conservatism of human institutions then explains why political development is frequently reversed by political decay, since there is often a substantial lag between changes in the external environment that should trigger institutional change, and the actual willingness of societies to make those changes.

In the end, however, this general framework amounts to something less than a predictive theory of political development. A parsimonious theory of political change, comparable to the theories of economic growth posited by economists, is in my view simply not possible.[26] The factors driving the development of any given political institution are multiple, complex, and often dependent on accidental or contingent events. Any causal factors one adduces for a given development are themselves caused by prior conditions that extend backward in time in an endless regression.

Let us take one example A well-known theory of political development argues that European state building was driven by the need to wage war.[27] The relationship between the need to wage war and the development of modern state institutions is fairly well established for early modern Europe, and as we will see applies equally well to ancient China. But before we can declare this to be a general theory of state formation, we need to answer some difficult questions: Why did some regions that experienced long-term warfare fail to develop state institutions (e.g., Melanesia)? Why did warfare in other regions seem to weaken rather than strengthen states (e.g., Latin America)? Why did some regions experience lower levels of conflict than others (e.g., India when compared to China)? Answering these questions pushes causality back to other factors such as population density, physical geography, technology, and religion. Warfare in places that are densely populated, with good physical communications (e.g., plains or steppe) and appropriate technologies (e.g., horses) has very different political effects from war in sparsely populated mountainous, jungle, or desert regions. So the theory of war and state formation dissolves into a series of further questions about why certain forms of warfare erupt in some places and not in others.

What I am aiming for in this book is a middle-range theory that avoids the pitfalls both of excessive abstraction (the vice of economists) and excessive particularism (the problem of many historians and anthropologists). I am hoping to recover something of the lost tradition of nineteenth-century historical sociology or comparative anthropology. I do not confront the general reader with a big theoretical framework at the outset. While I engage various theories in the course of the historical chapters, I reserve the more abstract treatment of political development (including definitions of some basic terms) for the last three chapters (chapters 28–30). This includes a general account of how political development happens as well as a discussion of how political development relates to the economic and social dimensions of development.

Putting the theory after the history constitutes what I regard as the correct approach to analysis: theories ought to be inferred from facts, and not the other way around. Of course, there is no such thing as a pure confrontation with facts, devoid of prior theoretical constructs. Those who think they are empirical in that fashion are deluding themselves. But all too often social science begins with an elegant theory and then searches for facts that will confirm it. This, hopefully, is not the approach I take.

There is a perhaps apocryphal story, retold by the physicist Stephen Hawking, about a famous scientist who was giving a public lecture on cosmology when he was interrupted by an old lady at the back of the room who told him he was speaking rubbish, and that the universe was actually a flat disc balanced on the back of a turtle. The scientist thought he could shut her up by asking what the turtle was standing on. She replied, "You're very clever, young man, but it's turtles all the way down."

This then is the problem with any theory of development: the particular turtle you pick as the starting point for your story is actually standing on the back of another turtle, or else an elephant or a tiger or a whale. Most purportedly general theories of development fail because they don't take into account the multiple independent dimensions of development. They are, rather, reductionist in seeking to abstract a single causal factor out of a much more complex historical reality. And they fail to push the story back far enough historically to the conditions that explain their own starting points and premises.

I push the story back very far. Before we get to state building in China, we need to understand not just where war comes from but also how human societies originated. The surprising answer is that they didn't come from anywhere. Both society and conflict have existed for as long as there have been human beings, because human beings are by nature both social and competitive animals. The primates from which the human species evolved practiced an attenuated form of politics. To understand this, then, we need to go back to the state of nature and to human biology, which in some sense sets the framework for the whole of human politics. Biology presents a certain degree of solid ground resting below the turtles at the bottom of the stack, though even biology, as we will see in the next chapter, is not an entirely fixed point.

2

THE STATE OF NATURE

Philosophical discussions of the state of nature; how the contemporary life sciences shed light on human nature and hence on the biological foundations of politics; politics among chimpanzees and other primates; what aspects of human nature undergird politics; when different parts of the world were first settled

In the Western philosophical tradition, discussions of the "state of nature" have been central to the understanding of justice and political order that underlies modern liberal democracy. Classical political philosophy distinguished between nature and convention or law; Plato and Aristotle argued that a just city had to exist in conformity with man's permanent nature and not what was ephemeral and changing. Thomas Hobbes, John Locke, and Jean-Jacques Rousseau developed this distinction and wrote treatises on the question of the state of nature, seeking to ground political rights in it. Describing the state of nature was a means and a metaphor for discussing human nature, an exercise that would establish a hierarchy of human goods that political society was meant to foster.

Aristotle differed from Hobbes, Locke, and Rousseau in one critical respect. He argued that human beings are political by nature, and that their natural capacities incline them to flourish in society. The three early modern philosophers, by contrast, argued that human beings are not naturally social, but that society is a kind of artifice that allows people to achieve what they cannot get on their own.

Hobbes's *Leviathan* begins with an extended catalog of natural human passions and argues that the deepest and most abiding one is the fear of violent death. From this he derives the fundamental right of nature, which is the liberty each man has to preserve his own life. Human nature also provides three causes of quarrel: competition, diffidence (fear), and glory;

"The first, maketh men invade for Gain; the second, for Safety; and the third, for Reputation." The state of nature is thus characterized by "Warre . . . of every man against every man." To escape from this perilous situation, human beings agree to give up their natural liberty to do as they please in return for other people respecting their right to life. The state, or Leviathan, enforces these reciprocal commitments in the form of a social contract by which human beings protect those rights which they have by nature but are not able to enjoy in the state of nature due to the war of every man against every man. The government, or Leviathan, secures the right to life by securing peace.[1]

John Locke, in his *Second Treatise on Government*, has a softer view of the state of nature than Hobbes; human beings are less occupied fighting one another than mixing their labor with the common things of nature to produce private property. Locke's fundamental law of nature, in contrast to that of Hobbes, gives human beings the right not just to life, but to "life, health, liberty, or possessions."[2] Unregulated liberty in the state of nature leads to the state of war, necessitating, as for Hobbes, a social contract for the preservation of natural liberty and property. Although the state, in Locke's view, is necessary, it can itself become the denier of natural rights, and so he posits a right to revolt against unjust authority. The right to life, liberty, and the pursuit of happiness posited by Thomas Jefferson in the American Declaration of Independence traces its ancestry directly back to Hobbes's right of nature, via Locke's amendment concerning the danger of tyranny.

Hobbes's violent state of nature, wherein the life of man is famously "solitary, poore, nasty, brutish, and short," is traditionally contrasted with Rousseau's more peaceful version, given in his *Discourse on the Origin and the Foundation of Inequality Among Mankind*. Indeed, Rousseau explicitly criticizes Hobbes at several points: "But above all things let us beware concluding with Hobbes, that man, as having no idea of goodness, must be naturally bad; that he is vicious because he does not know what virtue is; that he always refuses to do any service to those of his own species, because he believes that none is due to them; that, in virtue of that right which he justly claims to everything he wants, he foolishly looks upon himself as proprietor of the whole universe."[3] Rousseau argues that Hobbes has not in fact uncovered natural man; the violent creature described in *Leviathan* is actually the product of the contaminating effects of centuries of social development. Natural human beings for Rousseau are indeed solitary, but they are also timid, fearful, and more likely to flee one another than to fight. Savage man's "desires never extend beyond his physical wants; he knows no goods but food, a female, and rest"; he fears pain and hunger but not the abstraction of death. Thus the rise of political society does not represent salvation from the "warre of every man against every man" but a bondage to other human beings through ties of mutual dependence.

Rousseau says at the beginning of the *Discourse on Inequality* that "the researches, in which we may engage on this occasion, are not to be taken for historical truths, but merely as hypothetical and conditional reasonings, fitter to illustrate the nature of things, than to show their true origin." For Rousseau and Hobbes, the state of nature was less a historical account than a heuristic device for uncovering human nature—that is, the deepest and most abiding characteristics of human beings, when shorn of behaviors brought about by civilization and history.

Yet the intention of Rousseau's *Discourse* is clearly to provide a developmental account of human behavior. He talks about man's perfectibility, and speculates on how human thoughts, passions, and behavior have evolved over time. He adduces considerable evidence about the Caribs and other indigenous peoples of the New World, as well as arguments based on observations of animal behavior, to try to understand what is human by nature and what is human by social convention. It is always risky to think one understands the true intentions of great thinkers. But given the foundational importance of the accounts of the state of nature offered by Hobbes, Locke, and Rousseau to Western political self-understanding, it is not unfair to contrast them with what we actually know today about human origins as a result of recent advances in a range of life sciences.

This knowledge exists in several distinct domains, including primatology, population genetics, archaeology, social anthropology, and, of course, the overarching framework of evolutionary biology. We can rerun Rousseau's thought experiment using much better empirical data, and what we find confirms certain of his insights while throwing others into question. The recovery of human nature by modern biology, in any case, is extremely important as a foundation for any theory of political development, because it provides us with the basic building blocks by which we can understand the later evolution of human institutions.

Rousseau was brilliantly correct in certain of his observations, such as his view that human inequality had its origins in the development of metallurgy, agriculture, and, above all, private property. But he, Hobbes, and

Locke were wrong on one very important point. All three thinkers saw human beings in the state of nature as isolated individuals, for whom society was not natural. According to Hobbes, early human beings relate to one another primarily through fear, envy, and conflict. Rousseau's primitive human is even more isolated: while sex is natural, the family is not. Mutual human dependence comes about almost accidentally, as a result of technological innovations like agriculture that require greater cooperation. For both, human society emerges only with the passage of historical time, and involves compromises of natural liberty.

This is not the way things actually happened. In his 1861 book *Ancient Law*, the English legal scholar Henry Maine criticizes the state-of-nature theorists in the following terms:

> Yet these two theories [of Hobbes and Locke], which long divided the reflecting politicians of England into hostile camps, resemble each other strictly in their fundamental assumption of a non-historic, unverifiable condition of the race. Their authors differed as to the characteristics of the prae-social state, and as to the nature of the abnormal action by which men lifted themselves out of it into that social organization with which alone we are acquainted, but they agreed in thinking that a great chasm separated man in his primitive condition from man in society.[4]

We might label this the Hobbesean fallacy: the idea that human beings were primordially individualistic and that they entered into society at a later stage in their development only as a result of a rational calculation that social cooperation was the best way for them to achieve their individual ends. This premise of primordial individualism underpins the understanding of rights contained in the American Declaration of Independence and thus of the democratic political community that springs from it. This premise also underlies contemporary neoclassical economics, which builds its models on the assumption that human beings are rational beings who want to maximize their individual utility or incomes. But it is in fact individualism and not sociability that developed over the course of human history. That individualism seems today like a solid core of our economic and political behavior is only because we have developed institutions that override our more naturally communal instincts. Aristotle was more correct than these early modern liberal theorists when he said that human beings were political by nature. So while an individualistic understanding of human motivation may help to explain the activities of commodity traders and libertarian activists in present-day America, it is not the most helpful way to understand the early evolution of human politics.

Everything that modern biology and anthropology tell us about the state of nature suggests the opposite: there was *never* a period in human evolution when human beings existed as isolated individuals; the primate precursors of the human species had already developed extensive social, and indeed political, skills; and the human brain is hardwired with faculties that facilitate many forms of social cooperation. The state of nature might be characterized as a state of war, since violence was endemic, but the violence was not perpetrated by individuals so much as by tightly bonded social groups. Human beings do not enter into society and political life as a result of conscious, rational decision. Communal organization comes to them naturally, though the specific ways they cooperate are shaped by environment, ideas, and culture.

Indeed, the most basic forms of cooperation predate the emergence of human beings by millions of years. Biologists have identified two natural sources of cooperative behavior: kin selection and reciprocal altruism. With regard to the first, the name of the game in biological evolution is not the survival of a given organism but the survival of that organism's genes. This produces a regularity that was formulated by the biologist William Hamilton as the principle of inclusive fitness or kin selection, which holds that individuals of any sexually reproducing species will behave altruistically toward kin in proportion to the number of genes they share.[5] Parents and children, and full brothers and sisters, share 50 percent of their genes, and so will behave more altruistically toward each other than toward first cousins, who share only 25 percent. This behavior has been observed in species ranging from ground squirrels, which discriminate between full and half sisters in nesting behavior, to human beings, for whom nepotism is not only a socially but a biologically grounded reality.[6] The desire to pass resources on to kin is one of the most enduring constants in human politics.

The ability to cooperate with genetic strangers is referred to by biologists as reciprocal altruism, and in addition to kin selection is the second major biological source of social behavior found in many species of animals. Social cooperation depends on an individual's ability to solve what game theorists label repeated prisoner's dilemma games.[7] In these games, individuals potentially benefit by being able to work together, but they can often benefit more if they let other individuals do the cooperating and free-ride off of their efforts. In the 1980s, the political scientist Robert Axelrod staged a tournament of computer programs that mechanically implemented strategies for solving repeated prisoner's dilemma games. The winning strategy was called tit-for-tat, in which a player reciprocated cooperation if the other player had cooperated in an earlier game but refused to cooperate with a player who had failed to cooperate previously.[8] Axelrod demonstrated that a form of morality could evolve spontaneously as rational decision makers interact with one another over time, even though motivated in the first instance by nothing more than self-interest.

Reciprocal altruism occurs in a wide variety of species besides human beings.[9] Vampire bats and baboons have been observed feeding and protecting offspring within a colony not their own,[10] while in some cases like cleaner fish and the fish they clean, bonds of reciprocity exist between completely different species. The interactions between dogs and human beings suggests a similar set of evolved behaviors on the part of both species.[11]

CHIMPANZEE POLITICS AND ITS RELEVANCE TO
HUMAN POLITICAL DEVELOPMENT

Evolutionary biology provides the broad framework for understanding how the human species evolved from primate predecessors. We know that both human beings and modern chimpanzees are descended from a common chimplike ancestor, with humans branching off approximately five million years ago. The human and chimp genomes overlap by some 99 percent, matching each other more closely than any other pair of primates.[12] (That diverging 1 percent accounts for language, religion, abstract thought, and the like, not to speak of certain significant anatomical differences, however, so it's rather important!) We of course have no way of studying the behavior of the common chimp-human ancestor. But primatologists have spent a great deal of time observing the behavior of chimps and other primates both in their natural habitats and in zoos, behavior that reveals striking continuities with that of human beings.

The biological anthropologist Richard Wrangham in his book *Demonic Males* describes groups of male chimpanzees in the wild ranging beyond their territories to attack and kill chimps from neighboring communities.

These males cooperate with one another to stalk, surround, and then kill an isolated neighbor, and then go on to eliminate all of the other males in the colony. The females are then captured and incorporated into the raiding chimps' group. This is very similar to the kind of raiding done by human males in places like the New Guinea highlands, or among the Yanomamö Indians observed by the anthropologist Napoleon Chagnon. According to Wrangham, "Very few animals live in patrilineal, male-bonded communities wherein females routinely reduce the risks of inbreeding by moving to neighboring groups to mate. And only two animal species are known to do so with a system of intense, male-initiated territorial aggression, including lethal raiding into neighboring communities in search of vulnerable enemies to attack and kill."[13] These two species are chimps and human beings.

According to the archaeologist Steven LeBlanc, "Much of noncomplex society human warfare is similar to chimpanzee attacks. Massacres among humans at that social level are, in fact, rare occurrences, and victory by attrition is a viable strategy, as are buffer zones, surprise raids, taking captive females into the group, and mutilation of victims. The chimp and human behaviors are almost completely parallel."[14] The primary difference is that human beings are more deadly because they are able to use a wider and more lethal suite of weapons.

Chimpanzees defend their ranges like human groups do, but in other respects they are very different. Males and females do not come together in families to raise children; they create separate male and female hierarchies. The politics of dominance within those hierarchies, however, is reminiscent of politics within human groups. An alpha male in a chimp colony is not born to that status; like the Big Man in Melanesian society, he has to earn it by building coalitions of supporters. While physical size and strength matter, dominance is ultimately achieved through an ability to cooperate with others. The primatologist Frans de Waal, observing a colony of captive chimps in the Arnhem Zoo in the Netherlands, describes an older alpha male being displaced from his position by an alliance of two younger chimps. No sooner had one of the usurpers achieved alpha male status than he turned on his erstwhile ally and eventually murdered him.[15]

Once male or female chimps have achieved dominance within their respective hierarchies, they exercise what can only be described as *authority*—the ability to settle conflicts and set rules based on their status within the hierarchy. Chimps recognize authority through a submissive greeting, a series of short grunts followed by deep bows, the holding out of a hand to the superior, and kissing of feet.[16] De Waal describes a dominant female chimp named Mama, whom he compares to a grandmother in a Spanish or Chinese family. "When tensions in the group reach their peak, the combatants always turn to her—even the adult males. Many a time I have seen a major conflict between two males end up in her arms. Instead of resorting to physical violence at the climax of the confrontation, the rivals run to Mama, screaming loudly."[17]

Building coalitions in chimp society is not a straightforward process and requires something like an ability to judge character. Like humans, chimps are capable of deception and have to evaluate potential allies for their trustworthiness. Longtime observers of chimp behavior at Arnhem noted that each individual chimp had a distinct personality, and that some were more trustworthy than others. De Waal describes a female named Puist who was observed attacking fellows when least expected, or feigning a reconciliation, only to take advantage of the other chimp's relaxed guard. As a result of this behavior, low-ranking chimps learned to avoid her.[18]

Chimpanzees seem to understand that there are social rules they are expected to follow. They do not always do so, and the violation of group norms, or the defying of authority, is accompanied by what seem to be feelings of guilt or embarrassment. De Waal described an incident in which a graduate student named Yvonne had a young chimp named Choco staying with her:

> Choco was becoming more and more mischievous, and it was time she was checked. One day when Choco had taken the phone off the hook for the nth time, Yvonne gave her a good scolding while at the same time gripping her arm unusually tightly. The scolding seemed to have the desired effect on Choco, so Yvonne sat down on the sofa and started to read a book. She had forgotten the whole incident when suddenly Choco leapt on to her lap, threw her arms around Yvonne's neck and gave her a typical chimpanzee kiss (with open mouth) smack on the lips.[19]

De Waal notes the danger of human beings anthropomorphizing animal behavior, but the chimp's closest observers became completely convinced of the emotional undercurrents behind Choco's behavior.

The relevance of chimpanzee behavior to human political development is clear. Human beings and chimpanzees were both descended from an ancestral ape, and both modern chimpanzees and human beings, especially those living in hunter-gatherer or other relatively primitive societies, display similar forms of social behavior. For the account of the state of nature given by Hobbes, Locke, or Rousseau to be correct, we would have to postulate that in the course of evolving into modern humans, our ape ancestors somehow momentarily lost their social behaviors and emotions, and then evolved them a second time at a somewhat later stage in development. It is much more plausible to assume that human beings never existed as isolated individuals, and that social bonding into kin-based groups was part of their behavior from before the time that modern humans existed. Human sociability is not a historical or cultural acquisition, but something hardwired into human nature.

SPECIFICALLY HUMAN

What else is contained in that 1 percent of DNA that distinguishes human beings from their chimplike forebears? Our intelligence and cognitive abilities have always been regarded as key to our identity as a species. The label we have given the human species is *Homo sapiens*, animals of genus *Homo* who are "knowing." In the five million years since the *Homo* line broke off from the human-chimp ancestor, the size of the brain tripled, an extraordinarily fast development in evolutionary terms. The growing size of a woman's birth canal could barely keep up with the need to accommodate the enormous heads with which human infants are born. Where did this cognitive power come from?

At first glance, it may appear that cognitive abilities were required for human beings to adapt to and master their physical environments. Greater intelligence offers advantages with regard to hunting, gathering, making tools, surviving harsh climates, and the like. But this explanation is unsatisfying since many other species also hunt, gather, and use tools without having developed anything like a human being's cognitive abilities.

Many evolutionary biologists have speculated that the human brain grew as rapidly as it did for a different reason: to be able to cooperate and compete with other human beings. The psychologist Nicolas Humphrey and the biologist Richard Alexander have separately suggested that human beings in effect entered into an arms race with one another, the winners of which were those groups that could create more complex forms of social organization based on new cognitive abilities to interpret each other's behavior.[20]

Game theory, as indicated earlier, suggests that individuals who interact with one another repeatedly tend to gravitate toward cooperation with those who have shown themselves to be honest and reliable, and shun those who have behaved opportunistically. But to do this effectively, they have to be able to remember each other's past behavior and to anticipate likely future behavior based on an interpretation of other people's motives. This isn't so easy to accomplish, since it is the appearance of honesty and not honesty itself that is the marker of a potential collaborator. That is, I will agree to work with you if you seem to be honest based on experience. But if you have deliberately built up a fund of trust in the past, you can put yourself in a position to take even greater advantage of me in the future. So while self-interest propels individuals to cooperate in social groups, it also creates incentives for cheating, deceiving, and other forms of behavior that undermine social solidarity.

Chimpanzees can achieve a band level of social organization of a few dozen individuals because they possess some of the cognitive skills required to solve basic repeated prisoner's dilemma games. For example, Puist in the Arnhem Zoo was shunned by other chimps because of her history of unreliable behavior, while Mama achieved leadership status due to her reputation for impartiality in mediating disputes. Chimps thus have sufficient memory and communications skills to interpret and predict each other's likely behavior, out of which evolve leadership and cooperation.

But chimps are unable to move to higher levels of social organization because they do not have language. The emergence of language among early human beings opened up huge new opportunities for both improved cooperation and cognitive development in an intimately linked fashion. Having language means that knowledge of who was honest and who deceitful no longer depends on direct experience but can be passed on to others as social knowledge. But language can also be the medium for lying and deceit. Any social group that evolved a slightly better cognitive capacity to use and interpret language, and therefore to detect lying, achieved advantages over its competitors. The evolutionary psychologist Geoffrey Miller has argued that it was the specific cognitive demands of courtship that gave special impetus to the development of the neocortex, since the differing reproductive strategies of men and women create strong incentives for deceit and the detection of qualities signaling reproductive fitness.

Male reproductive strategy maximizes success by seeking out as many sexual partners as possible, while the female reproductive strategy involves harboring the resources of the fittest male for her offspring. Since these strategies work at cross-purposes, the argument goes, there is a strong evolutionary incentive to develop capacities for outwitting the partner, in which language plays a large role.[21] Another evolutionary psychologist, Steven Pinker, argues that language, sociability, and mastery of the environment all reinforced one another and created evolutionary pressures for further development.[22] This then explains the need for increased brain size, since a very large portion of the neocortex, which is the part of the brain possessed by behaviorally modern humans but not by chimps or archaic humans, is devoted to language.[23]

The development of language not only permits the short-term coordination of action but also opens up the possibility of *abstraction* and *theory*, critical cognitive faculties that are unique to human beings. Words can refer to concrete objects as well as to abstract classes of objects (dogs, trees) and to abstractions that refer to invisible forces (Zeus, gravity). Putting the two together makes possible mental models—that is, general statements about causation ("it gets warm because the sun shines"; "society forces girls into stereotyped gender roles"). All human beings engage in the construction of abstract mental models; our ability to theorize in this fashion gives us huge survival advantages. Despite the warnings of philosophers like David Hume and countless professors in first-year statistics classes that correlation does not imply causation, human beings are constantly observing correlations between events in the world around them and inferring causation from them. By not stepping on the snake or eating the root that killed your cousin last week, you avoid being subject to the same fate, and you can quickly communicate that rule to your offspring.

The ability to create mental models and to attribute causality to invisible abstractions is in turn the basis for the emergence of religion. Religion—or the belief in an invisible, supernatural order—exists in all human societies. The paleo-anthropologists and archaeologists who have tried to reconstruct the lineage of early human beings unfortunately have relatively little to say about their spiritual life, since all they have to go on is the material record of fossils and campsites. But we know of no historical primitive societies without religion and have archaeological clues that suggest that Neanderthals and other protohuman groups may have had religious beliefs.[24]

Some people today argue that religion is primarily a source of violence, conflict, and social discord.[25] Historically, however, religion has played the opposite role: it is a source of social cohesion that permits human beings to cooperate far more widely and securely than they would if they were the simple rational and self-interested agents posited by the economists. Those agents playing repeated prisoner's dilemma games with one another should be able to arrive at some degree of social cooperation, as we have seen. But as the economist Mancur Olson has shown, collective action begins to break down as the size of the cooperating group increases. In large groups, it becomes harder and harder to monitor the individual contributions of members; free riding and other forms of opportunistic behavior become much more common.[26]

Religion solves this collective action problem by presenting rewards and punishments that greatly reinforce the gains from cooperation in the here and now. If I believe that my tribe's chief is just another fellow like me following his own self-interests, I may or may not decide to obey his authority. But if I believe that the chief can command the spirits of dead ancestors to reward or punish me, I will be much more likely to respect his word. My sense of shame is potentially much greater if I believe I am being observed by a dead ancestor who might see into my real motives better than a live kinsman. Contrary to the views of both religious believers and secularists, it is extremely difficult to prove or falsify any given religious belief. Even if I am skeptical that the chief is really in touch with dead ancestors, I may not want to take the risk that he really is. Pascal's wager that one should believe in God because he may actually exist has been operative throughout human history, though in its earlier stages the number of skeptics was probably small.[27]

Religion's functional role in strengthening norms and buttressing communities has long been recognized.[28] Tit-for-tat, or returning favors for favors and harms for harms, is not just the rational outcome of repeated interaction but also the foundation of biblical morality and an almost universal moral rule among human societies. The Golden Rule mandating that you treat others as you want them to treat you is simply a variation on tit-for-tat, one that emphasizes the benefit rather than the harm side. (The Christian principle of returning a favor for a harm in this respect is highly unusual and, one might note, more often than not unimplemented in Christian societies. No society I know of approves returning a harm for a favor as a general moral rule within the group.)

Indeed, some evolutionary psychologists have argued that the survival benefits conferred by enhanced social cohesion is the reason that a propensity for religious belief seems to be hardwired into the human brain.[29] Religion is not the only way that ideas can reinforce group solidarity—today we have nationalism and secular ideologies like Marxism as well—but in early societies it played a critical role in making possible more complex forms of social organization. It is hard to see how human beings could have evolved beyond small band-level societies without it.[30]

From a cognitive point of view, any given religious belief can be described as a type of mental model of reality, in which causality is attributed to invisible forces that exist in a metaphysical realm beyond the phenomenal world of everyday experience. This generates theories about how to manipulate the world: for example, a drought is caused by the anger of the gods; it can be appeased by spilling the blood of babies into the furrows of the earth. This then leads to ritual, the repetitive performance of acts linked to the supernatural order, by which human societies hope to gain agency over their environment.

Ritual in turn helps to delineate communities, marking their boundaries and distinguishing them from one another. Because of its role in building social solidarity, ritual can become disconnected from the cognitive theory that led to its creation, as in the Christmas celebrations that contemporary secular Europeans continue to observe. The ritual itself and the beliefs supporting it are invested with tremendous intrinsic value. They no longer represent a mental model or theory that can be discarded when a better one comes along, but become ends of action in themselves.

THE BEAST WITH RED CHEEKS

Mental models and norms that help human beings cooperate and thus survive may be generated rationally, as the economists assert. But religious beliefs are never held by their adherents to be simple theories that can be discarded if proved wrong; they are held to be unconditionally true, and there are usually heavy social and psychological penalties attached to asserting their falsehood. One of the great cognitive advances offered by modern natural science is to give us a systematic empirical means for testing theories, which allows us to manipulate our environment more successfully (for example, by using irrigation systems rather than human sacrifice to promote agricultural productivity). This then raises the question of why human beings saddle themselves with theoretical constructs that are so rigid and hard to change.

A proximate answer to this question is that rule following for human beings is not primarily a rational process but one that is grounded in the emotions. The human brain has developed certain emotional responses that amount to autopilot mechanisms promoting social behavior. When a nursing mother sees an infant, she lactates, not because she consciously thinks to herself that her child needs food, but because the sight of her child involuntarily triggers her brain to order the production of certain hormones that in turn trigger lactation. Gratitude for a kindness done by a stranger, and anger at a gratuitous harm, are neither calculated responses nor emotions that are necessarily learned (though they can be reinforced or suppressed through practice). Similarly, when someone shows us disrespect by belittling us in front of our friends, or making comments about our mother's or sister's virtue, we don't launch into a mental calculation about the accuracy of the comment or how we need to defend our reputation for the sake of future transactions. We just get angry and try to slug the person who disrespected us. These actions—altruism toward genetic kin, defense of one's reputation—can be explained in terms of rational self-interest, but they are lived as emotional states. In average circumstances, the emotional reaction produces the rationally correct response, which is why the evolutionary process has programmed human beings to react in this fashion. But since the action is more often the product of the emotions than calculation, we often get things wrong and slug someone even though he's bigger and likely to retaliate.

These emotional responses make human beings conformist, norm-following animals. While the specific content of norms is culturally determined ("don't eat pork"; "respect your ancestors"; "don't light up a cigarette at a dinner party"), the faculties for norm following are genetically based, just as languages vary across cultures while being rooted in a universal human faculty for language. All human beings, for example, feel the emotion of embarrassment when they are seen violating a norm or rule followed by their peers. Embarrassment is clearly not a learned behavior, since children are often far more easily embarrassed than their parents by small failures to follow the rules. Human beings are able to put themselves in the position of other people and to observe their own behavior through the eyes of others. A child who is unable to see himself or herself in this fashion is today diagnosed as having the pathological condition of autism.

Norm following is embedded in human nature via the specific emotions of anger, shame, guilt, and pride. We feel anger when a norm is violated, such as when a stranger goes out of his way to disparage us, or when a religious ritual shared by our group is mocked or neglected. We feel shame when we ourselves fail to live up to the norm, and we feel pride when we have the approbation of the community for achieving a collectively valued goal. Human beings can invest so much emotion in following a norm that it becomes irrational with respect to self-interest, as when a gang member takes revenge on a member of another gang for an insult (real or perceived), knowing full well that this will lead to an escalating cycle of violence.

Human beings also invest emotion in metanorms, norms about how to properly formulate and enforce norms, and can display what the biologist Robert Trivers labels "moralistic aggression" when proper metanorms are not carried out.[31] They want to see that "justice is done," even when they have no direct self-interest in the outcome of a particular case. This explains the extraordinary popularity of crime shows and courtroom dramas on television, and the often obsessive attention with which people follow certain high-profile scandals or crimes.

The grounding of normative behavior in the emotions promotes social cooperation and has clearly conferred survival benefits as the human species evolved into its present form. Economists argue that blindly following rules can be economically rational, since calculating optimal outcomes in every situation is often costly and counterproductive. If we had to constantly negotiate new rules with our fellow human beings at every turn, we would be paralyzed and unable to achieve routine collective action. The fact that we become attached to certain rules not as means to short-term goals but as ends in themselves greatly enhances the stability of social life. Religion simply reinforces that stability and widens the circle of potential cooperators.

The problem this poses for politics, however, is that rules that have a clear utility when applied over a large number of cases may not be useful under specific short-run circumstances and frequently become dysfunctional when the conditions that gave rise to them change. Institutional rules are "sticky" and resistant to change, which is one of the chief sources of political decay.

THE STRUGGLE FOR RECOGNITION

When norms are invested with intrinsic meaning, they become objects of what the philosopher Georg W. F. Hegel called the "struggle for recognition."[32] The desire for recognition is fundamentally different from the desire for material resources that underlies economic behavior. Recognition is not a good that can be consumed. Rather, it is an intersubjective state of mind by which one human being acknowledges the worth or status of another human being, or of that human being's gods, customs, and beliefs. I may believe in my own worth as a pianist or a painter but feel greater satisfaction when that sense is validated through a prize or the sale of a painting. Since human beings organize themselves into social hierarchies, recognition is usually of relative rather than absolute worth. This makes the struggle for recognition fundamentally different from struggles over economic exchange, since the conflict is zero sum rather than positive sum. That is, one person's recognition can come only at the expense of the dignity of someone else; status can only be relative. In contests over status, there are no win-win situations as in trade.[33]

The desire for recognition has biological roots. Chimps and other primates compete for alpha male or alpha female status within their small bands. The hierarchical organization of a troop of chimps confers reproductive advantages on its members, since it controls internal violence within the group and permits the group to cooperate against other groups. The individual who achieves alpha male status also receives greater access to sexual partners and therefore more reproductive success. Status-seeking behavior has become genetically coded for a wide variety of animals, including humans, and is associated with biochemical changes in the brains of individuals who compete for status. When a monkey or a human being succeeds in achieving high status, levels of serotonin, a critical neurotransmitter, are elevated.[34]

But human recognition differs from primate recognition because of the greater complexity of human cognition. An alpha male chimp seeks recognition only for himself; a human being can seek recognition for an abstraction, like a god, a flag, or a holy place. A great deal of contemporary politics revolves around demands for recognition, particularly on the part of groups that have historical reasons for believing their worth has not been adequately acknowledged: racial minorities, women, gays, indigenous peoples, and the like. While these demands may have an economic component, like equal pay for equal work, economic resources are often seen more as markers of dignity rather than ends in themselves.[35]

Today we label demands for recognition "identity politics." This is a modern phenomenon that arises primarily in fluid, pluralistic societies where people are able to take on multiple identities.[36] But even before the rise of the modern world, recognition was a crucial driver of collective behavior. People struggled not just for individual gain but also on behalf of communities that wanted to have their way of life—their customs and gods and traditions—respected by others. Sometimes this took the form of dominion over other people, but in many cases it meant the opposite. A fundamental meaning of human freedom is the ability of a people to rule themselves, that is, to avoid subordination to people who are less worthy. It is this freedom that has been celebrated by the Jews every Passover since their release from captivity in Egypt more than three thousand years ago.

At the base of the phenomenon of recognition are judgments about the intrinsic worth of other human beings, or about the norms, ideas, and rules that human beings create. Coerced recognition isn't meaningful; the admiration of a free individual is far more satisfying than the obeisance of a slave. Political leadership emerges initially because members of a community admire a particular individual who demonstrates great physical prowess, courage, wisdom, or the ability to adjudicate disputes fairly. If politics is a struggle over leadership, it is also a story about followership and the willingness of the great mass of human beings to accord leaders higher status than themselves and subordinate themselves to them. In a cohesive and therefore successful community, this subordination is voluntary and based on belief in the leader's right to rule.

As political systems develop, recognition is transferred from individuals to institutions—that is, to rules or patterns of behavior that persist over time, like the British monarchy or the U.S. Constitution. But in either case, political order is based on *legitimacy* and the *authority* that arises from legitimate domination. Legitimacy means that the people who make up the society recognize the fundamental justice of the system as a whole and are willing to abide by its rules. In contemporary societies, we believe that legitimacy is conferred by democratic elections and respect for the rule of law. But democracy is hardly the only form of government that has been regarded as legitimate historically.

Political power is ultimately based on social cohesion. Cohesion may arise out of calculations of self-interest, but simple self-interest is frequently not enough to induce followers to sacrifice and die on behalf of their communities. Political power is the product not just of the resources and numbers of citizens that a society can command but also the degree to which the legitimacy of leaders and institutions is recognized.

FOUNDATIONS OF POLITICAL DEVELOPMENT

We now have in place all of the important natural building blocks out of which we can construct a theory of political development. Human beings are rational, self-interested creatures, and will learn to cooperate out of pure self-interest as economists assert. But beyond this, human nature provides certain structured paths toward sociability that give human politics its particular character. These include:

- Inclusive fitness, kin selection, and reciprocal altruism are default modes of sociability. All human beings gravitate toward the favoring of kin and friends with whom they have exchanged favors unless strongly incentivized to do otherwise.
- Human beings have a capacity for abstraction and theory that generates mental models of causality, and a further tendency to posit causation based on invisible or transcendental forces. This is the basis of religious belief, which acts as a critical source of social cohesion.
- Humans also have a proclivity for norm following that is grounded in the emotions rather than in reason, and consequently a tendency to invest mental models and the rules that flow from them with intrinsic worth.
- Human beings desire intersubjective recognition, either of their own worth, or of the worth of their gods, laws, customs, and ways of life. Recognition when granted becomes the basis of legitimacy, and legitimacy then permits the exercise of political authority.

These natural characteristics are the basis for the evolution of increasingly complex forms of social organization. Inclusive fitness and reciprocal altruism are not unique to human beings but shared among many animal species, and they explain the forms of cooperation evident among small groups of (mainly) genetic kin. In its early stages, human political organization is similar to the band-level society observed in higher primates like chimpanzees. This may be regarded as a default form of social organization. The tendency to favor family and friends can be overridden by new rules and incentives that mandate, for example, hiring a qualified individual rather than a family member. But the higher-level institutions are in some sense quite unnatural, and when they break down, humans revert to the earlier form of sociability. This is the basis for what I label patrimonialism.

The human capacity for abstract theorizing soon produces a host of new rules for mastering the environment and regulating social behavior that go well beyond anything that exists among chimpanzees. In particular, ideas concerning dead ancestors, spirits, gods, and other invisible forces create new rules and powerful incentives for following them. Religious ideas of various sorts enormously increase the scale on which human societies can be organized and constantly generate new forms of social mobilization.

The highly developed suite of emotions related to norm following ensure, however, that no mental model of how the world works is ever regarded as a simple theory that can be discarded when it no longer conforms to observed reality. (Even in the domain of modern natural science, where there are clear rules for hypothesis testing, scientists develop emotional attachments to theories and resist empirical evidence indicating that their pet theories are wrong.) The tendency to invest mental models and theories with intrinsic worth promotes social stability and allows societies to bulk up enormously in size. But it also means that societies are highly conservative and will fiercely resist challenges to their dominant ideas. This is most obvious in the case of religious ideas, but secular rules also tend to be invested with great emotion under the headings of tradition, ritual, and custom.

The conservatism of societies with regard to rules is then a source of political decay. Rules or institutions created in response to one set of environmental circumstances become dysfunctional under later conditions, but they cannot be changed due to people's heavy emotional investments in them. This means that social change is often not linear—that is, a process of constant small adjustments to shifting conditions—but rather follows a pattern of prolonged stasis followed by catastrophic change.

This in turn explains why violence has been so central to the process of political development. As Hobbes points out, the fear of violent death is a very different emotion from the desire for gain or economic motivation. It is extremely difficult to put a price tag on one's own life, or the life of a loved one, which is why fear and insecurity typically motivate people to do things that mere material self-interest does not. Politics emerges as a mechanism for controlling violence, yet violence constantly remains as a background condition for certain types of political change. Societies can get stuck in a dysfunctional institutional equilibrium, in which existing stakeholders can veto necessary institutional change. Sometimes violence or the threat of violence is necessary to break out of the equilibrium.

Finally, the desire for recognition ensures that politics will never be reducible to simple economic self-interest. Human beings make constant judgments about the intrinsic value, worth, or dignity of other people or institutions, and they organize themselves into hierarchies based on those valuations. Political power ultimately rests upon recognition—the degree to which a leader or institution is regarded as legitimate and can command the respect of a group of followers. People may follow out of self-interest, but the most powerful political organizations are those that legitimate themselves on the basis of a broader idea.

Biology gives us the building blocks of political development. Human nature is largely constant across different societies. The huge variance in political forms that we see both at the present time and over the course of history is in the first instance the product of variance in the physical environments that human beings came to inhabit. As societies ramify and fill different environmental niches across the globe, they develop distinctive norms and ideas in a process known as specific evolution. Groups of humans also interact with each other, and this interaction is as much a driver of change as is the physical environment.

But widely separated human societies have come up with strikingly similar solutions to the problem of political order. Virtually every society was at one time organized on the basis of kinship, whose rules increased steadily in complexity. Most societies then went on to develop states and impersonal forms of administration. Agrarian societies from China and the Middle East to Europe and India all developed centralized monarchies and increasingly bureaucratized forms of government. Societies enjoying little cultural contact nonetheless evolved similar institutions, down to the salt monopolies created by governments in China, Europe, and South Asia. In more recent times, democratic accountability and popular sovereignty have become widespread normative ideals, if unevenly implemented. Different societies reached these converging outcomes by a wide variety of pathways, but the fact of convergence suggests an underlying biological similarity among human groups.

EVOLUTION AND MIGRATION

Paleoanthropologists have been able to trace the descent of man from primate forebears to what are labeled "behaviorally modern human beings," while population geneticists have done a remarkable job tracing the movements of human populations as they migrated through the different regions of the planet. There is broad agreement that the transition from ape to human being took place in Africa, but the exit out of Africa that led to the populating of the rest of the world happened in two separate waves. What are labeled archaic human beings—species like *Homo erectus* and *Homo ergaster*—left that continent as much as 1.6–2 million years ago and found their way to northern Asia. An *ergaster* descendant, *Homo heidelbergensis*, may have left Africa and reached Europe around 300,000–400,000 years ago, and was the progenitor of later species like the famous Neanderthals who inhabited much of Europe.[37]

Anatomically modern human beings—that is, humans who had the same rough size and physical characteristics as contemporary humans—appeared on the scene approximately two hundred thousand years ago. It was only about fifty thousand years ago, however, that behaviorally modern humans emerged—human beings who had the ability to communicate using language and who therefore could begin to evolve much more complex forms of social organization.

Virtually all modern human beings outside of Africa are believed, by one current theory, to be descended from a single small group of behaviorally modern humans, perhaps as few in number as 150 individuals, who left Africa and crossed what is now the Bab al-Mandab into the Arabian peninsula approximately fifty thousand years ago. Because of recent advances in population genetics, paleoanthropologists can trace many of these developments in the absence of written records. The human genetic endowment includes both the Y chromosome and mitochondrial DNA that contain clues to the history of the species. Only men have a Y chromosome. Unlike the other parts of human DNA, which are randomly recombined from the mother and father's chromosomes and thus change from generation to generation, the Y chromosome is handed down from fathers to sons largely intact. Mitochondrial DNA, by contrast, is the vestige of bacteria that were trapped within human cells, which were put to work millions of years ago providing, among other things, energy to power the cell's activities. Mitochondria have their own DNA, which in a manner comparable to the Y chromosome is passed down largely intact from mothers to daughters each generation without being recombined. Both Y chromosomes and mitochondrial DNA tend to accumulate random mutations that are then inherited by subsequent generations of sons or daughters. By counting these mutations and seeing which are prior to others, population geneticists can reconstruct the lineage of different human groups around the planet.

This is how it is postulated that all human populations outside of Africa were descended from a single small group of individuals, since all non-African populations from China to New Guinea to Europe to South America can be traced back to the same male and female lineages. (There is a greater variety of lineages in Africa itself, since the rest of the world was seeded from one of several existing there at the time.) From the Arabian peninsula these modern humans branched out. One group followed the coastline around Arabia and India, and crossed over into the now nonexistent continents of Sunda (linking the islands of what is now Southeast Asia) and Sahul (which included New Guinea and Australia). Their movement was greatly facilitated by the glaciation that occurred then, which locked up a large part of the earth's water in ice caps and glaciers, and lowered sea levels hundreds of feet below what they are today. We know from genetic dating that the Melanesian and Austronesian populations currently inhabiting Papua New Guinea and Australia have been there for nearly forty-six thousand years, meaning that they reached this remote part of the world in a remarkably short time after the original group's departure from Africa.

Other human beings left Arabia for the northwest and northeast. Those in the former group moved through the Near East and Central Asia, and eventually reached Europe, where they encountered the descendants of the archaic human beings like the Neanderthals who had left Africa in the previous exodus. The group that went northeast populated China and other parts of northeast Asia, walked across the land bridge then connecting Siberia and North America, and migrated thence down the Americas, where some reached the southern part of Chile by approximately 12,000 B.C.[38]

The biblical story of the Tower of Babel, in which God scatters a unified human race and makes them speak different languages, is thus metaphorically true. As little bands of human beings migrated and adapted to different environments, they began their exit out of the state of nature by developing new social institutions. As we will see in the following chapters, the first complex forms of social organization continued to be based on kinship, but they could emerge only with the assistance provided by religious ideas.

3

THE TYRANNY OF COUSINS

Disputes over the fact and nature of human social evolution; family- or band-level social organization, and the transition to tribalism; an introduction to lineages, agnation, and other basic anthropological concepts

Since Rousseau's *Discourse on the Origins of Inequality* (1754), there has been a vast amount of theorizing about the origins of early human institutions. This was driven first in the late nineteenth century by the accumulation of empirical knowledge about existing primitive societies by founders of the new discipline of anthropology, such as Lewis Henry Morgan and Edward Tylor.[1] Morgan did field research on the dwindling populations of indigenous North American peoples and developed an elaborate classificatory system for describing their forms of kinship, a system he broadened to apply to European prehistory as well. In his book *Ancient Society*, he devised an evolutionary scheme that divided human history into three stages—savagery, barbarism, and civilization—through which, he argued, all human societies passed.

Morgan was read by Karl Marx's collaborator Friedrich Engels, who used the American anthropologist's ethnographic studies to develop a theory of the origins of private property and the family that later became gospel in the Communist world.[2] Together, Marx and Engels propagated the most famous developmental theory of modern times: they posited the existence of a series of evolutionary stages—primitive communism, feudalism, bourgeois society, and true communism—all driven by an underlying conflict between social classes. The misconceptions and oversimplifications of the Marxist development model led generations of later scholars down blind alleys, looking for an "Asiatic mode of production" or trying to find "feudalism" in India.

The second important impetus to theorizing about early political development was the publication of Charles Darwin's *On the Origin of Species* in 1859 and the elaboration of his theory of natural selection. It made logical sense to apply the principles of biological evolution to social evolution, which theorists like Herbert Spencer did at the beginning of the twentieth century.[3] Spencer saw human societies as engaging in a competition for survival, in which superior ones came to dominate their inferiors. Non-European societies were ones whose development was stunted or arrested. Indeed, development theory in the immediate post-Darwin period succeeded in justifying the existing colonial world order, with northern Europeans occupying a place at the top of a global hierarchy that stretched through various shades of yellow and brown down to black Africans at the bottom.[4]

The judgmental and racist character of evolutionary theorizing led to a counterrevolution in the 1920s whose impact is still felt in anthropology and cultural studies departments around the world. The great anthropologist Franz Boas argued that human behavior was not rooted in biology but was socially constructed to the core. In one famous study, he used empirical data from an analysis of immigrant head sizes to prove that much of what social Darwinists attributed to race was actually the product of environment and culture. Boas made the case that the study of early societies needed to be purged of all value judgments about higher and lower forms of social organization. Methodologically, ethnographers should immerse themselves in the societies they examined, evaluating their internal logic and divesting themselves of prejudices based on their own cultural backgrounds. Through the practice of what Clifford Geertz later labeled "thick description," different societies could only be described, not compared to one another or ranked in any way.[5] Boas's students Alfred Kroeber, Margaret Mead, and Ruth Benedict then went on to reshape the discipline of cultural anthropology in a nonjudgmental, relativistic, and decidedly non-evolutionary direction.

Early evolutionary theories, including those of Marx and Engels, had other problems. They often posited a relatively linear and rigid progression of social forms, in which one stage of development necessarily preceded the one following, and in which one factor (like Marx's "mode of production") determined the characteristics of the stage as a whole. With accumulating knowledge of actual primitive societies, it became increasingly clear that the evolution of political complexity was not linear: a given stage of development often contained characteristics of earlier ones, and there were multiple dynamic mechanisms moving societies from one stage to another. In fact, as we will see in later chapters, an early stage of development is never fully superseded by later ones. China made a transition from kinship-based forms of organization to state-level organization more than three thousand years ago, and yet complex kinship organizations still characterize parts of Chinese society today.

Human societies are so diverse that it is very difficult to make truly universal generalizations from the comparative study of cultures. Anthropologists delight in discovering obscure societies that violate purportedly general laws of social development. This does not mean, however, that regularities and similarities in evolutionary forms do not exist across different societies.

STAGES OF PREHISTORY

Coming against the backdrop of nineteenth-century social Darwinism, Boasian cultural relativism was an understandable development. But it has left an enduring legacy of political correctness in the field of comparative anthropology. Strict cultural relativism is at odds with evolutionary theory, since the latter necessitates identifying different levels of social organization and the reasons why one level gets superseded by another. The obvious reality is that human societies evolve over time. The two basic components of biological evolution—variation and selection—apply to human societies as well. Even if we scrupulously avoid value judgments about later civilizations being "higher" than earlier ones, they clearly become more complex, richer, and more powerful. Those that succeed in adapting usually win out over ones that don't, just as individual organisms do. Our continuing use of terms like "developing" or "development" (as in "developing countries" or the "US Agency for International Development") is testimony to the widespread view that existing rich countries are the product of a prior evolution of socioeconomic forms, and that poor countries would participate in this process if they could. Human political institutions are transmitted across time culturally rather than genetically and are subject to a great deal more intentional design than biological evolution. But there is an obvious analogy between Darwin's principle of natural selection and competitive human social evolution.

This recognition led to a revival of evolutionary theorizing at midcentury by anthropologists such as Leslie White,[6] Julian Steward,[7] Elman Service,[8] Morton Fried,[9] and Marshall Sahlins,[10] who argued that there was clear progression over time in the complexity, scale, and energy use of societies.[11] According to Sahlins and Service, the great diversity of social forms was the result of what they labeled "specific evolution" as human groups adapted to the myriad ecological niches that they came to occupy. But it was clear that a converging "general evolution" was also at work, as disparate societies came up with similar solutions to common problems of social organization.[12]

The methodological problem anthropologists face is that no one has ever directly observed the evolution of human societies from the earliest forms of society into more complex tribal- or state-level ones. All they can do is assume that existing hunter-gatherer or tribal societies are instances of earlier levels of development, observe their behavior, and speculate about the forces that would have caused one form of organization, like a tribe, to evolve into a different one, like a state. It is perhaps for this reason that theorizing about early social evolution has migrated from anthropology to archaeology. Unlike anthropologists, archaeologists can trace dynamic changes in societies over hundreds or thousands of years through the material record left behind by different civilizations. By investigating, for example, changes in the residential patterns and dietary habits of Pueblo Indians, they can reconstruct the way that warfare and environmental stress shaped the nature of social organization. The weakness of their approach, relative to anthropologists, is obviously that they lack the contextual detail available in an ethnographic study. Reliance on the archaeological record also leads to a bias toward materialist explanations for change, since much of the spiritual and cognitive world of prehistoric civilizations is effectively lost.[13]

Since the days of Tylor, Morgan, and Engels, systems for classifying the evolutionary stages of social development have themselves evolved. Terms with heavy moral implications like "savagery" and "barbarism" have been shunned in favor of more neutrally descriptive ones like Paleolithic, Neolithic, Bronze Age, Iron Age, etc., which refer to the dominant form of technology. A parallel system refers to the chief mode of production, as in the distinctions among hunter-gatherer, agricultural, and industrial societies. Evolutionary anthropologists have designated stages based on the form of social or political organization, which I will use here since this is my subject matter. Elman Service developed a four-level taxonomy involving bands, tribes, chiefdoms, and states.[14] For bands and tribes, social organization is based on kinship, and these societies are relatively egalitarian. Chiefdoms and states, by contrast, are organized hierarchically and exert authority on a territorial rather than a kinship basis.

FAMILY- AND BAND-LEVEL ORGANIZATION

Many believe that the primordial form of human social organization was tribal. This view extends back to the nineteenth century, when early comparative anthropologists like Numa Denis Fustel de Coulanges and Sir Henry Maine argued that early social life had to be understood in terms of complex kinship groups.[15] Tribal organization did not arise, however, until the emergence of settled societies and the development of agriculture around nine thousand years ago. The hunter-gatherer societies that preceded agricultural ones were organized for tens of thousands of years in a much simpler fashion, based on small groups of nomadic families comparable in scale to primate bands. Such societies still exist in marginal environments, and they include the Eskimos, the Bushmen of the Kalahari Desert, and Australian Aborigines.[16] (There are some exceptions to this, like the indigenous tribes of the U.S. Pacific Northwest, who were hunter-gatherers but lived in an area of extraordinary resource abundance that could support complex social organization.)

Rousseau pointed out that the origin of political inequality lay in the development of agriculture, and in this he was largely correct. Since band-level societies are preagricultural, there is no private property in any modern sense. Like chimp bands, hunter-gatherers inhabit a territorial range that they guard and occasionally fight over. But they have a lesser incentive than agriculturalists to mark out a piece of land and say "this is mine." If their territory is invaded by another group, or if it is infiltrated by dangerous predators, band-level societies may have the option of simply moving somewhere else due to low population densities. They also tend to have fewer investments in cleared land, houses, and the like.[17]

Within a band-level local group, there is nothing resembling modern

economic exchange and, indeed, nothing resembling modern individualism. There was no state to tyrannize over people at this stage of political
development; rather, human beings experienced what the social anthropologist Ernest Gellner has labeled the "tyranny of cousins."[18] That is, your
social world was limited to the circles of relatives surrounding you, who
determined what you did, whom you married, how you worshipped, and
just about everything else in life. Both hunting and gathering are done on
a group basis by families or groups of families. Hunting in particular leads
to sharing, since there is no technology for storing meat, and hunted animals must be consumed immediately. There is considerable speculation on
the part of evolutionary psychologists that the almost universal contemporary practice of meal sharing (Christmas, Thanksgiving, Passover) is derived from the millennia-long practice of sharing the proceeds of hunts.[19]
Many of the moral rules in this type of society are not directed at individuals who steal other people's property but rather against those who refuse to
share food and other necessities. Under conditions of perpetual scarcity,
the failure to share can often affect the group's prospects for survival.

Band-level societies are highly egalitarian. The major social distinctions are based on age and sex; in hunter-gatherer societies, the men hunt
and the women gather, and there is a natural division of labor in reproductive matters. But within the band, there is relatively little differentiation
between families, no permanent leadership, and no hierarchy. Leadership
is vested in individuals based on qualities like strength, intelligence, and
trustworthiness, but it tends to migrate from one individual to another.
Apart from parents and their children, opportunities for coercion are very
limited. In the words of Fried,

> It is difficult, in ethnographies of simple egalitarian societies, to find cases
> in which one individual tells one or more others, "Do this!" or some com-
> mand equivalent. The literature is replete with examples of individuals
> saying the equivalent of "If this is done, it will be good," possibly or pos-
> sibly not followed by somebody else doing it . . . Since the leader is unable
> to compel any of the others to carry out his wish, we speak of his role in
> terms of authority rather than power.[20]

In this type of society, leaders emerge based on group consensus; they have
no right to their office and cannot hand it down to their children. Since

there is no centralized source of coercion, there can obviously be no law in the modern sense of third-party enforcement of rules.[21]

Band-level societies are built around nuclear families and are typically what anthropologists label exogamous and patrilocal. Women marry outside of their immediate social group and move to their husband's place of residence. This practice encourages movement and contact with other groups, increasing genetic diversity and setting up the conditions for the emergence of something like intergroup trade. Exogamy also plays a role in mitigating conflict: disputes over resources or territory between groups can be smoothed over through the exchange of women, just as European monarchs made strategic marriage alliances for political purposes.[22] The composition of groups tends to be more fluid than in later tribal societies: "The food supply in any locality, whether it be a harvest of pinyon nuts or wild grass seeds among the Pauite, or the seal population at winter and spring hunting grounds, and the caribou herd migrating through an inland valley among the Central Eskimos, is so unpredictable or so widely scattered that the tendency for particular kinfolk in any generation to form coherent exclusive groups is frustrated by the opportunism enforced on the individual and the household by the ecological situation."[23]

FROM BAND TO TRIBE

The transition from band-level societies to tribal societies was made possible by the development of agriculture. Agriculture was invented in widely separated parts of the world, including Mesopotamia, China, Oceania, and Mesoamerica nine to ten thousand years ago, often in fertile alluvial river basins. The domestication of wild grasses and seeds took place gradually and was accompanied by large increases in population. While it might seem logical that new food technologies drove higher population densities, Ester Boserup has argued that the causality went the other way around.[24] Either way, the social impact was enormous. Depending on climatic conditions, hunter-gatherer societies have a population density from 0.1 to 1 person per square kilometer, while the invention of agriculture permits densities to rise to 40–60 per square kilometer.[25] Human beings were now in contact with one another on a much broader scale, and this required a very different form of social organization.

The terms "tribes," "clans," "kindreds," and "lineages" are all used to describe the next stage of social organization above the band. These terms are often used with considerable imprecision, even by anthropologists whose bread and butter it is to study them. Their common characteristic is that they are first, segmentary, and second, based on a principle of common descent.

The sociologist Émile Durkheim used the term "segmentary" to refer to societies based on the replication of identical small-scale social units, much like the segments in an earthworm. Such a society could grow by adding segments, but it had no overall centralized political structure, and was not subject to a modern division of labor and what he characterized as "organic" solidarity. In a developed society, no one is self-sufficient; everyone depends on a wide range of other people throughout the society. Most people in developed societies do not know how to grow their own food, or repair their cars, or fabricate their own cell phones. In a segmentary society, by contrast, each "segment" is a self-sufficient unit, able to feed, clothe, and defend itself, and thus is characterized by what Durkheim called "mechanical" solidarity.[26] The segments can come together for common purposes, like self-defense, but are otherwise not dependent on one another for survival; no one can be a member of more than one segment at the same level.

In tribal societies, these units are based on a principle of common descent. The most basic unit is a lineage, a group of individuals who trace their descent to a common ancestor who may have lived many generations ago. In the terminology used by anthropologists, descent can be either unilineal or cognatic. In the first case, descent is traced exclusively through the father and is labeled patrilineal, or exclusively through the mother, when it is called matrilineal. In cognatic systems, by contrast, descent can be traced through either or both parents. A moment's reflection will indicate that segmentary societies can arise only under conditions of unilineal descent. For the segments to be nonoverlapping, every child must be assigned exclusively to either the father's or the mother's descent group.

The most common form of lineage organization, which was prevalent in China, India, the Middle East, Africa, Oceania, Greece, Rome, and among the barbarian tribes that conquered Europe, was what the Romans labeled *agnatio*, and what anthropologists following them call "agnation." Agnation is the tracing of common descent exclusively through the male line.

When a woman marries, she leaves her descent group and joins that of her husband. In the agnatic systems of China and India, this involved severing her ties with her birth family almost completely. Marriages were thus often a moment of sadness for the wife's parents, compensated only by the bride price they were paid for their daughter. The woman had no status in the husband's family until she gave birth to a male offspring, at which point she became fully integrated into the husband's lineage, praying and offering sacrifices at her husband's ancestral tomb and protecting her son's future inheritance.

While the most common by far, agnation is not the only form of unilineal descent. In a matrilineal society, descent and inheritance are traced through the mother's family. Matrilineal societies are not the same as matriarchal ones, in which women hold power and dominate men; there does not seem to be any evidence that a true matriarchal society has ever existed. Matriliny simply means that it is the husband who leaves his descent group upon marriage and joins that of his wife. Power and resources are still largely controlled by men; the authority figure in the family is often the wife's brother rather than the child's biological father.[27] While matrilineal societies are rarer than patrilineal ones, they are still found all over the world, in South America, Melanesia, Southeast Asia, the Southwest United States, and Africa. Elman Service points out that they are typically found under one specific set of environmental conditions, such as rainfall horticulture where gardening is done primarily by women, though this theory does not account for why the Hopis of the southwestern American desert are matrilineal and matrilocal.[28]

One of the fascinating characteristics of lineages is that they can be aggregated upward into much larger superlineages simply by tracing descent back to an earlier ancestor. For example, I may be a member of a small lineage that traces its descent only to my grandfather, and live next to another lineage whose grandfather was different. But both of our lineages are related at the level of a fourth-, fifth-, or higher-generation ancestor, which allows us to consider ourselves kin, and under the right circumstances we might collaborate.

The classic description of such a society, one that has been read by generations of anthropology students, is E. E. Evans-Pritchard's studies of the Nuer, a pastoral cattle-raising people living in southern Sudan.[29] In the late twentieth century, the Nuer and their traditional rivals the Dinka were engaged in a long-term struggle with the central government in

Khartoum over autonomy for South Sudan, led for a long time by John Garang and the Sudan People's Liberation Army. But in the 1930s when Evans-Pritchard studied the region, Sudan was still a British colony, and the Nuer and Dinka were organized in a much more traditional way.

According to Evans-Pritchard, "Nuer tribes are split into segments. The largest segments we call primary tribal sections and these are further segmented into secondary tribal sections which are further segmented into tertiary tribal sections . . . A tertiary tribal section comprises a number of village communities which are composed of kinship and domestic groups."[30]

Nuer lineages fight with one another constantly, usually involving conflicts over cattle, which are central to their culture. Lineages fight with other lineages at the same level, but they can then combine with one another to fight at a higher level. At the top level, the Nuer tribes can combine to fight with the Dinka, who are similarly organized. As Evans-Pritchard explains,

> Each segment is itself segmented and there is opposition between its parts. The members of any segment unite for war against adjacent segments of the same order and unite with these adjacent segments against larger sections. Nuer themselves state this structural principle clearly in the expression of their political values. Thus they say that if the Leng tertiary section of the Lou tribe fights the Nyarkwac tertiary section—and, in fact, there has been a long feud between them—the villages which compose each section will combine to fight; but if there is a quarrel between the Nyarkwac tertiary section and the Rumjok secondary section, as has occurred recently over water rights at Fading, Leng and Nyarkwac will unite against their common enemy Rumjok which, in its turn, forms a coalition of the various segments into which it is divided.[31]

While segments can aggregate at a high level, they are prone to immediate fissioning once the cause of their union (such as external threat) disappears. The possibility of multilevel segmentation is seen in many different tribal societies and is reflected in the Arab saying, "Me against my brother, me and my brother against my cousin, me and my cousin against the stranger."

In Nuer society, there is no state, no centralized source of authority that can enforce law, and nothing approaching institutionalized hierarchical leadership. Like band-level societies, the Nuer are highly egalitarian. There is a division of labor between men and women, and within lineages there are age grades that separate people generationally. There are so-called leopard-skin chiefs who play a ritual role and help to settle conflicts, but they have no ability to coerce people within the lineage: "On the whole we may say that Nuer chiefs are sacred persons, but that their sacredness gives them no general authority outside specific social situations. I have never seen a Nuer treat a chief with more respect than they treat other people or speak of them as persons of much importance."[32]

The Nuer are a particularly well-developed and pure example of segmentary lineage organization, where genealogical rules precisely determine social structure and status. Many tribal societies are more loosely organized. Common descent is less a strict biological rule than a convenient fiction for establishing social obligation. Even among the Nuer, it is possible to take complete strangers into a lineage and treat them as kin (something that anthropologists label fictive kinship). Oftentimes biology is an *ex post* justification for political association rather than a driver of community. Chinese lineages often have memberships in the thousands; entire villages share the same surname, which suggests the fictive and inclusive nature of Chinese kinship. And while the Sicilian Mafia speaks of itself as a "family," the blood oath only symbolizes consanguinity. The modern concept of ethnicity pushes common descent so far back in time as to make the actual tracing of genealogy extremely difficult. When we speak of groups like the Kalenjin or Kikuyus in Kenya as being "tribes," we are using the term extremely loosely, since these are aggregates of tens or hundreds of thousands of people.[33]

ANCESTORS AND RELIGION

Since virtually all human societies organized themselves tribally at one point, many people are tempted to believe that this is somehow a natural state of affairs or biologically driven. It is not obvious, however, why you should want to cooperate with a cousin four times removed rather than a familiar nonrelative just because you share one sixty-fourth of your genes with your cousin. No animal species behaves in this manner, nor do human beings in band-level societies. The reason that this form of social organization took hold across human societies was due to religious belief, that is, the worship of dead ancestors.

Worship of dead ancestors begins in band-level societies; within each small group there may be shamans or religious specialists whose job it is to communicate with those ancestors. With the development of lineages, however, religion becomes more complex and institutionalized, which in turn affects other institutions like leadership and property. It is belief in the power of dead ancestors over the living and not some mysterious biological instinct that causes tribal societies to cohere.

One of the most famous descriptions of ancestor worship was provided by the nineteenth-century French historian Numa Denis Fustel de Coulanges. His book *The Ancient City*, first published in 1864, came as a revelation to generations of Europeans brought up to associate Greek and Roman religion with the Olympian gods. Fustel de Coulanges pointed to a much older religious tradition that was shared by other Indo-European groups including the Indo-Aryans who settled northern India. For the Greeks and Romans, he argued, the souls of the dead did not move into a celestial realm but continued to reside underneath the ground where they were buried. For this reason, "They never failed to bury [a dead man] with the objects of which they supposed he had need—clothing, utensils, and arms. They poured wine upon his tomb to quench his thirst, and placed food there to satisfy his hunger. They slaughtered horses and slaves with the idea that these beings, buried with the dead, would serve him in the tomb, as they had done during his life."[34] The spirits of the dead—the *manes* in Latin—required continual maintenance by their living relatives, who had to provide them with regular offerings of food and drink lest they become angry.

Fustel de Coulanges was one of the first comparative anthropologists, whose domain of knowledge ranged far beyond European history. He noted that the Hindus practiced a form of ancestor worship similar to the Graeco-Roman variety before the advent of the doctrine of metempsychosis (the passing of the soul at death into another body) and the rise of Brahmanic religion. This point was also emphasized by Henry Maine, who argued that ancestor worship "influences the everyday life of that vast majority of the people of India who call themselves in some sense Hindus, and indeed in the eyes of most of them their household divinities are of more importance than the whole Hindu pantheon."[35] Had he ranged even farther afield, he would have discovered identical burial practices in ancient China, where the graves of high-status people were filled with bronze and ceramic tripods, food, and the bodies of horses, slaves, and concubines that were intended to accompany the dead person into the afterlife.[36] The Indo-Aryans, like the Greeks and Romans, maintained a sacred fire in the household that represented the family and was never supposed to be extinguished unless the family line itself was extinguished.[37] In all of these cultures, the fire was worshipped as a deity that represented the health and well-being of the family—not just the living family, but also the family's dead ancestors stretching back over many generations.

Religion and kinship are closely connected in tribal societies. Ancestor worship is particularistic: there are no gods worshipped by the whole community. You have duties only to *your* ancestors, not those of your neighbors or your chief. Typically, the ancestor was not a terribly ancient one like Romulus, regarded as the progenitor of all Romans, but rather a progenitor three or four generations back who might be directly remembered by older members of the family.[38] According to Fustel de Coulanges, it was in no way comparable to Christian worship of saints: "The funeral obsequies could be religiously performed only by the nearest relative . . . They believed that the dead ancestor accepted no offerings save from his own family; he desired no worship save from his own descendents." Moreover, each individual has a strong interest in having male descendants (in an agnatic system), since it is only they who will be able to look after one's soul after one's death. As a result, there is a strong imperative to marry and have male children; celibacy in early Greece and Rome was in most circumstances illegal.

The result of these beliefs is that an individual is tied both to dead ancestors and to unborn descendants, in addition to his or her living children. As Hugh Baker puts it with regard to Chinese kinship, there is a rope representing the continuum of descent that "stretches from Infinity to Infinity passing over a razor which is the Present. If the rope is cut, both ends fall away from the middle and the rope is no more. If the man alive now dies without heir, the whole continuum of ancestors and unborn descendants dies with him . . . His existence as an individual is necessary but insignificant beside his existence as the representative of the whole."[39]

In a tribal society, ideas, in the form of religious beliefs, have a huge impact on social organization. Belief in the reality of dead ancestors binds individuals together on a far larger scale than is possible in a family- or band-level society. The "community" is not only the present members of the lineage, clan, or tribe; it is the whole rope of descent from one's ancestors to one's unborn descendants. Even the most distantly related kin feel they have some connection and duties toward each other, a feeling that is reinforced by rituals that apply to the community as a whole. Individuals do not believe they have the power of choice to constitute this kind of social system; rather, their roles are defined for them by the surrounding society before they are even born.[40]

RELIGION AND POWER

Tribal societies are far more powerful militarily than band-level ones, since they can mobilize hundreds or thousands of kinsmen on a moment's notice. It is likely, then, that the first society that was able to knit together large kindreds through religious belief in ancestors would have had enormous advantages over its rivals, and would have stimulated imitation the moment this form of social organization was invented. Thus war did not just make the state, it made the tribe as well.

Since religion plays an important functional role in facilitating large-scale collective action, the question naturally arises: Was tribal organization a consequence of previously formulated religious beliefs, or were the religious beliefs somehow added later to reinforce a preexisting form of social organization? Many nineteenth-century thinkers including Marx and Durkheim believed some version of the latter. Marx was famous for believing that religion was the "opiate of the masses," a fairy tale invented by elites to solidify their class privileges. He did not, as far as I know, express any views on ancestor worship in classless tribal societies, but one could easily extend his argument to posit that the anger of dead ancestors was manipulated by patriarchal household heads to reinforce their authority over the living. Or it may be that the leader of a small family band, needing help from neighboring bands against a common enemy, invoked the spirit of a legendary or mythological long-dead common ancestor to win their support, planting an idea that subsequently took on a life of its own.

We unfortunately can only speculate about the ways ideas and material interests were causally connected, because no one has ever witnessed the transition from a band-level to a tribally organized society. Given the importance of religious ideas in later history, it would be surprising if causality didn't flow in both directions, from religious creativity toward social organization, and from material interests toward religious ideas. It is important to note, however, that tribal societies are not "natural" or default forms of social organization to which all societies revert if higher-level organization breaks down. They were preceded by family- or band-level forms of organization, and flourished only under specific environmental conditions. Tribes were created at a particular historical juncture and are maintained on the basis of certain religious beliefs. If those beliefs change due to the introduction of a new religion, then the tribal form of social organization can break down. As we will see in chapter 19, this is precisely what started to happen after the advent of Christianity in barbarian Europe. Tribalism in an attenuated form never disappeared, but it was replaced by other more flexible and scalable forms of organization as time went on.

4

TRIBAL SOCIETIES: PROPERTY, JUSTICE, WAR

How kinship is related to the development of property rights; the nature of justice in a tribal society; tribal societies as military organizations; strengths and weaknesses of tribal organization

One of the biggest issues separating Right and Left since the French Revolution has been that of private property. Rousseau in his *Discourse on Inequality* traced the origins of injustice to the first man who fenced off land and declared it his own. Karl Marx set a political agenda of abolishing private property; one of the first things that all Communist regimes inspired by him did was to nationalize the "means of production," not least land. By contrast, the American Founding Father James Madison asserted in Federalist No. 10 that one of the most important functions of governments was to protect individuals' unequal ability to acquire property.[1] Modern neoclassical economists have seen strong private property rights as the source of long-term economic growth; in the words of Douglass North, "Growth will simply not occur unless the existing economic organization is efficient," which "entails the establishment of institutional arrangements and property rights."[2] Since the Reagan-Thatcher revolution of the late 1970s and early 1980s, one of the top agenda items pursued by market-oriented policy makers has been privatization of state-owned enterprises in the name of economic efficiency, something that has been fiercely resisted by the Left.

The experience of communism strongly reinforced the contemporary emphasis on the importance of private property. Based in part on a misreading of anthropologists like Lewis Henry Morgan, Marx and Engels argued that an early stage of "primitive communism" existed prior to the rise of exploitative class relationships, an idealized state that communism sought to recover. Morgan had described customary property owned by tightly bonded kin groups; real-world Communist regimes in the former USSR and China forced millions of unrelated peasants into collective farms. By breaking the link between individual effort and reward, collectivization undermined incentives to work, leading to mass famines in Russia and China, and severely reducing agricultural productivity. In the former USSR, the 4 percent of land that remained privately owned accounted for almost one-quarter of total agricultural output. In China, once collective farms were disbanded in 1978 under the leadership of the reformer Deng Xiaoping, agricultural output doubled in the space of just four years.

A good deal of theorizing about the importance of private property rights concerns what is called the tragedy of the commons. Grazing fields in traditional English villages were collectively owned by the village's inhabitants; since no one could be excluded from access to these fields, whose resources were depletable, they were overused and made worthless. The solution to the risk of depletion was to turn the commons into private property, whose owners would then have a strong incentive to invest in its upkeep and exploit its resources on a long-term, sustainable basis. In an influential article, Garrett Hardin argued that the tragedy of the commons exists with respect to many global resources, such as clean air, fisheries, and the like, and that in the absence of private ownership or strong regulation they would be overexploited and made useless.[3]

In many contemporary ahistorical discussions of property rights, one often gets the impression that in the absence of modern individual property rights, human beings always faced some version of the tragedy of the commons in which communal ownership undermined incentives to use property efficiently.[4] The emergence of modern property rights was then postulated to be a matter of economic rationality, in which individuals bargained among themselves to divide up the communal property, much like Hobbes's account of the emergence of the Leviathan out of the state of nature. There is a twofold problem with this scenario. The first is that many alternative forms of customary property existed before the emergence of modern property rights. While these forms of land tenure may not have provided the same incentives for their efficient use as do their modern counterparts, very few of them led to anything like the tragedy of the commons. The second problem is that there aren't very many examples of modern property rights emerging spontaneously and peacefully out of a bargaining process. The way customary property rights yielded to modern ones was much more violent, and power and deceit played a large role.[5]

KINSHIP AND PRIVATE PROPERTY

The earliest forms of private property were held not by individuals but by lineages or other kin groups, and much of their motivation was not simply economic but religious and social as well. Forced collectivization by the Soviet Union and China in the twentieth century sought to turn back the clock to an imagined past that never existed, in which common property was held by nonkin.

Greek and Roman households had two things that tied them to a particular piece of real estate: the hearth with its sacred fire, which resided in the household, and nearby ancestral tombs. Land was desired not simply for its productive potential but also because it was where dead ancestors and the family's unmovable hearth resided. Property needed to be private: strangers or the state could not be allowed to violate the resting place of one's ancestors. On the other hand, these early forms of private property lacked a critical characteristic of what we regard today as modern property: rights were generally usufructuary (that is, they conveyed the right to use land but not to own it), making it impossible for individuals to sell or otherwise alienate it.[6] The owner is not an individual landlord, but a community of living and dead kin. Property was held as a kind of trust on behalf of the dead ancestors and the unborn descendants, a practice that has parallels in many contemporary societies. As an early twentieth-century Nigerian chief said, "I conceive that land belongs to a vast family of which many are dead, few are living and countless members are still unborn."[7] Property and kinship thus become intimately connected: property enables you to take care of not only preceding and succeeding generations of relatives, but of yourself as well through your ancestors and descendants, who can affect your well-being.

In some parts of precolonial Africa, kin groups were tied to land because their ancestors were buried there, much as for the Greeks and Romans.[8] But in other long-settled parts of West Africa, religion operated differently. There, the descendants of the first settlers were designated Earth Priests, who maintained Earth Shrines and presided over various ritual activities related to land use. Newcomers acquired rights to land not through individual buying and selling of properties but through their entry into the local ritual community. The community conferred access rights to planting, hunting, and fishing not in perpetuity but as a privilege of membership in the community.[9]

In tribal societies, property was sometimes communally owned by the tribe. As the historical anthropologist Paul Vinogradoff explained of the Celtic tribes, "Both the free and the unfree are grouped in [agnatic] kindreds. These kindreds hold land in communal ownership, and their possessions do not as a rule coincide with the landmarks [boundaries] of the villages, but spread spider-like through different settlements."[10] Communal ownership never meant that land was worked collectively, however, as on a twentieth-century Soviet or Chinese collective farm. Individual families were often allocated their own plots. In other cases, properties were individually owned but severely entailed by the social obligations that individuals had toward their kin—living, dead, and yet to be born.[11] Your strip of land lies next to your cousin's, and you cooperate at harvesttime; it is unthinkable to sell your strip to a stranger. If you die without male heirs, your land reverts to the kin group. Tribes often had the power to reassign property rights. According to Vinogradoff, "On the borders of India, conquering tribes have been known to settle down on large tracts of land without allowing them to be converted into separate property even among clans or kindreds. Occasional or periodical redivisions testified to the effective overlordship of the tribe."[12]

Customary property held by kin groups still exists in contemporary Melanesia. Upward of 95 percent of all land is tied up in customary property rights in Papua New Guinea and the Solomon Islands. When a mining or palm oil company wants to acquire real estate, it has to deal with entire descent groups (wantoks).[13] Each individual within the descent group has a potential veto over the deal, and there is no statute of limitations. As a result, one group of relatives may decide to sell their land to the company; ten years later, another group may show up and claim title to the same property, arguing that the land had been unjustly stolen from them in previous generations.[14] Many individuals are unwilling to sell title to their land under any conditions, since the spirits of their ancestors dwell there.

But the inability of individuals within the kin group to fully appropriate their property's resources, or to be able to sell it, does not necessarily mean that they neglect it or treat it irresponsibly. Property rights in tribal societies are extremely well specified, even if that specification is not formal or legal.[15] The extent to which tribally owned property is well or poorly cared for is a function not of tribal ownership as such but of the inner cohesion of the tribe. It is not even clear to what extent the tragedy of the commons described by Hardin was a real problem in English history. The open-field system ended by the Parliamentary Enclosure Movement was not the most efficient use of land, and the wealthy private landowners who drove peasants off communal property in the eighteenth and nineteenth centuries had strong motives for doing so. But in the open-field system, which was "based on the solidarity of the groups of neighbour cultivators, [which] was originally conditioned by kinship,"[16] land was not as a rule overexploited or wasted.[17] To the extent it was, it was likely due to the decline of social solidarity within rural English villages. In other parts of the world, it is hard to find documented cases of the tragedy of the commons unfolding in well-functioning tribal societies with communal property.[18] This is certainly not a problem that afflicts Melanesia.

Tribal societies like the Nuer that are pastoral rather than agricultural operate by different rules. They do not bury their ancestors in tombs that they must perpetually protect, since they range over a very wide territory as they follow their herds. Their rights to a particular piece of land are not exclusive, as in the case of land for Greek and Roman families, but rather ones of access.[19] The fact that rights were not fully private did not, as in other customary arrangements, mean that pasture lands were inevitably overexploited. The Turkana and Masai of Kenya, and the Fulani pastoralists of West Africa, all developed systems whereby segments shared pasturage with each other while excluding outsiders.[20]

The failure of Westerners to understand the nature of customary property rights and their embeddedness in kinship groups lies in some measure at the root of many of Africa's current dysfunctions. European colonial officials were convinced that economic development could not occur in the absence of modern property rights, that is, rights that were individual, alienable, and formally specified through the legal system. Many were convinced that Africans, left to their own devices, did not know how to manage land efficiently or sustainably.[21] They were also motivated by self-interest, either for the sake of natural resources, commercial agricultural interests, or on behalf of European settlers. They wanted to be able to acquire legal title to land and assumed that local chiefs "owned" the tribe's land, much like a feudal lord in Europe, and could convey it to them.[22] In other cases, they set up the chief as their agent, not just for the purposes of acquiring land but also as an arm of the colonial administration. Traditional African leaders in tribal societies found their authority severely constrained by the checks and balances imposed by complex kinship systems. Mahmood Mamdani argues that the Europeans deliberately empowered a class of rapacious African Big Men, who could tyrannize their fellow tribesmen in a totally nontraditional way as a consequence of the Europeans' desire to create a system of modern property rights. They thus contributed to the growth of neopatrimonial government after independence.[23]

LAW AND JUSTICE

Tribal societies have weak centralized sources of authority—the Big Man or chief—and therefore much less ability than states to coerce individuals. They have no system of third-party enforcement of rules that we associate with a modern legal system. As Paul Vinogradoff points out, justice in a tribal society is a bit like justice between states in contemporary international relations: it is a matter of self-help and negotiation between decentralized units that constitute effectively sovereign decision makers.[24]

E. E. Evans-Pritchard describes justice among the Nuer in the following terms:

> Blood-feuds are a tribal institution, for they can only occur where a breach of law is recognized since they are the way in which reparation is obtained. Fear of incurring a blood-feud is, in fact, the most important legal sanction within a tribe and the main guarantee of an individual's life and property . . . When a man feels that he has suffered an injury there is no authority to whom he can make a complaint and from whom he can obtain redress, so he at once challenges the man who has wronged him to a duel and the challenge must be accepted.[25]

Evans-Pritchard is obviously using the terms "law" and "legal sanction" in an expansive sense, since there is little connection between tribal justice and law in a state-level society.

There are, however, rules about how blood feuds are to be pursued. The kinsman of a slain Nuer man may go after the perpetrator, and also any of the perpetrator's close male kin, but has no right to touch the mother's brother, father's sister, or mother's sister, since they are not members of the slayer's lineage. Disputes are mediated by the leopard-skin chief, to whose house a murderer repairs to seek sanctuary and cleanse himself ritually of the blood of his victim. Parties to a dispute go through elaborate rituals to prevent escalation, such as sending the spear that injured a man to the victim's village, so that it can be magically treated to prevent the wound from becoming fatal. The leopard-skin chief enjoys a certain authority as a neutral party, and along with other elders of the defendant's village he hears the different sides of a dispute. But he has no authority to enforce a judgment, any more than international mediators like the United Nations have the power to enforce judgments between modern states. And as in the case of international relations, power makes a difference; it is harder for a weak lineage to obtain redress from a strong one.[26] To the extent justice is served, it is based on calculations of self-interest on the part of the disputing parties not to see a feud escalate and become more damaging.

Virtually all tribal societies have comparable institutions for seeking justice: obligations on kinsmen to seek revenge or restitution for wrongs committed; a nonbinding system of arbitration for helping to settle disputes peacefully; and a customary schedule of payments for wrongs committed, which among the Germanic tribes of Northern Europe were called the wergeld. The *Beowulf* saga is an epic account of a murder and the attempt of kinsmen to seek revenge or wergeld from the perpetrators. Tribal societies differed, however, in the degree to which arbitration was institutionalized. Among the Indians living on the Pacific Coast's Klamath River, for example, "If a Yurok wanted to process a legal claim, he would hire two, three, or four 'crossers'—nonrelatives from a community other than his own. The defendant in the claim would also hire crossers, and the entire group hired by both parties would act as go-betweens, ascertaining claims and defenses and gathering evidence. The crossers would render a judgment for damages after hearing all the evidence."[27] As in the case of the Nuer leopard-skin chief, the crossers had no formal authority to enforce their judgments. They had to rely on the power of the threat of ostracism for failure to accept the crossers' verdict, something made more powerful by the organization of the males of the tribe into coresidential "sweathouse groups." Perpetrators of offenses calculated that they would need the support of the sweathouse group in the future if they were wronged, and thus they had an incentive to pay compensation to their victims.[28]

Similarly, the Law of the Salian Franks (the *Lex Salica*), which prevailed among the Germanic tribes at the time of Clovis from the sixth century on, established rules for justice: if "a tribesman of the Salian Franks wished to prefer a claim against one of his neighbours, he was obliged to adopt a precise method in summoning his opponent. He had to go to the house of his adversary, state his claim in the presence of witnesses and 'set the sun,' that is, name a day on which the party summoned was required to appear before the Mall, the judicial assembly. If the defendant did not appear, it was necessary to repeat the ceremony over and over again." Vinogradoff concludes, "We see most clearly the inherent weakness of tribal jurisdiction, for execution, the practical enforcement of legal decision, was not effected, as a rule, by sovereign authority, but left to a great extent in the hands of the individual litigant and his friends: it amounted to little more than self-help juridically sanctioned and approved by the tribe."[29]

Third-party enforcement of judicial decisions had to await the emergence of states. But tribal societies did develop increasingly complex institutions for rendering judgments in civil and criminal disputes. Tribal law was usually not written; it nonetheless needed custodians for the sake of applying precedents and establishing wergelds. Scandinavia developed the institution of the *laghman*, a legal expert elected from among the people, whose job it was to deliver discourses or lectures on legal custom to be read at trials.

Popular assemblies originated in the need to adjudicate tribal disputes. The *Iliad*'s account of the shield of Achilles describes a dispute over the blood price for a slain man, argued before a crowd in a marketplace, and a final verdict being read out by the tribe's elders. On a local level, the Salic Law was administered by a Teutonic institution known as the Court of the Hundred, consisting of assemblies of local villagers or moots (from which the contemporary "moot court" is derived). The Court of the Hundred met in the open air, and its judges were all local freemen living within the Hundred's jurisdiction. The president of the Hundred, the Thingman, was elected, and he presided over what was essentially a court of arbitration. According to Henry Maine, "Their great function was to give hot blood time to cool, to prevent men from redressing their own wrongs, and to take into their own hands and regulate the method of redress. The earliest penalty for disobedience to the Court was probably outlawry. The man who would not abide by its sentence went out of the law. If he were killed, his kinsmen were forbidden, or were deterred by all the force of primitive opinion, from taking that vengeance which otherwise would have been their duty and their right."[30] Maine points out that English kings were represented at similar courts, initially to collect a share of the fines imposed. But with the emergence of the English state, the king gradually asserted his authority to make judgments and, more important, to enforce the court's will (see chapter 17). The Hundred and the Thingman disappeared as juridical institutions, but survived, as we will see, as instruments of local government that would eventually emerge as units of modern democratic representation.

WARFARE AND MILITARY ORGANIZATION

I have thus far theorized little about why human beings made the transition from band-level to tribal societies, except to say that it was historically associated with the increased productivity made possible by the invention of agriculture. Agriculture made possible higher population densities, which in turn created a need for organizing societies on a larger scale. Agriculture also created the need for private property, which then became heavily intertwined with complex kinship structures, as we have seen.

But there is another reason that human beings transitioned to tribal societies: the problem of warfare. The development of settled agricultural societies meant that human groups were now living in much closer proximity. They could generate surpluses well above the minimum required for survival and thus had more real goods and chattels to protect or steal. Tribal societies were organized on a far larger scale than band-level ones and thus could overwhelm the latter based on sheer numbers. But they had other advantages as well, the most important being their organizational flexibility. As we have seen in the case of the Nuer, tribal societies can scale up very rapidly during emergencies, with segments at various levels able to mobilize in tribal federations. Caesar, describing the Gauls he conquered, noted that when war broke out the tribes elected a common authority for the whole confederation, who only then had the power of life and death over his followers.[31] It is for this reason that the anthropologist Marshall Sahlins described the segmentary lineage as "an organization of predatory expansion."[32]

The propensity for violence would seem to be one of the important points of continuity between ancestral apes and human beings. Hobbes is famous for his assertion that the state of nature was a state of war of "every man against every man." Rousseau, by contrast, argued explicitly that

Hobbes was wrong, that primitive human beings were peaceful and isolated, and that violence developed only at a later stage when society had
begun to corrupt human morals. Hobbes is far closer to the truth, albeit
with the important qualification that violence took place not between isolated individuals but between social groups. Human beings' highly developed social skills and ability to cooperate are not contradicted by the
prevalence of violence in both chimp and human societies; rather, they are
the precondition for it. That is, violence is a social activity engaged in by
groups of males and sometimes females. The vulnerability of both apes
and humans to violence by their fellow species members in turn drives the
need for greater social cooperation. Isolated individuals, whether chimp
or human, tend to get picked off by marauding gangs from neighboring
territories; those who were able to work with their fellows to defend themselves would survive and pass their genes to the next generation.

The idea that violence is rooted in human nature is difficult for many
people to accept. Many anthropologists, in particular, are committed, like
Rousseau, to the view that violence is an invention of later civilizations,
just as many people would like to believe that early societies understood
how to live in balance with their local environments. Unfortunately, there
is little evidence to support either view. The anthropologist Lawrence
Keeley and the archaeologist Steven LeBlanc have documented at great
length how the archaeological record shows a continuous use of violence
by prehistoric human societies.[33] Keeley notes that in cross-cultural surveys, from 70 to 90 percent of primitive societies—at the level of band,
tribe, or chiefdom—have engaged in warfare in the past five years, compared to 86 percent of states. Only a small minority of such societies report low levels of raiding or violence, and those are usually explained by
environmental conditions that shield them from neighbors.[34] Surviving
groups of hunter-gatherers, like the Bushmen of the Kalahari Desert or
the Copper Eskimos in Canada, had rates of homicide four times that of
the United States when left to their own devices.[35]

The origins of warfare for both chimpanzees and human beings seem to
lie in hunting.[36] Chimps organize themselves in groups to hunt monkeys
and transfer these same skills to the hunting of other chimps. The same is
true for human beings, with the difference that human prey is larger and
more dangerous, requiring higher degrees of social cooperation and better
weapons. The transferability of hunting skills to human predation is evident
in groups for which we have historical records, like the Mongols, whose

riding and horseback hunting skills were turned on human victims. The skills that human beings developed hunting large animals explains why paleoarchaeologists often date the arrival of human beings in a particular territory to the extinction of that region's megafauna. Mastodons, saber-toothed tigers, the giant flightless emu, giant sloths—all of these species appear to have been wiped out by well-organized bands of primitive human hunters.

It is only with tribal societies, however, that we see the emergence of a separate caste of warriors, along with what became the most basic and enduring unit of political organization, a leader and his band of armed retainers. Such organizations became virtually universal in subsequent human history, and continue to exist today in the form of warlords and their followers, militias, drug cartels, and street gangs. Because of their specialized skills in using weapons and organizing for war, they began to wield the power to coerce that did not exist at the band level of organization.

Getting rich was obviously a motive for making war in tribal societies. Of the Viking or Varangian elite that conquered Russia toward the end of the first millennium A.D., the historian Jerome Blum says:

> In return for the services his retainers gave [the Viking chieftain], the prince supported and protected them. Originally, they lived with him as part of his household, and depended for their maintenance upon the booty won in the prince's wars and the tribute he exacted . . . Prince Vladimir's retinue complained because they had to eat with wooden spoons instead of with silver ones. Whereupon the prince hastened to order that silver spoons be provided "remarking that with silver and gold he could not secure a retinue, but that with a retinue he was in a position to secure silver and gold."[37]

During the 1990s, Sierra Leone and Liberia collapsed into warlordism as a result of Foday Sankoh and Charles Taylor building retinues of retainers, which they then used to acquire not silver spoons but blood diamonds.

But war is not motivated by the acquisitive impulse alone. Although warriors may be greedy for silver and gold, they also display courage in battle not so much for the sake of resources, but for honor.[38] Honor has to do with the willingness to risk one's life for a cause, and for the recognition of other warriors. Consider Tacitus's account of the German tribes written in the first century A.D., one of the few contemporaneous accounts of these progenitors of modern Europeans:

> And so there is great rivalry among the retainers to decide who shall have the first place with his chief, and among the chieftains as to who shall have the largest and keenest retinue. This means rank and strength, to be surrounded always with a large band of chosen youths . . . when the battlefield is reached it is a reproach for a chief to be surpassed in prowess; a reproach for his retinue not to equal the prowess of a chief: but to have left the field and survived one's chief, this means lifelong infamy and shame: to defend and protect him, to devote one's own feats even to his glorification, this is the gist of their allegiance: the chief fights for victory, but the retainers for the chief.[39]

A warrior will not trade places with a farmer or a tradesman even if the returns to agriculture or trade prove higher, because he is only partly motivated by the desire for wealth. Warriors find the life of a farmer contemptible because it does not partake of danger and community:

> Should it happen that the community where they are born be drugged with long years of peace and quiet, many of the high-born youths voluntarily seek those tribes which are at the time engaged in some war; for rest is unwelcome to the race, and they distinguish themselves more readily in the midst of uncertainties: besides, you cannot keep up a great retinue except by war and violence . . . you will not so readily persuade them to plough the land and wait for the year's returns as to challenge the enemy and earn wounds: besides, it seems limp and slack to get with the sweating of your brow what you can gain with the shedding of your blood.[40]

Tacitus remarks that in the periods between wars, these youthful warriors spend their time in idleness, because engaging in civilian occupations would be demeaning to them. It was only with the rise of a bourgeois class in seventeenth- and eighteenth-century Europe that the warrior ethic was replaced by an ethic that placed gain and economic calculation above honor as the mark of a virtuous individual.[41]

Part of what makes politics an art rather than a science is the difficulty of judging beforehand the strength of the moral bonds between a group of retainers and their leader. Their common interests are often heavily economic, since they are organized primarily for predation. But what binds followers to a leader is never simply that. When the United States fought Saddam Hussein's Iraq in 1991 and 2003, it believed on both occasions that battlefield defeat would lead to Saddam's rapid overthrow because his inner circle would calculate they were better off without him. But that inner circle hung together in a remarkably durable way, as a result of family and personal ties, as well as fear.

Among the noneconomic sources of cohesion is simple personal loyalty through the reciprocal exchange of favors over time. Tribal societies invest kinship with religious meaning and supernatural sanctions. Militias, moreover, are typically made up of young men without families, land, or assets, but with raging hormones that incline them toward lives of risk and adventure. For them, economic resources are not the only objects of predation. We should not underestimate the importance of sex and access to women as a driver of political organization, particularly in segmentary societies that routinely use women as a medium of exchange. In these relatively small-scale societies, one could often follow the rules of clan exogamy only through external aggression due to the lack of nonrelated women. Genghis Khan, founder of the great Mongol Empire, was reported to have said, "The greatest pleasure . . . is to vanquish your enemies and chase them before you, to rob them of their wealth and see those dear to them bathed in tears, to ride their horses and clasp to your bosom their wives and daughters."[42] He succeeded quite well at satisfying the last of these aspirations. Through DNA testing, it is estimated that 8 percent of the present-day male population of a very large region of Asia are descendants of him or his lineage.[43]

A leader and his retinue in a tribal society are not the same as a general with his army in a state-level society, because the nature of leadership and authority is very different. Among the Nuer, the leopard-skin chief is primarily an arbitrator and assumes no power of command, nor is his authority hereditary. The same is true for the Big Man in contemporary Papua New Guinea or the Solomon Islands, who is traditionally chosen by his kinsmen as leader but who can by the same token lose his leadership position. Among the German tribes, writes Tacitus, "the authority of their kings was not unlimited or arbitrary; their generals control the people by example rather than command, and by means of the admiration which attends upon energy and a conspicuous place in front of the line."[44] Other tribal peoples were even more loosely organized: "The Comanche of the nineteenth century had no political unit that could be called a tribe with powerful chiefs leading their subjects . . . the Comanche population was distributed among a large number of loosely organized, autonomous bands with no formal organizations for warfare. 'War chiefs' were outstanding fighters with long records of accomplishments against enemies. Anyone was free to organize a war party if he could convince others to follow him, but such individuals had leadership roles only when others voluntarily followed, and only for the period of the raid."[45] It was only under military pressure from advancing European settlers that some Indian tribes like the Cheyenne began to develop more durable, centralized command-and-control structures such as a permanent tribal council.[46]

The loose, decentralized system of organization is a source of both strength and weakness for tribal societies. Their networked organization can at times generate enormous striking power. When equipped with horses, tribes of pastoral nomads were able to range over enormous distances and conquer huge territories. One example were the Almohads, Berber tribesmen who came out of nowhere to conquer all of North Africa and al-Andalus in southern Spain in the twelfth century. None could rival the Mongols, who, from their sanctuaries in inner Asia, managed to conquer Central Asia and much of the Middle East, Russia, parts of Eastern Europe, northern India, and the whole of China in a little over a century. But their lack of permanent leadership, the looseness of the ties binding segments, and the absence of clear rules of succession doomed tribal societies to long-run weakness and decline. Without permanent political authority and administrative capacity they could not govern the territories they conquered but were dependent on settled societies to provide routine administration. Virtually all conquering tribal societies—at least, the ones that did not quickly evolve into state-level societies—ended up disintegrating within a generation or two, as brothers, cousins, and grandsons vied for the founding leader's patrimony.

When tribal-level societies were succeeded by state-level societies, tribalism did not simply disappear. In China, India, the Middle East, and pre-Columbian America, state institutions were merely layered on top of tribal institutions and existed in an uneasy balance with them for long periods of time. One of the great mistakes of early modernization theory, beyond the error in thinking that politics, economics, and culture had to be congruent with one another, was to think that transitions between the "stages" of history were clean and irreversible. The only part of the world where tribalism was fully superseded by more voluntary and individualistic forms of social relationship was Europe, where Christianity played a decisive role in undermining kinship as a basis for social cohesion. Since most early modernization theorists were European, they assumed that other parts of the world would experience a similar shift away from kinship as part of the modernization process. But they were mistaken. Although China was the first civilization to invent the modern state, it never succeeded in suppressing the power of kinship on social and cultural levels. Hence much of its subsequent two-thousand-year political history revolved around attempts to block the reassertion of kinship structures into state administration. In India, kinship interacted with religion and mutated into the caste system, which up to the present day has proved much stronger than any state in defining the nature of Indian society. From the Melanesian wantok to the Arab tribe to the Taiwanese lineage to the Bolivian ayllu, complex kinship structures remain the primary locus of social life for many people in the contemporary world, and strongly shape their interaction with modern political institutions.

FROM TRIBALISM TO PATRONS, CLIENTS, AND POLITICAL MACHINES

I have defined tribalism in terms of kinship. But as tribal societies themselves evolved, the strict genealogical basis of the segmentary lineage gave way to cognatic tribes, and tribes that accepted members that could make no claim of actual kinship. If we define tribe more broadly to include not just kin claiming common descent but also patrons and clients linked through reciprocity and personal ties, then tribalism remains one of the great constants of political development.

In Rome, for example, the agnatic descent groups described by Fustel de Coulanges were known as *gentes*. But already by the time of the early Republic the gentes began to accumulate large numbers of nonkin followers known as *clientes*. These consisted of freedmen, tenants, household retainers, and in later periods poor plebeians willing to offer their support in return for cash or other favors. From the late Republic through the early Empire, Roman politics revolved around the efforts of powerful leaders like Caesar, Sulla, or Pompey to capture state institutions through the mobilization of their clientes. Networks of clientes were mobilized as private armies by rich patrons. In reviewing Roman politics at the end of the Republic, the historian S. E. Finer caustically notes that "if you strip personalities away . . . you will find no more sophistication, disinterestedness, or nobility than in a Latin-American banana republic. Call the country the Freedonian Republic; set the time in the mid-nineteenth century; imagine Sulla, Pompey, Caesar as generals Garcia Lopez, Pedro Podrilla, and Jaime Villegas and you will find clientelist factions, personalist armies, and military struggle for the presidency that parallel at every point the collapsing Republic."[47]

Tribalism in this expanded sense remains a fact of life. India, for example, has been a remarkably successful democracy since the country's founding in 1947. Yet Indian politicians are still heavily dependent on personalistic patron-client ties to get elected to parliament. Sometimes these ties are tribal in a strict sense, since tribalism still exists in some of the poorer and less-developed parts of the country. At other times, support is based on caste or sectarian grounds. But in each case, the underlying social relationship between the politician and his or her supporters is the same as in a kinship group: it is based on a reciprocal exchange of favors between leader and followers, where leadership is won rather than inherited, based on the leader's ability to advance the interests of the group. The same is true of patronage politics in American cities, where political machines are built up on the basis of who scratches whose back and not some "modern" motivation like ideology or public policy. So the struggle to replace "tribal" politics with a more impersonal form of political relationships continues in the twenty-first century.

5

THE COMING OF THE LEVIATHAN

How state-level societies differ from tribal ones; "pristine" versus competitive state formation; different theories of state formation, including some dead ends like irrigation, leading to an explanation of why states emerged early on in some parts of the world and not in others

State-level societies differ from tribal ones in several important respects.[1]

First, they possess a centralized source of authority, whether in the form of a king, president, or prime minister. This source of authority deputizes a hierarchy of subordinates who are capable, at least in principle, of enforcing rules on the whole of the society. The source of authority trumps all others within its territory, which means that it is *sovereign*. All administrative levels, such as lesser chiefs, prefects, or administrators, derive their decision-making authority from their formal association with the sovereign.

Second, that source of authority is backed by a monopoly of the legitimate means of coercion, in the form of an army and/or police. The power of the state is sufficient to prevent segments, tribes, or regions from seceding or otherwise separating themselves. (This is what distinguishes a state from a chiefdom.)

Third, the authority of the state is territorial rather than kin based. Thus France was not really a state in Merovingian times when it was led by a king of the Franks rather than the king of France. Since membership in a state does not depend on kinship, it can grow much larger than a tribe.

Fourth, states are far more stratified and unequal than tribal societies, with the ruler and his administrative staff often separating themselves off from the rest of the society. In some cases they become a hereditary elite. Slavery and serfdom, while not unknown in tribal societies, expand enormously under the aegis of states.

Finally, states are legitimated by much more elaborate forms of religious belief, with a separate priestly class as its guardian. Sometimes that priestly class takes power directly, in which case the state is a theocracy; sometimes it is controlled by the secular ruler, in which case it is labeled caesaropapist; and sometimes it coexists with secular rule under some form of power sharing.

With the advent of the state, we exit out of kinship and into the realm of political development proper. The next few chapters will look closely at how China, India, the Muslim world, and Europe made the transition out of kinship and tribalism and into more impersonal state institutions. Once states come into being, kinship becomes an obstacle to political development, since it threatens to return political relationships to the small-scale, personal ties of tribal societies. It is therefore not enough merely to develop a state; the state must avoid retribalization or what I label repatrimonialization.

Not all societies around the world made this transition to statehood on their own. Most of Melanesia consisted of acephalous tribal societies (that is, lacking centralized authority) prior to the arrival of European colonial powers in the nineteenth century, as did roughly half of sub-Saharan Africa, and parts of South and Southeast Asia.[2] The fact that these regions had no long history of statehood very much affected their development prospects after they achieved independence in the second half of the twentieth century, especially when compared to colonized parts of East Asia where state traditions were deeply embedded. Why China developed a state at a very early point in its history, while Papua New Guinea did not, despite the latter having been settled by human beings for a longer period of time, is one of the questions I hope to answer.

THEORIES OF STATE FORMATION

Anthropologists and archaeologists distinguish between what they call "pristine" and "competitive" state formation. Pristine state formation is the initial emergence of a state (or chiefdom) out of a tribal-level society. Competitive formation occurs only after the first state gets going. States are usually so much better organized and powerful than the surrounding tribal-level societies that they either conquer and absorb them, or else are emulated by tribal neighbors who wish not to be conquered. While there are many historical examples of competitive state formation, no one has ever observed the pristine version, so political philosophers, anthropologists, and archaeologists can only speculate as to how the first state or states arose. There are several categories of explanation, including social contract, irrigation, population pressure, war and violence, and circumscription.

The State as a Voluntary Social Contract

Social contract theorists like Hobbes, Locke, and Rousseau were not in the first instance trying to give empirical accounts of how the state arose. They were attempting, rather, to understand a government's basis of legitimacy. But it is still worth thinking through whether the first states could have arisen through some form of explicit agreement among tribesmen to establish centralized authority.

Thomas Hobbes lays out the basic "deal" underlying the state: in return for giving up the right to do whatever one pleases, the state (or Leviathan) through its monopoly of force guarantees each citizen basic security. The state can provide other kinds of public goods as well, like property rights, roads, currency, uniform weights and measures, and external defense, which citizens cannot obtain on their own. In return, citizens give the state the right to tax, conscript, and otherwise demand things of them. Tribal societies can provide some degree of security, but can provide only limited public goods because of their lack of centralized authority. So if the state arose by social contract, we would have to posit that at some point in history, a tribal group decided voluntarily to delegate dictatorial powers to one individual to rule over them. The delegation would not be temporary, as in the election of a tribal chief, but permanent, to the king and all his descendants. And it would have to be on the basis of consensus on the part of all of the tribal segments, each of which had the option of simply wandering off if it didn't like the deal.

It seems highly unlikely that the first state arose out of an explicit social contract if the chief issue motivating it were simply economic, like the protection of property rights or the provision of public goods. Tribal societies are egalitarian and, within the context of close-knit kinship groups, very free. States, by contrast, are coercive, domineering, and hierarchical, which is why Friedrich Nietzsche called the state the "coldest of all cold monsters." We could imagine a free tribal society delegating authority to a single dictator only under the most extreme duress, such as the imminent danger of invasion and extermination by an outside invader, or to a religious figure if an epidemic appeared ready to wipe out the community. Roman dictators were in fact elected in this fashion during the Republic, such as when the city was threatened by Hannibal after the Battle of Cannae in 216 B.C. But this means that the real driver of state formation is violence or the threat of violence, making the social contract an efficient rather than a final cause.

The State as a Hydraulic-Engineering Project

A variant of the social contract theory, over which a lot of unnecessary ink has been spilled, is Karl Wittfogel's "hydraulic" theory of the state. Wittfogel, a former Marxist turned anticommunist, expanded on Marx's theory of the Asiatic mode of production, providing an economic explanation for the emergence of dictatorships outside the West. He argued that the rise of the state in Mesopotamia, Egypt, China, and Mexico was driven by the need for large-scale irrigation, which could be managed only by a centralized bureaucratic state.[3]

There are many problems with the hydraulic hypothesis. Most early irrigation projects in regions with nascent states were small and locally managed. Large engineering efforts like the Grand Canal in China were undertaken only after a strong state had already been constructed and thus were effects rather than causes of state formation.[4] For Wittfogel's hypothesis to be true, we would have to imagine a group of tribesmen getting together one day and saying to each other, "We could become a lot richer if we turned over our cherished freedom to a dictator, who would be responsible for managing a huge hydraulic-engineering project, the likes of which the world has never seen before. And we will give up that freedom not just for the duration of the project, but for all time, because future generations will need a good project manager as well." If this scenario were plausible, the European Union would have turned into a state long ago.

Population Density

The demographer Ester Boserup has argued that population increase and high population densities have been important drivers of technological innovation. The dense populations around river systems in Egypt, Mesopotamia, and China spawned intensive systems of agriculture involving large-scale irrigation, new higher-yielding crops, and other tools. Population density promotes state formation by permitting specialization and a division of labor between elites and nonelite groups. Low-density band- or tribal-level societies can mitigate conflict simply by moving away from one another, hiving off segments when they find they can't coexist. Dense populations in newly created urban centers do not have this option. Scarcity of land or access to certain key public resources are much more likely to trigger conflicts, which then might require more centralized forms of political authority to control.

But even if higher population density is a necessary condition for state formation, we are still left with two unanswered questions: What causes population density to increase in the first place? And what is the mechanism connecting dense populations with states?

The first question might seem to have a simple Malthusian answer: population increase is brought about by technological innovation such as the agricultural revolution, which greatly increases the carrying capacity of a given piece of land, which then leads parents to have more children. The problem is that a number of hunter-gatherer societies operate well below their local environment's long-term productive capacity. The New Guinea highlanders and the Amazonian Indians have developed agriculture, but they do not produce the food surpluses of which they are technically capable. So the mere technological *possibility* of increased productivity and increased output, and therefore increased population, does not necessarily explain why it actually came about.[5] Some anthropologists have suggested that in certain hunter-gatherer societies, increases in food supply are met with decreasing amounts of work because their members value leisure over work. Inhabitants of agricultural societies may be richer on average, but they also have to work much harder, and the trade-off may not seem appealing. Alternatively, it may simply be the case that hunter-gatherers are stuck in what economists call a low-level equilibrium trap. That is, they have the technology to plant seeds and shift to agriculture, but the social expectations for sharing surpluses quickly quash private incentives to move to higher levels of productivity.[6]

It could be that the causality here is reversed: people in early societies would not produce a surplus on their own until compelled to do so by rulers who could hold a whip hand over them. The masters, in turn, might not want to work harder themselves but were perfectly happy to compel others to do so. The emergence of hierarchy would then be the result not of economic factors but rather of political factors like military conquest or compulsion. The building of the pyramids in Egypt comes to mind.

Hence, population density may not be a final cause of state formation but rather an intervening variable that is the product of some other as yet unidentified factor.

States as the Product of Violence and Compulsion

The weaknesses and gaps in all of the explanations that are primarily economic in focus point to violence as an obvious source of state formation. That is, the transition from tribe to state involves huge losses in freedom and equality. It is hard to imagine societies giving all this up even for the potentially large gains of irrigation. The stakes have to be much higher and can be much more readily explained by the threat to life itself posed by organized violence.

We know that virtually all human societies have engaged in violence, particularly at the tribal level. Hierarchy and the state could have emerged when one tribal segment conquered another one and took control of its territory. The requirements of maintaining political control over the conquered tribe led the conquerors to establish centralized repressive institutions, which evolved into an administrative bureaucracy of a primitive state. Especially if the tribal groups differ linguistically or ethnically, it is likely that the victor would establish a relationship of dominance over the vanquished, and that class stratification would become entrenched. Even the threat of this kind of conquest by a foreign tribe would encourage tribal groups to establish more permanent, centralized forms of command and control, as happened with the Cheyenne and Pueblo Indians.[7]

This scenario of a tribe conquering a settled society has unfolded countless times in recorded history, with waves of Tanguts, Khitai, Huns, Rurzhen, Aryans, Mongols, Vikings, and Germans founding states on this basis. The only question, then, is whether this was how the very first states got their start. Centuries of tribal warfare in places like Papua New Guinea and southern Sudan have not produced state-level societies. Anthropologists have argued that tribal societies have leveling mechanisms to redistribute power after conflict; the Nuer simply absorb their enemies rather than rule them. So it appears that still other causal factors are needed to explain the rise of states. It was only when violent tribal groups spilled out of the steppes of inner Asia or the Arabian desert or the mountains of Afghanistan that more centralized political units formed.

Circumscription and Other Geographical-Environmental Factors
The anthropologist Robert Carneiro has noted that although warfare may be a universal and necessary condition for state formation, it is not a sufficient one. He argues that it is only when increases in productivity take place within a geographically circumscribed area like a river valley, or when other hostile tribes effectively circumscribe another tribe's territory, that it is possible to explain the emergence of hierarchical states. In uncircumscribed, low-population-density situations, weaker tribes or individuals can simply run away. But in places like the Nile valley, bounded by deserts and the ocean, or in the mountain valleys of Peru, that were bounded by deserts, jungles, and high mountains, this option didn't exist.[8] Circumscription would also explain why higher productivity led to greater population density, since people didn't have the option of moving away.

The tribes of the New Guinea highlands have agriculture and live in circumscribed valleys, so those factors alone cannot explain the rise of states. Absolute scale might also be important. Mesopotamia, the Nile valley, and the Valley of Mexico were all relatively large agricultural areas that were nonetheless circumscribed by mountains, deserts, and oceans. Larger and more concentrated military formations can be raised, and can project their power over larger areas, particularly if they have domesticated horses or camels. So it was not just circumscription, but also the size and accessibility of the area being circumscribed, that determined whether a state would form. Circumscription would help early state builders in another way as well, by protecting them from external enemies outside the river valley or island while ever-larger forces were being marshaled. Across Oceania, chiefdoms and protostates were formed only on the larger islands like Fiji, Tonga, and Hawaii, not on the smaller ones like the Solomon Islands, Vanuatu, or the Trobriands. New Guinea is a large island, but it is extremely mountainous and cut up into a myriad of tiny microenvironments.

The State as the Product of Charismatic Authority
Archaeologists who speculate about the origins of politics tend to be biased in favor of materialistic explanations like environment and level of technology, rather than cultural factors like religion, simply because we know more about the material environment of early societies.[9] But it seems ex-

tremely likely that religious ideas were critical to early state formation, since they could effectively legitimate the transition to hierarchy and loss of freedom enjoyed by tribal societies. Max Weber distinguished what he called *charismatic* authority from either its traditional or modern-rational variants.[10] The Greek word *charisma* means "touched by God"; a charismatic leader asserts authority not because he is elected by his fellow tribesmen for leadership ability but because he is believed to be a designee of God.

Religious authority and military prowess go hand in hand. Religious authority allows a particular tribal leader to solve the large-scale collective action problem of uniting a group of autonomous tribes. To a much larger degree than economic benefit, religious authority can explain why a free tribal people would be willing to make a permanent delegation of authority to a single individual and that individual's kin group. The leader can then use that authority to create a centralized military machine that can conquer recalcitrant tribes as well as ensure domestic peace and security, which then reinforces the leader's religious authority in a positive-feedback loop. The only problem, however, is that you need a new form of religion, one that can overcome the inherent scale limitations of ancestor worship and other kinds of particularistic forms of worship.

There is a concrete historical case of this process unfolding, which was the rise of the first Arab state under the Patriarchal and Umayyad caliphates. Tribal peoples inhabited the Arabian peninsula for many centuries, living on the borders of state-level societies like Egypt, Persia, and Rome/Byzantium. The harshness of their environment and its unsuitability for agriculture explained why they were never conquered, and thus why they never felt military pressure to form themselves into a centralized state. They operated as merchants and intermediaries between nearby settled societies but were incapable of producing a substantial surplus on their own.

Things changed dramatically, however, with the birth of the Prophet Muhammad in A.D. 570 in the Arabian town of Mecca. According to Muslim tradition, Muhammad received his first revelation from God in his fortieth year and began preaching to the Meccan tribes. He and his followers were persecuted in Mecca, so they moved to Medina in 622. He was asked to mediate among the squabbling Medinan tribes, and did so by drafting the so-called Constitution of Medina that defined a universal umma, or community of believers, that transcended tribal loyalties. Muhammad's polity did not yet have all the characteristics of a true state, but it made a break with kinship-based systems not on the basis of conquest but through the writing of a social contract underpinned by the prophet's charismatic authority. After several years of fighting, the new Muslim polity gained adherents and conquered Mecca, uniting central Arabia into a single state-level society.

Normally in conquest states the lineage of the founding tribal leader evolves into the ruling dynasty. This didn't happen in Muhammad's case because he had only a daughter, Fatima, and no sons. Leadership of the new state thus passed to one of Muhammad's companions in the Umayyad clan, a parallel segment in Muhammad's Quraysh tribe. The Umayyads did evolve into a dynasty, and the Umayyad state under Uthman and Mu'awiya quickly went on to conquer Syria, Egypt, and Iraq, imposing Arab rule over these preexisting state-level societies.[11]

There is no clearer illustration of the importance of ideas to politics than the emergence of an Arab state under the Prophet Muhammad. The Arab tribes played an utterly marginal role in world history until that point; it was only Muhammad's charismatic authority that allowed them to unify and project their power throughout the Middle East and North Africa. The tribes had no economic base to speak of; they gained economic power through the interaction of religious ideas and military organization, and then were able to take over agricultural societies that did produce surpluses.[12] This was not a pure example of pristine state formation, since the Arab tribes had the examples of established states such as Persia and Byzantium all around them that they could emulate and eventually take over. Moreover, the power of tribalism remained so strong that subsequent Arab states were never able to overcome it fully or to create state bureaucracies not heavily influenced by tribal politics (see chapter 13). This forced later Arab and Turkish dynasties to resort to extraordinary measures to free themselves from the influence of kinship and tribal ties, in the form of slave armies and administrators recruited entirely from foreigners.

While the founding of the first Arab state is a particularly striking illustration of the political power of religious ideas, virtually every other state has relied on religion to legitimate itself. The founding myths of the Greek, Roman, Hindu, and Chinese states all trace the regime's ancestry back to a divinity, or at least to a semidivine hero. Political power in early states cannot be understood apart from the religious rituals that the ruler controlled and used to legitimate his power. Consider, for example, the following ode to the founder of China's Shang Dynasty, from the *Book of Odes*:

Heaven commissioned the swallow
To descend and give birth to the [father of our] Shang
[His descendants] dwelt in the land of Yin and became great.
[Then] long ago Ti appointed the martial T'ang
To regulate the boundaries through the four quarters . . .

Another poem asserts:

Profoundly wise were [the lords of] Shang
And long had there appeared the omens [of the dynasty];
When the water of the deluge spread vast abroad,
Yü arranged and divided the regions of the land.[13]

We seem to be getting closer to a fuller explanation for pristine state formation. We need the confluence of several factors. First, there needs to be a sufficient abundance of resources to permit the creation of surpluses above what is necessary for subsistence. This abundance can be natural: the Pacific Northwest was so full of game and fish that the hunter-gatherer-level societies there were able to generate chiefdoms, if not states. But more often abundance is made possible through technological advances like agriculture. Second, the absolute scale of the society has to be sufficiently large to permit the emergence of a rudimentary division of labor and a ruling elite. Third, that population needs to be physically constrained so that it increases in density when technological opportunities present themselves, and in order to make sure that subjects cannot run away when coerced. And finally, tribal groups have to be motivated to give up their freedom to the authority of a state. This can come about through the threat of physical extinction by other, increasingly well-organized groups. Or it can result from the charismatic authority of a religious leader. Taken together, these appear to be plausible factors leading to the emergence of a state in places like the Nile valley.[14]

Thomas Hobbes argued that the state or Leviathan came about as a result of a rational social contract among individuals who wanted to solve the problem of endemic violence and end the state of war. At the beginning of chapter 2 I suggested that there was a fundamental fallacy in this, and all liberal social contract theories, insofar as it presupposed a presocial state of nature in which human beings lived as isolated individuals. Such a state of primordial individualism never existed; human beings are social by nature and do not have to make a self-interested decision to organize themselves into groups. The particular form that social organization takes is frequently the result of rational deliberation at higher levels of development. But at lower ones, it evolves spontaneously out of the building blocks created by human biology.

But there is a flip side to the Hobbesean fallacy. Just as there was never a clean transition from an anomic state of nature to an orderly civil society, so there was never a complete solution to the problem of human violence. Human beings cooperate to compete, and they compete to cooperate. The birth of the Leviathan did not permanently solve the problem of violence; it simply moved it to a higher level. Instead of tribal segments fighting one another, it was now states that were the primary protagonists in increasingly large-scale wars. The first state to emerge could create a victor's peace but over time faced rivals as new states borrowing the same political techniques rose to challenge its predominance.

WHY WEREN'T STATES UNIVERSAL?

We are now in a position to understand why states failed to emerge in certain parts of the world like Africa and Oceania, and why tribal societies persist in regions like Afghanistan, India, and the uplands of Southeast Asia. The political scientist Jeffrey Herbst has argued that the absence of indigenous states in many parts of Africa flows from the confluence of several familiar factors: "The fundamental problem facing state-builders in Africa— be they colonial kings, colonial governors, or presidents in the independent era—has been to project authority over inhospitable territories that contain relatively low densities of people."[15] He points out that, contrary to popular imagination, only 8 percent of the continent's land has a tropical climate, and that 50 percent receives inadequate rainfall to support regular agriculture. Though the human species got its start in Africa, human beings have thrived better in other parts of the world. Population densities had always been low throughout the continent until the arrival of modern agriculture and medicine; it was not until 1975 that Africa reached the population density that Europe enjoyed in the year 1500. Parts of Africa that are exceptions to this generalization, like the fertile Great Lakes region and the Great Rift Valley, have supported much higher population densities and indeed saw the early emergence of centralized states.

The physical geography of Africa has also made the projection of power difficult. The continent has few rivers that are navigable over long stretches (again, exceptions to this rule like the lower Nile support this point, since it was home to one of the world's first states). The great deserts of the Sahel are a huge barrier to both trade and conquest, in contrast to the less arid steppe lands of Eurasia. Those mounted Muslim warriors who did manage to cross this obstacle soon found their horses dying of encephalitis from the tsetse fly, which explains why the Muslim parts of West Africa are limited to the northern parts of Nigeria, Cote d'Ivoire, Ghana, and the like.[16] In the parts of Africa that are covered by tropical forests, the difficulty of building and maintaining roads was an important obstacle to state building. The hard-surfaced roads the Romans built in Britain were still being used more than a millennium after the collapse of Roman power there; few roads can last more than a few seasons in the tropics.

There are relatively few regions in Africa that are clearly circumscribed by physical geography. This has made it extraordinarily difficult for territorial rulers to push their administration into the hinterland and to control populations. Low population density has meant that new land was usually available; people could respond to the threat of conquest simply by retreating farther into the bush. State consolidation based on wars of conquest never took place in Africa to the extent it did in Europe simply because the motives and possibilities for conquest were much more limited.[17] This meant, according to Herbst, that the transition from a tribal to a territorial conception of power with clearly conceived administrative boundaries of the sort that existed in Europe did not take place.[18] The emergence of states in parts of the continent that were circumscribed, like the Nile valley, is an exception fully consistent with the underlying rule.

The reason for the absence of states in aboriginal Australia may be similar to that which pertains to Africa. Australia is for the most part an extremely arid and undifferentiated continent; despite the length of time that human beings have lived there, population density has always been extremely low. The absence of agriculture and of naturally circumscribed regions may explain the failure of political structures above the level of tribe and lineage to emerge.

The situation in Melanesia is rather different. The region consists entirely of islands, so there is natural circumscription; in addition, agriculture there was invented long ago. Here the problem is one of scale and the difficulties of power projection, given the mountainous nature of most of the islands. The mountain valleys into which the islands are divided are small and capable of supporting only a limited population, and it is extremely difficult to project power over long distances. As noted earlier, the larger islands with more extensive fertile plains, such as Fiji and Hawaii, did see the emergence of chiefdoms and states.

Mountains also explain the persistence of tribal forms of organization in many of the world's upland regions, including Afghanistan; the Kurdish regions of Turkey, Iraq, Iran, and Syria; the highlands of Laos and Vietnam; and Pakistan's tribal agencies. Mountains simply make these regions very difficult for states and their armies to conquer and hold. Turks, Mongols, and Persians, followed by the British, Russians, and now the Americans and NATO forces have all tried to subdue and pacify Afghanistan's tribes and to build a centralized state there, with very modest success.

Understanding the conditions under which pristine state formation occurred is interesting because it helps to define some of the material conditions under which states emerge. But in the end, there are too many interacting factors to be able to develop one strong, predictive theory of when and how states formed. Some of the explanations for their presence or absence begin to sound like Kipling Just So stories. For example, in parts of Melanesia the environmental conditions are quite similar to those of Fiji or Tonga—large islands with agriculture supporting potentially dense populations—where no state emerged. Perhaps the reason has to do with religion, or particular accidents of unrecoverable history.

It is not clear how important it is to develop such a theory, however, since the vast majority of states around the world were the products of competitive rather than pristine state formation. Many states were formed, moreover, in historical times for which we have a written record. Chinese state formation, in particular, began extremely early, somewhat after Egypt and Mesopotamia, and contemporaneously with the rise of states around the Mediterranean and in the New World. There are extensive written and archaeological records of early Chinese history, moreover, that give us a far more contextualized sense of Chinese politics. But most important, the state that emerged in China was far more modern in Max Weber's sense than any of its counterparts elsewhere. The Chinese created a uniform, multilevel administrative bureaucracy, something that never happened in

Greece or Rome. The Chinese developed an explicit antifamilistic political doctrine, and its early rulers sought to undermine the power of entrenched families and kinship groups in favor of impersonal administration. This state engaged in a nation-building project that created a powerful and uniform culture, a culture powerful enough to withstand two millennia of political breakdown and external invasion. The Chinese political and cultural space extended over a far larger population than that of the Romans. The Romans ruled an empire, limiting citizenship initially to a relatively small number of people on the Italian peninsula. While that empire eventually stretched from Britain to North Africa to Germany to Syria, it consisted of a heterogeneous collection of peoples who were allowed a considerable degree of self-rule. By contrast, even though the Chinese monarch called himself an emperor rather than a king, he ruled over something that looked much more like a kingdom or even a state in its uniformity.

The Chinese state was centralized, bureaucratic, and enormously despotic. Marx and Wittfogel recognized this characteristic of Chinese politics by their use of terms like "the Asiatic mode of production" and "Oriental despotism." What I argue in succeeding chapters is that so-called Oriental despotism is nothing other than the precocious emergence of a politically modern state. In China, the state was consolidated before other social actors could institutionalize themselves, actors like a hereditary, territorially based aristocracy, an organized peasantry, cities based on a merchant class, churches, or other autonomous groups. Unlike in Rome, the Chinese military remained firmly under the state's control and never posed an independent threat to its political authority. This initial skewing of the balance of power was then locked in for a long period, since the mighty state could act to prevent the emergence of alternative sources of power, both economic and political. No dynamic modern economy emerged until the twentieth century that could upset this distribution of power. Strong foreign enemies periodically conquered parts or the whole of the country, but these tended to be tribal peoples with less-developed cultures, who were quickly absorbed and Sinified by their own subjects. Not until the arrival of the Europeans in the nineteenth century did China really have to contend with foreign models that challenged its own state-centered path of development.

The Chinese pattern of political development differs from that of the West insofar as the development of a precociously modern state was not offset by other institutionalized centers of power that could force on it something like a rule of law. But in this respect it also differed dramatically from India. One of Marx's biggest mistakes was to lump China and India together under a single "Asiatic" paradigm. Unlike China but like Europe, India's institutionalization of countervailing social actors—an organized priestly class and the metastacization of kinship structures into the caste system—acted as a brake on the accumulation of power by the state. The result was that over the past twenty-two hundred years, China's default political mode was a unified empire punctuated by periods of civil war, invasion, and breakdown, whereas India's default mode was a disunited system of petty political units, punctuated by brief periods of unity and empire.

The chief driver of Chinese state formation was not the need to create grand irrigation projects, nor the rise of a charismatic religious leader, but unrelenting warfare. It was war and the requirements of war that led to the consolidation of a system of ten thousand political units into a single state in the space of eighteen hundred years, that motivated the creation of a class of permanent trained bureaucrats and administrators, and that justified the move away from kinship as the basis for political organization. As Charles Tilly said of Europe in a later period, for China, "war made the state, and the state made war."

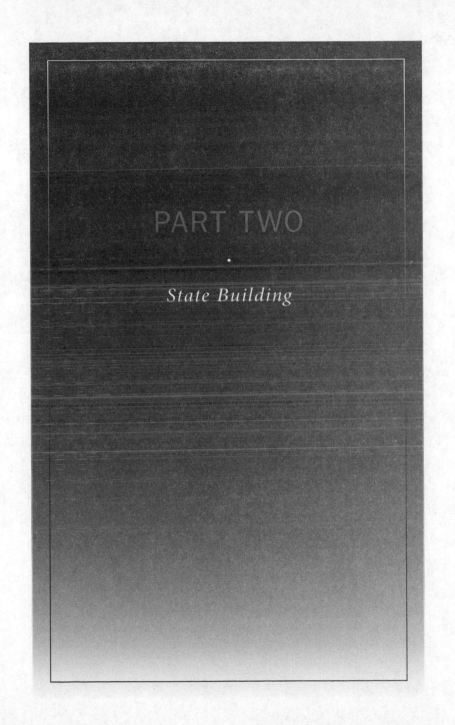

PART TWO

·

State Building

6

CHINESE TRIBALISM

The origins of Chinese civilization; organization of tribal society in ancient China; characteristics of Chinese family and kinship; spread of feudalism under the Zhou and the nature of political authority

Tribalism has existed in China from the beginning of its recorded history. Segmentary lineages still remain in parts of southern China and Taiwan. When historians speak of Chinese "families," they are often referring not to nuclear units consisting of two parents and their children but to much broader groups of agnates that can number in the hundreds or even thousands. Since early Chinese history is relatively well documented, we have a rare opportunity to observe the crystallization of states out of a tribal-level society.

Human beings have lived in China for a very long time. Archaic humans like *Homo erectus* were present there as much as eight hundred thousand years ago, and *Homo sapiens* appeared first a few thousand years after their exit from Africa. Millet (in the north) and rice (in the south) were first cultivated at a very early point, and metallurgy and settled communities first appeared during the predynastic Yangshao period (5000–3000 B.C.). Walled cities and clear evidence of social stratification appeared during the Longshan period (3000–2000 B.C.). Before this point, religion was based on ancestor or spirit worship presided over by shamans who, as in most band-level societies, were not specialists but simply ordinary members of the community. But with the emergence of more stratified societies during the Longshan period, rulers began to monopolize control over shamanism and use it to bolster their own legitimacy.[1]

After the development of agriculture, perhaps the most critical technological development was the domestication of the horse. This may have happened first in Ukraine in the fourth millennium B.C., and spread to Western and Central Asia by the early second millennium. The transition to pastoral nomadism was completed by the beginning of the first millennium, which is when the first mounted tribal peoples started pushing their way into China.[2] Much of subsequent Chinese history is dominated by this phenomenon.

The periodization of ancient China can be confusing (see Table 1).[3] Yangshao and Longshan are archaeological rather than dynastic categories, named after settlements on the middle and lower Yellow River in northern China. Dynastic China begins with the Three Dynasties, the Xia, Shang, and Zhou. The Zhou Dynasty in turn is divided into the Western and Eastern Zhou, a split that occurred in 770 B.C. when the Zhou moved their capital from Haojing in Shaanxi to Luoyang in modern western Henan province. The Eastern Zhou is then itself divided into two subperiods, the Spring and Autumn and Warring States periods.

Table 1. Ancient China

YEAR (B.C.)	DYNASTY	PERIOD	NO. OF POLITIES
5000		Yangshao	
3000		Longshan	
2000	Xia	Three Dynasties	3,000
1500	Shang		1,800
1200	Western Zhou		170
770	Eastern Zhou	Spring and Autumn (770–476)	23
		Warring States (475–221)	7
221	Qin		1

Ancient China refers to the period from earliest prehistory up to the beginning of the Qin Dynasty, which marked the unification of China as a single empire. What we know about this period comes from extensive archaeological data, including large numbers of inscriptions on oracle bones (usually the shoulder bones of sheep), which were used for divination; inscribed bronze vessels; and bamboo strips on which court officials kept records of state affairs.[4] Another source of information is the great classics of Chinese literature composed in the last few centuries of the Eastern Zhou. Most important are the five canonical works whose study constituted the foundation of a Chinese Mandarin's education in later centuries: the *Shi Jing*, or *Book of Odes*; the *Li Chi*, or *Book of Rites*; the *Shu Jing*, or *Book of History*; the *I Jing*, or *Book of Changes*; and the *Chun Qiu*, or *Spring and Autumn Annals*. The five classics were said to have been compiled, edited, and transmitted by Confucius, and they and their voluminous interpretations were the basis of Confucian ideology, which shaped Chinese culture for millennia. The classics were composed against the backdrop of growing civil war and political breakdown during the Eastern Zhou; the *Spring and Autumn Annals* is an account of the reigns of twelve successive rulers of the state of Lu that to Confucius demonstrated the growing degeneracy of this period. The classics, as well as works written by Confucius, Mencius, Mozi, Sun Tzu, and others in this time, contain a great deal of historical information, though the accuracy of these primarily literary works is unclear.

There is clear evidence, however, that there was a tremendous reduction in the total number of political units in China, from approximately ten thousand at the beginning of the Xia Dynasty to twelve hundred at the onset of the Western Zhou, to seven at the time of the Warring States.[5] Groundwork for the first truly modern state was laid in the western polity of Qin under Duke Xiao and his minister, Shang Yang. The process of state consolidation reached a conclusion when the king of Qin conquered all of his rivals and established a single empire, uniformly imposing institutions first developed in Qin on much of northern China.

TRIBAL CHINA

The transition from a tribal to a state-level society took place gradually in China, with state institutions being layered on top of kinship-based social structures. What are sometimes referred to as "states" during the Xia and Shang dynasties are actually better characterized as chiefdoms or tribes with increasingly higher levels of stratification and centralized leadership. Up through the end of the Shang Dynasty, kinship remained the primary form of Chinese social organization. This began to change only under the Zhou Dynasty, when true states with standing armies and administrative structures began to emerge.

In this early phase of Chinese history, society was organized as lineages, agnatic groups claiming descent from a common ancestor. The basic military unit consisted of males from approximately one hundred households making up a lineage, grouped under a flag or banner and led by the lineage chief. Lineages could flexibly combine into clans or higher-order lineages, and the king was the supreme head of all lineages in a particular area.[6]

During the period of the Three Dynasties, ritual behavior within lineages was codified in a series of laws. The rites revolved around worship of the lineages' common ancestor and took place at the ancestral temple that held the tablets inscribed with the ancestor's name. There were several sections of these temples, corresponding to the level of lineage or sublineage organization. Lineage leaders reinforced their authority through their control over the rites; failure to correctly observe either the rites or military orders led to severe punishment by the king or higher lineage heads. Correspondingly, if an enemy was to be truly vanquished, it was important to break up its ancestral temple, loot its symbolic treasures, and then kill off the enemy's male progeny to break the "rope of descent."[7]

As in other tribal societies, China in this period was subject to increasing and decreasing levels of social organization. On the one hand, lineages, based in settled villages, combined for purposes of war, self-defense, or commerce. Sometimes alliances were voluntary and based on common economic interest; sometimes they were due to the ritual respect of a particular leader; quite often they were due to coercion. Warfare became increasingly common, as evidenced by the spread of rammed-earth-walled towns that began to proliferate during the Longshan period.[8]

On the other hand, lineage society was subject to constant fission, as younger descendants sought new land and established their own branches of the kindred. At this time, China was sparsely populated, and families could escape the authority of an established lineage simply by moving to a new place.[9] Thus, as the theories of state formation predict, low population density and lack of circumscription worked against the formation of states and hierarchy.

Nonetheless, in the older parts of the Yellow River valley, population densities rose, along with agricultural productivity. Increasing levels of hierarchy during the Shang Dynasty are seen in the severe punishments that could be imposed by leaders on their followers, and by the spread of slavery and human sacrifice. Oracle bone inscriptions mention five types of punishment: branding the forehead, cutting off the nose, cutting off the feet, castration, and death.[10] Many burial sites from this period contain eight to ten prostrate, headless skeletons, probably of slaves or prisoners of war. Higher-level leaders were buried with as many as five hundred sacrificial victims; as many as ten thousand sacrificial victims have been uncovered in burial pits in Yinxu, along with large numbers of horses, chariots, tripods, and other valuable artifacts. Appeasing dead ancestors thus deprived the living of huge amounts of resources, human, animal, and material.[11] Clearly, a shift was beginning to take place from a tribal to a more hierarchical form of polity.

CHINESE FAMILY AND KINSHIP

One of the great constants in Chinese history is the importance of family and kinship to social organization. The rulers of Qin tried to suppress kin ties in favor of a more impersonal form of administration, both in their own kingdom and for China more broadly once they had established a unified empire. When the Chinese Communist Party came to power in 1949, it too tried to use its dictatorial power to eliminate traditional Chinese familism and bind individuals to the state. Neither of these political projects worked as well as their authors hoped; the Chinese family proved very resilient, and agnatic descent groups still exist in parts of China.[12] After the brief Q Dynasty, impersonal administration was finally established during the Former Han Dynasty (206 B.C.–A.D. 9). But kinship made a big comeback toward the end of the Later Han, Sui, and Tang dynasties. Impersonal state administration was restored only during the Song and Ming dynasties beginning in the second millennium A.D. Particularly in southern China, lineages and clans remained strong up to the twentieth century. On a local level, they played a quasi-political function and partially displaced the state itself as a source of authority over many matters.

There is a huge literature on Chinese kinship, much of it written by anthropologists who have studied contemporary communities in Taiwan and southern China, and have made use of kinship records going back to the nineteenth century for these areas.[13] There are also studies of family relationships for earlier periods of Chinese history based on the extraordinarily detailed records that individual kin groups have left behind. We have much less information on kinship in ancient China, and there is some danger in projecting modern trends that far back in time. Some scholars argue that contemporary lineages were the product of deliberate policies engineered by neo-Confucians during the Tang–Song transition and that kinship was different prior to the second millennium A.D.[14] Nonetheless, certain features of kinship organization have remained constant over the centuries of Chinese history.

Kinship in Chinese society is strictly patrilineal or agnatic. The lineage has been defined by one anthropologist as "a *corporate group* which celebrates *ritual unity* and is based on *demonstrated descent* from a common ancestor."[15] While some modern lineages trace ancestry to an ancestor twenty generations removed, historical ones usually went no deeper than five generations. By contrast, the clan was a much broader grouping of kin encompassing several lineages and often based on fictive kinship. They and related surname associations often existed only to define exogamy.[16]

As in other agnatic societies, succession and inheritance pass only through males. A woman is not considered a permanent part of her own lineage but is rather a resource to be used by the family in arranging alliances with other important families. When she marries, she breaks her ties with her birth family, and in many periods of Chinese history could return to visit them only on carefully prescribed days. The wife no longer worships at her birth family's temple but at that of her husband. Because the "rope of descent" passes only through males, she has no status in her new family until she herself bears a male offspring. Indeed, her soul is not secure until she has sons who will pray for her spirit along with her husband's once she is dead. In more practical terms, her sons are her source of social security in old age.

There is a high degree of tension between the young wife and her mother-in-law, documented in countless Chinese novels and plays over the centuries, since the latter is allowed to tyrannize the former until a son is born. But after bearing a son, a woman can achieve very high status as the mother of the heir in an important lineage. Many of the court intrigues in Imperial China revolved around the efforts of powerful dowagers to improve their sons' political standing. In the Former Han Dynasty, empress dowagers were able to choose the heir to the throne on at least six occasions.[17]

One of the sad truths about premodern societies was the difficulty of producing a male offspring who survived into adulthood. In an era before modern medicine, high status and wealth made very little difference in this quest. The history of monarchies around the world attests to the state of perpetual political crisis that attended the failure of queens or other royal consorts to produce male offspring. Many contemporary Japanese anxiously followed the travails of Crown Prince Naruhito's wife, Masako, in trying to conceive a son after their marriage in 1993. This paled in comparison to a string of earlier emperors, however: only three of the fifteen children of Emperor Ninko (1800–1846) survived past the age of three, and only five of Emperor Meiji's (1852–1912) fifteen offspring reached adulthood.[18]

In China, as in other societies, this problem was traditionally addressed through concubinage, by which high-status men could effectively acquire second, third, and even more wives. China developed a complex, formalized system for determining succession in such situations. For example, the son of a primary wife had superior inheritance rights to the son of a concubine, even if he were younger, though some emperors violated this rule. Despite the system of rules, uncertainties about succession fueled a great deal of court politics. In 71 B.C., Huo Xian, wife of a prominent official, had the empress Xu murdered while pregnant and had her own daughter substituted. In A.D. 115, the emperor Andi's childless empress Yan had a secondary consort put to death for having given birth to a son.[19]

As in the case of the Greeks and Romans described by Fustel de Coulanges, the Chinese kinship system was intimately connected with the system of private property. Initially during the Zhou Dynasty, all land was declared to be the property of the state, but Zhou kings were too weak to enforce this, and property increasingly became private and subject to sale or alienation.[20] The lineage as a whole owned the property housing the ancestral temple or hall. In addition, the richer lineages could invest in common property like dams, bridges, wells, and irrigation systems. Individual families owned their own plots, but their ability to alienate them was severely entailed by the ritual obligations of the lineage.[21]

Growth of the lineage always posed problems with regard to inheritance of property. A system of primogeniture existed during the early Zhou Dynasty, but it was replaced by a rule of splitting inheritances equally among male children that prevailed for most of the rest of Chinese history down to the twentieth century.[22] Under this system, family land often got divided into smaller and smaller parcels, leading to economically unviable holdings. The Chinese developed the ideal of the joint family, in which multiple generations of male descendants lived under the same roof. As the sons grew older, they started their own residences on subdivided family land, or else sought to acquire new land nearby. Descendants, however, still had a stake in the lineage's common property and owed worship duties to common ancestors, which could prevent them from moving too far away or freely selling their land.[23]

Strong regional differences later emerged with regard to property and coresidence. In northern China, the power of lineages declined over time; members of lineages moved to different, widely separated villages and lost their common sense of identity. In the south, however, lineage and clan members continued to live and work near each other, sometimes with entire villages bearing the same clan surname. There has been a great deal of speculation on the reasons for these different outcomes, including the fact that the south was an unsettled frontier for many centuries, which facilitated lineages remaining together even as they expanded, and the constant wars and displacement that occurred in the north, which tended to break up coresident kinship groups.

It is important to remember that lineage organization was in many respects a privilege of the well-to-do. Only they could afford large estates capable of subdivision, communal property, and the multiple wives and concubines sometimes required to produce heirs. In fact, when the rules of the lineage system were first codified during the Zhou Dynasty, they applied only to certain elite families. Poor families could afford fewer children, and in some cases compensated for the absence of a male heir by adopting a son who would give up his lineage name in favor of his wife's—a practice that became common in Japan but was frowned upon in China.[24]

CHINA'S "FEUDAL" PERIOD

The Shang people were conquered by the Zhou tribes who had settled to their west along the Wei River (in contemporary Shaanxi province), a process that began early in the eleventh century B.C. The conquest took several years to complete, the Shang forces having to simultaneously battle horse-mounted nomads to their east in Shandong. The Zhou king killed the Shang heir and murdered his own brothers to seize power, and in the end established a new dynasty.[25]

This conquest set the stage for what many scholars have labeled China's feudal period, in which political power was held on a highly decentralized basis by a series of hierarchically ranked clans and lineages. Throughout the Western and early Eastern Zhou dynasties, kinship remained the primary principle of social organization. But states began to coalesce all over China as a result of the incessant wars that were fought between these kinship groupings during the Spring and Autumn and Warring States periods. We can follow in great detail the factors driving Chinese state formation, based increasingly not on archaeological reconstructions but on historical evidence.

The process of Chinese state formation is particularly interesting in a comparative perspective, since it sets precedents in many ways for the process Europe went through nearly one thousand years later. Just as the Zhou tribes conquered a long-settled territory and established a feudal aristocracy, so too did the Germanic barbarian tribes overrun the decaying Roman Empire and create a comparably decentralized political system. In both China and Europe, state formation was driven primarily by the need to wage war, which led to the progressive consolidation of feudal lands into territorial states, the centralization of political power, and the growth of modern impersonal administration.[26]

There were a number of important differences between China and Europe, however, which are masked by the use of terms like "feudal," "family," "king," "duke," and "nobility" to label parallel Chinese institutions in English-language histories of dynastic China. We therefore need to define these terms carefully and indicate both where there were important parallels and where the civilizations diverged.

Among the most confusing and misused terms are "feudal" and "feudalism," which have been rendered largely meaningless as a result of promiscuous use by both scholars and polemicists.[27] In a tradition that starts with Karl Marx, "feudalism" is often taken to refer to an exploitative economic relationship between lord and peasant that existed in medieval Europe, centering around the manor. The rigidity of a lot of Marxist historiography has made scholars in that tradition look for a feudal stage of development as an inevitable precursor to the rise of modern capitalism in a host of societies where the concept is not relevant.[28]

A more historically accurate definition of feudalism was laid out by the historian Marc Bloch, focusing on the institutions of the fief and vassalage as they existed in medieval Europe. The fief was a contractual agreement between lord and vassal by which the latter was given protection and a plot of land in return for serving the lord in a military capacity. The contract was solemnized in a ceremony in which the lord placed the vassal's hands within his own and sealed the relationship with a kiss. The relationship of dependency entailed clear obligations on both sides and needed to be renewed annually.[29] The vassal could then create subfiefs out of his lands and enter into relationships with his own vassals. The system generated its own complex set of ethical norms concerning honor, loyalty, and courtly love.

From the standpoint of political development, the critical aspect of European feudalism was not the economic relationship between lord and vassal but the decentralization of power it implied. In the words of the historian Joseph Strayer, "Western European feudalism is essentially political—it is a form of government . . . in which political authority is monopolized by a small group of military leaders, but is rather evenly distributed among members of the group."[30] This definition, also associated with Max Weber, is the one I will use throughout this volume. The core of the institution was the grant of the fiefdom, benefice, or appanage, a delineated territory over which the vassal exerted some degree of political control. Despite the theoretical revocability of feudal contracts, European vassals over time turned their fiefdoms into patrimony, that is, property that they could hand down to their descendants. They acquired political rights over these territories to raise armies, tax residents, and administer justice free from interference of the nominal lord. They were thus in no way the lord's agent but rather lords in their own right. Marc Bloch points out that the patrimonial character of later feudalism actually represented a degeneration of the institution.[31] But it is precisely this distributed character of political power within a feudal system that makes it unique.

In this sense, the Zhou Dynasty China was a feudal society.[32] It bore no resemblance to a centralized state. Like many conquest dynasties before and after, the Zhou king found that he did not have the forces or resources under his personal control to rule the territories he had acquired. This was particularly true in the west, where the Zhou were under pressure from steppe nomads, and in the frontier areas to the south that would later become the state of Chu. So he distributed fiefdoms or appanages to his retainers and cowarriors who, given the tribal nature of Zhou society, were his kinsmen. The Zhou king set up seventy-one fiefdoms, of which his kinsmen ruled fifty-three. The others were distributed to defeated Shang lords who pledged loyalty to the new dynasty, or to other Zhou administrators or military commanders. The vassals to whom these lands were granted thereby obtained substantial autonomy to rule them as they pleased.[33]

There were a number of important differences between Chinese feudalism under the Zhou and its European variant. In Europe, segmentary, tribal institutions were destroyed at the beginning of Europe's feudal period, usually within a couple of generations after a barbarian tribe's conversion to Christianity. European feudalism was a mechanism for binding unrelated lords to unrelated vassals, facilitating social cooperation in a society where complex kinship no longer existed. In China, by contrast, the primary political actors were not individual lords but lords *and their kinship groups*. Within a European lord's domain, impersonal administration had already begun to take root, in the form of the feudal contract between lord and peasant. Authority was vested in the lord himself and not in the lord's clan. The fief was a possession of his family but not of a larger corporate descent group.

In China, on the other hand, fiefdoms were granted to kinship groups, who could then subinfeudate their lands to sublineages or collateral branches of the tribe. The authority of an individual Chinese noble was therefore less hierarchical and weaker than that of a European lord, because he himself was embedded in a larger kinship framework that limited his discretion. I noted earlier that in tribal societies, leadership is often achieved rather than ascribed—it has to be earned by the leader rather than being given by birth. In Zhou China, leadership was evolving in a more hierarchical direction, but it still remained constrained by kin networks and thus appeared more "tribal" than its European variant. According to one observer, during the Spring and Autumn period, "The state resembled an enlarged household; the ruler reigned but did not rule. Ministers were important not because they held their offices; they were important and received offices because they were kin to the ruler or because they were heads of prominent families."[34] The king was more first among equals than a true sovereign: "Various stories tell of nobles who upbraided the ruler in public and spat at him without being reprimanded or punished, who rejected requests for precious objects, who played board games with the ruler in the midst of his harem, who helped themselves uninvited from the ruler's table, or who called on the ruler to share dinner, only to find him out back shooting birds."[35]

In the clan-based organization of Zhou society, armies were themselves segmented, with no centralized command and control. Each lineage raised its own forces and combined (like Nuer segments) into larger units. "Accounts of campaigns reveal that in the field these levies remained under their own commanders, that major decisions were generally made by group consultation among the leaders, and that the detachments were only loosely bound together so that a commander might lead off his own men without regard for the rest of the army."[36] There were numerous cases in which a subordinate overrode the orders of a nominal lord because no strict command-and-control hierarchy existed. According to the anthropological categories developed in chapter 5, early Zhou polities were tribes or at best chiefdoms and not states.

Chinese feudal society in the Zhou Dynasty was similar to its European counterpart insofar as it developed sharp class divisions and an aristocracy set off by a moral code built around honor and the risk of life in violent struggle. Early tribal societies start off relatively egalitarian, with various leveling mechanisms to prevent the emergence of sharp status differences. Then certain individuals begin to distinguish themselves in the hunt. There is a continuity, stretching as we have seen all the way back to the human species' primate ancestors, between the hunt and warfare. In hunting and conquest, hierarchy asserts itself because some individuals and groups are simply better hunters and warriors than others. Those who excel in the hunt tend to excel in war; the cooperative skills needed for hunting evolve into military tactics and strategy. Through victory in battle, some lineages acquire higher status than others, and within each lineage, warriors who distinguish themselves emerge as leaders.

So too in China. The continuity between hunting and warfare was preserved in a series of rituals that served to legitimate the social status of the warrior aristocracy. Mark Lewis argues that during the Spring and Autumn period, "The actions that set the rulers apart from the masses were the 'great services' of those altars, and these services were ritually directed violence in the form of sacrifices, warfare, and hunting."[37] Hunting brought animals to be sacrificed to the ancestors, while warfare brought human sacrifices, a Shang practice that was continued under the Zhou until the fourth century B.C. Military campaigns began at temples with sacrifices and prayers to ensure the success of the campaign. Meat was ritually shared during the rites, prisoners' blood was shed to consecrate war drums, and particularly hated enemies were turned into a meat sauce to be consumed by members of the court or army.[38]

Aristocratic warfare in early Zhou China became highly ritualized. Wars were fought for the purpose of making another clan recognize one's dominance, or to avenge slights to one's honor. Armies went forth to defend the "inherited achievements of ancestors"; failure to do so would deny a leader the proper rites when he became a dead ancestor. They could achieve this through ceremonial tests of strength and honor rather than an all-out fight to the death. Battles were often prearranged between groups of aristocrats, who observed a complex set of rules. The appearance of the enemy on the battlefield required an army to engage or suffer dishonor, and it was sometimes regarded as dishonorable not to attack the enemy's strongest point. Conversely, armies would withdraw from the field of battle when the opposing lord died, so as not to increase the other side's mourning duties. In the early Spring and Autumn period, aristocrats did most of the fighting from chariots that were expensive and required a high degree of skill to operate and maintain.[39] Obviously, the military strategist Sun Tzu's advice to use the "indirect method," in which surprise and deceit were important components, came from a later period in Chinese history.

China during the early Zhou Dynasty had evolved into something between a tribal and a chiefdom-level society. None of the units commonly referred to as "states" in the histories were true states. Zhou China was a textbook example of a patrimonial society. That is, the entire country was "owned" by a series of local lords and their kin groups. Within the constraints of China's agnatic kinship rules, the land and the people living on it were patrimony or heritable property that was passed down to descendants. There was no distinction in this society between public and private; each ruling lineage raised armies, imposed taxes, and dispensed justice as it saw fit. All this, however, soon changed.

7

WAR AND THE RISE OF THE CHINESE STATE

How the Chinese state arose out of military competition; Shang Yang's modernizing reforms; the doctrine of Legalism and its critique of Confucian familism; why political development was not accompanied by economic or social development

During the Eastern Zhou Dynasty (770–256 B.C.), genuine states began to coalesce in China. They established standing armies that were capable of enforcing rules throughout a defined territory; they created bureaucracies to collect taxes and administer laws; they mandated uniform weights and measures; and they created public infrastructure in the form of roads, canals, and irrigation systems. One state in particular, the kingdom of Qin, embarked on a remarkable modernizing project whose direct target was the kinship-based, patrimonial social order of the early Zhou. It democratized the army by bypassing the warrior aristocrats and directly conscripting masses of peasants, it engaged in large-scale land reform by dispossessing patrimonial landowners and giving land directly to peasant families, and it promoted social mobility by undermining the power and prestige of the hereditary nobility. As "democratic" as these reforms sound, their only purpose was to increase the power of the Qin state and thus create a remorseless dictatorship. The strength of these modern political institutions allowed Qin to defeat all of the other contending states and unify China.

WAR AND STATE BUILDING

The political scientist Charles Tilly has famously argued that European state building was driven by the need of European monarchs to wage war.[1]

The correlation between war and state building is not a universal one; this process has not, by and large, played out in Latin America.[2] But war was without question the single most important driver of state formation during China's Eastern Zhou Dynasty. Between the beginning of the Eastern Zhou in 770 B.C. and the consolidation of the Qin Dynasty in 221 B.C., China experienced an unremitting series of wars that increased in scale, costliness, and lost human lives. China's transition from a decentralized feudal state to a unified empire was accomplished entirely through conquest. And virtually every modern state institution established in this period can be linked directly or indirectly to the need to wage war.

When compared to other warlike societies, China's bloody record during the Eastern Zhou stands out. One scholar has calculated that in the 294-year duration of the Spring and Autumn period, more than 1,211 wars were fought between and among Chinese "states." Throughout this entire period, there were only 38 years of peace. More than 110 political units were extinguished during this time. During the 254 years of the subsequent Warring States period, 468 wars took place, with only 89 peaceful years. The total number of wars declined only because the number of states had fallen dramatically through conquest and incorporation. During the Warring States period, sixteen states were extinguished by the seven that survived during this period. But the wars that did occur increased dramatically in scale and duration. During the Spring and Autumn period, some wars consisted of a single battle and were concluded in a day. Toward the end of the Warring States period, sieges could last for months and wars for years, and involve armies as large as five hundred thousand troops.[3]

Compared to other militaristic societies, China under the Zhou was remarkably violent. By one estimate, the state of Qin succeeded in mobilizing 8 to 20 percent of its total population, compared to only 1 percent for the Roman Republic and 5.2 percent for the Greek Delian League. Rates of mobilization were even lower in early modern Europe.[4] Casualties were also of unprecedented scale. Livy reports that the Roman Republic lost approximately 50,000 soldiers in their defeats at Lake Trasimene and Cannae; a Chinese memorialist claims that 240,000 soldiers died in one battle in 293 B.C. and 450,000 in another in 260. In all, the state of Qin was said to have killed more than 1.5 million soldiers of other states between 356 and 236 B.C. All of these figures are regarded by historians as wildly inflated and unverifiable, but it is still remarkable that the Chinese ones are a full order of magnitude higher than their Western counterparts.[5]

INSTITUTIONAL INNOVATIONS BROUGHT
ON BY CONSTANT WARFARE

Intensive warfare created incentives powerful enough to lead to the destruction of old institutions and the creation of new ones to take their place. These occurred with regard to military organization, taxation, bureaucracy, civilian technological innovation, and ideas.

Military Organization

The first consequence of this high level of warfare was, unsurprisingly, an evolution in the military organizations of the warring states.

As noted earlier, wars in the early Spring and Autumn period were fought by aristocrats riding chariots. Each chariot required a driver and at least two warriors, and was accompanied by an extensive logistics train of up to seventy soldiers. Driving a chariot and firing from it were difficult skills requiring substantial training and thus suitable as aristocratic occupations.[6] Infantry in this period served only as auxiliaries.

The transition from chariot to infantry/cavalry warfare took place gradually at the end of the Spring and Autumn period. Chariots were of limited use in the southern states of Wu and Yue, which had many lakes and swamps, and they were not effective in mountainous areas. Cavalry made its first appearance at the beginning of the Warring States period, evidently based on experience with the mounted western steppe barbarians. Infantry became more useful with the proliferation of iron weapons, crossbows, and lamellar (plated) armor. The western state of Qin was one of the first to reorganize its army and eliminate chariots in favor of a mixture of cavalry and foot soldiers, due partly to terrain and partly to constant pressure from barbarians. The state of Chu was the first to conscript the people of another state when it defeated Chen and forced its farmers into military service. These troops were not organized by kinship group but by administrative units arranged in clear hierarchies with fixed numbers of subordinate units.[7] The first all-infantry army was deployed in the mid-sixth century B.C. and infantry completely displaced chariot armies over the next two centuries. Mass conscription of peasants became common practice by the beginning of the Warring States period.[8]

The shift from chariots to infantry as the core of a Chinese army's striking power has clear parallels with the shift from the heavily armored mounted knights to infantry armies made up of bowmen and pikemen in Europe.

Neither of these developments enhanced the social position of the aristocracy, who constituted the charioteers and knights. In both civilizations, it was only the aristocratic elite that could afford to equip themselves for the older style of warfare and who had the requisite specialist training for these roles. While this shift would seem to be driven primarily by changes in technology, it is also likely that the ranks of the aristocracy were being continually thinned in China, leaving fewer highly trained military specialists.

Physical losses to the ranks of the aristocracy also had the effect of encouraging promotion within the military based on merit. In the early Zhou, positions of military leadership were claimed entirely on the basis of kinship and status within the clan. But as time went on, an increasing number of nonaristocratic leaders were promoted on the basis of their valor in battle. States began to offer explicit incentives of land, titles, and serfs as inducements to soldiers, and it soon became common for obscure commoners to rise to the position of general.[9] In a field army at war, meritocracy is not a cultural norm but a condition for survival, and it is very likely that the principle of merit-based promotion began in military hierarchies before it was introduced into the civilian bureaucracy.

Taxation and Population Registration

The mobilization of large conscripted peasant armies necessitated resources to pay for and equip them. Between 594 and 590 B.C., the state of Lu began to tax agricultural land, not as a possession of a kin group but on the basis of an allotment of land to groups of individual peasant families known as *qiu*. This occurred due to invasions from the neighboring state of Qi, which required Lu to rapidly increase the size of its conscripted army. Between 543 and 539, Zi Chan reorganized the fields of the state of Zheng into a regular grid with irrigation channels, restructured rural households into groups of five families, and imposed on them a new tax. In 548, the state of Chu performed a cadastral survey of its lands, registering salt ponds, fishponds, marshes, and forests, as well as population. This survey was done in anticipation of the reorganization of the tax base and also as a means of drafting the rural population as soldiers.[10]

The Growth of Bureaucracy

It is safe to say that the Chinese invented modern bureaucracy, that is, a permanent administrative cadre selected on the basis of ability rather than kinship or patrimonial connection. Bureaucracy emerged unplanned from the chaos of Zhou China, in response to the urgent necessity of extracting taxes to pay for war.

Administration in the first years of Zhou, like administration in other early states such as Egypt, Sumer, Persia, Greece, and Rome, was patrimonial. Administrative positions were granted to kinsmen of the ruler and considered part of the ruler's household. Decision making was not strictly hierarchical but based on consultation and personal loyalties. The ruler could therefore not always control his ministers or fire them when they disagreed. Indeed, like the Big Man in the wantok, a Zhou lord facing a strong consensus that he should be replaced by someone else often could not prevent this from happening. His only alternative, like Duke Xian of Qin in the year 669 B.C., was to massacre all of the relatives plotting against him. Since court intrigue was carried out by lineages rather than individuals, entire families had to be killed off in order to break the "rope of descent."[11]

Bureaucratization began in the army with the expansion of service from aristocrats to commoners. The army hierarchy needed to conscript, equip, and train large numbers of people, which required record-keeping and logistics services. The need to fund the army then increased demand for a civilian bureaucracy, in order to collect taxes and ensure the continuity in conditions of large-scale mobilization. The military bureaucracy also served as a training ground for civilian bureaucrats and facilitated growth of a command-and-control infrastructure.[12] The self-immolation of the Zhou aristocracy in internecine conflicts in the meantime created great opportunities for the upward social mobility of ministerial families. Though ministers were traditionally chosen from the noble class, they often came from social circles far distant from the ruler and his relatives. The shi class was a stratum somewhat below that of the nobility that included soldiers or other meritorious commoners, and they as well found themselves being promoted into positions of responsibility in place of the patrimonial ministers. Hence the principle of promotion by merit rather than birth began to take hold slowly as the ranks of the nobility became depleted.[13]

Civilian Technological Innovation

Both intensive and extensive economic growth took place in China from the fourth to the third century B.C. Intensive growth was fueled by a number of technological innovations, including the shift from bronze tools to iron, and then the development of iron-casting techniques based on double-action piston bellows; better techniques for yoking animals to plows; and improved land and water management. Commercial interactions increased between different parts of China, and population began to grow dramatically. Extensive growth was driven by population increase and the settling of new frontier areas like Sichuan.

This economic growth was to some extent what economists call "exogenous," meaning that it occurred as a result of fortuitous technological innovations that were not driven by the internal logic of the economic system. One of the critical external drivers was military insecurity. All states in the Warring States period felt huge pressures to increase levels of taxation, and therefore levels of agricultural productivity; all of them copied innovations and used them to increase their own relative power positions.[14]

Ideas

It is notable that the extremely violent centuries of the late Spring and Autumn and the Warring States era produced one of the greatest cultural outpourings in China's history. The extreme social dislocation created by perpetual wars occasioned considerable reflection on political and moral matters, and also created opportunities for talented teachers, writers, and advisers to make their mark. One of the many itinerant teachers attracting students in this period was Confucius, who came out of the gentry but had to make his own way as a scholar and teacher. There were many other writers as well during the so-called Hundred Schools of Thought period of the early Warring States era, including Mozi, Mencius, Sun Tzu, Han Fei, and Xun Zi, each of whom left writings that influenced Chinese politics over succeeding centuries. The political instability of the period seems to have created a kind of intellectual rootlessness, which was reflected in the physical mobility of intellectuals who moved from one jurisdiction to another offering their services to whatever political authority showed an interest in their teaching.[15]

The political significance of this intellectual ferment was twofold. First, it created something like an ideology, that is, a received set of ideas for the proper ordering of government by which later generations of Chinese could judge the performance of their political leaders. The best-known ideology was Confucian doctrine, but Confucianists engaged in bitter intellectual debates with other schools of thought, such as Legalism—a conflict that mirrored the political struggles taking place. Scholars and literati were enshrined as the highest human type, higher than even the warrior or the priest. There was in fact a melding of the roles of intellectual and bureau-crat in a way that does not have a clear counterpart in other civilizations.

Second, the mobility of intellectuals across China encouraged the growth of something that looked increasingly like a national culture. The great Chinese classics composed in this period became the basis of elite education and the foundation of subsequent Chinese culture. National identity came to be anchored in knowledge of the classics; their prestige was such that they penetrated into the remotest parts of the empire and indeed well beyond the empire's borders. Although nomad kingdoms on the frontier at times were militarily stronger than China, none could match its intellectual tradition. The non-Chinese people who attacked and periodically ruled parts of China seldom imposed their own institu-tions on the latter; rather, they tended to rule China using Chinese institu-tions and techniques.

SHANG YANG'S CAMPAIGN AGAINST THE FAMILY

Modern state institutions were gradually implemented all over China in the later years of the Zhou Dynasty, but nowhere more so than in the western state of Qin. In most cases the adoption of new institutions came haphaz-ardly, as the result of trial and error and dire necessity on the part of differ-ent governments. Qin, by contrast, formulated an ideology of state building that explicitly laid out the logic of the new centralized state. The Qin state builders saw clearly that the kinship networks of earlier ages were impedi-ments to the accumulation of power, so they implemented policies deliber-ately intended to replace them with a system that tied individuals directly to the state. This doctrine was called Legalism.

Shang Yang began his career as a minister in the state of Wei before moving to what was then the relatively backward state of Qin and becom-ing the chief adviser to its leader, Duke Xiao. Upon his arrival, he struggled with the existing patrimonial administration. He attacked their inherited privileges and eventually succeeded in replacing hereditary office with a system of twenty ranks that were to be awarded on the basis of merit—meaning, in the case of this frontier state, military merit. Land, retainers, women slaves, and clothing were all to be allocated by the state on the basis of performance.[16] Conversely, failure to obey the state's laws would be met with a series of draconian punishments. Most important, offices given out under this system could not be converted into heritable property like the positions of the patrimonial aristocracy but were periodically redistributed by the state.[17]

One of Shang Yang's most important reforms was abolition of the so-called well-field system and redistribution of land to individual families under the direct tutelage of the state. Under the well-field system, agricultural land was laid out in blocks of nine squares resembling the Chinese character for "well," with eight families working one square each around a central communal plot. Each noble family owned a certain number of well-fields, to whom the peasants working on them owed taxes, corvée labor, and other duties, much like peasants in feudal Europe. The squares were crossed at right angles with various pathways and irrigation channels, which facilitated supervision, and the eight families constituted a kind of commune under the protection of the landowner.[18] Abolition of the well-field system released peasants from their traditional social obligations to their lords and allowed them to resettle on new land being opened up by other landowners, or to own land themselves. This allowed the state to bypass the aristocracy by directly imposing a new, uniform land tax, to be paid in kind by all property owners.

In addition, Shang Yang implemented a poll tax on all adult males for the express purpose of funding military operations. The state decreed that if a household had several sons, they had to live separately once they attained a certain age, or pay a double tax. Shang Yang thus struck directly at the traditional Confucian ideal of the joint family and encouraged nuclear families. The system imposed severe hardships on poor families who didn't have large patrimonies to divide. The purpose of this change may have been to individualize incentives, but it also served to increase the state's control over individuals.

This reform was connected with a new family registration system. Instead of the sprawling kin networks of traditional China, Shang Yang divided families up into groups of five and ten households, which were then called upon to mutually supervise each other. Similar reforms were being implemented in other states, such as Lu, under the *qiu* system, but in Qin it was implemented with characteristic ferocity. Failure to report criminal activity within this group was punished by slicing in two, while those who reported crimes were rewarded as if they had obtained the head of an enemy in battle. A version of this system would be resurrected during the Ming Dynasty as the bao-jia system.

The political scientist James Scott in his book *Seeing Like a State* argues that all states have common characteristics: they seek to control their societies, which means that they want to make them "legible" in the first instance.[19] This is why they bulldoze old neighborhoods that grew up spontaneously as warrens of crooked streets and alleyways, and replace them with geometrical, orderly grids of streets. The broad boulevards that Baron Haussmann constructed over the rubble of medieval Paris during the nineteenth century were built not simply for aesthetic reasons but also with population control in mind.

Something very similar happened in Qin under Shang Yang. In addition to abolishing the well-field system, the minister extended the prefectural system through the kingdom. Forty-one new prefectures were created by amalgamating existing towns, districts, and villages, presided over by a prefect not selected by the locality but appointed by the central government. They were initially located in frontier regions, indicating their origin as military districts. The well-field system was replaced by much larger, evenly spaced rectangular blocks, oriented on an east-west/north-south axis. Modern topographical studies show the whole territory of what was the state of Qin to be covered with these rectilinear layouts.[20] Shang Yang also decreed a uniform system of weights and measures be used throughout Qin, which replaced the diverse standards used under the feudal system.[21]

Shang Yang's massive effort at social engineering replaced the traditional kinship-based system of authority and landownership with a far more impersonal form of rule centering on the state. It obviously generated tremendous opposition on the part of the patrimonial aristocracy within the state of Qin itself. When Shang Yang's protector, Duke Xiao, died, his successor turned against him, and Shang Yang had to go into hiding. He was ultimately turned in by a citizen acting on the basis of a law that Shang Yang had himself promoted requiring severe punishments for those sheltering criminals. He was reportedly executed by being pulled apart by four chariots, and the rest of his lineage was killed along with him.

Every one of the institutional innovations undertaken in China during the Eastern Zhou can be linked directly to the requirements of war. The expansion of military service to the general male population, the rise of first a military and then a civilian permanent bureaucracy, the decline of patrimonial officeholders and their replacement by newcomers chosen on the basis of merit, population registration, land reform and the reshuffling of property rights away from patrimonial elites, the growth of better communications and infrastructure, the imposition of a new, impersonal hierarchy of administrative offices, and uniform weights and measures all had their origins in military requirements. While war was not the only engine of state formation in China, it certainly was the major force behind the growth of the first modern states in China.

CONFUCIANISM VS. LEGALISM

The policies implemented by Shang Yang in Qin were justified and turned into a full-blown ideology known as Legalism by later writers like Han Fei. Much of China's subsequent history up through the Communist victory in 1949 can be understood in terms of the tensions between Legalism and Confucianism, a tension that revolved in part around the appropriate role of the family in politics.[22]

Confucianism is an intensely backward-looking doctrine that roots legitimacy in ancient practices. Confucius compiled his classics at the end of the Spring and Autumn period, looking back nostalgically at the Zhou social order, which was rapidly decaying as a result of China's incessant wars. Family and kinship were at the core of that patrimonial order, and Confucianism can in many ways be seen as an ideology that builds a broad moral doctrine of the state outward from a model based on the family.

All tribal societies practice some form of ancestor worship, but Confucianism gave the Chinese version a particular ethical cast. Confucian moral precepts dictated that one owed much stronger obligations to one's parents, and particularly to one's father, than to one's wife or children. Failure to act respectfully toward one's parents, or to fail to care for them economically, was severely punished, as was a son who showed greater concern for his immediate family than for his parents. And if there was a conflict between one's duty to one's parents—for example, if one's father was accused of a crime—and one's duty to the state, the father's interest clearly trumped that of the state.[23]

This tension between the family and the state, and the moral legitimacy that Confucianism gives to family obligations over political ones, has persisted throughout Chinese history. Even today, the Chinese family remains a powerful institution that jealously guards its autonomy against political authority. There has been an inverse correlation between the strength of the family and the strength of the state. During the decrepitude of the Qing Dynasty in the nineteenth century, southern China's powerful lineages took over control of most local affairs.[24] When China decollectivized under Deng Xiaoping's household responsibility reforms in 1978, the peasant family sprang back to life and became one of the chief engines of the economic miracle that subsequently unfolded in the People's Republic.[25]

The Legalists, by contrast, were forward looking and saw Confucianism and its glorification of the family as obstacles to the consolidation of political power. They had little use for Confucianism's delicate moral injunctions and obligations. In its place, they sought to implement a set of straightforward rewards and punishments—especially punishments—to make subjects obey. In the words of the Legalist ideologist Han Fei,

> Loving mothers have prodigal sons, whereas contumacious slaves are not found in a household that maintains strict discipline. . . . According to the laws of Lord Shang persons throwing ashes on the roads were subjected to corporeal punishment. Now dumping ashes is a minor crime and corporeal punishment is a heavy penalty. Wise rulers alone are capable of dealing severely with those who commit minor crimes, [making it clear that] even minor crimes are severely punished and that much more severely would those who commit major crimes be dealt with. Consequently, the people dare not transgress . . .
>
> The only way in which wise and sage rulers can long occupy the throne, hold the imperial authority, and enjoy exclusively the benefits of the empire, is to rule autocratically with deliberation, and to implement the policy of surveillance and castigation by inflicting heavy punishments without exception.[26]

The Legalists were proposing to treat subjects not as moral beings to be cultivated through education and learning but as *Homo economicus*, self-interested individuals who would respond to positive and negative incentives—especially punishments. The Legalist state therefore sought to undermine tradition, break the bonds of family moral obligation, and rebind citizens to the state on a new basis.

There are obvious parallels between Legalism and the social engineering attempted by the Chinese Communist Party after 1949. Mao, like Shang

Yang before him, saw traditional Confucian morality and the Chinese family as obstacles to social progress. His anti-Confucian campaign sought to delegitimize familistic morality; party, state, and commune were the new structures that would henceforth bind Chinese citizens to one another. It is not surprising, therefore, that the legacy of Shang Yang and Legalism was revived during the Maoist period and seen by many Communist scholars as a precedent for modern China.

In the words of one scholar, "With its ideal of the sage-king Confucian philosophy may be described as absolutism imbued with moral values; in contrast, Legalism may be characterized as naked absolutism which denied the relevancy of morality to human government."[27] Confucianism did not envisage any institutional checks on the power of the emperor; rather, it sought to educate the prince, to moderate his passions and make him feel accountable to his people. Good government achieved through princely education is not unknown in the Western tradition; this is in effect the system outlined by Socrates in his description of a just city in Plato's *Republic*. The degree to which Chinese emperors actually felt accountable to their subjects, rather than simply using Confucian morality to legitimate their self-interest in rule, is a subject I take up in subsequent chapters. But even the pretense of moral government was stripped away by the Legalists, who openly argued that the ruled existed for the sake of the rulers and not the other way around.

We should not be fooled by the Legalists' emphasis on law into thinking that their doctrine had anything to do with rule of law in the sense I use that term in this book. In the West, in India, and in the Muslim world, there was a body of preexisting law, sanctified by religion and safeguarded by a hierarchy of priests and clerics, that was prior to and independent of the state. This law was seen as being older, higher, and more legitimate than the current ruler and therefore binding on him. That is the meaning of the rule of law: even the king or emperor is bound by law and not free simply to do as he pleases.

Rule of law in this sense never existed in China, and least of all for the Legalists. For them, law was simply the codification of whatever the king or ruler dictated, commands rather than law in Friedrich Hayek's sense. They were meant to reflect the interests of the ruler alone and not a consensus of the moral rules governing the community as a whole.[28] The only sense in which Legalism's ordinances shared anything in common with modern rule of law was Shang Yang's view that a punishment, once established, should apply impartially to all members of society—aristocrats should not be able to exempt themselves from generally applicable laws.[29]

The new state institutions created by Shang Yang allowed Qin to mobilize resources on a far higher level than previously, and more effectively than its neighbors. But there was no inevitability to its final victory, since intense competition among the warring states led them to rapidly copy one another's institutions. The story of the rise of the Qin state to hegemony over the whole of China therefore belongs more to the realm of international relations than to the realm of development.

Qin was in fact a minor actor in the consolidating state system of the late Spring and Autumn period, playing the role of balancer between stronger rivals. It was the westernmost of the warring states and was as a result geographically protected to some extent (see map on page 123). Qin initiated only 11 of 160 wars involving the other major states between 656 and 357 B.C. This began to change after Shang Yang's reform of the state under Duke Xiao; between 356 and 221, Qin initiated 52 of 96 great power wars, and was victorious in 48. Qin inflicted defeat on the large southern state of Chu in the last decade of the fourth century B.C., and its two immediate neighbors to the east, Wei and Han, in 293. The state of Qi in the east, which remained the major opposing power, was defeated in 284. By 257, all other states had lost great power status, and the final wars of unification in 236 led to the emergence of a single Qin Dynasty over the whole of China in 221 B.C.[30]

What were the warring states fighting over? To some extent, a background issue in the conflicts of the Eastern Zhou had to do with the decline of the old aristocratic order and the replacement of those elites with commoners who found new opportunities to rise to positions of power. This was the ideological issue argued out between the Confucianists and Legalists. Yet this conflict took place as much within each individual state as between states, and was as much a consequence as a cause of the fighting. While Qin may have seen itself as the bearer of Legalism, the doctrine was adopted more out of utilitarian concerns than as a matter of deep principle.[31]

The dominant idea at stake here was different, centering around the old Shang-Zhou concept of kingship uniting the whole of China. The actuality of a unified China had always been more of a myth than a reality, but the internal divisions of the Eastern Zhou Dynasty were always seen

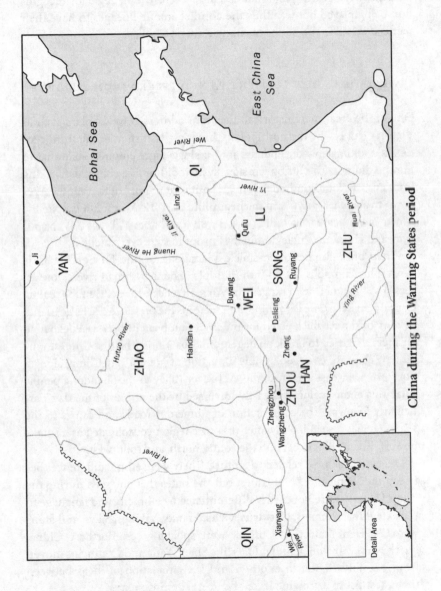

China during the Warring States period

as a prolonged anomaly that needed to be corrected by the lineage that would emerge bearing the Mandate of Heaven. The struggle for recognition being played out was thus the conflict among lineages to have their name attached to the honor of ruling a single China.

WHY CHINA'S DEVELOPMENT PATH DIFFERED FROM EUROPE'S

One of the great metahistorical questions addressed by scholars such as Victoria Hui is why the multipolar Chinese state system of the third century B.C. ultimately consolidated into a single large empire, while that of Europe did not. The European state system did in fact consolidate, going from perhaps four hundred sovereign entities at the end of the Middle Ages down to about twenty-five at the beginning of World War I. But despite the efforts of conquerors including the Habsburg Charles V, Louis XIV, Napoleon, and Hitler, no single dominant European state ever emerged.

There are a number of possible explanations for this. First on the list is geography. Europe is cut up into multiple regions by broad rivers, forests, seas, and high mountain ranges: the Alps, Pyrenees, Rhine, Danube, Baltic, Carpathians, etc. One very important factor is the presence of a large island, Britain, offshore, which acted for much of European history as a deliberate balancer that tried to break up hegemonic coalitions. The first Chinese empire, by contrast, emerged in only a portion of present-day China, along a northerly west-east axis from the Wei River valley to the Shandong peninsula. This entire region was easily traversed by the armies of the day, particularly following the construction of numerous roads and canals in the Warring States period. Only after this core region consolidated as a single, powerful state did it expand to the south, north, and southwest.

A second factor is related to culture. There were ethnic differences between the Shang and Zhou tribes, but the states that emerged during the Zhou Dynasty were not clearly differentiated by ethnicity and language to the extent that Romans, Germans, Celts, Franks, Vikings, Slavs, and Huns were. Different dialects of Chinese were spoken across northern China, but the ease with which individuals like Shang Yang and Confucius moved from one jurisdiction to another, and the circulation of ideas between them, testifies to a growing level of cultural homogeneity.

A third factor is leadership, or the lack thereof. As Victoria Hui points out, a multipolar system is not a mechanical, self-regulating machine that always achieves balance to prevent the emergence of a hegemonic power. States are run by individual leaders who interpret their self-interest. Qin's leaders exercised acute statecraft in using divide-and-rule tactics to break up hostile coalitions, and their opponents often fought suicidal wars among themselves without recognizing the danger that Qin represented.

But the final reason has to do directly with the different paths that political development took in China and in Europe. Europe never saw the emergence of a powerful absolutist state like Qin except for the Duchy of Muscovy, which developed late and was peripheral to European politics until the second half of the eighteenth century. (When Russia did enter the European state system, it quickly proceeded to overrun a good deal of Europe, both under Alexander I in 1814 and then under Stalin in 1945.) Those states like France and Spain in the late seventeenth century that are commonly spoken of as "absolutist" were, as we will see, considerably weaker in their power to tax and mobilize their societies than was the state of Qin in the third century B.C. When would-be absolutist monarchs began their state-building projects, they were checked by other well-organized social groups: an entrenched hereditary aristocracy, the Catholic church, a sometimes well-organized peasantry, and independent, self-governing cities, all of which could operate flexibly across dynastic boundaries.

Things were very different in China. Because it was based on an extended kinship system, the Chinese feudal aristocracy never established the same kind of local authority that European lords did. The Chinese nobles' power base in a lineage was geographically diffused and intertwined with other kin groups, in contrast to the strong hierarchical local political sovereignties that developed under European feudalism. They were, moreover, unprotected by law, the ancient rights and privileges that the latter enjoyed. The aristocrats' ranks were depleted by centuries of incessant tribal war, leaving the field open for political entrepreneurs to organize peasants and other commoners into powerful armies that could overwhelm the nobility-based formations of earlier centuries. China during the Zhou Dynasty thus never developed a powerful, hereditary landed aristocracy comparable to the one that would develop in Europe. The three-way struggle among monarch, aristocracy, and Third Estate that was so important to the development of modern European political institutions never happened in China. Instead, there was a precociously modern centralized state that defeated all of its potential rivals early on.

The state of Qin had many if not all of the characteristics that Max Weber defined as quintessentially modern. It is therefore something of a mystery why Weber, who knew a great deal about China, nonetheless described Imperial China as a patrimonial state.[32] Perhaps one reason for Weber's confusion lies in the fact that the coming of political modernity to China was not accompanied by economic modernization, that is, the rise of a capitalist market economy. Nor was it accompanied by social modernization: kinship was not superseded by modern individualism but continued to coexist with impersonal administration, up to the present day. Like other modernization theorists, Weber believed that the different dimensions of development—economic, political, social, and ideological—were tightly interconnected. It may be that because the other dimensions of modernization did not appear in China, Weber didn't recognize the presence of a modern political order. Political, economic, and social modernization were in fact not closely connected temporally in European development either; but the sequence was different, with social modernization preceding growth of a modern state. Europe's experience was thus a unique one that would not necessarily be replicated in other societies.

MANY MODERNIZATIONS

Why didn't political modernization lead to modernization in the economy and society after the Qin unification? The emergence of a modern state is a necessary condition for intensive economic development, but it is not a sufficient one. Other institutions needed to be in place for capitalism to emerge. The capitalist revolution in the West was preceded by a cognitive revolution in early modern times that created the scientific method, modern universities, technological innovations that produced new wealth from scientific observations, and a system of property rights that incentivized people to innovate in the first place. Qin China was in many ways an intellectually fertile place, but its major scholarly traditions tended to be backward looking and incapable of the abstraction needed by modern natural science.

In addition, no independent commercial bourgeoisie had developed in Warring States China. Cities were political and administrative hubs, not commercial centers, with no traditions of independence and self-government. There was no social prestige attached to being a merchant or craftsman; status was associated with landownership.[33] Property rights existed, but they were not configured to support development of a modern market economy. The Qin dictatorship dispossessed huge numbers of patrimonial landowners in its efforts to break their power, and taxed the new landowners very heavily to support its military ambitions. Instead of creating incentives for private individuals to work their land more productively, the state set output quotas (as the Communists would do two millennia later) and punished peasants for failing to meet them. While the initial Qin land reform broke up entailed estates and created a market in land, no class of smallholders emerged, the land instead being absorbed by a new class of wealthy families.[34] And there was ultimately no rule of law to limit the sovereign's ability to confiscate property further.[35]

Social modernization is the breakdown of kin-based relationships and their replacement with more voluntary, individualistic forms of association. This did not happen after the Qin unification for two reasons. First, the failure of a capitalist market economy to develop meant that there was no extensive division of labor that would mobilize new social groups and identities. Second, the effort to undermine kinship in Chinese society was undertaken as a top-down project by a dictatorial state. In the West, by contrast, kinship was undermined by Christianity, both on a doctrinal level and through the power that the church commanded over family matters and inheritance (see chapter 16). The roots of Western social modernization were thus laid several centuries before the rise either of the modern state or the capitalist market economy.

Top-down social engineering often fails to meet its goals. In China, the institutions of the agnatic lineage and patrimonial government based on it took a body blow but were not killed. As we will see, they made a big comeback after the short-lived Qin Dynasty and continued to rival the state as a source of authority and emotional attachment in the centuries following.

8

THE GREAT HAN SYSTEM

The first Qin emperor and why the dynasty he founded collapsed so quickly;
how the Han Dynasty restored Confucian institutions but retained Legalist
principles; how China was governed under the Qin and Han

The founder of the first unified Chinese state, Ying Zheng (also known by
his posthumous temple name Qin Shi Huangdi, 259–210 B.C.), was an
energetic megalomaniac who used political power to reshape Chinese society. The world-famous army of terra-cotta warriors, unearthed in 1974,
was created on his behalf and buried near a gigantic mausoleum within a
larger mausoleum precinct of more than two square miles. The Han Dynasty
historian Sima Qian claimed that seven hundred thousand workers were
mobilized to build the emperor's tomb; even if this is an exaggeration, it is
clear that the state he created disposed of a huge surplus and was able to
mobilize resources on a breathtaking scale.

Qin Shi Huangdi extended the institutions of his native Qin to the
whole of China and thereby created not just a state but what would become, under his Han Dynasty successors, a unified Chinese elite culture.
This was something much different from modern nationalism, which is a
mass phenomenon. Nonetheless, the new consciousness linking the elites
of Chinese society was so powerful that it always managed to reconstitute
itself after the fall of a dynasty and a period of internal political disintegration. While China was conquered several times by foreigners, the latter
failed to change the Chinese system but were instead absorbed by it, up
until the arrival of the Europeans in the nineteenth century. Neighboring
Korea, Japan, and Vietnam remained independent of Chinese power but
borrowed heavily from Chinese ideas.

The methods that the first Qin emperor used to unify China were based on naked political power, applying the Legalist principles first elaborated by Shang Yang when Qin was just a frontier state. The assault on existing traditions and the ambitious social engineering undertaken verged on the totalitarian and provoked such heavy opposition from virtually all segments of the population that the dynasty collapsed and was replaced a mere fourteen years after its founding.

The Qin Dynasty left a complex legacy for later Chinese rulers. On the one hand, the Confucianists and traditionalists whom the Qin rulers targeted execrated it for centuries to come as one of the most immoral and despotic regimes in Chinese history. The Confucianists returned to power in the succeeding Han Dynasty and tried to roll back many of the Qin innovations. On the other hand, Qin's use of political power succeeded in establishing powerful modern institutions that survived the restoration, and in fact came to define many important aspects of subsequent Chinese civilization. Though Legalism was never an approved ideology in later dynastic China, its legacy lived on in the institutions of the Chinese state.

THE QIN STATE AND ITS DEMISE

The first Qin emperor's policies were implemented by his grand councilor, Li Si, a fellow student of the Legalist ideologist Han Fei who nonetheless conspired to have Han discredited and driven to suicide. On coming to power, one of the first acts of the new state builders was to divide the empire into a two-level administrative structure, with thirty-six commanderies (districts) that were in turn divided into prefectures. The governors of the commanderies and the prefects were appointed by the emperor from his capital of Xianyang, and were intended to displace the power of local patrimonial elites. The already weakened feudal nobility was directly targeted, with the histories saying that 120,000 families were forcibly removed from around the country and relocated to a district close to the capital, where they could be kept under tight surveillance.[1] At this early period in human history, it is hard to find many precedents for this kind of use of concentrated political power, which shows how far China had evolved from a tribal society.

The Confucian officials inherited by the Qin emperor resisted state centralization and in 213 B.C. advised the emperor to reinfeudate the state, a move that not coincidentally provided them with a new power base in the countryside. Li Si understood that this would undermine their state-building project:

> If such conditions are not prohibited, the imperial power will decline above, and partisanships will form below. It is expedient that these be prohibited. Your servant requests that all persons possessing works of literature, the Shih [*Book of Odes*], the Shu [*Book of History*] and the discussions of the various philosophers should destroy them with remission of all penalty. Those who have not destroyed them within thirty days after the issuing of the order, are to be banned and sent to do forced labor.[2]

The Qin emperor agreed and ordered the burning of the classical books, and then was reported to have ordered that four hundred resisting Confucian scholars be buried alive. These acts understandably earned his regime the undying hatred of later Confucians.

Weights and measures had been standardized already under Shang Yang in the original state of Qin; this standardization was now extended to the whole of China. The first Qin emperor also standardized the written Chinese language based on the great seal script of Grand Historian Zhou, extending again a reform that had been undertaken in Qin before unification. The purpose of the reform was simply to promote consistency in preparing government documents.[3] While different dialects continue today to be spoken all over China, unification of the written language had incalculable consequences for Chinese identity. Not only was there a unified language of administration, but the same corpus of cultural classics could be shared across the different regions of China.

Strictly following Legalist methods, Qin rule was so harsh that it provoked a series of uprisings all over China and ultimately collapsed after the death of the Qin emperor in 210 b.c. The backlash began in earnest when a group of convicts on their way to a military camp were held up by rain. Since the law decreed the death penalty for delay, whatever the cause, the leaders of the group decided they wouldn't be any worse off if they revolted.[4] Mutinies then quickly spread to other parts of the empire. Many of the surviving ex-kings and feudal aristocrats, seeing that the dynasty was weakening, declared their independence from the new state and raised their own armies. Meanwhile, the grand councilor Li Si conspired with a court eunuch to put Qin Shi Huangdi's second son on the throne, only to be killed by the eunuch, who was in turn murdered by the third son, whom he had tried to install as emperor. An aristocrat, Xiang Yu, descendant of a noble family from the extinct kingdom of Chu, and one of his lieutenants, a commoner named Liu Bang, mobilized new armies, occupied the Qin capital, and ended the Qin line. Xiang Yu tried to return China to Zhou feudalism by distributing lands to his kinsmen and supporters. Liu Bang (whose posthumous name was Han Gaozu) turned against him, and after a four-year civil war emerged victorious. He established a new dynasty, the Former or Earlier Han, in 202.[5]

The regime created by the new emperor Gaozu represented a halfway house between the full feudal restoration attempted by Xiang Yu and the modern dictatorship of the first Qin emperor. Gaozu did not have a power base in a preexisting state as did Qin Shi Huangdi; his legitimacy was based entirely on his charisma as the successful leader of a rebel army fighting a hated tyranny. He led an alliance of different forces, including many traditional families and former ruling houses, in order to win power. In addition, he had to worry about incursions by the nomadic Xiongnu in the north. Hence his initial ability to reshape Chinese society was much more limited than that of his Qin predecessor.

Gaozu consequently created a two-track system. Part of the realm reverted to Zhou feudalism. He restored to rule in subordinate kingdoms several of the old ruling families and their generals who had helped him in the civil war, and enfeoffed members of his own family with new appanages. The other part of the realm retained the impersonal commandery/prefecture structure of the Qin monarchy, which constituted the core of Gaozu's own power.[6] The dynasty's control of the new subkingdoms was tenuous for a number of years. The Qin Dynasty unification of China had never been complete, and the early years of the Han Dynasty were spent finishing up the work of creating a uniform national state. Gaozu began this process by gradually removing from power rulers of localities with a surname other than Liu. The last feudal state in Changsha was abolished under a successor, the emperor Wen, in 157 B.C. The states run by royal family members lasted longer and grew more distant from the central government, now located in the western city of Chang'an, and seven of them revolted in 154 in bids to achieve full independence. Successful suppression of the rebellion led Emperor Jing to declare that the remaining feudal lords had no authority over their territories. The government imposed high taxes on them and forced the division of the domains by splitting them among siblings. A hundred years after the founding of the Former Han Dynasty, the last vestiges of feudal rule were finally rendered powerless and local authorities were now more uniformly appointed by the central government.[7]

Zhou-style feudalism, in which a family acquired a local power base independent of the central government, recurred periodically in subsequent Chinese history, particularly in the chaotic periods between dynasties. But once the central government regained its footing, it always had the ability to reassert control over these entities. There was never a period in which the territorial barons were powerful enough to force a constitutional compromise on the monarch, as happened in England under the Magna Carta. Local power holders never had the legal legitimacy that they did in feudal Europe. As we will see, when the hereditary aristocracy in later years tried to gain power in China, it was not by building a localized power base but by capturing the central government. The early centralization of a powerful Chinese state thus succeeded in perpetuating itself over time.

The eradication of patrimonial rule in the different regions of China and its replacement with a uniform national administration was, in effect, a victory for Legalism and the Qin tradition of building a powerful, centralized state. But in other respects, Confucian traditionalism made a comeback. This was particularly true on an ideological level. Under Emperor Wu (141–87 B.C.), Confucian scholars were reinstated to administrative positions and a Confucian college was founded with five faculties, one devoted to the study of each of the classics. Immersion in these books was seen to be the gateway to bureaucratic office, and the first rudimentary form of what was to become the famous Mandarin examination system was established at this time.[8]

An important change occurred on the level of ideas as well. The Legalist principles of Shang Yang and Han Fei that advocated the unsentimental use of the ruled for the sake of the rulers was discredited, and the older Confucian view that power ought to be exercised in the interest of the ruled regained respectability. This was far from an argument in favor of democracy: no Confucian believed that there should be formal institutional checks on an emperor's power or authority, much less anything like popular elections or individual rights. The only check on an emperor's power was a moral one. That is, emperors ought to be raised with the proper moral values that would make them exhibit benevolence toward their people and were exhorted constantly to live up to these ideals.

The early emperors' power was limited by the fact that it was institutionalized in the Confucian bureaucracy surrounding the palace. The bureaucracy served as agents of the emperor and had no formal ability to check his power. But like all bureaucrats, they exercised considerable informal influence, because of their expertise and knowledge of the actual workings of the empire. Like all leaders of hierarchical organizations from armies to corporations to modern nations, the emperor at the top of the Han government depended on a legion of advisers to frame policies, implement orders, and judge cases being brought before the court. These officials were responsible for training young princes and advising them when they grew up and exercised power as emperors. Tradition and cultural prestige reinforced the ability of senior Han bureaucrats to sway the emperor, and there are many recorded cases of councilors and secretaries upbraiding or criticizing their leaders, or getting them to reverse controversial decisions.[9]

The ultimate sanction for a bad emperor was armed rebellion, justified under the doctrine of the loss of the Mandate of Heaven. The Mandate of Heaven had first been introduced to justify the Zhou usurpation of the Shang Dynasty's throne in the mid-tenth century B.C. and was subsequently invoked to justify rebellion against unjust or corrupt emperors. There were no precise rules for knowing who possessed the Mandate of Heaven, which tended to get awarded after a successful revolt (see the more complete discussion of this issue in chapter 20). This was obviously an extreme check on princely power that could be undertaken only at great risk.

The Confucian idea that a ruler ought to rule in the interests of his people thus introduced a principle of accountability into the government of China. As noted, accountability was not formal or procedural but based rather on the emperor's own moral sense as shaped by the bureaucracy. Levenson and Schurmann argue that the kinds of moral injunctions fostered by the bureaucracy reflected primarily the interests of the bureaucrats themselves. That is, they were strongly opposed to the raw exercise of state power under Legalist rulers because Confucian bureaucrats were the first victims of that power. They sought nothing more than to protect their positions during the Han restoration. These bureaucrats were custodians not of a public interest but of a hierarchical, kinship-based social system at whose pinnacle they stood.[10] Nonetheless, there is something to be said for a governing ideology that asserts, at least in principle, that the ruler ought to be accountable to the ruled and that seeks to preserve existing social institutions against the power of the state.

THE NATURE OF HAN GOVERNMENT

The government administration that emerged during the Han Dynasty achieved a much better balance between the Qin Dynasty's despotic centralization and the kinship-based social system of the early Zhou Dynasty. Its central administration was increasingly rationalized and institutionalized, and over time moved against local pockets of patrimonial rule. But until Wang Mang's attempt at land reform at the end of the Former Han Dynasty, it never attempted to use its power to engage in large-scale social engineering. It left largely intact existing social networks and property rights. Although it exacted taxes and corvée labor for public projects, it did not try to bleed the population dry the way its Qin predecessor did.

During the Han Dynasty, the Chinese government became increasingly well institutionalized. In a patrimonial system, whether of Zhou China or a contemporary African or Central Asian state, government officials are appointed on the basis not of qualifications but due to their kinship or personal ties with the ruler. Authority resides not in the office but in the officeholder. As political systems modernized, bureaucracy replaced the patrimonial system. Among the characteristics of modern bureaucracy, according to Max Weber's classic definition, are offices defined by functional area with a clearly defined sphere of competence, organization of offices into a clearly defined hierarchy, candidates selected impersonally on the basis of qualifications, officials lacking an independent political base and subject to strict discipline within a hierarchy, and salaried offices treated as careers.[11]

The Chinese government of the Former Han Dynasty fulfilled virtually all of these criteria of modern bureaucracy.[12] There were many holdover patrimonial appointees within the government, particularly in the early days of Gaozu's reign when the emperor needed the help of his anti-Qin and civil war allies to consolidate his rule. But particularly within the central administration, patrimonial officeholders were gradually replaced by officials selected on a more impersonal basis. An increasingly sharp distinction was made between dignitaries of the court and the permanent bureaucracy that was charged with implementing the ruler's decisions.

Beginning in 165 B.C., decrees were issued calling on senior officials throughout China to nominate fixed quotas of young men of distinction for service in the bureaucracy. Under the reign of Emperor Wu, officials were ordered to vouch for their nominee's sense of family responsibility and integrity. In 124, pupils nominated from the provinces were sent to the Imperial Academy in the capital of Chang'an for testing. The best ones went on for another year's training with academicians and scholars based on the approved Confucian texts, and then were tested again for entry into high government service. Other sources of recruitment evolved as well, such as roving commissions that traveled around the empire looking for talented individuals, or contests in which the public was invited to respond with essays on the moral or material state of the empire. This type of impersonal recruitment allowed people of non-Han ethnic stock to rise to high positions, like the military commander Gongsun Hunye, who was of Xiongnu origin.[13]

In the year 5 B.C., when the registered population of China was sixty million, there were already about 130,000 bureaucrats serving in the capital and provinces. Schools were set up to train young men, beginning at age seventeen, for government service, where they would be tested for their ability to read different styles of script, to keep accounts, and the like. (The examination and recruitment system for the civil service would grow far more sophisticated during the Tang and Ming dynasties.) There was still a strong patrimonial element in Han times: high officials could recommend a son or brother for high office, and the nomination system was clearly not protected against personal influences. As in later dynasties, the degree of meritocracy was sharply limited by the educational requirements: only high-status families would have sons who were literate and therefore liable for nomination or examination.

Despite some surviving vestiges of the patrimonial system,[14] the central government became increasingly bureaucratized in Weberian terms over time. The three highest officials were the chancellor, the counselor, and the supreme commander, who ranked in that order. Sometimes the office of chancellor was split between two, one of the Left and one of the Right, where the two occupants of these powerful offices could watch over each other and balance each other's power. Underneath them were nine ministers of state, each with his own staff and budget. Among the most important officials were the superintendent of ceremonials, who was responsible for the rituals performed by the court; the superintendent of the palace, who controlled access to the palace and was responsible for the safety of the emperor; the superintendent of the guards, who commanded the palace guard and the military units of the capital; the superintendent of transport, who was in charge of logistics; the superintendent of trials, who managed the justice system; and the superintendent of agriculture, who was responsible for the collection of taxes. This last office was obviously important in this agrarian society; the superintendent of agriculture himself presided over a huge bureaucracy and posted senior officials from sixty-five subordinate offices to the provinces to manage granaries, agricultural work, and water supplies.[15]

Rational bureaucracy does not necessarily have to serve rational purposes. Among the high offices under the superintendent of ceremonials were directors for music, prayer, sacrificial meats, astrology, and divination. The director of astrology advised the emperor on auspicious and inauspicious days for holding events and rituals, and also supervised the examinations for entry into the civil service. The size of the Han government is evident in the fact that the director of prayer alone had a staff of 35, and the director of music controlled 380 musicians.[16]

One of the most remarkable features of government, which has been consistent from the earliest periods of Chinese history, is the strong control that civilian authorities have exercised over the military. In this respect China differed substantially from Rome, where ambitious generals like Pompey and Julius Caesar were constantly making bids for political power, or from contemporary developing countries with their frequent military coups.

This is not for lack of military authority or charisma in China. China's history is full of victorious generals and tales of martial greatness. Even after the close of the Warring States period, China continued to fight frequent wars, primarily against steppe nomads, but also against the Koreans, Tibetans, and tribal peoples to the south. Virtually all of the founding emperors of dynasties gained their positions initially as a result of military leadership. As we have seen, Liu Bang rose from being the son of a peasant to become Emperor Gaozu based on his skill as a military organizer and strategist, and he would not be the last to do so. Ambitious generals like An Lushan in the Tang Dynasty made bids for power; the dynasty eventually fell because the frontier forces needed to defend the country from barbarians to the north escaped the central government's control.

But in general, successful dynastic founders who rose through military conquest quickly donned their mufti when they achieved power, and ruled by virtue of their civilian office. They and their successors were able to keep generals out of politics, exiling ambitious soldiers to distant frontier posts and suppressing others who tried to organize rebel armies. Unlike the Roman Praetorian Guards or the Ottoman Janissaries, the emperor's palace guards never played big roles as kingmakers over the course of Chinese history. Given the importance of war to the formation of the Chinese state, it is important to understand why civilian control became as strong as it did.

One reason has to do with the relatively weak institutionalization of the military hierarchy compared to its civilian counterpart. Positions of supreme commander, and generals of the van, the rear, the right, and the left, all ranked theoretically higher than the ministers of state, but these posts were often left vacant. They were regarded more as ceremonial positions than ones conferring real military authority, and were frequently occupied by civilians with no military background. At this point in time, there was no professionalization of the military; officials from the emperor on down moved readily between military and civilian posts and were expected to be qualified for both. Once the civil wars at the beginning of the dynasty had ended, military service often involved being posted to distant steppe or desert garrison towns far removed from civilization. This was not the sort of career that ambitious up-and-comers sought.[17]

These considerations just beg the question, though, of why the military received so little prestige in the Chinese system. And here the answer is likely to be normative: somehow, in the crucible of the Spring and Autumn and Warring States periods, the idea arose that true political authority lies in education and literacy rather than in military prowess. Military men who wanted to rule found they had to garb themselves in Confucian learning if they were to be obeyed and have their sons educated by learned academics if they were to succeed them as rulers. If it seems unsatisfying to think that the pen is mightier than the sword, we should reflect on the fact that all successful efforts by civilian authorities to control their militaries are ultimately based on normative ideas about legitimate authority. The U.S. military could seize power from the president tomorrow if it wanted; that it has not done so reflects the fact that the vast majority of officers wouldn't dream of overturning the U.S. Constitution, and that the vast majority of soldiers they command would not obey their authority if they tried to do so.

The initial Han equilibrium was based on a balance between the interests of all parties in creating a strong, unified central Chinese state to avoid the turmoil and warfare of the Eastern Zhou, and the interests of the local elites across China who wanted to hold on to as much of their power and privilege as possible. The first Qin emperor tried to push the institutional balance too far in the direction of a strong, centralized state, which rode roughshod over the interests not just of the patrimonial elites but also of ordinary peasants who exchanged the tyranny of a local lord for the tyranny of the state. The Han Dynasty shifted the balance back to take account of the interests of the royal and aristocratic families targeted by the Qin, while working to reduce their influence over time. It relegitimated itself in a Confucianism informed by certain unacknowledged Legalist premises. The state that was created in the Former Han was stable because it was based on compromise. But it was also considerably weaker than the Qin state and never sought head-to-head confrontation with the surviving pockets of aristocratic influence. The new equilibrium nonetheless worked. With a brief interruption brought on by the regent Wang Mang (45 B.C.–A.D. 23), who declared himself emperor of a short-lived Xin Dynasty, the Han managed to survive for more than four centuries, from 202 B.C. to A.D. 220. This was a remarkable political achievement, but one that was not, unfortunately, fated to last.

9

POLITICAL DECAY AND THE RETURN OF PATRIMONIAL GOVERNMENT

Why the four-hundred-year-old Han Dynasty collapsed; significance of the growth of latifundia and inequality in a Malthusian society; how great families captured the government and weakened the state; the Chinese sense of nation

There should be no general presumption that political order, once it emerges, will be self-sustaining. Samuel Huntington's *Political Order in Changing Societies* began its life as an article titled "Political Order and Political Decay," in which Huntington argued that, contrary to modernization theory's progressive assumptions, there was no reason to assume that political development was any more likely than political decay. Political order emerges as a result of the achievement of some equilibrium among the contending forces within a society. But as time goes on, change occurs internally and externally: the actors who established the original equilibrium themselves evolve or disappear; new actors appear; economic and social conditions shift; the society is invaded from the outside or faces new terms of trade or imported ideas. As a result, the preceding equilibrium no longer holds, and political decay results until the existing actors come up with a new set of rules and institutions to restore order.

The reasons for the Han Dynasty's eventual breakdown were multiple and involved shifts in all aspects of the original political equilibrium. The unity of the Han ruling family and its legitimacy were severely compromised in the second century A.D. because of the influence of the families of empresses and of the court eunuchs. Eunuchs played important roles in many imperial courts in addition to China's: since they had been castrated, they no longer had sexual feelings or ability, so they could be trusted as personal staff. Without families of their own, they were psychologically dependent on their masters and would not scheme to advance their (non-existent) children's interests. They played a critical role in allowing Chinese emperors to bypass the strong and autonomous bureaucracy, but they in turn began developing corporate interests of their own.

All of this came to a head when the leader of the empress Liang's clan succeeded in naming a weak emperor, Huan (A.D. 147–167), which allowed her lineage to claim a host of government offices and privileges. They were stopped by what contemporary Latin Americans call an *auto-golpe* (a self-coup) initiated by the emperor against his own government with the help of his eunuchs, who then massacred the empress's clan. The eunuchs in turn became a powerful force in their own right, rewarded by the emperor with titles, tax exemptions, and the like. Their rise threatened in turn the position of the bureaucracy and of the Confucians, who began an antieunuch campaign in 165 and eventually succeeded in having them exterminated.[1]

Environmental conditions also intervened. There were epidemics in 173, 179, and 182; famines in 176, 177, 182, and 183; and floods in 175. Misery on a popular level led to the growth of Daoism, a religion that found numerous adherents among the peasantry and other common people. Confucianism, an ethic rather than a transcendental religion, was always the code of the elite, and Daoism, which had evolved out of ancient folk beliefs, served as a kind of protest religion for nonelites. Daoism became the animating principle behind the great Yellow Turban peasant rebellion (they wore yellow scarves on their heads) that broke out in 184. The rebellion was inflamed by all of the accumulated hardships endured by the peasantry in the preceding decade. Although it was suppressed after twenty years with great bloodshed (five hundred thousand people reportedly died), it succeeded in destroying a good deal of the empire's state infrastructure and productive capacity.[2] The cumulative effect of these disasters was a reported drop in China's population of an astonishing forty million people, or two-thirds of the total, between 157 and 280.[3]

From the standpoint of China's political development, however, one of the most important causes of the decline of the Han Dynasty was the recapture of the state by different patrimonial elites and the consequent weakening of the central government. The Qin effort to eliminate feudalism and create an impersonal modern state was undone; kinship returned as the primary avenue to power and status in China, a situation that lasted until the later years of the Tang Dynasty in the ninth century.[4]

This was not a restoration of Zhou feudalism, however. Too much had changed since the Qin, including the creation of a powerful centralized state and bureaucracy, and a court invested with enormous ceremonial legitimacy. The Former Han had gradually eliminated territorially based pockets of patrimonial influence, so when aristocratic families reasserted themselves, they did so not by rebuilding local power bases but by inserting themselves directly into the apparatus of the central government. The difference between the Zhou and Han aristocracies was thus a bit like the difference between the British and French nobilities in the late seventeenth century: the English lords still lived on their estates and commanded authority locally, while their French counterparts were forced to go to Versailles and seek power through proximity to the court and king. In China, power at court was a route to landownership: powerful officials could acquire land, retainers, peasants, and exemptions from taxes.

THE RICH GET RICHER

Over time, China saw the growth of increasingly large estates, or latifundia, controlled by aristocratic families working in high offices either in the central government in Chang' an or in one of its provincial arms. This had the consequence of increasing the overall disparities in wealth and concentrating it in the hands of a small group of noble families, and of steadily depriving the government of revenue as these landowners were able to shield more and more of the country's productive agricultural land from state taxation. These families were thus an early version of what we could today label a rent-seeking elite, who made use of their political connections to capture the state and use state power to enrich themselves.

There is something like an iron law of latifundia in agrarian societies that says that the rich will grow richer until they are stopped—either by the state, by peasant rebellions, or by states acting out of fear of peasant rebellions. In premodern agrarian societies, disparities in wealth do not necessarily reflect natural disparities in abilities or character. Technology is fixed and no one is rewarded for being entrepreneurial or innovative. Before the mechanization of agriculture, there were no particular economies of scale to be had, either, that would explain the growth of large latifundia in terms of efficiency. Even large landowners had their fields worked by individual peasant families farming on small plots. But small initial differences in resources reinforced themselves through the mechanism of debt peonage. A wealthier peasant or landowner would lend money to a poorer one; a single bad season or crop failure would then reduce the debtor to serfdom or slavery, with the forfeiture of his family's property.[5] Over time, the advantages of greater wealth became self-reinforcing, since larger landowners could then buy influence in the political system to protect and expand their holdings.

This is why the anachronistic application of contemporary property rights theory to historical situations leads to fundamental misunderstandings. Many economists believe that strong property rights promote growth because they protect private returns to investment, thereby stimulating investment and growth. But economic life in Han Dynasty China resembled the world described by Thomas Malthus in his *Essay on the Principle of Population* much more than the world that has existed since the beginning of the Industrial Revolution of the last two hundred years.[6] Today, we expect increases in labor productivity (output per person) as the result of technological innovation and change. But before 1800, productivity gains were much more episodic. The invention of agriculture, the use of irrigation, the invention of the printing press, gunpowder, and long-distance sailing ships all led to productivity gains,[7] but between them there were prolonged periods when population growth increased and per capita income fell. Many agrarian societies were operating at the frontier of their technological production possibilities, where further investment would not yield higher output. The only kind of economic growth possible was extensive growth, in which new land was settled and brought into cultivation, or else simply stolen from someone else. A Malthusian world is thus zero sum, in which a gain for one party means a loss for another. A wealthy landowner was therefore not necessarily more productive than a small one; he simply had more resources to tide him over rough periods.[8]

In a Malthusian economy where intensive growth is not possible, strong property rights simply reinforce the existing distribution of resources. The actual distribution of wealth is more likely to represent chance starting conditions or the property holder's access to political power than productivity or hard work. (Even in today's mobile, entrepreneurial capitalist economy, rigid defenders of property rights often forget that the existing distribution of wealth doesn't always reflect the superior virtue of the wealthy and that markets aren't always efficient.)

Left to their own devices, elites tend to increase the size of their latifundia, and in the face of this, rulers have two choices. They can side with the peasantry and use state power to promote land reform and egalitarian land rights, thereby clipping the wings of the aristocracy. This is what happened in Scandinavia, where the Swedish and Danish monarchs made common cause with the peasantry at the end of the eighteenth century against a relatively weak aristocracy (see chapter 28). Or the rulers can side with the aristocracy and use state power to reinforce the hold of local oligarchs over their peasants. This happened in Russia, Prussia, and other lands east of the Elbe River from the seventeenth century on, as a generally free peasantry was reduced to serfdom with the collusion of the state. The French monarchy under the Old Regime was too weak to dispossess the aristocracy or remove their tax exemptions, so it ended up placing the burden of new taxes on the peasantry until the whole system exploded in the French Revolution. Which course the monarch chose—to reinforce the existing oligarchy or to lean against it—depended on a host of contextual factors like the cohesiveness of both the aristocracy and the peasantry, the degree of external threat faced by the state, and rivalries within the court.

The Chinese monarchy during the Han Dynasty initially chose to side with the peasantry against the increasingly powerful landowners. During the Former Han there were periodic calls to return to the well-field system abolished by Shang Yang. The well-field system by that time was seen not as a feudal institution but as a symbol of agrarian communalism, and demands for its restoration were driven by the plight of poor peasants being driven off their lands by large latifundists. In 7 B.C., a proposal was put forward to limit estates to three thousand *mou* (a unit of land of approximately 0.165 acre). The proposal died because of opposition by large landowners. Wang Mang, the court official who usurped the throne from the Liu family and brought the Former Han to a close, also tried to implement land reform by nationalizing large estates. But he too faced tremendous opposition and eventually exhausted himself dealing with a peasant uprising known as Red Eyebrows (for the color they painted their brows).[9]

The failure of Wang Mang's land reform enabled the patrimonial aristocracy to extend its holdings and consolidate its power when the Later Han was restored. Owners of large estates succeeded in controlling hundreds or thousands of retainers, tenants, and kinsmen; they often commanded private armies as well. They secured tax exemptions for themselves and their dependents, reducing the empire's tax base and rural population available for corvée labor and military conscription.

The central government was further weakened by decay in the military. The bulk of the Chinese army was preoccupied fighting the tribal Xiongnu in the far northwest, where it had to operate from remote garrisons with long supply lines. It was hard to conscript peasants for this kind of service, and the government progressively turned either to mercenaries recruited from among the local barbarian populations or to slaves and convicts. Soldiers increasingly constituted a separate class of military households who lived and farmed near the frontier garrisons, and who passed on their occupations to their sons. Under these conditions, soldiers were more likely to be loyal to local commanders like the warlords Cao Cao and Dong Zhuo than to the distant central government.[10]

When growing land disparities were combined with the environmental disasters and epidemics of the 170s, the Yellow Turban revolt exploded. The collapse of order and the disintegration of the central government in factional struggles then induced these powerful families to entrench themselves behind walled compounds and districts, where they were effectively beyond the weak state's control. In the final decades of the Han Dynasty, the central state disintegrated completely and power passed to a series of regional warlords who turned from trying to place their own candidates on the throne to ruling in their own names.[11]

CHINA DISINTEGRATES AND PATRIMONIALISM RETURNS

China's longest enduring dynasty after the Qin unification, the Han, ultimately collapsed in A.D. 220, and with one brief exception no unified Chinese state existed for the next three hundred years. The period from the Later Han to the short-lived Jin Dynasty that appeared in 280 was the subject of one of the greatest Chinese historical novels, *The Romance of the Three Kingdoms*. The novel is attributed to Luo Guanzhong and was written early in the Ming Dynasty (perhaps in the late fourteenth century, though the dating is not certain), after the Ming had freed China from the Mongols and reunited the country once again under native Han Chinese rule.[12] One of the underlying themes of this novel is how China's disunity (*neiluan*) invites chaos and foreign invasion (*weihuan*); it sets forth the conditions under which national unity can be restored. The significance of *The Romance of the Three Kingdoms* in shaping the historical consciousness of modern Chinese has been compared to that of the historical plays

of Shakespeare, and the novel has been turned into video games and countless movies. The bad historical memories of disunity that underlie Beijing's
demand for the reincorporation of Taiwan date back to this period.

From the standpoint of China's political development, what is note-
worthy about the dynastic interregnum between the Han and the Sui
(when China was finally reunited in 581) is the way kinship and patrimonialism reinserted themselves as the organizing principles of Chinese politics. There is an inverse correlation between the strength of the centralized
state and the strength of patrimonial groups. Tribalism in its various forms
remains a default form of political organization, even after a modern state
has been created.

The period following the end of the Han is extremely complex, but
details are not important from the standpoint of the larger developmental
story. China initially broke up into the so-called Three Kingdoms, Wei,
Shu Han, and Wu. Wei managed to reunify the country briefly under the
Western Jin Dynasty, but the empire broke up again in civil war and the
Jin capital of Luoyang was sacked and occupied by the tribal Xiongnu in
311. The Xiongnu king created the first of many alien dynasties in northern China, while the survivors of Western Jin fled south and established
the first of several southern dynasties, the Eastern Jin, in Jiankang (modern Nanjing) on the Yangtze River. The north and the south remained
separate and both experienced continuing turmoil. In the north, the sack
of Luoyang led to a chaotic period of tribal warfare known as the Sixteen
Kingdoms. Two more barbarian invasions followed, first by the proto-
Tibetan Di and Qiang tribes, and then by the Tuoba or Tabgach, a branch
of the Turkic Xianbei. The latter established the Northern Wei Dynasty
(386–534), which over time became increasingly Sinicized, with tribes taking on Chinese surnames and intermarrying with Chinese families. Tensions among the Tuoba led, however, to civil war and the splitting of the
state into the Eastern and Western Wei in the first decades of the sixth
century. In the south, the old northern court was reestablished in the Eastern Jin Dynasty, to which large numbers of aristocratic families and their
retainers had fled. This dynasty was overthrown in a military coup in the
mid-fourth century, to be succeeded by other weak dynasties founded by
military men.[13]

The Wei kingdom, founded by the Han warlord Cao Cao and his son
Pei in 220, accelerated the late Han tendency toward patrimonialism by
establishing the Nine Rank system, in which an arbiter was appointed to

each commandery and prefecture to classify candidates for bureaucratic office according to character and ability. Unlike the earlier Han system of recommendation, the arbiters were chosen not by the central government but regionally, where they would obviously be much more subject to influence by local elites. The new recruitment system ranked all elite families in a single formal system and tied access to government office to those ranks. Whereas in the Han a man could have high status without being a bureaucrat, under the Nine Rank system, office became the sole route to high status. This was accompanied by a growing respect for pedigree, with sons now being far more likely to succeed their fathers in office.[14]

In the hands of a strong central government, recruitment through the Nine Rank system might have been a method of weakening a strong aristocracy and tying it to the state. In the seventeenth and early eighteenth centuries, the French monarchy sold an elaborate hierarchy of titles and ranks to the aristocracy, the effect of which was to undermine the capacity of the class as a whole for collective action. Each aristocratic family was too busy looking down at the people below them to be able to cooperate to defend their broader class interests. In third-century China, however, the Nine Rank system seems rather to have been a means by which the aristocracy could capture the state. No longer would it be possible for a talented commoner to rise to a position of high office through recommendation or examination; these offices would be reserved for the children of existing officeholders, just as if they were conquering tribal chiefs. Evidence that real power lay with the aristocratic families and not the state lies in the fact that an emperor in this period often could not secure the appointment of a favorite to high office because his candidate lacked the appropriate family pedigree.[15]

With the fall of the Western Jin, patrimonialism evolved in different ways in the north and the south. In the south, the Eastern Jin court was dominated by locally prominent families and by the aristocratic émigrés who had moved there from Luoyang. They brought with them the Nine Rank system and a government dominated by Wangs, Lus, and Changs, all cousins of a close degree from highly ranked lineages.[16]

Aristocratic domination was bolstered by the continuing growth of large latifundia. Already in the late third century the Western Jin had passed a land law declaring the right of all peasant families to a certain minimum amount of land, in return for their being subject to taxes and corvée labor. It also limited the size of holdings for aristocratic families, and the number of tenants and retainers they could shield from national taxation. But this law, as well as a similar one decreed in the Eastern Jin, was never enforced; like Wang Mang's abortive land reform, its failure was testament to the growing power of the latifundists and the degree to which they threatened the state's control and resources.[17]

In the north, the conquering Tibetans and Turkmen were organized tribally to begin with, and simply inserted their own leading lineages into positions of authority. In the early days of continuing strife and intertribal warfare, these foreign families constituted the leadership elite of the entire region. The aristocratic Chinese families that had risen to prominence during the Han Dynasty either fled south to the Eastern Jin court or else retreated to their estates. They held power locally but otherwise steered clear of court politics. Things began to change as the Northern Wei Dynasty centralized its power in the second half of the fifth century, and particu larly after it moved its capital to the historic city of Luoyang in the 490s. The emperor Xiao-wen forbade the use of Xianbei language and clothing at court, encouraged intermarriage between Xianbei and Chinese families, and invited leading aristocratic families to serve in the court. He succeeded in creating a unified aristocracy that ranked leading families much like the Nine Rank system of the south. This led to a situation where large numbers of high officials were all members of the same lineage and where aristocratic rank was a necessary condition to enter into the highest levels of the bureaucracy.[18] The consolidation of land into large latifundia accompanied by the expanding power of the aristocracy was also a problem in the north, as evidenced by a decree issued in 485 aimed at limiting large estates and guaranteeing peasants certain minimum holdings.[19]

THE STRONG CHINESE STATE

The northern states of Eastern and Western Wei were replaced by Northern Qi and Northern Zhou in the mid-sixth century. Yang Jian, of Xianbei extraction, whose wife was of a powerful Xiongnu clan, rose to prominence as a military commander when his state of Northern Zhou attacked and defeated Northern Qi in 577. After an internal struggle, Yang Jian defeated his rivals and established the Sui Dynasty in 581. His forces went on to defeat the southern states of Liang in 587 and Chen in 589. For the first time since the fall of the Han Dynasty in 220, China was reunified under a single central government (though the actual territory controlled did not correspond exactly to that of the Qin or Han dynasties). The new emperor, known posthumously as Wendi, moved the capital back to its old location in Chang'an and reconstituted a strong central government modeled on that of the Han Dynasty. His son and successor, Yangdi, had a megalomaniacal penchant for canal building and initiated a rash and unsuccessful attack on the Korean kingdom of Koguryo; the Sui Dynasty disappeared after his death in 618. This time, however, the interregnum was very short: another northern aristocrat named Li Yuan raised a rebel army in 617 and the following year captured Chang'an, proclaiming a new dynasty. The Tang Dynasty would be one of China's greatest and would last for almost three hundred years until the beginning of the tenth century.

The refounding of a centralized Chinese state under the Sui and Tang dynasties did not end the influence of the aristocratic families that had captured the governments of the different states of the previous interdynastic period. As we will see in chapters 20 and 21, the struggle against patrimonialism continued on for another three centuries, and it was not until the Song Dynasty in the eleventh century that public administration was put back on the more "modern" basis it arguably enjoyed during the Han Dynasty. Recentralization of the Chinese state eventually served to invigorate institutions like the examination system and the merit-based bureaucracy, which had steadily lost ground to wellborn aristocrats over the preceding centuries.

One of the most interesting questions raised by the chaotic events taking place in the three hundred years between the fall of the Han and the rise of the Sui is not why China fell apart, but rather why it came together again. The issue of how to maintain political unity over so large a territory is hardly trivial. The Roman Empire was never reconstituted after its decline, despite the efforts of Charlemagne and various Holy Roman Emperors to bring this about in later years. It would have been perfectly conceivable for the multistate system of the post-Han period to have congealed into a quasi-permanent system of competing states as Europe eventually did.

Part of the answer to this question has already come into view. The precocious modernization of the Chinese state left it as the most powerful organized social actor in the society. Even when the central state fell apart, it was succeeded by a host of would-be dynasties that tried as best they could to replicate the Han Dynasty's centralized institutions within their own borders and to reunify China under their own leadership. Legitimacy would ultimately come from inheriting the Mandate of Heaven, not in ruling a little local satrapy. By replicating Han institutions within their own borders, the successor states moreover prevented their further disintegration into ever-smaller units. There was nothing like the process of subinfeudation that took place in Europe.

A second and perhaps more important reason why China reunified has implications for contemporary developing countries. During the Qin and Han dynasties, China developed a common culture in addition to creating a strong state. This culture was not the basis for anything that could be called nationalism in the modern sense, since it existed for only the thin layer of elites that made up China's governing class and not the broad mass of the population. But there was a strong feeling that China was defined by a shared written language, a classical literary canon, a bureaucratic tradition, a shared history, empirewide educational institutions, and a value system that dictated elite behavior at both the political and social levels. That sense of cultural unity remained even when the state disappeared.

The strength of that common culture became most evident when it encountered foreign barbarians with different traditions. Virtually all invaders that conquered part of China—the Xiongnu, Xianbei, Tuoba, or later the Rurzhen (Manchus), Mongols, Tanguts, Xi Xia, and Khitan—at first sought to keep their tribal traditions, culture, and language. But they quickly found that they could not administer China without adopting China's more sophisticated political institutions. More than that, the prestige of Chinese culture was such that they either became Sinified themselves or else had to retreat into the steppes or forests from which they came if they were to maintain their indigenous cultural identity.

China reunified because the Qin and Han dynasties established the precedent that rule over the whole was more legitimate than rule over any of the component parts. Who had the right to claim that title, however, was a complicated question, and one we cannot fully answer until we have looked more closely at Chinese notions concerning political legitimacy. The interdynastic periods in Chinese history are particularly revealing in this regard, because during them a free-for-all broke out in which complete outsiders to political power—sons of peasants, foreigners with suspect ethnic backgrounds, and uneducated military men with no Confucian training—had the opportunity to rise to the very top of the system. The Chinese have been willing to bestow legitimacy and absolute power on them and their descendants for reasons that are in many ways bewildering. I will return to this question later, when we will have looked at other dynastic transitions.

China was the first world civilization to create a modern state. But it created a modern state that was not restrained by a rule of law or by institutions of accountability to limit the power of the sovereign. The only accountability in the Chinese system was moral. A strong state without rule of law or accountability amounts to dictatorship, and the more modern and institutionalized that state is, the more effective its dictatorship will be. The Qin state that unified China embarked on an ambitious effort to reorder Chinese society that amounted to a form of prototototalitarianism. This project ultimately failed because the state did not have the tools or the technology to carry out its ambitions. It had no broadly motivating ideology to justify itself, nor did it organize a party to carry out its wishes. The communications technology of the time did not permit it to reach very far into Chinese society. Where it was able to exercise power, its dictatorship was so harsh that it provoked a rebellion that led to its quick demise.

Later Chinese governments learned to moderate these ambitions and to live with existing social forces. In this respect they were authoritarian rather than totalitarian. Compared to other world civilizations, the Chinese ability to concentrate political power was remarkable.

In this respect, the path that Chinese political development followed was utterly different from that of India. These two societies have often been lumped together as "Asian" or "Oriental" civilizations. But while they displayed certain similarities early on, their later path of development could not be more different. The default Chinese political condition over the past two millennia was to be a centralized bureaucratic state punctuated by periods of disunity and decay; India's default situation was to be a series of small, squabbling kingdoms and principalities, punctuated by brief periods of political unity. If we look at the long sweep of Indian history, the fact that it is a democracy is perhaps not so unexpected. It is not that democratic ideas arose early on in Indian history and established a precedent, but rather that autocracy has always been very difficult to establish in Indian politics. The reasons for this lie in the realm of religion and ideas, as we will see in the following chapters.

10

THE INDIAN DETOUR

How India's early development diverged from China's due to the rise of Brahmanic religion; *varnas* and *jatis*; tribal society in early India; peculiarities of Indian kinship; the Indian detour on the road to statehood

Early Indian political development diverged markedly from that of China. Both societies started out with segmentary, tribal forms of social organization. In the middle of the first millennium B.C., the first chiefdoms and states began crystallizing in northern India out of these tribal formations, not too much later than occurred in China. In both civilizations, chiefdoms and states began exerting coercive powers through hierarchical administrations on a territorial rather than a kinship basis.

The two trajectories diverged, however, with respect to warfare. India never experienced a centuries-long period of continuous violence comparable to China's Spring and Autumn and Warring States periods. The reasons for this are unclear. It could be that population densities in the Indus and Ganges river valleys were much lower than those in China, and less circumscribed, so that people subject to coercion could simply migrate rather than having to submit to a hierarchical social order.[1] Whatever the reason, the early Indian states never faced the extreme requirements for social mobilization that China experienced.

More important than this was the fact that in India a unique pattern of social development unfolded that would have huge implications for Indian politics down to the present day. Right around the time that states were first being formed, a fourfold division of social classes emerged known as varnas: Brahmins, who were priests; Kshatriyas, warriors; Vaishyas, merchants; and Sudras, everyone else not in the first three varnas (at that time, mostly peasants). From the standpoint of politics, this was an extremely important development because it separated secular and religious authority. In China, there were priests and religious officials, like the superintendant of rites who officiated over the court's numerous ritual observances and the emperor's ancestral tombs. But they were all employees of the state and strictly subservient to royal authority. The priests had no independent corporate existence, making the Chinese state what would later be labeled "caesaropapist." In India, on the other hand, the Brahmins were a separate varna from the Kshatriyas and recognized as having a higher authority than the warriors. The Brahmins did not constitute a corporate group as well organized as the Catholic church, but they nonetheless enjoyed a comparable degree of moral authority independent of the power of the state. Moreover, the Brahmin varna was regarded as the guardian of the sacred law that existed prior to and independently of political rule. Kings were thus regarded as subject to law written by others, not simply as the makers of law as in China. Thus in India, as in Europe, there was a germ of something that could be called the rule of law that would limit the power of secular political authority.

A second critical social development was the emergence of jatis, or what came to be known as castes. Jatis subdivide all of the varnas into hundreds of segmentary endogamous occupational groups, from priests of different types to traders and shoemakers and farmers. They represent what one observer labeled the sacralization of the occupational order.[2] The jatis were superimposed on top of the existing lineage structure, fixing limits on clan exogamy. That is, exogamous agnatic lineages had to marry within the limits of the jati, so that a shoemaker's daughter would have to marry the son of another shoemaker of a different clan. The jatis retained some of the segmentary features of other tribal societies, insofar as the members of the jati cooperated and often lived together in self-contained communities. But they were also mutually interdependent because they were all part of a broader division of labor. This division was limited in degree when compared to an industrial society, but nonetheless was more complex than in a purely tribal society. The jatis thus displayed characteristics of both mechanical and organic solidarity in Durkheim's terms—that is, individuals were members of identical self-replicating units and participated in a broader interdependent society.

In China, the emergence of the state during the Zhou Dynasty displaced segmentary or tribal organization at the top levels of society. Although lineages remained important forms of social organization, there was an inverse correlation between the power of the state and the power of kinship groups: when one got stronger, the other got weaker. Ultimately, it was the state that decisively shaped Chinese civilization. In India, the new social categories of varna and jati formed the bedrock organization of society and severely limited the power of the state to penetrate and control it. Indian civilization, defined by varna and jati, spread all the way from the Khyber Pass to Southeast Asia and unified a diverse range of linguistic and ethnic groups. But this huge territory was never once ruled by a single political power and never developed a single literary language as China did. Indeed, the history of India before the late twentieth century is much more one of persistent political disunity and weakness, with some of the most successful unifiers being foreign invaders whose political power rested on a different social basis.

INDIAN TRIBAL SOCIETY

Our knowledge of tribal India and the transition to statehood is much more limited than in the case of China. At equivalent stages of social development, India was a far less literate society: there is nothing comparable to the voluminous oracle bone inscriptions documenting political transactions during the Shang Dynasty, or the lengthy historical chronicles of the Eastern Zhou Dynasty. For the earliest Indian settlements, the Harappan civilization at Mohenjo-Daro in western Punjab, we have only archaeological information.[3] Much of what we know about social organization in early India has to be inferred from the Vedic texts, which were hymns or prayers with their interpretive glosses dating back to the second or third millennium B.C. but transmitted orally until they were finally written down in the middle of the first millennium B.C.[4] The first and in many ways greatest indigenous Indian empire, the Mauryas (321–185 B.C.), was documented only through a handful of rock edicts scattered around the subcontinent, or from the writings of Greek, Chinese, and other foreign sources. There is a likely cause-and-effect relationship here: the lack of a widespread literary culture, particularly among the Indian rulers and administrators, constituted a major obstacle to the development of a powerful centralized state.

Indian political development starts with the migration of the Indo-

Aryan tribes out of an area in southern Russia between the Black and Caspian seas. Some of the tribes turned west and became the progenitors of Greeks, Romans, Germans, and other European groups. Another group went south into Persia, and a third turned east into eastern Afghanistan, through the Swat Valley in northwest Pakistan, and on into the Punjab and Indo-Gangetic watershed. While the consanguinity of the Indo-Aryans can now be traced through the Y chromosome and mitochondrial DNA, the relationship was first established by linguists through the linguistic similarities between Sanskrit, the language of the Indian tribes, and languages spoken to the west that were part of a larger Indo-European group.

The early Indo-Aryan tribes were nomadic pastoralists who raised and ate cattle, and who had already domesticated the horse. When they first moved into the Indo-Gangetic Plain, they encountered other settled communities they called *dasas*, which may have been ethnically different and spoke Dravidian or Austro-Asiatic languages.[5] In this period the behavior of these tribes was very similar to that of tribes elsewhere. They spent their time raiding the dasas and stealing their cattle, or fighting other tribes. If they encountered military resistance that was too strong, they could simply move on to a new area, since the region was still relatively thinly populated. The earliest of the Vedas, the Rg Veda, mentions numerous intertribal conflicts, the emergence of rajas or tribal chiefs, and priests who ensured the success of tribal campaigns. The Indo-Aryans began to settle in the Gangetic plain and shifted from pastoralism only to a mixture of pastoralism and agriculture. There were improvements in agricultural technology with a shift from wheat to rice cultivation, which made possible larger surpluses and thus more prominent gift giving and ritual prestations. It was around this time that the cow began to change in status, from the Indo-Aryans' chief source of protein (as with the Nuer) to a totemic animal that was an object of veneration.[6]

Indo-Aryan society at this stage of development does not seem to have been distinctive in any particular way from other segmentary societies we have already discussed. The term "raja," for example, while often translated as king, was actually nothing more than a tribal chief in this early period. The historian Romila Thapar points out that "raja" is derived from a root that means "to shine" or "to lead," and is also associated with another root, "to please." This suggests the more consensual nature of the tribal raja's authority.[7] The raja was a military leader who helped protect the community and led it on raids on neighboring tribes to acquire booty.

His power was checked by assemblies of kinsmen known as *vidatha, sabha,* and *samiti,* the first of which was responsible for the division of booty within the community. Like the Melanesian Big Man, the raja's status was determined by his ability to redistribute resources in sacrifices and feasts. Rajas competed with one another to demonstrate how much wealth they could put on display and ultimately waste, much like the potlatches of the Kwakiutl and other Northwest Pacific Coast Indians.[8]

As in other tribal societies, there were no legal institutions; disputes were settled through wergeld payments (one hundred cows being the price for killing a man). Rajas did not have any taxing authority, nor did they own land in a modern sense. Ownership was vested in families and entailed by kin obligations. As in other segmentary societies, the Indo-Aryan tribes could unite in larger confederations like that of the Panchalas, which could in turn unite with other higher-level segments.

INDIAN FAMILY AND KINSHIP

The Indo-Aryan tribes were organized into agnatic lineages much like the Greeks, Romans, and Chinese. Nineteenth-century historical anthropologists including Fustel de Coulanges and Henry Maine made a lot of the similarities between kinship structures in Greece, Rome, and Celtic and Teutonic peoples, and those of contemporary Hindus. I have already noted the sacred fire that was maintained in household altars in both Greece and Rome, and among the early Hindus (see chapter 3). Maine spent the years 1862 to 1869 in India as law member of the Council of the Governor General, where he studied Indian sources intensively. He became convinced that there was a single, unified "Aryan" civilization encompassing both the Romans and the Hindus, whose legal provisions for property, inheritance, and succession were remarkably similar due to their common historical origin. He also believed that India had somehow preserved ancient forms of legal and social practice intact, and that one could see Europe's past in India's present.[9]

Maine was heavily criticized by later generations of anthropologists for oversimplifying Indian kinship and imposing on it an inappropriate evolutionary framework. He did seem to have a strong interest in showing the common racial origins of European and Indian peoples, perhaps because it provided a historical basis for British rule there. But he was nonetheless one of the great founders of comparative anthropology and showed, through his vast learning, how different civilizations had evolved very similar solutions to problems of social organization. Although contemporary anthropologists are aware of all of the incredibly nuanced differences in kinship structures across societies, they are sometimes guilty of missing the forest for the trees and fail to adequately recognize the degree to which different societies at similar levels of social development resemble one another.

We can no more project contemporary Indian kinship organization backward in time on the early Indo-Aryans than we can in the case of China. Nonetheless, as in China, kinship never disappeared in India the way it did in the West as a basic structuring principle of the society. There is thus an underlying continuity in Indian social organization that we need to understand if we are to explain the dynamics of political development.

There are three broad areas of kinship organization in India, corresponding to the three large ethnolinguistic regions of the subcontinent: (1) the northern zone, populated by Sanskrit speakers descended from the Indo-Aryans; (2) a southern zone of Dravidian-language speakers; and (3) an eastern zone that shares much in common with Burma and other parts of Southeast Asia.[10] Almost all kinship groups in India form segmentary lineages, and the vast majority are patrilineal. However, in southern and eastern India there are some important groups that are matrilineal and matrilocal, like the Nayar of Malabar.[11] As in China, descent groups are organized around common ancestors and have corporate identities through ownership of some forms of joint property.

Indian kinship differs from its Chinese counterpart, however, insofar as it is overlaid with the hierarchical system of varnas and jatis. The latter determine the boundaries of exogamy, meaning that a person normally cannot marry someone outside of his or her varna or jati. Because the varna/jati system is so hierarchical, there are elaborate rules for lower-status women "marrying up" to higher-status men or, less frequently, lower-status men marrying up to higher-status women (known to anthropologists as hypergamy and hypogamy, respectively). Because each varna and jati is itself differentiated into an elaborate system of status ranks, there are sharp restrictions on whom one can marry even within their confines. For example, Brahmins are divided between those who do not have to officiate at domestic rituals and those who do; those who officiate at funerals and those who do not. A Brahmin man of the first class would never marry a daughter of a Brahmin of the lowest class (that is, those officiating at funerals).[12]

The major differences in kinship rules between the Sanskritic north and Dravidian south related to cross-cousin marriage, which may have had consequences for political organization. In the north, a son must marry outside the father's lineage, and one cannot marry a first cousin. In the south also a son must marry outside the father's lineage; however, he is not simply permitted but positively encouraged to marry his father's sister's daughter. (This practice is called cross-cousin marriage; parallel cousin marriages, or marrying one's father's brother's daughter, are not permitted, since this violates the rule of clan exogamy. Men are also permitted to marry their eldest sister's daughter, or their maternal uncle's daughter.) In other words, southern Indian tribes, like many Arab ones, tend to keep marriages (and hence inheritances) within a very narrow circle of kin. Related lineages consequently tend to live close to each other, while in the north, families are forced to cast their nets over a wider circle to find appropriate marriage partners for their children. The Dravidian practice of cross-cousin marriage reinforces the small-scale, inward-looking characteristic of social relationships that exist in all tribal societies.[13] These marriage practices presumably lowered the incentives for kings in the south to seek far-flung marriage alliances, like the one that united the crowns of Aragon and Castile to produce modern Spain.

This brief overview of Indian kinship does not begin to scratch the surface of its complexity. Even though it is possible to make generalizations about the Sanskritic north and Dravidian south, each of these regions exhibits a huge degree of internal variance in kinship rules by geographic subregion, caste, and religion.[14]

TRANSITION TO STATEHOOD

We have even less information on the forces that drove the initial Indian transition from a tribal society to a state than we do in the case of China. We have two mythic accounts of state formation that correspond to the alternative violence and social contract theories of the anthropologists. The first, from a later Vedic text known as the *Aitareya Brahmana*, explains that "the gods and demons were at war, and the gods were suffering badly at the hands of their enemies. So they met together and decided that they needed a *raja* to lead them in battle. They appointed Indra as their king, and the tide soon turned in their favour." This legend suggests that in the earliest times kingship in India was thought to be based upon human need and military necessity, and that the king's first duty was to lead his subjects in war.[15] The second version comes from Buddhist sources and explains that

> As men lost their primeval glory distinctions of class (*varna*) arose, and they entered into agreements one with another, accepting the institutions of private property and the family. With this theft, murder, adultery, and other crime began, and so the people met together and decided to appoint one man among them to maintain order in return for a share of the produce of their fields and herds. He was called "the Great Chosen One" (*Mahasammata*), and he received the title of raja because he pleased the people.[16]

Buddhism was always a kinder and gentler version of Hinduism, stressing nonviolence and greater possibilities for access to reincarnation, so it is perhaps not surprising that the Buddhists would see state formation as consensual. But neither story constitutes a historical account.

The actual transition to statehood probably partook of all of the conditions that have produced states in other societies. The first was conquest: the Rg Veda talks about the Indo-Aryans encountering dasas, fighting with them, and ultimately subjugating them. The first references to varnas were not the familiar fourfold division but a twofold one of arya-varnas and dasa-varnas, so the shift from an egalitarian tribal society to a stratified state-level one clearly begins with military conquest. The dasas may have originally been differentiated from their conquerors by ethnicity and language, though the word "dasa" itself later came to be associated with anyone who was subordinate or enslaved. This transition took place gradually after the Indo-Aryans' transition from a pastoral to an agricultural society.[17] Exploitation of a subservient class also resulted in a surplus of crops that could be extracted as a rent rather than through one's tribe's own labor, and there is a change in the meaning of "raja" from tribal chief to "he who enjoys an income from land or from a village."[18] Growing class stratification is also associated with the shift to permanent settlements, incipient urbanism, and landownership by about the early sixth century B.C.[19] Land is no longer worked by families laboring collaboratively in kinship groups but by peasants who have no kin connection with the landowners.[20] The need to keep an underclass in permanent subjection creates a requirement for standing military forces and political control over any territory to which the subjected may flee.

There were also technological changes, as in China, that promoted political consolidation. One was the increasing use of iron in the period after 800 B.C. Iron could be used for axes to clear dense forests, and for plowshares used in planting. The state didn't control the production of iron, but the use of iron implements conferred prestige and increased the overall level of available surplus that was appropriable by the state.[21]

Like Chinese and other societies making the transition from tribalism to a state-level society, the power of the tribal chief was greatly enhanced by his growing legitimation by a distinct and permanent set of priests, the Brahmins. The raja wielded political power, which the priests legitimated through ritual. The rajas repaid these services by supporting the priests and offering them resources. Early rajas were endowed with attributes of divinity by the priests, which allowed them to turn their positions into patrimonies that they could hand down to their sons through the growing practice of primogeniture. Obviously, a semigod is not just the first among equals in a group of tribal elders, and so the sabhas or tribal assemblies lost their ability to decide who would be the clan's leader and came to play more of an advisory role. Ritual investitures of kings developed into a year-long consecration ceremony in which the raja underwent purification and symbolic rebirth, at the end of which he was invested with office and divinity by the Brahmins.[22]

By the end of the sixth century B.C., society on the Indo-Gangetic Plain had made the transition from tribalism either to an early state or to a form of chiefdom known as the *gana-sangha*. Northern states such as Anga, Magadha, Kuru, and Panchala were fully sovereign entities that controlled defined territories and ruled over relatively dense populations centered on urban areas. They were highly stratified, had hereditary kingships, and their elites extracted rents from peasant labor. The gana-sanghas, by contrast, retained certain characteristics of tribal-level societies: lower levels of stratification, more diffuse leadership, and an inability to use coercion in the manner of true states.[23]

THE DETOUR

Up to this point, there are no important differences between the pattern of political development taking place in northern India and the changes that took place in China under the Western Zhou Dynasty two or three centuries earlier. Both societies were initially organized as federations of agnatic clans, both worshipped ancestors, and both shifted to greater hierarchy, hereditary leadership, and a division of labor between ruler and priest at around the time that they made the transition to settled agriculture. It is possible that the Shang rulers exercised a bit more authority than their Indian counterparts, but the differences are not striking.

But the evolution of Indian politics diverged from the Chinese pattern in dramatic ways right around the time of the emergence of the first real states on the Indo-Gangetic Plain. The Indian states did not pass through a five-hundred-year period of continuous warfare on an increasing scale the way that early Chinese states had done during the Western Zhou Dynasty. The Indian states fought with each other and with the gana-sanghas throughout the following centuries, but never to the bitter degree of mutual extinction that the Chinese states did. China, as we have seen, saw a steady drop in the total number of independent political units from more than a thousand at the beginning of the Eastern Zhou to one at its conclusion. India, by contrast, saw fewer and less-intensive wars and a smaller degree of consolidation. It is very revealing that the more primitive gana-sangha form of organization survived in India up through the middle of the first millennium A.D. without being absorbed by more powerful states. No Chinese political entity during the Warring States period could afford not to copy its neighbors in developing modern state-level institutions; Indian political entities obviously did not feel anything like this pressure. The Mauryas by the third century B.C. were able to unite a large part of the subcontinent in a single empire, but there were parts of the region they never conquered, and they never fully consolidated their rule even over core areas. The empire lasted for only 136 years, and a political entity of its size was never again reconstituted under an indigenous regime until the birth of the Indian Republic in 1947.

The second big area of divergence concerns religion. The Chinese developed a professional priesthood to preside over the rites that legitimated kings and emperors. But state religion in China never developed beyond the level of ancestor worship. The priesthood presided over the worship of the emperor's ancestors, but they did not have a universal jurisdiction. When emperors lost legitimacy at the end of a dynasty, or when there was no legitimate ruler in the interdynastic periods, it was not up to the priesthood to declare, as an institution, who held the Mandate of Heaven. Legitimacy in that sense could be bestowed by anyone, from peasant to soldier to bureaucrat.

Religion took a very different turn in India. The original religion of the Indo-Aryan tribes may have been based on ancestor worship as in China. But in the period beginning in the second millennium B.C. when the Vedas were composed, it evolved into a much more sophisticated metaphysical system that explained all aspects of the phenomenal world in terms of an invisible transcendent one. The new Brahmanic religion shifted the emphasis from one's genetic ancestors and descendants to a cosmological system encompassing the whole of nature. Access to this transcendent world was guarded by the class of Brahmins, whose authority was important to safeguard not only the lineage of the king but also the welfare of the lowliest peasant in a future life.

Under the influence of this Brahmanic religion, the twofold division of varnas into aryas and dasas evolved into the fourfold division of Brahmins, Kshatriyas, Vaishyas, and Sudras, with the priestly class clearly established at the top of the hierarchy. They were the ones who generated the ritual prayers that constituted the Vedas. As the religion developed, the prayers were committed to memory by generations of Brahmins; this memorization of ritual incantations became their specialty and the source of their comparative advantage in the struggle for social status with the other varnas. Out of these rituals sprang law, customary and oral at first, but eventually written down in law books like the Manava-Dharmasastra, or what the English called the *Laws of Manu*. Thus law, in the Indian tradition, did not spring from political authority as it did in China; it came from a source independent of and superior to the political ruler. Indeed, the Dharmasastra makes very clear that the king exists to protect the system of the varnas, and not the other way around.[24]

If we use the Chinese case as a baseline for political development, Indian society takes a big detour by around 600 B.C. India does not experience prolonged warfare of the sort that would drive it to develop a modern, impersonal centralized state.[25] Instead of concentrating authority in an emperor, it is split between a well-differentiated class of priests and a class of warriors, who need each other to survive. Even though India does not develop a modern state like China's in this period, it does create the beginnings of a rule of law that limits the power and authority of the state in a way that has no counterpart in China. India's persistent inability to concentrate political power in the manner of China is thus clearly rooted in Indian religion, at which we need to look more closely.

11

VARNAS AND JATIS

Economics versus religion as a source of social change; how Indian social life becomes comprehensible in light of religious ideas; implications of Indian religion for political power

One of the oldest controversies among social theorists concerns the relative priority of economic interests versus ideas as sources of social change. In a tradition that runs from Karl Marx to modern rational-choice economists, material interests are given priority. It was Marx who said that religion was the "opiate of the masses," a fairy tale that was cooked up by elites to justify their domination of the rest of society. While somewhat less acerbic than Marx, many modern economists have maintained that their rational utility-maximizing framework is sufficient to understand virtually all forms of social behavior. Those who think otherwise, the Nobel laureate Gary Becker once implied, just weren't looking hard enough.[1] Ideas are held to be endogenous, that is, they are created after the fact to justify material interests rather than being independent causes of social behavior.

On the other side of this argument lie some of the founders of modern sociology, including Max Weber and Émile Durkheim, who saw religion and religious ideas as primary, both as motivators of human action and as sources of social identity. Weber maintained that the entire framework in which modern economists operate, a framework that sees the individual as the primary decision maker and material interest as the chief motive, was itself the product of religious ideas coming out of the Protestant Reformation. After writing *The Protestant Ethic and the Spirit of Capitalism*, Weber went on to produce books on China, India, and other non-Western civilizations to show that religious ideas were necessary to understand how their economic life was organized.

If one wanted an example of a religion that, à la Marx, justified the dominance of a single, small elite over the rest of society, one would choose not Christianity or Islam, with their underlying messages of universal equality, but rather the Brahmanic religion that appeared in India in the last two millennia B.C. According to the Rg Veda,

> When the gods made a sacrifice with the Man as their victim . . . when they divided the Man, into how many parts did they divide him? What was his mouth, what were his arms, what were his thighs and his feet called?
>
> The brahman was his mouth, of his arms were made the warrior. His thighs became the vaisya, of his feet the shudra was born. With Sacrifice the gods sacrificed to Sacrifice, these were the first of the sacred laws. These mighty beings reached the sky, where are the eternal spirits, the gods.[2]

Not only did the Brahmins put themselves at the top of this fourfold social hierarchy; they also awarded themselves perpetual monopoly power over the prayers and texts that would be necessary for all legitimating rituals, from the highest investiture of kings to the lowliest wedding or funeral.

But a wholly materialistic account of the function of religion in Indian society is very unsatisfying. For one thing, it fails to account for the actual content of the fairy tale. As we have seen, Chinese society on the eve of the transition to statehood bore many structural similarities to Indian society. The Chinese elite, like elites in every known human society, also made use of legitimating rituals to enhance their power. But the Chinese never thought up a metaphysical system of the depth and complexity of the one that emerged in India. Indeed, they were able to seize and hold power quite effectively without the use of any transcendental religion whatsoever.

Moreover, in India it was not the elites holding coercive and economic power but the elites holding ritual power who ended up on top. Even if one believed material causes were primary, one would still need to answer the question of why the Kshatriyas and the Vaishyas—the warriors and the merchants—agreed to subordinate themselves to the Brahmins, giving them not just land and economic resources but also control over intimate aspects of their personal lives.

Finally, economic or materialist explanations of Indian society need to answer the question of why the system remained so durable over time.

Brahmanic religion suited the interests of a small elite in 600 B.C., but it did not suit the interests of many other classes or social groups in Indian society over time. Why didn't a counterelite arise, proclaiming an alternative set of religious ideas that justified universal equality? In a certain sense, Buddhism and Jainism were such protest religions. But both of them continued to share many of the metaphysical assumptions of the Brahmanic religion, and both failed to win broad acceptance in the subcontinent. The biggest challenges to the hegemony of the Brahmanic religion had to be forcibly imported by foreign invaders—the Moguls bringing Islam and the British bearing Western liberal and democratic ideas. Religion and politics must therefore be seen as drivers of behavior and change in their own right, not as by-products of grand economic forces.

THE RATIONALITY OF INDIAN RELIGION

It is hard to imagine a social system less compatible with the demands of a modern economy than the Brahmanic religion's system of jatis. Modern labor market theory demands that individuals should be free, in Adam Smith's phrase, to "better their condition" through investments in education and skills, and by contracting for their services to whomever they want. In a flexible labor market with good information, this should maximize everyone's well-being and lead to an optimal allocation of resources. Under the system of jatis, by contrast, individuals are born into a limited set of occupational categories. They must follow the occupation of their fathers and must marry someone from the same occupational group. It makes no sense to invest in education, since one can never better oneself in any fundamental way in this life. Social mobility is possible under the jati system, but only on the part of the community as a whole and not by individuals. Thus the jati may decide to move to or open a business in a new area, but there is no room for individual entrepreneurship. The system creates huge obstacles to social cooperation: for certain Brahmins, the simple act of laying eyes on an Untouchable would require going through a lengthy ritual of purification.

But what seems irrational from the standpoint of modern economics is totally rational if one accepts the Brahmanic religion's starting premises. Indeed, the entire social system down to the most minute rules of caste behavior makes perfect sense as logical outgrowths of the larger metaphysical system. Modern observers have frequently tried to explain Indian social rules in terms of their functional or economic utility—for example, that the prohibition on eating cows started out as a hygienic measure to avoid contaminated meat. Quite apart from the fact that the early Indo-Aryans were cow eaters like the Nuer, such explanations fail to penetrate the subjectively experienced coherence of the society and reflect nothing more than the secular biases of the observers themselves.

Max Weber recognized the high degree of rationality that lay behind the Brahmanic religious teaching—a theodicy, or justification of God, that he labeled "a stroke of genius."[3] This genius is often sensed by Western converts who go to study in Indian ashrams. The starting point is the denial of the reality of the phenomenal world. In the words of one observer,

> All Indic religious systems have as their ultimate purpose life-transcendence (*moksha*) because all assume that sentient existence is a false perception of reality (*maya*), the facade behind which lies The One (*tat ekam*), *brahman*, who, formless, and because formless eternal, is the sole reality. All that is perceived by the senses, all that we are attached to by virtue of our physical existence, is transitory (subject to death and decay) and therefore unreal (*maya*). The "purpose" of existence is actually not to "attain" identity with this ultimate being, as some interpreters claim, but to simply tear away all impediments standing in the way of discovering that what is true and permanent in individual being (*atman*) is already nothing more than ultimate being *brahman*.[4]

Mortal existence involves immersion in a material, biological existence that is the opposite of the disembodied, true existence that lies beyond the here and now. As the early Brahmins saw it, "The blood and gore associated with birth, the suffering and deformations associated with disease and violence, the repugnancies associated with waste effusions from the human body, and the decay and putrefaction associated with death" were all associated with the mortal life, which needed to be transcended. This was the justification for awarding themselves a privileged role in the social hierarchy: "Mortal existence was permeated with polluting substances whose control and systematic reduction through time, requiring Brahman-supervised rituals in one's present life and upward-spiraling rebirth (*sam-*

sara) over the long pull, were the essential ingredients for finding a way out (*moksha*)."[5]

The jati system arises out of the concept of karma, or what one does in this life. Occupations have a higher or lower status depending on how close they are to sources of pollution—to the blood, death, dirt, and decay of biological life. Occupations like hide tanner, butcher, barber, sweeper, midwife, or dealing with the disposal of dead animals or humans were regarded as the most impure. Brahmins by contrast were the most pure, because they could rely on other people to perform services for them that involved contact with blood, death, and dirt. This then may explain the practice of vegetarianism among Brahmins, since to eat meat is to eat a corpse.[6]

The only possibilities for social mobility existed not in this life but between lifetimes, since one's karma can change only from one lifetime to the next. An individual was thus trapped in his or her karma for life. But whether one moved up or down in the hierarchy of jatis depended on how one fulfilled the dharma, or rules governing good conduct, for the jati one was born into. Failure to abide by these rules could cause one to fall lower in the hierarchy in the next life, and hence farther away from true existence. The Brahmanic religion thus sacralized the existing social order, making the fulfillment of one's existing jati or occupation a religious duty.

The order of varnas grew out of the same metaphysical premises. The first three varnas—the Brahmins, Kshatriyas, and Vaisyas—were all regarded as "twice born" and were permitted, as a result of their second birth, to be initiated into ritual status. The Sudras, who included the vast majority of the population, were "once born" and could hope for ritual status only in the next life. It is not clear historically whether varnas preceded jatis or the reverse as Indian society evolved out of its initial stage of tribal organization. It is possible that lineages evolved into jatis, which they resemble in many ways due to their elaborate kinship rules, but it is also possible that the varnas evolved first and set the framework within which jatis then emerged.[7]

The system of jatis generated by these religious beliefs thus produced a remarkable combination of segmentary separation and social interdependence at one and the same time. Each jati became an inherited position that modified the existing lineage system. Since the jatis set the outer limits of clan exogamy, they tended to become self-sufficient communities in a sea of other segmentary units. On the other hand, each occupation was also part of a larger division of labor and thus mutually dependent on one another, from the high priest to the funeral undertaker.[8] The French anthropologist Louis Dumont, quoting E.A.H. Blunt, gives some examples:

> The Barbers boycott dancing girls who refused to dance for their marriages.
>
> In Gorakhpur, a planter tried to end the trade of the Chamars [manufacturers of leather goods], who, he believed, were poisoning the cattle (as they are often suspected of doing); he ordered his tenants to lacerate the hide of every animal which died of no apparent cause. The Chamars retorted by ordering their women to stop serving as mid-wives; the planter gave in.
>
> In Ahmedabad (Gujerat), a banker who was having his house re-roofed had a quarrel with a confectioner. The confectioners came to an agreement with the tile makers who refused to provide the banker with tiles.[9]

This was not simply economic interdependence, because each jati performing its function also had a ritual significance for the other jatis.

IDEAS AND THEIR POLITICAL CONSEQUENCES

The varna system had immense implications for politics since it subordinated the Kshatriyas, warriors, to the Brahmins.[10] There was, according to Harold Gould, a "symbiotic interdependence . . . between Brahman and Kshatriya. This arises from the need for royal power to be continuously resanctified by priestly (i.e., ritual) power in order for the former to retain its sacred legitimacy."[11] Each ruler would need to establish a personal relationship with a *purohita*, or court priest, who would have to sanctify each action he took as a secular leader.

How this theoretical separation between religious authority and secular power worked to limit the latter in practice is not entirely clear at first glance. The Brahmin hierarchy was not organized into an institution with a central, formal source of authority like the Catholic church. It resembled rather a vast social network, where individual Brahmins communicated and cooperated with one another without being able to exercise institutional authority as such. The Brahmins individually owned land, but the priesthood as an institution did not control territory and resources the way the church did in Europe. The Brahmins certainly could not raise their own armies in the manner of medieval popes. There is nothing in Indian history comparable to Pope Gregory VII's excommunication of the Holy Roman Emperor in the year 1076 and his forcing of the emperor to come barefoot to Canossa to plead for clemency. While secular rulers needed purohitas to bless their political plans, it does not seem to have been difficult for them to buy them off to get what they wanted. We need to look for other mechanisms by which India's hierarchical, segmented religious and social system made the concentration of political power difficult.

One obvious channel of influence was through the limitations that the varna/jati system placed on the development of military organization. The warriors or Kshatriyas were a constituent part of the fourfold varna system, which automatically limited the degree of military mobilization of which Indian society was capable. One reason that armed pastoral nomads like the Xiongnu, Huns, and Mongols became such potent military powers was that they could mobilize close to 100 percent of their able-bodied male population. Armed predation and pastoral nomadism are not especially different activities in terms of requisite skills or organizational requirements. Although this may have been true of the Indo-Aryans in their days of pastoral nomadism, it ceased to be so once they became a settled society divided into varnas. Warrior status became a specialty of a small, aristocratic elite, entry into which was not just a matter of specialized training and birth but also was invested with considerable religious significance.

This system didn't always work to limit entry in practice. While many of India's rulers were born into the Kshatriya class, many also started out as Brahmins, Vaisyas, and even Sudras. Having achieved political power, the new rulers tended to be awarded Kshatriya status retroactively; it was easier to become a Kshatriya in this fashion than to become a Brahmin.[12] All four varnas fought in wars, and Brahmins were known to hold high military rank. The Sudras tended to fight as auxiliaries, however, and the military hierarchy reproduced the social hierarchy in terms of the subordination of the lower orders.[13] Indian polities were never able to achieve general mobilization of a large part of their peasantries in the manner of the state of Qin and other Chinese states during the later Eastern Zhou Dynasty.[14] Given the ritual aversion to blood and dead bodies, one does not imagine that wounded soldiers received much succor from their highborn comrades. Such a conservative social system was also evidently slow to adopt new military technologies. Fighting chariots were abandoned only after the start of the Christian era, many centuries after the Chinese had given up on them; elephants continued to be used in war long after their utility was thrown into question. Indian armies also never developed effective cavalry forces with mounted archers, which led to defeats by the Greeks in the fourth century B.C. as well as by the Muslims in the twelfth century A.D.[15]

The second way Brahmanism limited political power was by providing an impetus for the organization of small, tightly knit corporate entities that extended all the way from top to bottom of the society, based on the jati. These units were self-governing and did not require the state to organize them. Indeed, they resisted the state's efforts to penetrate and control them, leading to the situation that the political scientist Joel Migdal characterizes as a weak state and a strong society.[16] This situation persists down to the present day, where caste and village organizations remain the backbone of Indian society.

The self-organizing character of Indian society was noted by many nineteenth-century Western observers, including Karl Marx and Henry Maine. Marx asserted that the king owned all land but then noted that villages in India tended to be economically autarchic and based on a primitive form of communism (a rather self-contradictory interpretation). Maine referred to the unchanging, self-regulating Indian village community, a notion that became widespread in Britain in Victorian times. British administrators in the early nineteenth century described the Indian village as a "little republic" that could survive the ruin of empires.[17]

In the twentieth century, Indian nationalists, drawing partly on these interpretations, imagined an idyllic picture of an indigenous village democracy, the *panchayat*, which was said to have been the source of political order until it was undermined by the British colonial administration. Article 40 of the modern Indian constitution has detailed provisions for the organization of revived panchayats that were intended to promote democracy on a local level, something that was given particular emphasis by Rajiv Gandhi's government in 1989 when it sought to decentralize power further within India's federal system. The actual nature of local governance in early India was not, however, democratic and secular, as later commentators and nationalists claimed, but based on jati or caste. Each village tended to have a dominant caste, that is, a caste that numerically outnumbered the others and owned the greater part of the village's land. The panchayat was simply the traditional leadership of that caste.[18]

Individual villages had local governance institutions and did not depend on a state to provide services from the outside. One of the chief functions of the panchayat was juridical; it arbitrated disputes between members of the jati based on customary law. Property rights within the village were not communal in the sense imagined by Marx. As in other segmentary lineage-based societies, property was held by a complex patchwork of kin, with many entails and restrictions on the ability of individual families to alienate land. This meant that the king did not "own" the land of the village over which he was nominally sovereign. As we will see in the following chapter, the power of different Indian political rulers to tax or appropriate land was often very limited.

Commercial activity was also based on jatis, which acted like closed corporations that needed little external support. A great deal of trade in southern India from the ninth to the fourteenth century was controlled by merchant guilds like the Ayyvole, which had representatives throughout the subcontinent and dealt extensively with Arab merchants outside India. Gujerati merchants, both Muslim and Hindu, have long dominated trade across the Indian Ocean, in East Africa, southern Arabia, and into Southeast Asia. The merchants of Ahmedabad were organized into a large, citywide corporation on which sat members of all of the major occupational groups.[19] In China, trade networks were based on lineages but were not nearly as well organized as their Indian counterparts.

Unlike Chinese lineages, whose jurisdiction tended to be limited to the regulation of family law, inheritance, and other domestic matters (especially in periods when the government was strong), the Indian jatis took on much more overt political functions in addition to being local social regulators. According to Satish Saberwal, "The *jati* provided the social field for mobilizing variously: aggressively, to secure dominance and rulerships . . . ; defensively, to resist the larger states' and empires' attempts to wedge into the dominant *jati's* domain . . . ; and subversively, to take office in one of these larger entities, and use its authority and stature to advance, rather, one's own private interests."[20] The jatis provided their members with opportunities for physical and social mobility. For example, the Kaikolar, a Tamil weaver caste, shifted to trading and soldiering when the opportunity arose under the Chola kings; Sikh carpenters and blacksmiths left their native

Punjab for Assam and Kenya in the late nineteenth century.[21] These decisions would be taken collectively by groups of families who would rely on one another for support in their new surroundings. In northern India, the Rajput jati was particularly successful in expanding its domain and came to control substantial territory.

A third mechanism by which the Brahmanic social system limited political power was by controlling literacy, a legacy that extends up to the present moment and consigns huge numbers of Indians to poverty and lack of opportunity. Contemporary India is something of a paradox. On the one hand, there are large numbers of extremely well-educated Indians who have risen to the top of global rankings in a variety of fields, from information technology to medicine to entertainment to economics. Indians outside of India always enjoyed a high degree of upward social mobility, a fact noted many years ago by the novelist V. S. Naipaul.[22] Since the economic reforms of the late 1980s and 1990s, they have been prospering inside India as well. On the other hand, the educated remain a minority in a country with extremely high levels of illiteracy and poverty. Next to fast-growing cities like Bangalore and Hyderabad are vast rural hinterlands whose human development outcomes rank among the lowest in the world.[23]

The historical roots of these disparities lie ultimately in the system of varnas and jatis. The Brahmins of course controlled access to learning and knowledge through their role as guardians of ritual. Through the end of the first millennium B.C., they had a very strong aversion to the writing down of the most important Vedic texts. According to Saberwal, "Memorizing the hymns for use in ritual—for oneself and for one's clients—has been the most characteristic form of Brahminical learning. Efficacy in the ritual, and therefore the process of learning, did not necessarily require that the meanings of what was memorized be understood . . . A great many Brahmins devoted large parts of their lives to memorization on a prodigious scale or to logical analyses and debates."[24] Exact memorization of the Vedic texts was necessary if they were to have their desired ritual effects; small mistakes in recitation, it was believed, could lead to disaster.

Perhaps not accidentally, the Brahmanic commitment to the oral transmission of the Vedas reinforced their own social supremacy by creating additional barriers to entry into their varna. Unlike Jews, Christians, and Muslims, who were all "people of the book" from the start of their religious traditions, the Brahmins strongly resisted the introduction of writing and technologies related to it. Chinese travelers to India in the fifth and seventh centuries A.D. looking for sources of Buddhist tradition were hard-pressed to find any written documents. Long after both the Chinese and Europeans had switched to writing on parchment, the Indians were still writing on palm leaves and bark. The aversion to durable parchment was religious in origin, since it was made from animal skin. But the Brahmins were also slow to adopt paper when that technology became available in the eleventh century.[25] In rural Maharashtra, paper was not used in routine administration until the middle of the seventeenth century, and when it did arise, it immensely improved the efficiency of accounting and oversight.[26]

It wasn't until the second millennium A.D. that writing became more common and spread beyond the Brahmins to other groups in Indian society. Merchants began to keep commercial records, and individual jatis recorded family genealogies. In Kerala, the Nayars "of royal and noble lineages" began to learn written Sanskrit, and the political class in that state began to produce voluminous records of political and commercial transactions. (In the late twentieth century, Kerala, under a local Communist government, emerged as one of the best-governed states in India; one wonders whether this performance had deeper roots in the tradition of literacy of the political class there in earlier centuries.)

Compared to the Chinese, the Brahmins' monopoly on learning and their resistance to the adoption of writing had an incalculable impact on the development of a modern state. From the Shang Dynasty onward, Chinese rulers used the written word to communicate orders, record laws, keep accounts, and write detailed political histories. The education of a Chinese bureaucrat centered on literacy and immersion in a long and complex literary tradition. Training for administrators, while limited by modern standards, involved prolonged analysis of written texts and the drawing of lessons from earlier historical events. With the adoption of the examination system beginning in the Han Dynasty, recruitment into the government was based on mastery of literary skills and was not restricted to people of a certain class. While the effective access of ordinary Chinese to high government office was limited in many practical ways, the Chinese were long aware that education was one important route to upward social mobility. Lineages and local communities therefore invested heavily in educating sons to take advantage of the system.

Nothing like this existed in India. Rulers were themselves illiterate and relied for administration on a similarly uneducated cadre of patrimonial officials. Literacy was a privilege of the Brahmin class, which had a strong self-interest in maintaining their monopoly over access to learning and ritual. As in the case of the military, the hierarchical system of varnas and jatis severely restricted the access of the great majority of the population to education and literacy, and therefore reduced the pool of competent administrators available to Indian states.

The final way religion affected political power in Indian development was through the establishment of the foundations for something that might be called a rule of law. The essence of the rule of law is a body of rules reflecting the community's sense of justice that is higher than the wishes of the person who happens to be the king. This was the case in India, where the law laid out in the different Dharmasastras was created not by kings but by Brahmins acting on the basis of ritual knowledge. And the laws make very clear the fact that the varnas are not there to serve the king; rather, the king can gain legitimacy only by being the protector of the varnas.[27] If the king violates the sacred law, the epic Mahabharata explicitly sanctions revolt against him, saying that the king is not a king at all but rather a mad dog. In the *Laws of Manu*, the locus of sovereignty lies in the law and not in the person of the king: "In essence, it is the law (*danda*) that is the king, the person with authority, the person who keeps the order of the realm, and provides leadership to it (*Manusmrti*, ch. 7. s. 17)."[28]

A number of classic sources tell the cautionary tale of King Vena, who forbade all sacrifices except to himself and enforced intercaste marriages. As a result, the divine sages attacked him and killed him with divine blades of grass that had miraculously been turned into spears. Many of India's dynasties, including the Nandas, Mauryas, and Sungas, were weakened by Brahmanic intrigue.[29] It is of course difficult to know when the Brahmins were simply defending their own interests as opposed to upholding a sacred law, much as in the case of the medieval Catholic church. But like Europe and unlike China, authority in India was split in a way that placed meaningful checks on political power.

The social system that grew out of Indian religion thus severely constrained the ability of states to concentrate power. Rulers could not create a powerful military instrument capable of mobilizing a large proportion of the population; they could not penetrate the self-governing, highly organized jatis that existed in every village; they and their administrators lacked education and literacy; and they faced a well-organized priestly class that protected a normative order in which they were consigned to a subordinate role. In every one of these respects their situation was very different from that of the Chinese.

12

WEAKNESSES OF INDIAN POLITIES

How the Mauryas were the first and most successful indigenous rulers of India; the nature of the Indian state under the Mauryas; the character of Ashoka; decline, disunity, and revival under the Guptas; why India subsequently fell to foreign conquerors

Indian social development outran both political and economic development early on. The subcontinent acquired a common culture under a set of religious beliefs and social practices that marked it as a distinctive civilization long before anyone ever tried to unify it politically. And when that unification was attempted, the strength of the society was such that it was able to resist political authority and prevent the latter from reshaping society. So whereas China developed a strong state that kept society weak in a self-perpetuating manner, India had a strong society that prevented a strong state from emerging in the first place.

Of the hundreds or thousands of tiny states and chiefdoms that crystallized out of tribal society at the beginning of the first millennium B.C. on the Indian subcontinent, three kingdoms—Kashi, Kosala, and Magadha—and the chiefdom or gana-sangha of Vrijjis, became the preeminent contenders for power on the Indo-Gangetic Plain. Of these, Magadha (whose core was in the contemporary state of Bihar) was destined to play the role of the state of Qin in unifying much of the subcontinent under a single house. Bimbisara became king in the second half of the sixth century B.C. and through a series of strategic marriages and conquests established Magadha as the dominant state in eastern India. Magadha began to extract taxes on land and produce in place of the voluntary payments made in prestate days by junior lineages. This required in turn the recruitment of an administrative staff to preside over tax collection. Taxes were said to be one-sixth of agricultural output, which if true was extremely high for an early agrarian society.[1] The king could not claim ownership of all land in his kingdom, but only of the wasteland, which at that period of low population density must have been quite extensive.

Bimbisara was later murdered by his son Ajatashatru, who annexed Kosala and Kashi to the west, and conducted a prolonged struggle with Vrijjis, which he eventually won by sowing dissention among the gana-sangha's leaders. By the time Ajatashatru died in 461 B.C., Magadha controlled the Ganges delta and much of the lower course of the river, with a new capital at Pataliputra. Rule then passed to a series of other kings, including the short-lived Nanda dynasty, which rose to power from Sudra status. Alexander the Great encountered the Nandas' army, before his troops mutinied and forced him to turn back toward Punjab. Greek sources claim that it consisted of twenty thousand cavalry, two hundred thousand infantry, one thousand chariots, and three thousand elephants, though these numbers were certainly exaggerated to justify the Greek retreat.[2]

The Nandas were succeeded in Magadha by Chandragupta Maurya, who vastly extended their domains and founded India's first great subcontinental polity, the Mauryan empire, in 321 B.C. He was a protégé of the Brahmin writer and minister Kautilya, whose book the *Arthasastra* is regarded as a classic treatise on Indian statecraft. Chandragupta conquered the northwest in a campaign against Alexander's successor, Seleucus Nicator, bringing Punjab and parts of eastern Afghanistan and Baluchistan under Mauryan control. His empire now stretched from Persia in the west all the way to Assam in the east.

Conquest of the Dravidian south of India was left to Chandragupta's son, Bindusara, and grandson, the great emperor Ashoka. Bindusara extended the empire into the southern Deccan plateau as far south as Karnataka, and Ashoka, in what was by all accounts a long and bloody campaign, conquered Kalinga in the southeast (comprising the modern states of Orissa and parts of Andhra Pradesh) in 260 B.C. Due to India's nonliterary culture at the time, Ashoka's accomplishments were never chronicled in a history like the Chinese *Book of History* or *Spring and Autumn Annals*. He was not recognized as a great king by later generations of Indians until 1915, when the script in which a large number of rock edicts were written was deciphered and archaeologists pieced together the extent of his empire.[3]

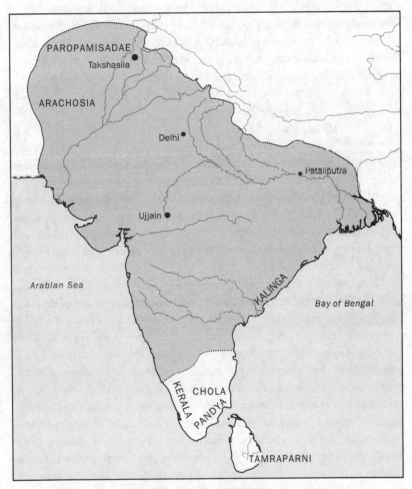

The Empire of Ashoka

The empire assembled by the Mauryas in three generations comprised the whole of north India south of the Himalayas from Persia in the west to Assam in the east, and southward to Karnataka. The only parts of the subcontinent not included were territories in the far south in what are now Kerala, Tamil Nadu, and Sri Lanka. No indigenous Indian regime would ever again unite this much territory under a single ruler.[4] The Delhi sultanate of the Moghuls was considerably smaller. The British ruled a larger empire in the subcontinent, but this begs the question: What does it mean to say that Ashoka, or Akhbar, or the British viceroy "ruled" India?

THE MAURYAN EMPIRE: WHAT KIND OF STATE?

Historians have debated at great length the question of what kind of state existed in ancient India.[5] We might gain better insight into this question if we put it in comparative perspective, and in particular contrast the Indian empire of Ashoka with the Chinese empire founded by Qin Shi Huangdi. These empires came into being at virtually the same time (mid- to late third century B.C.), but in terms of the nature of their polities, they could not have been more different.

Each empire was built around a core unit, the states of Magadha and Qin. The Qin state deserves to be called a true state, with many of the characteristics of modern state administration as defined by Max Weber. The patrimonial elite running the state had largely been killed off in the wars the state fought over the centuries and replaced by newcomers who were selected on an increasingly impersonal basis. Qin had upended traditional property rights through its abolition of the well-field system, and replaced the patrimonial districts with a uniform system of commanderies and prefectures. When Qin defeated its rival warring states and established a unified empire, it tried to extend this centralized public administration to the whole of China. The system of commanderies and prefectures was broadened to encompass the territory of the other conquered states, as were uniform weights and measures and a common written script. As we saw in chapter 8, the Qin dynasts were ultimately unsuccessful in their project, and patrimonial rule returned to some extent under the Former Han Dynasty. But the Han rulers persisted in the project to centralize administration, picking off the remaining feudatories one by one until they had established what could reasonably be called not an empire but a uniform, centralized state.

Very little of this happened under the Mauryan empire. The core state of Magadha does not appear to have had any modern features whatsoever, though we know much less about the nature of administration there than we do in the case of Qin. Recruitment to state administration was completely patrimonial and sharply limited by the caste system. Kautilya in the *Arthasastra* says that the chief qualification for high office should be noble birth, or that one's "father and grandfather" were *amatyas* or high officials. These officials were almost entirely Brahmins. Pay scales within the bureaucracy were very hierarchical, with the ratio of lowest-to-highest salaries being 1:4,800.[6] There is no evidence that bureaucratic recruitment was done on the basis of merit, or that public office was open to anyone outside of the top three varnas, a fact confirmed by the Greek traveler Megasthenes.[7] The wars that brought Magadha to dominance were not the prolonged brutal affairs experienced by the state of Qin; the old elites were not killed off, nor does Magadha's situation ever appear to have been so dire as to require total mobilization of the male population. The Mauryan state as far as we know did not make any efforts to standardize weights and measures, or to introduce uniformity into the languages spoken in areas under its jurisdiction. Indeed, as late as the sixteenth century A.D., Indian states were still struggling to impose uniform standards, and that did not finally occur until under the British Raj, nearly two full millennia after the Mauryas.[8]

The relationship between the core state of Magadha and the rest of the empire acquired through marriage and conquest was also quite different from those within China. Conquest of one Chinese state by another often resulted in the extermination or exile of an entire ruling lineage and the absorption of its territory under another ruling house. The number of Chinese elite lineages dropped substantially during the Eastern Zhou Dynasty. The Mauryan empire was built by much gentler means. The only war that seems to have produced large numbers of casualties and a scorched-earth policy was the incorporation of Kalinga, which had a traumatic effect on the conqueror, Ashoka. In most other cases conquest simply meant that the existing ruler after defeat in battle accepted the nominal sovereignty of the Mauryas. The *Arthasastra* advises weak kings to submit and voluntarily render homage to stronger neighbors. There was no "feudalism" in the Chinese or European sense where a conquered domain would be dispossessed of its existing rulers and donated as a benefice to a royal kinsman or household retainer. Indian historians sometimes speak of "vassal" kingdoms, but these had none of the contractual significance of European vassalage.[9] It is not accurate to say that the Mauryas redistributed power, since it was never really centralized in the first place. Needless to say, the Mauryas made no effort to impose their state institutions on anything but the core areas of the empire. Government on a local level throughout the empire remained completely patrimonial, with no attempt to establish a permanent, professional cadre of administrators. This meant that every new king brought with him a different set of loyalties and a turnover in administrators.[10]

Evidence of the Mauryan empire's light control over the territories it nominally ruled lies in the survival of tribal federations or chiefdoms—the gana-sanghas—throughout the period of its hegemony. Indian historians sometimes refer to these as "republics" because their political decision making was more participatory and consensual than in the hierarchical kingdoms. But this puts a modern gloss on what were simply surviving tribal polities still grounded in kinship.[11]

Kautilya in the *Arthasastra* discusses fiscal policy and taxation at great length, though it is not clear the extent to which his recommendations were actually put into effect. Contrary to believers in "Oriental despotism," the king did not "own" all the land in his realm. He had his own domains and asserted direct control over wasteland, uncleared forests, and the like, but he generally did not challenge existing customary property rights. The state did assert rights to collect taxes from landowners, of which there was a large variety. Taxes could be imposed on individuals, on land, on produce, on villages, or on rulers of more peripheral territories, and had to be collected largely in kind or through corvée labor.[12] No Indian ruler ever seems to have attempted anything like Shang Yang's abolition of the well-field system, or Wang Mang's ambitious though failed land reform efforts.

Ashoka died in 232 B.C., and his empire went into immediate decline. The northwest fell to the Bactrian Greeks, the tribal gana-sanghas reasserted themselves in Punjab and Rajasthan in the west, while Kalinga, Karnataka, and other territories to the south broke away and returned to their status as independent kingdoms. The Mauryas retreated to their original kingdom of Magadha in the central Ganges plain, and the last of the Mauryas, Brihadratha, was assassinated in 185. More than five hundred years passed before another dynasty, the Guptas, was able to reunify India on anything like the scale of the Mauryan empire. The subcontinental empire lasted for only a generation, and the dynasty for 135 years. The end of the Maurya saw the disintegration of the empire into hundreds of separate polities, many of them at a prestate level of development.

The fact that the Maurya empire lasted such a short time is prima facie evidence that it never exerted strong control over its constituent territories in the first place. This is not just a matter of post hoc ergo propter hoc. The Mauryas never established strong state institutions and never made the leap from patrimonial to impersonal administration. It maintained a strong network of spies throughout the empire, but there is no evidence of any of the road or canal building to facilitate communications like that of the early Chinese governments. It is remarkable that the Mauryans left no monuments to their power anywhere except in their capital city of Pataliputra, which is perhaps one reason why Ashoka failed to be remembered by later generations as an empire builder.[13]

It never occurred to any Maurya ruler to engage in anything resembling nation building, that is, to try to penetrate the whole society and imbue it with a different, common set of norms and values. The Mauryas had no real concept of sovereignty, that is, a right to impose impersonal rules over the whole of their territory. There was no uniform Indian Penal Code in the subcontinent until one was introduced by the poet and politician Thomas Babington Macaulay under British rule.[14] The monarchy did not engage in massive social engineering but rather protected the existing social order in all of its variety and complexity.

India never developed a set of ideas like Legalism in China, that is, a doctrine that set the naked accumulation of power as the goal of politics. Treatises like the *Arthasastra* did offer advice to princes that could be Machiavellian, but it was always in the service of a set of values and a social structure that lay outside of politics. More than that, Brahmanic spiritualism spawned ideas that were distinctly nonmilitary in character. The doctrine of ahimsa, or nonviolence, has its roots in Vedic texts, which suggests that the killing of living beings can have negative consequences for karma. Some texts criticized meat eating and the sacrificial slaughter of animals, though others approved it. As we have seen, nonviolence was even more central to protest religions like Jainism and Buddhism.

The first Maurya king, Chandragupta, became a Jain and abdicated his

throne in favor of his son Bindusara in order to become an ascetic. Together with a group of monks, he moved to southern India, where he was
said to have ended his life through slow starvation in the orthodox Jain
manner.[15] His grandson Ashoka started off as an orthodox Hindu, but he
was converted to Buddhism later in life. The loss of life during the Kalinga
campaign, when 150,000 Kalingans were reportedly killed or deported,
provoked deep feelings of remorse in Ashoka. According to one of his
Rock Edicts, "After that, now that the Kalingas had been annexed, began
His Sacred Majesty's zealous practice of the Law of Piety." He declared that
"of all the people who were slain, done to death, or carried away captive in
Kalinga, if the hundredth part or the thousandth part were now to suffer
the same fate, it would be a matter of regret to His Sacred Majesty. Moreover, should anyone do him wrong, that too must be borne with by His
Sacred Majesty, so far as it can possibly be borne with." Ashoka went on to
urge that unsubdued peoples on the frontiers of the empire "should not be
afraid of him, that they should trust him, and should receive from him
happiness not sorrow," and he called on his sons and grandsons to eschew
further conquests.[16] Expansion of the empire stopped abruptly; whether
Ashoka's descendants were following his wishes or were simply poor
statesmen, they presided over a crumbling domain. One wonders what
would have happened to Ashoka's empire had India developed a power
doctrine like Chinese Legalism, rather than Brahmanism, Jainism, or
Buddhism—but it if had, it wouldn't be India.

THE VICTORY OF SOCIETY OVER POLITICS

India, particularly in the north, experienced political decay after the decline of the Mauryan empire. Tribal polities reappeared in Rajasthan and
Punjab in the west, which was also beset by new tribal invaders coming
out of Central Asia. This was in part a consequence of the Chinese empire's superior level of political development. The Qin Dynasty had begun
the process of building one of many Great Walls to keep these invaders
out, which forced the nomadic Xiongnu back into Central Asia, where they
displaced a series of other tribes. In a chain reaction, this led the Scythians
or Shakas to invade northern India, to be followed by the Yuezhi, who
established the Kushana dynasty in what is now Afghanistan. No kingdom
in northern India was sufficiently well organized to contemplate a massive

engineering project like the Great Wall, and as a result these tribes occupied part of the north Indian plain.[17]

Farther south, local chiefdoms evolved into kingdoms, like the Satavahana dynasty that ruled in the western Deccan in the first century B.C. But this polity did not survive long and did not evolve strong centralized institutions any more than the Mauryas. They clashed with other small kingdoms for control of the northern Deccan, as did a series of small kingdoms including the Cholas, Pandyas, and Satiyaputras. This history is very complex and rather unedifying to study, since it is hard to place into a larger narrative of political development. What emerges from it is a picture of general political weakness. Southern states were often not able to perform the most basic functions of government such as collecting taxes, due to the strong, self-organized character of the communities they ruled.[18] Not one of these states succeeded in enlarging its domain and achieving hegemony on a permanent basis, or in evolving more sophisticated administrative institutions that would allow it to wield power more effectively. This region continued on in this state of political fragmentation for more than another millennium.[19]

The second successful attempt to create a large empire in India was that of the Guptas, beginning with Chandra Gupta I, who came to power in A.D. 320 in Magadha, the same power base as the Mauryas. He and his son Samudra Gupta succeeded in once again unifying a good deal of northern India. Samudra annexed numerous gana-sangha chiefdoms in Rajasthan and other parts of northwestern India, bringing to an end that form of political organization, conquered Kashmir, and forced the Kushanas and Shakas to pay tribute. Cultural life flourished under Samudra's son Chandra Gupta II (375–415), when many Hindu, Buddhist, and Jain temples were built. The dynasty continued for another two generations until the death of Skanda Gupta in the second half of the fifth century. By this time India was being invaded by a new group of tribal nomads from Central Asia, the Huns or Huna, who took advantage of the weakened chiefdoms in the northwest. The Guptan empire exhausted itself in this fight, eventually losing Kashmir, Punjab, and much of the Gangetic plain to the Huns by 515.[20]

Whatever their cultural accomplishments, the Guptas made no political innovations with regard to state institutions. They never tried to integrate the political units they conquered into a uniform administrative structure. In typical Indian fashion, defeated rulers were left in place to pay tribute and continue the actual governing of their territories. The Guptan bureaucracy was, if anything, less centralized and capable than its Mauryan predecessor. It collected taxes on agrarian output and owned key productive assets like salt works and mines but otherwise did not seek to intervene in existing social arrangements. The Guptan empire was considerably smaller as well, since it never succeeded in conquering territories in southern India. It lasted for some two hundred years, before dissolving into a welter of small, competing states, giving rise to another period of political decay.

NATION BUILDING BY FOREIGNERS

After the tenth century, the political history of India ceases to be one of indigenous development and is dominated by a series of foreign conquerors, first Muslim and then British. Political development from this point forward becomes a matter of the foreigners' efforts to transplant their own institutions onto Indian soil. They succeeded at this only partially. Each foreign invader had to contend with the same fragmented but tightly organized society of "little kingdoms" that were easy to conquer due to their disunity but hard to rule once they had submitted. They left layers of new institutions and new values that were in many ways transformative. Yet in many respects the exercise of power by outsiders left the internal social order untouched.

A series of Turko-Afghan Muslims invaded northern India from the end of the tenth century onward. Since the emergence of Islam in the seventh century, the Arabs and then the Turks had made the transition from tribal to state-level societies and in many respects developed more sophisticated political institutions than the indigenous Indian polities. The most important of these was the system of slave-soldiers and administrators (to be discussed in the following chapters) that allowed the Arabs and Turks to move beyond kinship and engage in merit-based recruitment. The armies of the Indian states resisted the repeated onslaughts of Muslim invaders coming out of Afghanistan, most notably the Rajputs, but were simply too weak and disorganized to prevail. By the early thirteenth century, the Mamluk dynasty of Qutb-ud-din Aybak had established itself in the sultanate of Delhi.

The sultanate held on for 320 years, longer than any indigenous Hindu empire. But while the Muslims were able to create a durable political order, their state too was limited in its ability to shape Indian society. Like the Gupta dynasty, they never extended their territorial reach very far into southern India. And in the words of Sudipta Kaviraj, "Islamic political rulers implicitly accepted limitations on political authority in relation to the social constitution, which parallel those of Hindu rulers . . . The Islamic state saw itself as limited and socially distant as the Hindu state."[21] The legacy of Muslim rule is felt today in the existence of the states of Pakistan and Bangladesh, as well as in the more than 150 million Indian citizens who are Muslim. But the Muslim political legacy in terms of surviving institutions is not terribly large, apart from some practices like the *zamindari* landholding system.

The same is not true of the British, whose lasting effect on India has been much more profound. In many respects, modern India is the result of a foreign nation-building project. Kaviraj argues that, contrary to the Indian nationalist narrative, "The British did not conquer an India which existed before their conquest; rather, they conquered a series of independent kingdoms that became political India during, and in part as a response to their dominion."[22] This echoes the view of Sunil Khilnani, that the "idea of India" as a political, as opposed to a social, entity did not exist before the British Raj.[23] The important institutions that bind India together as a polity—a civil service, an army, a common administrative language (English), a legal system aspiring to the application of uniform and impersonal laws, and of course democracy itself—were the result of Indians interacting with the British colonial regime and assimilating Western ideas and values into their own historical experience.

On the other hand, the British impact on social as opposed to political India has been much more limited. The British did succeed in modifying certain social practices that they found abhorrent, like sati (the immolation of a widow at her husband's funeral). They introduced Western notions of universal human equality, which induced Indians to rethink the philosophical premises of the caste system and unleashed demands for social equality. A liberal and nationalist Indian elite was then able to turn British ideas against their authors in the twentieth-century struggle for independence. But the caste system itself, the self-sufficient village community, and the highly localized social order remained largely intact and untouched by the power of the colonial authority.

CHINA VERSUS INDIA

In the early twenty-first century a voluminous literature was produced on the relative prospects of China and India as fast-growing emerging market countries.[24] Much of this discussion centered around the nature of their political systems. China, as an authoritarian country, has been much more successful than India in promoting large infrastructure projects like highways, airports, power plants, and gigantic hydroelectric projects like the Three Gorges Dam that required moving more than a million people from the floodplain. China manages to store five times as much water per capita as India, largely through large dam and irrigation projects.[25] When the Chinese government decides to bulldoze a neighborhood to make way for a new factory or condo project, it simply forces out the residents, who have little recourse to protect their rights or make their wishes known. India, on the other hand, is a pluralistic democracy in which a huge variety of social groups are able to organize and make use of the political system to get their way. When an Indian municipal or state government wants to build a new power plant or airport, it is likely to meet resistance from groups ranging from environmental nongovernmental organizations to traditional caste associations. In the view of many, this paralyzes decision making in India and reduces its prospects for long-term economic growth.

The problem with many of these comparisons is that they fail to take into account how the political systems of these countries are rooted in their social structure and in their histories. Many people believe, for example, that contemporary Indian democracy is a by-product of relatively recent and somewhat accidental historical developments. According to certain theories of democracy, for example, many people find it surprising that India has maintained a successful democracy at all since its independence in 1947. India meets none of the "structural" conditions for being a stable democracy: it has been, and in many ways remains, an extremely poor country; it is highly fragmented religiously, ethnically, linguistically, and in class terms; it was born in an orgy of communal violence that reappears periodically as its different subgroups rub up against each other. In this view, democracy is seen as something culturally foreign to India's highly inegalitarian culture, brought by a colonial power and not deeply rooted in the country's traditions.

This is a very superficial view of contemporary Indian politics. It is not that democracy in its modern institutional manifestations is deeply rooted in ancient Indian practices, as observers like Amartya Sen have suggested.[26] Rather, the course of Indian political development demonstrates that there was never the social basis for the development of a tyrannical state that could concentrate power so effectively that it could aspire to reach deeply into society and change its fundamental social institutions. The type of despotic government that arose in China or in Russia, a system that divested the whole society, beginning with its elites, of property and personal rights, has never existed on Indian soil—not under an indigenous Hindu government, not under the Moghuls, and not under the British.[27] This led to the paradoxical situation that protests against social injustice, of which there were a huge number, were typically never aimed against India's ruling political authorities, as was the case in Europe and in China. Rather, they were aimed at the social order dominated by the Brahmin class, and often expressed themselves as dissident religious movements like Jainism or Buddhism that rejected the metaphysical foundations of the worldly order. The political authorities were simply regarded as too distant and too irrelevant to daily life to matter.[28]

The same was not the case in China, where a strong state with modern institutions developed early on. That state could aspire to wide-ranging interventions against the existing social order, which succeeded in shaping a sense of national culture and identity. The state's early predominance then gave it a leg up when new social formations arose and challenged its supremacy. While there are signs of a Chinese civil society coming into view today as a result of economic development and exposure to a larger globalized world, social actors in China have always been much weaker than their Indian counterparts and much less able to resist the state. This contrast was apparent in the third century B.C. when Qin Shi Huangdi and Ashoka were building their empires, and it remains true today.

The strong, precociously developed Chinese state has always been able to carry out tasks that India could not, from building a Great Wall to keep out nomadic invaders, to mounting huge hydroelectric projects in the twenty-first century. Whether this has made the Chinese people better off in the long run is a different story. For the strong Chinese state has never been constrained by a rule of law that limited the whims of its rulers. Its visible accomplishments, from the Great Wall to the Three Gorges Dam, have come at the expense of the lives of ordinary Chinese who were (and are) largely powerless to resist the state and its plans to draft them into its service.

Indians experienced a kind of tyranny as well, not so much political tyranny in the Chinese style as what I earlier labeled the "tyranny of cousins." Individual freedom in India has been limited much more by things like kinship ties, caste rules, religious obligations, and customary practices. But in some sense, it was the tyranny of cousins that allowed Indians to resist the tyranny of tyrants. Strong social organization at the level of society helped to balance and keep in check strong organization at the level of the state.

The experiences of China and India suggest then that a better form of freedom emerges when there is a strong state *and* a strong society, two centers of power that are able to balance and offset each other over time. This is a theme to which I will return. But in the meantime, I will investigate the emergence of the state in the Muslim world and the unique institutions developed there that allowed Arab and Turkish polities to make their exit out of tribalism.

13

SLAVERY AND THE MUSLIM
EXIT FROM TRIBALISM

The Ottoman institution of military slavery; how tribalism was the main obstacle to political development among the Arabs; how military slavery first arose under the Abbasid dynasty; why tribesmen make good conquerors but poor administrators; Plato's solution to the problem of patrimonialism

In the early sixteenth century, at the height of the greatness of the Ottoman Empire, a highly unusual procedure unfolded roughly every four years. The Byzantine capital of Constantinople had fallen to the Turks in 1453; Ottoman armies had conquered Hungary in the Battle of Mohács in 1526 and were turned back at the gates of Vienna in 1529. Throughout the Balkan provinces of the empire, a group of officials would spread out, looking for young boys between the ages of twelve and twenty. This was the *devshirme*,[1] or levy of Christian youths. Like football scouts, these officials were expert at judging the physical and mental potential of young males, and each had a quota to fulfill that was set back in Istanbul, the Ottoman capital. When an official visited a village, the Christian priest was required to produce a list of all male children baptized there, and those of the appropriate age would be brought before the officials for inspection. The most promising boys were forcibly taken from their parents and led off in groups of 100 to 150. Their names were carefully inscribed in a register both when they were taken from their villages and when they arrived in Istanbul, and the registers compared, since parents occasionally tried to buy their children out of the levy. Some parents with particularly strong and healthy sons might have all of them taken from them; the official would return to Istanbul with his captives and the families would never see their children again. It is estimated that about three thousand boys a year were taken in this fashion in this period of the empire.[2]

These boys were not destined for lives of degradation and humiliation. Just the contrary: the top 10 percent served in the palaces of Istanbul and Edirne, where they received the finest training available in the Islamic world and were prepared for lives as senior administrators within the empire. The rest were raised as Turkish-speaking Muslims and were recruited into the famous Janissary corps, an elite infantry that fought by the sultan's side in his constant military campaigns in Europe and Asia.

The elite palace recruits received training lasting from two to eight years under the supervision of eunuchs. The most outstanding were given further training in the Topkapi, the sultan's residence in Istanbul. There they were trained in the Koran, and learned Arabic, Persian, Turkish, music, calligraphy, and mathematics. They received tough physical training in horsemanship, archery, and weapons handling, and were also taught arts like painting and bookbinding. But even those who failed to make the grade in the Inner Palace were destined for high-ranking positions in the household cavalry, the *sipahis* of the Porte.[3] If the young slave-soldiers proved strong and competent, they could rise through the ranks of the military to become generals, senior officials (viziers), provincial governors, or even the grand vizier of the empire, the highest official under the sultan, who was in effect the regime's prime minister. After serving in the sultan's household troops, many of the soldiers would be settled on estates where they could live off the taxes they collected from the inhabitants.

There was a parallel system for girls as well, who were not subject to the devshirme but were bought in slave markets from raiders in the Balkans and southern Russia. These girls served as wives and concubines for high-ranking Ottoman officials. They, like the boys, were raised in the palace harem under highly institutionalized rules supervising their upbringing and education. Many sultans were sons of slave mothers who, like other imperial mothers, could exercise considerable influence through their sons.[4]

There was one important restriction on these slaves, however: neither their offices nor the land they were given were private property; their holdings could not be sold, nor could they be passed down to their children. Indeed, many of these soldiers were forced to remain celibate their whole lives. Others had families with slave girls who were also forcibly taken from Christian provinces, but their children could not assume their father's status or position. And no matter how powerful they became, they remained slaves of the sultan, who could have them demoted or executed on the slightest whim.

The institution of military slavery in the Ottoman Empire was extremely peculiar in many respects. Since no Muslim could be legally enslaved, no Muslim inhabitant of the empire could aspire to enter high government service. As in China, both the military and the civilian bureaucracy were highly meritocratic, with systematic procedures in place for recruiting and promoting the best possible soldiers and officials. But unlike the Chinese bureaucracy, it was open only to foreigners, who were ethnically different from the society they governed. These slave-soldiers and bureaucrats grew up in an official bubble, bonding with their masters and with each other, but otherwise living apart from the society they governed. As is true of many people who work in closed castes, they developed a high degree of internal solidarity and could act as a cohesive group. In later stages of the empire, they could act as kingmakers, deposing and installing sultans of their own choosing.

Not surprisingly, Christian Europeans who were subject to the levy of boys, as well as those farther afield who simply heard about the practice, regarded it with horror. The image of a massively powerful empire run by a hierarchy of slaves came to symbolize in the Christian West the epitome of Oriental despotism. By the nineteenth century, when the Ottoman Empire was in full decline, the Janissaries appeared to many observers to be a weird and obsolete institution that was blocking the ability of the Turkish empire to modernize. They deposed Sultan Selim III in 1807 and elevated Mahmud II to the throne the following year. Mahmud II consolidated his position over the following years, and in 1826 he had the entire corps of Janissaries, some four thousand strong, killed by setting fire to their barracks. With the Janissaries out of the way, the Ottoman ruler could now reform the Turkish military and organize an army along modern European lines.[5]

Obviously, an institution that took children involuntarily from their parents, turned them into slaves, and forcibly converted them to Islam is a very cruel one that is incompatible with modern democratic values, regardless of the privileged lives these slaves may have led. No comparable institution ever developed outside of the Muslim world, which has led observers such as Daniel Pipes to argue that it was ultimately created for religious reasons specifically rooted in Islam.[6]

On closer examination, however, the Muslim system of military slavery evolved not out of any kind of religious imperative but as a solution to the problem of state building in the context of strongly tribal societies. Military slavery was invented in the Arab Abbasid dynasty because the Abbasid rulers found they could not rely on tribally organized forces to hold on to their empire. Tribal levies could be quickly mobilized and scaled up for rapid conquest; when unified and inspired by the new religion of Islam, they succeeded in overrunning much of the Middle East and the southern Mediterranean world. But, as we have seen, the tribal level of organization was displaced by state-level organization in China, India, and Europe because it could not achieve sustained collective action. Tribal societies are egalitarian, consensus based, and fractious; they have great difficulty holding territory over prolonged periods and are subject to internal disagreement and rupture.

The system of military slavery emerged as a brilliant adaptation designed to create a strong state-level institution against the backdrop of one of the most powerfully tribal societies on earth. It was so successful as a means of concentrating and consolidating state power that, in the view of the philosopher Ibn Khaldun, it saved Islam itself as a major world religion.[7]

CREATION OF A MUSLIM STATE

The Prophet Muhammad was born into the Quraysh tribe in a stateless part of western Arabia. As noted in chapter 5, he used a combination of social contract, force, and his own charismatic authority to unify first the quarreling tribes of Medina, and then those of Mecca and other surrounding towns as well into a state-level society. The Prophet's teachings were in a certain sense deliberately antitribal, insofar as they proclaimed the existence of a universal umma or community of believers whose first loyalty was to God and God's word, and not to their tribe. This ideological development was critical in creating the basis for a much wider scope for collective action and a hugely enhanced radius of trust among what had been a segmented and internally quarrelsome society.

But maintaining political unity has always been an uphill struggle in the context of Arab tribalism. The issue came to the fore immediately upon Muhammad's death in 632. The Prophet's charismatic authority had been sufficient to hold together the polity he created, but it threatened to split apart again into its constituent parts, like the Mecca-based Quraysh, the Ansar, or "supporters" from Medina, and the other tribal converts. It was only some skillful politicking on the part of one of Muhammad's companions that persuaded the tribes to accept Abu Bakr as the first caliph or successor. Abu Bakr was, among other things, an expert on tribal genealogy who used his knowledge of tribal politics to win consensus in favor of his leadership.[8]

Under the first three caliphs—Abu Bakr (632–634), Umar (634–644), and Uthman (644–656)—the Muslim empire expanded at a breathtaking rate, incorporating the whole Arabian peninsula and major parts of what are now Lebanon, Syria, Iraq, Iran, and Egypt.[9] The most spectacular victory was over the Persian Sasanian Empire at the Battle of Qadisiyyah, an event greatly celebrated by Saddam Hussein at the time of the Iraq-Iran War in the 1980s. With the establishment of the Umayyad dynasty in Damascus in 661, expansion continued, with further conquests in North Africa, Anatolia, Sind, and Central Asia. Arab armies reached Spain by 711 and conquered it; they continued their conquests north of the Pyrenees until finally stopped in France by Charles Martel at the Battle of Poitiers in 732.

Although the Arab tribesmen had religious motives, economic incentives were critical here as well since conquest of rich, long-settled agrarian societies yielded huge amounts of land, slaves, women, horses, and movable property. The initial governance problem was that of all purely predatory nomads: dividing the booty in ways that did not lead to fights among the various tribes over the spoils. Movable booty was usually divided up on the spot, with one-fifth being reserved for the caliph and sent back to Medina. Vacant land in conquered territories was taken over as state land under the control of the caliph, though a lot of it ended up in the hands of different tribes that had participated in the military campaign.[10]

Before very long, Arab tribesmen had to shift from being conquerors to rulers administering rich agricultural lands with settled populations. The caliphs did not need to reinvent the wheel with regard to state institutions, since all around them were examples of well-developed states or empires. The Sasanian Empire furnished the most immediate model of centralized administration since it had come under Arab control. Byzantine practices were well understood as well from the many Christians living in territories taken from Constantinople, many of whom worked for the new Muslim administration.

At what point did a true Muslim state emerge? The relative lack of documentary, as opposed to literary, sources makes this hard to judge precisely. Certainly by the time of the Umayyad 'Abd al-Malik (685–705), and possibly by the time of the second Umayyad caliph, Mu'awiya (661–680), a polity existed that maintained a standing army and police, extracted taxes from its subjects on a regular basis, maintained a bureaucracy to collect those taxes, administered justice and resolved disputes, and was capable of commissioning public works like grand mosques.[11] It is harder to assert that the Prophet Muhammad himself founded a state, as opposed to a tribal coalition, since none of these institutional elements existed in his time.

The Persian ideal of absolute monarchy posited a king so powerful that he could impose peace and restrain the armed, rapacious elites that were the major source of conflict and disorder in agrarian societies. Looking at such societies from a modern democratic perspective, we tend to see monarchs in agrarian societies as just other members of a predatory elite, perhaps designated by other oligarchs to protect their rents and interests.[12] In fact, there was almost always a three-sided struggle going on in these societies, among the king, an aristocratic or oligarchic elite, and nonelite actors like peasants and townsmen. The king often took the side of the nonelite actors against the oligarchy, both to weaken potential political challenges and to claim his share of tax revenues. In this, we can see the germ of the notion of the monarchy as the representative of a general public interest. In China, we have seen how emperors felt threatened by the growth of latifundia under the control of oligarchic elites and used the power of the state to try to limit or break them up. So in the Sasanian Empire, where absolute monarchy was seen as a bulwark of order against the different elites whose quarrels would hurt the interests of ordinary citizens. There was thus a strong emphasis on the monarch's enforcement of law as a hallmark of justice.[13]

In making the transition from a tribal to a state-level society, then, the early Arab rulers had several things going for them. They had a model of absolute monarchy and centralized bureaucratic administration as the norm for the state-level societies that surrounded them. More important, they had a religious ideology that emphasized universal human equality under God. In a sense, the group that drew the most logical conclusion from the Prophet's teachings was the Kharijites, who established bases of power in Basra and in the Arabian Peninsula. They argued that it did not matter whether the successor to Muhammad was Arab or non-Arab, or what tribe he came from, as long as he was a Muslim. Had Muhammad's successors built upon this idea, they might have tried to create a transnational, multiethnic empire based on ideology rather than kinship along the lines of the Holy Roman Empire. But maintaining the unity of the empire, much less creating a single centralized administration across all of its different parts, proved an uphill task for the Umayyad dynasty. Powerful tribal loyalties trumped purely ideological considerations, and the Muslim state continued to be undermined by kinship quarrels and animosities.

One of the most important of these conflicts broke out shortly after the Prophet's death. Muhammad was part of the Hashemite lineage within the Quraysh tribe, related to a competing lineage, the Umayyads, via a common ancestor, Abd Munaf, great-great-grandfather of the Prophet. The Umayyads and Hashemites quarreled bitterly before and during the Prophet's lifetime, with the former taking up armed opposition to Muhammad and his Muslim followers in Medina. After the conquest of Mecca, the Umayyads converted to Islam, but the animosity between the lineages continued unabated. Muhammad had no son, but rather a daughter, Fatima, by his first wife, Khadija, who married the Prophet's cousin Ali. The third caliph, Uthman, was an Umayyad who brought many of his kinsmen to power, and was later assassinated. He was succeeded by Ali, who was himself forced out of Arabia and killed by a Kharijite while praying in Kufa (in present-day Iraq). A series of *fitnas* or civil wars broke out among the Hashemites, Kharijites, and Umayyads, with the latter finally consolidating their rule and dynasty after the death of Ali's son Husain at the Battle of Karbala in southern Iraq. The partisans of Ali, who would come to be known as Shiites, were legitimists who believed that the caliphate should have been awarded to Muhammad's direct descendants.[14] The followers of the Umayyad caliph Mu'awiya would evolve into the Sunnis, who claimed to be the partisans of orthodox theory and practice.[15] The great split between Sunnis and Shiites, which in the twenty-first century still leads to car bombings and terrorist attacks on mosques, originated as an Arab tribal rivalry.

The early caliphs tried to create state structures that transcended tribal loyalties, particularly in the army, where units of tens and hundreds were created that spanned tribal boundaries. But in the words of one historian, the new Muslim elite "realized that the tribal identification was too well rooted in Arabian society simply to be abolished by decree or swept aside by a few measures that tended to transcend the exclusiveness of the tribal bond. The success of their integration of the tribesmen into a state, then, depended as much upon their ability to use tribal ties for their own ends as it did upon their ability to override those ties."[16] As the Americans occupying Iraq's Anbar province after the 2003 invasion discovered, it was easier to control tribal fighters using the traditional authority of the tribal chief than to create new impersonal units that did not take account of underlying social realities. A tribesman who quarreled with his commanding officer might simply decide to slip away and return to his kinsmen; not so if his officer was also his sheikh.

But a state built on tribal foundations is inherently weak and unstable. Tribal leaders were famously touchy and ill disciplined, often disappearing with their kinsmen as a result of a slight or quarrel. The early caliphs were highly distrustful of tribal leaders they had recruited and often refused to put them in important command positions. The new state was moreover constantly threatened by unincorporated tribal nomads, for whom the Muslim leadership felt considerable disdain; the caliph Uthman was said to have dismissed the opinion of an important tribal leader as the word of an "imbecile Bedouin."[17]

THE ORIGINS OF MILITARY SLAVERY

The system of military slavery was developed in the Abbasid dynasty in the mid-ninth century as a means of overcoming the persistent weaknesses of tribal levies as the basis of Muslim military power.[18] The Abbasids, who were of the Hashemite lineage, deposed the Umayyads in 750 with the help of Shiite and Khorasani forces based in Persia, and moved the capital from Damascus to Baghdad.[19] The early Abbasids were ruthless in their use of force to consolidate their rule, wiping out as much of the Umayyad lineage as they could and suppressing their erstwhile Shiite and Khorasani allies. State centralization increased, with the concentration of power in the hands of a prime minister known as a vizier. The size and luxury of the court grew as well, increasing the separation between the settled, urban empire and the tribal areas from which they sprang.[20]

Early on, the Abbasid rulers had intimations that military slavery might be a way of overcoming the fickleness of political power based on kinship ties. The caliph al-Mahdi (775–785) gave preference to a group of *mawali*,

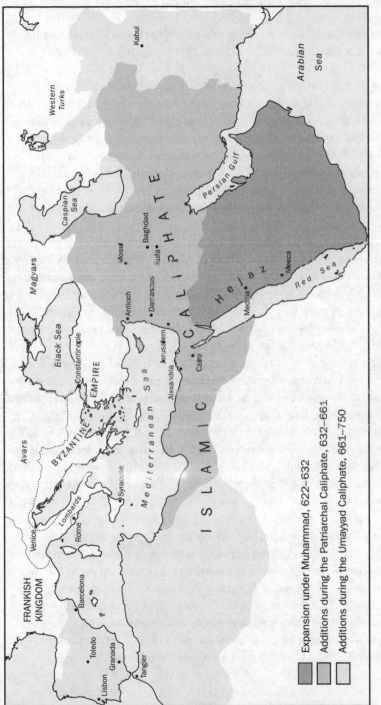

Arab expansion under the early Caliphates

Expansion under Muhammad, 622–632

Additions during the Patriarchal Caliphate, 632–661

Additions during the Umayyad Caliphate, 661–750

or manumitted slaves, over kinsmen or his Khurasani allies as servants or assistants, explaining that

> when I sit in a public audience, I may call a *Mawla* and raise him and seat him by my side, so that his knee will rub my knee. As soon, however, as the audience is over, I may order him to groom my riding animal, and he will be content with this, and will not take offence. But if I demand the same thing from somebody else, he will say: "I am the son of your supporter and intimate associate," or "I am a veteran in your [Abbasid] cause (*da'wa*)" or "I am the son of those who were the first to join your [Abbasid] cause." And I shall not be able to move him from his [obstinate] stand.[21]

But the use of foreigners as the core of the state's military power did not come until the conquest of Transoxania in Central Asia under the caliphs al-Ma'mun (813–833) and al-Mu'tasim (833–842), when large numbers of Turkish tribesmen were incorporated into the empire. Arab expansion was checked when they ran into Turkish tribes living in the Central Asian steppe, whose superior fighting abilities many Arab authors recognized.[22] But the Turks could not be recruited as tribal units to fight on the caliph's behalf, since they too shared in the defects of tribal organization. Rather, they were taken as individual slaves and trained as soldiers in a nontribal army. Al-Ma'mun created a guard of four thousand Turkish slaves known as Mamluks, a core that grew to nearly seventy thousand under al-Mu'tasim.[23] These tribesmen were tough nomads, recently converted to Islam and full of enthusiasm for the Muslim cause. They became the core of the Abbasid army "because of their superiority over other races in prowess, valour, courage, and intrepidity." One observer of al-Ma'mun's campaigns saw

> two lines of horsemen on both sides of the road near the halting place. . . . The line on the right-hand side of the road was composed of 100 Turkish horsemen. The line on the left-hand side of the road was composed of 100 horsemen of "others" [i.e., Arabs] . . . All were arrayed in battle-order, awaiting the arrival of Ma'mun . . . It was midday and the heat became intense. When Ma'mun reached the place he found all the Turks sitting on the backs of their horses, with the exception of three or four, whereas "all that medley" . . . have thrown themselves on the ground.[24]

Al-Mu'tasim organized the Turks into a Mamluk regiment and moved the capital from Baghdad to Samara because of violence between the local inhabitants and the Turkish fighters. He gave them special training in their own academies, bought Turkish slave girls for them to marry, and forbade them from mixing with any local people, thus creating a military caste sharply separated from its surrounding society.[25]

The idea that there is a tension between loyalty to the family and a just political order goes back a long way in Western political philosophy. Plato's *Republic* is a discussion between the philosopher Socrates and a group of young men about the nature of a "just city" that they are attempting to create "in speech." Socrates leads them to agree that the just city would need a class of guardians who are particularly spirited or proud in their defense of the city. The guardians are warriors whose first principle is to do good to friends and harm to enemies; they must be carefully trained to be public-spirited through the proper use of music and gymnastics.

Book V of the *Republic* contains the famous discussion of the communism of women and children of the guardians. Socrates points out that sexual desire and the desire for children are natural, but that ties to the family compete with loyalty to the city that the guardians protect. It is for that reason, he argues, that they must be told the "noble lie" that they are children of the earth, and not of biological parents. He argues that they must live in common, and that they not be allowed to marry individual women but rather have sex with different partners and raise their children in common. The natural family is the enemy of the public good:

> So, as I am saying, doesn't what was said before and what's being said now form them into true guardians, still more and cause them not to draw the city apart by not all giving the name "my own" to the same thing, but different men giving it to different things—one man dragging off to his own house whatever he can get his hands on apart from the others, another being separate in his own house with separate women and children, introducing private pleasures and griefs of things that are private?[26]

It is not at all clear that either Socrates or Plato believed that such a communism is possible; indeed, Socrates' interlocutors later express considerable skepticism as to whether the just city "in speech" can be constructed as a real city. The purpose of the discussion was to highlight the permanent tensions that exist between people's private kinship ties and their obligations to a broader public political order. The implication is that any successful order needs to suppress the power of kinship through some mechanism that makes the guardians value their ties to the state over their love for their families.

It is doubtful whether al-Ma'mun, al-Mu'tasim, or any of the other early Muslim leaders read Plato or knew of his ideas. But the institution of military slavery responded to the same imperatives as Plato's just city. The slaves were not told they were born of the earth; rather, they were born very far away and told they had no other loyalty than to their caliph, who was the embodiment of the state and the public interest. The slaves did not know their biological parents; they knew their master only and were intensely loyal to him alone. They were given nondescript new names, usually Turkish, that left them unconnected to any lineage in a society based on lineage. They did not practice a communism of women and children, but they were segregated from Arab society and not allowed to sink roots into it. In particular, they were not permitted to set up private households to which they could drag off "whatever they could get their hands on"; the problem of nepotism and conflicting tribal loyalties that was pervasive in traditional Arab society was thus overcome.

The development of the Mamluks as a military institution came too late in the Abbasid dynasty to secure its position or prevent its decline. Already by the mid-ninth century the empire was breaking down into a series of independent sovereignties. This began in 756 when a fleeing Umayyad prince set up an independent caliphate in Spain. In the late eighth and early ninth centuries, independent dynasties were established in Morocco and Tunisia, as well as in eastern Iran in the late ninth and early tenth centuries. By the mid-tenth century, Egypt, Syria, and Arabia were lost as well, reducing the Abbasid state to ruling only over parts of Iraq. Never again would an Arab regime, dynastic or modern, unite either the Muslim or Arab worlds. This would happen only under the Turkish Ottomans.

But while the Abbasid empire did not survive, the institution of military slavery did, and in fact became crucial to the survival of Islam itself in subsequent centuries. Three new power centers emerged, each based on the effectiveness of military slavery. The first was the Ghaznavid empire centered in Ghazni (Afghanistan), discussed in the previous chapter, which united parts of eastern Persia and Central Asia. The Ghaznavids penetrated northern India and paved the way for the Muslim domination of the subcontinent. The second was the Mamluk sultanate in Egypt, which played a crucial role in stopping both the Christian Crusaders and the Mongols, and in so doing arguably saved Islam as a world religion. And finally there were the Ottomans themselves, who perfected the institution of military slavery and used it as the basis for their rise as a world power. In all three cases, military slavery solved the problem of creating a durable military instrument in what were fundamentally tribal societies. But in the Ghaznavid and Egyptian Mamluk cases, the institution declined because kinship and patrimonialism reinserted themselves within the Mamluk institution itself. Moreover, the Mamluks, as the most powerful social institution in Egyptian society, failed to remain under civilian control and succeeded in taking over the state in a manner prefiguring the military dictatorships of twentieth-century developing countries. Only the Ottomans saw clearly the need to banish patrimonialism from their state machinery, which they did for nearly three centuries. They also kept the military under firm civilian control. But they too began to decline when patrimonialism and the hereditary principle reasserted themselves from the late seventeenth century onward.

14

THE MAMLUKS SAVE ISLAM

How the Mamluks came to power in Egypt; the curious fact that power in the
Arab Middle East lay in the hands of Turkish slaves; how the Mamluks saved
Islam from the Crusaders and Mongols; defects in the Mamluk implemen-
tation of military slavery that led to the regime's ultimate decline

The institution of military slavery anchored Muslim power in Egypt and
Syria for three hundred years, from the end of the Ayyubid dynasty in
1250 up to 1517, when the Mamluk sultanate was defeated by the Ottomans. Today we take the existence of Islam and a large global community
of Muslims—now numbering about a billion and a half people—for granted.
But the spread of Islam did not depend simply on the appeal of its underlying religious ideas. It depended also very much on political power. The
extent of Muslim belief was determined in the first instance by Muslim
armies waging jihad, or holy war, against nonbelievers in the Dar-ul Harb
(Land of War), bringing them into the Dar al-Islam (Land of Islam). Just
as the Muslims themselves eliminated Christianity and Zoroastrianism as
major religions in the Middle East, so too might Islam have been relegated
to the status of a minor sect had the Christian Crusaders succeeded in
dominating the region, or had the Mongols swept all the way to North Africa.
The border of Muslim communities in the northern parts of Nigeria, Cote
d'Ivoire, Togo, and Ghana was determined by the reach of Muslim armies.
The countries of Pakistan and Bangladesh, and the sizable Muslim minority
in India, might not exist but for the fighting ability of Muslim armies. That
military prowess in turn did not emerge only on the basis of a fanatical
commitment to religion. It was based on states that were able to organize
effective institutions to concentrate and use power—and above all, the institution of military slavery.

The opinion that the survival of Islam itself depended on the use of military slavery was shared by the great Arab historian and philosopher Ibn Khaldun, who lived in North Africa in the fourteenth century, contemporaneously with the Mamluk sultanate in Egypt. In the *Muqadimmah*, Ibn Khaldun says the following:

> When the [Abbasid] state was drowned in decadence and luxury and donned the garments of calamity and impotence and was overthrown by the heathen Tatars, who abolished the seat of the Caliphate and obliterated the splendor of the lands and made unbelief prevail in place of belief, because the people of the faith, sunk in self-indulgence, preoccupied with pleasure and abandoned to luxury, had become deficient in energy and reluctant to rally in defense, and had stripped off the skin of courage and the emblem of manhood—then, it was God's benevolence that He rescued the faith by reviving its dying breath and restoring the unity of the Muslims in the Egyptian realms, preserving the order and defending the walls of Islam. He did this by sending to the Muslims, from this Turkish nation and from among its great and numerous tribes, rulers to defend them and utterly loyal helpers, who were brought from the House of War to the House of Islam under the rule of slavery, which hides in itself a divine blessing. By means of slavery they learn glory and blessing and are exposed to divine providence; cured by slavery, they enter the Muslim religion with the firm resolve of true believers and yet with nomadic virtues unsullied by debased nature, unadulterated with the filth of pleasure, undefiled by the ways of civilized living, and with their ardor unbroken by the profusion of luxury.[1]

The Mamluk institution was created at the end of the Kurdish Ayyubid dynasty that ruled Egypt and Syria briefly in the late twelfth and early thirteenth centuries, and whose most famous offspring was Salah al-Din, known in the West as Saladin. The Ayyubids had used Turkish slave soldiers in their wars against the Crusaders in Palestine and Syria, but it was the last sultan, al-Salih Ayyub, who created the Bahri regiment, named after a fortress on an island in the Nile River where it was headquartered. He reportedly turned to the Turks because of the unreliability of his Kurdish soldiers.[2] The regiment, consisting of eight hundred to one thousand cavalry soldiers, were slaves of primarily Kipchak Turkish origin. Turkish tribes like the Kipchaks were coming to play an increasing role in the

Middle East due to the pressure they were feeling from another powerful group of pastoral nomads, the Mongols, who were pushing them out of their traditional tribal ranges in Central Asia.

The Bahri regiment proved its fighting abilities very early on. The French king Louis IX launched the Seventh Crusade, landing in Egypt in 1249. He was met and defeated the following year by the Bahri regiment, led by a Kipchak Turk named Baybars who had been captured by the Mongols, sold as a slave in Syria, and recruited as a leader of the new Mamluk force. The Crusaders were expelled from Egypt, and Louis had to be ransomed for an amount equal to a year's national product of France.

Baybars and the Bahri regiment won a far more important victory, however, when they defeated a Mongol army at the Battle of Ayn Jalut in Palestine in 1260. The Mongol tribes, united by Genghis Khan prior to his death in 1227, had conquered much of Eurasia by this point. They destroyed the Jin Dynasty, which had been ruling the northern third of China in the 1230s, defeated the Khwarazm empire in central Asia, as well as kingdoms in Azerbaijan, Georgia, and Armenia the same decade; invaded and occupied much of Russia, sacking the city of Kiev in 1240; and advanced into Eastern and Central Europe in the 1240s. They were stopped there not so much by the power of Christian armies, but because the Great Khan Ogedei (Genghis's son) died and the Mongol commander withdrew to consult over the succession. Hulagu Khan, grandson of Genghis, had been ordered to conquer the Middle East by his brother the Great Khan Mongke in 1255. He occupied Iran, where he established the Ilkhanid dynasty, and pushed on toward Syria with the intention of eventually conquering Egypt. Baghdad was occupied and utterly devastated in 1258, and the last Abbasid caliph executed there.

The Mamluk victory at Ayn Jalut was partly due to numbers, since Hulagu had to withdraw with the bulk of his army on the death of Mongke. Nonetheless, he left a substantial force under one of his best commanders to attack the Mamluks. The Mongols were superb tacticians and strategists, using their high degree of mobility and lean logistics trains to maneuver around their enemies. The Mamluks, by contrast, were better equipped, riding larger horses than the Mongols' ponies, having heavier armor and bows, lances, and swords. They were also extremely well disciplined.[3] The victory at Ayn Jalut was no fluke: the Mamluks defended Syria from the Ilkhanids in a series of battles until the end of the war in 1281, and fended off three further Mongol invasions, in 1299, 1300, and 1303.[4]

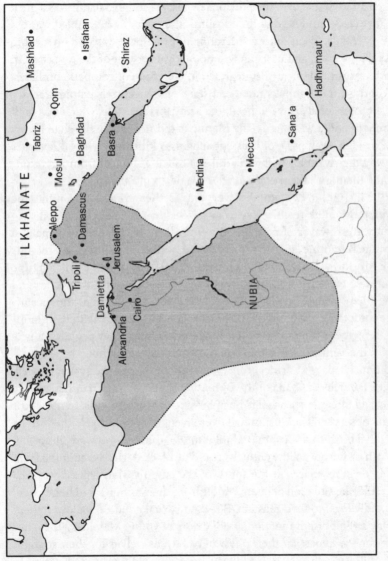

Mamluk sultanate, Bahri dynasty, 1250–1392

The Mamluks had displaced the Ayyubids and taken power in their own right at the beginning of the war with the Ilkhanids, with Baybars as their first sultan.[5] The regime that was set up on the basis of Mamluk power was far more stable than the previous dynasty. Though Saladin was a great military leader and hero to the Muslims, the polity he assembled was extremely fragile. It was more a federation of principalities based on kinship links than a state, and its army was not a loyal servant of the dynasty. On Saladin's death, his army disintegrated into a group of competing militias. By contrast, the Mamluks ran a real state, with a centralized bureaucracy and a professional army—indeed, the army *was* the state, which was both a strength and a weakness.[6] The Mamluks did not divide the state in any way, or give away parts of it as appanages to kinsmen or royal favorites the way the Ayyubids did. Syria did not quickly split off from Egypt under the Mamluks, the way it did after the death of Saladin.[7]

The institution of Mamluk slavery was further strengthened under the Egyptian Mamluk regime. Key to its success was the sultanate's ability to capture fresh waves of new recruits from the Central Asian steppe and from the Byzantine lands to the north and northwest. Some of the recruits were Muslim already, others were still pagan, and others Christian. The process of conversion to Islam was vital to remaking their loyalties and tying them to their new masters. Key too was the fact that the recruits were completely cut off from access to or communication with their families and tribes. As a result of their boyhood training, they acquired a new family, the family of the sultan and the Mamluk brotherhood.[8]

Eunuchs played a critical role in the functioning of the system as well. Unlike eunuchs in China or the Byzantine Empire, Muslim eunuchs were almost all foreigners who were born outside of Muslim lands. In the words of one observer, "No Muslim had ever given birth to him. Neither did he ever give birth to a Muslim."[9] Unlike the Mamluks, who were almost all Turkish or European, the eunuchs could be black Africans recruited from Nubia or other places to the south of the empire. They shared with the Mamluks the situation of being cut off from their families and hence were devotedly loyal to their masters. But their sexual condition allowed them to play an important function as educators of young Mamluks. The latter were chosen in part for their physical beauty, as well as for their strength and military prowess; as a military fraternity with restricted access to women, homosexual advances by older Mamluks were a constant problem against which the eunuchs could act as a barrier.[10]

In addition to the way they were educated, a key to the success of the Mamluks as a political institution was the fact that they were a one-generation nobility. They could not pass on their Mamluk status to their children; their sons would be ejected into the general population and their grandsons would enjoy no special privileges at all. The theory behind this was straightforward: a Muslim could not be a slave, and all of the Mamluks' children were born Muslims. Moreover, the Mamluk children were born in the city and raised without the rigors of nomadic life on the steppe, where the weak died young. Were Mamluk status to become hereditary, it would violate the strict meritocratic grounds on which young Mamluks were selected.[11]

MAMLUK DECAY

There were at least two problems in the design of Mamluk political institutions that weakened them over time. The first was that there was no well-institutionalized governance mechanism within the Mamluk fraternity itself. There was a hierarchical chain of command descending from the sultan but no clear rules for selection of a sultan. Indeed, there were two competing principles at play, a dynastic principle in which rule was passed down to a son chosen by the current sultan, and a nonhereditary one under which the various Mamluk factions sought to reach consensus even as they jockeyed for power.[12] The latter was the more powerful; sultans often acted as figureheads chosen by the senior emirs who headed the factions.

The second key defect in the structure of the Mamluk state was the lack of an overarching political authority. The Mamluks were created as the Ayyubid's military instrument, but when the last Ayyubid sultan died, the Mamluks stepped forward and took over the state themselves. This created a kind of reverse agency problem. In most political hierarchies, principals hold authority and delegate the implementation of their policies to agents whom they appoint. Many governance dysfunctions arise because the agents have different agendas from the principals, and the problem of institutional design is related to incentivizing the agents to do the principals' bidding.[13]

In the Mamluk case, by contrast, the agents *were* the principals; they were simultaneously part of a military hierarchy serving the sultan and contenders for the role of sultan. This meant that they had to do their jobs as officers while conspiring to gain power and weaken the influence of rival Mamluks. This naturally had a terrible effect on discipline and hierarchy, not unlike the situation that emerges in contemporary developing countries run by military juntas. This problem became acute in 1399, when the Mongol Tamerlane invaded Syria and sacked Aleppo; the Mamluks were too busy feuding with each other to mount a defense, and retreated to Cairo. They also lost control of Upper Egypt to the local tribes there, and were saved in the end only by the fact that Tamerlane needed to turn his attention to the threat posed by a new power, the Ottomans.[14] Had the Mamluks been subordinated to a civilian political authority, as was the case in the Ottoman Empire, the civilians could have taken steps to fix this problem.[15]

It was the decay of the antihereditary principle that eventually led to the breakdown of the Egyptian Mamluk state. As time went on, hereditary succession came to be practiced not just within the sultan's family but by other Mamluks as well who sought to establish dynasties of their own. The one-generation nobility principle worked against the basic imperatives of human biology, just as the impersonal Chinese examination system did: each Mamluk sought to protect the social position of his family and descendants. Wealthy Mamluks found they could get around the one-generation principle by endowing Islamic charities or *waqfs* in the form of mosques, madrassas (schools), hospitals, or other kinds of trusts, putting their descendants in charge of their administration.[16] Furthermore, while Mamluks had no immediate family, they developed ethnic ties as a basis for solidarity. Sultan Qalawun began importing Circassian and Abkhaz slaves rather than Kipchaks and formed them into an alternative Burji regiment. The Circassian faction was ultimately to take over the sultanate from the Kipchaks.[17]

Serious deterioration of the Mamluk institution was evident by the middle of the fourteenth century. The background condition was actually the peace and prosperity of the time, which had a disastrous effect on Mamluk discipline. The Christian presence in the Holy Land had largely disappeared by this time, and the Mamluks signed a peace treaty with the Mongols in 1323. The sultan al-Nasir Muhammad, himself not a Mamluk, began appointing non-Mamluks loyal to himself to senior military positions and purging the ranks of capable officers whose loyalty he doubted.[18]

The regime was briefly reinvigorated with the rise of Sultan Barquq in

1390, who came to power with the help of the Burji or Circassian Mamluks and restored the old system of foreign recruitment. But problems of a different sort emerged when later sultans, using resources from a number of state monopolies, greatly expanded the recruitment of younger Mamluks, which created a generational rift. The older Mamluks began to evolve into a military aristocracy, beating back the challenge from the younger recruits and, like tenured professors in contemporary American universities, entrenching their positions in the hierarchy. The average age of senior emirs began to rise, the turnover of personnel slowed markedly, and the elder aristocracy began dividing up into clans. Mamluks started to promote their families and establish their status through sumptuous displays of wealth, and women began to play a greater role in promoting the interests of their offspring. Thus the Mamluk system, which was originally created to overcome tribalism in military recruitment, managed to retribalize itself.[19] The new tribes were not necessarily kinship based, but they reflected a deep-seated human urge to promote and protect the interests of descendants, friends, and clients against the requirements of an impersonal social system.

As time went on, the Mamluk system degenerated from a centralized state to something resembling a rent-seeking coalition of warlord factions. The younger Mamluks were no longer bound by ties of personal loyalty to their sultan. They had become, in the words of one historian,

> an interest group whose field reliability was dubious but whose propensity for revolt was endemic. The chronicles compiled from daily accounts of events in Cairo during the sultanate's final decades tell a tale of unremitting pressure on the monarch for payments in return for a modicum of domestic tranquility. Pillaging by his mamluk recruits . . . greeted al-Ghawri [a late sultan] on the day of his accession; the trainees burned the palaces of five senior officers, a gesture of their irritation over their perception of low wages received, in contrast to the immense fortunes grand amirs routinely amassed.[20]

The moral ties that had bound the Mamluks to earlier sultans were replaced by a purely economic calculus. Senior Mamluks bought the loyalty of junior recruits, who then expected their patrons to reward them through their ability to extract rents from the state or from the civilian population. The sultan was simply the first among equals; several had been assassinated or removed by Mamluk cliques, and all of the later sultans had to watch their backs for conspiracies.

In addition to political instability, the regime faced a fiscal crisis in the late fifteenth century. As a result of disruption of the spice trade by Portuguese naval primacy in the Indian Ocean, the sultan's revenues began to decline toward the end of the fourteenth century and he turned to increasingly higher rates of taxation. This then compelled economic agents—farmers, traders, and craftsmen—to hone their skills in hiding assets and evading taxes. The civilian bureaucrats who administered the tax system lowered tax rates in return for kickbacks; the result was that higher attempted tax rates yielded lower actual levels of tax revenues. The regime resorted to sweeping confiscations of whatever assets could be found, including those of the charitable Islamic waqfs that Mamluk grandees had used to shelter wealth for their descendants.[21]

STATES AS ORGANIZED CRIMINALS

A number of political scientists have compared the early modern European state to organized crime. They mean that rulers of states seek to use their expertise in the organization of violence to extract resources from the rest of the society, what economists call rents.[22] Other writers use the term "predatory state" to describe a range of more recent developing world regimes like Zaire under Mobutu Sese Seko or Liberia under Charles Taylor. In a predatory state, the elites in charge seek to extract the highest level of resources they can from the underlying society and divert them to their own private uses. The reason these elites seek power in the first place is the access that power gives them to economic rents.[23]

There is no question that some states are highly predatory, and that all states are predatory to some degree. An important question in understanding political development, however, is whether all states seek to maximize rents from predation, or whether they are driven by other considerations to extract rents at a level well below the theoretical maximum. This predatory, rent-maximizing model of state behavior was not necessarily characteristic of mature agrarian societies like Ottoman Turkey, Ming China, or France under the Old Regime. But it is certainly an accurate picture of certain political orders, such as the conquest regimes set up by tribal nomads like the Mongols. And it increasingly came to characterize the late Mamluk regime. The confiscatory and arbitrary taxes imposed by Mamluk sultans clearly made any long-term investment unthinkable and induced property owners to put their assets into less than optimally productive uses like religious waqfs. It is interesting to speculate whether commercial capitalism was thereby smothered in its crib in Egypt, just at a moment when it was beginning to take off in other places such as Italy, the Netherlands, and England.[24]

On the other hand, the fact that these high levels of taxation were reached only toward the end of a three-hundred-year period of rule by the Egyptian Mamluks suggests that earlier sultans were taxing at levels well below the highest possible rate. In other words, maximum rent extraction was not an inevitable characteristic of premodern states ruling over agrarian societies. In the Persian theory of the Middle Eastern state that was adopted by the Arabs, one of the monarch's functions was in fact to protect the peasantry from the rapacious behavior of landlords and other elites who wanted to maximize their rents, in the interests of justice and political stability. The state was thus less a stationary bandit than a guardian of an incipient public interest. The Mamluk state was eventually driven to fully predatory behavior, but only by a constellation of internal and external forces.

There were many causes contributing to the political decay of the Mamluk regime and its destruction at the hands of the Ottomans in 1517. Egypt endured twenty-six years of plagues between 1388 and 1514. One of the immediate consequences of the rise of the Ottomans was that it became harder and harder for the Mamluks to recruit young slave-soldiers since the Ottomans sat directly astride the trade routes to Central Asia. And finally, the Mamluk system proved too inflexible to adopt new military technologies, particularly the use of firearms by infantry forces. The Ottomans, facing a European enemy, began to use firearms in 1425, perhaps a century after the innovation was first explored in Europe.[25] They quickly mastered these weapons, and cannons played a key role in the fall of Constantinople in 1453. The Mamluks, by contrast, did not seriously begin to experiment with firearms until the sultanate of Qansuh al-Ghawri (1501–1516), just prior to their defeat by the Ottomans. The Mamluk cavalry found the use of firearms beneath their dignity, and the regime was constrained by its lack of access to iron and copper deposits. After some abortive tests (in one, fifteen of fifteen cannons exploded on being fired), the sultanate managed to deploy a limited number of cannons and recruited a non-Mamluk Fifth Corps armed with muskets.[26] But these technological innovations came too late to save a cash-strapped, corrupt, and tradition-bound regime.

The Ayyubid sultan who recruited the initial Bahri regiment was trying to solve the same problem as the early Chinese state builders: how to create an army that would be loyal to the state, represented by his person, rather than to their tribe, in a highly tribal society. He did this by buying young foreigners and breaking their loyalties to their families. Once they entered the Mamluk slave family, promotion within the Mamluk hierarchy was done on a meritocratic basis; new entrants would feed into the system every year and rise on the basis of ability. The military machine built on this basis was very impressive. It was able to withstand a two-generation-long war with the Mongols, expel the Crusaders from the Holy Land, and defend Egypt from Tamerlane. As Ibn Khaldun said, the Mamluks saved Islam itself at a historical moment when the religion might have been marginalized.

On the other hand, the design of the Mamluk institution contained the seeds of its own undoing. The Mamluks took power directly, rather than remaining agents of the state. There was no principal to discipline them; each Mamluk could aspire to become sultan himself and spent time conniving to achieve power. A dynastic principle reinserted itself early on among the top leadership and soon spread to the entire Mamluk upper ranks, which became entrenched as a hereditary aristocratic elite. At the same time, this elite did not have secure property rights and spent a great deal of energy trying to figure out how to shield income from the sultan so as to be able to turn it over to descendants. Under the Burji Mamluks, the elite split along age lines, and younger Mamluks were recruited into the patrimonial networks of the older ones. The training that once bonded a young Mamluk to the state gave way to outright rent seeking on the part of factions within the elite, who used their coercive power to extract resources from the civilian population and from each other. The Mamluk elite became so consumed with these internal power struggles that it by necessity had to adopt an extremely cautious foreign policy. By luck it faced no powerful external threats from the invasion of Tamerlane early in the fifteenth century until the appearance of the Ottomans and Portuguese at the century's end. But its resources were declining through plague-induced depopulation and loss of external trade. Absence of outside threats also provided no incentives for military modernization. So the Mamluks' 1517 defeat by the Ottomans, who perfected the use of the institution of military slavery and organized a much more powerful state, was overdetermined.

15

THE FUNCTIONING AND DECLINE
OF THE OTTOMAN STATE

How the Ottomans centralized power in a way that eluded European monarchs; how the Ottomans perfected the system of military slavery; instability of the Turkish state and its reliance on continued foreign expansion; causes of the decay of the Ottoman system; military slavery as a developmental dead end

Niccolò Machiavelli's famous treatise on politics, *The Prince*, was written in 1513. The Ottomans were then at the height of their power, about to conquer Hungary and to launch their first assault on Vienna, the seat of the Habsburg Empire. In chapter 4 Machiavelli makes the following observation:

> In our times the examples of these two diverse kinds of government are the Turk and the king of France. The whole monarchy of the Turk is governed by one lord; the others are his servants. Dividing his kingdom into sanjaks [provinces], he sends different administrators to them, and he changes and varies them as he likes. But the king of France is placed in the midst of an ancient multitude of lords, acknowledged in that state by their subjects and loved by them: they have their privileges, and the king cannot take them away without danger to himself. Thus, whoever considers the one and the other of these states will find difficulty in acquiring the state of the Turk, but should it be conquered, great ease in holding it. So inversely, you will find in some respects more ease in seizing the state of France, but great difficulty in holding it.[1]

Machiavelli captures the essence of the Ottoman state: it was far more centralized and impersonally managed than France in the early sixteenth century, and in that way more modern. Later in the sixteenth century,

French monarchs would seek to create a similarly centralized and administratively uniform regime by attacking the privileges of the landed aristocracy. Like the Turkish bey (governor) governing a sanjak, the French king sent out intendents—the forerunners of modern prefects—from Paris to administer the kingdom directly in place of the local patrimonial elites. The institutions used by the Ottoman state were different, being based on the devshirme and the military slave system. But the Ottomans succeeded in creating a highly powerful and stable state that was the rival of any power in Europe at the time, and presided over a huge empire larger than anything created by an Arab caliph or sultan. Ottoman society resembled China at the time of the contemporaneous Ming Dynasty insofar as it combined a strong, centralized state with relatively weak and unorganized social actors outside the state. (It differed from China, however, insofar as political power was limited by law.) The institutions of the Ottoman state were a curious mixture of modern and patrimonial, and it decayed when the patrimonial elements entrenched themselves at the expense of the modern ones. The Ottomans perfected the military slave system of the Mamluks, but they too eventually succumbed to the natural human desire of their elites to pass on status and resources to their children.

A ONE-GENERATION ARISTOCRACY

The administrative system described by Machiavelli, whereby the Turkish monarch could appoint administrators to rule each province and remove them at will, had its origins in the fact that the Ottoman state was a relatively recent conquest dynasty that had not inherited ancient institutions but could start afresh in creating new ones. The Mongol conquests of the thirteenth century had pushed a series of Turcoman tribes out of Central Asia and the Middle East, and into a frontier region of western Anatolia where they were sandwiched between the Byzantine Empire to the west and the Seljuk sultanate (from 1243, a vassal state of the Mongol Ilkhanids) to the east. These frontier tribes organized themselves to wage *gaza*, or war, against the Byzantines. One of these gazi leaders, Osman, succeeded in defeating a Byzantine army at Baphaeon in 1302, thus establishing his fame and elevating him above all of the other frontier lords who then flocked to his banner. Thus the Osmanli, or Ottoman, dynasty was established as a parvenu frontier state that could borrow institutions from the established states surrounding it as it conquered new territory to the east and west.[2]

The Ottoman system of provincial administration as it developed in the fifteenth century was based on a cavalryman, the sipahi, and the appanage he was given, the *timar* (which means horse grooming). The smallest timars consisted of a village or villages with tax revenues sufficient to support a single cavalryman with horse and equipment. A larger appanage called a *zeamet* was given to middle-ranking officers known as *zaims*, while senior officers received an estate called a *has*. Each sipahi or zaim lived on his estate and collected taxes in kind from the local peasantry, usually a wagonload of wood and fodder and half a wagonload of hay per peasant per year. This system was used by the Byzantines and simply adopted by the Ottomans. Like the manor lord in Europe, the timar holder provided local government functions like security and the dispensing of justice. It was the responsibility of the sipahi to convert the in-kind payments he received into cash and to use the money to equip himself and journey to the front in time for the campaigning season. Holders of large estates were required to produce a second mounted soldier together with grooms and equipment. The whole system was known as *dirlik*, or livelihood, indicating its function: in an only partially monetized economy, the sultan's army could be sustained without having to raise tax revenues to pay the troops.[3]

Provincial-level government was organized around the sanjak, a district encompassing several thousand square miles and perhaps a population of one hundred thousand. As new territories were conquered, they were organized into sanjaks and subjected to detailed provincial cadastral surveys, which meticulously listed human and economic resources, village by village. The purpose of these surveys was to establish the tax base and to divide up land for distribution as timars. At first, the regulations applied to each province differed according to the province's circumstances, but as time went on and new territories were rapidly added, a more uniform system of laws and regulations was applied.[4] The beys who acted as governors of the sanjak were not recruited locally but were appointed by the central administration in Istanbul and, like the Chinese prefects, rotated to new assignments after serving tours of three years.[5] The *sanjakbey* was the officer who led the cavalry of his district into battle.[6] Above the level of sanjaks was a higher level of administration known as the *beylerbeyilik*, which constituted the major regions of the empire.

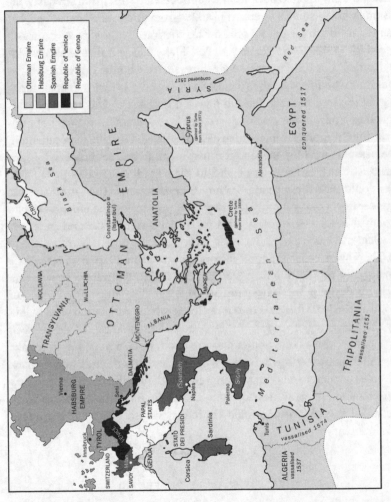

Ottoman Empire in the 1500s

Legend:
- Ottoman Empire
- Habsburg Empire
- Spanish Empire
- Republic of Venice
- Republic of Genoa

Red Sea

SYRIA

conquered 1517

EGYPT
conquered 1517

Cyprus
(gained by Turks
from Venice 1571)

CRIMEA

Black Sea

Constantinople
(Istanbul)

ANATOLIA

Alexandria

Crete
(gained by Turks
from Venice 1669)

MOLDAVIA

WALLACHIA

TRANSYLVANIA

OTTOMAN EMPIRE

Mediterranean Sea

MOREA

ALBANIA

MONTENEGRO

DALMATIA

Vienna

HABSBURG EMPIRE

Seni

TRIPOLITANIA
vassalised 151

Innsbruck

TYROL

SWITZERLAND

SAVOY

Milan

FRANCE

GENOA

Corsica

STATO
DEI PRESIDI

PAPAL
STATES

(Spanish)

Naples

Sardinia

Palermo

Sicily

Tunis

TUNISIA
vassalised 1574

ALGERIA
vassalised
1537

The single most important difference between the dirlik system and European feudalism was, as Machiavelli recognized, the fact that unlike in Europe, the Turkish appanages could not be turned into heritable property and given to the sipahi's descendants. Owing to the fact that most land in the empire had been recently conquered by an upstart dynasty, the vast bulk of it—some 87 percent in 1528—remained state owned and was granted to the timar holder only for his lifetime. Timars were granted in return for military service; they could be taken away if that service wasn't performed, but only by the sultan himself. The holders of large estates could not subinfeudate their lands, as in Europe. When the sipahi grew too old to serve or died, his land reverted to the state and could be reassigned to a new cavalryman. Indeed, the status sipahi itself was not heritable; the children of military men had to return to the civilian population.[7] The peasants working the land for the timar and zeamet holders, by contrast, had only usufructuary rights to their land, but unlike their lords, they could pass these rights down to their children.[8] The Ottoman state thus created a one-generation aristocracy, preventing the emergence of a powerful landed aristocracy with its own resource base and inherited privileges.[9]

There were other practical factors that prevented the emergence of a territorially rooted nobility. The Ottomans were constantly at war, and each cavalryman was expected to report for duty during the summer months. The local lord was thus away for several months each year, relieving the peasantry of some of its burdens and attenuating the tie between the sipahi and his land. Sometimes the cavalryman was required to take up winter quarters elsewhere than in his timar. His wife and children back at home were left to fend for themselves, and the soldier often took on new consorts and opportunities offered by camp life. All of this served to break the link between aristocrat and land that was so critical in European development.[10]

MILITARY SLAVERY PERFECTED

The dirlik system rested on the system of military slavery, without which it could not be properly managed. The Ottomans built on the military slave systems created by the Abbasids and Mamluks, as well as those used by other Turkish rulers, but eliminated many of the features that made the Mamluk system so dysfunctional.

First and most important was that there now was a clear distinction between civilian and military authority, and a strict subordination of the latter to the former. The military slaves emerged initially as an outgrowth of the sultan's household, as in the case of the Ayyubid Mamluks. Unlike the latter, however, the Ottoman ruling house remained in control of the slave hierarchy until much later in the empire. The dynastic principle applied only within the Ottoman ruling family; no slave, no matter how high ranking or talented, could aspire to become sultan himself or hope to found his own minidynasty within the military institution. As a result, the civilian authorities could establish clear rules for recruitment, training, and promotion that focused on building an effective military and administrative institution, without having to worry constantly about that institution trying to seize power in its own name.

The effort to prevent dynasties from forming within the military led to strict rules regarding children and inheritance. The sons of Janissaries were not allowed to become Janissaries, and indeed, in the early days of the empire, Janissaries were not allowed to marry and have families. The sons of the elite sipahis of the Porte were allowed to enter the corps of sipahioghlans as pages, but their grandsons were rigidly excluded. The Ottomans from the beginning seemed to understand the logic of military slavery as designed to prevent the emergence of an entrenched hereditary elite. Recruitment and promotion in the slave system were based on merit and service, for which the slaves were rewarded with tax exemptions and estates.[11] Ogier Ghiselin de Busbecq, ambassador of Holy Roman Emperor Charles V to the court of Suleiman the Magnificent, noted that the lack of a blood nobility allowed the sultan to pick his slaves and advance them according to their abilities. "The shepherd who rose to become an illustrious grand vezir was a figure that never ceased to fascinate European observers."[12]

The Ottomans improved on the Mamluk system by maintaining a strict distinction between the people recruited into the ruling institution as non-Muslim slaves—the *askeri*—and the rest of the empire's Muslim and non-Muslim citizens, the *reaya*. A member of the reaya could have a family, own property, and bequeath his property and rights to land to his children and all later descendants. The reaya could also organize themselves into semiautonomous, self-governing communities based on sectarian affiliation known as *millets*. But none among the reaya could aspire to become a member of the ruling elite, to bear arms, or to serve as a soldier or bureaucrat in the Ottoman administration. The cadres of the askeri had to be constantly renewed from year to year by new Christian recruits who had broken all of their ties to their families and were loyal to the Ottoman state. There were no guilds, factions, or self-governing associations among the askeri; they were supposed to have loyalties to the ruling dynasty alone.[13]

THE OTTOMAN STATE AS A GOVERNING INSTITUTION

There is evidence to suggest that the Ottomans in their prime did not seek to extract taxes at the maximum rate but rather saw their role as preserving a certain basic level of taxation, while protecting the peasantry from exactions by other elites who were more likely to behave like organized criminals. We know this because there were later periods in Ottoman history when fiscal distress caused sultans to raise levels of taxation to far more burdensome levels.

But the need for restraint was built into the Ottoman theory of the state itself, which was inherited from earlier Middle Eastern regimes. The Persian ruler Chosroes I (531–579) was quoted as saying, "With justice and moderation the people will produce more, tax revenues will increase, and the state will grow rich and powerful. Justice is the foundation of a powerful state."[14] "Justice" in this context means moderation in rates of taxation.[15] We might recognize this as an early Middle Eastern version of the Laffer curve popularized during the Reagan administration, which held that lower tax rates would produce higher total tax revenues by giving individuals greater incentives to produce. This sentiment was echoed by a number of early Turkish writers[16] and inscribed into the so-called circle of equity, which was built around eight propositions:

1. There can be no royal authority without the military.
2. There can be no military without wealth.
3. The reaya produce the wealth.
4. The sultan keeps the reaya by making justice reign.
5. Justice requires harmony in the world.
6. The world is a garden, its walls are the state.

7. The state's prop is the religious law.
8. There is no support for the religious law without royal authority.

These propositions were usually written around a circle, with the eighth leading back to the first, indicating that religious legitimacy (point 8) was necessary to support royal authority (point 1).[17] This is an unusually succinct statement about the interrelationships of military power, economic resources, justice (including rates of taxation), and religious legitimacy. It suggests that Turkish rulers did not see their objectives as the narrow maximization of economic rents, but rather the maximization of overall power through a balance of power, resources, and legitimacy.[18]

One great vulnerability of the Ottoman system that made it potentially less stable than contemporaneous European monarchies was the lack of a well-established system of primogeniture or other procedures for determining succession. By an old Middle Eastern tradition, succession in the ruling family was in the hands of God, and to establish a rule of succession was to go against God's will.[19] During periods of succession, different candidates needed the support of the Janissaries, court officials, ulama (the religious bureaucracy), and administrative machinery. At puberty, the sultan's sons were sent out to different provinces with their tutors to gain experience as governors; the ones closest to the capital had a leg up in influencing the politics of the Janissaries and the court in their favor. This led to periodic civil wars among the sons upon the sultan's death and occasional efforts to jump the gun by seizing power when the father was still alive. Under these conditions, fratricide was virtually assured. Mehmed III (1595–1603) had his nineteen brothers executed in the palace when he seized power. He ended the practice of sending his sons out to the provinces, instead keeping them trapped in a special quarter of the palace where they lived as virtual prisoners.[20] One might explain this system as designed to ensure that the toughest and most ruthless son eventually emerged as the new sultan. But lack of an institutionalized mechanism for succession also created great weaknesses, leaving the empire vulnerable to foreign threats during succession struggles and giving undue influence to actors in the system like the Janissaries who were supposed to be no more than agents of the sultan.

The chaotic Ottoman succession mechanism raises the question of exactly how institutionalized their system was as a whole. As in the case of China, Max Weber characterizes the Ottoman system as patrimonial rather than modern. This is true if one defines "patrimonial" to mean that the whole of the government emanates from the ruler's household and is subject to the ruler's whims. This was obviously true of the Ottoman system. The fact that virtually all of the employees of the state had the formal status of slave indicates that the sultan had total discretionary control over the bureaucracy. Like the Chinese emperor, he could order the execution of any official up to grand vizier at will. Sultans had the power to change major institutional rules as they wished, such as the decision of Suleiman to relax the rules about Janissaries having families.

On the other hand, whatever the theoretical powers of the sultan, it is clear that the system over which he presided was highly rule bound and predictable in the way it made decisions. In the first place, the Ottoman sultan was bound by Muslim religious law—the sharia—both in theory and in practice. Like Christian monarchs in the Middle Ages, the sultan formally recognized the sovereignty of God and God's law; his powers were granted only by way of delegation. The custodian of the law was a large and venerable institution, the ulama or scholars who interpreted the law and operated the system of religious courts that had jurisdiction over family, marriage, inheritance, and a host of other matters of personal status. The sultan did not presume to interfere in the quotidian administration of law at this level. Private property rights and usufructuary rights to state land were similarly protected (see chapter 19). Even the chaotic succession struggles were prescribed, in a certain way, by Islamic law, which forbade primogeniture as a principle of succession.

The system became increasingly rule bound, moreover, as a result of the requirements of delegation. It is a simple fact of life that all absolute rulers have to delegate power and authority to agents, and that the agents as a result of their expertise and abilities come to exert authority in their own right. This is all the more true when one has to rule over a large, diverse, and complex domain like the Ottoman Empire.

Curiously, the devshirme and the system of military slavery was one of the most modern features of the Ottoman system. Functionally, it served the same purpose as the Chinese examination procedure for entry into the bureaucracy: it was a source of impersonal recruitment into the state system that would ensure a supply of candidates loyal to the state and free of ties to family and kin, and it ruthlessly selected only the most fit for promotion to high levels of leadership. It was less rational than the Chinese system insofar as it restricted entrants to foreigners. On the other hand, the motive for this restriction was to prevent patrimonialization of the system by negating the need for reliance on local elites who would have strong ties to family or locality.[21]

Another measure of the system's degree of modernity was the uniformity of administrative laws and procedures across the empire. The Chinese of course set the gold standard for this, having created from a very early period a remarkably uniform administrative system that allowed relatively few exceptions to general rules. The Ottoman system permitted more diversity. The central regions of the empire, Anatolia and the Balkans, came to be governed under a reasonably consistent set of rules regarding land tenure, taxation, justice, and the like. Even though the Ottomans forcibly converted their military slaves to Islam, they did not seek to impose their own social system in their provincial administration. The Greek and Armenian Christians, and the Jews, while not having the same legal rights as the Muslim reaya, were permitted a degree of autonomy under the millet system. The religious leaders of these communities were responsible for fiscal matters, education, and legal administration, particularly issues having to do with family law and personal status.[22] The farther one moved from the center of the empire, the more the system diverged from the core. After the defeat of the Mamluks in 1517, important areas of the Middle East, including Egypt, Syria, and the Hejaz (the west side of present-day Saudi Arabia, along the Red Sea), were added to the empire. The Mamluks were allowed to keep their own slave-soldier system while recognizing Ottoman sovereignty. The Hejaz had to be administered under its own special rules, since it contained the Muslim holy cities of Mecca and Medina, of which the Ottomans were now custodians.

REPATRIMONIALIZATION AND DECAY

The decay of the Ottoman system was due to both external and internal factors. The external factors were related to the physical limits of the empire and the broad demographic and environmental changes that affected not just the Turkish lands but all large agrarian empires during the late sixteenth and early seventeenth centuries. The internal factors had to do with the breakdown of the military slave system and the evolution of the Janissaries from an instrument of state power to an entrenched interest group.

As we have seen, the Ottoman system started as a conquest dynasty and was dependent on continued territorial expansion as a source of tax revenues and land for new timars. By the end of the third decade of the sixteenth century, the Ottomans were engaged on two major fronts separated by almost two thousand miles: with the Austrians in Eastern Europe, and with a newly invigorated Persian Empire under the Safavids. The Ottomans were able to mobilize a very large proportion of the empire's manpower, but they could not keep an army in the field for an entire year. They did develop a sophisticated logistics system given the technology of the time, but armies still had to be marshaled in the spring and road-marched several hundred miles to the front. The first attempted conquest of Vienna failed because the army did not reach the outskirts of that city until September 27, 1529; the siege had to be broken off less than three weeks later so that the troops could return home to their lands and families before the onset of winter. Similar constraints existed with regard to the Persian front.[23]

The Ottomans responded by garrisoning Hungary year-round and by improving their naval arm for operations in the Mediterranean. They continued to make conquests (such as the islands of Cyprus and Crete) well into the seventeenth century. But the days of easy territorial gains came to a close by the middle of the sixteenth century; armed external predation ceased to be a good source of economic rents for the regime. This had important internal governance consequences, since higher levels of resource extraction would now have to come from the core areas of the empire instead of the frontiers. And the lack of new Christian territories reduced the influx of new slaves under the devshirme.

The other big external development was a prolonged price inflation and rise in population, phenomena that were related to each other. From 1489 to 1616, grain prices in Anatolia in constant silver units rose by 400 percent. Many scholars have attributed the price rise to the influx of gold and silver from Spain's New World possessions, but as Jack Goldstone argues, there are good reasons to think that the Ottoman inflation was not a monetary event. There is little evidence of new bullion coming into the Ottoman lands; in fact, the government had to repeatedly debase its coinage for lack of silver. Rather, the inflation was driven by a rise in demand due to rapid population growth. In Asia Minor, population increased between 50 and 70 percent between 1520 and 1580, with the population of Istanbul alone increasing from one hundred thousand to seven hundred thousand between 1520 and 1600. The causes of this increase in population, which occurred also in China and in Europe, are unclear. One factor was certainly the receding of the waves of plague that had decimated populations all over Eurasia during the fifteenth century, which Goldstone argues may have been in turn related to climate change as well as the growing disease immunity of populations.[24]

The impact of these changes on Ottoman institutions was dramatic. Inflation made the timar system of land tenure increasingly unviable. Although the timar-holding cavalrymen lived off the land, they had monetary expenses related to their lands and military equipment, which they were increasingly unable to meet. Many of them refused to go on campaigns; others abandoned their holdings and began to form bandit groups that preyed on peasants and landlords in the countryside. The urban-based Janissary corps, to make ends meet, were allowed to take on civilian occupations as craftsmen or merchants, eroding the bright line that had formerly existed between the askeri and reaya classes. Certain Janissaries also secured appointments as financial officers, where they could manipulate the timar registers to their own advantage, granting lands to themselves or even to reaya who paid them for the privilege.[25]

The central state also faced a fiscal crisis in the late sixteenth century. The introduction of firearms was making cavalry, which had been the backbone of fifteenth-century Ottoman armies, obsolete. The state had to rapidly expand the infantry at the expense of the cavalry; the number of Janissaries increased from 5,000 to 38,000 between 1527 and 1609, and then to 67,500 by 1669. In addition, the regime started to recruit landless peasants known as *sekbans* as musketeers on a temporary basis.[26] Unlike the old cavalry forces, which were self-sustaining, these new infantry forces needed to be equipped with modern weapons and paid cash salaries. The government desperately needed to convert its revenues from in-kind payments into cash, which was taking over as the basis for transactions within the economy as a whole. The numbers of cavalry had fallen by as much as the infantry increased, and the abandoned timars were now converted into rented estates given over to private civilian entrepreneurs. This allowed cash taxes to be collected by tax farmers, who were recruited from outside the askeri class. Former restraints on exploitation of the peasantry were relaxed as the regime desperately started searching for revenues.[27]

Given these fiscal stringencies, it was perhaps inevitable that the internal rules governing the system of military slavery would erode. We saw in the case of the Mamluks that rules preventing slave-soldiers from passing on their status and resources to their children were very hard to enforce, since it came up against certain realities of human nature. The original Ottoman system was even more severe, enforcing celibacy among the Janissaries and forbidding them to have families. There was constant pressure from inside the institution to relax these rules. As the regime faced increasing financial pressure, this is precisely what happened. The process began under Selim the Grim (1512–1520) and Suleiman the Magnificent (1520–1566), who first allowed the Janissaries to marry and have families. These Janissaries then pressured the court to allow their sons to enter military service. This happened under Selim II (1566–1574), when a quota for the sons of Janissaries was established. Sultan Murad IV formally abolished the devshirme as a recruitment system in 1638, simply confirming the existing situation in which Janissaries replenished their ranks with their own children. Indeed, some reaya were now allowed to enter the military class.[28] Advancement was increasingly based on personal connections within the state system rather than on rules. Patrimonialism, which had formerly been restricted only to the higher levels of palace politics, now spread throughout the system as a whole.[29]

Like the Burji Mamluks, the Janissaries' moral ties to the sultan eroded as they became preoccupied with their own well-being and that of their families, and began to act like just another self-seeking interest group. Discipline broke down and the Janissaries began to riot regularly in the capital over demands for back pay or to protest payment in debased coinage. Like the Mamluks, they developed ties to the civilian economy, acquiring trade or commercial interests, or extracting rents out of the abandoned timars that they came to control.[30]

Many historians have objected to the idea that the Ottomans were in inevitable decline from the early seventeenth century on. The regime, indeed, hung on for three hundred more years, until the rise of the Young Turk movement in 1908. The Ottomans could display surprising vigor, such as under the vizirate of the Köprülüs in the second half of the seventeenth century, when order was firmly restored throughout the central provinces of the empire and expansion resumed in the Mediterranean with the conquest of Crete and another attempted attack on Vienna in 1683.[31] But this revival was itself reversed. The rise of the Shiite Safavid dynasty in Persia led to a prolonged struggle that had strong Sunni-versus-Shia overtones and encouraged an enforcement of Sunni orthodoxy throughout the empire that closed it off to new ideas coming from the outside. The Ottomans found themselves increasingly unable to keep up with the technological and organizational innovations being pioneered by neighboring European empires, and decade by decade they found themselves ceding territory to them. Even so, Turkey managed to defeat the British at Gallipoli and remained a major player in European politics into the twentieth century.

THE OTTOMAN LEGACY

The Ottomans were by far the most successful regime ever to emerge in the Muslim world. They were able to concentrate power on a scale unprecedented for the region on the basis of the institutions they created. They made the shift from a tribal to a state-level society in a remarkably short period of time and then developed state institutions that incorporated several notably modern features. They established a centralized bureaucracy and military which, while resting on a limited foreign recruitment base, selected and advanced people on impersonal criteria of merit. This system was able to surmount the limitations imposed by the tribal organization of Middle Eastern societies.

Moreover, the Ottomans created a system of provincial administration that they could control from the center. Through this system they were able to impose a relatively uniform set of rules that defined the day to day workings of the economy and kept the peace throughout an enormous empire. The Ottomans never permitted the emergence of a locally rooted blood nobility that would fragment political power, as occurred under European feudalism. For that reason, the sultans never had to reclaim power from that aristocracy in the manner of early modern European monarchs. Ottoman institutions were far more sophisticated than those of many contemporaneous European polities in the fifteenth century.

With regard to its ability to centralize power and dominate the society over which it presided, the Ottoman state in its prime was much closer to the Chinese imperial state than to either contemporary European states, or to any of the indigenous Hindu states created on the Indian subcontinent. As in China, there were relatively few well-organized social groups independent of the state. There was, as Machiavelli noted, no ancient blood nobility; there were no independent commercial cities with their own charters, militias, and systems of law. Unlike India, villages were not organized according to ancient religious social rules.

The one area in which the Ottoman state and its Arab precursors differed from China was in the existence of a lawmaking religious establishment that was, theoretically at least, independent of the state. How much this limited the centralization of state power would come to depend, in the end, on the degree to which religious authority was itself institutionalized. (This is a subject to which I will return in the discussion of the origins of the rule of law in chapter 21.)

The institution of military slavery that lay at the core of Ottoman power represented a dead end with respect to global political development. It was motivated by the same concerns that led the Chinese to invent the Mandarin examination system for entry into the bureaucracy. Today, the functional equivalent of the Chinese system remains in place in the requirements for entry into modern European and Asian bureaucracies, as well as in more general qualification tests like the Scholastic Aptitude Tests in the United States or the *baccalauréate* in France. By contrast, military slavery disappeared as an institution from world politics and left no traces. No one outside the Muslim world ever thought that it was legitimate to enslave and then elevate foreigners to high positions in government. The problem wasn't slavery per se; this institution was considered legitimate in the West, as everyone knows, until well into the nineteenth century. What never occurred to any European or American was to turn their slaves into high government officials.

While the military slave system served as the basis for the Ottomans' rapid rise to power from the fourteenth to the sixteenth century, it was subject to internal contradictions and could not survive the changing external conditions faced by the empire in the late sixteenth century. The Ottomans never developed an indigenous capitalism capable of sustained productivity growth over long periods, and hence they were dependent on extensive growth for fiscal resources. Economic and foreign policy failure fed off each other and made their indigenous institutions impossible to sustain. Their survival into the twentieth century was explained by the adoption of Western institutions by reforming sultans, and at the very end, by the Young Turks. This was ultimately not sufficient to preserve the regime, and the Turkish Republic that succeeded it was based on entirely different institutional principles.

16

CHRISTIANITY UNDERMINES THE FAMILY

How the European exit from kinship was due to religion rather than politics; common misunderstandings about the nature of the European family; how the Catholic church destroyed extended kinship groups; how English individualism was extreme even in a European context

In the three regions of the world I have covered so far, state institutions were formed directly out of tribal societies. Early social organization in China, India, and the Middle East was based on agnatic lineages; the state was created to overcome the limitations imposed by tribal-level societies. In each case, state builders had to figure out how to make individuals loyal to the state rather than to their local kin group. Institutions based on territory and centralized legal authority had to be layered on top of strongly segmentary societies. The most extreme response to this problem was that of the Arabs and Ottomans, who literally kidnapped children and raised them in artificial ouseholds so they would be loyal to the state and not to their kin.

In none of these cases did the top-down state-building effort succeed in abolishing kinship as a basis for local social organization. Indeed, much of the history of institutional development in all of these societies revolved around the effort of kin groups to reinsert themselves into politics—what I have labeled repatrimonialization. Thus the impersonal state institutions created in the Qin and Former Han dynasties were recaptured by powerful lineages by the time of the collapse of the Later Han Dynasty; these families remained important players in Chinese politics through the Sui and Tang dynasties. Indian polities made much less headway in creating powerful impersonal institutions in the first place, and these institutions remained largely irrelevant to social life in Indian villages organized around segmentary jatis. The Turkish state was most successful in reducing the influence of tribal organization in its Anatolian and Balkan heartland, but much less so in the more lightly governed Arab provinces. Indeed, the Ottoman state exercised little authority over peripheral Bedouin communities, whose tribal organization remains untouched to the present day. In all of these regions—China, India, and the Middle East—family and kinship remain far stronger today as sources of social organization and identity than they do in Europe or North America. There are still full-blown segmentary lineages in Taiwan and southern China, Indian marriages remain more a union of families than of individuals, and tribal affiliations remain omnipresent throughout the Arab Middle East, particularly among people of Bedouin stock.

EUROPEAN EXCEPTIONALISM

Kinship in Europe assumed a different shape. In a 1965 article, the demographer John Hajnal noted the striking contrast between marriage patterns in Western Europe and virtually every other part of the world.[1] In Western Europe, both men and women tended to marry later, and there was a higher overall degree of individuals who never married. Both of these factors were linked to relatively low crude birth rates. There were also more young women in the labor force, and more equality within households, due to the fact that women, by virtue of their late marriages, had more opportunities to acquire property. This was not simply a contemporary phenomenon; Hajnal dated this pattern back to a period between 1400 and 1650.

Other important differences between Western Europe and the rest of the world stood out. Local communities organized around tightly bonded kinship groups claiming descent from a common ancestor disappeared from Europe much earlier than is suggested by Hajnal's dating. Kinship and descent mattered to Europeans, but primarily to kings and aristocrats who had substantial economic resources to pass on to their children. Yet they were not embedded in a tyranny of cousins the way that Chinese aristocrats were, since the principles of partible inheritance and primogeniture became well established. During medieval times, individual Europeans had much more freedom to dispose of their land and chattels as they saw fit, without having to get permission from a host of kinsmen.

European society was, in other words, *individualistic* at a very early point, in the sense that individuals and not their families or kin groups could make important decisions about marriage, property, and other personal issues. Individualism in the family is the foundation of all other individualisms. Individualism did not wait for the emergence of a state declaring the legal rights of individuals and using the weight of its coercive power to enforce those rights. Rather, states were formed on top of societies in which individuals already enjoyed substantial freedom from social obligations to kindreds. In Europe, *social development preceded political development.*

But when did the European exit from kinship occur, and what, if not politics, was the driving force behind this change? The answers are that the exit occurred very shortly after the Germanic tribes that overran the Roman Empire were first converted to Christianity, and the agent was the Catholic church.

MARX'S MISTAKE

It is clear that all of the component peoples whose descendants constitute modern Europeans were once organized tribally. Their forms of kinship, laws, customs, and religious practices were documented, to the extent that records were available, by the great historical anthropologists of the nineteenth century, such as Numa Denis Fustel de Coulanges, Henry Maine,[2] Frederick Pollock and Frederic Maitland,[3] and Paul Vinogradoff. All of these men were comparativists with a wide range of knowledge of different cultures, and all were struck by the similarities in agnatic kinship organization in societies as widely separated as the Hindus, Greeks, and Germans.[4]

The nineteenth-century historical anthropologists all believed that kinship structures evolved over time, and that there was a general pattern of development in human societies from large corporate kin groups to smaller families based on voluntary unions by individual men and women. In Henry Maine's famous concept, modernization involved the shift from "status to contract."[5] That is, early societies ascribed social status to individuals, specifying everything from marriage partners to occupations to religious beliefs. In modern societies, by contrast, individuals could freely contract with one another to enter into different kinds of social relationships, the most central of which was the marriage contract. Maine did not, however, have a dynamic theory of how and when the shift from status to contract occurred.

There is in fact much misunderstanding about both the dating of the shift in European kinship patterns and the causative agent. Many people believe that Europeans, much like other peoples around the world, lived in tribes or large, extended family groups right up until the Industrial Revolution, when the pressures of machine production and the need for social mobility broke them up. By this view, the economic changes we associate with industrialization and the emergence of smaller nuclear families were part of the same process.[6]

This opinion most likely comes from early modernization theory. Karl Marx in the *Communist Manifesto* talks about the bourgeois family and how the bourgeoisie "has torn away from the family its sentimental veil, and has reduced the family relation to a mere money relation." The rise of the bourgeoisie is driven, in turn, by changes in technology and the material modes of production. Max Weber postulated a sharp break between traditional and modern societies. Traditional societies were characterized by extensive kinship ties, restrictions on market transactions due to religious or kinship constraints, lack of individual social mobility, and informal social norms rooted in tradition, religion, and charisma. Modern societies, by contrast, were individualistic, egalitarian, merit and market oriented, mobile, and structured by rational-legal forms of authority. Weber argued that all of these characteristics were part of a single package: it was impossible to develop an efficient, market-based economy in a society in which priests set prices or property was entailed by kin obligations. He believed that this kind of rational modernity emerged only in the West and dated the transition to modernity to a sequence of events that took place in the sixteenth and seventeenth centuries, encompassing the Protestant Reformation and the Enlightenment. Thus Marxists tended to see the rise of individualism and the nuclear family driven by economic change, whereas Weberians saw Protestantism as the main driver. Either way, in their views, the change was not more than a few hundred years old.

FROM STATUS TO CONTRACT

Twentieth-century social historians and anthropologists have pushed the dating of the shift from status to contract steadily backward in time. I already noted Hajnal's view that the distinctive European pattern dated from the fifteenth and sixteenth centuries. Alan MacFarlane's study of the origins of English individualism shows that the right of individuals to freely alienate their property while still alive and disinherit their children in testamentary wills was already well established in the English Common Law by the early sixteenth century.[7] This is significant because in what he labels "peasant societies" that were characteristic of Eastern Europe and much of the rest of the world, kinship obligations imposed severe entails on the ability of property owners to sell their land. What he labels a peasant society is one characterized by extended families, in which property rights are either held communally or else tied up in complex relations of interdependence between different degrees of relatives. In such societies, peasants are tied to the land they work by many noneconomic factors, such as the fact that their ancestors are buried on it.

But MacFarlane notes that the right of seisin, or freehold possession of land, had already become widespread in England at least three centuries before this. One study of land transfers in an English district during the late fifteenth century showed only 15 percent going to the owner's family during his lifetime, and 10 percent at death.[8] But all the way back at the end of the twelfth and beginning of the thirteenth century, English villeins (tenants legally tied to their lands) were buying, selling, and leasing property without the permission of their lords.[9]

One important measure of the decay of complex kinship structures is the legal right of women to hold and dispose of property. In agnatic societies, women achieve legal personhood only by virtue of their marriage to and mothering of a male in the lineage. While widows and unmarried daughters may have certain rights of inheritance, they are usually required to keep the lineage's property within the agnatic line. Yet Englishwomen had the right to hold and dispose of property freely and to sell it to individuals outside the family from a point not long after the Norman Conquest in 1066. Indeed, from at least the thirteenth century, they could not only own land and chattels, they also could sue and be sued, and make wills and contracts without permission of a male guardian. Granting such rights in a patrilineal society would have the effect of undermining the lineage's ability to control property, and would thus undermine the social system as a whole.[10] Hence the ability of women to own and bequeath property is an indicator of the deterioration of tribal organization and suggests that strict patrilineality had already disappeared by this early point.

One of the fascinating indicators of early English individualism cited by MacFarlane is the appearance of "maintenance contracts" between children and their parents as early as the thirteenth century. Tribal societies organized around groups claiming descent from a common ancestor typically worship those ancestors. A great deal of Confucian morality is built around the obligations of children, particularly sons, to look after their parents. Confucian moralists were clear that individuals had stronger obligations to their parents than to their own children, and Chinese law severely punished children who behaved in unfilial ways.

Things were rather different in England, where parents who foolishly passed legal title to their possessions to their children while still alive had no customary residual rights to their property. One medieval poem cites the case of a father who turned over his property to his son, who then began to feel his father was too heavy a burden and started to mistreat him. When his father was shivering with cold, he told his young son to cover his grandfather with a sack. "The boy cut the sack in two, covered his grandfather with half of it, and showed his father the other half, to signify that just as his father had mistreated his grandfather, so the boy when his turn came would mistreat his father in his old age and cover him when he was cold with only half a sack."[11] To avoid situations like this, parents signed maintenance contracts with their children obliging the latter to care for them once they had inherited their parents' property. "For surrendering the property a couple in Bedfordshire in 1294 were promised, in return, food and drink and a dwelling in the main messuage [house], but if the two couples started to quarrel, then the old couple were to have another house and 'six quarters of hard corn at Michaelmas, namely three quarters of wheat, a quarter and a half of barley, a quarter and a half of beans and peas, and a quarter of oats' and all the goods and chattels, movable and immovable, of the said house."[12]

The reduction of relationships in the family to "a mere money relation" that Marx thundered against was not, it appears, an innovation of the eighteenth-century bourgeoisie but appeared in England many centuries before that class's supposed rise. Putting one's parents out to pasture in a nursing home has very deep historical roots in Western Europe. This suggests that, contrary to Marx, capitalism was the consequence rather than the cause of a change in social relationships and custom.

But even the thirteenth century is too late to date the European shift away from complex kinship, or from status to contract. The great French historian Marc Bloch noted that blood ties were the basis of social organization before the rise of feudalism in the ninth and tenth centuries. The vendetta, or feud between two rival tribal lineages, has a long history in European society, something with which we are familiar from Shakespeare's *Romeo and Juliet*. In addition, Bloch confirms that in this period, groups of kinsmen or large extended families owned property in common, and that even when land started to become freely alienable by individuals, it was still entailed by requirements that the seller obtain the permission of a circle of kinsmen.[13]

However, Bloch notes, the huge agnatic lineages tracing descent to a single ancestor characteristic of China, India, and the Middle East had long ago disappeared in Europe: "The Roman *gens* had owed the exceptional firmness of its pattern to the absolute primacy of descent in the male line. Nothing like this was known in the feudal epoch." As evidence, he points out that Europeans in the Middle Ages never traced their descent unilineally through the father, as would be necessary to maintain the boundaries between lineage segments in a tribal society. Throughout medieval times it was common for mothers to give their daughters their own surnames, something forbidden in an agnatic society like China. Individuals often thought of themselves as belonging equally to both the mother's and the father's family, and the offspring of two prominent families would join the surnames of both lineages (for example, Valéry Giscard d'Estaing, or the present-day Spanish practice of using the family names of both parents). By the thirteenth century, nuclear families very similar to contemporary ones had already started to emerge all over Europe. It was harder to carry on blood feuds, because the circle of vengeance kept getting smaller, and there were many individuals who felt themselves related to both sides of the quarrel.[14]

According to Bloch, the entire institution of feudalism can in some sense be understood as a desperate adaptation to social isolation in a society that could not fall back on kinship ties as a source of social solidarity. From the late seventh century on, Europe suffered a series of devastating external invasions: the Vikings from the north, the Arabs or Saracens coming up through North Africa and Spain from the south, and the Hungarians from the east. Even if the Arabs were turned back at Poitiers, Muslim control of the Mediterranean cut Europe off from the trade with Byzantium and North Africa that had been the basis of the Roman economy.[15] With the decay of the Carolingian Empire in the ninth century, cities began to wither, and populations, beset by innumerable warlords, retreated into the self-sufficiency of individual villages.

During this nadir of European civilization, kinship did make something of a comeback due to the collapse of larger political structures. But already by then, the structure of the European peoples' agnatic lineages had been too weakened to be a source of social support. Feudalism arose as an *alternative* to kinship:

> Yet to the individual, threatened by the numerous dangers bred by an atmosphere of violence, the kinship group did not seem to offer adequate protection, even in the first feudal age. In the form in which it then existed, it was too vague and too variable in its outlines, too deeply undermined by the duality of descent by male and female lines. That is why men were obliged to seek or accept other ties. On this point history is decisive, for the only regions in which powerful agnatic groups survived—German lands on the shores of the North Sea, Celtic districts of the British Isles— knew nothing of vassalage, the fief and the manor. The tie of kinship was one of the essential elements of feudal society; its relative weakness explains why there was feudalism at all.[16]

Feudalism was the voluntary submission of one individual to another, unrelated, individual, based on the exchange of protection for service: "Neither the State nor the family any longer provided adequate protection. The village community was barely strong enough to maintain order within its own boundaries; the urban community scarcely existed. Everywhere, the weak man felt the need to be sheltered by someone more powerful. The powerful man, in his turn, could not maintain his prestige or his fortune or even ensure his own safety except by securing for himself, by persuasion or coercion, the support of subordinates bound to his service."[17]

But we still have not arrived at the proper date for the European transition out of kinship, nor an adequate causal mechanism.[18] The most convincing explanation for the shift has been given by the social anthropologist Jack Goody, who pushes the date for the beginnings of the transition all the way back to the sixth century, and attributes responsibility to Christianity itself—or, more specifically, to the institutional interests of the Catholic church.[19]

Goody notes that the distinctive Western European marriage pattern began to branch off from the dominant Mediterranean pattern by the end of the Roman Empire. The Mediterranean pattern, which included the Roman gens, was strongly agnatic or patrilineal, leading to the segmentary organization of society. The agnatic group tended to be endogamous, with some preference for cross-cousin marriage. (I noted the prevalence of cross-cousin marriage in the Dravidian culture of southern India in chapter 11; it is also widely practiced in the Arab world and among Pashtuns, Kurds, and many Turkic peoples.) There was a strict separation of the sexes and little opportunity for women to own property or participate in the public sphere. The Western European pattern was different in all of these respects: inheritance was bilateral; cross-cousin marriage was banned and exogamy promoted; and women had greater rights to property and participation in public events.

This shift was driven by the Catholic church, which took a strong stand against four practices: marriages between close kin, marriages to the widows of dead relatives (the so-called levirate), the adoption of children, and divorce. The Venerable Bede, reporting on the efforts of Pope Gregory I to convert the pagan Anglo-Saxons to Christianity in the sixth century, notes how Gregory explicitly condemned the tribe's practices of marriage to close relatives and the levirate. Later church edicts forbade concubinage, and promoted an indissoluble, monogamous lifetime marriage bond between men and women.[20]

The reasons for these prohibitions, Goody argues, are not firmly anchored in the Scriptures, or in Christian doctrine more generally. The prohibited practices were common in the Palestine of Jesus' birth; Jesus himself may have been the product of a cross-cousin marriage, and the levirate was common among the Jews. The Gospels, it is true, take an antifamilistic stand: in Matthew, Jesus says, "He that loveth father or mother more than me is not worthy of me: and he that loveth son or daughter more than me is not worthy of me." But these, Goody argues, are the words of a millenarian prophet seeking to recruit people away from the security of their kin groups into a new schismatic sect. The theological arguments in favor of the new prohibitions were often taken from Old Testament sources that the Jews interpreted quite differently.

The reason that the church took this stand, in Goody's view, had much more to do with the material interests of the church than with theology. Cross-cousin marriage (or any other form of marriage between close relatives), the levirate, concubinage, adoption, and divorce are all what he labels "strategies of heirship" whereby kinship groups are able to keep

property under the group's control as it is passed down from one generation to another. Life expectancy in Europe and the Mediterranean world
at the time was less than thirty-five. The probability of a couple's producing a male heir who survived into adulthood and who could carry on the
ancestral line was quite low. As a result, societies legitimated a wide range
of practices that allowed individuals to produce heirs. Concubinage has
already been discussed in this regard in the discussion of China; divorce
can be seen as a form of serial concubinage in monogamous societies. The
levirate was practiced when a brother died before he produced children;
his wife's marriage to a younger brother ensured that his property would
remain consolidated with that of his siblings. Cross-cousin marriage ensured that property would remain in the hands of close family members.
Whatever the case, the church systematically cut off all available avenues
that families had for passing down property to descendants. At the same
time, it strongly promoted voluntary donations of land and property to
itself. The church thus stood to benefit materially from an increasing pool
of property-owning Christians who died without heirs.[21]

The relatively high status of women in Western Europe was an accidental by-product of the church's self-interest. The church made it difficult
for a widow to remarry within the family group and thereby reconvey her
property back to the tribe, so she had to own the property herself. A woman's right to own property and dispose of it as she wished stood to benefit
the church, since it provided a large source of donations from childless
widows and spinsters. And the woman's right to own property spelled the
death knell for agnatic lineages, by undermining the principle of unilineal
descent.[22]

The Catholic church did very well financially in the centuries following these changes in the rules, though this was not simply a case of post
hoc ergo propter hoc. By the end of the seventh century, one-third of the
productive land in France was in ecclesiastical hands; between the eighth
and ninth centuries, church holdings in northern France, the German
lands, and Italy doubled.[23] These donations turned the church into a for-
midable economic and political institution, and paved the way for the investiture conflict of Gregory VII (described in chapter 18). There is some
parallel between these donations and the waqf donations to charitable
foundations by wealthy Muslims. But while many of the waqfs were stratagems by wealthy individuals to shield their property from taxation and
hand it down to their children, the lands donated by childless widows and

spinsters came with no strings attached. The church thus found itself a large property owner, running manors and overseeing the economic production of serfs throughout Europe. This helped the church in its mission of feeding the hungry and caring for the sick, and it also made possible a vast expansion of the priesthood, monasteries, and convents. But it also necessitated the evolution of an internal managerial hierarchy and set of rules within the church itself that made it an independent political player in medieval politics.

These changes had a correspondingly devastating impact on tribal organization throughout Western Europe. The German, Norse, Magyar, and Slavic tribes saw their kinship structures dissolve within two or three generations of their conversion to Christianity. It is true that these conversions were rooted in politics, like the Magyar monarch István's (St. Stephen) acceptance of Holy Communion in the year 1000. But the actual change in social mores and family rules was enforced not by political authorities but by the church on a social and cultural level.

THE SOCIAL BACKGROUND TO STATE BUILDING IN EUROPE

Europe (and its colonial offshoots) was exceptional insofar as the transition out of complex kinship occurred first on a social and cultural level rather than on a political one. By changing marriage and inheritance rules, the church in a sense acted politically and for economic motives. But the church was not the sovereign ruler of the territories where it operated; rather, it was a social actor whose influence lay in its ability to set cultural rules. As a result, a far more individualistic European society was already in place during the Middle Ages, before the process of state building began, and centuries before the Reformation, Enlightenment, and Industrial Revolution. Rather than being the outcome of these great modernizing shifts, change in the family was more likely a facilitative condition for modernization to happen in the first place. An emerging capitalist economy in Italy, England, and the Netherlands in the sixteenth century did not have to overcome the resistance of large corporately organized kinship groups with substantial property to protect, as in India and China. Instead, it took root in societies that already had traditions of individualized ownership where property routinely changed hands between strangers.

This is not to say that European state builders faced a clear-cut terrain free of entrenched social institutions. Quite the contrary: when I resume the story of the origins of the European state in chapter 21, we will see that a whole variety of powerful social actors were in place that were critical to the creation of a rule of law and of accountable government. There were no clans or tribes, but there was an entrenched blood nobility that had accumulated wealth, military power, and legal standing during the feudal period.

The fact that these social institutions were feudal rather than kinship based made a huge difference to the subsequent political development of Europe. The feudal relationship of vassalage was a contract entered into voluntarily between a stronger and a weaker individual, and it entailed legal obligations on both sides. Although it formalized a highly unequal and hierarchical society, it nonetheless set precedents for both individualism (since the contracts were entered into by individuals and not by kin groups) and for the broadening of the understanding of legal personhood. The historian Jenö Szücs argues that the relationship between landlord and peasant had come to acquire a contractual character by the year 1200, which created the basis for an expanded application of human dignity to this broader class of persons. From that point on, "every peasant revolt in the West was an expression of enraged human dignity at the landlord's breach of contract, and a demand for the right to 'freedom.'"[24] This did not happen in societies where land rights were kin based and customary, or else based on the physical domination of one kin group over another.

The replacement of kinship-based local institutions with feudal ones had another important political impact with regard to the efficacy of local government. Both lineages and feudal institutions took on functions of sovereignty and governance at various points, particularly when central states were weak. They could provide for local security, the administration of justice, and the organization of economic life. But feudal institutions were inherently more flexible because they were based on contract, and they were capable of organizing more decisive collective action because they were more hierarchical. Once a feudal lord's rights were legally established, they were not subject to constant renegotiation in the way that authority within a lineage was. Legal title to property, whether held by the strong or the weak, conveyed a clear power to buy or sell it without restrictions imposed by a kin-based social system. A local lord could speak decisively on behalf of the community he "represented" in a way that a tribal leader could not. As we have seen, a mistake commonly made by European colonialists in India and Africa was assuming that tribal leadership amounted to the same thing as the authority of a local lord in a feudal society, when the two were actually quite different.

One of Max Weber's legacies is the tendency to think of the impact of religion on politics and the economy in terms of values, for example, the Protestant work ethic, which was said to directly influence the behavior of individual entrepreneurs during the Industrial Revolution through sanctification of work. Values were certainly important; the Christian doctrine of the universal equality of all human beings under God made it much easier to justify equality of rights for women as property owners.

But this type of explanation often begs the question of why certain religious values get promoted and rooted in societies in the first place. Such is the case with the church's assault on extended kinship. These values do not obviously stem from Christian doctrine; after all, the no less Christian Eastern church in Constantinople made no parallel effort to change marriage and inheritance laws. As a result, tightly knit kin communities survived in most of the lands ruled by Byzantium. The famous multigenerational Serbian *zadruga*, or the Albanian clans with their prolonged and intricate feuds, are just two examples. The fact that these institutions died out in Western Europe has much more to do with the material interests and powers of the church, whose control over social values was an instrument it used to its own benefit. So from one point of view, the economic turtle is standing on the back of a religious turtle, while from another point of view the religious turtle is standing on the back of an economic one farther down the stack.

Whether one regards the Catholic church's motives as primarily religious or economic, it came to be institutionalized as an independent political actor to a far greater degree than the religious authorities in any of the other societies under consideration. China never developed an indigenous religion more sophisticated than ancestor or spirit worship. India and the Muslim world, by contrast, were shaped from the beginning by religious innovation. Religion in both cases served as an important check on political power. But in the world of Sunni Islam, and in the Indian subcontinent, religious authority never coalesced into a single, centralized bureaucratic institution outside the state. How this happened in Europe is intimately bound up with the development of the modern European state, and with the emergence of what we today call the rule of law.

PART THREE

·

The Rule of Law

17

THE ORIGINS OF THE RULE OF LAW

European exceptionalism evident in the role of law in early state formation; definitions and disagreements about the rule of law; Hayek's theories about the priority of law over legislation; how English Common Law was based on royal power, and how that bolstered the legitimacy of the English state

European political development was exceptional insofar as European societies made an early exit from tribal-level organization, and did so without the benefit of top-down political power. Europe was exceptional also in that state formation was based less on the capacity of early state build ers to deploy military power than on their ability to dispense justice. The growth of the power and legitimacy of European states came to be inseparable from the emergence of the rule of law.

Early European states dispensed justice but not necessarily law. Law was rooted elsewhere, either in religion (as in the edicts regulating marriage and the family discussed in the last chapter) or in the customs of tribes or other local communities. Early European states occasionally legislated—that is, created new laws—but their authority and legitimacy rested more on their ability to impartially enforce laws not necessarily of their own making.

This distinction between law and legislation is critical to understanding the meaning of the rule of law itself. As with a term like "democracy," it sometimes seems as if there are as many definitions of "rule of law" as there are legal scholars.[1] I use it in the following sense, which corresponds to several important currents in thinking about the phenomenon in the West: The *law* is a body of abstract rules of justice that bind a community together. In premodern societies, the law was believed to be fixed by an authority higher than any human legislator, either by a divine authority, by immemorial custom, or by nature.[2] *Legislation*, on the other hand, corresponds to what is now called positive law and is a function of political power, that is, the ability of a king, baron, president, legislature, or warlord to make and enforce new rules based ultimately on some combination of power and authority. The rule of law can be said to exist only where the preexisting body of law is sovereign over legislation, meaning that the individual holding political power feels bound by the law. This is not to say that those with legislative power cannot make new laws. But if they are to function within the rule of law, they must legislate according to the rules set by the preexisting law and not according to their own volition.

The original understanding of the law as something fixed either by divine authority, by custom, or by nature implied that the law could not be changed by human agency, though it could and had to be interpreted to fit novel circumstances. With the decline of religious authority and belief in natural law in modern times, we have come to understand the law as something created by human beings, but only under a strict set of procedural rules that guarantee that they conform to a broad social consensus over basic values. The distinction between law and legislation now corresponds to the distinction between constitutional and ordinary law, where the former has more stringent requirements for enactment, such as supermajority voting. In the contemporary United States, this means that any new law passed by Congress must be consistent with a prior and superior body of law, the Constitution, as interpreted by the Supreme Court.

Up to this point, I have discussed political development in terms of state building, the ability of states to concentrate and use power. The rule of law is a separate component of political order that puts limitations on a state's power. The first checks on executive power were not those imposed by democratic assemblies or elections. Rather, they were the result of societies believing that rulers had to operate under the law. State building and the rule of law therefore coexist in a certain tension. On the one hand, rulers can enhance their authority by acting within and on behalf of the law. On the other hand, the law can prevent them from doing things they would like to do, not just in their own private interest but in the interest of the community as a whole. So the rule of law is constantly threatened by the need to generate political power, from seventeenth-century English monarchs who wanted to raise revenues without going through Parliament to Latin American governments in the twentieth century fighting terrorism with extralegal death squads.

CONTEMPORARY CONFUSIONS CONCERNING
THE RULE OF LAW

In contemporary developing countries, one of the greatest political deficits lies in the relative weakness of the rule of law. Of all the components of contemporary states, effective legal institutions are perhaps the most difficult to construct. Military organization and taxing authority arise naturally out of people's basic predatory instincts. It is not difficult for a warlord to throw together a militia and use it to extract resources from the community. At the other end of the spectrum, democratic elections are relatively easy (if expensive) to stage, and there is today in place a large international infrastructure to help facilitate them.[3] Legal institutions, on the other hand, must be spread throughout the entire country and maintained on an ongoing basis. They require physical facilities as well as huge investments in the training of lawyers, judges, and other officers of the court, including the police who will ultimately enforce the law. But most important, legal institutions need to be seen as legitimate and authoritative, not just by ordinary people but also by powerful elites in the society. Bringing this about has proved to be no easy task. Latin America today is overwhelmingly democratic, but rule of law is extremely weak, from the bribe-taking police officer to a tax-evading judge. The Russian Federation still stages democratic elections, but particularly since the rise of Vladimir Putin, its elites from the president on down have been able to break the law with impunity.

There is a large literature that links the establishment of the rule of law to economic development.[4] This literature reflects at base an important insight, namely, that the emergence of the modern world, including the emergence of a capitalist economy, was broadly dependent on the prior existence of a rule of law. The absence of a strong rule of law is indeed one of the principal reasons why poor countries can't achieve higher rates of growth.

But this literature is highly confused and inconsistent with regard to the basic definition of the rule of law and how to measure its presence or absence. In addition, the theory that links the different components of the rule of law to economic growth is empirically questionable, and becomes doubly so when projected back onto societies that existed under Malthusian economic conditions. Before we can proceed with the historical account of the origins of the rule of law, then, we need to clear away some of the baggage left by contemporary discussions of this subject.

When economists talk about the rule of law, they are usually referring to modern property rights and contract enforcement.[5] Modern property rights are those held by individuals, who are free to buy and sell their property without restrictions imposed by kin groups, religious authorities, or the state. The theory by which property rights and contract are related to economic growth is straightforward. No one will make long-term investments unless he knows that his property rights are secure. If a government suddenly raises taxes on an investment, as Ukraine in the early 1990s did after signing an agreement for cell phone infrastructure, the investors may pull out and will be deterred from future projects. Similarly, trade requires a legal machinery to enforce contracts and to adjudicate the disputes that inevitably arise among contracting parties. The more transparent the contracting rules, and the more even-handed their enforcement, the more trade will be encouraged. This is why many economists emphasize the importance of "credible commitments" as a hallmark of a state's institutional development.

This definition of the rule of law overlaps, but only partially, with the one presented at the beginning of this chapter. Obviously, if a government does not feel bound by a preexisting rule of law, but considers itself fully sovereign in all respects, nothing will prevent it from taking the property of its citizens, or of foreigners who happen to be doing business with it. If general legal rules are not enforced in the cases of powerful elites, or against the most powerful actor of all, the government, then there can be no ultimate certainty about the security of either private property or trade. As the political scientist Barry Weingast has noted, a state strong enough to enforce property rights can also take them away.[6]

On the other hand, it is perfectly possible to have "good enough" property rights and contract enforcement that permit economic development without the existence of a true rule of law in the sense of the law being the final sovereign.[7] A good example is the People's Republic of China. There is no true rule of law in China today: the Chinese Communist Party does not accept the authority of any other institution in China as superior to it or able to overturn its decisions. Although the PRC has a constitution, the party makes the constitution rather than the reverse. If the current Chinese government wanted to nationalize all existing foreign investments, or renationalize the holdings of private individuals and return the country to Maoism, there is no legal framework preventing it from doing so. The

Chinese government chooses not to do so out of self-interest, which seems to be regarded by most parties as a sufficiently credible assurance to future good behavior. An abstract commitment to "rule of law" has not been necessary for the country to achieve double-digit rates of growth for more than three decades. When the party disbanded collective farms in 1978 under the Household Responsibility law, it did not restore to Chinese peasants full modern property rights (that is, the full right of individuals to alienate real property). Rather, it gave them heritable usufructuary rights to their land (rights to long-term leases), similar to the rights possessed by peasants in the central provinces of the Ottoman Empire. These rights, however, were "good enough" to lead to a doubling of agricultural output just four years after the change in property rules.

Dynastic China did not have a rule of law any more than Communist China. On the other hand, imperial China in normal times may well have had "good enough" property rights at a local level to promote agricultural productivity up to at least the frontier of then-existing technology, rights not terribly different from those enjoyed by Chinese peasants today. The constraints on property rights were less those imposed by a grasping, predatory state than the continuing connection between property and kinship. Property was entailed by myriad rights and duties imposed by agnatic lineages, which up through the Chinese Republic in the twentieth century still recognized the rights of families to restrict the alienation of land.[8]

It is not clear, moreover, that even the best-specified modern property rights would be sufficient in themselves to raise productivity substantially, or to create the modern capitalist economic world out of a Malthusian society. Before the introduction of other institutions necessary to sustain continuous technological advance (such as the scientific method, universities, human capital, research laboratories, a cultural milieu that encouraged risk and experimentation, and so forth), there were limits to the kinds of productivity gains that good property rights on their own could induce, and thus no assumption that continuous technological advances would occur.[9]

Thus the economists' emphasis on modern property rights and contract enforcement under a rule of law may be misplaced in two respects. First, in the contemporary world where continuous technological innovation is possible, "good enough" property rights with no sovereign rule of law are at times sufficient to produce high rates of economic growth. Second, in a Malthusian world, such rates of growth are not achievable even presuming the existence of modern property rights and a rule of law, because the binding constraint on growth lies elsewhere.

There is yet another definition of the rule of law that likely had as great an impact on economic life in premodern as in contemporary times. This is the simple security of persons, the ability to exit from the violent state of nature and go about one's daily business without fear of being killed or robbed. We tend to appreciate this aspect of the rule of law more when it is absent than when it is present and we can take it for granted.

Finally, it is not possible to talk about the rule of law without specifying *to whom* the law applies, that is, the circle of people who are considered legal persons protected by the law. Societies seek to enforce basic social rules universally, but a rule of law that protects citizens against arbitrary actions of the state itself is often initially applied only to a minority of privileged subjects. The law, in other words, protects the interests of the elites who are close to the state or who control the state, and in that sense law resembles what Socrates in Plato's *Republic* labels the "justice of a band of robbers."

Take, for example, a letter from Mme. de Sévigné, one of the greatest salon patrons of seventeenth-century France, to her daughter. This witty and sensitive woman describes how soldiers in Brittany were enforcing a new tax, turning old men and children out of their houses in search of assets to seize. Some sixty townspeople were to be hanged the following day for nonpayment. She goes on: "The fiddler who had begun the dance and the stealing of stamped paper was broken on the wheel; he was quartered [cut into four pieces] and his four quarters exposed in the four corners of the town."[10]

Obviously, the French state would not enforce such drastic penalties on Mme. de Sévigné and her circle. As we will see in chapter 23, it imposed onerous taxes on commoners precisely because it was too respectful of the property rights and personal security of the aristocracy. It is therefore not true that there was no rule of law in seventeenth-century France, but the law did not regard commoners as legal persons entitled to the same rights as the aristocracy. The same was true of the United States at its founding, which denied African Americans, women, Native Americans—anyone who wasn't a white male property owner—the right to vote. The process of democratization gradually expands the rule of law to include all persons.

One of the consequences of these confusions about the meaning of the rule of law is that programs designed by rich countries to improve rule of law in poor ones seldom produce useful results.[11] People lucky enough to live in countries with a strong rule of law usually don't understand how it arose in the first place, and they mistake the outward forms of the rule of law for its substance. Thus, for example, "checks and balances" is taken to be a hallmark of a strong rule-of-law society, since the branches of government check the behavior of one another. But the mere existence of a formal check is not the same thing as strong democratic governance. Courts can be used to frustrate collective action, as in contemporary India, where prolonged judicial appeals can bog down critical infrastructure projects, or they can be used to protect the interests of elites against the will of the government, as in the 1905 Supreme Court case of *Lochner v. New York*, which protected business interests against a legislative effort to limit working hours. Thus the form of separated powers periodically fails to correspond necessarily to the substance of a law-abiding society.

In the discussion that follows, we will look at the development of the rule of law in as broad a perspective as possible: Where did law itself—that is, a common set of rules of justice—originate? How did specific rules regarding property rights, contract enforcement, and commercial law develop? And how did the highest political authorities come to accept the sovereignty of law?

HAYEK'S THEORY THAT LAW IS PRIOR TO LEGISLATION

The great Austrian economist Friedrich A. Hayek developed a sophisticated theory of the origins of law that provides important insights into the meaning of the rule of law, and is the framework for how many people think about the law today. Hayek is known as the godfather of contemporary libertarianism, but libertarians are not opposed to rules as such: according to Hayek, "Only the existence of common rules makes the peaceful existence of individuals in society possible."[12] Hayek took aim at what he labeled the "rationalist" or "constructivist" understanding of the origins of law, namely, that it proceeded from the will of a legislator who rationally studied the problems of society and devised a law to establish what he thought was a better social order. Constructivism, Hayek argued, was a conceit of the last three hundred years, and particularly of a series of French thinkers including Descartes and Voltaire, who thought the human mind was sufficient to understand the workings of human society.

This led to what Hayek regarded as huge mistakes, such as the French and Bolshevik revolutions, in which top-down political power was used to re-order the whole of society based on a preconceived notion of social jus-tice. In Hayek's day (the middle decades of the twentieth century), this mistake was being repeated not only by Socialist countries such as the Soviet Union, which relied on rational planning and centralized authority, but by social democratic welfare states in Europe.

This was wrong, according to Hayek, for a number of reasons, the most important of which was the fact that no single planner could ever have enough knowledge about the actual workings of a society to rationally re-order it. The bulk of knowledge in a society was local in character and dis-persed throughout the whole society; no individual could master enough information to anticipate the effects of a planned change in the laws or rules.[13]

Social order was not, according to Hayek, the result of top-down ratio-nal planning; rather, it occurred spontaneously through the interactions of hundreds or thousands of dispersed individuals who experimented with rules, kept the ones that worked, and rejected those that didn't. The pro-cess by which social order was generated was incremental, evolutionary, and decentralized; only by making use of the local knowledge of myriads of individuals could a working "Great Society" ever appear. Spontaneous orders evolved in the manner Darwin posited for biological organisms—through decentralized adaptation and selection, and not through the pur-poseful design of a creator.

According to Hayek, the law itself constituted a spontaneous order, and "there can be no doubt that law existed for ages before it occurred to man that he could make or alter it." Indeed, "individuals had learned to observe (and enforce) rules of conduct long before such rules could be expressed in words." Legislation—the conscious decreeing of new rules—"came relatively late in the history of mankind," and the idea that "all law is, can be, and ought to be, the product of the free invention of a legislator . . . is factually false, an erroneous product of . . . constructivist rationalism."[14]

The model of spontaneous order that Hayek clearly had in mind was the English Common Law, in which law evolves as a result of the cumula-tive decisions of countless judges who try to apply general rules to the specific cases that are brought before them:

The freedom of the British which in the eighteenth century the rest of Europe came so much to admire was . . . a result of the fact that the law that governed the decision of the courts was the Common Law, a law existing independently of anyone's will and at the same time binding upon and developed by the independent courts; a law with which parliament only rarely interfered and, when it did, mainly only to clear up doubtful points within a given body of law.[15]

Hayek thus zeroed in on the essence of the rule of law: there is a preexisting body of law representing the will of the whole community that is higher than the will of the current government and that limits the scope of that government's legislative acts. His preference for English Common Law is shared by a number of contemporary economists, who regard it as more adaptive and market-friendly than the continental tradition of civil law.[16]

In laying out this theory of the origins of law, Hayek was making both an empirical and a normative assertion. He was arguing that law developed in an unplanned, evolutionary manner in most societies, and that this type of spontaneously generated law *ought* to be superior to consciously legislated rules. This interpretation was promoted by the great English jurist Sir Edward Coke, who argued that the Common Law dated from time immemorial, and was also taken up by Edmund Burke in his defense of incrementalism.[17] Hayek was a great enemy of a powerful state, not just of Soviet-style Communist dictatorships but also of European social democracies that sought to achieve "social justice" through redistribution and regulation. He was taking one side of a long-standing argument between what the legal scholar Robert Ellickson labels "legal centralists" and "legal peripheralists." The former think that formal legislated laws create and shape moral rules, while the latter argue that they simply codify existing informal norms.[18]

Hayek's normative preference for a minimal state seems, however, to have colored his empirical views about the origins of law. For although law did precede legislation in many societies, political authorities frequently stepped in to alter it, even in early societies. And the emergence of the modern rule of law was critically dependent on enforcement by a strong centralized state. This is evident even in the very origins of the Common Law that Hayek celebrates.

FROM CUSTOMARY TO COMMON LAW

Hayek's fundamental insight that law tends to develop based on the decentralized evolution of social rules is right in a broad sense, both in ancient and in modern times. But there have been major discontinuities in the development of law that can be explained only by the intervention of political authority and not as the result of a process of "spontaneous order." Hayek was simply wrong about certain of his historical facts.[19]

One of these transitions was the shift from customary to Common Law in England itself. Common Law is not just a formalized and written version of customary law. It is law of a fundamentally different sort. As we saw in chapter 4, a major change in the meaning of law occurs when societies make the transition from tribal to state-level forms of organization. In tribal societies, justice between individuals is a bit like contemporary international relations, based on the self-help of rival groups in a world where there is no higher third-party enforcer of rules. State-level societies, by contrast, are different precisely because such an enforcer exists, the state itself.[20]

England after the end of the Roman Empire was tribally organized, composed of various groups of Angles, West Saxons, Jutes, Celts, and others. There was no state. Households were grouped into villages, and villages into larger units called hundreds (an area large enough to sustain one hundred families) or counties. Above this level were kings, but these early monarchs did not have a monopoly of force and could not enforce rules on the tribal units. They saw themselves not as territorial rulers but as kings of peoples—e.g., the *Rex Anglorum*, or king of the Angles. As we saw in the last chapter, Christianity began to undermine Anglo-Saxon tribal organization when it appeared at the end of the sixth century with the arrival of the Benedictine monk Augustine. But the erosion of tribal law was gradual, and it continued to prevail through the chaotic centuries in the second half of the first millennium. There were strong bonds of trust within kin groups but hostility and mutual wariness between rival clans. Justice therefore revolved around the regulation of relationships between groups of kinsmen.

The first known compilation of Anglo-Saxon tribal law was the Laws of Ethelbert from around 600. It was similar to the slightly earlier *Lex Salica* of the Merovingian king Clovis, insofar as it consisted of a listing of wergeld penalties for various injuries:

The four front teeth were worth six shillings each, the teeth next to them four, the other teeth one; thumbs, thumbnails, forefingers, middle fingers, ring fingers, little fingers, and their respective fingernails were all distinguished, and a separate price, called a *hot*, was set for each. Similar distinctions were made among ears whose hearing was destroyed, ears cut off, ears pierced, and ears lacerated; among bones laid bare, bones damaged, bones broken, skulls broken, shoulders disabled, chins broken, collar bones broken, arms broken, thighs broken, and ribs broken; and among bruises outside the clothing, bruises under the clothing, and bruises which did not show black.[21]

One characteristic of wergeld penalties was their inequality. The compensation paid for different injuries varied depending on the social status of the harmed individual. Thus the murder of a freeman would be compensated at many times the rate of a servant or a slave.

Germanic tribal law was not different in essence from the law of any other tribal society, from the Nuer to contemporary wantoks in Papua New Guinea. If someone injures you or your kinsman, your clan needs to retaliate to defend the group's honor and credibility. Both injuries and retribution are collective: it is usually sufficient to retaliate not against the perpetrator of an injury but against a close kinsman. The wergeld exists as a means of settling disputes before they escalate into prolonged feuds or tribal vendettas.

Modern-day courts had their distant origins in the interclan assemblies used to mediate blood feuds. Among the Anglo-Saxon tribes, these were the moots. The moots heard testimony from the accuser and the accused, and deliberated on the appropriate form of compensation. They did not, however, have modern powers of subpoena to force witnesses to testify. Nor could their decisions be enforced except by mutual agreement of the parties. Legal proof was often based on ordeals, such as forcing defendants to walk barefoot over glowing coals or plowshares, or dunking them in cold or hot water to see whether they rose or sank.[22]

As Friedrich Nietzsche was to later observe, the introduction of Christianity was to have profound implications for morality after it was introduced among the Germanic tribes. Christian heroes were peaceful saints and martyrs, not warriors or vengeful conquerors, and the religion preached a doctrine of universal equality that ran counter to the hierarchy of an honor-based tribal society. Not only did new Christian rules on marriage and inheritance disrupt tribal solidarity, they also created the notion of universal community based on common faith rather than kin loyalties. The concept of kingship changed from the leader of a group claiming descent from a common ancestor to the leader and protector of a much broader Christian community. This shift, however, was very gradual.

The fact that tribalism broke down in Christian society did not mean that patrimonialism was dead, however. As in the Eastern church, priests and bishops in this period were allowed to marry and have children. They practiced a form of priestly concubinage known as nicolaism. With the growing properties of the church acquired through donation, it was inevitable that church leaders would seek to hand down their ecclesiastical benefices to their children and get drawn into local clan and tribal politics. With so much material wealth at stake, church offices became valuable properties that could be bought or sold under a practice known as simony.

The conversion of Germanic pagans to Christianity, like the conversion of infidels to Islam in Arab or Turkish tribal society, poses an interesting challenge for Hayek's theory of spontaneous order. A glance through Hayek's index shows not a single reference to religion, and yet religion is clearly a critical source of legal rules in Jewish, Christian, Hindu, and Muslim societies. The introduction of Christianity into Europe produced the first major discontinuity in the evolution of law as it emerged from tribal custom. The shift in marriage and property rules to allow female ownership was not a spontaneous experiment by some local judge or community but an innovation dictated by the hierarchy of a powerful institution, the Catholic church. The church did not simply reflect local values, which were quite different; neither the Eastern church nor Muslim religious authorities sought to change the existing kinship rules of their societies in a similar fashion. The church itself understood that it was not simply ratifying customary law: as Pope Urban II said to the count of Flanders in 1092, "Dost thou claim to have done hitherto only what is in conformity with the ancient custom of the land? Thou shouldst know, notwithstanding, thy Creator hath said: My name is Truth. He hath not said: My name is Custom."[23]

The second major discontinuity in the development of English law was the introduction of the Common Law itself. The Common Law did not emerge as some kind of spontaneous evolution of customary law. It was intimately associated with the rise of the early English state and dependent on state power for its eventual dominance. In fact, promulgation of a uniform Common Law across the whole of the English realm was the major vehicle for the expansion of state power in the period following the Norman Conquest. The great legal scholars Frederic Maitland and Frederick Pollock describe the origins of the Common Law:

> The custom of the king's court is the custom of England, and becomes the Common Law. As to local customs, the king's justices will in general phrases express their respect for them. We see no signs of any consciously conceived desire to root them out. None the less, if they are not being destroyed, their further growth is checked. Especially in all matters of procedure, the king's court, which is now obtaining a thorough control over all other courts, is apt to treat its own as the only just rules.[24]

This process cannot be understood without appreciating the role of early European kings. Kings in the eleventh century were not territorial rulers but still something more like first among equals in a decentralized feudal order. Monarchs like William I or Henry I spent most of their lives on the road, moving from one part of their realm to the other, since this was the only way they could assert their authority and maintain communications in a world that had retreated into an isolated village- and manor-level society. One of the major services the king could provide was to act as a court of appeals in cases where subjects were not satisfied with the justice provided by the local seigneurial or manor courts. The king for his part had an interest in expanding the jurisdiction of his courts, since he was paid fees for their services. But appeal to royal courts also increased the prestige of the king, who could undermine the authority of a local lord by overturning one of his judicial opinions.[25]

There was in the beginning competition among the various types of courts for judicial business, but over time the king's courts came to predominate. These were preferable to local courts for a number of reasons. The itinerant royal courts were seen as more impartial because they had fewer ties than the seigneurial courts to local litigants, and they also had certain procedural advantages, like their ability to compel citizens to serve on juries.[26] Over time they also benefited from economies of scale and scope. The administration of justice required manpower, expertise, and education. The first national bureaucracies were recruited by royal courts that had started to compile customary rules and to establish a system of precedents, for which writing was obviously a necessary precondition. With each passing decade, there was an increasing number of legal specialists trained in precedent, who were then appointed as judges across the realm.

The Common Law is called common because it is not particularistic. That is, the myriad customary rules that governed the different regions of England were replaced by a single Common Law, in which a precedent in one part of the realm was applicable to the rest of the kingdom (the principle of stare decisis). Law was applied by a network of judges, who worked within a unified legal system that was far more systematic and formal than the patchwork of customary rules that prevailed earlier. It is true that the Common Law built on precedents set by customary law, but the rise of state power created a whole new set of situations where customary rules were not adequate. For example, offenses that were previously compensated by the perpetrator's kin group through a wergeld payment were now criminally prosecuted by a higher third party, either the local manor lord or the king himself. The king's courts also came to serve as the venues for the recording of noncontentious issues like property registrations and land transfers.[27]

Thus the Common Law represented a discontinuity in English legal development. While it drew on earlier precedents, it would never have become the law of the land without the Norman Conquest, which displaced the older Danish and Anglo-Saxon nobility and established a single, increasingly powerful source of centralized authority. The later evolution of the Common Law may have been a spontaneous process, but its existence as a framework for legal decision making required centralized political power to bring it into being.[28]

The historian Joseph Strayer argues that in the medieval period, early states were built around legal and financial systems rather than around military organizations, even though the requirements of military mobilization drove state building in the later early modern period. Indeed, legal institutions in some sense preceded even financial ones, since the royal courts were one of the king's most important sources of revenue. It was the king's ability to administer equal justice—as opposed to the differential schedule of wergelds dependent on the social status of the victim of an offense under customary law—that increased his prestige and authority.[29] As in the Middle Eastern tradition of monarchy, the king was not necessarily seen as the biggest and most predatory warlord. He also was protector of the rights of those who might be victimized by the predation of local lords, and a dispenser of justice.

This legal function of the central state was to prove extremely important for the subsequent development of property rights in England and thereby the legitimacy of the English state itself. Seigneurial courts had exclusive jurisdiction over the dealings of local lords with their free and unfree tenants up through approximately the year 1400, which was a bit like having the fox guard the chicken coop when it came to disputes over property. Gradually, however, the royal courts asserted authority over these issues. In the early thirteenth century, the argument was put forth that the king exercised jurisdiction over all temporal matters in the realm, and that lesser courts were granted jurisdiction only by delegation. Plaintiffs preferred to have their cases taken to the royal courts, and over time the seigneurial courts lost their jurisdiction over land tenure disputes to them.[30] This market-driven preference suggests that the royal courts must have been perceived as being fairer and less biased in favor of the local lords, and better able to enforce their decisions.

A similar shift did not occur in other European countries. In France, in particular, seigneurial courts retained their jurisdiction over land tenure issues right up to the French Revolution. This is ironic, in a sense, since it was seventeenth-century French kings such as Louis XIII and Louis XIV who were perceived, in contrast to their English counterparts, as having emasculated the nobility in their assertion of absolute power. But the one power that was left to the provincial nobility was jurisdiction over local courts. Sir Henry Maine, in his essay "France and England," points out that after the outbreak of the revolution, chateaux were burned all over France, and the first object of the fires was the muniment room, in which property titles were stored. In contrast to the English peasantry, the French peasantry felt that the land titles held by the landlords were illegitimate because of the fundamental bias of the courts, which were controlled by local lords.[31]

This latter example illustrates an important point about the nature of the rule of law. The rule of law rests on the law itself and on the visible institutions that administer it—judges, lawyers, courts, and the like. It also rests on the formal procedures by which those institutions operate. But the proper functioning of a rule of law is as much a normative as an insti-

tutional or a procedural matter. The vast majority of people in any peaceful society obey the law not so much because they are making a rational
calculation about costs and benefits, and fear punishment. They obey because they believe that the law is fundamentally fair, and they are morally
habituated to follow it. They are much less inclined to obey the law if they
believe that it is unjust.[32]

Even a law perceived as fair will be regarded as unfair if it is unevenly
applied, if the rich and powerful are seen as exempting themselves from it.
This then would seem to put the burden back on institutions and procedures, and their ability to administer justice evenhandedly. But there is still
an important normative dimension at play here. For how can a mere institution constrain the rich and powerful if they don't at some level believe in
the need for self-constraint, or at least in the need to constrain others like
themselves? If the judges and prosecutors and police can be bought off or
intimidated, as happens in many countries where rule of law is weak, what
difference does the existence of the formal institution make?

Religion was essential to the establishment of a normative legal order
that was accepted by kings as well as by ordinary people. Pollock and
Maitland write that the king was not above the law: "The theory that in
every state there must be some man or definite body of men above the law,
some 'sovereign' without duties and without rights, would have been rejected . . . Nobody supposed that the king even with the consent of the
English prelates and barons could alter the Common Law of the catholic
church."[33] The king was constrained by the fact that his subjects would
rebel against any actions they regarded as unjust. But what they regarded
as unjust, and what would mobilize resistance against the king, were in
turn dependent on perceptions of whether the latter was acting within or
outside the law.[34]

But a fair normative order also requires power. If the king was unwilling to enforce the law against the country's elites, or lacked the capacity to
do so, the law's legitimacy would be compromised no matter what its
source in religion, tradition, or custom. This is a point that Hayek and his
libertarian followers fail to see: the Common Law may be the work of
dispersed judges, but it would not have come into being in the first place,
or been enforced, without a strong centralized state.

England made an early and impressive transition from a customary to
a modern legal system, which constituted the basis for the legitimacy of

the English state itself. Other European countries made a similar transition in the thirteenth century but based on a completely different legal system, the civil law derived from the Justinian Code. The key to this transition on the Continent was the behavior of the Catholic church. That story, and how the church differed from religious institutions in India and the Muslim world, are the subject of the following chapter.

18

THE CHURCH BECOMES A STATE

How the Catholic church was critical to the establishment of the rule of law in Europe; the investiture conflict and its consequences; how the church itself acquired statelike characteristics; the emergence of a domain of secular rule; how contemporary rule of law is rooted in these developments

The rule of law in its deepest sense means that there is a social consensus within a society that its laws are just and that they preexist and should constrain the behavior of whoever happens to be the ruler at a given time. The ruler is not sovereign; the law is sovereign, and the ruler gains legitimacy only insofar as he derives his just powers from the law.

Before our more secular modern age, the most obvious source of just laws outside the political order was religion. But religiously based laws constrained rulers only if religious authority was constituted independently of political authority. If religious authorities were poorly organized, if the state controlled their property and the hiring and firing of priests, then religious law was more likely to bolster political authority than to limit it. So to understand the development of the rule of law, one must look not to just the source and nature of religious rules themselves but also the specific ways religious authority is organized and institutionalized.

The rule of law in Europe was rooted in Christianity. Long before there were European states, there was a Christian pontiff in Rome who could establish authoritative laws of the church. European rules regarding marriage and the inheritance of property were dictated not initially by a monarch but by individuals like Pope Gregory I, who passed clear instructions to his delegate Augustine, sent to convert the pagan king Ethelbert of Britain to Christianity.

Especially since the rise of radical Islamism in the late twentieth century, a lot has been made of the fact that church and state are separated in the West but fused in Muslim countries like Saudi Arabia. This distinction does not withstand scrutiny. The Western separation of church and state has not been a constant since the advent of Christianity but rather something much more episodic.

Christianity began as a millenarian sect that was heavily persecuted first by Jewish and then by the Roman political authorities during the first three centuries of its existence. But with the conversion of Constantine to Christianity in A.D. 313, Christianity changed from a heterodox sect to the state religion of the Roman Empire. As the western part of the Roman Empire was conquered by pagan barbarians, religion and political authority were once again separated. The weakness of political authority in the West gave the Catholic church greater opportunities to assert its independence, as in the doctrine of Pope Gelasius (492–496), who argued that prelates had legislative authority that was higher than kingly executive power.[1] But with the recovery of political power at the end of the Dark Ages, they were fused a second time.

Caesaropapism denotes a system in which religious authority is completely subordinated to the state, as was the case when the Christian church became the state religion of Rome. The title pontifex maximus, now given to popes, was taken by Roman emperors in their capacity as heads of the Roman state religion. China was always caesaropapist (with the possible exception of the Tang Dynasty, when Buddhism became popular among the elite), as was most of the Muslim world outside of the areas where Shiism prevailed. The Eastern Roman Empire in Byzantium, progenitor of modern Orthodox Christianity, was the polity for which the term "caesaropapist" was invented, and it never ceased being such up through the conquest of Constantinople by the Turks in 1453. What is not so commonly recognized is that most of the world of western Christianity had also become effectively caesaropapist by the early eleventh century.

The practical meaning of caesaropapism is that political authorities have the power of appointment over ecclesiastical ones, and this was the case throughout Europe during the early medieval period. The emperor, and the various kings and feudal lords throughout Europe, appointed bishops of the church. They also had the power to call church councils and could promulgate church law. Although popes invested emperors, emperors also made and unmade popes. Of the twenty-five popes who held office immediately before 1059, twenty-one were appointed by emperors and five dismissed by them. Kings throughout Europe had veto power over the ability of church authorities to impose penalties on civil authorities.[2]

It is true that the church owned from a quarter to a third of all land in most European countries, which provided it with a lucrative source of income and autonomy. But since the political authorities controlled appointments to ecclesiastical benefices, the effective independence of the church was limited. Church lands were frequently regarded as just another source of royal patronage. Rulers often appointed their kinsmen to bishoprics, and since bishops and priests could marry, they were frequently drawn into the family and court politics of the jurisdictions where they lived. Church lands could become heritable property to be passed down to the children of bishops. Church officials also served in a host of political offices, increasing the connection between religious and political authority.[3] The church itself was hence a premodern, patrimonial organization.

THE CATHOLIC CHURCH DECLARES INDEPENDENCE

The Catholic church's declaration of independence from political authority came in the late eleventh century, led by a monk named Hildebrand who later became Pope Gregory VII from 1073 to 1085.[4] Hildebrand's group within the papal party, which included Peter Damiani, Cardinal Humbert, and Pope Paschal II, argued that popes should exercise legal supremacy over all Christians, including all political authorities, and that the pope had the right to depose the emperor. He asserted that the church, and not lay authorities, was the only institution that could appoint bishops. This came against the background of the machinations of the Holy Roman Emperor Henry III, who upon his arrival in Rome for his coronation had three rival popes deposed in favor of a candidate of his own choosing.[5]

But in Hildebrand's view, the church could not become independent of political authority unless it reformed itself, and the most important reform was to restrict the ability of priests and bishops to marry and have children. He attacked the common practices of simony and nicolaism, by which church offices were bought and sold, and could be turned into heritable property.[6] Hildebrand's party unleashed a pamphlet war urging Christians not to take sacraments from married priests or priests living in concubinage, and attacked the practice of taking money in return for ecclesiastical appointments.[7] As Gregory VII, he made celibacy of the priesthood official church doctrine and forced already married priests to choose between their duties to the church and their duties to their families. This challenged the entrenched practices of the priesthood and led to an enormous and often violent struggle within the church itself. Pope Gregory's goal was to end corruption and rent seeking within the church by attacking the very source of patrimonialism, the ability of bishops and priests to have children. He was driven by the same logic that led the Chinese and Byzantines to rely on eunuchs, or the Ottomans to capture military slaves and tear them from their families: if given the choice between loyalty to the state and to one's family, most people are driven biologically to the latter. The most direct way to reduce corruption was therefore to forbid officials to have families in the first place.

This reform was naturally opposed by the existing bishops, and Pope Gregory understood that he could not win this battle unless he and not the emperor had the right to appoint them. In a papal manifesto in 1075, he withdrew from the king the right of deposing bishops and of lay investiture. Holy Roman Emperor Henry IV responded by attempting to oust Gregory from the Apostolic See with the words "Descend, descend, thou ever accursed," to which Gregory responded in turn by excommunicating the emperor.[8] Many of the German princes, as well as a number of bishops, supported the pope and forced Henry in 1077 to come to Gregory's residence at Canossa. He waited for three days to present himself barefoot in the snow to receive the pope's absolution.

Certain historical events are catalyzed by individuals and cannot be explained without reference to their particular moral qualities. The investiture conflict was one such moment. Gregory had a titanic and inflexible will, and was once addressed by one of his associates in the papal party as "my holy Satan." Like Martin Luther four centuries later, he had a grand vision for a reformed church and its role in society. He could not be intimidated and was willing to see the conflict with the emperor escalate into outright war.

But this historic conflict cannot be explained simply as a matter of individual will. A critical background condition facilitating the emergence of the Catholic church as an autonomous political actor was the general political weakness throughout Europe. The Eastern church in Byzantium, and its Russian Orthodox successor, had no choice but to remain under the tutelage of the empires in whose seat they were headquartered. The

Western church, by contrast, was situated in the politically fragmented Italian peninsula. The closest states were the equally fragmented German ones to the north, whose unity under the Holy Roman Empire was no more than nominal. France was scarcely more unified in the eleventh century and incapable, at this juncture, of intervening decisively in papal politics. So while the church did not possess military forces of its own in this period, it could easily play off the rivalries of the surrounding polities.

Although Henry accepted the authority of the pope at Canossa, he did not concede the pope's right to appoint bishops and continued to reject Gregory's demands. Henry went on to occupy Rome, deposing Gregory and making his own candidate, Clement III, an antipope. Gregory called on the Norman kings of southern Italy for help; they availed him, but at the cost of sacking Rome and turning its population against them. Gregory was forced to retreat with his Norman allies to the south, where he died in Salerno in 1085, a defeated man. The conflict over the right of investiture continued for more than another generation, with Gregory's successors excommunicating Henry IV again, as well as his son Henry V, and the emperor deposing popes and setting up imperial candidates as antipopes. The matter was finally settled in 1122 by the Concordat of Worms, in which the emperor largely gave up the right of investiture, while the church recognized the emperor's authority in a range of temporal matters.

The investiture controversy was hugely important to subsequent European development in several respects. In the first place, it allowed the Catholic church to evolve into a modern, hierarchical, bureaucratic, and law-governed institution that, as the legal historian Harold Berman has argued, became the model for later secular state builders. One of Samuel Huntington's criteria for institutional development is autonomy, and no organization can be autonomous if it does not have control over the appointment of its own officials. This is why the controversy over investiture was so central. After the Concordat of Worms, the pope through the church hierarchy became, for the time being, its undisputed chief executive officer, who with the advice of the College of Cardinals could hire and fire bishops as he pleased.

The church cleaned up its own act. The celibacy of the priesthood removed the temptations of the patrimonial awarding of lucrative benefices to kinsmen and descendants, and set a new moral tone with regard to the sale of church offices. The church could also collect its own taxes in the form of the tithe, and with the disentangling of the priesthood from local clan politics it was better able to dispose of its own fiscal resources. The church took on many of the characteristics of a true state, marshaling at times its own military forces and claiming direct jurisdiction over a defined (if small) territory.

The church's involvement in temporal affairs did not end, of course, with the investiture conflict. Secular rulers continued to try to manipulate the papacy and establish their own candidates, like the Avignon popes of the fourteenth century. Over time new abuses arose that would eventually pave the way for the Protestant Reformation. But the Catholic church had become far more highly institutionalized in terms of its adaptability, complexity, autonomy, and coherence than the religious establishments of any of the other world religions.

The second important consequence of the investiture conflict was to clearly separate the domains of the spiritual and temporal, and thus to pave the way for the modern secular state. This separation, as noted earlier, was only latently present in Christianity. The Concordat of Worms conclusively ended the caesaropapist period in the history of the Western church, in a manner that never occurred in either the Eastern church or the Muslim lands.

The Gregorian reform sought to reduce the authority of political rulers by claiming universal authority over all matters spiritual and temporal, including the right to depose kings and emperors. The Christian pope was claiming, in effect, same authority that Brahmins in India exercised from the beginning. In practice, however, the church at the end of a long political and military struggle was forced to compromise. By carving out a clearly defined spiritual domain over which the church was to exercise unquestioned control, it conceded the right of temporal rulers to exercise power in their own separate sphere. This division of labor established the grounds for the subsequent rise of the secular state.[9]

Finally, the investiture conflict had great consequences for the development of both law and the rule of law in Europe. The first came about through the church's efforts to legitimate itself by formulating a systematic canon law, the second through the creation of a separate, well-institutionalized domain of spiritual authority.

THE REAPPEARANCE OF ROMAN LAW

In their conflict with the emperor, Gregory and his successors did not have armies of their own to deploy and sought instead to bolster their power through appeals to legitimacy. The papal party initiated a search for sources of law to bolster its case for the universal jurisdiction of the church. One of the consequences of this search was the rediscovery of the Justinian Code, the *Corpus Iuris Civilis*, in a library in northern Italy at the end of the eleventh century.[10] To this day, the Justinian Code remains the basis for the civil law tradition that is practiced throughout continental Europe and in other countries colonized by or influenced by countries there, from Argentina to Japan. Many basic legal concepts, like the distinction between civil and criminal law, and between public and private law, have their origins in it.

The Justinian Code was a highly sophisticated compilation of Roman law produced in Constantinople under the emperor Justinian at the beginning of the sixth century.[11] The newly recovered text consisted of four parts: the Digest, the Institutes, the Code, and the Novella, of which the Digest was by far the most important, covering issues like personal status, torts, unjust enrichment, contracts, and remedies. The Digest was a compilation of what Justinian's jurists believed were the most valuable legacies of the whole earlier body of Roman law (now lost) and became the subject of study for the new generation of European jurists who emerged in the twelfth century.[12]

The revival of Roman law was possible because legal studies had been established on a new institutional basis, in the emerging modern university. At the end of the eleventh century, the University of Bologna became a center where thousands of students flocked from all over Europe to hear professors like Irnerius lecture on the Digest.[13] The new legal curriculum exposed Europeans to a sophisticated legal system that they could readily use as a model for law in their own societies. Knowledge of the Code was thus carried to the remotest corners of the continent, and law faculties were established in other cities such as Paris, Oxford, Heidelberg, Cracow, and Copenhagen.[14] The recovery of Roman law had the effect, like English Common Law, of suddenly displacing the mass of particularistic Germanic customary law that prevailed through much of Europe and replacing it with a more consistent transnational body of rules.[15]

The first generation of expositors of the Justinian Code was known as the glossators, who saw their job primarily as one of reconstructing and reproducing Roman law. But subsequent generations of scholars, such as Thomas Aquinas, looked even farther back, to the ancient Greeks in their search for the intellectual foundations of law. Classical philosophers such as Aristotle argued that custom and received opinion needed to be subjected to human reason and measured against more universal standards of truth. Aquinas applied this principle to his own study of Aristotle, and the philosophical tradition he founded encouraged later generations of commentators on the law not to mechanically reproduce an existing body of law but instead to reason about the sources of law and how it was to be applied to novel situations.[16] The classical tradition that was revived in European universities was not simply one of appeal to the authority of certain static texts but also of rational inquiry into the meaning of those texts.

The new university produced a separate class of lawyers trained to interpret classical texts and master a special domain of knowledge. Both ecclesiastical and lay authorities came to understand that they needed to defer to the lawyers' specialized knowledge in making decisions, particularly in the commercial sphere, where contract and property rights were of paramount importance. The lawyers in turn developed their own institutional interests in protecting their domain from incursions by nonspecialists and self-interested political parties.

Prior to the Gregorian reform, church law consisted of a diverse range of decrees of church councils and synods, writings of church fathers, papal decrees, and decrees of kings and emperors speaking on behalf of the church. It was mixed up with remnants of Roman law and with customary Germanic law.[17] With the establishment of a unified hierarchy within the church, it was for the first time possible for the church to legislate authoritatively and bring unity to this body of law through the activities of an increasingly professionalized group of ecclesiastical legal specialists. The monk Gratian, trained in the legal curriculum, analyzed thousands of canons issued over the past centuries; he reconciled and synthesized them into a single body of canon law. This was published in 1140 in a massive legal treatise of some fourteen hundred pages, the *Concordance of Discordant Canons*, or the *Decretum*. Gratian established a hierarchy among divine, natural, positive, and customary law, and established rational procedures by which contradictions among them could be resolved. In the century following Gratian, canon law expanded enormously to cover a wide range of other topics including criminal, family, property, contract, and testamentary law.[18]

The Catholic church acquired statelike attributes through its concept of a single canon law. But it also became more statelike by developing a bureaucracy by which it could administer its affairs. Legal scholars have argued that the first model of the modern bureaucratic "office" as defined by Weber was created within the new, twelfth-century church hierarchy.[19] Among the hallmarks of the modern office are a separation between the office and the officeholder; the office is not private property; the officeholder is a salaried official subject to the discipline of the hierarchy within which he is embedded; offices are defined functionally; and officeholding is based on technical competence. All of these were, as we have seen, characteristic of Chinese bureaucracy from the time of the state of Qin, though many offices were repatrimonialized during later dynasties. They were also increasingly characteristic of the church bureaucracy after its liberation from lay investiture and the imposition of celibacy on the priesthood. The church, for example, began to distinguish between *officium* and *beneficium*—office and benefice—in the early twelfth century. No longer would officeholders necessarily receive feudal benefices; they could now simply be salaried employees of the church, who could be hired and fired based on their performance in their office. These bureaucrats began to staff new offices like the Papal Chancery that soon became the model for the chanceries of secular rulers.[20]

LAW AND THE RISE OF THE MODERN STATE

The political order in Europe at the time of the Gregorian reform saw the beginnings of a reversal of the extreme decentralization of power that had taken place after the breakup of the Carolingian Empire in the ninth century. Power had leached out to a series of regional leaders and then was further divided when local lords started building impregnable castles at the end of the tenth century. The manor—a largely self-sufficient productive and military unit centered around the lord's castle and lands—became the source of governance throughout Europe. On top of this system there began to appear a number of royal houses like that of the Capetians around the Île de France or the various Norman barons who conquered England

and southern Italy, whose domains were larger than those of their rivals and who formed the core of a new territorial state system.

The Gregorian reform not only provided territorial states with a model of bureaucracy and law but also encouraged them to develop their own institutions. Secular rulers were responsible for securing peace and order in their realms, and providing the rules that facilitated the emerging levels of commerce. This led to the formulation of not just one but several distinct domains of law, related to feudalism, the manor, the city, and long-distance trade. Harold Berman argues that this plurality of legal forms promoted the development of liberty in Europe by motivating competition and innovation between jurisdictions. Particularly important was the rise of independent cities, whose free populations and dependence on external trade stimulated new demands for commercial law.[21]

The church's move toward institutional independence stimulated the corporate organization of the other sectors of feudal society as well. In the eleventh century, the bishops Gérard de Cambrai and Aldabéron de Laon formulated a doctrine that society should be organized into three hierarchical orders: the aristocracy, the ecclesiastics, and the commons—those who fought, those who prayed, and those who worked to support those who fought and prayed. This functional rather than territorial organization provided an ideological basis for the formation of each of these groups into representative estates, which rulers called together periodically to grant taxes and deliberate on issues of importance to the realm as a whole. As will be seen in later chapters, it was the ability of these estates to stand up to centralizing monarchs that determined whether particular European countries developed either accountable or absolutist governments.[22]

One of the peculiar features of European state building was its heavy early dependence on law as both the motive and the process by which state institutions grew. Specialists have grown accustomed to thinking that war and violence were the great drivers of European political development. This certainly became true in the early modern period, when the rise of absolutism was built around the fiscal requirements of military mobilization. But in the medieval period, states gained legitimacy and authority by their ability to dispense justice, and their early institutions crystallized around the administration of justice.

Nowhere was this more true than in England. In the early twenty-first century, we are used to thinking of England and its offshoot the United

States as the home of Anglo-Saxon laissez-faire economic liberalism, and France as the birthplace of dirigiste centralized government. Up through the fourteenth century, however, exactly the opposite was true. Of all European polities, the English state was by far the most centralized and powerful. This state grew out of the king's court and its ability to offer justice across the whole realm. Already by the year 1200 it boasted permanent institutions staffed by professional or semiprofessional officials; it issued a rule saying that no case concerning the possession of land could be initiated without a writ from the king's court; and it was able to tax the entire realm.[23] Evidence of the central state's power lay in the Domesday Book, compiled shortly after the Norman Conquest, in which residents of every single shire in the realm were surveyed.[24]

There was also already an incipient sense of English national identity. When the barons confronted King John at Runnymede in 1215 and imposed on him the Magna Carta, they did so not as individual warlords seeking to exempt themselves from general rules. They expected a unified national government to better protect their rights through the king's courts, and in this respect saw themselves as representatives of a larger community.[25] France, by contrast, was a much less unified realm at the time. There were major linguistic and cultural differences among its various regions, and the king could not raise taxes beyond his own small domain around the Île de France.

HOW THE MEDIEVAL CHURCH SET PRECEDENTS FOR CONTEMPORARY RULE OF LAW

The emergence of the Catholic church as a modern bureaucracy and its promulgation of a coherent canon law in the twelfth century still leaves us very far from contemporary rule of law. In developed countries with a strong rule of law, the law that gives legitimacy to political rule is usually a written constitution. This higher law is not derived from religious authority, and many constitutions in fact mandate political neutrality with regard to the substantive moral issues to which religion speaks. The legitimacy of modern constitutions comes rather out of some kind of democratic ratification procedure. That higher law may be seen as rooted in timeless or universal principles, as Abraham Lincoln argued the U.S. Constitution was,[26] and most modern constitutions leave somewhat ambiguous the ultimate source of their legitimacy.[27] But as a practical matter, the interpretation of those principles is always subject to political contestation. In the end, the power of democratically legitimated executives and legislatures is checked by a constitutional law that is also democratically legitimated, albeit with more stringent requirements for social consensus through some form of supermajority voting. (In a more recent development, governments can also be checked by supranational legal bodies like the European Court of Human Rights or the International Criminal Court, whose basis of legitimacy is much murkier than those of national-level courts.[28]) In some liberal democracies including Israel and India, religious courts still exercise jurisdiction over certain issues like family law. But these are seen as exceptions to a general rule that excludes religious authority from participation in the legal system.

So why does it make sense to say that law based on religion created the foundations for modern rule of law?

The existence of a separate religious authority accustomed rulers to the idea that they were not the ultimate source of the law. The assertion of Frederic Maitland that no English king ever believed that he was above the law could not be said of any Chinese emperor, who recognized no law other than those he himself made. In this respect Christian princes were like Indian rajas and Kshatriyas, and Arab and Turkish sultans, who would agree that they were below the law.

In every society with religiously based law, political rulers legislated and tried to encroach on the domain of religious law. In many cases, this encroachment was necessary since there were many areas of life where religious law did not provide adequate rules. But the more dangerous encroachments were ones of principle. The great political struggles of early modern Europe (to be detailed in subsequent chapters) concerned the rise of monarchs who asserted novel doctrines of sovereignty that placed themselves rather than God at the top of the hierarchy. These kings, like Chinese emperors, asserted that they alone could make law through their positive enactments, and that they were not bound by prior law, custom, or religion. The story of the rise of modern rule of law concerns the success of resistance to these claims and a reassertion of the primacy of law. This resistance was obviously made much easier when a religious tradition gave law a sanctity, autonomy, and coherence that it otherwise might not have had.

The discontinuity between medieval and modern rule of law is more apparent than real, moreover, if one understands law as an embodiment of a broad social consensus regarding rules of justice. This is what Hayek meant when he said that law was prior to legislation. In a religious age like the twelfth century, or in the contemporaneous Muslim or Indian worlds, social consensus was expressed religiously because religion played a far greater role in people's daily lives than it does today. Religious laws were not something dropped on societies from outer space. Even when they were initially imposed through violence and conquest, they coevolved with their societies and were taken up by them as indigenous moral codes.[29] There was no separation between the religious and secular realms, and therefore no way to articulate social consensus other than in religious terms. Today, in an age when religion plays a much more restricted role, it is inevitable that social consensus has to be determined in other ways, such as by voting in democratic elections. But law remains an expression of broadly shared rules of justice regardless of whether it is expressed in religious or in secular terms.

The religious law that emerged from the twelfth century on had an important effect on modern rule of law by helping to institutionalize and rationalize the law. For rule of law to exist, it is not sufficient to establish a theoretical principle that political rulers are subject to law. Unless that law is embodied in visible institutions that exist with some degree of autonomy from the state, it is much less likely to inhibit the state's discretion. Moreover, if the law is not a coherent and clearly stated body of rules, it cannot be used to limit executive authority. The idea of a constitutional separation of powers has to be based on the reality of a legal system that has strong influence over its own recruitment and promotion, sets its own professional standards, trains its own lawyers and judges, and is granted genuine power to interpret the law without interference from political authority. Even though the English king was responsible for creating a common law based on the final authority of the royal courts, he also delegated a huge amount of authority to judges and permitted the growth of a strong legal profession that was not exclusively dependent on the state for its employment and income. In continental Europe, the Justinian civil law tradition meant that the interpretation of law remained more centralized, but there was a parallel development of an autonomous legal profession—in fact, multiple legal professions for the multiple forms of law that appeared. In either case, Western law was rationalized to a greater degree than either Indian or Sunni Muslim law. Neither of these traditions saw the emergence of someone like Gratian, who would take the whole body of religious edicts and make them internally consistent.

The legal tradition that emerged in Western Europe was distinctly different from the one that existed in the lands under the influence of the Eastern church. It was not Christianity per se, but the specific institutional form that Western Christianity took, that determined its impact on later political development. In the Eastern Orthodox church, bishops continued to be appointed by the emperor or by local political rulers, and the church as a whole never declared independence from the state. While the Eastern church never lost the tradition of Roman law the way the Western church did, it also never asserted the same kind of primacy over the Byzantine emperor.

The emergence of a rule of law is the second of three components of political development that together constitute modern politics. As in the transition out of tribal or kinship-based social organization, the dating of this shift in Europe needs to be pushed back to a point well before the beginning of the early modern period—in the case of rule of law, to at least the twelfth century. This underlines one of the central themes of this book, namely, that the different components of modernization were not all part of a single package that somehow arrived with the Reformation, Enlightenment, and Industrial Revolution. While modern commercial law codes were driven by the requirements of independent cities and burgeoning trade, the rule of law in the first instance was the product not of economic forces but of religious ones. Thus two of the basic institutions that became crucial to economic modernization—individual freedom of choice with regard to social and property relationships, and political rule limited by transparent and predictable law—were created by a premodern institution, the medieval church. Only later would these institutions prove useful in the economic sphere.

19

THE STATE BECOMES A CHURCH

How the rule of law developed in India and the Middle East but not in China; how authority was effectively split between secular and religious authorities in the Middle East; how premodern Middle Eastern regimes observed property rights; why the Muslim ulama were never able to check state power in the manner of the Christian church; why no rule of law exists in the contemporary Arab world; the modern rules of law compared

In China, religion didn't reflect social and cultural consensus, but tended rather to be a source of social protest. This was true from Daoism in the Han and Buddhism in the Tang Dynasty, to the Christian-influenced Taipings in the nineteenth century, to Falun Gong today. The Chinese state has never recognized a source of religious authority higher than itself and has easily controlled whatever priesthoods existed.

There was thus no historical grounding for a religiously based rule of law in China. In a tradition anchored by Legalism, the Chinese thought of their law primarily as positive law. The law was whatever the emperor decreed. Major legal codes were published during the Qin, Han, Sui, Tang, and Ming dynasties, many of which were simply lists of punishments for various infractions. The Tang Code, issued in several different versions in the seventh and eighth centuries, contains no reference to a divine source for the law; rather, it makes clear that laws are made by earthly rulers to control persons whose misbehavior would upset the balance of nature and society.[1]

Things were totally different in India, where the Brahmanic religion that developed contemporaneously with or slightly before the period of Indian state formation subordinated the political/warrior class—the Kshatriyas—to the priestly class, the Brahmins. Indian religion was built around the fourfold hierarchy of varnas that put priests at the top, and all Indian rulers had to turn to the Brahmins for legitimacy and social sanction. Law was therefore deeply rooted in religion rather than in politics; the earliest law tracts, the Dharmasastras, were not edicts of emperors as in China but documents written by religious authorities.[2] Subsequent Indian law developed a bit like English Common Law, based not strictly on these legal texts but on case law and linked precedents generated by panditas, or religious experts on law.[3] Not only were their rulings often enforced by Brahmins rather than by the political authorities, but they did not permit a separate secular realm of rule making. Law had many of the specific characteristics mentioned by Hayek: it was generally unalterable, or could be changed only by reference to an even more ancient precedent from which the current law was said to be a degeneration.[4] As a conservative Hindu was reported to have said in response to the postindependence Indian parliament's effort to modify the marriage and divorce laws, "The authority of Parliament cannot override the dictates of the Shastras, God's Spoken Words, written down for our benefit by all-seeing Rishis. No Hindu can accept any other authority than that of the Shastras."[5]

The Brahmin class was not organized, however, into a single hierarchy that could give orders to kings and emperors. There was no Hindu pope and no Hindu church. The Brahmin class represented more of a network whose members communicated with one another horizontally across the myriad villages and cities where they lived. But the Brahmins were themselves riven by class distinctions defined by the jatis into which they were divided. A Brahmin who presided over royal investitures might not be willing to consort with one who presided over funeral rites. Religious authorities therefore exercised tremendous influence at a local level, where their services were needed for virtually every social event. They were never subordinated to the state or made into state employees. But they also were incapable of collective action through an institutional hierarchy. The jati-induced fragmentation of authority affected not just political power but religious power as well.

RULE OF LAW IN THE MIDDLE EAST

In addition to India and Europe, the other world civilization in which a rule of law came into being was the Islamic Middle East. Many people today inside and outside the region are aware that many regimes, particularly in the Arab world, are cruel dictatorships unconstrained by any sense of higher law or justice.[6] Westerners often think that the fusion of church and state is intrinsic to Islam while being foreign to Christian Europe, and that the kind of theocratic regime set up in Iran after the 1979 revolution somehow constitutes a reversion to a traditional form of Muslim rule. None of this is accurate.

The emergence of modern Muslim dictatorships is a result of the accidents of the region's confrontation with the West and subsequent transition to modernity. Political and religious authority were frequently united in Christian Europe. In the Muslim world, they were effectively separated through long historical periods. Law played the same function in Muslim lands that it did in Christian ones: acting as a check—albeit weaker—on the power of political rulers to do as they pleased. Rule of law is basic to Muslim civilization, and in fact defines that civilization in many respects.

Let us begin by cataloging the similarities between the Muslim and Christian worlds with regard to the role of law in society. Law is rooted in religion in both traditions; there is only one God, who exercises universal jurisdiction and is the source of all truth and justice. Both traditions, along with Judaism, are deeply scriptural, with basic social rules being codified from a very early point. In the case of Islam, those rules are not just the Holy Koran but also the sunna and the hadith, which incorporated stories and sayings from the life of Muhammad that could serve as guidance for behavior. The interpretation of these rules, however, was in many cases uncertain and had to be delegated to a special class of priests—clergy of the church, in the case of Christianity, and to the ulama, or scholars, in the case of Islam. In both cases, law comes not from political power, as in China, but from God, who has dominion over political authorities. While Muhammad may have become a tribal ruler in his lifetime, his authority over his fellow Arabs did not rest merely on his command of force but also on his role as the transmitter of the word of God.

The first few caliphs united, like Muhammad, religious authority and political power in their own persons, a practice that continued through the Umayyad dynasty. But political and caliphal power began to part ways at the dynasty's end, when an Umayyad prince fleeing the Abbasids set up a separate western caliphate in Spain. Different provinces of the empire peeled off over time, reducing the authority of the caliph in Baghdad to the area immediately around the capital, and even there he became a puppet of the military commander who held real power.[7] The Fatimids in Tunisia and then in Egypt set up their own schismatic caliphate, and the

Baghdad caliph's authority was never recognized in the first place by the Shiites and the Kharijites. While caliphs may have claimed universal spiritual authority, their effective jurisdiction fell far short of it.

By the eleventh century, power was effectively split between the caliph and whoever was in control of political power in a particular territory. The real power holder—that is, the secular prince—assumed the title "emir of emirs." Through a legal sleight of hand, the caliph claimed to have delegated authority to him, in return for securing his own authority over more narrowly religious matters.[8] The legal scholar Abu al-Hasan al-Mawardi explained that this was legitimate because the caliph continued to exercise temporal authority through his deputy, though the truth was exactly the opposite: the caliph had become a puppet of the emir.[9] The world of Islam was effectively caesaropapist rather than theocratic: secular rulers held power and hosted on their territory a caliph and an ulama who administered the sharia.[10]

What never happened in the Sunni Muslim world was the formal extrication of the caliph and the ulama from the polities in which they were embedded into a single, separate institution with its own clear hierarchy, jurisdiction, and control over its own personnel. No one, that is, ever established a single Muslim "church" comparable to the Catholic church that emerged after the Gregorian reform. Like the Catholic church before the Investiture conflict, the Muslim clerisy was a distributed network of priests, judges, and scholarly interpreters who read and applied Muslim case law. Within the Sunni tradition, there were four major competing schools of Muslim law that were philosophically heterogeneous and whose rise and fall were dependent on political favor. Because the ulama never institutionalized itself around a hierarchy, it was not possible to generate a single legal tradition. Nor was it possible for a Muslim hierarchy to contest political power in the manner of Roman popes.

SEPARATION OF MOSQUE AND STATE

This did not mean, however, that there was *no* functional separation of religious and secular authority. In the fifteenth-century Ottoman Empire, Tursun Bey wrote that the sultan could make positive law on his own initiative, independently of the sharia. This body of secular law became known as the *kanunname* (derived from the term "canon law" used in Europe), and was used in areas where traditional Islamic jurisprudence failed to establish adequate rules, such as public and administrative law. Rules involving taxation and property rights in newly conquered territories, as well as rules regulating the issuance of currency and trade, fell under the kanunname.[11] The traditional sharia, focusing primarily on marriage, family, inheritance, and other personal matters, was applied by a network of *kadis* and *mujtahids*, jurisconsults who were learned in the Muslim classics and could apply this diffuse body of law to specific cases, much like the Hindu panditas.[12] This then required the establishment of two parallel judicial establishments, one secular and the other religious. The kadis applied the sharia but had to rely on secular authorities to enforce their judgments.[13]

In theory, the growing body of secular law used in the Ottoman Empire was subordinate to the body of sharia and reviewable by the religious authorities. But just as the caliph's theoretical authority over the sultan belied an actual relationship of dependence, so too the religious law was squeezed by the expanding requirements for regulation of a growing commercial society. The independence of the religious authorities was further restricted when the Ottoman court created the position of grand mufti. Previously, the government had appointed kadis from among the community of scholars but left determination of the content of the law up to them. The new mufti and the bureaucracy under him were authorized to issue nonbinding opinions, or fatwas, regarding the content of the sharia. Turkey moved in the opposite direction from Europe, toward increasing political control over religion.[14] If the Roman church took on attributes of a state, the Turkish state took on attributes of a church.

To what extent was a rule of law actually observed in the premodern Middle East? As noted in chapter 17, there are at least two separate meanings of the rule of law commonly in use today, the first having to do with the day-to-day observance of property rights and contract law that permits commerce and investment to take place, and the second related to the willingness of the ruler and the ruling class to observe the limits set by law. The second meaning has implications for the first, because if a society's elites do not observe the rule of law, they will be tempted to use their power to arbitrarily seize property from people weaker than them. But as also noted, it is possible for rulers to have large theoretical powers to arbitrarily violate property rights and yet respect a day-to-day rule of law in practice.

For the two Middle Eastern regimes we have looked at in depth, the Egyptian Mamluks and the Turkish Ottomans, a rule of law in the first sense existed as a default condition. That is, there were well-established rules regarding property and inheritance that permitted both long-term investment and predictable commercial transactions. Rule of law in the second sense existed as well, since both Mamluk and Ottoman sultans conceded the principle that their powers were limited by a prior law established by God. In practice, however, they had considerable latitude to interpret that law in their favor, particularly in periods of fiscal stringency where their search for revenues induced them to violate long-standing legal norms.

While full, modern property rights didn't exist in either case, it is not clear that their absence was the binding constraint on economic development in the Muslim world.[15] Most land in the Ottoman Empire was owned by the state and given out to sipahis only during their term of active military service. The peasants who worked the sipahis' land, however, did have usufructuary rights that they could pass on to their children. Other reaya, like craftsmen and merchants, had private property rights and could accumulate large fortunes if they were lucky and skillful. All traditional Middle Eastern rulers were well aware of the dangers of excessively high and burdensome taxes, which they sought to avoid in the name of "justice." In addition, they, like other monarchs, saw their role as protectors of common people from the predatory instincts of wellborn elites. Not even the sultan could simply go around the law. If the sultan's sipahis came to execute a punishment on his orders, they nonetheless needed to bring the accused into a kadi's presence and obtain a judgment against him. In cases when an individual died intestate, the property remained in the hands of an executor before it could be claimed by the state. Property of deceased non-Muslim foreigners was similarly recorded by a kadi and held until an heir appeared.[16]

One clear piece of evidence of how law limited the power of traditional Muslim governments was in the role of charitable waqfs. As we have seen, the elite military slaves who ran the regime were initially forbidden to have descendants or to accumulate property. Both the Mamluks and Turkish Janissaries got around these rules first by acquiring families, and then by establishing charitable foundations to be run by their children or other designees, and whose income would guarantee their descendants' livelihoods. Arab and Turkish rulers left many of these waqfs intact over many generations, though strict restrictions on modifying the bequest limited their economic usefulness.[17]

But if the waqf defines the limits of the state's ability to take private property, its frequent use as a shelter for assets suggests that other, less religiously protected forms of property were subject to arbitrary taxation. Even if not every state deserves to be called predatory, all states are tempted to become predatory when circumstances demand it. The fifteenth-century Circassian Mamluk regime fell into increasingly dire fiscal straits as time went on, leading their sultans to seek desperate stratagems to raise revenues. Ordinary tax rates were raised arbitrarily and fortunes seized, leading wealthy individuals to look for ever more creative ways to hide their wealth rather than investing it. Similarly, the fiscal crisis that the Ottomans faced in the second half of the sixteenth century led to increases in tax rates and threats to traditional property rights. The long-held institutional rules regarding Janissary employment and the prohibition against families were relaxed, and state timars were corruptly sold off by insiders to the highest bidder rather than being retained as rewards for military service. The Mamluks even raided the waqfs in their search for funds, just as Christian rulers constantly tried to get their hands on the rich holdings of monasteries and other church properties.

The Pope's Divisions

Joseph Stalin was said to have contemptuously asked, "How many divisions has the pope?" Since, as I have argued, the rule of law is rooted in religion, we can ask a similar question of judges and lawyers: How many divisions do they deploy in a state ruled by law? What powers of enforcement do they have to make rulers obey the laws according to their interpretations?

The answer, of course, is none. The separation of powers between an executive and a judiciary is only metaphorical. The executive has real coercive powers and can call up armies and police to enforce his (or her) will. The power of a judicial branch, or of religious authorities who are the custodians of the law, lies only in the legitimacy that they can confer on rulers and in the popular support they receive as protectors of a broad social consensus. Gregory VII could force Henry to come to Canossa, but he could not actually depose him as emperor. For this, he had to rely on military allies like the German princes who were jealous of Henry, or the Norman kings of southern Italy. The pope's ability to attract worldly allies was dependent, in turn, on their views of the legitimacy of his cause, as well as of their own calculations of short-term self-interest. The outcome of the investiture conflict was a complex mixture of both material and moral factors. In the end, a temporal ruler with access to military and economic resources was forced to compromise with a spiritual leader with some economic resources but no coercive power. The pope's authority was thus real, but it didn't rest on his divisions.

The power of the Muslim ulama was founded, like the power of the pope, on its ability to confer legitimacy on the sultan. This power was particularly great during succession struggles. In Muslim lands, both Islamic and Turkish tribal custom forbade the establishment of clear rules of dynastic succession like primogeniture. Sultans could designate heirs, but the actual succession process often turned into a free-for-all among the sultan's sons or, in the case of the Mamluks, the major factional leaders. In this situation, the power of the ulama to grant or withhold its support gave it considerable leverage. But if the intervention in the power struggle became too overt, as in the case of the caliphs during the period of the Circassian Mamluks, they could undermine their own position.

We should not, however, exaggerate the strength of the rule of law in premodern Muslim societies. The law operated in a "good enough" fashion for the protection of property rights and commerce, but it did not constitute anything like a constitutional guarantee of rights against rulers who were determined to violate them. The fact that the grand mufti and the network of kadis were all selected and employed by the state significantly lessened their autonomy, quite differently from the independent jurists employed by the Catholic church after the twelfth century. The Ottoman state remained caesaropapist to the end, and indeed increased its degree of control over the Muslim scholars as time went on.

HOW THE RULE OF LAW FAILED TO SURVIVE CONTACT WITH THE WEST IN BOTH INDIA AND ISLAM

There are many similarities between the rule of law in India and in the Middle East before they were either colonized or heavily influenced by the West. In both cases there was a traditional written law protected by religious authorities and a complex body of case law created over the centuries by religious judges—panditas in the Hindu case and kadis in the Muslim—

which was passed down as precedents. In both cases, the religious law was the ultimate source of justice; political rulers were, theoretically at least, only authorized or deputized to carry it out.

In this respect, both India and the Middle East were far closer to Christian Europe than any of these three regions was to China. Where both India and the Middle East differed from Europe was in the fact that their religious establishments did not extract themselves from the political order. There was never anything like a Brahmin pope, and while there was a Muslim caliph, after the Umayyads he was largely a captive of the dominant political ruler in the Islamic lands. Not being independent of governments, neither religious establishment could set itself up as a hierarchical, modern bureaucracy with autonomous control over cadres and promotions. And without autonomy, it was hard for the religious-legal establishment to act as a powerful check on the state. Since the religious establishment remained interpenetrated with the state, the state itself could not evolve as a separate secular institution.

The traditional rule of law did not survive modernization either in India or in the Muslim world, and that failure is particularly tragic in the latter case. In India, the presidency of the East India Company led by Warren Hastings decided in 1772 to apply the Dharmasastra to the Hindus, Islamic law to the Muslims, and some version of English "Justice, Equity, and Good Conscience" to all other cases.[18] In their application of "Hindu" law, the British simply misunderstood the role of law in Indian society. They believed that the Dharmasastra was the equivalent of European ecclesiastical law, that is, religious as opposed to secular law that was codified in written texts and uniformly applicable to all Hindus. Canon law in Europe had turned into this, as we have seen, after a long period of development, but Indian law never went through a similar evolution. It was less a textually based law than a living and evolving body of rules overseen by panditas and applied contextually in different parts of India.[19] The British rulers were hobbled by, among other things, their limited ability to read Sanskrit. The British made use of panditas as if they were scholarly experts on the Dharmasastra, but distrusted them and tried to circumvent them as more Sanskrit texts became available in English. The use of panditas was abolished altogether in 1864, replaced by British judges who sought to interpret traditional Hindu law on their own. (A parallel break in the use of sharia by Indian Muslims occurred as well.[20]) At that point, traditional Hindu law as a living tradition collapsed. It was revived under the Republic of India, but the continuity of the tradition had by then been broken.

An even more radical break occurred in the tradition of Muslim rule of law. The Ottoman government sought to do what the British had done to Indian law in a reform called the Mecelle that was compiled between 1869 and 1876. The aim was to codify the sharia and to systematize it into a single, coherent set of laws, seeking in effect to achieve what Gratian had done with canon law in 1140. In the process, they undercut the traditional social role of the ulama, since the role of judge in a strictly codified legal system is very different from and less important than that in a more amorphous system. The Ottoman constitution of 1877 reduced the sharia to one form of law among several, depriving it of its former role as the legitimating framework for political rule as a whole. The traditional class of scholars was gradually displaced by judges trained in Western law. With the rise of Kemal Ataturk and the Turkish Republic after World War I, the caliphate was abolished and the Islamic basis of the Turkish state replaced by secular nationalism.[21] The Arabs, for their part, never accepted the Mecelle as fully legitimate, and they developed an increasingly separate sense of identity as the Ottoman and Young Turk movements unfolded. After independence, they found themselves stranded between a truncated system of traditional sharia and a Western legal system brought to them by the colonial powers.

The Indian and Arab paths diverged greatly after the transition from colonialism to independence. The Indian Republic established a constitutional order in which executive authority was limited by both law and legislative elections. Postindependence Indian law has never been pretty to look at—it is a patchwork of modern and traditional forms of law, notorious for being overly procedural and slow. But it is at least law, and with the brief exception of the state of emergency declared by Indira Gandhi in the 1970s, Indian leaders have been willing to work within its constraints.

The Arab world turned out very differently. The traditional monarchs put in place by the British, French, and Italian colonial authorities in countries including Egypt, Libya, Syria, and Iraq were quickly replaced by secular nationalist military officers, who proceeded to centralize authority in powerful executives that were limited by neither legislatures nor courts. The traditional role of the ulama was abolished in all of these regimes, and was replaced with a "modernized" law that emanated solely from the executive. The only exception to this was Saudi Arabia, which had not been colonized and maintained a neofundamentalist regime whose executive authority was balanced by a Wahhabi religious establishment. Many of the executive-dominated Arab regimes turned into oppressive dictatorships that failed to produce either economic growth or personal freedom for their people.

The legal scholar Noah Feldman argues that the rise of Islamism in the early twenty-first century and the widespread demand for a return to the sharia throughout the Arab world reflect a grave dissatisfaction with the lawless authoritarianism of contemporary regimes in the region and a nostalgia for a time when executive power was limited by a genuine respect for law. He maintains that the demand for sharia should be seen not simply as a reactionary turning back of the clock to medieval Islam, but rather as a desire for a more balanced regime in which political power would be willing to live within predictable rules. The repeated demand for "justice," incorporated into the names of many Islamist parties, reflects not so much a demand for social equality as a demand for equal treatment under the law. Powerful, modern states that are not offset by rule of law or accountability simply succeed in being more perfect tyrannies.[22]

Whether modern Islamists can achieve a democratic regime limited by a rule of law is a delicate question. The experience of the Islamic Republic of Iran after the 1979 revolution is not encouraging. Since the nineteenth century, Shia Iran has had a better-organized clerical hierarchy than anything existing in the Sunni world. This hierarchy, led by Ayatollah Khomeini, took control of the Iranian state and turned it into a genuine theocracy in which the clerical hierarchy controlled the state apparatus. That state developed into a clerical dictatorship that routinely jailed and killed opponents and has been willing to bend the law to suit its purposes as it went along.

In theory, the Iranian Republic's 1979 constitution could be the basis for a moderate, democratic, law-governed state. It permits legislative and presidential elections, limited by decisions of an unelected supreme leader and a Guardian Council composed of senior clerics who are the human representatives of God. In itself, this type of arrangement is not necessarily "medieval" or premodern. The constitution of Wilhelmine Germany that Max Weber took to be the quintessence of a modern, rational state had an elected legislature with powers that were limited by an unelected kaiser. If the supreme leader or Guardian Council simply saw their role as a supercharged traditional ulama with Supreme Court–like powers to periodically declare un-Islamic laws passed by a democratically elected Majlis, it could make a more plausible claim to be an updated form of Islamic rule of law. The 1979 constitution, however, grants the supreme leader not just judicial powers but substantial executive ones as well. He has control over the Islamic Revolutionary Guard Corps and the paramilitary Basij; he is able to intervene actively to disqualify candidates running for elective office and, evidently, to manipulate elections to produce favorable outcomes.[23] Like the Bismarck constitution, or the constitution of Meiji Japan that was modeled on it, the Iranian constitution carves out a reserved sphere of executive powers, given not to an emperor but to the clerical hierarchy. As in Japan and Germany, these executive powers are corrupting and have led to increasing control of the clerisy by the armed forces rather than the reverse relationship specified in the constitution.

State building concentrates political power, while rule of law limits it. For that reason alone the development of a rule of law will be politically contested and driven by the political interests of particular actors like the early English kings or an ambitious pope, or by opposition Islamist groups demanding the return of sharia. The foundations for European rule of law were established in the twelfth century, yet its eventual consolidation depended on the outcome of several more centuries of political struggle. The story of the rule of law in later years begins to merge with the story of the rise of accountable government, since the proponents of accountable government initially demanded not democratic elections but an executive that would abide by the law. This story will be taken up again in chapter 27.

WHY THE RULE OF LAW WAS STRONGER IN WESTERN EUROPE

Rule of law existed in medieval Europe, the Middle East, and India well before any of these regions made a transition to modernity. Rulers in all of these societies acknowledged that they lived under a law that they themselves did not create. And yet, the degree to which this would impose real restrictions on their behavior depended not just on this theoretical acknowledgment but also on the institutional conditions surrounding the formulation and enforcement of law. The law would become a more binding constraint on rulers under certain specific conditions: if it was codified into an authoritative text; if the content of the law was determined by specialists in law rather than political authorities; and finally if the law was protected by an institutional order separate from the political hierarchy, with its own resources and power of appointment.

Rule of law was institutionalized to a greater degree in Western Europe than in the Middle East or India. This was probably less a function of the underlying religious ideas than of historically contingent circumstances of European development, since the Eastern Orthodox church never went through a comparable development. A critical factor was the extreme fragmentation of power in Europe, which gave the church tremendous leverage. It led to an unusual situation in which rule of law became embedded in European society even before the advent not just of democracy and accountable government but also the modern state-building process itself. This is evident in all the dimensions of institutionalized law.

Codification

In contrast to India, where the Vedas were transmitted orally and written down only at a relatively late point, the three monotheistic religions of Judaism, Christianity, and Islam were all based from a very early point on authoritative Scriptures. The latter were all "people of the Book." But only in Western Europe was the confusing welter of written texts, decrees, interpretations, and commentaries systematized with a view toward making them logically consistent. There was no equivalent of the Justinian Code or Gratian's *Decretals* in the Muslim, Hindu, or Eastern Orthodox traditions.

Legal specialization

Christianity does not differ essentially from the other traditions in this respect, since all of them created a cadre of legal specialists to interpret and administer the law. However, the degree to which legal education was developed in a sophisticated university system and formalized was probably greater in Western Europe than elsewhere.

Institutional autonomy

By Huntington's categories, autonomy is a hallmark of institutional development, and here law in the West became far more developed than its counterparts elsewhere. No other part of the world experienced the equivalent of the Gregorian Reform and the investiture conflict, in which the entire hierarchy of the church engaged in a prolonged political conflict with the temporal ruler and ended up stalemating the latter. The resulting settlement, the Concordat of Worms, ensured autonomy for the church as an institution and gave it considerable incentive to develop its own bureaucracy and formal rules.

Thus, in premodern times, the rule of law became a far more powerful check on the power of temporal rulers in Western Europe than was the case in the Middle East, India, or in the Eastern Orthodox church. This had significant implications for the later development of free institutions there.

In Europe, the rule of law survived, even as the basis of its legitimacy changed during the transition to modernity. This was the result of an internal, organic process, as the Reformation undermined the authority of the church and the secular ideas of the Enlightenment eroded belief in religion as such. New theories of sovereignty, based on the authority of king, nation, or people, began to replace the sovereignty of God as the basis for legal legitimacy. As many observers have pointed out, in the West the rule of law predated modern democracy by many centuries, and so it was possible to have a Rechtsstaat (state of law) eighteenth-century Prussia that checked executive authority well before the principle of popular sovereignty was admitted. But by the late nineteenth century, the democratic idea had gained legitimacy, and law increasingly came to be seen as the positive enactment of a democratic community. The habits engendered by the rule of law had by this time become deeply embedded in Western society. The idea that civilized life was coterminous with law, the existence of a large and autonomous legal establishment, and the needs of a burgeoning capitalist economy all served to strengthen rule of law even as its basis of legitimacy changed.

I have repeatedly stressed that the one great world civilization where the rule of law did not exist was China. Chinese emperors certainly were capable of acts of tyranny, like the first Qin emperor, who created a unified Chinese state on the basis of harsh Legalist punishments. And yet dynastic China was not renowned for the harshness of its rule. The Chinese state observed certain clear limits with respect to property rights, taxation, and the degree to which it was willing to intervene to reshape traditional social practices. If these limitations did not come from law, what was their origin? China's governance as a mature agrarian society is the subject of the following two chapters.

20

ORIENTAL DESPOTISM

How a modern state was reconsolidated in China after the Tang Dynasty; the usurpation of the empress Wu and what it tells us about the Chinese political system; what the Mandate of Heaven was and how political legitimacy was established in dynastic China

With the possible brief exception of the late-twentieth-century Republic of China (since 1949 moved to Taiwan), no Chinese government has accepted a true rule of law. While the People's Republic of China has a written constitution, it is the Chinese Communist Party that is sovereign over the constitution. Similarly, in dynastic China, no emperor ever acknowledged the primacy of any legal source of authority; law was only the positive law that he himself made. There were, in other words, no judicial checks on the power of the emperor, which allowed enormous scope for tyranny.

All of this raises at least four basic questions about the nature of the Chinese political system. The first concerns the implications of the lack of a rule of law for politics. There is a long tradition in the West of categorizing China as an "Oriental despotism." Is this line of thinking a matter of ignorance, hubris, and Eurocentrism? Or did Chinese emperors exercise greater powers than their counterparts in Western Europe?

Second, what was the source of legitimacy in the Chinese system? The history of China was characterized by innumerable revolts, usurpations, civil wars, and attempts to establish new dynasties. And yet the Chinese always returned to an equilibrium wherein they delegated huge authority to their sovereign. On what grounds were they willing to do this?

The third question is why, despite the periodic despotism of Chinese emperors, did Chinese rulers often not use their theoretical power to its

full extent? In the absence of law, there were practical checks on their authority, and long periods of Chinese history when emperors presided over
a stable, rule-bound polity without infringing terribly much on the everyday rights and interests of their subjects. Indeed, there were many times
when emperors were weak and clearly failed to enforce rules on a recalcitrant society. What, then, furnished the real limits of state power in traditional China?

And finally, what broader lessons does Chinese history teach us about
the nature of good governance? The Chinese invented the modern state,
but they could not prevent that state from being repatrimonialized. The
subsequent centuries of imperial Chinese history constituted a continual
struggle to maintain these institutions against decay, to prevent powerful
individuals from patrimonializing power by carving out privileges for themselves and their families. What were the forces promoting political decay,
and its reversal?

I will try to answer the first two of these questions in the present chapter, and the second two in the following chapter. But first, a brief overview
of Chinese history from the Tang to the Ming dynasties is necessary.

CHINA'S MODERNITY AFTER THE TANG-SONG TRANSITION

When I last discussed China in chapter 9, we had followed its development up through its reunification under the Sui and Tang dynasties following a three-hundred-year period of political decay from the third to
the sixth century. I noted that the modern state institutions put in place in
Qin and Han China had undergone considerable breakdown, which led to
the repatrimonialization of government. The successor states to the Later
Han Dynasty were largely ruled by aristocratic families that placed their
kinsmen in key offices and competed to capture larger shares of power.
Yang Jian and Li Yuan, founders of the Sui and Tang dynasties that reunified China, came out of this class. The former was from a leading aristocratic family of the state of Northern Zhou, while the latter was the duke
of Tang, descended from the noble Li clan in northwestern China.[1] Like
most of the Han successor states, the Sui and early Tang dynasties were
dominated by noble families who staffed the bureaucracy, commanded
the army, and held power at a local level. This elite consisted of northern
military aristocrats whose families had intermarried extensively with Xian-

bei and other barbarian lineages. While an examination system was rein-stituted in 605, it was perfunctory and a poor avenue for nonelite recruit-ment into the bureaucracy.[2]

The Tang Dynasty lasted almost three hundred years but in its later years proved highly unstable. (See Table 2 for a listing of the dynasties.) The aristocratic elites succeeded in killing off many of their fellows, begin-ning with the rise of the "evil" empress Wu in the mid-seventh century. In the middle of the eighth century, a Soghdian-Turkish military commander on the empire's northeast frontier named An Lushan launched a rebellion, during which the Tang emperor and the heir apparent had to flee their capital of Chang'an in different directions in the dead of night. The rebel-lion was eventually put down eight years later, but the civil war, occurring as it did in the heart of the empire, led to enormous population losses and economic decline. The empire never recovered; power leached out to a series of military commanders on the periphery who could act with in-creasing autonomy. The Chinese political system had always exercised strong civilian control over the military, but in this period it began to re-semble the Roman Empire, where powerful generals in provincial com-mands looked to use them as power bases from which to launch political

Table 2. Later Chinese Dynasties

YEAR	DYNASTY	FOUNDER/TEMPLE NAME
618	Tang	Li Yuan/Gaozu
907	Later Liang	Zhu Wen
923	Later Tang	Li Keyong
936	Later Jin	Shi Jingtang
947	Later Han	Liu Zhiyuan
951	Later Zhou	Guo Wei
960	Northern Song	Zhao Kuangyin/Taizu
1127	Southern Song	Zhao Gou/Gaozong
1272	Yuan	Kublai Khan
1368	Ming	Zhu Yuangzhang/Taizu
1644	Qing	

careers. The Tang Dynasty finally collapsed amid revolts and civil war in the first decade of the tenth century, whereupon a series of five short-lived dynasties led by military men took power in the north, and ten separate kingdoms came and went in the south.

Despite a nearly fifty-year interruption, however, the legitimacy of a centralized state had become so widely accepted by the end of the Tang that one of those military commanders, Zhao Kuangyin, was able to re-unify the country in 960 as the emperor Taizu, founder of the great Song Dynasty. In many ways the Song was the most intellectually fertile of them all. While Buddhism and Daoism had made great inroads among both the Chinese people and elites during the Sui and Tang dynasties, Confucian-ism saw a huge revival at their expense during the Northern Song. Neo-Confucianism was a powerful intellectual movement that spread to the neighboring countries of Korea and Japan and greatly influenced intellec-tual life throughout East Asia.[3]

At the same time, China began to experience a new series of invasions by tribal peoples that succeeded in conquering large parts of its territory, and finally the country as a whole.[4] This began with the Khitan, a Turco-Mongol group from the Mongolian border region that set up the enormous Liao Empire to China's north and conquered sixteen key northern prefec-tures with ethnic Han Chinese populations. To the west of the Liao Empire, the Tanguts established the Xi Xia state, which included border regions that had been under Chinese control during earlier dynasties. Next to emerge were the Rurzhen (ancestors of the Manchus), a tribal people coming out of Manchuria who destroyed the Liao Empire and pushed the Khitan back into Central Asi. (They were pushed so far west that they eventually bumped into the Russians, who thereafter referred to all Chinese as "Ki-taiskiy.") In 1127, the Rurzhen sacked the Song capital of Kaifeng, took prisoner both the recently abdicated emperor and his son, and forced the entire Song court to move to southern China, inaugurating the Southern Song Dynasty. The Rurzhen state of Jin at its peak controlled roughly one-third of China, until it was in turn smashed in 1234 by another no-madic invader, the Mongols.[5] After taking northern China, the Mongols under Kublai Khan invaded from the southwest, and this time occupied the entire country. In 1279, the Mongols chased the Southern Song court down to Yaishan, an island in the far southeast, where thousands of court-iers committed suicide by jumping off of a cliff into the sea when finally surrounded by Mongol forces.[6] Kublai Khan became the first emperor of the new Yuan Dynasty until these foreign rulers were finally driven out in a nationalist uprising and replaced by a new indigenous Chinese dynasty, the Ming, in 1368.

While the prolonged period of military competition during the Spring and Autumn and Warring States periods initiated an intense round of state building, foreign invasion during the Song Dynasty did not have remotely comparable effects on the Chinese political order. Despite the intellectual brilliance of the neo-Confucian school that arose during the Northern Song Dynasty, this was a rather dispiriting time when internal factional struggles within the Chinese court prevented the regime from preparing adequately to meet the clear and present danger arising on its borders. The reasons for this complacency lay in the fact that the source of military pressure was pastoral nomads at decidedly lower levels of social development than China itself. At this point in human history, political development did not necessarily confer on state-level societies decisive military advantages over tribal-level peoples organized as light cavalry. In the particular geography of China, the Middle East, and Europe, bordering as they did on the vast steppes of Central Asia, this led to the repeated cycle of decadence, barbarian conquest, and civilized renewal noted by the Arab philosopher Ibn Khaldun. The Khitans, Tanguts, Rurzhen, and Mongols all eventually adopted Chinese institutions once they conquered Chinese territory; not one left behind a significant political legacy. It would take conquest by far more developed "barbarians" from Europe to stimulate the Chinese political system into more fundamental reform.

One of the broadest political developments to occur in China between the founding of the Sui in 581 and the later years of the Song Dynasty in the twelfth century was the reversal of patrimonial government and the restoration of centralized power operating through something that looked like the classical bureaucracy of the Former Han Dynasty. By the end of this period, Chinese government was no longer dominated by a small circle of aristocratic families but was rather ruled by a gentry elite recruited from a much broader swath of society. The integrity of the bureaucracy as the guardian of Confucian values had been restored, laying the basis for the impressive governmental system of the Ming Dynasty in the fourteenth century. China's population had also increased enormously over this period, growing to fifty-nine million in 1000 and then to one hundred million by the year 1300.[7] China's land area also expanded to something far closer to its present-day extent with the settlement of large frontier areas in the south. Commerce and communications across the whole of this huge region increased substantially through the building of canals and roads. And yet, despite the size of the polity, China developed a centralized political structure that set rules and extracted taxes from across this complex society. No European state was to come close to governing so large a territory for more than another half millennium.

The idea that China had established (or reestablished) a far more modern political system not after its contact with the West in the seventeenth-eighteenth centuries but during the Tang–Song transition, was first put forward by the Japanese journalist-scholar Naito Torajiro after World War I.[8] Naito argued that rule by aristocrats was swept away during the turbulent period after 750 when the Tang Dynasty experienced a number of internal rebellions and wars that empowered a series of military strongmen of nonnoble background. After the Song Dynasty came to power in 960, the emperor's position was no longer threatened by noble families, and a much purer form of centralized despotism resulted. The examination system became a more open method of recruitment into the elite, and the position of commoners was improved by the ending of their serflike obligations to aristocratic landlords. A common mode of life was established throughout China, one less dependent on inherited privilege; the highly formal writing of the Tang period was replaced with a vernacular literature and easily accessible popular novels and histories. Naito drew explicit parallels to the early modern period in European history when feudal privileges were ended and equality of citizenship was introduced under the aegis of a strong absolutist state.[9] While much about the Naito hypothesis has been debated (particularly his effort to fit East Asian history into a Western periodization), many of his broad conclusions have been accepted by more recent scholars.[10]

We can now turn to the four questions about China's political order posed at the beginning of the chapter, starting with the issue of despotism, and whether it was more severe in China than in other civilizations.

THE EVIL EMPRESS WU

The story of Wu Zhao (624–705), known to later Chinese memorialists as the "evil empress Wu," is compelling enough to deserve retelling quite apart from what it teaches us about the nature of Chinese politics. Empress

Wu was the only woman to rule China in her own name and to establish her own dynasty. Her rise and fall is a chronicle of intrigue, brutality, terror, sex, mysticism, and female empowerment. She was an extraordinarily gifted politician who gained power through sheer will and cunning, an achievement all the more striking given the resolutely antifemale nature of Confucian ideology.[11]

In the earlier discussion of the rule of law, I noted that it often applies initially to elites rather than to the broad mass of the population, who are not considered fully human beings subject to the law's protection. Where the rule of law does not exist, on the other hand, it is frequently the case that it is at times more dangerous to be a member of the elite than to be an ordinary person, given the high stakes and intense competition for power at the top. This was the situation that played out under the reign of Empress Wu, who unleashed a wide-ranging terror against China's old aristocratic families.

A number of historians, particularly Marxist ones, have seen great social implications in the ascent of Empress Wu. Some have argued that she represented a rising bourgeois class; others, that she was a champion of the masses; still others, that she played an important role in pushing aside the patrimonial elites of the Sui and early Tang Dynasty period, replacing them with nonaristocratic officials. It is not clear that any of these theories is ultimately correct: she herself had an impeccable aristocratic lineage, being related to the royal Yang family of the Sui Dynasty. Far from promoting able commoners, she canceled the examinations for several years so she could pack the bureaucracy with her own favorites. To the extent that she contributed to the broader Tang–Song transition, it was because her purges of real and suspected aristocratic opponents decimated their numbers and weakened that class as a whole, paving the way for a rebellion by An Lushan that marked the beginning of the end of the Tang Dynasty and set in train enormous social transformations of Chinese society.

Wu Zhao got her start, like many other women in the Chinese court, as a lowly concubine of the second Tang emperor, Taizong. Her father had been a supporter and later high official of the first Tang emperor, Gaozu, and her mother as noted was descended from the Sui royal family. She was rumored to have had an affair with Taizong's son Gaozong even before his father died. On her husband's death, she shaved her head and entered a Buddhist nunnery, but the new emperor Gaozong's senior consort, the empress Wang, wanted to distract him from another concubine and deliberately brought her to court as a rival.

This proved to be a deadly mistake. Emperor Gaozong was infatuated with Wu Zhao, and in the course of his long reign proved to be weak and easily manipulated by her. Wu Zhao had a daughter with the emperor, whom she arranged to have smothered after the childless Empress Wang had visited the child in the palace. The empress was accused of murdering Wu Zhao's daughter; Wang and a former favorite were demoted to commoner status and their families were exiled to a distant southern province. Wu Zhao then advanced to the position of senior consort. Upon becoming empress herself in 655, she had the former empress Wang and rival concubine chopped into pieces and stuffed in a wine vat. One by one, the court officials who had supported the former empress and opposed Wu Zhao's rise, including many who had loyally served former Tang emperors, found themselves exiled, or ended up dead.

While many Chinese women have exercised de facto power as regents or powers behind the throne for their sons or husbands, Empress Wu was determined to rule as a true coemperor and made increasingly public displays of her autonomous power. When the emperor accused her of witchcraft and sorcery as a means of getting out from under her domination, she confronted him and forced him to kill her accusers and purge all of their supporters from the court. She shocked the court by reviving a number of ancient ceremonials by which she honored herself as well as her husband, and moved the capital from Chang'an to Luoyang to escape ghosts of the many opponents she had murdered there. The empress had the heir apparent poisoned, then framed her own son who was next in line for the throne, on a charge of conspiracy to usurp his father, whereupon he was exiled and forced to commit suicide. When her husband finally died in 683, she had his successor (and her third son), Zhongzong, dragged from the throne and sequestered.

The empress's rise, not surprisingly, led to open rebellion in 684 on the part of a group of Tang aristocrats whose families she had degraded. The empress acted quickly to suppress the uprising and then unleashed a reign of terror against the entire noble class by setting up a network of spies and informants who were lavishly rewarded for denouncing conspiracies. Her secret police engaged in what would now be called widespread "extrajudicial killings," and when the terror had run its course, she turned on her police officials and had them executed as well. This paved the way for her declaration of a new Zhou Dynasty in 690, ruling in her name alone and not that of any male relative.

Empress Wu promoted a number of populist policies, reducing taxes and corvée labor, cutting back on lavish public expenditures, and distributing support to the aged and poor. She also promoted the writing of histories of Chinese women, raised the mourning duties owed mothers, and canonized her own mother as empress dowager. She did succeed in effecting a social revolution insofar as she killed off a large number of Tang aristocrats and Confucian scholars who had staffed the old administrative system. She replaced them, however, not with a cadre of talented commoners but with a series of favorites and sycophants, for whom she had to relax the examination and education requirements. The end of her reign was marked by mysticism, a series of lovers (often connected to her religious passions), and openly venal patronage that she did not attempt to control. Nearly eighty years old, she was finally forced from power by a conspiracy that restored her son Zhongzong and the Tang Dynasty to power.

The empress Wu's behavior was hardly typical of all Chinese rulers, and subsequent Confucian moralists inveighed against her as a particularly bad ruler. But she was neither the first nor the last Chinese sovereign to behave despotically and to unleash a massive reign of terror against the regime's own elites. Most European monarchs behaved in a more rule-bound way, even if their treatment of peasants and other commoners was often much crueler.

The empress Wu's rise also constituted a setback for the empowerment of Chinese women, since later writers took her to be an example of the bad things that happen when women get involved in politics. The Ming emperor had a metal plaque posted in his palace warning him and his successors against the intrigues of palace women. The latter had to return to the practice of manipulating their sons or husbands from behind the scenes.[12]

THE MANDATE OF HEAVEN

The empress Wu's attempt to seize the throne and create her own dynasty raises the question of how Chinese monarchs acquired legitimacy in the first place. In *Leviathan*, Thomas Hobbes argues that the sovereign derives his legitimacy from an unwritten social contract by which each individual gives up his natural liberty to do as he pleases in order to secure his own natural right to life, which would otherwise be threatened by the "warre of every man against every man." If we substitute "group" for "man," it is clear that many premodern societies operated on the basis of such a social contract, China's included. Human beings were willing to give up a huge amount of freedom and delegate a corresponding amount of discretion to an emperor who would rule them and guarantee social peace. They found this preferable to a state of war, which they had experienced repeatedly in their history, when powerful oligarchs fought each other and exploited their own people without restraint. This, then, was the meaning of the Mandate of Heaven: it was a conferral by Chinese society of legitimacy on a particular individual and his descendants to rule them with dictatorial authority.

What is perplexing about the Chinese system was not that the Mandate of Heaven existed in the first place, since a functional equivalent to it existed in all princely societies. The issue was rather procedural: How did a pretender to the throne know when he (or in the empress Wu's case, she) had the Mandate of Heaven? And once conferred, why did not other ambitious pretenders try to take it away at the first opportunity, given the enormous power and wealth that came along with being emperor?

The legitimacy of rulers in premodern societies can come from a number of sources. In hunter-gatherer and tribal societies, it usually is the result of some form of election, if not by the people as a whole, then by the leading lineages or tribal elders who hold a council and often vote on who will lead them. In feudal Europe, some form of elective procedure survived into early modern times, when bodies bearing names like the Estates-General or Cortes would be called upon to ratify the coming to power of a new dynasty. This occurred even in Russia, where a *zemskiy sobor* (assembly) of nobles was called to legitimate the transfer of power to the Romanov dynasty in 1613.

The other major source of dynastic legitimacy was religion. In Christian Europe, the Middle East, and India, there were powerful religious establishments that could confer legitimacy on a ruler, or at times take it away (as in Gregory VII's conflict with the Holy Roman Emperor). Often these religious establishments were under the heel of the political authorities and had little choice but to confirm the ruling house. But in times of leadership struggle, these religious authorities could often tilt the balance in one direction or another through their ability to confer legitimacy on one of the contenders.

China was different from all of these other civilizations insofar as the Mandate of Heaven involved neither election nor religious legitimation. There was no Chinese institutional equivalent of the Estates-General by which the elites of Chinese society could meet to formally ratify the selection of a new dynastic founder. Nor was there religious legitimation awarded by a religious hierarchy. There was no transcendental God in the Chinese system. The "heaven" in the Mandate of Heaven was not conceived of as a deity in the sense of the monotheistic religions Judaism, Christianity, and Islam, which laid down a clear set of written rules. Rather, it was more like Nature or the "grand order of things" that could be upset and required a return to equilibrium. Furthermore, there was no religious institution that could award the mandate on behalf of heaven, the way that a Christian pope or Muslim caliph could legitimate a king or sultan.[13]

A change of dynasty always poses a major problem of legitimacy, since it is very frequently the case that the new dynasty has come to power through simple usurpation or violence. The concept of the Mandate of Heaven first appeared after the Shang–Zhou transition in the twelfth century B.C., since the Zhou kings clearly usurped the throne from its legitimate holder. China subsequently experienced a huge number of changes in dynasty during its more than four millennia of history. Not only were there major dynasties like the Qin, Han, Tang, Song, and Ming, but countless other lesser ones like the Three Dynasties following the fall of the Han, and the Five Dynasties succeeding the Tang. In addition, during the periods when China fell apart into separate regional states, each was ruled by its own dynasty.

There were no social prerequisites for becoming a dynastic founder. Some, like the founders of the Sui and Tang dynasties, were aristocrats and high officials in the previous regime. But others, like Liu Bang who founded the Han Dynasty, or Zhu Yuangzhang, who founded the Ming Dynasty, were commoners. Indeed, the first Ming emperor started out his life as an orphaned son of a peasant who barely survived famine and pestilence as a child, and went on to serve as a novice in a Buddhist monastery. He became a military commander in the Red Turban uprising, a religious movement of peasants, bandits, and adventurers who fought the injustices of local authorities. From there he went on to command ever larger armies of the growing anti-Mongol movement. Late Yuan China had fallen under the control of a series of local warlords, of whom Zhu Yuangzhang was one. Like many other dynastic founders, he was in some sense the warlord who proved to be the smartest and toughest and ended up on top.

Did might then make right for the Chinese? Was the Mandate of Heaven simply an after-the-fact ratification of a power struggle between warlords? To a large extent, it was. Characteristically, there is a large Chinese literature on the subject, such as the essay of Ban Biao from the first century A.D. that explains why certain rulers deserved the Mandate and others did not. But it is very hard to extract from these writings a clear set of principles or procedures for awarding the Mandate that could not be applied afterward to any particular holder of the office who succeeded in coming to power.[14] The awarding of the title "dynasty" to the rule of a particular leader was often conferred by historians long afterward, legitimating a regime that had been regarded as highly dubious at the time. The historian Frederick Mote points out that there was very little to distinguish the usurpations of Guo Wei, founder of the little-noted Later Zhou Dynasty, and Zhao Kuangyin, who a decade later founded the mighty Song Dynasty. Both came to power as a result of betrayal and deceit; Guo Wei's dynasty folded early only because his son Guo Rong died unexpectedly at the age of thirty-eight. Had the latter lived, Zhao Kuangyin might have gone down in history as an able commander who tried to stage a treasonable putsch.[15]

But the moral distance between an emperor and a powerful warlord is still enormous. The former is a legitimate ruler whose authority is willingly obeyed; the latter is a violent usurper. The Chinese elites themselves had a sense of which leaders were qualified to hold the Mandate of Heaven and which were not, even if this could not be articulated in a precise set of procedural rules. The Confucian idea of the Rectification of Names meant that emperors had to live up to ideal types of predecessors. They had to possess something like Machiavelli's quality of *virtù* that characterized the successful prince. A would-be emperor obviously had to be a born leader, someone who could inspire others to follow his authority, and could take risks to achieve his goals. Leadership was most often exercised in the domain of military affairs, which is why so many dynastic founders got their start as military officers. But China prized military prowess to a much lesser degree than did other civilizations. The Confucians very much had in mind an ideal of an educated scholar-bureaucrat and not an uncouth warlord. A pretender who did not exhibit both deference toward Confucian values and a certain subtlety born of education would not attract the support of the various factions around the court. Mote contrasts the Ming founder Zhu Yuangzhang to another warlord-pretender against whom he successfully competed, Zhang Shicheng:

> Zhang Shicheng's liability in the eyes of potential elite advisors and political associates was that he was a smuggler and a bandit, a ruffian whose career had given little evidence that he could become more than that . . . Zhu Yuangzhang took great pleasure in a literati joke played on Zhang Shicheng by some of his early scholar-advisors. In devising elegant-sounding formal names for Zhang and his brothers, they had given Zhang the name Shicheng, not telling him that in the book of *Mencius* there is a well-known line where those two words appear in sequence. With a slight adjustment in the punctuation the line in *Mencius* can be made to read: "Shicheng is a cad." This ingenious display of contempt toward Zhang Shicheng made Zhu laugh, until he grew suspicious that his literati advisers in all likelihood had similarly ingenious ways of denigrating him.[16]

While elites in Chinese society did not vote to ratify a new dynasty, they exercised considerable behind-the-scenes influence in the power struggles between potential rulers. The Mandate of Heaven was not simply something always awarded to the most ruthless and brutal warlord, though such people did periodically come to power in China.

Many would-be dynastic founders, like the empress Wu, went through the rituals required to invest themselves with imperial authority—choosing a temple name for themselves as well as the name of the age that their dynasty was to initiate—but were then quickly deposed. The Chinese system was, however, capable of extraordinary institutionalization. Once there was a general consensus within the society that a particular individual held the Mandate of Heaven, the emperor's legitimacy was not generally challenged except under extraordinary circumstances. In this respect the Chinese political system was far more developed than that of the tribal societies surrounding it.

When an emperor received the Mandate of Heaven, his power was virtually unlimited. And yet, Chinese emperors seldom used their powers to the fullest extent possible. Tyranny was always a possibility, but often not a reality. Why that is so is the subject of the following chapter.

21

STATIONARY BANDITS

Whether all states are predatory, and whether the Chinese state in Ming times deserved to be called that; examples of arbitrary rule drawn from later periods in Chinese history; whether good government can be maintained in a state without checks on executive authority

In an influential article, the economist Mancur Olson posited a simple model of political development.[1] The world was initially ruled by "roving bandits," like the various warlords of early twentieth-century China, or the ones operating in Afghanistan and Somalia at the beginning of the twenty-first century. These bandits were purely predatory and sought to extract as many resources from the population as possible, often with very short time horizons so they could quickly move on to other victims. At a certain point one bandit would emerge stronger than all the others and come to dominate the society: "These violent entrepreneurs naturally do not call themselves bandits but, on the contrary, give themselves and their descendants exalted titles. They sometimes even claim to rule by divine right." In other words, the king, who claimed a legitimate title to rule, was simply a "stationary bandit" with motives no different from those of the roving bandits he displaced. The stationary bandit realizes, however, that he can become even richer if, instead of going for short-term plunder, he provides stability, order, and other public goods to his society, thereby making it richer and liable to higher taxes in the long run. From the standpoint of the ruled, this represents an advance on the roving bandits. But "exactly the same rational self-interest that makes a roving bandit settle down and provide government for his subjects also makes him extract the maximum possible amount from the society for himself. He will use his monopoly of coercive power to obtain the maximum take in taxes and other exactions."

Olson goes on to posit that there is a rate of tax extraction at which the stationary bandit can maximize his revenues, comparable to the monopolist's price in microeconomics. If rates are raised beyond this limit, they undermine incentives to produce, thereby causing total tax revenues to fall. Olson argues that autocratic rulers inevitably set taxes at that maximum rate, but that democratic regimes, because they have to appeal to a "median voter" who bears the brunt of taxation, tax at a lower rate than their autocratic counterparts.

Olson's view of rulers as stationary bandits who extract as much as they can from society in taxes unless somehow politically prevented from doing so is a pleasingly cynical concept of the way that government works. It very much fits with the efforts of economists to extend their model of rational, utility-maximizing behavior into the political realm and to see politics as nothing more than an extension of economics. It also accords nicely with the antistatist traditions of American political culture, which have always regarded both government and taxation with great suspicion. And it provides an elegant predictive model of both political economy and political development, one that has been greatly expanded by other social scientists in recent years.[2]

The only problem with Olson's theory is that it isn't correct. The rulers of traditional agrarian societies often failed to tax their subjects at anything close to Olson's posited maximizing rate. It is of course extremely difficult to do a retroactive estimate of what a maximal tax rate would have been for incompletely monetized societies with poor historical data on incomes and tax revenues. But we do know that premodern rulers often raised their tax rates substantially to meet specific spending needs like financing wars and lowered them again once the emergency had passed. Only at certain points did rulers push their societies toward a counterproductive breaking point, and this usually occurred in response to desperate conditions at the end of a dynasty. During normal times they must have been taxing their societies at levels well below the maximum.

There is no better illustration of the inadequacies of Olson's model than China during the Ming Dynasty, where there is a broad scholarly consensus that tax rates were set far below their theoretical maximum, and indeed far below a level that was necessary to provide the minimal public goods, particularly defense, that were needed to keep the society viable. What was true for Ming China was true for other agrarian societies as well, like the Ottoman Empire and the various monarchies in Europe, and provides the components of an alternative theory as to why these traditional regimes seldom taxed subjects at maximal rates.[3]

It was not only on matters of taxation that emperors did not use their powers to the degree theoretically possible. Despotism of Empress Wu's sort was a periodic but not a continual phenomenon. Many Chinese rulers exhibited what might charitably be labeled leniency or forbearance toward their subjects, or what a Confucian would call "benevolence." China has had a long history of tax protests, and a strong Confucian tradition maintained that high taxes represented a moral failing of the state. The *Shi Jing*, or *Book of Odes*, contains the following poem:

> *Big rat, big rat,*
> *don't eat my millet!*
> *Three years I've served you*
> *but you won't care for me.*
> *I'm going to leave you*
> *and go to that happy land,*
> *happy land, happy land*
> *where I'll find my place.*[4]

Whatever the constraints on the power of the Chinese emperor in Ming times, they were *not* based on law. As we have seen in the case of the empress Wu, Chinese rulers, unlike their European counterparts, did not have to seek permission from sovereign courts or parliaments in order to raise taxes. Not only could they arbitrarily set tax rates through simple executive order, they could also confiscate property at will. Unlike the "absolutist" monarchs of early modern France and Spain who had to proceed very gingerly when confronting powerful elites (see chapters 23 and 24), the first Ming emperor, Taizu, simply confiscated the lands of the largest landowners in the realm. He was said to have liquidated "countless" affluent households, particularly in the Yangtze delta, where he believed he faced particularly strong opposition.[5]

The real constraints on Chinese power were different, and were of three basic sorts. The first was a simple lack of incentives to create the administrative capacity to carry out orders and in particular to extract a high level of taxes. China was already a huge country at the beginning of the Ming Dynasty, with a population of more than 60 million in 1368 that grew to 138 million by the seventeenth century.[6] The challenges of collecting taxes over so vast a territory were daunting. In the fourteenth century there was very little money in circulation, so the basic agricultural tax that was supposedly leveled on every inhabitant of China was collected in kind.[7] In-kind payments were usually made in grain, but they could take the form of silk, cotton, timber, or other goods. There was no consolidated monetary system for recording these payments or converting them into a common unit of measure. Many payments were consumed (that is, "budgeted") locally; others had to be physically shipped to granaries at successively higher levels of administration and ultimately to the capital (first at Nanjing, and later in Beijing). Taxpayers were charged the costs of shipping their taxes to the government, a surcharge that often exceeded the value of the underlying goods. There were no clear distinctions between local and central revenues and budgeting. One scholar has compared the system to an old-fashioned telephone switchboard, in which wires would come out of different holes and into others in a system of confusing spaghetti-bowl-like complexity.[8] The ministry of revenue was so understaffed that it was unable to control or even understand this system. The cadastral surveys that were supposed to be the basis of the land tax were incompletely performed early on in the dynasty, and not updated, so that with subsequent population growth, changes in ownership, or even physical geography (flooding or the reclaiming of land), the basic population registers soon became hopelessly out of date. The Chinese, like other peoples, were extremely good at hiding assets from the tax collector and engaging in schemes to in effect launder income.[9]

The draconian powers of taxation and confiscation held by the emperor also tended to be a wasting commodity. It could be used early on in a dynasty when the emperor was consolidating power and settling scores with former opponents. But as time went on, the palace found it often needed the cooperation of those same elites and dramatically reduced tax rates in the areas it had earlier confiscated property.

Lack of administrative capacity limited tax revenues not only on the supply side; there were also limitations to the amounts of revenues demanded by different emperors. Olson's assumption that any ruler would want to maximize revenues reflects the common assumption of modern economics that maximization is a universal characteristic of human behavior. But this is an anachronistic projection of modern values backward onto a society that didn't necessarily share them. The first Ming emperor,

Taizu, was an austere autocrat who cut the size of the central government and avoided foreign wars; his granaries actually ran surpluses. This was not true of his successor, Chengzu (1360–1424), who launched an ambitious program of canal construction and palace building. Chengzu was also the emperor who funded the voyages of the eunuch naval commander Zheng He (1371–1435), who sailed a fleet of giant ships as far as Africa and possibly beyond. Expenditures ran at two to three times the level of the first Ming emperor. Surtaxes and labor requisitions were raised accordingly, which led to tax revolts and discontent throughout the empire. As a result, the third emperor and his successors lowered tax rates to a level closer to those of the first emperor and made other political concessions to an offended gentry class.[10] For much of the dynasty, the land tax was set at a low 5 percent of total yield, a figure significantly lower than those of other agrarian societies.[11]

Chinese monarchs, no less than rulers of other premodern societies, often exhibited what the economist Herbert Simon has labeled "satisficing" rather than maximizing behavior.[12] That is, in the absence of an urgent need for revenue, such as a war, they were often content to let sleeping dogs lie and collect only the amount of revenues required for their regular needs.[13] A truly determined emperor could decide to behave like a maximizer, and some, like Chengzu, did, but the idea that all autocratic political leaders automatically maximize is manifestly not true.

A third limitation on the power of Chinese emperors operated in domains well beyond taxation and fiscal policy, which was the need for delegation. All large organizations, whether governments or private corporations, have to delegate authority, and when they do, the "leader" sitting at the top of the administrative hierarchy loses an important degree of control over the organization. The delegation can be to functional specialists like budgeting officers or military logisticians, or it can be regional, to a cadre of provincial, prefectural, municipal, and local authorities. These delegations are necessary because no ruler can ever have enough time or knowledge to make all of the important decisions in his realm.

But with the delegation of authority goes power. The agents to whom power has been delegated have authority over the delegator in the form of knowledge. This can be either the technical knowledge that goes with the running of a specialized ministry or agency or the local knowledge of particular conditions existing in a certain region. It is for this reason that organizational specialists like Herbert Simon have argued that authority in any large bureaucracy does not flow only from the top to the bottom, but oftentimes in a reverse direction as well.[14]

Chinese emperors experienced this problem much as modern presidents and prime ministers do, in the form of unresponsive and sometimes outright rebellious bureaucracy. Ministers objected to policies proposed by their boss, or quietly failed to implement them. Of course, Chinese rulers had certain tools that modern executives don't: they could administer vicious floggings on the bare buttocks of even their most senior ministers, or casually imprison or execute them.[15] But this kind of coercive solution to the principal-agent problem didn't solve the underlying issue of information. Bureaucrats often didn't carry out the wishes of their leader because they had better knowledge of the real conditions of the empire—and could hide their activity from him.

A large country like China had to be governed by delegation to local authorities, but then these local authorities would commit abuses, become corrupt, or even conspire against the central government. The normal administrative hierarchy was not adequate to deal with this problem, because while orders flowed downward, information did not necessarily flow back up. The most dictatorial emperor would not be able to discipline a wayward official if he didn't know an abuse was occurring.

This limitation of princely power was discussed in premodern China under the heading of the relative merits of the "feudal" versus the "prefectural" forms of administration. Feudal (*fengjian*) in this sense carries none of the complex connotations of European feudalism; it simply means that authority was decentralized, compared to the prefectural system, where local officials were agents of the center. According to the Ming scholar Gu Yanwu (1613–1682),

> The fault of feudalism was its concentration of power on the local level, while the fault of the prefectural system is its concentration of power at the top. The sage rulers of antiquity were impartial and public-minded in their treatment of all men, parceling out land to them and dividing up their domains. But now the ruler considers all the territory within the four seas to be his own prefecture, and is still unsatisfied. He suspects every person, he handles every affair that comes up, so that each day the directives and official documents pile higher than the day before. On top of this, he sets up supervisors, provincial governors and governors-general, supposing

that in this way he can keep the local officials from tyrannizing over and harming the people. He is unaware that these officials in charge are concerned only in moving with utmost caution so as to stay out of trouble until they have the good fortune to be relieved of their posts, and are quite unwilling to undertake anything of profit to the people.[16]

The typical solution that Chinese rulers devised to get around the problem of unresponsive administrative hierarchies was to superimpose on them a parallel network of spies and informants who were completely outside the formal governmental system. This explains the great role played by eunuchs. Unlike normal bureaucrats, eunuchs had direct access to the imperial household and often came to be trusted to a far greater degree than the regular administrators. The palace therefore sent them out on missions to spy on and discipline the regular hierarchy. By the end of the Ming Dynasty, there were an estimated one hundred thousand eunuchs associated with the palace.[17] From 1420 on they were organized into an Orwellian secret police organization known as the Eastern Depot, under the direction of the eunuch director of ceremonial, which became "an organ of totalitarian terrorism" in the later years of the dynasty.[18] But the emperor found he could not control the eunuchs themselves, who made their own policy, staged coups, and conspired against him despite the existence of a "Eunuch Rectification Office."[19] The political system didn't have any downward mechanisms of political accountability—that is, there were no local elections or independent media to keep officials honest. As a consequence, the emperor had to pile one centralized system of top-down control on top of another. Even so, he was not able to achieve a strong degree of control over his realm.

The Ming Dynasty's unwillingness and inability to extract the taxes it needed led ultimately to its collapse. Whereas China had been largely free of foreign threats for the first two centuries of Ming rule, the security situation began to deteriorate sharply toward the end of the sixteenth century. Japanese pirates began to raid the wealthy southeastern seaboard, and the shogun Toyotomi Hideyoshi invaded Korea in 1592. The same year a war started in Inner Mongolia, and there were uprisings by aboriginal peoples in the south. The most serious development of all was that the Manchu to the north were becoming stronger and better organized, and making incursions along the northeastern frontier.

The government's response to the crisis was completely feckless. In the face of rising expenses, it depleted its silver reserves but refused to raise taxes on the gentry class until too late. Accumulated tax delinquencies continued to rise through the first decades of the seventeenth century as the military threat became more intense. The emperor even declared a number of tax amnesties, apparently in recognition of the fact that the state had no chance of collecting back taxes. The soldiers on the frontier, who had formerly been organized into self-sufficient military colonies, could no longer support themselves but became dependent on payments from the central government that had to be delivered over long supply lines. The regime failed to organize an adequate logistics system and thus failed to pay its soldiers on time. The dynasty stumbled on until 1644, when the government in Beijing was weakened by the Han Chinese rebel Li Zicheng, and then finally fell to a Manchu army from the north working together with disgruntled remnants of the Ming army.

GOOD GOVERNMENT, BAD GOVERNMENT

The Ming Dynasty was the last fully indigenous regime to rule China until the twentieth century, in which the traditional Chinese political system developed to its greatest extent. It was characterized by institutions that in retrospect were amazingly modern and effective, and others that were unbelievably backward and dysfunctional.

In the first category was the recruitment system into the imperial bureaucracy. The examination system's roots went all the way back to the Han Dynasty, but throughout the Sui, Tang, and early Song dynasties entry into the bureaucracy tended to be controlled by a small circle of elite families. It was only during the Ming Dynasty that the examination system became the main avenue for entry into government and acquired a level of prestige and autonomy that made it a model for all subsequent exam systems.

The examination system was linked to a much broader educational establishment. There was a network of Confucian schools all over the country, to which ambitious parents could send their children. The best students were recommended by their teachers to go on to the national universities in Beijing and Nanjing, where they would prepare to take the civil service exams. (Teachers who recommended students who failed to perform well were punished, something that modern universities might consider as a means of combating grade inflation.) It was still possible for elite families to get their children placed within the system through a category known as "students by purchase." But these Chinese precursors of contemporary legacy admittees to Harvard or Yale (that is, children of wealthy alumni) seldom made it to the highest reaches of the bureaucracy, which remained heavily meritocratic.[20] The highest possible honor was to place first in the three successive levels of exams: provincial, metropolitan, and palace. Only one individual, Shang Lu, managed to achieve this in the entire history of the dynasty; he went on to reach the very top of the hierarchy as senior grand secretary in the late fifteenth century.[21]

The Chinese bureaucracy established a model that would eventually be replicated by virtually all modern bureaucracies. There was a centralized system of appointment and promotion, based on ranks from 1 at the top to 9 at the bottom (much like the General Service schedule in the American bureaucracy). Each of these ranks was divided into an upper and lower section, so one would expect a promotion from, say, rank 6a to 5b. Officials making it through the examination system were appointed to low-ranking offices in various parts of the country, always in a region different from the one in which he grew up. If relatives happened to be assigned to the same office, the junior one usually had to withdraw. After three years, a bureaucrat was rated by the head of his agency, who passed the evaluation on to the central personnel office. Lateral entry into the bureaucracy was discouraged. The officials who survived this system and were promoted to the top of the hierarchy tended to be extraordinarily well qualified.[22]

These highly qualified and well-organized bureaucrats served, however, at the whim of an autocrat who was not himself rule bound in any way and could with the stroke of a pen undermine carefully formulated policies. They were subject to capricious punishments and purges by the sovereign, and only a minority of senior bureaucrats succeeded in finishing their terms without being humiliated in one way or another. Some of the worst decisions were those made by the first Ming emperor, Taizu, who, growing suspicious of his own grand counselor, not only abolished the office but also forbade any of his successors to reestablish the office on pain of death. This meant that no succeeding Ming emperor was allowed to have the equivalent of a prime minister but instead had to deal directly with the tens of ministries and agencies that did the actual work of government. This system was barely workable for an extremely energetic and detail-oriented emperor like Taizu, and a disaster for subsequent rulers of lesser capabilities. In one ten-day period, Taizu had to respond to 1,660 different official documents dealing with 3,391 separate matters.[23] One can imagine what his successors thought about the work load he imposed on them.

Many later emperors were not up to snuff. By tradition, one of the worst was the emperor Shenzong (otherwise known as the Wanli emperor), whose long rule between 1572 and 1620 corresponded to the period of the dynasty's decline.[24] In the second half of his rule, he refused to see ministers or preside over the court. He allowed thousands of reports and memoranda to pile up in his office, unread and unanswered. Indeed, he failed to come out of his palace at all for years at a time, during which important governmental decisions simply failed to be made. He was also extremely greedy, raiding the state treasury to meet personal expenses like building a magnificent tomb. At the time of the early seventeenth-century military crisis, when state reserves were reduced to some 270,000 taels of silver, the emperor had accumulated more than two million taels in his personal account. Despite repeated requests from the minister of revenue, he refused to release more than nominal amounts of funds to the government for purposes like paying the troops.[25] His actions led directly to the growth of Manchu power, which would ultimately destroy the dynasty.

THE "BAD EMPEROR" PROBLEM

Of the three components of political development that we have been following—state building, rule of law, and accountability—the Chinese got the first right at a very early point in their history. In a sense, they invented good government. They were the first to design an administrative system that was rational, functionally organized, and based on impersonal criteria for recruitment and promotion. Perhaps because Chinese society is so familistic, Chinese state builders saw their particular task as freeing the government from patrimonial or nepotistic influences that were the source of enormous corruption.

Creating such a system in the cauldron of the Warring States period was one thing; keeping it going over the next two millennia was another. The modernity of the bureaucracy, achieved early on, fell victim to decay and repatrimonialization as the state fell apart and was appropriated by wealthy aristocratic families. Decay of the state took place over many centuries, and restoration of the bureaucracy to something like the design originally intended by its Qin and Han creators also took centuries to accomplish. By the time of the Ming Dynasty, the classical system had been perfected in many ways. It was more meritocratic and exercised control over a society that was far larger and more complex than the one that had existed in Han times.

In other respects, however, the Chinese political system was underdeveloped. It never generated a rule of law or mechanisms of political accountability. Society outside the state continued as before to be far less organized for political action than its counterparts in Europe or India. There was no landed, independent aristocracy, and no independent cities. The dispersed gentry and peasantry could passively resist the government's orders, and periodically broke out into violent uprisings that were suppressed with great savagery. But it was never able to institutionalize itself as a corporate group to demand rights from the state, as the peasantry in Scandinavia was to do. Independent religious orders had sprung up during the Sui and Tang dynasties, with the spread of Buddhism and Daoism. At different times in Chinese history, these religious orders acted to oppose the state, from the Red Turbans to the Taiping rebels. But religion continued to be a sectarian phenomenon that was viewed with suspicion by the orthodox Confucian authorities and never represented a powerful social consensus that could limit the state's power through its custodianship of law.

One of dynastic China's great legacies, then, is high-quality authoritarian government. It is no accident that virtually all of the world's successful authoritarian modernizers, including South Korea, Taiwan, Singapore, and modern China itself, are East Asian countries sharing a common Chinese cultural heritage. It is very hard to find authoritarian rulers with qualities like those of Lee Kuan Yew of Singapore or Park Chung Hee of South Korea in Africa, Latin America, or the Middle East.

But the experience of the Ming Dynasty, as well as other periods of Chinese history, raises troubling questions about the durability of good governance under conditions where there is no rule of law or accountability. Under the leadership of a strong and capable emperor, the system could be incredibly efficient and decisive. But under capricious or incompetent sovereigns, the enormous powers granted them often undermined the effectiveness of the administrative system. The empress Wu purged the bureaucracy and packed it with her own unqualified supporters; the emperor Taizu abolished the prime ministership and locked his successors into this awkward system; the emperor Shenzong ignored the bureaucracy altogether and government collapsed. The Chinese recognize this as the problem of the "bad emperor."

There was a form of accountability in the Chinese system. Emperors were trained to feel responsibility to their people, and good ones tried to be responsive to their demands and complaints. Responsible rulers were constantly chastising their own officials on behalf of the people, relying on their networks of eunuch spies to find out who was doing his job and who not. But the only kind of formal accountability in the system was upward toward the emperor. Local officials had to worry about what the palace would think about their performance, but they could not care less about what ordinary people said since there were no judicial or electoral procedures that the latter could deploy against them. For an ordinary Chinese, the only recourse when faced with a bad official was to appeal to the top and hope that the emperor might listen. Even under a good emperor, the likelihood that one could get his attention in so vast an empire was low.

In certain ways, things are not all that different in contemporary China. Instead of an emperor, there is a Chinese Communist Party sitting at the top of the government hierarchy, keeping watch over a vast and complex bureaucracy that rules well over a billion people. Like the eunuch spy network, the party hierarchy constitutes a structure parallel to that of the government, monitoring it and reporting abuses. The quality of the bureaucracy, particularly in its upper reaches, is high; the Chinese leadership has been able to guide the country through a miraculous economic transformation in the decades after 1978 that few other governments could have pulled off.

However, neither rule of law nor political accountability exists in contemporary China any more than they did in dynastic China. The vast majority of abuses that take place are not those of a tyrannical central government but rather of a dispersed hierarchy of local government officials who collude in the stealing of peasants' land, take bribes from developers, overlook environmental and safety rules, and otherwise behave as local government officials in China have behaved from time immemorial. When a disaster happens, like shoddy school construction revealed by an earthquake, or the tainting of baby formula by a poorly regulated company, Chinese citizens' only recourse is upward to the central government. Like the emperor, the central government may or may not respond: sometimes it will take stern action against the offending official, but at other times it will be too busy or distracted, or will have other priorities.

The rule of law and political accountability are desirable in their own right. Sometimes, they can get in the way of good, effective government, as when an Indian state is unable to make a decision on a major infrastructure project due to litigation and public protests, or when the U.S. Congress cannot bring itself to deal with pressing problems like entitlements due to the influence of lobbyists and interest groups.

But at other times rule of law and accountability are necessary to preserve good government. Under the right conditions, a strong authoritarian system can produce extremely effective government. Political systems need to be able to endure changing external conditions and changing leaders. The checks on state authority provided by rule of law and accountability serve to reduce the variance in governmental performance: they constrain the best governments, but they also prevent bad ones from spiraling out of control. The Chinese, by contrast, were never able to solve the problem of the bad emperor.

INSTITUTIONS AREN'T ENOUGH

There is a huge literature addressing the question of why traditional China failed to develop indigenous capitalist institutions, including Max Weber's *Religion of China* and Joseph Needham's monumental *Science and Civilisation in China*. The purpose of this volume is not to contribute to this debate, except to say that the binding constraint on capitalist development in China was probably not its lack of good institutions.

China during the Ming Dynasty had most of the institutions now regarded as critical for modern economic development. It had a strong and well-organized state that provided stability and predictability. The sale of offices and other overt forms of corruption existed but were much less prominent than in seventeenth-century France and Spain (see chapters 23 and 24).[26] Violence was under control; compared to many contemporary developing countries, China achieved an extraordinary degree of civilian authority over its military. The one area of weakness was of course the fact that the absence of a rule of law left property rights vulnerable to the government's capriciousness. But as I argued in chapter 17, rule of law in the constitutional sense is not necessary for economic growth. Although landowners were periodically expropriated, particularly at the beginning of the dynasty, the country had "good enough" property rights for many decades, as well as an extraordinarily low level of taxation in the countryside. The People's Republic of China today does not have rule of law in the constitutional sense either, nor is property completely safe, but it does have property rights good enough to support extraordinary rates of growth.[27]

Ming China, of course, pursued many economically irrational policies. It placed excessive controls on merchants and commerce generally. Its monopoly on salt production artificially raised prices and led, as in France and the Ottoman Empire, to high levels of smuggling and corruption. But policies are much less fundamental to the growth story than are institutions; policies can be changed overnight, whereas institutions are much more difficult to build.

What China did not have was the spirit of maximization that economists assume is a universal human trait. An enormous complacency pervaded Ming China in all walks of life. It was not just emperors who didn't feel it necessary to extract as much as they could in taxes; other forms of innovation and change simply didn't seem to be worth the effort. The eunuch admiral Zheng He sailed across the Indian Ocean and discovered new trade routes and civilizations. This didn't provoke curiosity, however, and the voyages were never followed up. The next emperor cut the navy's budget as an economizing move, and the Chinese Age of Discovery was over almost before it had begun. Similarly, during the Song Dynasty, an inventor named Su Sung invented the world's first mechanical clock, a huge, multistory mechanism powered by a waterwheel, but it was abandoned when the Rurzhen conquered the Song capital of Kaifeng. The parts of the clock were scattered; knowledge of how to make it, and even of its existence, was lost within a few generations.[28]

Whatever the binding constraints that prevented rapid economic growth from taking off in Ming–Qing China, they no longer exist today. The cultural constraints that earlier generations of Western observers believed to be holding China back are not factors now. In the early twentieth century, it was common to deride the Confucian ideal of the gentleman-scholar with long fingernails who refused to work at anything other than government service as an obstacle to modernization. The specific ideal of the gentleman disappeared in the twentieth century, but the cultural legacy of an emphasis on education and personal achievement lives on in a manner that has been highly beneficial to Chinese economic growth. It endures in the countless Chinese mothers around the world who save money to send their children to the best possible schools and push them to excel in standardized examinations. The self-satisfaction that led Emperor Chengu's successors to cancel long-distance voyages has been replaced by an extraordinary willingness of Chinese leaders to learn from foreign experiences and adopt them when they seem practically useful. It was Deng Xiaoping, the statesman who inaugurated China's opening to the world, who said, "It doesn't matter whether the cat is white or black as long as it catches mice." It is far likelier that cultural attitudes toward science, learning, and innovation explain why China did so poorly in the global economic race in previous centuries, and is doing so well at the present, rather than any fundamental defect in its political institutions.

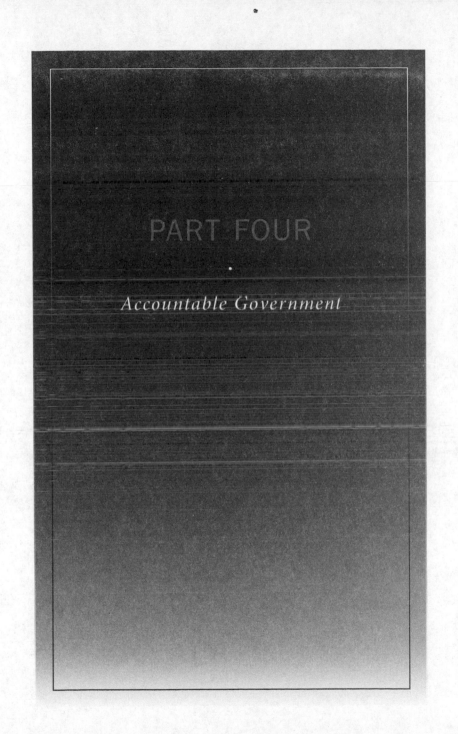

PART FOUR

Accountable Government

22

THE RISE OF POLITICAL ACCOUNTABILITY

What political accountability is; how the lateness of European state building was the source of subsequent liberty; what is wrong with "Whig history"
and how political development cannot be understood except by comparing
countries; five different European outcomes

Accountable government means that the rulers believe that they are responsible to the people they govern and put the people's interests above
their own.

Accountability can be achieved in a number of ways. It can arise from
moral education, which is the form it took in China and countries influenced by Chinese Confucianism. Princes were educated to feel a sense of
responsibility to their society and were counseled by a sophisticated bureaucracy in the art of good statecraft. Today people in the West tend to
look down on political systems whose rulers profess concern for their
people but whose power is unchecked by any procedural constraints like
rule of law or elections. But moral accountability still has a real meaning
in the way that authoritarian societies are governed, exemplified by the
contrast between the Hashemite Jordan and Ba'athist Iraq under Saddam
Hussein. Neither country was a democracy, but the latter imposed a cruel
and invasive dictatorship that served primarily the interests of the small
clique of Saddam's friends and relatives. Jordanian kings, by contrast, are
not formally accountable to their people except through a parliament with
very limited powers; nonetheless, they have been careful to attend to the
demands of the various groups that make up Jordanian society.

Formal accountability is procedural: the government agrees to submit
itself to certain mechanisms that limit its power to do as it pleases. Ultimately, these procedures (which are usually spelled out in constitutions)

allow the citizens of the society to replace the government entirely for malfeasance, incompetence, or abuse of power. Today the dominant form of procedural accountability is elections, preferably multi-party elections with universal adult suffrage. But procedural accountability is not limited to elections. In England, early demands for accountable government were made on behalf of the law, to which citizens believed the king should submit himself. The most important law was the Common Law, which was at that point heavily shaped by unelected judges, as well as statute laws passed by a parliament elected on the basis of restricted suffrage. Hence the earliest forms of political accountability were not to the people as a whole but to a traditional body of law that was seen as representing the consensus of the community, and to an oligarchic legislature. This is why I use the term "accountability" rather than "democracy" in this section.

Over time, democratization did take place. The franchise was extended and came to include broader classes of people, including men without property, women, and racial and ethnic minorities. In addition, it became clear that the law itself was no longer based on religion but needed to be democratically ratified, even if its application remained in the hands of professional judges. But in Britain, the United States, and Western Europe, the full democratization of procedural accountability did not occur until well into the twentieth century.

EUROPE'S LATE STATE BUILDING

In early modern times, European state builders embarked on the identical project as their Chinese and Turkish counterparts—to build a powerful, centralized state that would homogenize administration over their whole territory and be able to assert its sovereignty throughout. These efforts started late, beginning toward the end of the fifteenth century, and were not completed until the end of the seventeenth century. Theories of state sovereignty emerged from the pens of writers such as Hugo Grotius and Thomas Hobbes, who argued that it was not God but the king who was truly sovereign.

But European monarchs overall met far greater resistance in this project, because the other political actors in their society were better organized than those faced by the Chinese or Turks. State building proceeded, but it was often stymied by organized opposition, which forced rulers to seek allies and compromises. A landed nobility was deeply entrenched, living in physically impregnable castles with independent sources of income and their own military forces. The Chinese aristocracy never had this kind of independence, and the Ottomans, as we saw, did not allow such an aristocracy to emerge in the first place. Elements of a capitalist economy had also appeared in Western Europe by the time that the state-building project got into full swing. Large amounts of wealth were being generated by traders and early manufacturers, independent of state control. Autonomous cities had grown up, particularly in Western Europe, which lived by their own rules and deployed their own militias.

The early development of law in Europe was also very important in establishing limits to state power. Monarchs encroached on the property rights of their subjects constantly, but few rulers felt free simply to confiscate private property without legal cause. As a consequence, they did not have unlimited taxing authority and needed to borrow money from bankers to finance their wars. European aristocrats were also more secure in their persons against arbitrary arrest or execution. Apart from in Russia, European monarchs refrained from launching campaigns of outright terror and intimidation against the elites in their societies.

The very lateness of the European state-building project was the source of the political liberty that Europeans would later enjoy. For precocious state building in the absence of rule of law and accountability simply means that states can tyrannize their populations more effectively. Every advance in material well-being and technology implies, in the hands of an unchecked state, a greater ability to control society and to use it for the state's own purposes.

THE MARCH OF EQUALITY

At the beginning of *Democracy in America*, Alexis de Tocqueville talks about the "providential" fact that the idea of human equality had been gaining ground across the world for the past eight hundred years.[1] The legitimacy of aristocracy—the idea that certain people are better by birth—was no longer taken for granted. The relationship of lordship and bondage could not be upended without a change in the consciousness of the slave, and the slave's demand for recognition. There were many roots to this revolution in ideas. The notion that all human beings are equal in dignity or worth despite their evident natural and social differences is a Christian one, but it was not regarded by the medieval church as something to be implemented in the here and now. The Protestant Reformation, combined with the invention of the printing press, empowered individuals to read the Bible and find their way to faith without the interposition of intermediaries like the church. This reinforced the growing willingness of Europeans to question established authority that had started with recovery of the classics during the late medieval period and the Renaissance. Modern natural science—the ability to abstract general rules out of a mass of empirical data and to test causal theories through controlled experiments—created a new form of authority that was soon institutionalized in universities. Science and the technology it spawned could be put to use by rulers but could never be fully controlled by them.

Slaves were becoming empowered through increasing consciousness of their own worth. The political manifestation of this change was the demand for political rights, that is, the insistence on a share in common decision-making power that had once existed in tribal societies but had been lost with the rise of the state. This demand led to the mobilization of social groups like the bourgeoisie, the peasantry, and the urban "crowd" of the French Revolution, which had formerly been passive subjects of political power.

It was critical to the rise of modern accountable government that this demand was couched in universal terms—that it was based, as Thomas Jefferson would later put it in the Declaration of Independence, on the premise that "all men are created equal." Throughout all phases of prior human history, different individuals and groups had struggled for recognition. But the recognition they sought was for themselves, or their kin group, or their social class; they sought to be masters themselves and not to throw into question the entire relationship of lordship and bondage. The new universal understanding of rights meant that the political revolutions to follow would not simply replace one narrow elite group with another but would lay the grounds for the progressive enfranchisement of the entire population.

The cumulative effect of these intellectual changes was enormous. In France, there was the medieval institution of the Estates-General, which gathered representatives of the whole realm to decide questions of great national importance. When this body was called together in 1614 under the regency of Marie de Medicis, it grumbled and complained about corruption and taxes, but in the end it accepted the authority of the Crown. When it was called again in 1789 under the influence of the ideas of the Enlightenment and the Rights of Man, it provoked the French Revolution.[2]

But ideas by themselves are not sufficient to bring about stable liberal democracy in the absence of an underlying balance of political forces and interests that make it the least bad alternative for all of the actors. The miracle of modern liberal democracy, in which strong states capable of enforcing law are nonetheless checked by law and by legislatures, could arise only as a result of the fact that there was a rough *balance* of power among the different political actors within the society. If none of them was dominant, then they would need to compromise. What we understand as modern constitutional government arose as a result of this unwanted and unplanned compromise.

We have seen this dynamic unfold since the collapse of communism and the emergence of what Samuel Huntington labeled the third wave of democratization. The third wave began with the democratic transitions in Spain, Portugal, and Turkey during the 1970s, proceeded to Latin America and East Asia in the 1970s and '80s, and culminated with the collapse of communism in Eastern Europe after 1989. The idea that democracy was the most, or indeed the only, legitimate form of government spread to every corner of the world. Democratic constitutions were rewritten, or written for the first time, in Africa, Asia, Latin America, and the former Communist world. But stable liberal democracy was consolidated only in a subset of those countries undergoing democratic transitions, because the material balance of power in each society did not force the different actors to accept constitutional compromise. One or another actor—usually the one that had inherited executive authority—emerged as much more powerful than the others and expanded its domain at the expense of the others.

The Enlightenment ideas that underpinned modern democracy were broadly disseminated across Europe, all the way to Russia. Their reception, however, differed markedly from country to country depending on how different political actors saw those ideas impinging on their own interests. Understanding the emergence of accountable government requires, then, understanding the particular political forces that existed in the different parts of Europe and why some constellations of power promoted accountability while others proved no bar to the growth of absolutism.

HE WHO KNOWS ONLY ONE COUNTRY
KNOWS NO COUNTRIES

Although I have been speaking about Europe as if it were a single society to be compared to China or the Middle East, the fact is that there were multiple patterns of political development within it. The story of the emergence of modern constitutional democracy has frequently been told from the standpoint of the winners, that is, based on the experience of Britain and its colonial offshoot, the United States. In what has become known as "Whig history," the growth of liberty, prosperity, and representative government is seen as an inexorable progress of human institutions that begins with Greek democracy and Roman law, is enshrined early on in the Magna Carta, then threatened by the early Stuarts, but defended and vindicated during the English Civil War and the Glorious Revolution. These institutions then spread to the rest of the world via Britain's colonization of North America.[3]

The problem with Whig history is not that it is necessarily wrong in its fundamental conclusions. In fact, its emphasis on the role of taxation as the primary driver of accountability is broadly correct. The problem is rather that, like all single-country histories, it cannot explain why parliamentary institutions emerged in England but not in other similarly situated European countries. This kind of history often leads observers to conclude that what *did* happen *must* have happened, since they are not made aware of the complex concatenation of circumstances that led to a particular outcome.

To give one example, in 1222, seven years after Runnymede, the Hungarian king Andrew II was forced by the class of royal servants to concede the Golden Bull, a document that has been labeled an East European Magna Carta. The Golden Bull protected certain elites from arbitrary actions by the king and gave bishops and magnates the right to resist should the monarch fail to keep his promises. Yet the Golden Bull never became the foundation of Hungarian liberty. This early constitution limited the power of Hungarian kings so well that effective rule was placed in the hands of an undisciplined aristocracy. Instead of developing a political system in which strong executive power was balanced against that of cohesive legislature, the constitution that the Hungarian noble estate imposed on the monarchy prevented the emergence of a strong central executive to the point that the nation was not prepared to defend itself externally. Domestically, Hungarian peasants had no king to protect them from a rapacious oligarchy, and the country lost its freedom altogether to the Ottomans at the Battle of Mohács in 1526.

Any interpretation of the rise of accountable government thus needs to look not just at the successful cases but the unsuccessful ones as well and derive from these cases an explanation of why representative institutions appeared in one part of Europe while absolutism prevailed in other parts. Several efforts have been made to do this, beginning with the German historian Otto Hintze and continuing through the work of Charles Tilly, who sees external military pressure and capacity for tax extraction as the primary explanatory variables.[4] Perhaps the most sophisticated recent effort is the work of Thomas Ertman, who looks at a much broader range of cases than most comparative histories and provides plausible explanations for much of the observed variance.[5]

This literature falls short of being a real theory of political development, however, and it is not clear whether it will ever be possible to generate such a theory. The problem, to put it in social science terms, is that there are too many variables and not enough cases. The political outcome that the theory is trying to explain is not a simple binary choice between representative government and absolutism. As will be seen below, at least five significantly different types of state emerged in Europe whose provenance needs to be explained. The kind of absolutism that emerged in France and Spain, for example, was quite different from the variants that appeared in Prussia and Russia, and indeed, Prussia and Russia differed significantly from each other. The number of explanatory variables that can be empirically demonstrated to have played a role in producing these different outcomes is even larger, ranging from familiar ones like the external military threat and taxation capacity used by Tilly, to the structure of internal class relations, to international grain prices, to religion and ideas, and the way that they were received by broad populations and by individual rulers. The prospects of producing a predictive general theory out of this soup of causal factors and outcomes seem to be very slim indeed.

What I will attempt to do instead in the following chapters is to describe several important paths of European political development and the range of causal factors associated with each one. From this range of cases it may be possible to generalize about which factors were most and least important, but in ways that fall short of providing a genuine predictive theory.

EUROPE'S EASTERN ZHOU PERIOD

Feudal Europe in the year 1100 resembled China during the Zhou Dynasty in many ways. There was a nominal monarch or ruling dynasty, but de facto power was split among a highly decentralized number of feudal lords who maintained their own military forces, kept order, administered justice, and were largely self-sufficient economically. As in China, certain dynastic houses distinguished themselves through greater organizational ability, ruthlessness, or luck, and began to consolidate territorial states over ever wider domains.

Between the fifteenth and seventeenth centuries, a huge political transformation took place in Europe that led to the rise of strong national states, comparable to the state building that had occurred in China from the fifth to the third centuries B.C. A background condition for this change was a large increase in population, particularly during the sixteenth century, and also increases in per capita wealth. This is part of the same global phenomenon affecting the Ottoman Empire that we have already encountered, though its effects were probably more benign in Europe than in the Middle East. Europe's population rose from sixty-nine million in 1500 to eighty-nine million in 1600, an increase of almost 30 percent.[6] The monetization of its economy proceeded apace, with large imports of gold and silver from Spain's colonies in the New World. Trade began to grow much more quickly than GDP overall; between 1470 and the early nineteenth century, the size of the Western European merchant fleet grew seventeenfold.[7]

At the beginning of this period, most European polities were "domain states," in which the king derived the whole of his income from his own domain, which was but one of many in the territory he nominally ruled. Administrative staffs were small and arose out of the king's household. Actual power was diffused among subsidiary layers of feudal vassals who acted as autonomous political entities. They maintained their own armies, taxed their own subjects, and administered justice locally. They owed service to their lord, who might be the king if they were powerful barons, or might be a baron or some lesser lord for lower-ranking vassals. They paid this obligation in blood, either by fighting themselves or with their retainers, rather than in taxes, and indeed, most nobles were exempt from taxation for this reason. The king's domain could be a discontinuous collection of territories scattered across a wide area, and his kingdom a patchwork of subsidiary domains in which the lands of a lord owing service to a rival king could be interspersed.

By the end of this period, much of the European political order had been transformed into a system of states. The domain state had been transformed into a tax state, in which the monarchy's revenues were derived not just from the king's domain but also from his ability to tax the whole of his territory. Administration of this system required the creation of much larger state bureaucracies, beginning with chanceries and finance ministries to control the collection and disbursement of revenue. The autonomy of local lords was severely diminished. They now owed taxes rather than service, and the central government disrupted their traditional relationships with their peasants by directly taxing the latter. The domains directly controlled by states increased dramatically as well, since ecclesiastical properties all over Europe were seized and taken over as state lands. The territorial jurisdiction of states shifted from patchworks of discontinuous domains to contiguous blocks of land; France, for example, took on its now familiar hexagonal shape in this period. States increased in size also by absorbing, through conquest, marriage, or diplomacy, weaker and less viable political units. And states began to penetrate their societies to a far greater extent as well, reducing the numbers of local dialects in favor of the one used at court, homogenizing social customs, and creating common legal and commercial standards over increasingly large jurisdictions.

The speed and extent of this transformation was remarkable. It was comparable in many ways to what had happened to China during the Eastern Zhou Dynasty, though at the end of the process there were still multiple surviving states rather than a single empire. Consider taxation. In the Habsburg Empire, taxation increased from 4.3 million florins in 1521–1556 to 23.3 million in 1556–1607. Average annual tax revenues in England shot up from £52,000 during the years 1485–1490 to £382,000 in 1589–1600. Castile took in 1.5 million ducats in taxes in the year 1515, and 13 million by 1598.[8] This enlarged tax take was used to support a bigger and more professional public sector. France in the year 1515 had seven to eight thousand officeholders working for the king; by 1665, the royal administrative corps numbered eighty thousand. The Bavarian government had 162 officials on its payroll in 1508, and 866 by 1571.[9]

Whereas the early development of European states was rooted in their ability to provide justice, from the sixteenth century on the process was driven almost entirely by the need to finance war. Wars in this period were fought on increasingly large scales and were nearly continuous. The large ones included a prolonged conflict between France and Spain for control of Italy; the effort of Spain to subdue its Dutch provinces; the contest among England, Spain, Portugal, the Netherlands, and France over colonies in the New World; the attempted Spanish invasion of England; prolonged conflict in Germany following the Reformation, culminating in the Thirty Years' War; Swedish expansion into Central and Eastern Europe and Russia; and ongoing conflict among the Ottoman, Habsburg, and Russian empires.

States in the early modern period did not provide much by way of services other than basic public order and justice; the vast bulk of their budgets went to military expenses. Ninety percent of the budget of the Dutch Republic was spent on war in the period of their long struggle with the Spanish king; 98 percent of the Habsburg Empire's budget went to finance its wars with Turkey and the Protestant powers in the seventeenth century. From the beginning of the seventeenth century to its end, the budget of France rose five- to eightfold, while the British budget increased sixteenfold from 1590 to 1670.[10] The size of the French army increased proportionately, from 12,000 men in the thirteenth century to 50,000 in the sixteenth, to 150,000 in the 1630s, to 400,000 late in Louis XIV's reign.[11]

THE ROLE OF LAW IN EUROPEAN DEVELOPMENT

Sometime in the middle of the first millennium B.C., China made a transition from warfare based on small numbers of aristocrats riding chariots to much larger mass infantry armies based on general conscription. A similar technological transition took place in Europe in the twelfth and thirteenth centuries, as horse-mounted, heavy knights were replaced by large infantry armies using bows and pikes. Unlike early Chinese state builders, however, early modern European monarchs did not raise these armies by conscripting masses of peasants on their own territories. The great armies that the emperor Charles V put into the field were built around a core of Castillian troops known as *tercios* but included large numbers of mercenaries hired under contract from both their own lands and foreign jurisdictions.[12] Mass conscript armies appeared in Europe only in the eighteenth century, but they didn't really emerge as the basis for state power until the *levée en masse* of the French Revolution. By contrast, Chinese states like Qin went directly from horse-mounted aristocratic warfare to mass conscription, without passing through the mercenary stage.[13]

Why didn't these early modern European monarchs behave like their Chinese counterparts and simply conscript masses of peasants living on their territory? And why didn't they pay for these armies by hiking direct tax rates throughout their territories, instead of relying on loans and the sale of offices?

One of the chief reasons was the existence of a rule of law in Europe. We saw in chapter 18 how it evolved out of religious law and spread to a wide variety of other domains. The entire hierarchical structure of European feudalism, which effectively distributed sovereignty and power to a host of subordinate political units, was protected by inherited law. Peasants were bound by a whole range of feudal laws and obligations, primarily to their local lord. The king had no legal right to conscript them; indeed, he might not even have the right to conscript those working directly on his own domains because their duties were specified in great detail and might not include military service. European monarchs did not feel entitled simply to seize the property of their elite subjects, who would claim ancient rights based on feudal contract. States could impose taxation, but they would have to go through organized estates (like the French Estates-General) by which they justified the imposts to the payers and received their permission. Although absolutist monarchs tried to whittle away the power of these estates, they did this within the overall legal framework on which their own legitimacy rested. Nor did kings feel they had the right to violate the personal security of their rivals by arbitrarily seizing or killing them. (It is important to note, however, that these rules were much less rigorously applied to nonelites like peasants and other commoners up until a much later period in history.)

Early Chinese kings exercised tyrannical power of a sort that few monarchs in either feudal or early modern Europe attempted. They engaged in wholesale land reform, arbitrarily executed the administrators serving them, deported entire populations, and engaged in mad purges of aristocratic rivals. The only European court in which one saw this kind of behavior was that of Russia. This kind of unconstrained violence became much more prevalent only after the French Revolution, when modernization swept away all of the ancient inherited legal constraints of the old European order.

It is important to understand, then, that European state development had to take place against a well-developed background of law that limited state power. European monarchs tried to bend, break, or go around the law. But the choices they made were structured and checked by the preexisting body of law that was developed in medieval times.

A FRAMEWORK FOR STATE BUILDING

To engage in war, a state has to mobilize resources on a larger and larger scale. The need for resources drives higher levels of taxes and novel ways of extending the domain of the tax state to encompass more of the population and more of the society's resources. Administration of fiscal resources in turn drives increases in the size of the state bureaucracy and an increasing rationalization of that bureaucracy to squeeze the greatest possible value out of it. States need to be territorially large to increase their revenue base, and territorially contiguous for purposes of defense. Pockets of political dissidence can be exploited by enemies; hence the need to impose uniform administration over the entire territory of the state.

Certain parts of Europe—some of the German and Eastern European lands, and geographically isolated areas like Switzerland—did not face early military competition and therefore organized modern states relatively late. All of the other major powers—France, Spain, England, the Netherlands, Sweden, Russia, the Habsburg Empire, Poland, Hungary, and others—faced growing demands for military expenditures and thus centralization from the fifteenth century on.[14]

The story of political development from this point in European history is the story of the interaction between these centralizing states and the social groups resisting them. Absolutist governments arose where the resisting groups were either weak and poorly organized, or else were co-opted by the state to help in extracting resources from other social groups that weren't co-opted. Weak absolutist governments arose where the resisting groups were so strongly organized that the central government couldn't dominate them. And accountable government arose when the state and the resisting groups were better balanced. The resisting groups were able to impose on the state the principle of "no taxation without representation":

they would supply it with substantial resources, but only if they had a say in how those resources were used.

The outcome of these struggles was not a bilateral fight for rights between the state and society as a whole. In very general terms, the struggle tended to be a four-legged one among the central monarchy, an upper nobility, a broader gentry class (that is, small landowners, knights, or other free individuals), and a Third Estate that included city dwellers (the incipient bourgeoisie). Peasants, who accounted for the vast majority of the population in these societies, were not yet significant players because they were not socially mobilized into corporate bodies that could represent their interests.

The amount of resistance to state centralization depended on the degree to which the three groups outside the state—nobility, gentry, and Third Estate—were able to work together to resist royal power. It also depended on the internal cohesion that each one demonstrated. And finally, it depended on the cohesion and sense of purpose of the state itself.

FIGURE 1. POLITICAL POWER IN AN AGRARIAN SOCIETY

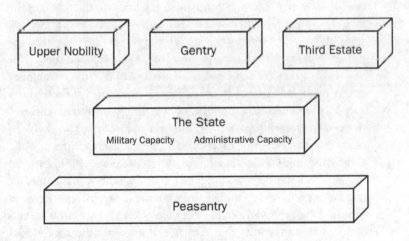

FOUR PATHWAYS

In the chapters that follow, I will present the stories of four European state-building outcomes and some of the reasons why these outcomes diverged from one another. This selection covers the most diverse set of cases from the most representative to the most absolutist. They are:

1. *Weak absolutism.* The French and Spanish monarchies of the six-teenth and seventeenth centuries epitomized the new absolutist state, and they were more centralized and dictatorial in certain ways than, say, their Dutch and English counterparts. On the other hand, neither was able to fully dominate the powerful elites in its society, and a heavier burden of taxation was placed on those least able to resist it. Their centralized administrations remained patrimonial, and indeed the level of patrimonialism increased over time.

2. *Successful absolutism.* The Russian monarchy succeeded in co-opting both its nobility and gentry, and turning them into a service nobility completely dependent on the state. They were able to do this in part by a common interest all three developed in binding the peasantry to the land and ruthlessly imposing the largest burden of taxation on them. The government remained patrimonial until a late point, which nonetheless did not prevent the Russian monarch from terror-izing and controlling the nobility to a far greater degree than the French or Spanish kings.

3. *Failed oligarchy.* The aristocracies of both Hungary and Poland suc-ceeded early on in imposing constitutional limits to the power of the king, who then remained weak and unable to construct a modern state. The weak monarchy was unable to protect the interests of the peasantry from the noble class, who ruthlessly exploited them. Nor was it able to extract sufficient resources to build a state machinery strong enough to resist external aggression. Neither of these states succeeded in building a modern, nonpatrimonial government.

4. *Accountable government.* Finally, England and Denmark were able to develop both strong rule of law and accountable government, while at the same time building strong centralized states capable of national mobilization and defense. England's development of parliamentary institutions is the most familiar story, but the same outcome occurred in Scandinavia through a rather different political process. By the end of the nineteenth century, one had a liberal state, the other the founda-tions for a social-democratic one, but the principles of law and ac-countability were extremely well anchored in both.

There were important variants and outcomes besides these. The Dutch Republic and the Swiss confederation represented alternative republican pathways to accountable government and rule of law, while the Prussian monarchy developed a strong modern state and rule of law in the absence of accountability. I am not able to cover these and other outlier cases. What is important, however, is to understand the broad conditions that tended to support the emergence of either accountable government or the different forms of absolutism.

23

RENTE SEEKERS

How fiscal crisis led to the rise of patrimonial government in France; the intendants and the growth of centralized government; how the French elite understood liberty as privilege, and how they were prevented from achieving collective action; the French government's ultimate weakness and inability to tax or control its own elites

France of the ancien régime presents a highly contradictory picture of both enormous strength and underlying weakness. Anyone who has visited Versailles outside Paris understands why Europeans of the age of Louis XIV held the French monarchy in such awe. Frederick the Great's Sanssouci in Potsdam seems like a mere hut in comparison. Louis's English and Dutch rivals regarded France in the late seventeenth century a bit the way Americans looked at the Soviet Union during the cold war, as an immense, rich, powerful, and ambitious land power that threatened the freedoms of the whole of Europe. The French monarchy was a pioneer in European state building and laid the basis for the modern, centralized administrative state. Alexis de Tocqueville, writing in the 1840s, noted how Frenchmen of his generation believed that this state appeared only with the French Revolution. But as he set out to prove, its foundations had been laid two centuries prior by kings of the ancien régime who "joined hands with modern France across the abyss of the Revolution."

At the same time, the entire edifice of the French state was built on rotten and crumbling foundations. When Louis XIV died in September 1715, his state was completely bankrupt. The royal debt amounted to almost two billion livres, not counting another six hundred million livres of short-term unfunded government paper. France's creditors had claims on future tax revenues stretching all the way up to 1721; debt service alone exceeded anticipated tax revenues for the foreseeable future.[1] This parlous fiscal state was not something new, though Louis XIV's aggressive foreign policy had greatly added to its scale. For more than a century, French kings had been constructing their centralized state based on a set of unimaginably complex deals with local power holders, who traded various privileges and immunities in return for cash. The state had gradually encroached on the freedom of all of its subjects, but only by mortgaging its own future to a legion of corrupt officeholders in an unsustainable way. It could not move to the higher state of absolutism that had been achieved by the Chinese state centuries earlier. Ultimately, it was normatively bound to respect the interests of the same social classes it was trying to dominate, and had to respect the laws inherited from the past. Only after those social classes were swept away by the revolution could a truly modern French state emerge.

In many respects, the situation of the French monarchy was very similar to that of certain contemporary developing countries insofar as it regarded the rule of law as an inconvenient obstacle to its purposes. The government was profligate, lavishing money not on subsidies or social programs, but on war. The resulting budget deficits had to be financed, and the monarchy's desperate search for revenues led it to stretch, bend, and break the law wherever it thought it could get away with it. But it was limited by the fact that in the end it had to go back to the same group of creditors for funds. The only way out of this situation would have been for the monarchy simply to expropriate the holdings of the elite en masse, which is what the revolution eventually did. But this was beyond the imagination or capabilities of the ancien régime, which therefore found itself stuck in a situation of perpetual economic crisis.

At the same time, the society from which the government sought to extract funds was unable to impose upon it a basic principle of accountability. The reason for this was a lack of social solidarity or social capital among the different economic classes. The aristocracy, bourgeoisie, and peasantry, while united at earlier times in their history, came to feel little sympathy for one another and did not believe, like their English counterparts, that they constituted parts of a single nation. Each of these classes was in turn internally stratified into a host of self-regarding ranks. Each rank was jealous of its privileges and more concerned to maintain its status relative to the next rank down than to protect the class itself or the nation from being dominated by the state. Liberty was interpreted as privilege, and the result was a society in which, according to Tocqueville, "there were not ten men willing to work together for a common cause" on the eve of the revolution.

Weak absolutism arises when neither the centralizing state nor the groups opposing it are able to organize themselves adequately in the struggle for dominance. The result in France was tilted more toward absolutism, but it was a fragile system that could not withstand the Enlightenment shift in ideas that based legitimacy on the Rights of Man.

THE BEGINNINGS OF PATRIMONIAL ABSOLUTISM

When the first Bourbon king, Henry IV, was crowned in 1594, France was very far from being either a unified nation or a modern state. From a power base in an area around Paris, earlier kings had assembled a realm out of other principalities, such as Burgundy, Normandy, Brittany, Navarre, and Languedoc, but there remained strong regional variations in language and customs. The kingdom was divided between the *pays d'élections* and the *pays d'états*. The former constituted the core of the country in the regions around Paris; the latter were more recently acquired territories at the extremities and operated under different legal rules. In addition, the Reformation had divided the country along sectarian lines. The religious civil war between the Catholic League and the Huguenots was brought to an end only when the Protestant Henry converted to Catholicism and granted the Edict of Nantes in 1598, establishing Catholicism as the state religion but granting equal rights to the Protestants.

From the beginning of the Bourbon line up until the Revolution in 1789, the story of French state building follows two parallel tracks. The first concerns the ever-increasing centralization of the French state and the reduction of the political rights of all the subordinate units that had existed in feudal times. These included all of the principalities and independent noble houses that had once constituted the locus of government in France, as well as municipalities, guilds, the church, even independent private business organizations that increasingly came under protection and control of the state.

The second track concerns the *manner* in which this centralization occurred. Unlike the early Chinese state, and unlike the German state that was to emerge in Brandenburg-Prussia in the eighteenth century, the centralized French state was not built around an impersonal, merit-based bureaucracy recruited on the basis of functional specialization and education. It was instead thoroughly patrimonialized. Government offices, from military commands to positions in the finance ministry to tax collection, were sold to the highest bidder by a state that was constantly short of cash and desperate for revenue. Government, in other words, was privatized down to its core functions, and public offices turned into heritable private property.[2]

If the problem of good governance is understood in principal-agent terms, where agents have to be properly incentivized to do the bidding of the principal, then the system created by the French government was an absolute nightmare. It virtually legitimized and institutionalized rent seeking and corruption by allowing agents to run their public offices for private benefit. Indeed, the very word "rente" originated in the French government's practice of selling off a public asset, like the right to collect a certain type of tax, that would produce a continuing stream of revenues.[3] If modern public administration is about the observance of a bright line between public and private, then the ancien régime represented a thoroughly premodern system. The French state was thus a curious and unstable combination of modern and patrimonial elements.

The development of a centralized administrative state and patrimonial officeholding was so intertwined that it is not possible to trace their development separately. The fiscal system of the ancien régime was highly complex, reflecting the piecemeal way it had developed. There were several kinds of taxes, the most important of which was the taille, a direct levy on agricultural output whose burden fell on the peasantry. There were a poll tax and a series of indirect taxes on items like wine and goods transiting from one part of the country to another. There was also a tax on salt manufactured by a state monopoly (the gabelle).[4] Later kings imposed a host of other taxes, including the capitation (per capita tax) and the vingtième (income tax).

Direct property taxes were hard to assess because the state did not have a system for maintaining an up-to-date census and registration of its population and their assets the way the Chinese, Ottoman, and English states had done.[5] There was natural resistance on the part of wealthy families to any kind of honest declaration of their assets, since this would simply increase their tax liabilities.[6] Collection of indirect taxes was made difficult by France's size (when compared, for example, to England) and the dispersed nature of its thousands of local markets. The French economy in the seventeenth century was incompletely monetized, and there was a perpetual shortage of coin in which money taxes could be paid. France was overwhelmingly agricultural in this period, and those taxes that were technically easy to collect, like customs duties, failed to produce substantial revenue.[7]

But the real complexities of the tax system were driven by a welter of special exemptions and privileges. Feudal France had developed a two-level system of estates in the late medieval period, a national Estates-General and a series of local or provincial estates—otherwise known as sovereign courts or *parlements*—that the king consulted to get approval for new taxes.[8] In order to secure the incorporation of various provinces into the realm, he had granted special favors to the provincial estates, confirming the local elites they represented in their customs and privileges. Tax regimes thus varied from region to region, especially between the pays d'élection and the pays d'état. The nobility used their leverage over weak kings to win themselves a variety of tax exemptions, from both direct taxes and excise taxes for goods produced on their own properties. These exemptions and privileges began to spread outside the nobility, to wealthy commoners in cities, royal officers, magistrates, and the like. The only people who could not win such exemptions were nonelites, the peasants and artisans who constituted the vast majority of the country's population.[9]

The practice of the sale of public offices—venality—began in the sixteenth century under the pressure of the state's need for revenue as a result of its prolonged struggle with Spain for control of Italy. French kings in this period could not cover war expenses from revenues from their own domains and so began borrowing large sums of money from the newly developing financial centers in Italy, Switzerland, and southern Germany. The state's credibility was never high, and it was undermined entirely when the government essentially repudiated its debts to a consortium of bankers known as the Grand Parti in 1557. It also defaulted on debts to those foreign mercenaries fighting its wars, like the Swiss. In 1602, it owed thirty-six million livres to Swiss towns and cantons, and to the Swiss colonels and captains commanding its troops. When the French government reneged, the Swiss stopped fighting.[10]

The state's solution to its credibility problem was to sell public offices to private individuals through the mechanism of the rente. Compared to an ordinary loan, the rente entitled its holder to a specific revenue stream that the officeholder controlled. Venal officeholders were put in charge of the collection of the *taille* (land tax) and other taxes, at least in the pays d'élections; since the monies passed through their hands, they had greater surety of having interest and principal repaid. Thus was created the system of "inside finance," whereby the chief source of state finance became not private bankers but rather wealthy individuals who were already part of the state apparatus and thus bound to it by prior investments.

It turned out that even the credibility of these rentes was low, since the government soon turned on their holders and asked for retroactive renegotiations of their terms. Under Henry IV and his finance minister, Sully, the state came up with an innovation in the early sixteenth century, the *paulette*, by which a rente holder could convert his office into what amounted to heritable property by bequeathing it to his descendants in return for a fee.[11] This return of outright patrimonialism was rooted in reforms of an earlier period, when the Catholic church had set a precedent for modern administration by dividing the beneficium from the officium (see chapter 18). The former was a claim to economic rents whose heritability was limited by the celibacy of the priesthood; the latter was a functional office held at will under control of a bureaucratic hierarchy. Once nonecclesiastical commoners began staffing state bureaucracies without the promise of benefices or feudal domains, they too started looking for ways of guaranteeing their jobs and taking care of their children. The French government in turn saw the incorporation of these commoners into the state system as a useful means of counteracting the influence of the old nobility. The single largest source of demand for offices came from the bourgeois members of the Third Estate, who hoped to better their condition through purchase of an official title. Full-scale patrimonialism had thus reinserted itself into the heart of French public administration.

The adoption of the paulette did not end the French state's machinations with regard to revenue. The state sold the right to collect indirect taxes to tax farmers who, in return for guaranteeing the state a certain fixed return, could keep any excess tax revenues for themselves. It also sold off the right to collect the new *droits aliénés*, surtaxes that soon dwarfed the traditional taille. In addition, the state could simply increase the number of offices for sale, which had the effect of depressing the price of existing offices and thus diluting the property rights of their holders. The constantly rising demand for offices surprised even the creators of the system.

Pontchartrain, the controller general for Louis XIV, was asked by his king how he succeeded in finding new purchasers of offices. Pontchartrain answered, "Your Majesty . . . as soon as the king institutes an office, God creates a fool who will buy it."[12]

The inefficiencies and opportunities for corruption that this system fostered were huge. The venal post of intendant of finance, usually bought by a private financier, could be very valuable because it would give him a leg up on his competition in knowing in advance what bids the French state was likely to make. The finance minister presided over a regular burning of money orders and other financial records in order to prevent later scrutiny of his accounts.[13] While England developed an advanced theory of public finance and optimal taxation, elucidated in Adam Smith's *Wealth of Nations*, French taxation was opportunistic and dysfunctional.[14] The gabelle, or tax on salt, for example, was unevenly applied across France, creating an artificial "salt boundary" that encouraged smuggling from low- to high-cost regions.[15] Most important, the French fiscal system deliberately encouraged rent seeking. Wealthy individuals, instead of investing their money in productive assets in the private economy, spent their fortunes on heritable offices that could not create but only redistribute wealth. Rather than focusing on technological innovation, they innovated with regard to new ways of outwitting the state and its tax system. This weakened private entrepreneurship and made its emerging private sector dependent on state largesse, just at the same moment that private markets were blossoming across the English Channel.

The French fiscal system that developed by the late seventeenth century was highly regressive, taxing the poor in order to support the rich and powerful. Virtually every elite group, from high aristocrats to guild members to bourgeois towns, had succeeded in securing for itself a tax exemption, leaving the greatest burden to fall on the peasantry. This naturally provoked a long series of peasant uprisings and revolts. Tax increases to support the wars of Louis XIV were met with revolts in 1661, 1662, 1663, 1664, 1665, 1670, 1673, and 1675, the last being the large and serious uprising of the Bonnets Rouges.[16] All were violently suppressed; for example, in the tax revolt of 1662, government troops took 584 rebels captive. Those over seventy and under twenty years of age were pardoned; the rest were condemned to the galleys.[17] Taxes were levied to pay for armies, but troops had to be pulled from the frontiers to coercively extract taxes in a self-defeating manner. This underlines a central lesson of tax policy, which is that extraction costs are inversely proportional to the perceived legitimacy of the authority doing the taxing.

THE INTENDANTS AND CENTRALIZATION

The fiscal crisis experienced by France in the first half of the seventeenth century under Louis XIII and his minister Richelieu, and then by Louis XIV and Mazarin, paved the way for administrative centralization under the tutelage of a new institution, the intendants. They were usually young officials with careers still to make who, according to Tocqueville, "did not exercise [their] powers by virtue of election, birth, or purchase." What was critical was that they lacked ties to either local elites or the hierarchy of venal officeholders responsible for administration of the fiscal system. The intendant was usually a recently ennobled man; his immediate subordinate, the subdelegate, was a commoner. Unlike the venal officeholders, both officials could be dismissed at will by the ministry in Paris. The French had discovered the same system used by the Chinese to staff their commanderies and counties, or the Turks to run their sanjaks. Tocqueville continues:

> These all-powerful officials were, however, eclipsed by the remnants of the old feudal aristocracy and virtually lost in the radiance the aristocracy still projected . . . In government, the nobility surrounded the king and made up his court; they commanded the fleets, directed the armies; they were, in short, that which most struck contemporaries' eyes and too often monopolizes posterity's attention. One would have insulted a great lord by suggesting he be named an intendant; the poorest gentleman of rank would have generally refused to accept the position.[18]

Prior to the middle of the seventeenth century, the intendants were dispatched without any systematic plan in mind. They were simply ad hoc representatives of the central government on specific issues.[19] They were increasingly used to collect taxes, particularly the taille, which traditionally had been supervised by local officials. Their usurpation of this role was the background to the constitutional crisis at midcentury.

The principal struggle over the allocation of powers between the central government and other regional and local actors concerned the role of the sovereign courts, or parlements. There were, as already noted, two levels of such traditional bodies, one representing each province (the most important of which was the Parlement de Paris), and the national-level Estates-General. In the late medieval period, French kings had called on the Estates-General periodically to approve taxes, in the manner of the English Parliament. But the ability of kings to rule without them was seen as the hallmark of absolutist power, and no Estates-General was called between the regency of Marie de Medicis in 1614 and 1789, just prior to the revolution. Any understanding of why representative institutions developed in England and not in France has to revolve around the question of why the sovereign courts failed to develop into powerful institutions in one country but did in the other.

The provincial sovereign courts, which represented the interests of local elites, were primarily judicial bodies. They met much more frequently than the Estates-General and could potentially act as a check on the king's power. When the king wanted to enact a new tax, it was brought before the court for registration. The sovereign court usually held a public debate, often quite heated when it turned on matters of taxation, and then could register the legislation unaltered, amend it, or fail to register it. Unpopular legislation was subject to oral or written remonstrances by local officials to the king's court. The power of the sovereign courts was limited, however, by the fact that the king could convene what was known as a *lit de justice* after a parlement's failure to register legislation and force the law through anyway.[20] The sovereign courts could do little more than embarrass the crown through their remonstrances.

The system faced a grave crisis after the Peace of Westphalia in 1648 when the accumulated arrears of the Thirty Years' War led the government to attempt to continue wartime levels of taxation in times of peace. The refusal of the Parlement de Paris to register new taxes initially led Mazarin to back down and withdraw the intendants from most provinces, but the subsequent arrest of the parlement's leaders sparked a general insurrection known as the Fronde.[21] The Fronde, which unrolled in two phases between 1648 and 1653, represented the ultimate sanction that both traditional local elites and the nobility held over the monarchy: armed resistance. The civil war could have gone either way, but in the end the disparate social actors made unhappy by the government's policies could not combine to produce a military victory.

The defeat of both the parlementaires and the nobility paved the way for a much more thoroughgoing centralization of the French political system. In the second half of the seventeenth century, Louis XIV and his controller general, Jean-Baptiste Colbert, deliberately turned the intendants into instruments by which the Royal Council extended its authority in a uniform way over the whole of France.[22] They were reinserted into each province, and their powers increased. They began to recruit and supervise local militias, they took over the management of public works, and they became responsible for general public order. The feudal aristocracy had long since given up its obligation to help the local poor; this too became a function of the central government through the mechanism of the intendant.[23]

Among the freedoms that were extinguished in the process of state building was that of towns and municipalities to govern themselves. The general population of French towns exercised the right to hold democratic elections for local magistrates up through the late seventeenth century. They were frequently supported by the Crown in the assertion of their rights as a means of weakening the local aristocracy.[24] But elections were abolished for the first time in 1692, and the magistrates' positions turned into offices controlled from the center. Tocqueville makes the following comment about this transformation:

> And what deserves all the contempt that history can bestow, this great revolution was accomplished without any political purpose in mind. Louis XI had limited municipal freedoms because their democratic character frightened him; Louis XIV destroyed them without being afraid of them. What proves this is that he returned their liberties to all the towns that could buy them back. In fact, he wanted less to abolish their rights than to buy and sell them, and if in fact he did abolish them, it was without intending to, purely because it was financially expedient; and oddly enough the same game went on for eighty years.[25]

Tocqueville makes a fascinating comment that the New England town parish that he so admired as the basis for American democracy and the medieval French town both had their origins in the same local feudal institution, and yet they diverged by the eighteenth century as a result of the efforts of the central state to buy the loyalty of individuals.[26] The government of the towns in France came to be controlled by a small oligarchy who increasingly came to hold their offices through purchase. They sought office to distinguish themselves from their fellow townsmen; the solidarity of the community was undermined and those outside of the officeholding elite fell into apathy.

The impact of political centralization was far reaching, producing the more homogeneous nation that we know today. The revocation of the Edict of Nantes in 1685 made Catholicism hegemonic and led to the emigration of many entrepreneurial and skilled Protestants to other parts of Europe as well as to places farther afield like North America and South Africa. The central government had much greater power to declare new taxes without opposition from the now-cowed sovereign courts; differences in the application of taxes across the country were reduced. Especially after their defeat in the Fronde, the nobility lost their bases of power in the countryside and were brought to court. There they could lobby directly for subsidies and exemptions, and could be manipulated through control over access to the king. The famous levée of Louis XIV, by which ancient nobles tripped over one another to attend to the monarch's early morning bathroom functions, is one example. The nobility retained their social status at the expense of real political power and wealth.[27] The one area in which the nobility retained their power was in their continuing control over seigneurial courts, which as we saw in chapter 17 had early on come under royal control in England. The French thus got uniformity in all the wrong places: the loss of local political autonomy to make decisions on issues of interest to the community, yet an uneven system of justice still under the dominance of local notables, which undermined belief in the fairness of the existing property rights system.

THE LIMITS OF CENTRALIZED POWER AND
THE IMPOSSIBILITY OF REFORM

The increased power of the French state by the early eighteenth century led it to trample on the rights of individuals, their property rights first and foremost. But it did so in a typically European way, through manipulation of the legal system rather than through the extralegal use of pure coercion. The abrogation of customary rights and constraints had to be argued at length and politically contested within limits set by the old feudal legal order. Thus the crushing of the power of the parlements took the better part of a century to accomplish. Whereas French kings were brutal toward peasants who resisted their power, they treated elite actors with remarkable respect. After suffering defeat in the Fronde, the two insurgent nobles who led the revolt, Turenne and Condé, asked for and received Louis XIV's forgiveness. Had they been Chinese aristocrats, they and all their families would have been summarily executed.

The death of Louis XIV in 1715 left the monarchy with crushing debts. In order to reduce this burden, the state resorted to what amounted to a protection racket. It summoned special courts it controlled called the *chambres de justice* and then threatened creditors with investigations into their personal finances. Since virtually all of the creditors were corrupt in one way or another, they agreed to reduce the amount owed the government in return for calling off the investigation.[28] The tactic of the selective use of anticorruption investigations to raise revenues and intimidate political opponents is still very much in use today.

Under a new finance minister, John Law, the state tried another novel approach to getting around its creditors. It created a national bank in which the state committed itself to exchange specie for banknotes at a fixed rate and coerced citizens into converting their specie into notes at this rate by threatening them with criminal prosecution, house searches, and seizure of their property. The bank then reneged on its commitment to repay and repeatedly reduced the value of the notes in terms of specie, trying in effect to force down the rate of interest it had to pay on its debt. Law asserted that all property held by individuals belonged to them only insofar as it was used in a manner deemed useful by the king, leading Montesquieu to label Law "one of the greatest promoters of despotism yet seen in Europe." Law's system, however, proved unenforceable and soon collapsed.[29] Like many dictatorships in more recent times, the French monarchy found it could not create investor confidence or repeal basic laws of economics by political fiat.

During the eighteenth century, there were some important shifts in the balance of power between France's different social and political actors. The growing capitalist world economy increased levels of productivity and led to the growing material wealth and size of France's bourgeois class. But these economic shifts were far less important than the intellectual developments that took place in this period, with the sudden victory of Enlightenment ideas about the Rights of Man and equality that spread rapidly all over Europe. When the convening of the Estates-General was brought up again during the 1780s, the justifications given were entirely different from previously: the right of the estates to limit the power of the king was based not on their ancient origin in feudal custom but rather on their ability to represent a broader public consisting of equal individuals with rights. There was a general recognition that the fiscal system of the ancien régime had grown hideously complex and unfair. The proposals of earlier generations of finance ministers to keep the system going through ever more novel ways of fleecing creditors and defaulting on obligations was replaced by a view that taxation ought to be made uniform, equitable, and legitimated by the French people through their representatives.

The story of the French Revolution and the coming of democracy is a familiar one that I will not deal with at great length in this volume. I bring it up here for a different purpose. When a generation of French politicians under the influence of these new ideas in the 1770s and '80s tried to change the old system through peaceful reform, they were completely stymied by the degree to which entrenched interests continued to have a lock on political power.

There were two such efforts. The first took place beginning in 1771 under Louis XV and his minister Maupeou. Maupeou initiated conflict with the parlements by forbidding them to have contact with one another or to go on strike, and when they refused to go along, he reorganized the entire judiciary, taking away much of the jurisdiction of the Parlement de Paris. Most important, he abolished the sale of judicial and official posts, and replaced venal officials with new magistrates to be paid directly by the Crown. A new and more equitable tax, the vingtième, was to be made permanent and imposed through a more rigorous and honest valuation of assets. The regime attacked frontally the entire system of venal office, threatening not only the political positions of the officeholders but also their invested family savings.[30]

This move aroused tremendous opposition, not just from the entrenched ranks of the venal officeholders but for once from other parts of a newly emerging democratic public as well, which rallied behind the oligarchy in opposition to this extension of absolutist power. The traditional patrimonial elites were able to portray their opposition to the reform as resistance to despotism. Louis XV died suddenly in 1774, a highly unpopular king, and his successor, Louis XVI (who would lose his head during the revolution), was eventually forced to restore all the old rights and privileges of the sovereign courts.[31]

The second attempt at reform came in the 1770s under the ministry of the physiocrat Anne-Robert-Jacques Turgot. Turgot was not interested in political reform, but he was strongly influenced by liberal economic ideas and hoped to rationalize the French economy. He was in this sense a forerunner of the technocratic neoliberal finance ministers who came to the fore in many developing countries during the late 1980s and '90s. Turgot abolished export controls on grain and complex market regulations that had stabilized the price of bread. He followed this with further edicts abolishing the trade guilds and converting the corvée into a tax on landowners. All of these could be regarded as modernizing, rational, and in some sense necessary economic reforms. But they were met with violent protest, not just by the urban poor who saw bread prices rise, but also by the guilds and other entrenched interests that lived off of rents granted by the state. Turgot fell, and the second effort at reform came to an end.[32]

The political system of the ancien régime was incapable of reforming itself. The authority of the state had been built by empowering a broad coalition of rent-seeking elites and entrenching them in tradition and law. Their property rights in public offices were irrational, dysfunctional, and in many cases unjustly gained. A modern France could not arise until venal officeholding was replaced by impersonal, merit-based bureaucracy. But the regime could not attack those rights frontally without delegitimating the entire system of law on which its own power rested. The rule of law, an important component of a modern political system, had developed early on in France, well before the rise of accountable political institutions and capitalism. As a result, it protected not a modern political system and a liberal market economy but rather traditional social privilege and an inefficient state-directed economic system. Even when those at the top of the hierarchy came to accept intellectually the bankruptcy of the old system and the need to change it fundamentally, they didn't have the power to upset the equilibrium established by the rent-seeking coalition. It would take a much greater force, the anger of nonelite groups left out of the system, to destroy it with the revolution.

THE FAILURE OF RESISTANCE TO ABSOLUTISM IN FRANCE

If absolutism didn't succeed fully in France, neither did the social groups opposing it succeed in forcing on the state some form of political accountability. Indeed, their failure was by far the greater of the two and was a result of their failure to act cohesively (see Figure 2). The locus of opposition should have been the sovereign courts at a provincial level and the Estates-General at a national one. These courts remonstrated, complained, debated, and resisted, and on many occasions forced the French monarchy to back off of proposals that they opposed. But until the final summoning of the Estates-General just prior to the revolution, the sovereign courts never forced the monarchy to accept the constitutional principle of their superiority over the executive. So the question naturally arises: Why were these traditional political assemblies, left over from feudal times, unable to achieve collective action in the manner of their English counterparts? The issue goes well beyond just the question of the sovereign courts. Municipalities were also organized as autonomous political bodies during the Middle Ages in both England and France. Why did one evolve into the New England township and the other into a passive administrative unit?

FIGURE 2. FRANCE

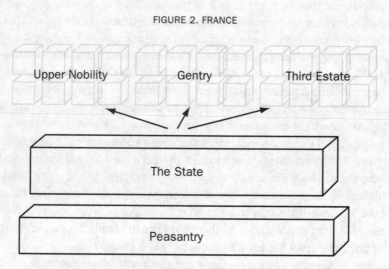

We cannot begin to answer these questions until we have gone through the other national cases on a comparative basis. We can, however, suggest some general categories of answers that might narrow the eventual search for causes. One type of explanation would locate the answer in the structure of French society, dating back to feudal times if not earlier. The political scientist Thomas Ertman argues that the rise of patrimonial absolutism in France, Spain, and the Norman kingdoms of southern Italy had to do with the type of top-down state building that occurred there after the collapse of the Roman Empire. In those parts of Europe that were not part of the Carolingian Empire—England, Scandinavia, and parts of Eastern Europe—there was greater social solidarity between commoners and nobles, and the development of strong grassroots political institutions that survived into early modern times. The weakness of these local institutions in Latin Europe, combined with the high level of warfare from the Middle Ages onward, then explains the failure of collective action on the part of the ancient feudal orders of society in the face of rising absolutism. Germany, which was part of the Carolingian Empire, developed a nonpatrimonial form of absolutism because it was not exposed to severe geopolitical competition from as early a date as Spain and France; when it faced military threats, it could avoid their mistakes and create a more modern bureaucratic type of state.[33]

A second type of explanation, favored by Tocqueville, would locate the French failure in much more recent times. Specifically, he argues that the lack of social solidarity on the part of the French aristocracy and commons was the product of deliberate monarchical manipulation. Tocqueville explains that feudal institutions were not all that different from one part of Europe to another; that the manor and the municipality and the peasant village all had similar laws and forms of social solidarity. In the great ninth and tenth chapters of the second book of *The Old Regime and the Revolution*, he gives many examples of this. On a local level, the French lord and his commoner vassals were called together every two weeks to judge cases in the lord's court, just as in the moots and hundreds of England. The bourgeoisie of the fourteenth century played an active role in both the provincial estates and the Estates-General, a more prominent role than this class would play in later centuries as social distinctions excluded them from governance. The principle of "no taxation without representation" was as well established in France in the Middle Ages as it was in England.[34]

For Tocqueville, the weak solidarity of French society in the face of growing absolutism was rooted not in ancient traditions but rather in the practice of patrimonialism itself. "But, of all the ways to make distinctions between people and classes, inequality of taxation is the most pernicious and most apt to add isolation to inequality." The problem dated from the second half of the fourteenth century:

I would dare to argue that from the day when the nation, tired of the long disorders that had accompanied the captivity of King John and the insanity of King Charles VI, permitted the kings to establish a general tax without its consent, and when the nobility had the cowardice to allow the Third Estate to be taxed provided that the nobility itself was exempted; on that day was planted the seed for almost all the vices and abuse which affected the old regime for the rest of its life, and finally caused its violent death.[35]

Tax exemption was the most hated of all privileges and became all the more so as the burden of taxation increased steadily throughout the sixteenth and seventeenth centuries. With the sale of public offices, tax exemption became the privilege not just of a broad social class but also of an individual family. The individuals who bought proprietary offices were willing to let the rights of their fellow citizens be compromised, as long as they themselves felt secure. In England, it was the poor who enjoyed tax privileges; in France, it was the wealthy.

Unequal taxation had a corrupting effect on both the nobility and the bourgeoisie. The former lost their real right to rule and as compensation clung all the more tenaciously to their inherited social status. Given that there were so many recently ennobled commoners who had bought their titles, the older nobility closed the doors to many offices to anyone who could not demonstrate "four quarters" noble descent, that is, from all four grandparents, while the parvenus tried to shut the door on those coming after them. The bourgeoisie, for their part, sought to separate themselves from the peasantry by moving to towns and securing some form of public office. Their energies and ambitions were diverted from entrepreneurship into the search for status and security as defined by public authority.[36]

This is not the end of the interpretive story, however. Venal offices and privileges existed in England as well, and yet the English monarchy was never able to split the solidarity of the groups represented in Parliament as effectively as did the French. Tocqueville himself admits that the English aristocracy from the beginning was less a hereditary caste than a true governing aristocracy (rule by the best). Talented commoners could join its ranks much more readily than in other European societies, for obscure reasons that are buried in a much earlier historical period. Again, we are back to the problem of the stacked turtles. It is possible that patrimonial officeholding itself rests on a set of prior social conditions even as it is fostered by deliberate government policy.

RENT-SEEKING SOCIETIES

Ancien régime France was an early prototype of what is today called a rent-seeking society. In such a society, the elites spend all of their time trying to capture public office in order to secure a rent for themselves—in the French case, a legal claim to a specific revenue stream that could be appropriated for private use.

Was this rent-seeking coalition a stable one? It lasted for almost two centuries and provided a political basis for France's emergence as the dominant continental power. On the other hand, we know that the grandeur of the French court masked enormous weaknesses. The most important was the vivid sense of anger and injustice felt by those left out of the coalition, which eventually erupted in the revolution. But even those inside the co alition were not committed to it in principle. The monarchy would have been perfectly happy to abolish venal officeholding altogether, and tried to do so toward the end of its existence. The officeholders themselves had little sympathy for anyone but themselves. But they could not tolerate the idea of reform because of their own deep personal stake in the system. This was, then, a perfect collective-action problem: the society as a whole would have benefited enormously from abolishing the system, but the individual interests of the parties making it up prevented them from cooperating to bring about change.

The French case teaches a lesson about the role of the rule of law in political development. The rule of law that had emerged in the Middle Ages before modern states existed acted as a constraint on tyranny, but it also acted as a constraint on modern state building since it protected old social classes and customs that would have to be abolished for a truly modern society to exist. The lawful defense of liberty against centralizing monarchs in the early modern period meant defense of a traditional feudal order and highly entailed, feudal property rights that were incompatible with a modern capitalist economic order. Patrimonial rule evolved precisely because governments felt they had to respect the property rights of traditional elites. They could not expropriate their assets directly and therefore had to resort to borrowing and increasingly bizarre financial chicaneries. Respect for the rule of law thus helped to create a highly unequal society in which the state tried but ultimately failed to get its hands on the wealth of the oligarchic elite. As a result, it had to raise revenues on the backs of the poor and the politically weak, exacerbating inequality and paving the way for its own demise.

The old French patrimonial system died in the revolution. But a very similar system was created by the old regime in Spain, which didn't experience a revolution and reform in the eighteenth century. Instead, that system was exported to Latin America, which has had to live with its legacy ever since.

24

PATRIMONIALISM CROSSES THE ATLANTIC

Why government in Latin America has characteristic features not found in other parts of the world; early modern Spain and how it developed patrimonial absolutism very similar to that of France; Spanish institutions and their transmission to colonies in the New World

Latin America is a continent of tremendous geographical, ethnic, cultural, and economic diversity. But the countries of the region also display common characteristics, and a mode of government that distinguishes Latin America from East and South Asia, the Middle East, and Africa.

By the early twenty-first century, a large majority of the population of Latin America lived in countries that had achieved what the World Bank labels "upper middle income" status. They had annual per capita incomes in the range of $4,000 to $12,000, putting them ahead of not just the bulk of Africa but also of fast-growing countries such as India and China.[1] Economic growth, however, has tended to be episodic and on average much lower than growth in East Asia since the middle of the twentieth century.[2] Since the third wave, the region as a whole has become one of the most democratic in the world, though there has been backsliding with the rise of populist governments in countries like Venezuela.[3]

Latin America performs less well in two areas. The first is equality, where the region leads the world in levels of both income and wealth inequality. While levels of inequality have come down slightly in some countries in the first decade of the twenty-first century, they have proved to be remarkably persistent.[4] The second area of weakness is rule of law. Although Latin American countries have been relatively good at holding elections and using democratic accountability mechanisms to get rid of unpopular leaders, the routine administration of justice lags far behind. This is manifested in everything from poor security and high levels of crime, clogged court dockets, weak or insecure property rights, and impunity for many of the rich and powerful.

These two phenomena—inequality and weak rule of law—are related. Rule of law protections often apply to only a small minority of people in Latin America, such as those who run big businesses or belong to trade unions. In Peru, Bolivia, and Mexico, as much as 60 to 70 percent of the population lives in what is known as the informal sector. These people often do not have legal title to the homes they occupy; they operate unlicensed businesses; if they are employed, they are not members of trade unions and do not receive formal labor protections. Many poor Brazilians live in vast *favelas*, where the formal authorities do not penetrate; justice is often provided privately, sometimes by criminal gangs. Economic inequality is promoted by the uneven application of law, since the poor live in a world largely unprotected by it. It makes no sense for them to invest in their homes, since they don't have clear legal title, nor can they trust the police when they are victimized by crime.[5]

The sources of this inequality are not hard to find. Much of it is simply inherited. Many well-to-do families of the older elite are large landowners, descendants of people who had established large latifundia and succeeded in passing down this wealth. The fiscal systems in many Latin American countries further entrench inequality. Within the group of rich countries comprising the Organization for Economic Cooperation and Development, fiscal systems are mostly used to redistribute income from rich to poor. This can happen through either a progressive tax system (as in the United States) or redistributive policies that provide income support and social services to the less well off (as in Europe). In Latin America, by contrast, the fiscal system does very little redistribution, and in some cases succeeds in redistributing income *toward* relatively privileged groups like unionized public sector workers or university students. Workers in the formal sector and elites of all sorts are able to protect their benefits and subsidies; indeed, most are quite successful at evading taxes. Unlike the United States, with its sharply progressive personal income tax, Latin American countries collect only a small amount of revenue from individuals. Wealthy Latin Americans have gotten very good at hiding their true income or moving it offshore to places beyond the reach of the tax collector. This means that the burden of taxation comes from excise, customs, or value-added taxes that fall disproportionately on the poor.

Latin American governments have gotten better at managing macroeconomic policy in the early twenty-first century. But this is a very recent development. For much of their history, Latin American governments were notorious for running budget deficits, heavy public sector borrowing, high rates of inflation, and ultimately sovereign debt defaults.[6] The last time this happened on a regionwide basis was in the early 1980s, when Mexico, Brazil, Argentina, Peru, Bolivia, and other countries declared moratoriums on debt payments and saw rates of inflation skyrocket. Argentina in the late 1980s experienced genuine hyperinflation, with annualized rates running at well over 1,000 percent, and faced another financial collapse and debt default in 2001.

Politically, governance in Latin America has also been distinctive. The region, as noted, has had a relatively good record of democracy in recent years. But all of the large countries succumbed to military dictatorship during the 1960s and '70s in the wake of the Cuban Revolution. Although democracy has roots going back to the first postindependence regimes in the early 1800s, not a single regime in Latin America has had a continuous history of democratic government. The region's dictatorships also have a special quality. With the sole exception of Fidel Castro's Cuba, no dictatorship in Latin America has succeeded in establishing a state powerful enough to be called totalitarian. None has generated sufficient coercive capacity to truly implement a social revolution by, for example, stripping wealthy elites of their assets and income. The region's authoritarian regimes have (fortunately) never been able to pull off something like the collectivization that occurred in Russia or China under their Communist regimes, or the mass killi ;s that characterized Mao's Cultural Revolution. This is true as well for "electoral authoritarian" regimes like Hugo Chávez's Venezuela, which has been unable to control crime or corruption within the regime itself.[7] The brunt of state power has tended to fall on nonelites, such as the terrible counterinsurgency war waged by Guatemala's government against a guerrilla movement based in its indigenous population during the 1980s. Wealthy elites have learned to live with nondemocratic governments and protect themselves from the state's authority, and often benefit from institutionalized corruption.

If any of this sounds familiar, that is because it is reminiscent of the pattern of governance that emerged in ancien régime France. In Latin America, these precedents come from a very similar patrimonial regime, early modern Spain. Like France, the absolutist Spanish state was built after 1492 out of tape and glue. The Spanish monarchy was perpetually broke as a result of endless wars. It tried to cover budget deficits through borrowing but quickly lost credibility with lenders and ultimately resorted to the same variety of stratagems as the French monarchy, including repeated debt reschedulings, debasing of the currency, and the sale of venal offices as a means of raising capital. Indeed, this outwardly powerful state sold off larger and larger pieces of its public sector, including much of its military, to private entrepreneurs in its quest for cash. The result was the same system of inside finance, whereby private individuals succeeded in capturing rights to rents generated by the state. Corruption was rife because venal officeholding completely eroded the distinction between public and private.

At the same time, resistance to absolutism was weakened in Spain by the same factors that Tocqueville described as operating in France. The aristocracy, gentry, and Third Estate that should have united to resist royal power were instead internally divided because of the opportunities that the state offered to individuals to partake in rents. The Spanish Cortes, which (like the French sovereign courts and the English Parliament) had to approve new taxes during the Middle Ages, ceased to function as a serious check on state power. Concern over officeholding and minute distinctions of rank obstructed collective action on the part of Spanish society.

This, then, was the political system that was transmitted to the New World through the viceroyalties of New Spain (Mexico) and Peru. Moreover, it sat on top of a social system that was far more unequal than any in Europe. Like Spain itself after the Reconquista, the New World had been acquired through military conquest, but unlike the former Moorish territories, it was inhabited by large numbers of indigenous peoples. The discovery of significant deposits of silver in Potosí (Bolivia) and Zacatecas (Mexico) in the 1540s led to the creation of a huge extractive empire in which the European rulers lived off of mining rents, while the work was done by enslaved indigenous laborers. The chroniclers of the time noted that the Spaniards who sailed to the New World went there not to work but to be masters: they "are sustained by the labour of the Indians and the work of their hands and are maintained thanks to their sweat."[8] The moral economy of Spanish America was therefore different from the start from that of the owner-farmers who settled the New England colonies to the north. The colonial government in Latin America was structured as if the political institutions of the United States had been built around only the Southern states in which black slavery had been well established.

THE BANKRUPT SPANISH STATE

The modern Spanish state emerged with extraordinary rapidity on the world scene following the marriage of Ferdinand and Isabella in 1469, which united the crowns of Aragon and Castile, including the Aragonese territories of Catalonia, Naples, and Sicily. The joint monarchy succeeded in conquering the last Moorish bastion in Grenada in 1492, the same year that Columbus set out for the New World and claimed the Indies for Spain. Their grandson Charles V added to these Spanish possessions Burgundy (including the Low Countries and the Franche-Comté), and, after his election as Holy Roman Emperor in 1519, the Austrian Habsburg lands as well.

By the 1520s, Charles V controlled the largest world empire of the time. But the fact that this empire had been acquired through dynastic alliance rather than conquest created fiscal constraints that decisively shaped the character of developing state institutions. Charles and his son Philip II had a secure tax base only in Castile (including Castile's valuable New World possessions); the Spanish monarch could not exploit the other parts of the empire for his own purposes.[9] Nonetheless, the Habsburg monarchy took on expensive commitments outside the peninsula. One of these was a prolonged war with France in the sixteenth century for control of Italy and particularly the Duchy of Milan. Another was an eighty-year war with the Netherlands. Finally, there was the devastating Thirty Years' War in the German lands, which became a pan-European war as the result of France's support under Richelieu of the Protestants. War in this period was made particularly expensive by the development of the *trace italienne*, a star-shaped fortress that was less vulnerable to siege artillery, making the investment of cities prolonged, grinding affairs.[10] Eighty percent of the costs of these wars were borne by taxpayers in Castile.[11]

All of these expensive foreign policy commitments strained the Spanish fiscal system enormously, despite the influx of precious metals from the New World. Government expenses always exceeded remittances from the American colonies severalfold throughout the sixteenth and seventeenth centuries. Imports of gold and silver rose from 200,000 to 300,000 ducats per year during the 1530s and '40s up to a maximum of 2.2 million by the end of the century. But these were outpaced by debts that had increased from 1.2 to 6 million ducats for the same period.[12]

The Spanish Crown early in the sixteenth century was much more eager to borrow than to tax and soon found itself straining its credibility as

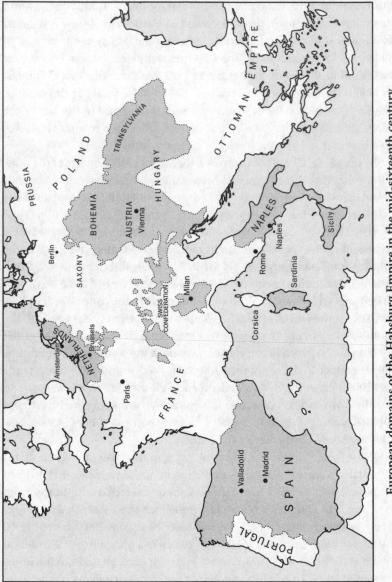

European domains of the Habsburg Empire in the mid-sixteenth century

a borrower. Already in the 1520s, debt service amounted to more than a third of revenues, and more than 100 percent by the end of the long war with France in 1560.[13] The failure to find adequate funds to finance deficits caused the Spanish Crown to declare bankruptcy in 1557, 1560, 1575, 1596, 1607, 1627, 1647, 1652, 1660, and 1662.[14] These bankruptcies were not full debt repudiations, but more like what today would be called debt reschedulings or workouts. The Crown would declare a moratorium on the payment of interest on short-term and floating debt on the grounds that it was usurious and then enter into a prolonged and rancorous negotiation with its creditors. In place of the old debt, the creditors would be forced to take on a new piece of paper, the *juro al quitar*, which was a claim on future tax revenues comparable to the French rente. The juros were undated and negotiable bonds that initially paid a rate of interest of 7 percent but were subject to periodic arbitrary adjustments in interest rates and principal repayment. By means of the juro, the monarchy tapped into the savings of the elites of Castilian society—the clergy, nobility, gentry, bureaucracy, and the like. The more powerful creditors were usually able to negotiate better terms, either by exempting themselves from the payment moratoriums, or by passing on the burden of the rescheduling to weaker partners. When the firm of Vitoria failed to receive payments from the government, it stiffed its own creditors, which included "friars, monasteries, almshouses, widows and orphans, and other such people who are not in business."[15] The government's perpetual failure to live up to debt obligations was an alternative to taxing these same elites directly, which the regime found much more difficult to do politically. It is a tradition carried on by contemporary governments in Latin America, such as that of Argentina, which after the economic crisis of 2001 forced not just foreign investors but also its own pensioners and savers to accept a massive write-down of its sovereign debt.

TAXATION AND NO REPRESENTATION

Many contemporary Europeans, particularly the English, who were threatened by Spanish power were in awe of the supposedly absolutist powers of the Spanish Crown and believed the king to have "Turk-like" powers of taxation and prerogative. But the foundations of Spanish power rested on an extremely precarious fiscal foundation, and the king's authority over his own elites was limited by both law and custom. Spanish absolutism was too weak to take on its own elites frontally, unlike the Chinese and Russian versions, nor was it able to develop a system of legitimate taxation based on consent as the English were to do.

Like other European countries, the kingdoms that came together to become Spain possessed a medieval institution of estates known as the Cortes. The kingdom of León had one of the earliest assemblies in Europe, while that of Aragon was one of the best organized and powerful.[16] The Cortes of Castile, which absorbed León, was less representative and more restricted than that of the English Parliament or the Estates-General in France, insofar as it did not regularly include the clergy or nobility as corporate bodies that would meet in a single assembly with the commons. By the fourteenth century, only the *procuradores* (proctors) of one hundred towns would be summoned to the Cortes, a number that fell to two representatives of eighteen cities by the fifteenth century. These thirty-six individuals claimed that they spoke on behalf of the entire realm, but in fact they were representatives of the oligarchic factions that ruled in each of Spain's major regions.[17]

The traditional powers of the Cortes were limited as well. It had no authority over legislation, which was a prerogative of the king. The Nueva Recopilacion (New Compilation), a collection of laws issued by Philip II in 1567, said that "no impositions, contributions, or other taxes are to be imposed on the whole Kingdom without the Cortes being summoned and without their being granted by the procuradores." But this authority was only over new, extraordinary taxes; existing taxes like the *alcabala* (a general excise tax), the *regalias* (customs duties), and the *quintos* (taxes on mines, salt, and the like) did not need to be approved. The king also asserted that the Cortes did not have the right to withhold assent to new imposts if the demand was just, the definition of "just" being up to him.

The relative power of king and Cortes did not come out of the blue but was the result of political struggle. The alcabala had been farmed out by the central authorities, a practice opposed by the cities, which preferred a system known as the *encabezamiento*, in which they were responsible for the collection and apportionment of taxes. The encabezamiento was granted by Isabella, and then abolished in 1519 by Charles V, which provoked a popular uprising known as the revolt of the *comuneros*. Charles had stacked the Cortes with his own clients, and over opposition forced through the new tax system; part of the opposition was due to the fact that he was perceived as a foreign king (he had been born in Flanders) and would use Castile's tax money for foreign wars of little interest to the people of Castile. Cities all across Castile erupted and organized popular militias, and moved to establish an alternative elective Cortes while promoting the candidacy of a new monarch, Queen Joanna. Charles might well have lost control of his kingdom but for the fact that the comuneros turned on the nobility. The latter shifted its support to the king, and Charles was finally able to reestablish military control.[18]

The aftermath of the comunero revolt was similar in certain ways to the consequences of the uprising of the Fronde in France that took place 130 years later. The king asserted his authority over the cities in a decisive military victory. The idea of an elected, independent Cortes that would be the protector of Spanish liberties was dead. At the same time, the king realized that he needed to deal with the underlying sources of discontent and did so through the progressive and piecemeal buying off of potential opponents. He reinstated the encabezamiento, whose withdrawal had sparked the revolt, and left new taxes like the *servicios* and the *millones* in the hands of local authorities. The latter tended to be patrimonial officeholders who could keep a percentage of the revenues they collected on behalf of the Crown.[19] The Cortes would be summoned and consulted in later years, but it would never demand or receive powers over the purse. Their preferences nonetheless could influence public finance. They didn't want to pay property taxes and so new taxes took the form of imposts on commerce, taxation that fell more heavily on the poor and hindered Spanish economic growth.

The patrimonialization of the Spanish state started in the 1560s and reached its peak under Philip IV (1621–1665). As in France, the process was driven by the continual wars that Spain fought and its unending budget deficits. This process began at the time of the first Spanish bankruptcy in 1557, when the king sent his friend and courtier, Ruy Gómez, to sell as many municipal offices as he could.[20] Unlike in France, venal offices in Spain tended at first to be those of the cities and regions. The practice was widely condemned, as it was understood that the offices sold could not provide an adequate return except through the access they gave to outright corruption.[21] But fiscal stringency drove the state to further sales, nonetheless. By one estimate, the government had created thirty thousand proprietary officeholders by 1650, a number twice as high in per capita terms as in the France of that period.[22] In addition, as much as 30 percent of the territory of Castile was returned to seigneurial jurisdiction, not for political purposes but simply as a result of the monarchy's need for ready cash. Authority over entire towns and cities, including the right to collect taxes and to administer justice, was sold to private individuals. Spanish state building went into reverse in a certain sense, with the central government losing control over much of its own territory as the simple consequence of fiscal improvidence.

Patrimonialism also affected military organization. Spain had liberated itself from the Moors over many centuries, and when the crowns of Castile and Aragon were united, the military was reformed into infantry units known as tercios that were armed with pikes and, later, arquebuses.[23] Spanish soldiers with this kind of training and equipment were the ones who conquered the indigenous empires of the New World under Cortés and Pizarro. They also served in many other parts of the empire, particularly from bases in northern Italy from which they could reach the Low Countries via the so-called Spanish Road.[24] Castilian soldiers participated in the defense of Vienna against the Ottomans in 1533, and Spanish sailors accounted for a small proportion of ships in the attack on Tunis in 1535, the failed attempt to conquer Algiers in 1538, and the great Battle of Lepanto in 1571. But in the seventeenth century, the raising of armies and navies was increasingly outsourced to private individuals who recruited troops using their own resources, or to coastal towns that outfitted their own galleys or ships. The logistical infrastructure that provisioned these forces came under the control of Genoese financiers and meant that by the mid-1600s the Spanish monarchy had little control over its own armed forces.[25]

As in other western European countries, the rule of law played an important role in limiting the authority of the Spanish king to simply do as he pleased with property rights and communal liberties. In Spain, the tradition of Roman law had not been extinguished as completely as in northern Europe, and after the recovery of the Justinian Code in the eleventh century it developed a very strong civil law tradition. The civil law was seen as a codification of divine and natural law. Although the king could make positive law, the Recompilacion made clear that he was subject to existing legal precedents and that edicts contradicting those laws had no force. The Catholic church remained the custodian of ecclesiastical law and often challenged royal prerogatives. Royal commands that were contrary to customary rights or privileges were resisted under the rubric *"Obédezcase, pero no se cumpla"* (obey, but do not put into effect), which was often invoked by the conquistadores in the New World when they received an order they didn't like from an imperial viceroy. Individuals who disagreed with royal commands had the right to appeal them to the Royal Council, which like its English counterpart constituted the highest judicial authority in the land. According to the historian I.A.A. Thompson, "The Council of Castile stood for legalism and due process against arbitrariness, and for a judicialist as against an administrative or executive mode of government, actively resisting any recourse to extraordinary or irregular procedures and consistently defending established rights and contractual obligations."[26]

The impact of this legal tradition can be seen in the way that Spanish kings dealt with domestic enemies and with the property rights of their subjects. There was no Spanish counterpart of Qin Shi Huangdi or Ivan the Terrible, who would arbitrarily execute members of their own courts together with their entire families. Like the French kings of this period, Spanish monarchs chipped away at property rights incessantly in their search for cash, but they did so within the framework of existing law. Rather than arbitrarily expropriate assets, they renegotiated interest rates and principal repayment schedules. Rather than risk confrontation over higher levels of direct taxes, they debased the currency and accepted a higher rate of inflation. Inflation via loose monetary policy is in effect a tax, but one that does not have to be legislated and that tends to hurt ordinary people more than elites with real rather than monetary assets.

TRANSFER OF INSTITUTIONS TO THE NEW WORLD

Conquest societies have different opportunities for institutional development and reform than do ones with ancient customs and long patterns of settlement. Conquest societies can be subject to what in contemporary corporate lingo is called "greenfield development"—a refoundation of institutions without the encumbrances of deeply entrenched stakeholders or patterns of behavior. The Ottomans could settle their sipahis (cavalry officers) on timars (estates) as a one-generation nobility because the land had been recently taken from its previous owners. It is not surprising that when the Spanish conquered the New World, they brought existing institutions with them. But they faced far fewer constraints from entrenched interests there than they did in Europe, as well as a different set of economic opportunities and resource endowments. So if governance in Latin America has come to resemble governance in old regime Spain, the process of institutional transfer was not necessarily straightforward or immediate.

The Spanish conquest of the Americas followed hard on the heels of the final acts of the Reconquista of the peninsula itself: Christopher Columbus witnessed Ferdinand and Isabella's triumphal entry into Grenada, and Cortés's uncle and father participated in the military campaign against the Moors. Cortés conducted his campaign against the Aztecs as if he were fighting the Moors and used similar strategies of divide and conquer.[27] Many of the same techniques of settlement, colonization, and political organization were simply lifted from the experience of colonizing southern Spain. Indeed, the conquistadores had a habit of referring to indigenous temples as "mosques."

These early expeditions were sponsored by the Spanish king but driven by the entrepreneurial energy of the private individuals who organized them. The development of Latin American institutions was the result of an interplay between the individuals on the ground in the new territories and an increasingly powerful government back in Madrid that tried to keep tight control over its colonies. Mining rights to the gold and silver that were discovered were of special interest; no land grants to private individuals included subsurface rights, which all stayed in state hands. The bulk of the new settlers in Peru and Mexico were not, however, involved in the extraction of specie; rather, they wanted to establish themselves as the overlords of land and the agricultural resources that land provided. The novel situation they faced was that the land they conquered was densely populated compared to southern Spain and therefore conducive to a different mode of exploitation.

The institution devised by the Spanish authorities to both reward and control the conquistadores was the *encomienda*, a grant of people rather than of land. As in the case of the Ottoman timar, the Crown's intention was to prevent the emergence of an entrenched local nobility; the grant of the encomienda was conditional and noninheritable.[28] Some 40 percent of the survivors of Cortés's conquest of the Aztec capital of Tenochtitlán were granted encomiendas, as were a substantial number of Pizarro's followers in Peru. The encomienda did not technically enslave the indigenous people given in grant, but it required their labor in return for the *encomenderos* instructing them in the Christian religion and treating them well. The Spanish Crown had a paternalistic concern about the mistreatment of indigenous workers by their new overlords, and by the precipitous decline in their numbers as a result of smallpox and other diseases to which the Indian population was particularly vulnerable. Thus a hierarchical relationship of lordship and bondage, based on race, was built into early Latin American institutions.

The Spanish quickly established a modern and, for the times, relatively efficient administrative system for ruling its American colonies. The legitimacy of the Spanish New World empire was based on the bull of Pope Alexander VI in 1493, which gave the Indies (of unspecified geographical extent) to the Crown of Castile and León in perpetuity. Authority rested with the Spanish king and his Council of the Indies in Madrid, and passed through the viceroyalties that had been established in Mexico and Peru. The laws that were applied in the New World were those of Castile alone, not other parts of the empire, despite the fact that many conquistadores and settlers were born elsewhere. Cortés began his conquest of Mexico in 1519, the year before the outbreak of the great comunero revolt; as a result of the outcome of that struggle, the political institutions transferred to the Americas would not include a strong Cortes or other types of representative bodies. The only early bid for political independence was the revolt of Francisco Pizarro's brother Gonzalo, who tried to set himself up as an independent king of Peru. He was defeated and executed by royal troops in 1548, and no further challenges to central authority from the New World Spaniards occurred until the wars of independence of the early nineteenth century.

The Spanish authorities did transfer their Roman legal system, establishing high courts or *audiencias* in ten places, including Santo Domingo, Mexico, Peru, Guatemala, and Bogotá. A large number of the administrators sent over to help govern the colonies were lawyers and judges with long experience in civil law. The administrators were not permitted to marry local women or establish family ties in their territories, much like the Chinese prefects or Ottoman sanjakbeys. Of the system of colonial administration as a whole, the historian J. H. Elliott writes, "If the 'modernity' of the modern state is defined in terms of its possession of institutional structures capable of conveying the commands of a central authority to distant localities, the government of colonial Spanish America was more 'modern' than the government of Spain, or indeed of that of almost every Early Modern European state."[29] It contrasts in this respect with the

rather laissez-faire attitude of the English monarchy to its new colonies in
North America.

THE IRON LAW OF LATIFUNDIA

Although Spain's administrative system in the New World seemed more
modern than contemporary European systems in the year 1570, this situation was not to last. The patrimonialization of Spain's own political system
kicked into high gear only in the seventeenth century, and it was inevitable that institutions like venal office would be transferred to the Americas.
The basic dynamic driving this process was, however, initiative on the part
of local actors in the colonies seeking to increase their rents and privileges,
and the fact that the central government back in Madrid was too weak and
too far away to prevent them from doing so.

The iron law of the large estate or latifundia—the rich tend to get richer,
in the absence of state intervention—applied in Latin America much as in
other agrarian societies like China and Turkey. The one-generation encomiendas were strongly resisted by the settler class, who not surprisingly
wanted to be able to pass on their entitlements to their children and who
in the 1540s revolted against a law mandating their automatic reversion to
the Crown. Title over people enabled certain encomenderos to get rich by
commanding their labor, and they began to purchase large tracts of land.
Unlike the encomienda, land was heritable. By the late sixteenth century,
the Americas were facing a depopulation crisis of the indigenous populations; Mexico went from 20 million to 1.6 million inhabitants in this
period.[30] This meant that a lot of lightly populated land suddenly became
available.

This new creole elite tended to live in cities, and they exploited their
land as absentee landlords using hired labor. Customary land tenure in
Latin America was not essentially different from what existed in other tribal
societies, being communal and tied to extended kinship groups. The remaining Indians were tricked into selling their lands, or else simply forced
off them. Communal lands were turned into private estates, and the environment was dramatically changed as native crops like maize and manioc
were replaced by European cash crops. A lot of agricultural land was given
over to cattle ranching, with often devastating effects on soil fertility. The
government back in Madrid was committed to protecting the rights of the

indigenous owners, but was far away and unable to control things on the ground. Oftentimes local Spanish authorities worked hand in hand with the new class of landowners to help them evade regulation. This was the origin of the Latin American latifundia, the hacienda, which in later generations would become the source both of inequality and persistent civil strife.[31]

The concentration of land in the hands of a small elite was promoted by the Spanish practice of *mayorazgo*, a system of primogeniture that prevented large haciendas from being broken up and sold piecemeal. The seventeenth century saw the accumulation of large landholdings, including entire towns and villages, by wealthy individuals, who then introduced the mayorazgo to prevent land from slipping out of family control through endless division to children. This practice was introduced into the New World as well. The Spanish authorities tried to limit the number of licenses for mayorazgos under the same theory that led them to take back encomiendas. The local creole or settler population responded by making use of the *mejora*, by which parents could favor one child over another in order to maintain the power and status of the family's lineage.[32]

A class of powerful landed families emerged, but they failed to operate as a coherent political actor. As in ancien régime France, the tax system helped to bind individual settlers to the state and to break up the solidarity they might have felt with any of their non-European fellow citizens. The large numbers of single men who constituted early waves of settlers ended up marrying or having children with indigenous women, producing a class of mestizos. The mulatto offspring of whites and the black slaves that were being transported to the New World in increasing numbers constituted yet another separate caste. Against these groups, the creole offspring of Hispanic settlers claimed tax exemptions for themselves, a status enjoyed in Spain only by nobles and hidalgos (lower gentry). As in North America, the simple fact of being white conferred status on people and marked them off from tribute-paying Indians and blacks.[33]

Given the dire fiscal condition of the Crown back in Madrid, it was perhaps inevitable that the European institution of venal office would eventually cross the Atlantic. Fiscal administration in Spanish America had been reasonably good through much of the sixteenth century, since the colonies were, after all, a major source of precious metals and, increasingly, agricultural goods. But mining output began to decline by the end of the century, and the Spanish king's need for revenues increased as the Thirty

Years' War got under way. The monarchy's efforts to prevent the formation of a New World aristocracy thus faded. J. H. Elliott describes this shift:

> Making use of their special connections to the royal administration, leading urban families built up their resources, established entails where it suited their purposes, and consolidated their dominance over the cities and their hinterland. They took advantage, too, of the crown's growing financial difficulties to buy their way into public office. Private traffic in *regimientos*—aldermanships—in city councils had long been standard practice, and from 1591 they were put up for public sale. From 1559 notarial posts were placed on the market, and these were followed in 1606 by almost all local offices. Philip II and Philip III had held the line against the sale of treasury offices, but in 1633 Philip IV began putting these too up for sale. Eventually, in the second half of the seventeenth century, even the highest posts came onto the market, with posts in the Audiencias being systematically sold from 1687.[34]

As in France and Spain, sale of public offices became a route to upward mobility for the merchant class, who could now think of themselves as caballeros and pass that status down to their children. The older families could still protect their relative status by buying their way into the Spanish nobility. The seventeenth-century Spanish monarchs opened the floodgates and permitted the entry of hundreds of creoles into the prestigious Spanish military orders, while making others marquises and counts.

By the eighteenth century, when doctrines of equality and the Rights of Man began to penetrate into New World colonies, the Spanish political and social system had succeeded in reproducing itself in Latin America. The irony was that this transfer of patrimonial institutions happened *despite* the wishes of colonial administrators in Madrid. Through much of the 1500s, they had tried to create a more modern, impersonal political order in the colonies, only to have these schemes undone by the deteriorating fiscal position of the Crown, which prevented them from exercising stronger control. The same erosion of boundaries between public and private interest that occurred in the peninsula took place in America.

In France, the capture of the state by rentiers and venal officeholders undermined the state's power and eventually produced the social explosion that was the French Revolution. In Spain, the same political evolution produced a long-term decline in Spanish power, but the equivalent political revolution never came to either the metropole or the colonies. The wars of independence from Spain that were fought in the early nineteenth century took up ideas of liberty and equality from the French and American revolutions. But they were led by a creole elite—exemplified by individuals like Simón Bolívar—that was heavily implicated in the patrimonial political system of the old regime.

The French Revolution was able to reestablish a bright line between public and private interest by simply expropriating all of the old venal officeholders' patrimonies and lopping off the heads of the recalcitrant ones. A new political system in which recruitment into public office was to be based on merit and impersonality—something the Chinese had discovered nearly two millennia earlier—was then brought to the rest of Europe by a man on horseback. Napoleon's defeat of a patrimonial Prussian army at Jena-Auerstadt in 1806 convinced a new generation of reformers like Baron vom Stein and Karl August von Hardenberg that the Prussian state would have to be rebuilt on modern principles.[35] The nineteenth-century German bureaucracy that became Max Weber's model for modern, rational public administration did not evolve out of patrimonial officeholding, but rather styled itself as a conscious break with that tradition.[36]

In Latin America, the social revolution never occurred before independence was achieved. Patrimonialism was left embedded in many of the postindependence regimes. Even though practices like the sale of offices and aristocratic titles were abolished, and formal democratic institutions established, the same mind-set lived on. Very few of the new states in nineteenth-century Latin America were strong enough to confront their own elites, or able to tax and regulate them. Those elites had succeeded in penetrating and controlling the state itself and found ways of passing on their social and political privileges to their children. Up through the late twentieth century, the fiscal bad habits of old regime Spain like persistent budget deficits, excessive borrowing, debt renegotiation, and taxation via inflation lived on in Argentina, Mexico, Peru, and Bolivia. Formal democracy and constitutionalism was not based on confrontation and negotiated consensus between social classes, but was granted from above by elites who could take it back when it no longer suited their interests. This led to the emergence of highly unequal and polarized societies in the twentieth century, a situation that generated truly revolutionary social forces—in the form of Mexican and Cuban revolutions. Periodically over the last century, Latin American states have been roiled by the demand for a fundamental renegotiation of the entire social contract.

Many new social actors have emerged in recent generations, like trade unions, business groups with strong international ties, urban intellectuals, and newly mobilized indigenous groups seeking to reclaim the status and power taken from them by colonization. Latin America's political systems, both democratic and authoritarian, have tended to accommodate them not through a genuine reordering of political power but by buying them off through their piecemeal incorporation into the state. For example, in Argentina, the rise of the working class in the early decades of the twentieth century was fiercely resisted by the traditional landed agrarian elite. In Europe, the working class was incorporated through the formation of broad social democratic parties pushing for redistributive agendas that laid the basis for modern welfare states. In Argentina, by contrast, the working class was represented by a military caudillo, Juan Perón, whose political party (the Partido Justicialista) provided selective benefits to networks of supporters. The country bounced from periods of populist fervor to military dictatorship, without putting in place a true European-style welfare state. Something similar happened in Mexico under the long dominance of the Institutional Revolutionary Party (the Partido Revolucionario Institucional, or PRI), which doled out patronage to select groups of organized supporters. Mexico was more stable than Argentina, but it similarly failed to solve its deep problems of social exclusion and poverty. The patrimonial legacy of old regime Spain thus lives on in the twenty-first century.

25

EAST OF THE ELBE

Why Hungary is of interest as an alternative route to failed accountability; how serfdom was imposed in Eastern Europe just as it was being abolished in the West; the emergence of constitutionalism and noble dominance in Hungary; why it is important to have a strong central state as well as constraints on that state if liberty is to flourish

Early modern France and Spain were examples of weak absolutism and failed accountability. The states that were formed in the sixteenth and seventeenth centuries were absolutist because their monarchies centralized power in a way that was not formally accountable to a parliament or any other representative body. There were political and social actors like the parlements and Cortes, the comuneros and Frondeurs, who opposed the state's centralizing project, but all were eventually defeated. The way they were defeated underscores a basic weakness of the absolutist authority. Elite actors had to be individually co-opted by offering them a piece of the state. This co-optation weakened their capacity for acting collectively, but it also limited the authority the state could exercise over them. Their property and privileges, while constantly challenged and eroded, remained largely intact.

Hungary and Russia, by contrast, offer two alternative paths of development that are different both from each other and from the French and Spanish models. All four of these cases ultimately terminate in an absence of political accountability. In Hungary, the absolutist project initially failed because a strong and well-organized noble class succeeded in imposing constitutional limits on the king's authority. The Hungarian Diet, like its English counterpart, made the Hungarian king accountable to itself. Accountability was not sought on behalf of the whole realm but rather on behalf of a narrow oligarchic class that wanted to use its freedom to squeeze its own peasants harder and to avoid onerous taxes to the central state. The result was the spread of an increasingly harsh serfdom for nonelites, and a weak state that ultimately could not defend the country from the Turks. Freedom for one class, in other words, resulted in a lack of freedom for everyone else and the carving up of the country among stronger neighbors.

We are taking the time to consider the Hungarian case for a simple reason: to show that constitutional limits on a central government's power do not by themselves necessarily produce political accountability. The "freedom" sought by the Hungarian noble class was the freedom to exploit their own peasants more thoroughly, and the absence of a strong central state allowed them to do just that. Everyone understands the Chinese form of tyranny, one perpetrated by a centralized dictatorship. But tyranny can result from decentralized oligarchic domination as well. True freedom tends to emerge in the interstices of a balance of power among a society's elite actors, something that Hungary never succeeded in achieving.

LORDSHIP AND BONDAGE

One of the great puzzles of European history is the very different development of relations between master and bondsman in the two halves of Europe at the beginning of the early modern period, in the sixteenth and seventeenth centuries. In the lands west of the Elbe River—that is, in the western German states, the Low Countries, France, England, and Italy—the serfdom that had been imposed on peasants during the Middle Ages was gradually abolished. It never existed in the first place in Spain, Sweden, and Norway. By contrast, east of the river (in Bohemia, Silesia, Hungary, Prussia, Livonia, Poland, Lithuania, and Russia), formerly free peasants were progressively enserfed at virtually the same historical moment.[1]

Serfdom, like feudalism, has been defined in a wide variety of ways. According to the historian Jerome Blum, "A peasant was recognized as unfree if he was bound to the will of his lord by ties that were degrading and socially incapacitating, and that were recognized as a fundamental part of the legal and social structure of the land, rather than the result of an agreement or contract between lord and peasant." It was the lord and not the state who had legal jurisdiction over the peasant, and while their relationship might be defined by detailed customary rules, lords could change the rules to the peasants' disadvantage. While the serf retained some minimal legal rights that distinguished him from a slave, the practical distinction was not very great.[2]

The serfs of Western Europe had won their freedom at different times and to different degrees from the twelfth century on. Serfs usually first graduated to the status of renters on the property of their lords, whose usufructuary rights might be limited to their lifetimes or sometimes transmissible to their children. Some rights to land were mainmortable—that is, they passed to their children only if their children lived with them; otherwise they reverted to the landowner. In the eighteenth century, the abolition of mainmort became one of the great causes of liberal reformers. In other cases, peasants graduated to the status of landowners with complete rights to buy, sell, and hand down their land as they saw fit. On the eve of the French Revolution, peasants owned 50 percent of the land in France, more than twice as much as the nobles.[3] Tocqueville points out that lords by then had long since ceased to play any real role in governing their peasants, which is why their residual rights to collect a variety of fees or to force the peasants to use their mills or winepresses was so bitterly resented.[4]

Precisely the opposite happened in Eastern Europe. There was a considerably higher degree of freedom there in the late Middle Ages than in the west, largely because much of this region was an underpopulated frontier zone where colonists from Western Europe and Eurasia could live under their own laws. But beginning in the fifteenth century, new rules were established throughout Eastern Europe limiting the peasants' mobility. Peasants were forbidden to leave their holdings, or were under threat of big fines; heavy punishments were set for those aiding runaways, and restrictions were put on cities' abilities to shelter peasants from manorial obligations.

Nowhere was the loss of peasant freedom greater than in Russia. There had been slaves and serfs going all the way back to Kievan Rus in the twelfth century, but with the rise of the Muscovite state in the fifteenth century, the obligations of peasants increased steadily. Their freedom of movement diminished until it was limited to a single yearly occasion around St. George's day (provided their debts were paid), though even this opportunity was canceled in the next century.[5] The rights that Russian lords had over their serfs steadily increased through the end of the eighteenth century, just as the doctrine of the Rights of Man was spreading throughout the West. Serfs were permanently bound to their owners; they had no rights of movement, and indeed could be arbitrarily moved from one property to another, or exiled to Siberia and then just as arbitrarily returned. The Russian ruling class began to measure its status by the numbers of serfs an individual owned. The upper reaches of the Russian nobility were staggeringly rich: Count N. P. Sheremetov owned 185,610 serfs, while his son, Count D. N. Sheremetov, managed to increase that number to more than 300,000. Count Vorontsov owned 54,703 serfs of both sexes at the end of the eighteenth century, while his successor had 37,702 male serfs alone in the decade prior to the abolition of serfdom in the mid-nineteenth century.[6]

Why did the institution of serfdom develop so differently in the two halves of Europe? The explanation lies in a combination of economic, demographic, and political factors that made serfdom untenable in the west and highly profitable in the east.

Western Europe was much more densely populated, with three times the population of the east in the year 1300. In the economic boom that had started in the eleventh century, it had also become much more urbanized. The existence of urban centers radiating from northern Italy up through Flanders was first and foremost the product of political weakness and the fact that kings found it useful to protect the independence of cities as a means of undercutting the great territorial lords who were their rivals. Cities were also protected by ancient feudal rights, and the urban tradition from Roman times had never been entirely lost. Thus sheltered, the cities evolved as independent communes that, through growing trade, developed their own resources independent of the manorial economy.[7] The existence of free cities in turn made serfdom increasingly difficult to maintain; they were like an internal frontier to which serfs could escape to win their freedom (hence the medieval saying, "Stadtluft macht frei"—City air makes you free).[8] In the less densely populated parts of Eastern Europe, by contrast, cities were smaller and served more as administrative centers for the existing political powers, as they did in China and the Middle East.

The trend toward freedom in the west and unfreedom in the east was stimulated by the disastrous population decline that occurred in the fourteenth century as recurring waves of plague and famine struck Western Europe harder and earlier than the east. As economic growth returned in the fifteenth century, Western Europe saw regeneration of towns and cities, which offered sanctuary and economic opportunities that prevented the nobility from squeezing its own peasantry harder. Indeed, to keep labor on the land, lords had to offer peasants greater freedom in what was becoming a modern labor market. The centralizing monarchies of the region found they could weaken their aristocratic rivals by protecting the rights of cities and towns. Increased demand had to be met instead by imports of food and precious metals from Eastern and Central Europe. But east of the Elbe, the weakness of both independent cities and kings permitted the nobility to develop export agriculture on the backs of their own peasantry. In the words of the historian Jenö Szücs, "The regions beyond the Elbe paid, in the long run, for the West's recovery . . . The legislative omens of the 'second serfdom' appeared with awesome synchrony in Brandenburg (1494), Poland (1496), Bohemia (1497), Hungary (1492 and 1498), and also in Russia (1497)."[9]

This, then, is the most salient explanation for the different pattern of peasant rights in the two halves of Europe. In the west, aristocratic power was offset by the existence of cities supported by increasingly powerful kings. In France and Spain, kings eventually prevailed in this long struggle, but the interelite competition opened up greater opportunities for peasants and other social actors who had grievances or conflicts with the local lords. In Eastern Europe, cities and kingly power were weak, leaving the noble class a free hand to dominate their peasants. This was the pattern that emerged in Hungary and Poland, where kings were elected by the noble class. States were strong in two places in the east: in Russia from the fifteenth century on, and in Brandenburg-Prussia after the eighteenth century. In both of these cases, however, the state did not act to counter the aristocracy on behalf of the commons. Instead, the state allied itself with the aristocracy against the peasantry and the bourgeoisie, and increased its own power through the recruitment of nobles into its own service.

In later years, peasants would be liberated in sweeping gestures like Tsar Alexander II's emancipation manifesto in 1861. But genuine freedom for nonelites—and this includes not just peasants but also artisans and the bourgeoisie of cities—depended on the existence of deadlock or balance of power among existing elite actors. These nonelite groups were crushed under two circumstances: when a decentralized oligarchy became too powerful, which was the case in Hungary and Poland, and when the central government became too powerful, the case in Russia.

CONSTITUTIONALISM AND DECLINE IN HUNGARY

Present-day Hungary constitutes only a truncated portion of what was once an extensive medieval kingdom that at various times included parts of what are now Austria, Poland, Romania, Croatia, Bosnia, Slovenia, Slovakia, and Serbia. The Hungarians were a tribal people who invaded Europe toward the end of the first millennium. Comprising seven tribes, the rulers of the leading one, the Megyeri, provided the ruling Árpád dynasty. An Árpád prince, István, was baptized a Christian and crowned king of Hungary in the year 1000; he oversaw the conversion of the country to Christianity and was later canonized as St. Stephen, Hungary's patron saint.[10]

The persistent pattern of oligarchic dominance in Hungary was the flip side of the dynastic struggles that consumed the monarchy and weakened it. The monarchy had initially come to possess sizable estates with the dissolution of the tribes' communal property, as well as income from royal mines that gave the Hungarian ruler resources comparable to those of the kings of France and England. Particularly toward the end of the reign of King Béla III (c. 1148–1196), the Crown began to give away royal estates, large segments of the counties into which the country was organized, income from customs and fairs, and the like. These donations were not feudal grants in exchange for service, as in Western Europe, but rather grants of allodial property owned outright by an emerging class of barons. The dissipation of royal property continued through the power struggles among Béla's successors, who vied with each other to bestow gifts on the aristocracy.[11]

This provided the setting for the proclamation by King Andrew II in 1222 of the Golden Bull, noted earlier (see page 326).[12] It was in fact a constitutional document limiting the king's power, though it was driven by a rather different set of social actors. In the case of the Magna Carta, the powerful English barons, speaking in the name of the entire realm, forced King John to accept limitations on his own authority over them. The Golden Bull was forced not by Hungary's barons but by the class of royal soldiers and the garrisons of the counties' castles, who actually wanted the king to protect them from the power of the barons.[13] The Hungarian church, supported by the powerful post-Gregorian papacy, was also a significant political actor pressing for changes in royal policy. The church wanted to protect its own lands and privileges from further erosion, and also sought the ouster of Muslim and Jewish merchants from the kingdom and their replacement with Christians. The politics of the Golden Bull thus illustrated the degree to which Hungarian society was already organized into powerful competing groups outside of the state, including the barons or upper nobility, the lower gentry, and the clergy.[14]

The first result of this weakness of central authority was Hungary's dev-

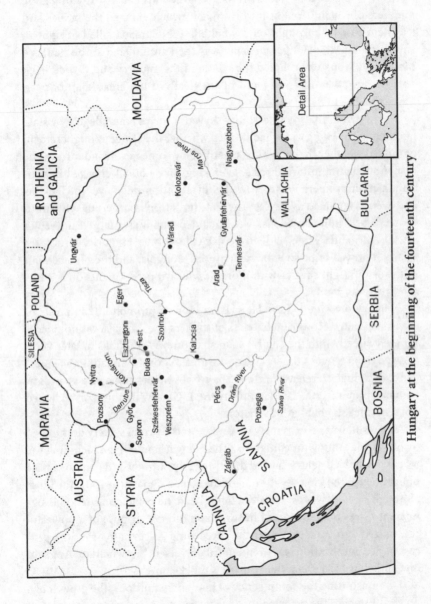

Hungary at the beginning of the fourteenth century

astation by the Mongols, who after conquering Russia entered Hungary in 1241.[15] King Béla IV had tried to strengthen his hand by inviting large numbers of pagan Cumans into Hungary, which enraged the nobles and led them to refuse to fight on his behalf. The Cumans failed to fight in any event, and the Hungarian army was then annihilated at the Battle of Mohi. The Mongols occupied the whole of the country and turned back only because they received word of the death of the great khan back in Mongolia.

Hungary's military vulnerability served to drive some degree of state building.[16] The Hungarians had no idea whether the Mongols might return, or indeed whether they might be assaulted by some new invader from the east. Anticipating future threats, later kings like Louis I engaged in substantial military operations to extend Hungary's dominion over the Balkans and even as far afield as Naples. The state undertook numerous reforms to protect itself from invasions. This included building a large number of stone castles and fortified cities to replace the wooden and brick structures that had proved to be so vulnerable to the Mongols, and the replacement of the army's light cavalry with more heavily armored knights on a Western European model.

Military pressure led the Hungarian king to promote the interests of the lower gentry. However, this class of soldiers and officials was not incorporated directly into the central state structure. Weak kings in later years allowed them to enter the service of the great barons, facilitating the emergence of a single, large noble class. The royal soldiers and castle guardians who had promoted the Golden Bull by the 1300s saw their interests aligned not with the king but with the barons.[17]

The result was an extremely weak state and a strong society dominated by oligarchic landowning interests. The Hungarian nobility, including the recently ennobled gentry, owned their property outright and had no service obligations to the king. By the end of the Árpád dynasty in 1301, the king, although elected, was essentially a figurehead; he could command no significant forces or resources of his own and did not dispose of a powerful centralized bureaucracy. Under the succeeding Angevin dynasty, the process of decentralization was momentarily reversed, but when the Angevin line ended in 1386, the nobility made a quick comeback.

Demonstrating the contingency of human institutions, the growth of a powerful state in the principality of Moscow was aided greatly by the fact that the founding dynasty consistently produced male heirs up through the end of the sixteenth century. Hungary, by contrast, faced repeated succession struggles due to its short-lived dynasties and the foreign origin of many of its kings.[18] Royal pretenders gained power only by turning back resources to the nobility; under King Sigismund, a large number of the monarchy's castles reverted to noble control.[19]

Indeed, the noble estate in Hungary succeeded in institutionalizing its power in the form of a diet, whose power exceeded that of the French sovereign courts, the Spanish Cortes, or the Russian zemskiy sobor.[20] In anticipation of John Locke, the noble estate "proclaimed their right to defend the welfare of the kingdom even against the king should he seek to act in opposition to the common interest," and even jailed a king on these grounds.[21] The precedent for holding diets went all the way back to the days of the Golden Bull, and by the mid-1400s a national diet met annually and held the power to select kings. Unlike the English Parliament, however, the Hungarian Diet was dominated by the large noble landowners and represented only the interests of the noble class. In the words of the historian Pal Engel, "The essence of the new system was the radical extension of the right of decision-making, in theory to all the landowners of the kingdom, but in practice to that part of them which was involved in politics—the nobility."[22] The cities had earlier been permitted to participate, but they gradually ceased doing so as their influence waned.[23] (The configuration of political power in medieval Hungary is shown in Figure 3.)

FIGURE 3. HUNGARY

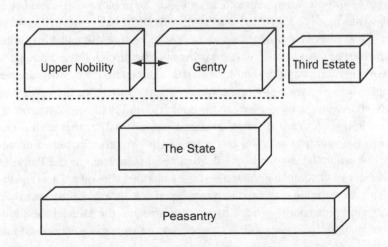

The last possibility for creating a more powerful state in Hungary occurred just as the Ottoman threat to the southeast was gathering in the second half of the fifteenth century. János Hunyadi, a noble landowner who was elected regent by the diet in 1446, gained enormous prestige by engineering a series of military victories over the Turks, including a heroic defense of Belgrade in 1456.[24] As a result, János's son Mátyás (Matthias Corvinus) was elected king in 1458, and in the course of a more than thirty-year rule he succeeded in modernizing the central Hungarian state. This included the creation of a powerful Black Army under the direct control of the king, replacing the poorly disciplined, semiprivate noble armies on which military capacity had been based; the development of the royal chancery and its staffing with university-trained officials, who replaced the old noble patrimonial officeholders; and the imposition of national customs and direct taxes, and a sharp rise in the tax burden levied by the central government.[25] Using these new instruments of power, Mátyás Hunyadi was able to score significant military victories against the Turks in Bosnia and Transylvania, as well as against the Austrians, Poles, and Silesians.[26]

Mátyás Hunyadi was driven by military necessity to do what other modernizing, absolutist monarchs of the period were doing. But unlike the kings of France and Spain, he still faced a highly powerful and well-organized noble estate. He was compelled to consult regularly with the diet that elected him. While his military successes forced the nobles to grant him considerable leeway, they resented the increasing tax burden he was imposing on them, as well as the erosion of their influence in decision making. As a result, when Mátyás died in 1490, the nobles took back most of the gains made by the central state in the preceding half century. They were angry at their loss of privileges and eager to restore the status quo ante. The barons placed a weak foreign prince on the throne, starved the Black Army of funds, and then sent it into battle against the Turks, whereupon it was destroyed. The noble estate succeeded in reducing its tax burden by 70–80 percent, at the expense of the country's ability to defend itself.

Hungary had reverted to a decentralized, aristocratic mean. The consequence was felt very soon thereafter, when a poorly disciplined noble-based army was defeated by Suleiman the Magnificent at the Battle of Mohács in 1526, and the Hungarian king was killed. The spectacle of squabbling barons more interested in pursuing an agenda against the state than defending the country, which had played a role in the Mongol conquest, repeated itself. Hungary lost its independent existence as a nation and was divided up into three parts controlled by the Austrian Habsburgs, the Ottomans, and a Turkish vassal state in Transylvania.

FREEDOM AND OLIGARCHY

I have covered the case of Hungary in some detail to make a relatively simple point: that political freedom is not necessarily achieved by a strong, cohesive, and well-armed civil society that is able to resist the power of the central government. Nor is it always achieved by a constitutional arrangement that puts strict legal limits on executive authority. Hungary was all of these things, and it succeeded in weakening central authority to the point that the country could not defend itself from a clear and present foreign enemy. A similar situation materialized in Poland, where weak kings were controlled by a noble council; Poland as well lost its national independence two centuries after Hungary.

Hungary's loss of national independence was not the only type of freedom lost. Hungary was facing, after all, a huge and well-organized Turkish empire that had absorbed most of the neighboring kingdoms and principalities in southeastern Europe. Even a more centralized, modern country might not have been able to withstand the Turkish onslaught. But the weakness of the central Hungarian state condemned the Hungarian peasantry and cities to servitude as well. After the chaos and depopulation brought on by the Mongol invasion, peasants were largely free people, particularly those living on the large royal domains. They had fixed rights and obligations as royal "guests," and could either serve as soldiers or pay a tax in lieu of service. The most important freedom they had was that of movement, as well as the right to elect their own judges and priests.[27]

But both the lay and ecclesiastical landowners wanted to tie their peasants to the land and turn them into a salable commodity. The transfer of royal lands to private hands that began in the thirteenth century had the effect of putting increasing numbers of peasants under the jurisdiction of the landowners and their arbitrary rule. The rise in food prices that began in the early sixteenth century induced landowners to increase the seigneurial dues in kind they were owed by their peasants. They were also forced to perform more corvée labor, from a day a week in the previous century to as many as three by 1520. The right of peasants to choose their own local judges and priests was limited and put under seigneurial control.[28]

Further, the landowners began to block the free movement of peasants from one lord to another, or to prevent their migration from the village to the market town. The worsening condition of the peasantry led to a major peasant uprising in 1514, which was brutally suppressed, the revolt leader being "enthroned" on a stake and his companions forced to eat his burning flesh.[29] This uprising came right on the eve of the Turkish invasion and was one factor contributing to the Ottoman success.[30]

Progressive enserfment was not, as noted at the beginning of this chapter, limited to Hungary. It occurred as well in Bohemia, Poland, Prussia, Austria, and Russia. Nobles throughout the region were pressing to increase taxation, take away freedoms, and restrict the movement of their dependent populations. The twentieth century has taught us to think about tyranny as something perpetrated by powerful centralized states, but it can also be the work of local oligarchs. In contemporary China, many of the worst abuses of peasant rights, violations of environmental and safety laws, and cases of gross corruption are the work not of the central government in Beijing but of local party officials or of the private employers who work hand in hand with them. It is the responsibility of the central government to enforce its own laws against the oligarchy; freedom is lost not when the state is too strong but when it is too weak. In the United States, the ending of Jim Crow laws and racial segregation in the two decades following World War II was brought about only when the federal government used its power to enforce the Constitution against the states in the South. Political freedom is not won, it would seem, only when the power of the state is constrained but when a strong state comes up against an equally strong society that seeks to restrict its power.

The need for such balance was understood by the American Founding Fathers. Alexander Hamilton, writing on the question of the rights of states versus the federal government in Federalist No. 17, said the following:

> In those instances in which the monarch finally prevailed over his vassals, his success was chiefly owing to the tyranny of those vassals over their dependents. The barons, or nobles, equally the enemies of the sovereign and the oppressors of the common people, were dreaded and detested by both; till mutual danger and mutual interest effected a union between them fatal to the power of the aristocracy. Had the nobles, by a conduct of clemency and justice, preserved the fidelity and devotion of their retainers and followers, the contests between them and the prince must almost always have ended in their favor, and in the abridgment or subversion of the royal authority.

Hamilton goes on to say that the states within a federal structure are comparable to feudal baronies. The degree to which they can maintain their independence from the central government depends on how they treat their own citizens. A powerful central government is neither intrinsically good nor bad; its ultimate effect on freedom depends on the complex interplay between it and the subordinate political authorities. This is a truth that played out in the history of the United States, much as it did in Hungarian and Polish history.

On the other hand, when a strong state sides with a strong oligarchy, freedom faces a particularly severe threat. This was the situation that emerged in Russia with the rise of the principality of Moscow in the same century that the Hungarian state came to an end.

26

TOWARD A MORE PERFECT ABSOLUTISM

The emergence of the Muscovite state and peculiarities of Russian political development; how the gradual enslavement of Russian peasants was the result of the monarchy's dependence on the aristocracy; why absolutism triumphed more completely in Russia than in other parts of Europe

The Russian Federation, particularly since the rise of Vladimir Putin in the early 2000s, has become what some political scientists label an "electoral authoritarian" regime.[1] The government is fundamentally authoritarian, controlled by a shadowy network of politicians, officials, and business interests, which nonetheless holds democratic elections to legitimate its continuation in power. The quality of Russian democracy is very low: the regime controls virtually all of the major media outlets and does not permit criticism of itself, it intimidates and disqualifies opposition candidates, and it provides patronage to its own candidates and supporters.

Worse than the quality of its democracy is its performance with regard to rule of law. Journalists who uncover official corruption or criticize the regime end up dead, and there is no real effort to find their killers; companies facing hostile takeovers by regime insiders are subjected to spurious charges from government agencies that force them to surrender their assets; important officials can literally get away with murder with no accountability. Transparency International, a nongovernmental organization that does systematic surveys of perceptions of levels of corruption around the world, ranks Russia at number 147 out of 180 countries, worse than Bangladesh, Liberia, Kazakhstan, and the Philippines, and only slightly better than Syria and the Central African Republic.[2]

Many people see a continuity between twenty-first-century Russia and the former Soviet Union, a view bolstered by the nostalgia frequently voiced by some Russians for Stalin and the Soviet past. Communism sank roots in Russia in the seventy years following the Bolshevik Revolution and clearly shaped the attitudes of contemporary Russians.

But many stacked turtles lie hidden beneath communism. To attribute contemporary authoritarianism simply to twentieth-century politics begs the question of why communism triumphed so thoroughly in Russia in the first place, as it did in China. There was, of course, a much older absolutist tradition at play. Russia prior to the Bolshevik Revolution had developed a strongly centralized state, in which executive power was only weakly constrained by either rule of law or accountable legislatures. The nature of the absolutism that was achieved in pre-Bolshevik Russia was qualitatively different from that of either old regime France or Spain, and much closer to the premodern Chinese or Ottoman variants. The reasons for this had much to do with Russia's physical geography and location, which has had a lasting impact on its political culture.

SOURCES OF RUSSIAN ABSOLUTISM

The Russian state originated in the area around Kiev (Ukraine) at the end of the first millennium, when it was a major trading depot connecting Northern Europe to the Byzantine Empire and Central Asia. But the continuity of that state was broken in the late 1230s, when Russia was invaded and occupied by the Mongols under Batu Khan and Subutai. Kiev was utterly devastated; the papal legate, Archbishop Carpini, wrote that when they passed through the city, "We found lying in the field countless heads and bones of dead people; for this city had been extremely large and very populous, whereas now it has been reduced to nothing: barely two hundred houses stand there, and those people are held in the harshest slavery."[3] Mongol occupation lasted for almost 250 years thereafter. Many contemporary Russians, when asked why their state and political culture differ so greatly from those of Western Europe, immediately blame the Mongols. There is also a long history of Western observers of Russia, like the Marquis de Custine, who insisted on seeing Russia as an "Asiatic" power that was shaped decisively by its interactions not just with the Mongols but also with the Ottomans, Cumans, and other Asiatic peoples.[4] More recently, with the emergence of an independent Mongolia, opinion has shifted, and a new wave of revisionism has emerged that casts the role of the Mongols in a much more positive light.[5]

In any event, the Mongol invasion exerted considerable influence over subsequent Russian political development in a number of mostly negative ways.[6] First, it cut Russia off from trade and intellectual contact with Byzantium and the Middle East, which had been the source of Russian religion and culture. It hindered contact with Europe as well, which meant that Russia did not participate in developments like the Renaissance and Reformation to the extent of lands farther to the west.

Second, the Mongol occupation greatly delayed Russian political development, which essentially had to start over again after the destruction of Kievan Rus, the area around contemporary Kiev in Ukraine that was the original Russian area of settlement. The Russian state had started to break up well before the Mongols' arrival, but the conquest confirmed the dispersion of political authority into a myriad of small appanages ruled by petty princes. Russia's center of gravity shifted from pontic Europe north of the Black Sea to the northeast, where the Grand Duchy of Moscow emerged as the central political player. Unlike European feudalism, which evolved over an eight-hundred-year period, appanage Russia existed for little more than two centuries—from the onset of the Tatar yoke in 1240 to the mid-1500s when Ivan III came to power—before the princes had to face the growing power of a centralizing monarchy.

Finally, the Mongols undermined any legal traditions inherited from Byzantium and made political life far harsher and more cruel. In sharp contrast to the Christian princes of Europe, Mongol rulers saw themselves as pure predators whose avowed purpose was to extract resources from the populations they dominated. They were a tribal-level people who had no developed political institutions or theories of justice to transmit to the populations they conquered. They made no pretense that lordship existed for the sake of the ruled; unlike rulers of traditional agrarian states, they had short time horizons and were willing to extract resources at unsustainable levels. They punished resistance harshly and were perfectly willing to execute the inhabitants of entire towns simply to make a point. They recruited Russian princes, including the Muscovite prince who would go on to create the Russian state, to act as their tax collectors. The Mongols thus trained several generations of Russian leaders in their own predatory tactics. Indeed, through intermarriage they merged genetically with the Russian population.

As in the case of almost all of the other polities we have looked at, Russian state building was driven by the need to wage war. Like the Capetians on the Île de France, the Rurik dynasty in Moscow used its central location as a hub for outward expansion, fighting and absorbing other appanage principalities as well as the Mongols, Lithuanians, and other foreign forces. The state emerged as a major power under Ivan III (1440–1505), who annexed Novgorod and Tver and assumed the title of the sovereign of all Russia. The principality of Moscow grew from six hundred square miles at the time of Ivan I (1288–1340), to fifteen thousand square miles under Basil II (1415–1462), to fifty-five thousand square miles by the end of Ivan III's reign.[7]

There were many similarities between the Russian state-formation process during the appanage period and that of both China and the Ottomans. Like the founding dynasty of the Western Zhou, the descendants of the Kievan princely family had proliferated all over Russia and, particularly after the Mongol invasion, disintegrated into a series of small principalities that constituted a Russian version of feudalism. Each prince controlled territory, economic resources, and troops, and could contract for the services of a free aristocratic boyar class.

The power of the Muscovite state was built around the middle service class, made up of cavalrymen who were paid not in cash but in grants of land known as *pomest'ia*. Each pomest'ia was supported by the labor of only five or six peasant households. Since land was so abundant, control over people was more important than control over land. The cavalry did not constitute a standing army but were called into service by the prince and had to return home to their lands after the end of the campaigning season. The similarities between the Russian pomest'ia and the Ottoman timar are striking and very likely not accidental, since the Russians came increasingly into contact with the Turks in this period. Like the Ottoman sipahis, the core of the Russian army was made up of a class of what would elsewhere in Europe be labeled lower gentry, soldiers who were dependent on the state for access to land and resources. The Russian cavalry army even resembled the Ottoman cavalry in their relatively light equipment and dependence on maneuver, both differing substantially from the heavily armored knights of Western Europe. The Moscow regime's motive

Russia in 1462

Territory added by 1533

Territory added by 1598

Novaya
Zemlya

*Barents
Sea*

Kara Sea

SIBERIA

NORWAY   SWEDEN

Ob River

•Archangel

DENMARK

NOVGOROD

MUSCOVY

KAZAN

LITHUANIA

•Moscow

HOLY
ROMAN
EMPIRE   POLAND

Dnieper River

Don River

Volga River

TURKISH
KHANATES

Aral
Sea

OTTOMAN

Black Sea

Caspian Sea

EMPIRE

The rise of Russia

for building this kind of army was similar to that of the Ottomans: it created a military organization dependent on it alone for status, which nonetheless did not have to be paid in cash. This force could be used to offset the power of the princes and boyars who held their own land and resources.[8]

Here, then, is one critical difference between Russia and Hungary. In Russia, the middle service class was recruited to work directly for the Muscovite state, whereas in Hungary it was incorporated into the noble class. This choice was probably sufficient to determine the subsequent paths of centralization and decentralization taken by the two societies. The fact that the middle service class was directly subordinated to the state rather than subenfeudated to the territorial nobles is one important reason why Russian society threw up far fewer obstacles to the Muscovite state-building project than did the societies of Western Europe.

Another reason for the failure of the Russian nobility to limit the power of the central state had to do with the fact that the Russian version of feudalism simply did not exist long enough to entrench itself. There has been a long standing debate in Russian historiography as to whether the country experienced feudalism at all, since Russian feudal domains did not have the same self-governing authority that their Western European counterparts did.[9] Russian princes and lesser nobles did not have the time to build castles; the flat Russian plains and steppe gave an advantage to highly mobile offensive forces over defensive ones.

The Muscovite state deliberately promoted disunity among the aristocracy by promulgating the *mestnichestvo*, a hierarchical ranking of boyar families as well as individuals within families. Like the French and Spanish sale of titles and privileges, the mestnichestvo undermined the internal cohesion of the nobility by putting them in direct competition with one another.[10] The result was that Russian nobles were far less cohesive as a class and developed few institutions that permitted them to collectively resist the centralized state. They were famous for the petty internal squabbles that constantly consumed them.

In Russia, the rule of law was from the start weaker than in Western Europe. The Russian Orthodox church never played the same role that the Catholic church did in establishing a canon law outside the purview of territorial sovereigns. The Byzantine Empire from which Russia drew its model of church-state relations was caesaropapist; the eastern emperor appointed the patriarch of Constantinople and intervened on issues of doctrine. The equivalent of the investiture conflict and the Gregorian reform never took place in the Byzantine world. The Eastern church failed to develop a state-like centralized bureaucracy by which it could promulgate law, and did not succeed in codifying its decretals into a uniform canon law in the manner of the Catholic church. When the Mongol invasion cut the Russian church off from its Byzantine sources, it found a new protector in the Muscovite state. The interests of church and state coincided: the latter gave the former patronage and power, while the former promoted the latter's legitimacy as the seat of the "Third Rome." The Russian church became fully caesaropapist with the deposing of Patriarch Nikon in 1666, and under Peter the Great's Spiritual Regulation of 1721 the patriarchate was abolished completely and replaced by a Holy Synod directly appointed by the tsar.[11]

If we doubt the importance of the protections that the rule of law gave the elite of Western Europe, we have only to consider the *oprichnina*, a dark period in Russian history that unfolded in the second half of the reign of Ivan IV (1530–1584), which had no real counterpart in Western European history. (He was subsequently known as Ivan Grozny, which can be translated either as Ivan the Terrible or Ivan the Great.) The death of Ivan's young and beloved wife, Anastasia, in 1560 caused the prince to fall into wild suspicions of the court officials surrounding him. He left Moscow unexpectedly, only to return in 1565 with the demand that the boyars accept the creation of a special administrative district known as the oprichnina in which the prince would have sole authority to deal with evildoers and traitors. They granted him this power only to see the prince turn on them in a reign of terror in which larger and larger numbers of boyars were arrested, tortured, and executed, along with their entire families. Ivan created a special police corps known as the *oprichniki*, who dressed in black and rode black horses, that became the instrument of his special, extra-legal rule. Private property within the oprichnina was confiscated by the state and more land added to it subsequently until this domain came to constitute half the territory of the state. It is estimated that anywhere from four thousand to ten thousand boyars were killed. Only nine of the old princely families were left alive, and most of their lands were confiscated.[12] Ivan seems to have completely lost his emotional balance, at one point mortally wounding his son and heir, and after his death the country could only be described as traumatized.[13] It is hard not to see in the oprichnina a precedent for Joseph Stalin's purges of the Soviet Communist Party in the mid- to late 1930s, when the party general secretary suspected plots all around him and killed off all of the old Bolsheviks who had worked with him to make the revolution.[14] It also harkens back to Chinese rulers like the empress Wu, who engaged in purges of aristocratic elites.

The puzzling question from the standpoint of Russian political development is why the boyars endangered themselves by granting Ivan these special powers. One answer seems to be that they did not think they could take power on their own and were terrified of the consequences if the monarch did not exercise strong authority. This possibility had been raised during Ivan's strange withdrawal from Moscow. The Russian fear of chaos and disintegration in the wake of a weak state was not absurd, for this is precisely what happened when Ivan's son Feodor died childless in 1598, ending the Rurik dynasty and inaugurating the so-called Time of Troubles. The Muscovite state was beset by famine and foreign invasion and fell apart as a series of "false Dmitris" vied for the throne. The state apparatus that the Moscow princes had created was not strong enough to withstand a prolonged succession struggle, nor was it possible to return to a more decentralized form of feudal administration now that the power of the princes had been broken. The result was anomic violence and foreign domination, which was ended only with the emergence of the Romanov dynasty in 1613.

FREE ALTERNATIVES

The rise of Russian absolutism was not foreordained by some inner logic of Russian culture. There were in fact precedents in Russian history for Western-style republican institutions, or for representative assemblies, which provide some vision of alternative Russian possibilities. The city of Novgorod in the far northwest was never conquered by the Mongols and remained a vigorous commercial republic through the early appanage period. It was tightly integrated with the Baltic trade and served as a gateway for European goods entering Russia. Novgorod's prince commanded the army but was limited in his powers by the *veche*, or popular assembly, that elected a mayor from among the city's aristocracy. All free citizens were given a vote. The veche had control over taxes, laws, and foreign affairs, and could dismiss the prince. Even within the city, neighborhoods exercised considerable autonomy in managing their own affairs. Novgorod was eventually conquered by Ivan III and added to the Muscovite state in 1478. He ended all of Novgorod's unique republican institutions, executed many of its leaders as traitors, and deported a large number of boyar and merchant families to other parts of his realm.[15]

The second representative institution was the zemskiy sobor, a council of nobles that bore some resemblance to the Estates-General or Cortes in the West. The zemskiy sobor met irregularly but played a critical role at certain moments, such as when it approved a number of Ivan IV's initiatives such as his war with Livonia. Another zemskiy sobor approved the succession of Ivan IV's son Feodor as tsar in 1584 and offered the throne to the regent Boris Godunov in 1598. Perhaps the most important act of a zemskiy sobor was to approve Mikhail Romanov as tsar in 1613, bringing to an end the Time of Troubles. The body continued to meet to approve war and taxes on numerous occasions during the seventeenth century, up until Peter the Great marginalized it.[16] Representative institutions then disappeared from Russian history, until the Duma or legislature that was granted in the aftermath of the Russo-Japanese War in 1906.

A final potential source of resistance to authority was the Russian church. For reasons noted above, the Russian church has often been denounced by critics as a pliant tool of the ruler in Moscow from tsarist times to the present. But during the period prior to the deposing of the Patriarch Nikon, there was potentially a different path. The Russian Orthodox church enjoyed autonomy due to its possession of nearly a quarter of all the land in Russia. It had a strong monastic tradition from the reform of St. Sergius, whose monastic orders were often distrusted by secular rulers. The metropolitan of Moscow was appointed not by the prince but by the patriarch in Constantinople, at least up until the crisis triggered by the Florentine Union in 1441, whereupon the metropolitan was appointed by a council of Russian bishops.[17] Individual church leaders took heroic stands against tyranny, such as Metropolitan Philip of Moscow, who denounced Ivan IV and was banished from his see and eventually strangled for his efforts.[18]

These examples suggest that the Russian tradition is not one of unremitting tyranny but one in which free alternatives have sprouted and periodically prospered. It is the promise of a freer society that reappeared after the fall of communism and may yet be realized in the future.

THE PEASANT-OWNING CARTEL

The Russian state at the end of the seventeenth century was centralized, but far less developed than its European counterparts. There was no coherent centralized bureaucracy, only a series of so-called *prikazy*, departments with overlapping and inconsistent mandates created out of a welter of individual orders (*prikaz*) made by the tsar.[19] Unlike the French system of intendants, local government up through Ivan IV was based on appointments by the tsar known as *kormlenie*, or "feedings." The name suggests the combination of oversight and predatory intent behind the institution. The forms of local self-government that had existed in the sixteenth century were abolished under Ivan IV, and the state relied on a system of *voevody*, or military governors, to execute its orders. The army was similarly primitive, still based on cavalry with new infantry units of dubious reliability organized in the capital.[20]

The next big round of Russian state building occurred under Peter the Great (1672–1725), who moved the capital from Moscow to St. Petersburg and imported a host of institutions from Europe. Peter was a giant, both physically and in terms of his leadership ability, and single-handedly pushed the limits of what was possible in terms of top-down social transformation of a society. War was again the chief motive for state building, especially the enormous pressures created by the Great Northern War with Sweden. Following defeat by Charles XII at the Battle of Narva in 1700, Peter began a thorough reorganization of the army along contemporary European lines and built a navy from scratch (beginning with a single ship and ending with a fleet of more than eight hundred that was capable of defeating the Swedish navy). He also modernized Russia's central administration by abolishing the old prikazy and replacing them with a system of colleges modeled on similar institutions in Sweden. The colleges were built around technical expertise—often, at this point, coming from foreigners—and exercised a deliberative function in debating and executing policies.

The first phase of state building in the fifteenth and sixteenth centuries was based on mobilization of the middle service class, which split the nobility and ensured that a large number of them would be directly dependent on the state. Peter went even further and drafted the entire aristocracy into state service. The gentry entered the army as boys, were promoted on modern merit criteria, and had to remain with the regiments for their entire lives. The idea of a service nobility thus lasted far longer in Russia than it had in Europe, though it was implemented very differently. The nobles who served the state did not come with their own retinues of vassals and retainers but were assigned positions by a centralized hierarchy. This led to an overall militarization of Russian society, with a moral emphasis placed on duty, honor, hierarchy, and obedience.[21]

The balance of internal political forces supporting Russian absolutism is illustrated in Figure 4.

FIGURE 4. RUSSIA

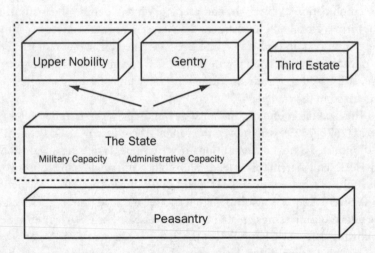

Peter replaced the old mestnichestvo with a Table of Ranks in 1722, a hierarchical system in which each of his subjects was entered into a legally defined order with its own privileges and obligations. By reaching a certain grade, a nonnoble servitor, whether bureaucrat or military man, was automatically entered into the ranks of the hereditary nobility. This provided a path for new entrants into the nobility, which was needed because of the state's enormous staffing needs. The Table of Ranks solidified the corporate identity of the nobility and its capacity for collective action. But it never saw itself as an opponent of monarchical power; its interests had become too tightly bound to the state for that.[22]

What the nobles got in return for service was exemption from taxation, exclusive rights to the ownership of land and people, and the opportunity to squeeze their serfs harder. The close relationship of the deteriorating condition of the peasantry and the rise of a service gentry is indicated by the fact that serfdom first appeared in the lands given by the prince to his gentry as pomest'ia. These tended to be in the south, southeast, and west, frontier regions where new land had been acquired from neighboring countries. In the great expanse of northern territories where there was no fighting, the condition of peasants was much better—they were for the most part state peasants with obligations to the state rather than a private landlord.[23]

Throughout the sixteenth and seventeenth centuries there was a continuing increase in the tax burden laid on peasants, but the more important legal restrictions were those placed on the right of movement. The peasant's right of departure had been an old tradition, but it was increasingly limited and then abolished altogether.[24] These limits on peasant movement were critical to both the formation of a cohesive Russian aristocracy and its alliance with the monarchy.

The reason for this was, ironically, related to Russia's geography, which as noted was highly *unfavorable* to the development of slavery due to its lack of circumscription. There are few natural barriers to movement such as impassable rivers or mountain ranges in Russia, and the country's borderlands stretched outward with the expansion of the country, particularly to the south and southeast. The free Cossack communities that grew up in southern Ukraine and in the Don basin were said to have been founded by escaped serfs. Just as in the American South, whose slave-owning territories abutted an open frontier, the institution of serfdom could be made viable only if there was strong agreement among serf owners to restrict their movement, to return runaways, and to severely punish not only serfs but also other landowners who violated the rules. If one major actor opted out of the system—whether a subset of landlords, or a group of free cities, or the king himself offering protection to runaways—then the whole system would collapse. Given the relative scarcity of labor in this period, it would be highly profitable for any individual landowner to defect from the coalition and attract serfs to his territory by offering them better terms. Hence the solidarity of the landowning cartel had to be reinforced through strong status privileges and binding commitments to enforce rules against peasant movement. Russian absolutism was founded on the alliance that emerged between the monarch and both the upper and lower nobility, all of whom committed themselves to binding rules at the expense of the peasantry.

The need to maintain this serf-owning cartel explains many things about Russian political development. The government put increasing restrictions on the free ownership of land by non-serf-owning individuals. To acquire property, one had to enter the nobility, whereupon one automatically acquired serfs and the obligations to maintain the system. This then constrained the growth of a bourgeoisie in independent commercial cities, which had played such an important role in promoting peasant freedom in the West. Hence capitalist economic development in Russia was spearheaded by nobles rather than an independent bourgeoisie.[25] The need to maintain the cartel also explains Russian expansion to the south and southeast, since the existence of free Cossack territories along the frontier presented a continuing lure and opportunity for peasant escape and needed to be suppressed.

AFTER PETER

Peter I was a great modernizer who "Europeanized" Russia in many ways and made it a major player in European politics. But his forced-march, top-down methods of reform ran into limitations posed by the underlying nature of Russian society. For example, his efforts at reforming government on a provincial, municipal, and local level through the creation of a two-tier system of provinces and districts and new municipal codes came to naught due to what in a contemporary developing country context would be called "lack of capacity." That is, there was an insufficient number of trained administrators at a local level, and those who existed lacked initiative. Statutes proclaimed from the center were not implemented, nor was it possible for the regime to put an end to corruption and arbitrary rule.[26]

Nor did Peter's efforts to create a modern, merit-based promotion system for the army and central bureaucracy last much beyond his death. Many of his reforms were dependent on his personal oversight and energy; for example, he sat in on the examinations of individual cadets entering government service. With his passing, the administrative system was repatrimonialized by the powerful families around the court. Under the weaker rulers who succeeded him, promotion to the highest ranks of the military and bureaucracy became dependent on patronage from one of the great families like the Dolgorukovs, Naryshkins, Golitsyns, or Saltykovs. The aristocrats, increasingly in control of state policy, succeeded in having their service obligations abolished in 1762 and also obtained further rights against the peasantry, such as the ability to move or deport them at will.[27] Rivalry between the families and their patronage networks extended into the military, where effectiveness was impaired by these struggles for control.

The rise of these aristocratic families diffused power within the Russian system and softened the tradition of absolutism bequeathed by Ivan IV and Peter. This, as well as the dominance of French culture among Russian elites, made the early nineteenth-century noble society described in Tolstoy's *War and Peace* seem recognizably European in a way it would not have been two hundred years earlier. But this diffusion of power should not be confused with the rise of a modern administrative state taking place in the West. According to the historian John LeDonne, "The existence of a national network of families and client systems made a mockery of the rigid hierarchy established by legislative texts in a constant search for administrative order and 'regularity.' It explained why the Russian government, more than any other, was a government of men and not of laws."[28]

ABSOLUTISM ACHIEVED

This account of Russia ends with the emergence of a consolidated absolutist state in the late eighteenth century. A lot obviously happened after that, both in terms of liberal experimentation in the nineteenth century and the rise of a totalitarian state in the twentieth century. Already by the time of the French Revolution, however, certain features of Russian governance distinguished it sharply from both the weak absolutisms of France and Spain on the one hand, and the Chinese and Ottoman states on the other.

The Russian state was stronger than its French or Spanish counterparts in several respects. The latter felt bound by respect for a rule of law, at least with regard to elites, which simply didn't exist in Russia. The French and Spanish governments nibbled away at property rights through debt defaults, currency manipulation, and trumped-up charges through court proceedings designed to extort money from their target. But at least they felt compelled to work through the existing legal system. The Russian government, by contrast, expropriated private property outright with no pretense of legality, forced the entire nobility into government service, and did away with enemies and traitors without attention to due process. Ivan IV's oprichnina was in some respects a one-time event that was not duplicated on the same scale until the Communist government of the twentieth century. But the fact that it happened created important precedents for subsequent Russian rulers, who understood that they had an extreme sanction against their elites that was unavailable to Western sovereigns. In this respect the Russian government was much closer to imperial China than to governments that emerged in the West. The Russian government developed absolutist institutions that paralleled those of the Ottomans, like the pomest'ia. But both the Ottomans and the Mamluks at their peak displayed a stronger respect for rule of law than did Russian rulers.

On the other hand, Russian absolutism was far more patrimonial than the Chinese or Ottoman versions. The Chinese, as we have seen, invented modern bureaucracy and centralized, impersonal rule. While Chinese history was largely a struggle over the repatrimonialization of the state, the ideal of impersonal, merit-based administration existed even prior to the emergence of a unified China in the third century B.C. The Ottoman system of military slavery succeeded in creating a merit-based administrative system that had, in its heyday, the admiration of visiting Europeans for its freedom from patrimonial influences. Peter the Great tried to create such a system in Russia, but he succeeded only partially. The Russian government was easily recaptured by patrimonial forces who operated in completely nontransparent ways behind the scenes to shape policy.

The parallels between contemporary Russia and the society that emerged in the hundred years following the death of Peter the Great are striking. Despite modern Russia's formal constitution and written laws, the country is run by shadowy elite networks that resemble the Saltykov and Naryshkin families that used to control imperial Russia. These elites have access to power in ways that are not defined either by law or regularized procedure. But unlike in China, Russia's most senior elites do not have a comparable sense of moral accountability to the nation as a whole. As one moves up the political hierarchy in China, the quality of government improves, whereas it gets worse in Russia. Contemporary elites are willing to use nationalism to legitimate their power, but in the end they seem to be in it largely for themselves.

Russia is in no way trapped by its history. The absolutist precedents set by Ivan IV, Peter, and Stalin were followed by periods of liberalization.

Society is mobilized today in a way that it was not under the old regime, and the introduction of capitalism permits the elite deck to be restacked periodically. The corrupt and messy electoral authoritarianism in place today is hardly the brutal dictatorship Russians have experienced in the past, and Russian history provides many alternative paths toward greater freedom that may serve as precedents for reform down the road.

27

TAXATION AND REPRESENTATION

How the preceding cases of failed accountability set a context for understanding the development of parliamentary institutions in England; sources
of political solidarity and their roots in pre-Norman England; the role of law
in legitimizing English institutions; what the Glorious Revolution actually
accomplished

The final case regarding the development of political accountability is
England, in which all three dimensions of political development—the
state, rule of law, and political accountability—were successfully institutionalized. I examine England last in order to avoid some of the pitfalls of
what is called "Whig history." Many accounts have been written about the
rise of representative government in England that make its development
seem like a logical, necessary, or inevitable outgrowth of a Western pattern of development stretching all the way back to ancient Athens. Because
these histories are seldom put in a comparative context, however, the
causal train of events adduced in them fails to account for a host of other
unobserved or more remote factors that played critical roles in the outcome. They fail, in other words, to observe the turtles lurking beneath the
ones at or near the top of the stack.

We avoid this problem because we have already covered four cases of
European states in which accountable government *failed* to emerge—indeed,
more than four if we consider also the non-Western cases discussed. By
looking at the ways England was both similar to and different from these
other cases, we can gain a better insight into what combination of factors
caused accountability to develop there.

England, like France, Spain, Hungary, and Russia, was first a tribal and
then a feudal society in which a centralizing state began to accumulate
power in the late sixteenth and early seventeenth centuries. The elites in

each of these societies were organized into estates—the English Parliament, the French sovereign courts, the Spanish Cortes, the Hungarian Diet, and the Russian zemskiy sobor—to which the modernizing monarch turned for support and legitimacy. In France, Spain, and Russia, these estates failed to coalesce into powerful, institutionalized actors capable of standing up to the centralizing state to impose on it a constitutional settlement that required the king to be accountable to a parliament. In England, by contrast, Parliament was both powerful and cohesive.

More specifically, unlike the Spanish Cortes, which represented primarily Castile's cities, or the French or Russian bodies, which were dominated by the aristocracy, the English body represented not just the aristocracy and clergy (the lords temporal and spiritual) but also the broad mass of gentry, townspeople, and property owners more generally who, as the Commons, were its soul and driving force. The English Parliament was strong enough to stymie the king in his plans to raise taxes, create new military instruments, and bypass the Common Law. Parliament created its own army and defeated the king in a civil war, executed him, and then forced the abdication of a second monarch, James II, in favor of a foreign pretender, William of Orange. At the end of the process, the English state was ruled not by an absolutist monarch like its continental rivals but by a constitutional monarch who formally conceded the principle of parliamentary accountability. The natural question then is why the English Parliament developed into this kind of body while its counterparts elsewhere in Europe were, until the eve of the French Revolution, divided, weak, co-opted, or indeed actively supportive of monarchical absolutism.

There is another respect in which England constitutes an interesting precedent for contemporary developing countries. The English state under the early Stuarts at the beginning of the seventeenth century was not only increasingly authoritarian, it was also very corrupt. The same sorts of practices that infected public administration in contemporary France and Spain, like venal officeholding and patrimonial appropriation, happened in England as well, even if on a more modest scale. In England, however, the problem of public corruption was, if not solved, at least substantially mitigated by the end of the century. The political system eliminated venal officeholding and established modern bureaucratic administration in a manner that increased the overall power and efficiency of the state. This didn't decisively solve the problem of corruption in English public life, but it did prevent the country from sinking into the same morass of venality that delegitimized and ultimately undermined the ancien régime in France. Present-day developing countries facing pervasive public corruption might look to how the English political system dealt with this problem.

THE ROOTS OF ENGLISH POLITICAL SOLIDARITY

We have seen how the French, Spanish, and Russian monarchies used various strategies to co-opt, intimidate, or neutralize potential opponents in the aristocracy, gentry, and bourgeoisie. English monarchs tried this as well, but the social classes represented in Parliament hung together sufficiently firmly to resist and ultimately defeat the king. The question then is where this solidarity came from.

There are at least three key components of an answer, some of which have been elaborated in earlier chapters. First, solidarity in English society was from a very early point more political than social. Second, the Common Law and English legal institutions were broadly regarded as legitimate and gave property owners a strong stake in defending them. Finally, religion, while bitterly dividing the English throughout this period, gave Parliament a strong sense of transcendent purpose that it would not have had were the contest with the king simply over property and resources.

Local Government and Solidarity

We noted in chapter 16 how tribal social organization had broken down in Europe under the impact of Christianity long before the modern state-building project began. Nowhere was this process more advanced than in England, where, starting with the mission of St. Augustine of Canterbury in the late sixth century, extended kin ties were replaced by a far more individualistic form of community. (This was not as true of the Irish, Welsh, or Scots, who retained tribal ties—for example, the Highland clans—into a much later period of history.) Communities of unrelated neighbors were common back in Anglo-Saxon times prior to the Norman invasion, and they made peasant society there quite different from its counterparts in Eastern Europe, not to speak of China and India.[1]

The weakness of kin-based social organization did not, however, preclude social solidarity overall. Strongly bonded kin groups can provide collective action within the limits of the group while serving as barriers to cooperation outside the lineage or tribe. Political institutions are needed precisely because of the narrowness of collective action typical of kin-based societies.

The early individualism of English society therefore did not mean that there was no social solidarity. It meant that solidarity took a more explicitly political rather than social form. Prior to the Norman Conquest, England was already organized into relatively uniform units called shires, which may at one time have been independent kingdoms but were now amalgamated into a larger English kingdom. The shire was presided over by an ancient official called an ealdorman who held his post on a hereditary basis. (The ealdorman, from a Danish root meaning "old man," survives in American local politics as the alderman.)[2] But increasingly real power was held by a royal official, the shire reeve (or sheriff), who was appointed by the king and represented royal authority. The shire reeve organized a shire moot or council, which all free men (later all free landowners) in the district were obliged to attend on the occasion of its biannual meetings.[3] The Norman Conquest did not destroy this system of governance but only renamed it, so that the shires became counties following continental Frankish practice. However, the power of the king's representative, the sheriff, increased greatly at the expense of the hereditary ealdorman. The shire moot evolved into the county court, where, in the words of Frederic Maitland, "the tenants in chief of the crown have to meet their own vassals on a footing of legal equality; a tenant may find himself sitting as the peer of his own lord."[4]

While the details of these institutions may seem of only antiquarian interest today, they are extremely important in explaining the evolution of Parliament as a political institution. The nature of feudalism in continental Europe, particularly in those regions that had been part of the Carolingian Empire, looked very different. In the latter regions, the territorial nobility had far greater control over the administration of justice than its English counterpart.[5] In England, the king had the advantage. After the Norman Conquest, the king used the county courts to check the feudal courts; if an individual felt he could not get justice from the lord, he could appeal to the sheriff to have the jurisdiction moved to the county court. In time, the growth of the royal courts (detailed in chapter 17) displaced the county courts as courts of first instance for important matters, while the county courts continued to preside over lesser cases involving land disputes up to forty shillings. Nonelites therefore had far greater access to these institutions in England than they did on the Continent.

Even as the county courts began to lose their judicial functions, they were gaining a political one as the locus of representation for the broader political system. As Maitland explains,

> When in the middle of the thirteenth century we find elected representatives called to form part of the national assembly, of a common council of the realm, or parliament, they are the representatives of the county courts. They are not the representatives of unorganized collections of men, they are the representatives, we might almost say, of corporations. The whole county is in theory represented by its court . . . The king's itinerant justices from time to time visit the counties; the whole county (*totus comitatus*), i.e., the body of freeholders, stands before them; it declares what the county has been doing since the last visitation; the county can give judgment; the county can give testimony; the county can be punished by fines and amercements when the county has done wrong.[6]

The county was thus a curious combination of top-down and bottom-up organization. It was created by the king and ruled by a sheriff he appointed who was accountable to him, but it was also based on broad participation by all of the free landholders regardless of inherited rank or feudal status. The sheriff was in turn checked by locally elected officials named coroners, which legitimated the idea that the county's interests ought to be represented by locally elected officials. Upward accountability to the king was increasingly balanced by downward accountability to the county's population.

Below the level of the shire or county there were the hundreds, smaller units of local administration comparable to the Carolingian centenae. (These units were also carried over into American local administration.) The hundreds had their own assemblies or courts called hundred moots or courts, which came to play an increasingly important role in the administration of justice. The hundreds were put under the authority of bailiffs or constables appointed by the sheriff, and were collectively responsible for police functions like the apprehension of criminals. The hundreds were also the basis of the English jury system, since they were required to produce panels of twelve men to decide criminal cases.[7]

Thus, even prior to the Norman Conquest, the whole of English society had been organized down to a village level into highly participatory political units. This was not a grassroots phenomenon of local social organization taking on a political role; rather, it was national government inviting local participation in a way that structured local life and became deeply rooted as a source of community.

The Role of the Common Law and Legal Institutions

It is notable that the building blocks of later English representative political institutions started out as judicial bodies like the county and hundred courts. In English history, the rule of law emerged well before there was anything like political accountability, and the latter was always closely tied to the defense of the law. The participatory nature of English justice, and the locally responsive nature of judicial rule-making under the Common Law, created a much greater feeling of popular ownership of the law in England than in other European societies. Public accountability meant in the first instance obedience to the law, despite the fact that neither judge-made nor statute law was produced in this period by a democratic political process.

One of the chief functions of the rule of law is the protection of property rights, and this the Common Law did much more effectively than law in other lands. This is due in part to the fact that the Common Law is, as Hayek observed, the product of decentralized decision making that is highly responsive to local conditions and knowledge. But paradoxically, it was also due to the fact that English kings were willing to support the property rights of nonelites against those of the nobility, something that depended in turn on the existence of a powerful centralized state. In England, plaintiffs early on could shift the venue of a property rights dispute to the king's courts or, if the amounts in question were small, to the county or hundred courts. There were many complex classes of traditional property rights in the Middle Ages, such as the copyhold, by which a villein or unfree tenant could in effect transfer property that was technically that of his lord to a son or relative. The king's courts tended to protect copyholders' rights against their lords, such that this form of property began to evolve into something closer to freehold or true private property.[8]

The existence of a multiplicity of courts at the county and hundred level, and the king's willingness to act as a neutral arbiter in local property rights disputes, strongly reinforced the legitimacy of property rights in England.[9] By the fifteenth century, the independence and perceived neutrality of the English judicial system allowed it to play an increasingly important role as a genuine "third branch" with competence to judge constitutional issues, like the right of Parliament to abrogate a royal patent. In the words of one observer, "It is hard to think of another place in medieval Europe where such issues would be settled—and indeed settled independently—by judges talking the common language of their profession rather than by the political maneuvering or coercion of the parties."[10] This degree of judicial competence and independence still eludes many countries in the developing world today.

By the time we get to the great constitutional crises of the seventeenth century, then, protecting the rule of law against monarchs who wanted to bend or break it had become a great rallying cry in the defense of English liberty and a source of solidarity for those groups in Parliament opposing the king. The threat to the law that emerged in the period of the early Stuarts (1603–1649) was the king's Court of Star Chamber, a court of obscure origin and jurisdiction that evaded the usual procedural protections of the ordinary courts (including trial by jury) in pursuit of more "efficient" prosecution of crimes. Under the second Stuart king, Charles I (1600–1649), it had become politicized and was used not simply for criminal prosecutions but also to go after perceived enemies of the Crown.[11]

There was no greater embodiment of the independence of English law than Sir Edward Coke (1552–1634), a jurist and legal scholar who eventually rose to be chief justice of the King's Bench. In his various legal roles, he unbendingly stood up to political authorities and to the king himself in support of the law against their encroachment. When James I sought to shift certain cases from Common Law to ecclesiastical jurisdiction, Coke greatly offended him by saying that the king did not have sufficient authority to interpret the law as he chose. The king asserted that it was treasonable to maintain that he should be under the law, to which Coke responded by quoting Bracton to the effect that *"quod Rex non debet esse sub homine set sub deo et lege"* (the king should not be under man but under God and the law).[12] For this and other confrontations with royal authority, Coke was eventually dismissed from his legal posts, whereupon he joined Parliament as a leader of the anti-Royalist side.

Religion as the Basis for Collective Action

Unlike the French, Spanish, Hungarian, and Russian cases, English resistance to absolutist power was overlaid with a religious dimension that immensely strengthened the solidarity of those on the parliamentary side. The first Stuart king, James I, was the son of the executed Mary Stuart, the Roman Catholic queen of the Scots, while his son Charles I was married to the French king Louis XIII's sister Henrietta Maria. While both James and Charles professed Protestantism, they were frequently suspected of having pro-Catholic sympathies. The Anglicanism of Archbishop Laud sought to bring the English national church back closer to Catholic practice with regard to emphasis on ritual, a shift that was bitterly resented by the Puritan sects. The early Stuarts' doctrine of absolutism and the divine right of kings echoed arguments being made by French and Spanish Catholic monarchs, and in this many Protestants saw a vast international popish conspiracy to deprive the English of their natural rights. The rebellion in Catholic Ireland of 1641 struck close to home; reports of atrocities committed against Protestant settlers seemed to confirm the worst fears of many English about the consequences of spreading international Catholicism. There was in this more than a grain of truth; the Spanish king had sent the Armada against England at the end of the sixteenth century and was involved in an eighty-year struggle to subdue the Protestant United Provinces of the Netherlands. This cause would be taken up again in the late seventeenth century by Louis XIV of France, who invaded Holland and had a secret sympathizer in the last Catholic king of England, James II.

In the enormous historiography on the English Civil War, there have been cycles of revisionism that have shifted scholarly understanding of the motives for the war in step with prevailing intellectual fashions, to the point that some historians have despaired of ever coming to a consensus.[13] Many of the twentieth-century interpretations downplayed the religious motivations of the actors in the war and saw religious ideology as a mask or justification for class or sectional economic interests. There was in fact a complex interplay between religion and class in this period, and no simple mapping between religion and political allegiance. There were Anglicans who took the side of Parliament, and Protestants who were royalists; many high church Anglicans saw the nonconformist sects like the Congregationalists and Quakers as a greater threat to the moral order than the Catholic church.[14] It was clear that the more radical Protestant sects served as vehicles for social mobilization and economic advancement, since they provided outlets for protest and community that were unavailable through more traditional and hierarchical religious channels.

On the other hand, even if one argues that the conflict was not primarily over religion, it is still clear that religion had a major effect in mobilizing political actors and increasing the scope of collective action. This was particularly true on the parliamentary side and in the New Model Army created by Parliament, which over time became a hotbed of antiroyalist radicalism in no small measure because of the religious convictions of many of its officers. During the Glorious Revolution, the willingness of the parliamentary side to accept a foreign pretender, William of Orange, as king in place of the country's legitimate monarch, James II, would have been much harder to explain but for the fact that the former was Protestant and the latter Catholic.

Thus the organization of England into local, self-governing bodies, the rootedness of law and belief in the sanctity of property rights, and the association of monarchy with a global Catholic conspiracy all contributed to a striking degree of solidarity on the parliamentary side.

FREE CITIES AND THE BOURGEOISIE

Contemporary conventional wisdom has it that democracy will not emerge without the existence of a strong middle class, that is, a group of people who own some property and are neither elites nor the rural poor. This notion finds its origins in English political development, which to a greater degree than any other European country (with the possible exception of Holland) saw the early emergence of cities and an urban-based bourgeoisie. The urban middle class played a key role in Parliament and gained substantial economic and political power well prior to the Civil War and Glorious Revolution. It was a powerful counterweight to the great lords and the king in their three-way contest for power. The rise of an urban bourgeoisie was part of a broader Western European shift that encompassed the Low Countries, northern Italy, and the Hanseatic port cities of northern Germany as well. This important phenomenon has been described at length by authors from Karl Marx to Max Weber to Henri Pirenne.[15] Marx made the "rise of the bourgeoisie" the centerpiece of his entire theory of modernization, a necessary and inevitable stage in the developmental process of all societies.

The existence of free cities explains, as we saw in chapter 25, the emancipation of the serfs in Western Europe. The emergence of a strong, cohesive bourgeois class was important to English political development and to the triumph of Parliament. But the role played by the bourgeoisie in English and Western European history was in many ways exceptional, the result of contingent circumstances that did not exist in other European

countries. Particularly east of the Elbe, there were relatively few independent, self-governing commercial cities living under their own laws and
protected by their own militias. Cities were rather more like Chinese ones,
administrative centers dominated by local lords, which also happened to
serve as commercial hubs. Marx's influence has been such that many generations of students have continued to see the "rise of the bourgeoisie" as
something that simply happens as a concomitant of economic modernization, without the need for further explanation, and to see that class's political power as flowing from its economic power.[16]

Writing almost seventy-five years before Marx, Adam Smith in *The
Wealth of Nations* provided a more nuanced and ultimately convincing
account of the provenance of the bourgeoisie, one that sees politics as
cause as much as consequence of its rise. At the beginning of book three
of the first volume, Smith notes that there should be a natural progression
in what he calls "opulence," or economic growth, starting with improved
agricultural productivity, leading to greater internal trade between countryside and town, and only in the end to increased international trade.
However, he notes, in the modern states of Europe the order was reversed:
international trade developed before inland trade; only after the former
flourished was there a breakdown in the political hegemony of the great
barons and landowners.[17]

There were, according to Smith, several reasons for this peculiar sequence. One was the fact that most land after the fall of the Roman Empire
was held by great barons who were more interested in preserving their
political power than in maximizing the returns on their property. For this
reason they created rules of primogeniture and entail to prevent the fragmentation of their estates. In addition, they reduced agricultural laborers
to the status of serfs or slaves, who according to Smith had no incentives
to work and invest in their lands. Another reason why they didn't maximize their returns was a simple lack of consumption items on which to
spend a surplus, given the collapse of trade in the Dark Ages. As a result,
anyone with wealth and power had no choice but to share it with a large
group of retainers.[18]

Smith goes on to note that the towns and cities that emerged in the
Middle Ages were at first inhabited by "tradesmen and mechanicks" who
were of lower class or fully servile status but who had escaped from the
control of their lords and found refuge in the city. Over time they were
granted privileges by kings to give away their own daughters in marriage,

to raise their own militias, and eventually to live under their own laws as a corporate entity. This was the origin of the bourgeois class, though Adam Smith does not use this term to describe them. Unlike Marx, however, Smith notes that there was an important political precondition for the rise of independent cities:

> The lords despised the burghers, whom they considered not only as of a different order, but as a parcel of emancipated slaves, almost of a different species from themselves. The wealth of the burghers never failed to provoke their envy and indignation, and they plundered them upon every occasion without mercy or remorse. The burghers naturally hated and feared the lords. The king hated and feared them too; but though perhaps he might despise, he had no reason either to hate or fear the burghers. Mutual interest, therefore, disposed them to support the king, and the king to support them against the lords.[19]

Smith adds that this is why the kings granted cities independent charters and laws, to allow them to act as a counterweight to the lords with whom they were locked in struggle.

Cities and the bourgeoisie, then, do not simply come into being as a result of economic growth and technological change, as Marx believed. They are initially weak and vulnerable, and unless they are granted political protection, they will be subordinated to the powerful territorial lords. This was exactly what happened in Poland, Hungary, Russia, and other lands east of the Elbe, where a different configuration of political power either made monarchs weak or induced them to side with one or another stratum of the aristocracy *against* the interests of the townsmen. For this reason, there was never a strong, independent bourgeoisie in Eastern Europe. A technologically advanced capitalist market was not introduced by townsmen but by progressive landowners, or by the state itself, and therefore failed to flourish to the same extent.

Once a city-based capitalist market economy appears, we leave the old Malthusian world and begin to enter into a modern economic system where productivity increases become much more routine. At that point, the conditions for political development change as well, through the mechanism of an increasingly wealthy bourgeois class that is more and more in a position to undermine the power of the old landed order. Smith suggests that the old elites were seduced into giving up their political power for the sake of money—a diamond buckle "fitter to be the playthings of children than the serious pursuits of men"—which the old agricultural economy was incapable of producing.[20] Thus began a truly modern system of political development in which political change could be induced by economic and social change. But there was a political precondition for the rise of a capitalist class in the first place—the mutual hatred of the townsmen and the king for the great lords. Where this condition did not prevail, as in many parts of Eastern Europe, no such class emerged.

THE STRUGGLE OVER TAXATION

English parliaments had begun meeting regularly since the thirteenth century on a far more regular basis than their French, Spanish, or Russian counterparts. Their original function was, as noted, judicial, but over time they came to play a much broader political role as joint rulers with the king. The role of Parliament in approving taxation was particularly important, since Parliament included a large majority of the realm's landowners whose assets and income served as a national tax base. In the fourteenth and fifteenth centuries, the House of Commons had worked closely with English monarchs to remove incompetent or corrupt officials, and took on a regular role in financial oversight of the monies it had appropriated.[21] The balance of forces that existed in England in 1641, on the eve of the Civil War, is illustrated in Figure 5.

In 1629, Charles I had dissolved Parliament and commenced an eleven-year period of "personal rule" in which he sought to expand state power at the expense of Parliament. This led to a struggle between Charles and his parliamentary opponents over a number of issues, some of which have been touched upon already. Many in Parliament disliked the authoritarian Anglicanism of Archbishop Laud and suspected Charles of pro-Catholic sympathies given his interest in building diplomatic ties to France and Spain. The religious issue converged with the defense of the rule of law, as novel bodies like the Star Chamber, the High Commission, and the Council of the North undertook prosecutions against anti-Episcopal Puritans. The Star Chamber's brutal arrest and torture of a Puritan preacher, Alexander Leighton, without benefit of due process, was regarded as a particularly egregious abuse of both religious and royal authority.

But two other issues loomed equally large at the time. One was the right

FIGURE 5. ENGLAND

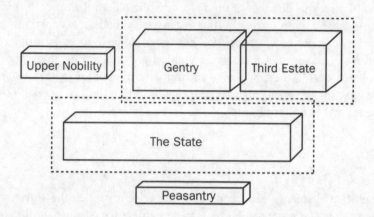

of the king to raise taxes without parliamentary approval. The king raised new customs duties, levied arbitrary penalties against landowners, reintroduced a host of monopolies in ways that circumvented an act prohibiting them, and raised "ship money" to pay for naval rearmament in a time of peace.[22] The English tax system had evolved in a very different way from that of the French. The English nobility and gentry had not bought themselves special privileges and exemptions in the manner of the French, with the result that the largest part of the tax burden actually fell on those relatively wealthy individuals represented in Parliament. With reasons possibly having to do with the greater sense of local solidarity in England, the wealthier classes did not conspire with the Crown to shift the tax burden onto the peasantry, artisans, or newly rich middle classes, and therefore had a direct stake in the powers and prerogatives of Parliament.

The second conflict concerned political corruption. England was no less exempt from the practice of patrimonialism and venal officeholding than were France and Spain. Beginning in Tudor times, royal offices were increasingly obtained on the basis of political patronage, with advancement coming not on the basis of merit but on one's membership in a variety of patron-client groups.[23] Offices were put up for sale and became heritable property, and under the early Stuarts the French practices of tax farming (for customs duties) and inside finance (borrowing from state officials) were introduced. The Crown established royal commissions of inquiry which, like the French chambers of justice, were used to shake down wealthy insiders on the grounds of personal corruption.[24]

The Civil War that broke out in 1641 dragged on for a decade and eventually led to victory for the parliamentary side and the beheading of Charles I in 1649. But the long struggle between king and Parliament was not ultimately settled by force of arms, though violence and the latent threat of violence were important determinants of the outcome.[25] The parliamentarians who emerged victorious discredited their own side by their execution of the king, and narrowed their political base by following increasingly radical policies during the Protectorate of Oliver Cromwell. It was therefore with a certain sense of relief that Charles's son was restored as Charles II in 1660, and the country returned to a sense of normality after two decades of intense political conflict.

The Restoration did succeed in resolving one of the issues that provoked the Civil War, which was the problem of corruption. Parliament had undertaken many governmental reforms during the Civil War and Protectorate, such as the creation of a well-organized, modern New Model Army and the purging of corrupt royalist officials. But Charles II's rule brought back many of the corrupt practices of the early Stuarts, including sale of offices, patronage appointments, and the like. A number of factors conspired, however, to create a reform coalition within the English government that succeeded in beating back these practices.

The first was the outbreak of the Second Dutch War (1665–1667), which, when combined with outbreaks of plague and the great fire of London, led to a serious deterioration of English defenses to the point that the Dutch were able to sail up the Thames and burn the English naval yards. France as well was gaining ground under Louis XIV with an aggressive foreign policy that threatened the existing balance of power on the Continent, and it was clear that military spending would have to rise. The second was the fact that Charles hoped to be able to live within his means in order to avoid having to go to Parliament for extraordinary revenue requests. Third was the emergence of a group of extremely talented and astute reformers within the government, including Sir George Downing and the diarist Samuel Pepys, who looked with concern at mounting foreign threats and recognized that the fiscal system and general administration needed to be made far more efficient.[26] And finally, there was Parliament, which had emerged from the Civil War and Protectorate suspicious of waste and corruption in a government that was diverting their own tax money to nonpublic purposes.

The confluence of these different pressures allowed the Second Treasury Commission, organized by Downing, to recommend and implement an important set of reforms that put English public administration on a much more modern and nonpatrimonial footing. It took power away from the exchequer, which since Tudor days had been a hotbed of corrupt officeholding, and put it in the hands of a reformed Treasury Department that became the master accountant for all of the government's spending departments. Instead of going to inside financiers, it floated new bonds called Treasury orders that were marketed to the general public and were thus subject to the discipline of the public bond market. And finally, it converted proprietary offices into "at pleasure" posts and eliminated the sale of further offices.[27]

The reform efforts that took place after 1667 dealt a serious blow to patrimonial practices and ensured that the English state would administer public finances far more efficiently than France or Spain. The struggle against corrupt government is never decisively won or lost, and many of the reforms initiated by Downing in the 1660s were not fully implemented until early in the eighteenth century. Nor did these early reform efforts obviate the need for subsequent commissions and inquiries, since patrimonialism always seeks to reinsert itself over time.

But the late seventeenth century does provide an important model of how patrimonialism can be reversed that has some relevance to present-day anticorruption efforts. All of the elements that came together to produce the late Stuart reforms are still critical: an external environment that puts fiscal pressure on the government to improve its performance; a chief executive who, if not personally leading the reform effort, is at least not blocking it; reform champions within the government who have sufficient political support to carry out their program; and finally, strong political pressure from below on the part of those who are paying taxes to the government and don't want to see their money wasted.

Many recent anticorruption efforts by international institutions like the World Bank or Britain's Department of International Development have foundered because one or another of these elements was not in place. One problematic characteristic of the contemporary world is that corrupt governments often do not have to go to their own citizens for revenues the way Charles II did and have no parliament or civil society watching over the way their money is spent. Instead, government income comes from natural resources or aid from international donors, who do not demand accountability for how their money is spent. Samuel Huntington has suggested that if the rallying cry of the English Parliament was "no taxation without representation," today's slogan ought to be "no representation without taxation," since it is the latter that best incentivizes political participation.[28]

THE GLORIOUS REVOLUTION

The denouement of the prolonged struggle between king and Parliament was the Glorious Revolution of 1688–1689, which forced James II to abdicate. William of Orange was brought from Holland and placed on the throne as King William III. The proximate cause of the crisis had been the Catholic James's efforts to increase the size of the military and to staff it with Catholic officers, which raised immediate suspicions that he intended to use the army to assert absolutist power in possible alliance with France and other Catholic powers. The larger issue at stake, however, was the same as the one that had driven the struggles of Parliament against the early Stuarts and led to the Civil War: that legitimacy should ultimately be based upon the consent of the governed, and that the king did not have the right to impose policies without it. The settlement that came out of the crisis had important constitutional, religious, financial, and military dimensions. Constitutionally, it established the principle that the king could not raise an army without Parliament's consent; the latter passed a bill defining the rights of Englishmen that the state could not contravene. Financially, the settlement firmly established the principle that new taxes could not be raised without the express consent of Parliament. Religiously, the settlement forbade Catholics from becoming king or queen of England, and included a toleration bill that increased the rights of dissenting Protestants (though not of Catholics, Jews, or Socinians).[29] Finally, the settlement made possible a huge expansion of the English state by allowing the government to issue much higher levels of debt. While the principle of full parliamentary sovereignty was not finally established until some years later, the Glorious Revolution is rightly seen as a major watershed in the development of modern democracy.[30]

The Glorious Revolution led to a major shift in ideas concerning political legitimacy. The philosopher John Locke, who was an observer and participant in all of these events, expanded on Thomas Hobbes's argument that the state was the result of a social contract entered into for the purpose of guaranteeing rights that existed universally by nature.[31] His *First*

Treatise of Government attacked Sir Robert Filmer's justification of monarchy on the basis of divine right, and his *Second Treatise* argued, against Hobbes, that a monarch who had become a tyrant by violating the natural rights of his subjects could be replaced by them. It was critical to the constitutional settlement of 1689 that these principles were stated in universal terms: the Glorious Revolution was not about one ruler or set of elites grabbing control of the state and its rents from another, but about the principle upon which all subsequent rulers would be chosen. There is a very short distance from Locke's *Second Treatise on Government* to the American Revolution and the constitutional theories of the Founding Fathers. While modern democracy has many complex dimensions, the fundamental principle that governments can legitimately rule only with the consent of the governed was firmly established by the events of 1688–1689.

Although the Glorious Revolution institutionalized the principle of political accountability and representative government, it did not yet herald the arrival of democracy. The English Parliament in this period was chosen by only a small proportion of the population. In it sat the upper classes, burgesses, and the gentry, the latter of whom were the most important political class in England and represented, according to Peter Laslett, perhaps 4 to 5 percent of the entire population.[32] A much broader group of people participated in local governance by sitting on juries and cooperating in the work of the hundreds and counties, and included a large part of the yeoman class of better-off farmers. Including this group would increase political participation to something closer to 20 percent of the male adult population.[33] Democracy as we understand it today—the right of all adult persons to vote regardless of sex, race, or social status—was not implemented in either Britain or the United States until well into the twentieth century. Like the American Declaration of Independence, however, the Glorious Revolution did establish the principle of popular consent, leaving it up to succeeding generations to widen the circle of those considered the "people" in a political sense.

The significance of the Glorious Revolution is not that it marked the onset of secure property rights in England, as some have argued.[34] Strong property rights had been established centuries earlier. Individuals, including women, exercised the right to buy and sell property as far back as the thirteenth century (see chapter 14). The Common Law and the multiplicity of royal, county, and hundred courts allowed nonelite landowners to litigate property disputes outside of the jurisdiction of the local lord. A strong capitalist economy had already emerged by the late seventeenth century, as had a growing middle class who were participants in the struggle against Stuart absolutism. The success of the Glorious Revolution was therefore more a consequence of the existence of strong, credible property rights than a cause of them. Englishmen with property felt they had something important to defend.

Nor did the Glorious Revolution give newly powerful taxpayers an excuse for cutting their own taxes, as Mancur Olson has suggested.[35] Exactly the opposite happened: government spending as a percentage of national income in England shot up from 11 percent of GDP in 1689–1697 to 17 percent in 1741–1748 and almost 24 percent in 1778–1783.[36] In peak years during the eighteenth century, Britain collected as much as 30 percent in taxes.

One of the Glorious Revolution's main accomplishments was to make taxation legitimate because it was henceforth clearly based on consent. Democratic publics do not necessarily always resist high taxes, as long as they think they are necessary for an important public purpose like defense of the nation. What they dislike is taxes being taken from them illegally, or public monies that are wasted or that go to corrupt purposes. In the years following the Glorious Revolution, England was plunged into two expensive wars with Louis XIV's France: the Nine Years' War (1689–1697) and the War of the Spanish Succession (1702–1713). Two decades of nearly continuous warfare proved enormously expensive, with the size of the English fleet nearly doubling between 1688 and 1697 alone. Taxpayers were willing to support the costs of this and later wars because they were consulted on the wisdom of the wars themselves and asked to approve the tax burden imposed. The much higher rates of British taxation did not, needless to say, stifle the capitalist revolution.[37]

The contrast with absolutist France was stark. Because France admitted no principle of consent, taxes had to be extracted by force. The government was never able to collect more than 12–15 percent of its national product in taxes over the same period, and often achieved much less. The elites in French society who could best afford to pay them succeeded in buying themselves special exemptions and privileges, which meant that the tax burden fell on the weakest members of society. As a result, France, with a population nearly four times that of Britain, found itself bankrupt on the death of Louis XIV in 1715.

The Glorious Revolution and the fiscal and banking reforms undertaken in its wake, such as the establishment of the Bank of England in 1694, did indeed revolutionize public finance. They allowed the government to borrow on transparent public debt markets in ways unavailable to France or Spain. As a result, levels of government borrowing shot up substantially in the eighteenth century, allowing the British state to grow much larger.

TO THE AMERICAN AND FRENCH REVOLUTIONS

I am ending the account of political development in this volume on the eve of the American and French revolutions at the end of the eighteenth century. There is a certain logic for stopping at this point. Alexandre Kojève, the great Russian-French interpreter of Hegel, argued that history as such had ended in the year 1806 with the Battle of Jena-Auerstadt, when Napoleon defeated the Prussian monarchy and brought the principles of liberty and equality to Hegel's part of Europe. In his typically ironic and playful way, Kojève suggested that everything that had happened since 1806, including the sturm und drang of the twentieth century with its great wars and revolutions, was simply a matter of backfilling. That is, the basic principles of modern government had been established by the time of the Battle of Jena; the task thereafter was not to find new principles and a higher political order but rather to implement them through larger and larger parts of the world.[38]

I believe that Kojève's assertion still deserves to be taken seriously. The three components of a modern political order—a strong and capable state, the state's subordination to a rule of law, and government accountability to all citizens—had all been established in one or another part of the world by the end of the eighteenth century. China had developed a powerful state early on; the rule of law existed in India, the Middle East, and Europe; and in Britain, accountable government appeared for the first time. Political development in the years subsequent to the Battle of Jena involved the replication of these institutions across the world, but not in their being supplemented by fundamentally new ones. Communism aspired to do this in the twentieth century but has all but disappeared from the world scene in the twenty-first.

England was the first large country in which all these elements came together at once. The three components were highly interdependent. Without a strong early state, there would not have been a rule of law and a broad perception of legitimate property rights. Without a strong rule of law and legitimate property rights, the Commons would never have been motivated to come together to impose accountability on the English monarchy. And without the principle of accountability, the British state would never have emerged as the great power it became by the time of the French Revolution.

A number of other European states, including the Netherlands, Denmark, and Sweden, also succeeded in putting together the state, rule of law, and accountability in a single package by the nineteenth century. The specific routes by which they got to this outcome differed substantially from that of Britain, but it is sufficient to recognize that once this package had been put together the first time, it produced a state so powerful, legitimate, and friendly to economic growth that it became a model to be applied throughout the world.[39] How the application of that model has fared in countries lacking the specific historical and social conditions of Britain will be the subject of the second volume of this work.

28

WHY ACCOUNTABILITY? WHY ABSOLUTISM?

The previous cases compared; why England's path to representative government was not the only one possible; getting to Denmark; how the historical discussion is relevant to democratic struggles in the present

We have now covered five European cases leading to four divergent outcomes with regard to accountability and representative institutions. France and Spain saw the emergence of a weak absolutism, in which no principle of parliamentary accountability was established. Both states achieved this result by selling themselves off piecemeal to a wide variety of elites, whose privileges and exemptions protected them—but not the rest of their societies—from arbitrary state power. In Russia, a more thoroughgoing Chinese-style absolutism was established, in which the monarchy could dominate its own elites by conscripting them into state service. In Hungary, a strong and cohesive elite succeeded in putting constitutional checks on the power of the monarch and established a principle of accountability. But these checks were so strong that they hobbled the ability of the state itself to function cohesively. Finally, only in England did a powerful Parliament succeed in imposing a principle of accountability on the king, but in a way that did not undermine a powerful and unified sovereignty. The question then is, What accounts for the difference in these outcomes?

A very simple model can explain this variance, which has to do with the balance of power among only four groups of political actors in the agrarian societies we have covered. These are the state itself, represented by the king; the upper nobility; the gentry; and what I call the Third Estate. This fourfold division oversimplifies things tremendously but is nonetheless helpful in understanding outcomes.

The state emerged in Europe when certain noble houses achieved a first-mover advantage in becoming more powerful than the others—the Capetians in France, the Árpáds in Hungary, the Rurik dynasty in Russia, the Norman royal house after the conquest. Their rise was due to some complex combination of favorable geography, good leadership, organizational competence, and the ability to command legitimacy. Legitimacy may have been the source of the ruler's initial advantage, as in the case of István leading the Magyars to Christianity, or it may have followed upon the military success of a prince in vanquishing rival warlords and bringing about peace and security for the society as a whole.

The upper nobility might well be described as residual warlords who possessed their own land, armies of retainers, and resources. This group effectively governed their own territories, which could be handed down to descendants or traded for other assets.

The gentry were lesser elites with social status but who did not necessarily possess significant land or resources. They were more numerous than the nobility and distinctly subordinate to them.

The Third Estate consisted of tradesmen, merchants, free serfs, and others who inhabited towns and cities and lived outside of the manorial economy and feudal legal system.

In addition to these four groups, there was the peasantry, which constituted the vast bulk of the population. The peasantry was not, however, a significant political actor until it emerged as such in certain parts of northern Europe in the eighteenth century. Dispersed, indigent, and poorly educated peasants could seldom achieve significant collective action. Agrarian societies from China to Turkey to France saw the periodic outbreak of violent peasant rebellions, and all were eventually suppressed, often with great savagery. Those revolts affected the behavior and calculations of other actors, for example by inducing caution on the part of the state when considering raising agricultural taxes. On other occasions, peasant uprisings could help overturn a Chinese dynasty. But the peasantry could seldom act as a corporate group or force long-term institutional change that would take its interests into account.

The relationships among these five groups were illustrated in Figure 1 (see page 333). Except for the peasantry, these social groups were mobilized to a greater or lesser extent and thus could behave as political actors and struggle for power. The state could try to expand its dominion, while the groups outside the state sought to protect and enlarge their existing privileges against the state and against one another. The outcome of these struggles depended largely on the collective action that any of these major actors could achieve. The need for solidarity extended to the state itself. State weakness could be the result of internal cleavages within the ruling dynasty, organizational failures, a loss of belief in the ruling house's legitimacy on the part of its retainers, or even the simple failure of a king to produce an heir. In addition, any number of alliances were possible among these different groups—between the king and gentry, between the king and the Third Estate, between the upper nobility and the gentry, between the gentry and the Third Estate, and so on.

In the cases where absolutism emerged, whether of a strong or weak variety, there were inevitably collective action failures on the part of groups resisting the state (see Figure 6). Where accountability was imposed, the state was relatively weak in relationship to the other political groups. Parliamentary government emerged when there was a relative balance of power between a cohesive state and an equally well-organized society that could defend its interests.

FIGURE 6. COLLECTIVE ACTION FAILURES

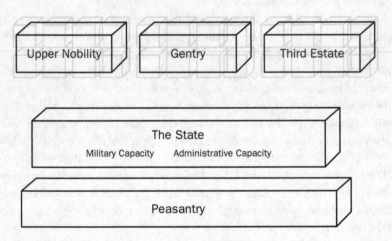

WEAK ABSOLUTISM

We are now in a position to summarize the outcomes described in the preceding chapters.

Weak absolutism emerged in France and Spain when a relatively weak state encountered a well-organized society and nonetheless succeeded in dominating it. In both cases, the power base of the state centered around a limited territory consisting of royal domains and associated lands where the state had direct taxing authority—the pays d'états in the regions surrounding Paris in the case of the French monarchy, and Castile for the Spanish Habsburgs. The state nevertheless sought to extend its authority over a far wider region through co-optation, dynastic intrigue, and outright conquest. The geography of Western Europe and the military technologies of the late sixteenth and early seventeenth centuries were not conducive to rapid military expansion, however—the trace italienne, it should be remembered, made siege warfare necessary and expensive—and both the French and Spanish monarchs quickly found themselves in deep financial trouble from military expenditures and imperial overextension.

In both cases, there were powerful local actors outside the state that sought to resist the centralization project. These included an ancient blood nobility with land and resources, a broad gentry class, and an urban bourgeoisie, which were organized into formal estates—the parlements in France and the Cortes in Spain. Both the French and Spanish states succeeded in the piecemeal co-optation of these groups. This seems to have started not as a deliberate state-building strategy but rather as a desperate innovation to stave off bankruptcy. The French state initially bought the loyalty of local elites in the pays d'élections by granting them special tax exemptions and privileges. After the bankruptcy and repudiation of debts to the Grand Parti in 1557, it began to sell offices to wealthy individuals, offices that became heritable in the early seventeenth century and were thereafter continually sold and resold up to the time of Louis XIV at the century's end. The Spanish state bankrupted itself early on through its prolonged dynastic wars in Italy and the Low Countries. While revenues from the New World kept it going through the end of the sixteenth century, it too resorted to the wholesale auctioning off of parts of the state in the seventeenth century.

The ability of both the French and Spanish monarchs to accumulate power was strictly limited by the prior existence of a rule of law in both countries. Their monarchs felt compelled to respect the feudal rights and privileges of their subjects. They sought to expand their taxing and conscription powers at every opportunity, and tried to bend, break, or go around the law whenever they could. They encouraged intellectuals to promulgate doctrines of absolutism and sovereignty to buttress their claims that they were the ultimate sources of law. But they did not try to abolish law itself or seek to ignore it. In the end, they were normatively constrained from acting in the arbitrary fashion of certain Chinese monarchs like the empress Wu, who implemented a bloody purge of her aristocratic rivals, or the first Ming emperor, who simply seized the land of leading aristocratic families.

The piecemeal co-optation of elites meant in effect a broadening of the rent-seeking coalition to include, first, the traditional aristocratic elites, and then newly mobilized social actors like the urban bourgeoisie. Rather than act cohesively to protect their interests as a class, these elites traded political power for social status and a share of the state—not in the form of parliamentary representation but rather as a claim on the state's taxing authority. In Tocqueville's phrase, liberty was understood not as genuine self-government but as privilege. This led to a weak form of absolutism because the state on the one hand faced no formal constitutional constraints on its power, but on the other hand had mortgaged its future to a host of powerful individuals against whom it had limited power to act.

State weakness ultimately proved deadly to both France and Spain. Because state building was based on exempting elites from taxes, the burden fell on the peasantry and ordinary tradesmen. Neither country could raise sufficient revenues to meet the imperial ambitions of their rulers. France could not compete with a smaller England whose tax base was secured by the principle of parliamentary accountability. Spain, for its part, went into a centuries-long military and economic decline. The states in both countries lost legitimacy because of the corrupt way they were put together in the first place, and France's failed efforts to reform itself paved the way for the revolution.

STRONG ABSOLUTISM

Russia was able to establish a strong form of absolutism much closer to that of China for reasons that become apparent when comparing its development to that of France or Spain. There were at least five important points of divergence.

First, the physical geography of Russia—a flat, open steppe with few physical barriers to cavalry-based armies—made it vulnerable to invasion from the southwest, southeast, and northwest, often simultaneously. This put a premium on military mobilization but also meant that the warlord who moved first to establish military dominance had great scale advantages over his rivals. The power of the Muscovite state was built on its recruitment of the middle service class—Russia's equivalent of a gentry—into direct military service. It could do this because of its position as a frontier state with poorly defined borders. As in the case of the Ottoman sipahis, members of the middle service class were rewarded by settling these cavalrymen on new lands as direct dependents of the Crown. (The closest equivalent of this practice in Western Europe was the Spanish Crown's granting of huge encomiendas in the New World to the conquistadores as a reward for service, a practice that led to a similarly hierarchical political system.) The Duchy of Muscovy obtained significant first-mover advantages by its early successes against the Tatars, which gave it considerable legitimacy over the other appanage princes.

Second, very little time elapsed between the lifting of the Mongol yoke and the state-building project undertaken by Moscow. In Western Europe, feudalism had had eight hundred years to sink roots, producing a proud blood nobility entrenched in the impregnable castles that dotted the landscape. Russia's appanage period by contrast lasted only a couple of centuries. Members of the noble boyar class were far less well organized to resist the power of the centralizing monarch, and they didn't live in castles. They, as well as independent cities like Novgorod, were less protected by physical geography than were their counterparts in Western Europe.

Third, Russia had no tradition of rule of law comparable to that of Western Europe. The Eastern church in Byzantium, which appointed the Russian patriarch, itself never went through the equivalent of the investiture conflict and remained caesaropapist until the fall of Constantinople. Law in the Byzantine Empire failed to be turned into a coherent body guarded by an autonomous legal profession the way it was in the West. The Russian Orthodox church, which was the spiritual heir of the Byzantine church, from time to time exhibited some political independence from the rulers in Moscow, but it also received great benefits from the state's patronage. Unlike the situation in Western Europe, where the Catholic church could play one ruler off against another in a fragmented political landscape, the Russian church had nowhere else to go but to Moscow and often ended up as a pliant supporter of the state. The lack of an independent ecclesiastical authority guarding a body of church law meant that there was no institutional home for legally trained specialists with their own corporate sense of identity. Ecclesiastical bureaucrats served as the administrative cadre for early Western European states; in Russia, the state apparatus was staffed by military men and patrimonial appointees (often one and the same person). Finally, the model of rulership available to many Russians was not the law-governed prince but the purely predatory Mongol conqueror.

Fourth, physical geography necessitated formation of a serf-owning cartel, and tightly bound the interests of the entire elite, nobles and gentry, to those of the monarchy. In the absence of physical circumscription, an institution like serfdom could be maintained only if serf owners showed great self-discipline in punishing and returning escaped serfs. The tsar could bind the elite to the state by supporting ever-tighter restrictions on serfs. In Western Europe, by contrast, free cities were refuges where escaped serfs could run to seek freedom from their lords and the manorial economy. The city served as the functional equivalent of the frontier—eventually closed— in Russia. In contrast to the Russian monarch and other rulers in Eastern Europe, Western European kings found free cities useful in their struggle against the great lords, and therefore protected them.

Finally, certain ideas simply failed to penetrate in Russia to the extent they did in lands farther to the west. This began with the idea of the rule of law but extended to the whole complex of ideas coming out of the Reformation and Enlightenment. At virtually the same moment that the Danish dowager queen Sophie Magdalene was freeing the serfs on her own domains, Catherine the Great, an erstwhile friend of Voltaire, was imposing even tighter restrictions on the movement of serfs in Russia. Many Enlightenment ideas were adopted by modernizing Russian monarchs like Peter the Great, of course, and in another three generations Tsar Alexander II would free the serfs. But modern ideas still had a slower and weaker impact there than in other parts of Europe.

WHY DIDN'T ENGLAND END UP LIKE HUNGARY?

Against the backdrop of these unsuccessful attempts to resist an absolutist state, the English achievement seems all the more striking. There was far more solidarity among key social groups in England to protect their rights against the king than there was elsewhere. The English Parliament included representatives of all of the country's propertied classes, from the great nobles down to yeoman farmers. Two groups were of particular importance, the gentry and the Third Estate. The former had not been recruited as a class into state service, as in Russia, and the latter were largely unwilling to trade their political rights for titles and individual privileges, as in France. The French, Spanish, and Russian monarchies succeeded in undermining the cohesion of their various elites by selling access and titles to individuals within the elite. The Russian mestnichestvo, or table of noble rankings, served a purpose very similar to that of French and Spanish venal offices in this regard. While English monarchs tried similar stratagems like the sale of offices, Parliament remained a cohesive institution for the reasons presented in the previous chapter—a common commitment to local government, the Common Law, and religion.

But it is not sufficient to explain why the English Parliament was strong enough to force the monarchy into a constitutional settlement. The Hungarian nobility represented in the diet was also very powerful and well organized. Like the English barons at Runnymede, the lesser Hungarian nobility forced their monarch into a constitutional compromise in the thirteenth century, the Golden Bull, and in subsequent years kept the central state on a very short leash.[1] After the death of Mátyás Hunyadi in 1490, the noble estate reversed the centralizing reforms that the monarchy had put into place in the previous generation and returned power to themselves.

But the Hungarian noble estate did not use their power to strengthen the country as a whole; rather, they sought to lower taxes on themselves and guard their own narrow privileges at the expense of the country's ability to defend itself. In England, by contrast, the constitutional settlement coming out of the Glorious Revolution of 1688–1689 vastly strengthened the state, to the point that it became, over the next century, the dominant power in Europe. So if the English Parliament was strong enough to constrain a predatory monarch, we need to ask why that Parliament did not itself evolve into a rent-seeking coalition and turn against itself like the Hungarian Diet.

There are at least two reasons why accountable government in England did not degenerate into rapacious oligarchy. The first has to do with England's social structure compared to that of Hungary. While the groups represented in the English Parliament were an oligarchy, they sat on top of a society that was much more mobile and open to nonelites than was Hungary's. In Hungary, the gentry had been absorbed into a narrow aristocracy, whereas in England they represented a large and cohesive social group, more powerful in certain ways than the aristocracy. England, unlike Hungary, had a tradition of grassroots political participation in the form of the hundred and county courts and other institutions of local governance. English lords were accustomed to sitting in assemblies on equal terms with their vassals and tenants to decide issues of common interest. Hungary, furthermore, had no equivalent of the English yeomanry, relatively prosperous farmers who owned their own land and could participate in local political life. And cities in Hungary were strictly controlled by the noble estate and did not generate a rich and powerful bourgeoisie the way that English ones did.

Second, despite English traditions of individual liberty, the centralized English state was both powerful and well regarded through much of the society. It was one of the first states to develop a uniform system of justice, it protected property rights, and it acquired substantial naval capabilities in its struggles with various Continental powers. The English experiment with republican government after the beheading of Charles I in 1649 and the establishment of Cromwell's Protectorate was not a happy one. The regicide itself seemed, even to the supporters of Parliament, an unjust and illegal act. The English Civil War witnessed the same sort of progressive radicalization experienced later during the French, Bolshevik, and Chinese revolutions. The more extreme anti-Royalist groups like the Levellers and the Diggers seemed to want not just political accountability but also a much broader social revolution, which frightened the property-owning classes represented in Parliament. It was thus with a great deal of relief that the monarchy was restored in 1660 with the accession of Charles II.[2] After the Restoration, the issues of political accountability reappeared under the Catholic James II, whose machinations again aroused suspicions and opposition from Parliament and ultimately led to the Glorious Revolution. But this time around, no one wanted to dismantle the monarchy or the state; they only wanted a king who would be accountable to them. They got one in William of Orange.

Ideas were again important. By the late seventeenth century, thinkers like Hobbes and Locke had broken free of concepts of a feudal social order based on classes and estates, and argued in favor of a social contract between state and citizen. Hobbes argued in *Leviathan* that human beings are fundamentally equal both in their passions and in their ability to inflict violence on one another, and that they have rights merely by virtue of the fact that they are human beings. Locke accepted these premises as well and attacked the notion that legitimate rule could arise from anything other than consent of the governed. One could overthrow a king, but only in the name of the principle of consent. Rights, according to these early liberals, were abstract and universal, and could not be legitimately appropriated by powerful individuals. Hungary had succumbed to the Turks and the Austrians long before ideas like these could spread there.

There is one simple lesson to be drawn from this comparison. Political liberty—that is, the ability of societies to rule themselves—does not depend only on the degree to which a society can mobilize opposition to centralized power and impose constitutional constraints on the state. It must also have a state that is strong enough to act when action is required. Accountability does not run in just one direction, from the state to the society. If the government cannot act cohesively, if there is no broader sense of public purpose, then one will not have laid the basis for true political liberty. In contrast to Hungary after the death of Mátyás Hunyadi, the English state after 1689 remained strong and cohesive, with a Parliament willing to tax itself and make sacrifices in the prolonged foreign struggles of the eighteenth century. A political system that is all checks and balances is potentially no more successful than one with no checks, because governments periodically need strong and decisive action. The stability of an accountable political system thus rests on a broad balance of power between the state and its underlying society.

GETTING TO DENMARK

One of the problems with Whig history is that it makes England's story paradigmatic for the rise of constitutional democracy as such. There were, however, other paths that states in Europe took to get to the same place where the English ended up. Since we began this long account of political development by raising the question of how Denmark got to be Denmark—a law-abiding, democratic, prosperous, and well-governed polity with some of the world's lowest levels of political corruption—we need to spend some time explaining this outcome.

In the year 1500, it was not obvious that Denmark (or any other country in Scandinavia) would turn out differently from other late medieval societies in Europe. Some observers have tried to trace Denmark's present all the way back to the Vikings who originally settled Scandinavia.[3] But it is hard to see how this particular group of tribal marauders distinguished

themselves fundamentally from the other Germanic barbarians that settled Europe after the end of the Roman Empire, other than the fact that
they sailed in longboats rather than rode horses.

The Danish monarchy, of very ancient lineage, was relatively weak from
the thirteenth century, when the king was forced to sign a Great Charter
requiring consultation with a noble parliament and special privileges for
the church.[4] The Danish economy, as in the rest of Europe, was based on
the manor, though Denmark's location at the entrance to the Baltic and its
proximity to the cities of the Hanseatic League made international trade a
relatively more important factor in its economic development.[5] After the
breakup of the Kalmar Union, which briefly united much of Scandinavia
in the mid-fifteenth century, Denmark remained a fairly important multinational power, controlling Norway, Iceland, the German-speaking territories of Schleswig and Holstein, and provinces across the Sound in what
is now western Sweden.

If there is a single event that sent Denmark and other parts of Scandinavia off on a distinct development path, it was the Protestant Reformation. As
in other parts of Europe, Martin Luther's ideas proved tremendously destabilizing, catalyzing long-standing popular grievances against the Catholic
church. In Denmark, a brief civil war led to a victory by the Protestant side
and the establishment of a Lutheran Danish national church in 1536.[6] This
outcome was driven as much by material as by moral factors: the Danish
king saw an important opportunity to seize the church's considerable assets,
which may have amounted to some 30 percent of the land in Denmark.[7]

The truly lasting political impact of the Reformation in Denmark came,
however, through its encouragement of peasant literacy. The Lutherans believed strongly in the need for ordinary people to have direct access to God
through their ability to read the Bible or, failing that, Luther's Lesser Cate-
chism. Beginning in the sixteenth century, the Lutheran church began to set
up schools in every village in Denmark, where priests taught peasants the
basics of reading and writing. The result was that, by the eighteenth century,
the peasantry in Denmark (and in other parts of Scandinavia) had emerged
as a relatively well-educated and increasingly well-organized social class.[8]

Social mobilization in contemporary societies usually takes place as a
result of economic development. This was also the route taken in medieval England, where extension of property rights under the Common Law
facilitated the transformation of the top layer of the English peasantry into
politically active yeoman farmers. In premodern sixteenth-century Den-

mark, by contrast, it was religion that drove social mobilization. Literacy allowed peasants not only to improve their economic condition, it also helped them to communicate among themselves and organize as political agents. It is hard to imagine a greater contrast than that between rural Scandinavia and Russia in the early nineteenth century, despite geographical proximity and similarities in climate.

Unlike the English case, representative democracy did not emerge out of the survival of a feudal institution (parliament) that was sufficiently well organized to resist the centralizing state. In Denmark, an absolutist state with an increasingly sophisticated bureaucracy had been established in 1660 following defeat in a war with Sweden.[9] The Danish Diet was abolished and there was no estate-based political structure to which the monarch had to go to receive permission to raise taxes.

The critical political revolution came in the period from 1760 to 1792, when an enlightened Danish monarchy progressively abolished a form of serfdom known as the Stavnsbånd, first on the royal domains and then for all landowners, and restricted the right of landlords to impose degrading punishments on peasants like flogging on a wooden horse.[10] Peasants were not enfranchised, but they were given the right to own land and freely engage in commerce on an equal basis.[11]

The Danish monarch saw peasant freedom as an opportunity to undermine the power of the noble landowners, who fiercely resisted his reforms. Freeing the peasants would allow him to conscript them directly into the national army. Ideas were important as well: Adam Smith's *Wealth of Nations* had been published in 1776, arguing that landowning farmers would ultimately be far more productive than unfree serfs. But equally important was the fact that the peasantry itself was increasingly educated, mobilized, and ready to take up the opportunities of economic freedom by moving into higher value-added activities like food processing.

The second major event making possible modern Danish democracy was externally driven. Denmark remained a middle-range, multinational European power at the end of the eighteenth century. It lost Norway in 1814 as a consequence of the Napoleonic Wars. The spread of the ideas of the French Revolution in the early decades of the nineteenth century had complex political consequences, since they stimulated both class-based demands for political participation on the part of the bourgeoisie and peasantry, as well as demands for national recognition on the part of Denmark's sizable German-speaking minority.

The Prussians solved the problem by taking the predominantly German-speaking duchies of Schleswig and Holstein away from the Danes in 1864 in a short but decisive war. Overnight, Denmark became a small, homogeneous, largely Danish-speaking country and realized that it would have to live within the confines of a much smaller state.

This, then, forms the context for the story of the emergence of democracy in the late nineteenth century and social democracy in the early twentieth. A farmer-based political movement inspired by the priest and educator N.F.S. Grundtvig took shape at first in the guise of a religious revival movement that broke away from the official Lutheran church and established schools throughout the country.[12] After a constitutional monarchy took power in 1848, the farmers' movement and the national liberals representing the bourgeoisie began pushing for direct political participation, which led to the granting of voting rights the following year. The emergence of the Danish welfare state in the twentieth century is beyond the scope of this volume. But when it finally arrived, it was based not solely on an emerging working class but also on the farmer class, whose mobilization was facilitated at key junctures not by economic growth but by religion.

The development of democracy and a modern market-based economy was far less conflictual and violent in Denmark than it was in England, not to mention France, Spain, and Germany. To get to modern Denmark, the Danes did indeed fight a number of wars with neighbors including Sweden and Prussia, and there were violent civil conflicts in the seventeenth and nineteenth centuries. But there was no prolonged civil war, no enclosure movement, no absolutist tyranny, no grinding poverty brought on by early industrialization, and a far weaker legacy of class conflict. Ideas were critical to the Danish story, not just in terms of Lutheran and Grundtvigian ideology but also in the way that Enlightenment views about rights and constitutionalism were accepted by a series of Danish monarchs in the eighteenth and nineteenth centuries.

The story of the rise of Danish democracy is full of historical accidents and contingent circumstances that cannot be duplicated elsewhere. The Danes took a much different route to get to modern liberal democracy than the English, but in the end they arrived at a very similar place. Both countries developed a strong state, rule of law, and accountable government. It would appear, then, that there are a number of different routes for "getting to Denmark."

PART FIVE

·

Toward a Theory of
Political Development

29

POLITICAL DEVELOPMENT AND POLITICAL DECAY

The biological foundations of politics; mechanisms by which political order evolves; what politics is and how it differs from economics; a definition of institutions; sources of political decay; the state, rule of law, accountability, and how they are related; how the conditions for political development have changed over time

This book provides an account of political development from prehuman times up to the eve of the French and American revolutions, the moment when fully modern politics emerged. From that point on, a number of polities appeared that encompassed all three important categories of political institutions: the state, rule of law, and accountable government.

Some readers may conclude that my account of political development is historically determinist. That is, by describing the complex and context-specific origins of institutions, I am arguing that comparable institutions can emerge in the present *only* under similar conditions, and that countries are locked into a single path of development by their unique historical pasts.

This is definitely not the case. Institutions that confer advantages to their societies are routinely copied and improved by others; there are both learning and institutional convergence across societies over time. Moreover, the historical story in this volume ends just on the eve of the Industrial Revolution, which changed enormously the conditions under which political development occurred. Both of these points will be elaborated in the concluding chapter. The second volume of this series will then describe and analyze how political development has taken place in the post-Malthusian world.

Given the enormous conservatism of human societies with regard to institutions, societies do not get to sweep the decks clear in every generation. New institutions are more typically layered on top of existing ones, which survive for extraordinarily long periods of time. Segmentary lineages, for example, are one of the most ancient forms of social organization and yet they continue to exist in many parts of the modern world. It is impossible to understand the possibilities for change in the present without appreciating this legacy, and the way that it often limits choices available to political actors in the present.

Moreover, understanding the complex historical circumstances under which institutions were originally created can help us see why their transfer and imitation are difficult even under modern circumstances. Oftentimes a political institution comes into being as a result of nonpolitical reasons (an economist would say these factors are *exogenous* to the political system). We have already seen several examples of this. Private property, to take one case, emerged not only for economic reasons but also because lineages needed a place to bury their ancestors and appease the souls of the dead. Similarly, the sanctity of the rule of law was historically dependent on the religious origins of law. The state itself came into being in China and Europe as the result of the desperate incentives created by unremitting warfare, something that the contemporary international system seeks to suppress. Trying to re-create these institutions without the help of these exogenous factors is therefore often an uphill struggle.

I will summarize some of the themes that have run through the historical account of institutional development given in this book and try to distill from them the outlines of a theory of political development and political decay. This may not amount to a genuine predictive theory, since outcomes are the result of so many interlocking factors. There is, moreover, the turtle problem: the turtle one chooses as an explanatory factor is always resting on another turtle farther down. One of the reasons I began this volume with an account of the state of nature and human biology is that it is an obvious starting point, a Grund-Schildkröte (base turtle) on which subsequent turtles can be placed.

THE BIOLOGICAL FOUNDATIONS OF POLITICS

Human beings are not completely free to socially construct their own behavior. They have a shared biological nature. That nature is remarkably uniform throughout the world, given the fact that most contemporary humans outside of Africa descended from a single relatively small group of individuals some fifty thousand years ago. This shared nature does not determine political behavior, but it both frames and limits the nature of institutions that are possible. It also means that human politics is subject to certain recurring patterns of behavior across time and across cultures. This shared nature can be described in the following propositions.

Human beings never existed in a presocial state. The idea that human beings at one time existed as isolated individuals, who interacted either through anarchic violence (Hobbes) or in pacific ignorance of one another (Rousseau), is not correct. Human beings as well as their primate ancestors always lived in kin-based social groups of varying sizes. Indeed, they lived in these social units for a sufficiently long period of time that the cognitive and emotional faculties needed to promote social cooperation evolved and became hardwired in their genetic endowments. This means that a rational-choice model of collective action, in which individuals calculate that they will be better off by cooperating with one another, vastly understates the degree of social cooperation that exists in human societies and misunderstands the motives that underlie it.[1]

Natural human sociability is built around two principles, kin selection and reciprocal altruism. The principle of kin selection or inclusive fitness states that human beings will act altruistically toward genetic relatives (or individuals believed to be genetic relatives) in rough proportion to their shared genes. The principle of reciprocal altruism says that human beings will tend to develop relationships of mutual benefit or mutual harm as they interact with other individuals over time. Reciprocal altruism, unlike kin selection, does not depend on genetic relatedness; it does, however, depend on repeated, direct *personal* interaction and the trust relationships generated out of such interactions. These forms of social cooperation are the default ways human beings interact in the absence of incentives to adhere to other, more impersonal institutions. When impersonal institutions decay, these are the forms of cooperation that always reemerge because they are natural to human beings. What I have labeled patrimonialism is political recruitment based on either of these two principles. Thus, when bureaucratic offices were filled with the kinsmen of rulers at the end of the Han Dynasty in China, when the Janissaries wanted their sons to enter the corps, or when offices were sold as heritable property in ancien régime France, a natural patrimonial principle was simply reasserting itself.

Human beings have an innate propensity for creating and following norms or rules. Since institutions are essentially rules that limit individual freedom of choice, one can equivalently say that human beings have a natural inclination to create institutions. Rules can be rationally derived by individuals calculating how to maximize their own self-interest, which requires that they enter into social contracts with other individuals. Human beings are born with a suite of cognitive faculties that allow them to solve prisoner's-dilemma-type problems of social cooperation. They can remember past behavior as a guide to future cooperation; they pass on information about trustworthiness through gossip and other forms of information sharing; they have acute perceptual faculties for detecting lies and untrustworthy behavior through vocal and visual cues; and they have common modes for sharing information through language and nonverbal forms of communication. The ability to make and obey rules is an economizing behavior in the sense that it greatly reduces the transaction costs of social interaction and permits efficient collective action.

The human instinct to follow rules is often based in the emotions rather than in reason, however. Emotions like guilt, shame, pride, anger, embarrassment, and admiration are not learned behaviors in the Lockean sense of being somehow acquired after birth through interaction with the empirical world outside the individual. Rather, they come naturally to small children, who then organize their behavior around genetically grounded yet culturally transmitted rules. Our capacity for rule making and following is thus very much like our capacity for language: while the content of the rules is conventional and varies from society to society, the "deep structure" of the rules and the ability to acquire them are natural.

This propensity of human beings to endow rules with intrinsic value helps to explain the enormous conservatism of societies. Rules may evolve as useful adaptations to a particular set of environmental conditions, but societies cling to them long after those conditions have changed and the rules have become irrelevant or even dysfunctional. The Mamluks refused to adopt firearms long after their usefulness had been demonstrated by the Europeans, because of their emotional investment in a certain form of cavalry warfare. This led directly to their defeat by the Ottomans, who were far more willing to adapt. There is thus a general principle of the conservation of institutions across different human societies.

Human beings have a natural propensity for violence. From the first moment of their existence, human beings have perpetrated acts of violence against other human beings, as did their primate ancestors. *Pace*

Rousseau, the propensity for violence is not a learned behavior that arose only at a certain point in human history. At the same time, social institutions have always existed to control and channel violence. Indeed, one of the most important functions of political institutions is precisely to control and aggregate the level at which violence appears.

Human beings by nature desire not just material resources but also recognition. Recognition is the acknowledgment of another human being's dignity or worth, or what is otherwise understood to be status. Struggles for recognition or status often have a very different character from struggles over resources, since status is relative rather than absolute, or what the economist Robert Frank calls a "positional good."[2] In other words, one can have high status only if everyone else has lower status. Unlike cooperative games, or the gains from free trade, which are positive sum and allow both players to win, struggles over relative status are zero sum in which a gain for one player is necessarily a loss for another.

A great deal of human politics revolves around struggles for recognition. This was true not just of would-be Chinese dynasts seeking the Mandate of Heaven but also of humble peasant rebels seeking justice under banners like the Yellow or Red Turbans, or the French Bonnets Rouges. Arab tribes were able to settle their differences and conquer much of North Africa and the Middle East because they sought recognition for their religion, Islam, much as European warriors conquered the New World under the banner of Christianity. In more recent times, the rise of modern democracy is incomprehensible apart from the demand for equal recognition that lies at its core. In England, there was a progressive shift in the nature of demands for recognition, from the rights of the tribe or village, to the rights of Englishmen, to Locke's rights of man.

It is important to resist the temptation to reduce human motivation to an economic desire for resources. Violence in human history has often been perpetrated by people seeking not material wealth but recognition. Conflicts are carried on long beyond the point when they make economic sense. Recognition is sometimes related to material wealth, but at other times it comes at the expense of material wealth, and it is an unhelpful oversimplification to regard it as just another type of "utility."

IDEAS AS CAUSE

It is impossible to develop any meaningful theory of political development without treating ideas as fundamental causes of why societies differ
and follow distinct development paths. In social science terms, they are
independent variables, or in turtle terminology, they are turtles far down
the stack that do not necessarily stand on the backs of turtles related to the
economy or physical environment.

People in all human societies create mental models of reality. These
mental models attribute causality to various factors—oftentimes invisible
ones—and their function is to make the world more legible, predictable,
and easy to manipulate. In earlier societies, these invisible forces were
spirits, demons, gods, or Nature; today, they are abstractions like gravity,
radiation, economic self-interest, social classes, and the like. All religious
beliefs constitute a mental model of reality, in which observable events are
attributed to or caused by non- or dimly observable forces. Since at least
the time of David Hume, we have understood that it is not possible to
verify causality through empirical data alone. With the rise of modern
natural science, however, we have moved toward theories of causation
that can at least be falsified, through either controlled experiments or sta-
tistical analysis. With better ways of testing causal theories, human beings
can more effectively manipulate their environment, using fertilizer and
irrigation, for example, rather than the blood of sacrificial victims to increase crop yields. But every known human society has generated some
type of causal model of reality, suggesting that this is a natural rather than
an acquired faculty.

Shared mental models—most particularly those that take the form of
religion—are critical in facilitating large-scale collective action. Collective
action based merely on rational self-interest is wholly inadequate in explaining the degree of social cooperation and altruism that actually exists
in the world.[3] Religious belief helps to motivate people to do things they
would not do if they were interested only in resources or material well-
being, as we saw in the case of the rise of Islam in seventh-century Arabia.
The sharing of belief and culture improves cooperation by providing common goals and facilitating the cooperative solution of shared problems.[4]

Many people, observing religious conflict in the contemporary world,
have become hostile to religion as such and regard it as a source of violence and intolerance.[5] In a world of overlapping and plural religious en-

vironments, this can clearly be the case. But they fail to put religion in its broader historical context, where it was a critical factor in permitting broad social cooperation that transcended kin and friends as a source of social relationships. Moreover, secular ideologies like Marxism-Leninism or nationalism that have displaced religious beliefs in many contemporary societies can be and have been no less destructive due to the passionate beliefs that they engender.

Mental models and rules are intimately intertwined, since the models often suggest clear rules for societies to follow. Religions are more than theories; they are prescriptive moral codes that seek to enforce rules on their followers. They, like the rules they enjoin, are invested with considerable emotional meaning and therefore are believed for intrinsic reasons and not simply because they are accurate or useful. While religious beliefs cannot be verified, they are also difficult to falsify. All of this reinforces the fundamental conservatism of human societies, because mental models of reality once adopted are hard to change in the light of new evidence that they are not working.

The universality of some form of religious belief among virtually all known human societies suggests that it is somehow rooted in human nature. Like language and rule following, the content of religious belief is conventional and varies from society to society, but the faculty for creating religious doctrines is innate.[6] Nothing of what I say here about the political impact of religion rests, however, on whether or not there is a "religion gene." Even if it were a learned behavior, it would still have a large effect on political behavior.

Thinkers like Karl Marx and Émile Durkheim, seeing the utilitarian role that religious beliefs play in binding communities together (whether the community as a whole, or a particular social class), believed that religion was therefore somehow deliberately created for that purpose. As we have seen, religious views evolve along with political and economic orders, moving from shamanism and magic to ancestor worship to poly- and monotheistic religions with highly developed doctrines.[7] Religious beliefs must obviously be related in some manner to the material conditions of existence of the groups that maintain them. Suicide cults or sects forbidding reproduction among their members like the Shakers tend not to survive for very long. It is therefore very tempting to see religion as somehow the product of those material conditions and wholly explicable in terms of them.

This would, however, be an enormous mistake. Religion can never be explained simply by reference to prior material conditions. We saw this most clearly with regard to the contrast between China and India. Up until the end of the first millennium B.C., both societies were similar in terms of social structure based on agnatic lineages and the kinds of political forms thereby produced. But thereafter Indian society took a sharp detour that could be explained only by the rise of Brahmanic religion. The specific metaphysical propositions that underlie that religion are highly complex and sophisticated, and it is a fool's errand to try to relate them in any detail to the specific economic and environmental conditions existing in northern India at that particular time.

I have traced many other instances where religious ideas played an independent role in shaping political outcomes. The Catholic church played a major role, for example, in the shaping of two major European institutions. It was critical in undermining the structure of property rights of kin groups among the barbarian Germanic tribes that took over the Roman Empire from the sixth century on, which in turn was crucial in weakening tribalism per se. Europe therefore made an exit out of kinship-based social organization through social rather than political means, in sharp contrast to China, India, and the Middle East. Then, in the eleventh century, the Catholic church declared its independence from secular authority, organizing itself as a modern hierarchy, and then promulgating a transnational European rule of law. While comparable independent religious institutions existed in India, the Middle East, and the Byzantine Empire, none succeeded to the extent of the Western church in institutionalizing an independent legal order. Without the investiture conflict and its consequences, the rule of law would never have become so deeply rooted in the West.

In none of these cases do religious values simply trump material interests. The Catholic church, just like the Brahmin class in India or the class of ulama in Muslim societies, constituted a social group with its own material interests. The changes in inheritance laws mandated by Gregory I appear to have been undertaken not for doctrinal but for self-interested reasons, as a means of diverting land away from their kin group owners toward the church itself. Nonetheless, the church was not simply another political actor like the warlords dominating Europe at the time. It could not readily convert its resources into military power, nor could it engage in predation without the help of secular authorities. On the other hand, it had a legitimacy that it could confer on the secular political actors, which they could not achieve on their own. Economists sometimes speak of political actors "investing" in legitimacy, as if legitimacy were a simple factor of production like land or machines.[8] But legitimacy has to be understood in its own terms, that is, in terms of the ideas people hold about God, justice, man, society, wealth, virtue, and the like.

One of the most important changes in values and ideology that define the modern world—the idea of the equality of recognition—appeared just at the end of the period covered in this volume. The idea of human equality has deep roots; writers from Hegel to Tocqueville to Nietzsche have traced modern ideas of equality to the biblical idea of man made in the image of God. The expansion of the charmed circle of human beings accorded equal dignity was very slow, however, and only after the seventeenth century came eventually to include the lower social classes, women, racial, religious, and ethnic minorities, and the like.

The passage from band- and tribal-level societies to state-level ones represented, in some sense, a huge setback for human freedom. States were wealthier and more powerful than their kin-based predecessors, but that wealth and power led to a huge amount of stratification that left some masters and many others slaves. Hegel would say that the recognition offered a ruler in such an unequal society was defective and ultimately unsatisfying even to the rulers, because it was offered by people who themselves lacked dignity. The rise of modern democracy gives all people the opportunity of ruling themselves, on the basis of the mutual recognition of the dignity and rights of their fellow humans. It thus seeks to restore, in the context of large and complex societies, something of what was lost in the original transition to the state.

The story of the emergence of accountable government cannot be told without reference to the spread of these ideas. We saw in the case of the English Parliament how its solidarity depended critically on a belief in the rights of Englishmen, and how the Glorious Revolution was shaped by a broader Lockean concept of universal natural rights. These were the ideas that would go on to animate the American Revolution. If the historical reasons I present for the rise of accountability seem at times rooted in the material interests of the actors in these struggles, they must in turn be seen against the backdrop of ideas that defined who the actors were and what their scope for collective action was.

THE GENERAL MECHANISM OF POLITICAL DEVELOPMENT

Political systems evolve in a manner roughly comparable to biological evolution. Darwin's theory of evolution is based on two very simple principles, variation and selection. Variation among organisms occurs due to random genetic combinations; those variants that are better adapted to their specific environments have greater reproductive success and therefore propagate themselves at the expense of those less well adapted.

In a very long historical perspective, political development has followed the same general pattern: the forms of political organization employed by different groups of human beings have varied, and those forms that were more successful—meaning those that could generate greater military and economic power—displaced those that were less successful. At this high level of abstraction, it is hard to see how political development could have proceeded in any other way. What is more important, however, is to understand the ways political evolution differs from its biological counterpart, of which there are at least three.

First, in political evolution, the units of selection are rules and their embodiments as institutions, rather than genes as in biological evolution. Although human biology facilitates the formulation and following of rules, it does not determine their content, and that content can vary enormously. Rules are the basis for institutions that confer advantages on those societies employing them and are selected through the interaction of human agents over less advantageous ones.

Second, in human societies, variation among institutions can be planned and deliberate, as opposed to random. Hayek argues strongly against the idea that human societies self-consciously design institutions, something he traces to the hubris of post-Cartesian rationalism.[9] He argues that most information in societies is local in nature and therefore cannot be comprehended by centralized human agents.[10] The weakness of Hayek's argument is that human beings successfully design institutions all the time, at all levels of society. He does not like top-down, centralized social engineering on the part of states, but he is willing to accept bottom-up, decentralized institutional innovation that is no less subject to human design. While large-scale design may work less frequently than smaller-scale projects, it still does periodically work. Human beings can rarely plan for unintended consequences and missing information, but the fact that they can plan means that the variance in institutional forms they create is more likely to produce adaptive solutions than simple randomness. Hayek is correct, however, that institutional evolution is not dependent on the ability of human beings to design successful institutions; random variation and the principle of selection by themselves can produce an adaptive evolutionary outcome.[11]

The third way political development differs from biological evolution is that the selected characteristics—institutions in one case, genes in the other—are transmitted culturally rather than genetically. This represents both an advantage and a disadvantage with respect to the adaptability of the system. Cultural traits, whether norms, customs, laws, beliefs, or values, can at least in theory be altered on the fly within the space of a single generation, as in the spread of Islam in the seventh century, or literacy among the Danish peasantry in the sixteenth. On the other hand, human beings tend to invest institutions and the mental models they arise from with intrinsic value, which leads to the conservation of institutions over time. A biological organism, by contrast, doesn't worship or reify its own genes; if they do not permit the creature to survive and reproduce, the principle of selection ruthlessly eliminates them. Institutional evolution can therefore be both faster and slower than biological evolution.

In contrast to biological evolution, institutions can spread through imitation. Some societies with weaker institutions are either conquered or eliminated by stronger ones, but in other cases they can adopt the institutions of their competitors in a process known as "defensive modernization."[12] During Japan's Tokugawa shogunate from the seventeenth to the nineteenth century, the feudal lords who ran the country knew about the existence of firearms from their early contacts with the Portuguese and other travelers. They engaged in what amounted to a long-term arms control arrangement, however, by which they agreed not to introduce firearms among themselves because they did not want to give up their traditional form of sword- and archery-based warfare. But when Commodore Matthew Perry showed up with his "black ships" in Tokyo Bay in 1853, the ruling elite realized that they would have to end this comfortable arrangement and acquire the same types of military technology possessed by the Americans if they were not to end up a Western colony like China. After the Meiji Restoration in 1868, Japan introduced not just firearms but also a new form of government, a centralized bureaucracy, a new educational system, and a host of other institutions borrowed from Europe and the United States.

Biological evolution is both specific and general. Specific evolution occurs as species adapt to very particular environments and differentiate, as
in the case of Darwin's famous finches. But general evolution also occurs
as certain successful categories of organisms proliferate across local environments. There were thus large general transitions from single-celled to
multicellular organisms, from asexual to sexual reproduction, from dino-
saurs to mammals and the like. So, too, in political development. As behaviorally modern humans left Africa some fifty thousand years ago and
spread over the world, they adapted to the different local environments
they encountered and developed different languages, cultures, and institutions. At the same time, certain societies hit upon forms of social organization that provided large advantages, and thus there were also general
transitions from band- to tribal- to state-level societies. Among state-level
societies, those that could organize themselves more effectively defeated
or absorbed less effective ones and thus proliferated their own form of
social organization. Hence there was both differentiation and convergence
among political institutions.

Competition is critical to the process of political development, just as
it is in biological evolution. If competition did not exist, there would be no
selection pressure on institutions, and therefore no incentives for institutional innovation, borrowing, or reform. One of the most important competitive pressures leading to institutional innovation has been violence
and war. The transition from band- to tribal-level societies was made possible by greater economic productivity, but it was directly motivated by
the superior ability of tribal societies to mobilize manpower. In chapter 5
I discussed various theories of pristine state formation, including economic self-interest, irrigation, population density, physical geography, religious authority, and violence. Although all these factors play a role, the
difficult transition from a free tribal society to a despotic state-level society seems far more plausibly motivated by the need for physical self-
preservation than by economic interest alone. And when we looked at the
historical record of state formation in China, India, the Middle East, and
Europe, violence once again played a central role in incentivizing not just
state formation but also the creation of the specific institutions we associate with modern states. For reasons detailed below, certain kinds of cooperative problems cannot be solved except through resort to violence.

SPANDRELS EVERYWHERE

In a 1979 article, the biologists Stephen Jay Gould and Richard Lewontin used the analogy of the spandrel to explain the unpredictable way that biological innovation works.[13] A spandrel is a curved architectural area formed by the intersection of arches holding up a dome. The spandrel was not deliberately designed by the architect but was an accidental by-product of other components that were deliberately put into place. Nonetheless, spandrels came to be decorated and took on their own character and meaning as time went on. Gould and Lewontin argued that many biological features of organisms evolve for one reason, but then prove to have adaptive benefits for completely different reasons at a later point in time.

We have seen many equivalents of spandrels in political evolution. The idea of the corporation—a permanently lived institution with an identity separate from the individuals who made it up—arose initially as a religious organization and not for commercial purposes.[14] The Catholic church upheld the right of women to inherit property not because it wanted female empowerment—something quite anachronistic in the seventh century— but because it had its eye on valuable real estate held by powerful clans and saw this as a way of getting it away from them. It is doubtful that any church leaders at the time could foresee the impact this would have on kin relationships as a whole. And finally, the whole idea of governments being limited by independent judiciaries was not present in the minds of those engaged in the investiture conflict, which was a moral and political struggle over the independence of the Catholic church. And yet, in the West, the independence won by a religious organization evolved over time into the independence of the judicial branch. The religious grounding of law was replaced by secular sources, and yet the structure of law remained as it was. Thus the rule of law itself was a kind of spandrel.

The actual historical roots of different institutions often seem to be the products of a long concatenation of historical accidents that one could never have predicted in advance. This might seem discouraging insofar as no contemporary society could ever be expected to pass through exactly the same sequence of events to arrive at a similar institution. But this ignores the role of spandrels in political development. The particular historical source of an institution matters less than the institution's functionality. Once discovered, it can be imitated and used by other societies in completely unanticipated ways.

INSTITUTIONS

In this book, I have been using Samuel Huntington's definition of institutions as "stable, valued, recurring patterns of behavior."[15] And with regard to the institution called the state, I have been using not only Max Weber's definition of the state (an organization deploying a legitimate monopoly of violence over a defined territory) but also his criteria for a modern state (states should be subject to a rational division of labor, based on technical specialization and expertise, and impersonal both with regard to recruitment and their authority over citizens). Impersonal modern states are difficult institutions to both establish and maintain, since patrimonialism—recruitment based on kinship or personal reciprocity—is the natural form of social relationship to which human beings will revert in the absence of other norms and incentives.

Modern organizations have other characteristics as well. Samuel Huntington lists four criteria for measuring the degree of development of the institutions that make up the state: adaptability-rigidity, complexity-simplicity, autonomy-subordination, and coherence-disunity.[16] That is, the more adaptable, complex, autonomous, and coherent an institution is, the more developed it will be. An adaptable organization can evaluate a changing external environment and modify its own internal procedures in response. Adaptable institutions are the ones that survive, since environments always change. The English system of Common Law, in which law is constantly being reinterpreted and extended by judges in response to new circumstances, is one prototype of an adaptable institution.

Developed institutions are more complex because they are subject to a greater division of labor and specialization. In a chiefdom or early state, the ruler may be simultaneously military general, chief priest, tax collector, and supreme court justice. In a highly developed state, all of these functions are performed by separate organizations with specific missions and a high degree of technical capacity to undertake them. During the Han Dynasty, the Chinese bureaucracy ramified into countless specialized agencies and departments at national, prefectural, and local levels. While much less complex than a modern government, it nonetheless represented an enormous shift away from earlier governments that were run as simple extensions of the imperial household.

The two final measures of institutionalization, autonomy and coherence, are, as Huntington points out, closely related. Autonomy refers to the degree to which an institution has developed its own sense of corporate identity, which insulates it from other social forces. In the account of the rule of law given in chapters 17–19, we saw that the degree to which law acts as a constraint on government power depends in good measure on the degree to which courts possess institutional autonomy. In this case, autonomy means the ability to train, hire, promote, and discipline members of the bar and judiciary free from political interference.[17] Autonomy is closely related to specialization, which is why it tends to characterize more developed institutions. An army that is allowed to control its own internal promotions will tend to do better, other things being equal, than one in which generals are appointed on political grounds or purchase their commissions.

Coherence, on the other hand, is more of a systemic measure of the degree to which the roles and missions of different organizations within a political system are well defined and agreed upon. An incoherent political system would have many organizations responsible for, say, collecting taxes or public safety, with no clear sense of who is really in charge. A state apparatus composed of many autonomous institutions is more likely to be coherent than one with subordinated institutions. In patrimonial societies, members of the leader's family or tribe will be given overlapping or ambiguous authority over different state functions, or else special positions of authority will be created for specific individuals. Loyalty is more important than talent in organizing public administration, a practice that continues in many developing countries (and not a few developed ones as well). The formal division of authority among ministries will not correspond to the real distribution of power, leading to institutional incoherence.

Implicit in this four-part definition of institutionalization is the notion that institutions are rules or repeated patterns of behavior that survive the particular individuals who operate them at any one time. The Prophet Muhammad bound together the Medinan tribes by force of his own charismatic personality during his lifetime, but he left behind no system for succession to the caliphate. The young religion barely survived the power struggles over leadership in the generation following, and in many respects is still living with that failed early institutionalization in the form of the Sunni-Shiite split. Regimes that later became successful in the Muslim world did so precisely because they set up institutions like the recruitment of military slaves under the devshirme employed by the Ottomans that were not dependent on the authority of individuals. In China, the emperor was virtually a prisoner of his own bureaucracy and its elaborate rules.

While individual leaders can shape institutions, more highly developed institutions not only survive poor individual leaders but also have a system for training and recruiting new and better ones.

POLITICAL DECAY

If there is a dynamic process by which competition among institutions produces political development, there is also a corresponding process of political decay, by which societies become less institutionalized. There arc two processes by which political decay occurs. Institutions are created in the first place to meet the competitive challenges of a particular environment. That environment can be a physical one, involving land, resources, climate, and geography, or it can be a social one, involving rivals, enemies, competitors, allies, and the like. Institutions once formed tend to be preserved, due to the biological proclivity noted above to invest rules and mental models with intrinsic significance. Indeed, institutions wouldn't be institutions—that is, "stable, valued, recurring patterns of behavior"— if they were not further reinforced by strong social norms, rituals, and other kinds of psychological investments in them. The conservation of institutions has a clear adaptive value: if people did not have a biological proclivity to conform to rules and patterns of behavior, the rules would have to be constantly renegotiated at enormous cost to the stability of the society in question. On the other hand, the fact that societies are so enormously conservative with regard to institutions means that when the original conditions leading to the creation or adoption of an institution change, the institution fails to adjust quickly to meet the new circumstances. The disjunction in rates of change between institutions and the external environment then accounts for political decay or deinstitutionalization.

Legacy investments in existing institutions lead to failures not simply in changing outmoded institutions but also in the very ability to perceive that a failure has taken place. This phenomenon is described by social psychologists as "cognitive dissonance," of which history is littered with examples.[18] If one society is getting more powerful militarily, or wealthier, as a result of superior institutions, members of a less competitive society have to correctly attribute those advantages to the underlying institutions if they are to have any hope of surviving. Social outcomes are inherently multicausal, however, and it is always possible to come up with alternative explanations for social weakness or failure that are plausible—but wrong. Societies from Rome to China attributed military setbacks to inadequate observance of religious obligations; instead of spending time reorganizing and reequipping the army, they devoted resources to increased rites and sacrifices. In more recent societies, it is easy to blame social failures on the machinations of various outsiders, whether Jews or American imperialism, rather than looking to indigenous institutions for the explanation.

The second form of political decay is repatrimonialization. The favoring of family or friends with whom one has exchanged reciprocal favors is a natural form of sociability and is a default manner of human interaction. The most universal form of human political interaction is a patron-client relationship in which a leader exchanges favors in return for support from a group of followers. In certain stages of political development, this constituted the *only* form of political organization. But as institutions evolved, new rules were put in place to recruit on the basis of function or talent—the Mandarin examination system, the devshirme in Turkey, the celibacy of the Catholic priesthood, or contemporary legislation outlawing nepotism in hiring. But there is constant pressure to repatrimonialize the system. Individuals initially recruited into an institution on impersonal grounds nonetheless often try to pass on their positions to their children or friends. When institutions come under stress, leaders often find they have to give in to these pressures in order to secure political primacy or meet fiscal needs.

We have seen numerous examples of both forms of political decay. In the first part of the seventeenth century, the Ming Dynasty in China faced increasing military pressure from well-organized Manchu forces to the north. Regime survival depended on the government's ability to marshal resources, rebuild a professional army, and deploy it on the northeastern frontier. None of these things happened, due to the government's unwillingness or inability to raise sufficient tax revenues to cover the cost of self-defense. At this point in the dynasty, the regime had fallen into a certain comfortable relationship with the elites that would have had to shoulder a higher tax burden, and it was simply easier for disengaged emperors to let sleeping dogs lie.

Repatrimonialization is a recurring phenomenon. The impersonal bureaucratic system set up during the Former Han Dynasty was gradually eroded by aristocratic families who sought to secure privileged places for themselves and their lineages in the central government. These families continued to dominate the Chinese bureaucracy during the Sui and Tang dynasties. Both the Egyptian Mamluks and the Turkish Janissaries undermined the impersonal slave recruitment system by demanding first to be allowed to have families, and then that their children be allowed to enter the military institution. In the case of the Mamluks, this happened in response to the receding of the Mongol threat in the late thirteenth century, combined with repeated plagues and worsening terms of trade. For the Ottomans, it was price inflation and severe budgetary pressures that led Sultans Selim the Grim and Suleiman the Magnificent to make similar concessions to the Janissaries. The Catholic church created modern bureaucracies by forbidding priests and bishops to have families, but the system broke down over time as ecclesiastical officers sought to rejoin the officium to the beneficium and make that heritable property. In France and Spain, this led to an overtly corrupt system of venal office, by which the public sector was privatized and made into heritable property.

The two types of political decay—institutional rigidity and repatrimonialization—oftentimes come together as patrimonial officials with a large personal stake in the existing system seek to defend it against reform. And if the system breaks down altogether, it is often only patrimonial actors with their patronage networks that are left to pick up the pieces.

VIOLENCE AND THE DYSFUNCTIONAL EQUILIBRIUM

We can be much more precise about why institutions are slow to adjust to changes in the environment beyond saying that there is a natural tendency toward the conservation of institutions. Any institution or system of institutions benefits certain groups in a society, often at the expense of others, even if on the whole the political system provides public goods like domestic peace and property rights. Those groups favored by the state may feel more secure in their persons and property, they may collect rents as a result of their favored access to power, or they may receive recognition and social status. Those elite groups have a stake in existing institutional arrangements and will defend the status quo as long as they continue to remain cohesive. Even when the society as a whole would benefit from an institutional change, such as raising the land tax in order to pay for defense against an external threat, well-organized groups will be able to veto change because for them the net gain is negative.

This kind of collective action failure is well understood by economists. The situation constitutes what game theorists call a stable equilibrium, since none of the players will individually gain from changing the underlying institutional arrangements. But the equilibrium is dysfunctional from the standpoint of the society as a whole. Mancur Olson has made the general argument that entrenched interest groups tend to accumulate in any society over time, which aggregate into rent-seeking coalitions in order to defend their narrow privileges.[19] They are much better organized than the broad mass of people in a society, whose interests often fail to be represented in the political system. The problem of a dysfunctional political equilibrium can be mitigated by democracy, which at least theoretically allows nonelites to have a greater share in political power. But even then there is usually a large disparity in the organizational capacity of elites and nonelites that prevents the latter from acting decisively.

We have seen numerous examples of rent-seeking coalitions that have prevented necessary institutional change and therefore provoked political decay. The classic one from which the very term rent derives was ancien régime France, where the monarchy had grown strong over two centuries by co-opting much of the French elite. This co-optation took the form of the actual purchase of small pieces of the state, which could then be handed down to descendants. When reformist ministers like Maupeou and Turgot sought to change the system by abolishing venal office altogether, the existing stakeholders were strong enough to block any action. The problem of venal officeholding was solved only through violence in the course of the revolution.

But the problem of dysfunctional equilibria goes much farther back in history than this. There is archaeological evidence of band-level societies that had access to agricultural technology and yet did not make the shift from hunting and gathering for many generations. The reason for this would again appear to be the vested interests of existing stakeholders. Band-level societies are egalitarian and engage in considerable food sharing, something that becomes impossible once agriculture and private property are adopted. The moment that one family settles down and starts growing food, it would have to be shared among the other members of the band, destroying the incentive for investing in agriculture in the first place. The shift from one form of production to another would make the society as a whole richer due to the higher productivity of agriculture over hunting and gathering, but it would also require the exclusion of certain members of the band from the free enjoyment of surpluses. The archaeologist Steven LeBlanc suggests that the slowness of some forager societies to adopt agriculture was due precisely to their inability to solve this type of cooperation problem.[20]

The ability of societies to innovate institutionally thus depends on whether they can neutralize existing political stakeholders holding vetoes over reform. Sometimes economic change weakens the position of existing elites in favor of new ones, who push for new institutions. The relative decline of returns to landed property when compared to commerce or manufacturing in England empowered the bourgeoisie to make political gains at the expense of the old aristocracy in the seventeenth century. Sometimes, new social actors are empowered by the rise of a new religious ideology, as in the case of Buddhism and Jainism in India. The peasantry in Scandinavia ceased being an inert mass of dispersed individuals after the Reformation, due to the promotion of literacy and lay access to the Bible. At other times, it is the sheer force of leadership and the ability to assemble winning coalitions of out-of-power groups that lead to change, as in the case of Gregory VII's organization of the papal party during the investiture conflict. This is, in effect, the essence of politics: the ability of leaders to get their way through a combination of authority, legitimacy, intimidation, negotiation, charisma, ideas, and organization.

The stability of dysfunctional equilibria suggests one reason why violence has played such an important role in institutional innovation and reform. Violence is classically seen as the problem that politics seeks to solve,[21] but sometimes violence is the only way to displace entrenched stakeholders who are blocking institutional change. The fear of violent death is a stronger emotion than the desire for material gain and is capable of motivating more far-reaching changes in behavior. We already noted in chapter 5 that economic motives like the desire to put in place a large irrigation system were highly implausible causes of pristine state formation. Incessant tribal warfare or fear of conquest by better-organized groups is, by contrast, a very understandable reason why free and proud tribesmen might agree to live in a centralized state.

In Chinese history, patrimonial elites stood in the way of the creation of modern state institutions both during the rise of the state of Qin and during the Sui and Tang dynasties when they had made a comeback. In the first case, incessant warfare led by aristocrats decimated their ranks and opened the way for nonelite military recruitment. In the latter case, the rise of the empress Wu to power early in the Tang Dynasty led to a general purge of traditional aristocratic families, and thus the empowerment of a broader elite. The two world wars performed a similar service for the democratic Germany that emerged after 1945 by eliminating the aristocratic Junker class, which could no longer block institutional change.

It is not clear that democratic societies can always solve this type of problem peacefully. In the United States in the period leading up to the Civil War, a minority of Americans in the South passionately sought to defend their "peculiar institution" of slavery. The existing institutional rules under the Constitution allowed them to do this as long as the westward expansion of the country did not lead to the admission of enough free states to permit an override of their veto. The conflict was ultimately one that could not be solved under the Constitution and necessitated a war that claimed more than six hundred thousand American lives.

In many respects, the norms and institutions of the contemporary world have closed off violence as a means of resolving political deadlocks. No one expects, or hopes, that the countries of sub-Saharan Africa will go through the same centuries-long process experienced by China and Europe in order to generate strong, consolidated states. This means either that the burden of institutional innovation and reform will fall on other, nonviolent mechanisms like the ones described above, or that societies will continue to experience political decay.

Fortunately, the world described here, in which the basic political institutions of the state, rule of law, and accountability were forged, is quite different from the contemporary world. In the slightly more than two centuries since the American and French revolutions, the world has experienced both the Industrial Revolution and the advent of technologies that have vastly altered the degree of interconnectedness that exists among societies. The political, economic, and social components of development interact with one another quite differently now than they did before the year 1806. What that interaction looks like is the subject of the final chapter of this book.

30

POLITICAL DEVELOPMENT, THEN AND NOW

How the conditions for political development have changed dramatically since the eighteenth century; the political, economic, and social dimensions of development, and how they interacted in a Malthusian world; how these dimensions interact now; anticipations of the contemporary world

The central insight of Samuel Huntington's 1968 book *Political Order in Changing Societies* was that political development had its own logic, which was related to but different from the logic of the economic and social dimensions of development. Political decay, he argued, occurred when economic and social modernization outran political development, with the mobilization of new social groups that could not be accommodated within the existing political system. This, he maintained, was what was causing instability among the newly independent countries of the developing world during the 1950s and '60s, with their incessant coups, revolutions, and civil wars.

The argument that political development follows its own logic and is not necessarily part of an integrated process of development needs to be seen against the backdrop of classic modernization theory. This theory had its origin in nineteenth-century thinkers like Karl Marx, Émile Durkheim, Ferdinand Tönnies, and Max Weber, who sought to analyze the momentous changes occurring in European society as a result of industrialization. Though there were significant differences among them, they tended to argue that modernization was of one piece: it included development of a capitalist market economy and a consequent large-scale division of labor; the emergence of strong, centralized, bureaucratic states; the shift from tightly knit village communities to impersonal urban ones; and the transition from communal to individualistic social relationships. All of these elements come together in Marx and Engels's *Communist Manifesto*, where the "rise of the bourgeoisie" affects everything from labor conditions to global competition to the most intimate family relationships. Classic modernization theory tended to date these changes from approximately the time of the Protestant Reformation in the early sixteenth century; they unfolded with incredible rapidity in the three centuries following.

Modernization theory migrated to the United States in the years before World War II, taking up residence in places like Harvard's Department of Comparative Politics, the MIT Center for International Studies, and the Social Science Research Council's Committee on Comparative Politics. The Harvard department, led by Weber's protégé Talcott Parsons, hoped to create an integrated, interdisciplinary social science that would combine economics, sociology, political science, and anthropology.[1] Modernization theorists placed a strong normative value on being modern, and, in their view, the good things of modernity tended to go together. Economic development, changing social relationships like the breakdown of extended kinship groups and the growth of individualism, higher and more inclusive levels of education, normative shifts toward values like "achievement" and rationality, secularization, and the development of democratic political institutions were all seen as an interdependent whole. Economic development would fuel better education, which would lead to value change, which would promote modern politics, and so on in a virtuous circle.[2]

Huntington's *Political Order in Changing Societies* played an important role in killing off modernization theory by arguing that the good things of modernity did not necessarily go together. Democracy, in particular, was not always conducive to political stability. Huntington's definition of political order corresponds to our category of state building, and his book became well known for its argument that political order ought to receive priority over democratization, a development strategy that came to be known as the "authoritarian transition."[3] This was the path followed by Turkey, South Korea, Taiwan, and Indonesia, which modernized economically under authoritarian rulers and only later opened up their political systems to democratic contestation.

The historical material presented in this volume confirms Huntington's basic insight that the different dimensions of development need to be separated from one another. As we have seen, the Chinese developed a modern state in the Weberian sense more than two millennia ago, without this being accompanied by either rule of law or democracy, not to speak of social individualism or modern capitalism.

European development, moreover, occurred in a manner very different from the accounts presented by Marx and Weber. The roots of European modernity stretch much farther back in time than the Protestant Reformation. As we saw in chapter 16, the exit out of kinship-based social organization had started already during the Dark Ages, with the conversion of Germanic barbarians to Christianity. The right of individuals, including women, to freely buy and sell property was already well established in England in the thirteenth century. The modern legal order had its roots in the fight waged by the Catholic church against the emperor in the late eleventh century, and the first European bureaucratic organizations were created by the church to manage its own internal affairs. The Catholic church, long vilified as an obstacle to modernization, was in this longer-term perspective at least as important as the Reformation as the driving force behind key aspects of modernity.

Thus the European path to modernization was not a spasmodic burst of change across all dimensions of development but rather a series of piecemeal shifts over a period of nearly fifteen hundred years. In this peculiar sequence, individualism on a social level could precede capitalism; rule of law could precede the formation of a modern state; and feudalism, in the form of strong pockets of local resistance to central authority, could be the foundation of modern democracy. Contrary to the Marxist view that feudalism was a universal stage of development preceding the rise of the bourgeoisie, it was in fact an institution that was largely unique to Europe. It cannot be explained as the outgrowth of a general process of economic development, and we should not necessarily expect to see non-Western societies following a similar sequence.

We need, then, to disaggregate the political, economic, and social dimensions of development, and understand how they relate to one another as separate phenomena that periodically interact. We need to do this, not least because the nature of these relationships is very different now than it was under the historical conditions of a Malthusian world.

THOMAS MALTHUS

The world changed very dramatically after approximately the year 1800, with the advent of the Industrial Revolution. Before then, economic growth in the form of continuously increasing productivity based on technological change could not be taken for granted. Indeed, it barely existed at all.

This is not to say that there weren't important increases in productivity taking place before 1800. Agriculture, the use of irrigation, the metal plow, the printing press, and long-distance sailing ships all increased output per person.[4] For example, the introduction of new varieties of corn tripled the productivity of agriculture in Teotihuacán (Mexico) between the third and second millennia B.C.[5] The difference between then and now was that steady, year-on-year increases in productivity, and thus in GDP per person, did not occur. We assume today that computers and the Internet will be much improved a mere five years down the road, and we are probably right. By contrast, agricultural techniques in China were not that much different in the former Han Dynasty shortly after the birth of Christ than they were in the late Qing Dynasty, prior to China's colonization in the nineteenth century.

Figure 7 shows estimates of per capita GDP for Western Europe and China between 400 and 2001. It indicates that incomes were rising gradually in the eight-hundred-year period between 1000 and 1800 but suddenly

FIGURE 7

COMPARATIVE LEVELS OF GDP PER CAPITA:
CHINA AND WEST EUROPE, 400–2001
(in 1990 international dollars)

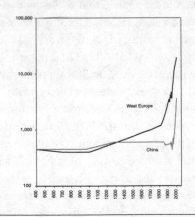

SOURCE: Maddison (1998, 2001, and 2003a).

Reprinted with the permission of the American Enterprise Institute for Public Policy Research, Washington, D.C.

accelerated thereafter. Chinese per capita income was largely flat over this same period, but when it began to increase after 1978, it took off at an even faster rate than Europe's.

The reasons for the massive increase in post-1800 productivity have always been at the core of studies of growth. They have to do with changes in the intellectual environment that promoted the emergence of modern natural science, the application of science and technology to production, development of techniques like double-entry bookkeeping, and supportive microeconomic institutions like patent law and copyright that permitted and encouraged continuous innovation.[7] But the understandable focus on developments of the last two hundred or so years has obscured our ability to comprehend the nature of political economy in premodern societies. The presumption that a high rate of continuous economic growth is possible puts a premium on investment in the sorts of institutions and conditions that facilitate such growth, like political stability, property rights, technology, and scientific research. On the other hand, if we assume that there are only limited possibilities for productivity improvements, then societies are thrown into a zero-sum world in which predation, or the taking of resources from someone else, is often a far more plausible route to power and wealth.

This low-productivity world was most notably analyzed by the English clergyman Thomas Malthus, whose *Essay on the Principle of Population* was first published in 1798 when the author was only thirty-two. Malthus, himself one of eight children, argued that while population grows at a geometrical rate (assuming a "natural" total fertility rate of fifteen children per woman), food production increased at only an arithmetic rate, meaning that food output per person tended to decline. Malthus accepted the possibility that there would be increases in agricultural productivity, but he did not think that they would ever be sufficient to keep up with the rate of population growth in the long run. There were some "virtuous" checks on population growth like marital "constraint" (this in a world before widespread birth control), but in the end the problem of human overpopulation would be solved only through the mechanisms of famine, disease, and war.[8]

Malthus's essay was published right on the eve of the Industrial Revolution, which led to the remarkable post-1800 increases in productivity noted above, particularly with regard to the unlocking of energy contained in fossil fuels like coal and oil. Worldwide energy availability increased sixfold between 1820 and 1950, while population "only" doubled.[9] With the emergence of the modern economic world, it has been common to disparage "Malthusian" economics as shortsighted and unduly pessimistic about the prospects for technological change.[10] But if Malthus's model did not work very well for the period 1800–2000, it is more plausible as a basis for understanding the political economy of the world prior to that period.

As a historical description of pre-1800 economic life, the Malthusian model would have to be revised in certain important ways. Ester Boserup, for example, has argued that population increase and high population densities have been responsible not for starvation but on occasion for productivity-enhancing technological innovation. Thus, for example, the dense populations around river systems in Egypt, Mesopotamia, and China spawned intensive modes of agriculture involving large-scale irrigation, new higher-yielding crops, and other tools.[11] Hence population growth per se is not necessarily a bad thing. Moreover, there is no direct correlation between levels of food availability and mortality, except in periods of extreme famine; disease has historically been far more important than hunger as a check on population.[12] Populations can also respond to the declining availability of food not by dying off but by individuals becoming smaller in stature and therefore requiring fewer calories.[13] Something like this appears to have happened in North Korea over the past generation in response to widespread famine.[14] Finally, local environmental exhaustion needs to be added to overpopulation as a source of declining per capita food output. Environmental damage is not something new in human societies (though its present scale is unprecedented); past societies killed off megafauna, eroded topsoils, and changed local microclimates.[15]

With these modifications, the Malthusian model provides a good framework for understanding economic development prior to the Industrial Revolution. Global population has expanded dramatically over the past ten thousand years, from perhaps six million individuals worldwide at the beginning of the Neolithic period to over six billion in 2001, a thousandfold increase.[16] But the bulk of that population increase took place in the twentieth century; indeed, much of it occurred in the last decades of that century. A great deal of economic growth prior to 1820 was extensive, that is, the result of human beings settling new lands, draining swamps, clearing forests, reclaiming land from the sea, and so on. Once new lands were settled and exploited up to the limits of available technology, life assumed a zero-sum character in which increasing resources for one person had to come at the expense of someone else. There were no continuous increases in per capita output; absolute growth would be followed by stagnation and absolute decline, both for the world as a whole and for local populations. Globally, world population experienced massive decreases as a result of disease. One such decline took place toward the end of the Roman Empire when it was swept by barbarian invasions, famine, and plague. Another happened as the Mongol invasions of Europe, the Middle East, and China in the thirteenth century brought the plague to new parts of the world. Between 1200 and 1400, the population of Asia declined from around 258 million to 201 million; between 1340 and 1400, Europe's population fell from 74 to 52 million.[17]

When technological advance comes this slowly, it has a two-edged character. In the short run, it improves living standards and benefits the innovators. But greater resources promote increases in population, which then reduce per capita output and leave human beings on average no better off than before the technological change occurred. This is why many historians have argued that the transition from hunter-gatherer to agricultural societies left people worse off in many ways. Although the potential for food production was much greater, human beings consumed a narrower range of foods, which adversely affected their health; they expended a greater amount of effort to produce food; and they lived in densely populated areas and were thus more subject to disease, and so on.[18]

POLITICS IN A MALTHUSIAN WORLD

Life in a zero-sum, Malthusian world has enormous implications for political development and looks very different from development today. In a Malthusian world, individuals with resources have few options for investing them in things like factories, scientific research, or education that will produce long-run economic growth. If they want to increase their wealth, it often makes much more sense to take a political route and engage in predation, that is, forcibly taking resources from someone else. Predation can take two forms: those with the power to coerce can take resources from other members of their own society, through taxation or outright theft, or they can organize their society to attack and steal from neighboring societies. Organizing for predation through increased military or administrative capacity is thus oftentimes a more efficient use of resources than investment in productive capacity.

Malthus himself recognized war as a factor restraining population, but the classic Malthusian model probably understates war's significance as a means of limiting overpopulation. It interacts strongly with famine and disease as population control mechanisms, since the latter usually follow conflict. But unlike famine and disease, predation is the one way of dealing with Malthusian pressures that is under deliberate human control. As the archaeologist Steven LeBlanc points out, the prevalence of warfare and violence in prehistoric societies can be explained by the perpetual problem of populations outrunning the economic carrying capacity of the local environment. Most human beings, in other words, would rather fight than starve.[19]

An expanded Malthusian model would thus look something like Figure 8. Any technological advance like a new crop or harvesting tool would temporarily increase output per person, but this increased output would in time be offset by either population growth or degradation of the local environment. Output per person would then decrease. Growing poverty could be offset by one of four major mechanisms: people could starve or grow physically smaller, they could die of disease, they could engage in internal predation, or they could go to war with other communities (external predation). Output per person would then increase, either as land and food became more readily available, or as the predators got richer at the expense of other individuals.

It is important not to overstate the degree to which zero-sum thinking

FIGURE 8. THE MALTHUSIAN TRAP

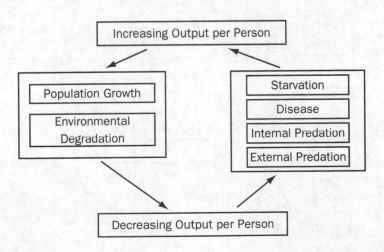

predominates in a broadly Malthusian world where continuous technological improvement does not take place. There are many opportunities to
gain from cooperation rather than from predation. Farmers and town dwellers can raise their joint welfare by trading with one another; governments
that promote broad public goods like public order and mutual defense
will benefit both themselves *and* their subjects. Indeed, predation itself
requires a substantial degree of cooperation; this very fact is one of the most
important motives for political organization.

Figure 9 illustrates the relationship between political institutions and
economic development in a preindustrial, Malthusian world. Intensive
economic growth is marooned by itself in the upper left. There are no arrows pointing to it. Intensive growth happened as a result of periodic technological advances, but these advances occurred unpredictably and were
often spaced at great intervals in time from one another. Technological innovation back then was what economists label exogenous to the system:
it occurred independently of any of the other aspects of development. (Ester Boserup's hypothesis that increasing population density periodically
spurred innovation and technological change makes the latter endogenous, but it was not related to growing population in a predictable or linear fashion.) The economic growth that took place was largely extensive
rather than intensive, meaning that total population and resources increased over time, but not on a per capita basis.

FIGURE 9. DEVELOPMENT UNDER MALTHUSIAN CONDITIONS

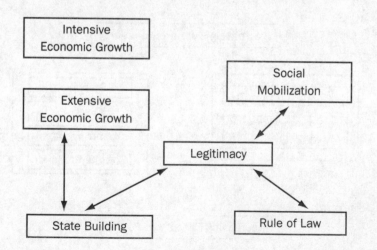

The critical political institution in a Malthusian world was the state, because it was the primary route to achieving extensive economic growth. Coercive capacity—armies and police—could be turned into resources through external predation—war and conquest. Coercion could also be used against domestic populations to maintain the ruler's hold on power. Conversely, resources collected through conquest or taxation could be converted into coercive capacity, so the lines of causation run in both directions. The state could improve economic productivity on a one-time basis by providing basic public goods like security and property rights— Olson's shift from the roving to the stationary bandit—but it had no way of promoting continuous improvements in productivity.

The power of states was in turn very much affected by legitimacy, which is the transmission belt by which rule of law and social mobilization affect politics. In most Malthusian societies, legitimacy took a religious form. China, the Byzantine Empire, and other caesaropapist states were directly legitimated by the religious authorities that they controlled. In societies where religiously based rule of law existed, religion legitimated an independently constituted legal order, which could then grant or withhold legal sanction to the state.

The possibilities for the mobilization of new social groups within an existing society were much more limited than in the contemporary world. Religious legitimacy played a very large role in mobilizing formerly inert social actors, like the Arab tribes of seventh-century Arabia and Buddhist and Daoist sects of Tang Dynasty China. Christianity played a similar role in mobilizing new elites during the Roman Empire. In agrarian societies, religion often served as a vehicle for social protest against the established political order and therefore constituted not just a legitimating but also a destabilizing force.

In a Malthusian world, the possibilities for political development existed in two primary channels. One revolved around the internal logic of state building and extensive economic growth. Political power generated economic resources, which in turn generated greater political power. This process fed upon itself, up to the point that the expanding polity ran into a physical limit like geography or available technology, or bumped up against another polity, or a combination of the two factors. This is the logic of state building and war that unfolded in China and Europe.

The other channel of political change has to do with legitimacy, which then affects the power of states either by establishment of a rule of law or through the empowerment of new social actors. The source of what I have called the Indian detour was the rise of a new Brahmanic religion that compromised the ability of Indian rulers to accumulate state power in the manner of their Chinese counterparts. New social actors empowered by religion could either contribute to the power of the state, as in the case of the Arabs, or constrain the sovereign's attempts to centralize power, as in the case of the English Parliament.

In a Malthusian world, the dynamic sources of change were relatively limited. The process of state building was very slow and took place, in both China and Europe, over a period of many centuries. It was also subject to periods of political decay in which polities returned to lower levels of development and had to begin the process over again nearly from scratch. New religions or ideologies appeared from time to time, but just like technological innovation they could not be counted on to provide continual dynamic inputs to the system. In addition, technology constrained the ability of people and ideas to move from one part of the world to another. News of Qin Shi Huangdi's invention of the Chinese state never reached the ears of the leaders of the Roman Republic. While Buddhism succeeded in making its way across the Himalayas to China and elsewhere in East Asia, other institutions remained bottled up in their countries of origin. The separate traditions of law in Christian Europe, the Middle East, and India all developed without influencing one another to any large degree.

DEVELOPMENT UNDER CONTEMPORARY CONDITIONS

Let us consider now how the dimensions of development have interacted since the onset of the Industrial Revolution. The most important change is the emergence of continuous intensive economic growth, which shapes virtually all the other dimensions of development. Extensive economic growth continues to occur, but it is much less important as a driver of political change than is increasing per capita output. In addition, democracy has joined state building and the rule of law as a component of political development. These dimensions are illustrated in Figure 10.

There has been substantial research on the empirical linkages among these different dimensions in the contemporary world, which can be summarized in a series of relationships.

FIGURE 10. DIMENSIONS OF DEVELOPMENT

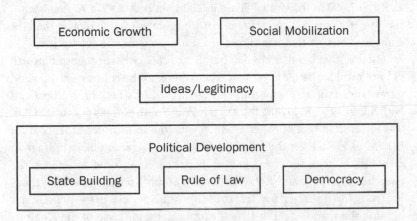

Between state building and economic growth

Having a state is a basic precondition for intensive economic growth. The economist Paul Collier has demonstrated the converse of this proposition, namely, that state breakdown, civil war, and interstate conflict have very negative consequences for growth.[20] A great deal of Africa's poverty in the late twentieth century was related to the fact that states there were very weak and subject to constant breakdown and instability. Beyond the establishment of a state that can provide for basic order, greater administrative capacity is also strongly correlated with economic growth. This is particularly true at low absolute levels of per capita GDP (less than $1,000); while it remains important at higher levels of income, the impact may not be proportionate. There is also a large literature linking good governance to economic growth, though the definition of "good governance" is not well established and, depending on the author, sometimes includes all three components of political development.[21]

While the correlation between a strong, coherent state and economic growth is well established, the direction of causality is not always clear. The economist Jeffrey Sachs has maintained that good governance is endogenous: it is the product of economic growth rather than a cause of it.[22] There is a good logic to this: government costs money. One of the reasons why there is so much corruption in poor countries is that they cannot afford to pay their civil servants adequate salaries to feed their families, so they are inclined to take bribes. Per capita spending on all government services, from armies and roads to schools and police on the street, was about $17,000 in the United States in 2008 but only $19 in Afghanistan.[23] It is therefore not a surprise that the Afghan state is much weaker than the American one, or that large flows of aid money generate corruption.

On the other hand, there are a number of cases where economic growth did not produce better governance, but where, to the contrary, it was good governance that was responsible for growth. Consider South Korea and Nigeria. In 1954, following the Korean War, South Korea's per capita GDP was lower than that of Nigeria, which was to win its independence from Britain in 1960. Over the following fifty years, Nigeria took in more than $300 billion in oil revenues, and yet its per capita income declined in the years between 1975 and 1995. In contrast, South Korea grew at rates ranging from 7 to 9 percent per year over this same period, to the point that it became the world's twelfth-largest economy by the time of the Asian financial crisis in 1997. The reason for this difference in performance is almost entirely attributable to the far superior government that presided over South Korea compared to Nigeria.

Between rule of law and growth

In the academic literature, the rule of law is sometimes considered a component of governance and sometimes considered a separate dimension of development (as I am doing here). As noted in chapter 17, the key aspects of rule of law that are linked to growth are property rights and contract enforcement. There is a large literature demonstrating that this correlation exists. Most economists take this relationship for granted, though it is not clear that universal and equal property rights are necessary for this to happen. In many societies, stable property rights exist only for certain elites, and this is sufficient to produce growth for at least certain periods of time.[24] Furthermore, societies like contemporary China with "good enough" property rights that yet lack traditional rule of law can nonetheless achieve very high levels of growth.

Between economic growth and stable democracy

The correlation between development and democracy was first noted by the sociologist Seymour Martin Lipset in the late 1950s, and ever since then there have been many studies linking development to democracy.[25] The relationship between growth and democracy may not be linear—that is, more growth does not necessarily always produce more democracy. The economist Robert Barro has shown that the correlation is stronger at lower levels of income and weaker at middle levels.[26] One of the most comprehensive studies of the relationship between development and democracy shows that transitions into democracy from autocracy can occur at any level of development but are much less likely to be reversed at higher levels of per capita GDP.[27]

Whereas growth appears to favor stable democracy, the reverse causal connection between democracy and growth is much less clear. This stands to reason if we simply consider the number of authoritarian countries that have piled up impressive growth records over recent years—South Korea and Taiwan while they were ruled dictatorially, the People's Republic of China, Singapore, Indonesia under Suharto, and Chile under Augusto Pinochet. Thus, while having a coherent state and reasonably good governance is a condition for growth, it is not clear that democracy plays the same positive role.

Between economic growth and social development, or the development of civil society

A lot of classic social theory links the emergence of modern civil society to economic development.[28] Adam Smith in *The Wealth of Nations* noted that the growth of markets was related to the division of labor in society: as markets expand and firms take advantage of economies of scale, social specialization increases and new social groups (for example, the industrial working class) emerge. The fluidity and open access demanded by modern market economies undermine many traditional forms of social authority and force their replacement with more flexible, voluntary forms of association. The theme of the transformative effects of the expanding division of labor was central to the writings of nineteenth-century thinkers like Karl Marx, Max Weber, and Émile Durkheim.

Between social mobilization and liberal democracy

From Alexis de Tocqueville onward there has been a large body of democratic theory arguing that modern liberal democracy cannot exist without a vigorous civil society.[29] The mobilization of social groups allows weak individuals to pool their interests and enter the political system; even when social groups do not seek political objectives, voluntary associations have spillover effects in fostering the ability of individuals to work with one another in novel situations—what is termed social capital.

The correlation noted above linking economic growth to stable liberal democracy presumably comes about via the channel of social mobilization: growth entails the emergence of new social actors who then demand representation in a more open political system and press for a democratic transition. When the political system is well institutionalized and can accommodate these new actors, then there is a successful transition to full democracy. This is what happened with the rise of farmers' movements and socialist parties in Britain and Sweden in the early decades of the twentieth century, and in South Korea after the fall of the military dictatorship in 1987.

A highly developed civil society can also pose dangers for democracy and can even lead to political decay. Groups based on ethnic or racial chauvinism spread intolerance; interest groups can invest effort in zero-sum rent seeking; excessive politicization of economic and social conflicts can paralyze societies and undermine the legitimacy of democratic institutions.[30] Social mobilization can lead to political decay. The Huntingtonian process whereby political institutions failed to accommodate demands of new social actors for participation arguably happened in Bolivia and Ecuador in the 1990s and 2000s with the repeated unseating of elected presidents by highly mobilized social groups.[31]

Between democracy and rule of law

There has always been a close historical association between the rise of democracy and the rise of liberal rule of law.[32] As we saw in chapter 27, the rise of accountable government in England was inseparable from the defense of the Common Law. Extension of the rule of law to apply to wider circles of citizens has always been seen as a key component of democracy itself. This association has continued through the third-wave democratic transitions after 1975, where the collapse of Communist dictatorships led to both the rise of electoral democracy and the creation of constitutional governments protecting individuals' rights.

Among ideas, legitimacy, and all of the other dimensions of development

Ideas concerning legitimacy develop according to their own logic, but they are also shaped by economic, political, and social development. The history of the twentieth century would have looked quite different without the writings of an obscure scribbler in the British Library, Karl Marx, who systematized a critique of early capitalism. Similarly, communism collapsed in 1989 largely because few people any longer believed in the foundational ideas of Marxism-Leninism.

Conversely, developments in economics and politics affect the kinds of ideas that people regard as legitimate. The Rights of Man seemed more plausible to French people because of the changes that had taken place in France's class structure and the rising expectations of the new middle classes in the later eighteenth century. The spectacular financial crises and economic setbacks of 1929–1931 undermined the legitimacy of certain capitalist institutions and led the way to the legitimization of greater state control over the economy. The subsequent growth of large welfare states, and the economic stagnation and inflation that they appeared to encourage, laid the groundwork for the conservative Reagan-Thatcher revolutions of the 1980s. Similarly, the failure of socialism to deliver on its promises of modernization and equality led to its being discredited in the minds of many who lived under communism.

Economic growth can also create legitimacy for the governments that succeed in fostering it. Many fast-developing countries in East Asia, such as Singapore and Malaysia, have maintained popular support despite their lack of liberal democracy for this reason. Conversely, the reversal of economic growth through economic crisis or mismanagement can be destabilizing, as it was for the dictatorship in Indonesia after the financial crisis of 1997–1998.[33]

Legitimacy also rests on the distribution of the benefits of growth. Growth that goes to a small oligarchy at the top of the society without being broadly shared often mobilizes social groups against the political system. This is what happened in Mexico under the dictatorship of Porfirio Díaz, who ruled the country from 1876 to 1880 and again from 1884 to 1911. National income grew rapidly in this period, but property rights existed only for a wealthy elite, which set the stage for the Mexican Revolution of 1911 and a long period of civil war and instability as underprivileged groups fought for their share of national income. In more recent times, the legitimacy of democratic systems in Venezuela and Bolivia has been challenged by populist leaders whose political base is poor and otherwise marginalized groups.[34]

THE MODERN DEVELOPMENT PARADIGM

Multiple connections among the different dimensions of development mean that there are many potential paths to modernization possible today, most of which were unavailable under Malthusian conditions. Let us take as an example South Korea, in which the development components came together in a particularly favorable way (see Figure 11).

FIGURE 11. SOUTH KOREA, 1954–1999

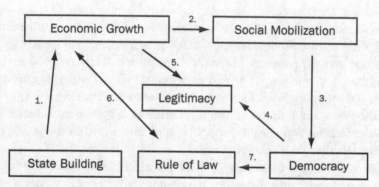

South Korea at the end of the Korean War possessed a relatively strong government. It inherited a Confucian state tradition from China and had put many modern institutions in place during the period of Japanese colonialism from 1905 to 1945.[35] This state, under the leadership of General Park Chung-Hee, who came to power in a coup in 1961, used industrial policy to promote rapid economic growth (arrow 1). South Korea's industrialization transformed the country from an agrarian backwater into a major industrial power in the space of a generation, setting in motion the social mobilization of new forces—trade unions, church groups, university students, and other civil society actors who had not existed in traditional Korea (arrow 2). Following the delegitimization of the military government of General Chun Doo-Hwan after the Kwangju massacre in 1980, these new social groups began agitating for the military to step down from power. With some gentle nudging from its ally the United States, this happened in 1987, when the first democratic elections for president were announced (arrow 3). Both the country's rapid economic growth and its transition to democracy helped strengthen the regime's legitimacy, which in turn helped, among other things, to strengthen its ability to weather the severe

Asian financial crisis of 1997–1998 (arrows 4 and 5). Finally, both economic growth and the advent of democracy helped to strengthen South Korea's rule of law (arrows 6 and 7).

In South Korea's case, all of the different dimensions of development tended to fortify one another, as modernization theory suggested, though there was a definite sequencing of stages that delayed the onset of electoral democracy and rule of law until industrialization had occurred. South Korea's pattern is not necessarily a universal one, however; there are many other possible paths to modernization. In Europe and America, rule of law existed before the state was consolidated, and in England and the United States, some form of democratic accountability predated industrialization and economic growth. China has thus far followed South Korea's path, but left out arrows 3, 4, and 7. The People's Republic of China inherited a reasonably competent state from the Maoist period when it began to liberalize its economy under Deng Xiaoping's leadership in 1978. Open economic policies powered rapid economic growth for the next thirty years, leading to a major social transformation of the society as millions of peasants left the countryside for industrial employment in the cities. Growth has helped to legitimize the state and created a nascent Chinese civil society, but it has neither destabilized the political system nor put much pressure on it to democratize. In addition, growth has led to some improvement in rule of law as China seeks to bring its legal system up to the standards mandated by the World Trade Organization. The big question in China's future is whether the huge social mobilization engendered by rapid development will one day lead to irresistible demands for greater political participation.

WHAT HAS CHANGED

If we consider the prospects for political development during historical periods characterized by Malthusian economic conditions with the situation that has existed since the onset of the Industrial Revolution, we immediately see a host of differences. The key is the possibility of sustained intensive economic growth. Growth in per capita output does far more than put larger resources in the hands of states. It stimulates a broad transformation of society and mobilizes a host of new social forces that over time seek to become political actors as well. In the Malthusian world, by contrast, social mobilization was much rarer, being stimulated largely by changes in the world of legitimacy and ideas.

Social mobilization is one important key to breaking out of the dysfunctional equilibria represented by traditional elites locked in rent-seeking coalitions. The Danish king was able to undermine the power of the entrenched aristocracy in the 1780s because of the emergence of an educated, well-organized peasantry—something new in world history, which had known only anomic, disorganized peasant revolts. Being a preindustrial society, the source of this mobilization was religion, specifically in the form of the Protestant Reformation and its insistence on universal literacy. In South Korea during the 1980s, the power of the interlocked military and business elites was broken by the emergence of a host of new social actors, almost none of which had existed at the beginning of South Korea's period of post–World War II growth. Political change thus came to both Denmark and South Korea. Denmark's mobilization, however, seemed an almost accidental fluke of history—the fact that Danish kings had opted for Lutheranism—while South Korea's was a much more predictable consequence of economic growth in a Malthusian world. In both cases, social mobilization had benign effects with regard to the spread of democracy, but in other respects it led to political instability.

The other hugely important difference between political development then and now is the degree to which international factors affect the evolution of national institutions. Almost all of the stories told in this book involve single societies and the interplay among different domestic political actors within them. International influences appear largely as a result of war, conquest or the threat of conquest, and the occasional spreading of religious doctrines across borders. There were "transnational" institutions at this time like the Catholic church and the Islamic caliphate, which were important in facilitating the diffusion of institutions including the Justinian Code or sharia across political boundaries. There was in addition diachronic learning as early modern Europeans tried to recover their classical Graeco-Roman past. But looking at the globe as a whole, development tended to be highly compartmentalized by geography and region.

The situation in this regard is very different today. The phenomenon we now label globalization is only the latest iteration of a process that has been taking place continuously over the past several centuries with the spread of technologies related to transportation, communications, and information. The possibility that any society will develop on its own with relatively little input from the outside world is highly unlikely today. This is true even of the most isolated and difficult regions of the world like Afghanistan or Papua New Guinea, where international actors in the form of foreign troops, Chinese logging companies, or the World Bank manage to show up, invited or not. Even they face an accelerating pace of change from what they have known in the past.

The greater integration of societies around the world has increased the level of competition among them, and ipso facto produced both a higher rate of political change and convergence of political forms. Specific evolution—that is, speciation and increasing biological diversity—occurs when organisms proliferate into distinct microenvironments and lose contact with one another. Its converse, biological globalization, has been occurring as species are transported, either deliberately or accidentally in the bilge tanks of ships, from one ecological zone to another. Zebra mussels and kudzu and Africanized killer bees now compete with indigenous species. These, together with the biggest competitor of all, human beings, have led to a dramatic reduction in the number of species around the globe.

So too in politics. Any developing country is today free to adopt whatever development model it wishes, regardless of its indigenous traditions or culture. During the cold war, both the United States and the Soviet Union sought to export their political and economic models, something the United States still does through its democracy promotion programs. There is also an East Asian model of state-directed development and the path of authoritarian capitalism offered by China. International institutions like the World Bank, the International Monetary Fund, and the United Nations have been ready with advice on institution building as well as resources and technical support for capacity building. It is not necessary for modern late developers to reinvent the wheel with regard to institutions or policies.[36]

On the other hand, bad things cross borders as well—drugs, crime, terrorism, weapons of all sorts, illicit money, and the like. Globalization has been called the "twilight of sovereignty."[37] This is surely an exaggeration, but technology and increased mobility have made it much harder for states to enforce laws on their own territory, collect taxes, regulate behavior, or do many of the other things associated with traditional political order. In the days when most wealth was held in the form of land, states could exercise considerable leverage on wealthy elites; today, that wealth can easily flee to offshore bank accounts.[38]

It is therefore no longer possible to speak simply about "national develop-ment." In political science, comparative politics and international rela-tions have traditionally been regarded as distinct subfields, the one dealing with things that happen within states, the other with relationships among states. Increasingly these fields will have to be studied as an integrated whole. How we got to this point, and how political development takes place in the contemporary world, will be the subject of the second volume of this work.

Ultimately, societies are not trapped by their historical pasts. Economic growth, the mobilization of new social actors, integration of societies across borders, and the prevalence of competition and foreign models all provide entry points for political change that either did not exist, or existed in a much attenuated form, before the Industrial Revolution.

And yet societies are not simply free to remake themselves in any given generation. It is easy to overstate the degree to which globalization has truly integrated societies around the world. While levels of social inter-change and learning are far higher than they were three hundred years ago, most people continue to live in a horizon shaped largely by their own traditional culture and habits. The inertia of societies remains very great; while foreign institutional models are far more available than they once were, they still need to be overlaid on indigenous ones.

The present historical account of the origins of political institutions needs to be seen in proper perspective. No one should expect that a con-temporary developing country has to replicate all of the violent steps taken by China or by societies in Europe to build a modern state, or that a modern rule of law needs to be based in religion. We have seen how institutions were the products of contingent historical circumstances and accidents that are unlikely to be duplicated by other differently situated societies. The very contingency of their origins, and the prolonged historical strug-gles that were required to put them in place, should imbue us with a cer-tain degree of humility in approaching the task of institution building in the contemporary world. Modern institutions cannot simply be transferred to other societies without reference to existing rules and the political forces supporting them. Building an institution is not like building a hy-droelectric dam or a road network. It requires a great deal of hard work to persuade people that institutional change is needed in the first place, build a coalition in favor of change that can overcome the resistance of existing stakeholders in the old system, and then condition people to accept the new set of behaviors as routine and expected. Oftentimes formal institutions need to be supplemented by cultural shifts; electoral democracy won't work well, for example, if there isn't an independent press and a self-organizing civil society to keep governments honest.

The environmental and social conditions that gave rise to democracy were unique to Europe. However, once constitutional government emerged through a seemingly accidental concatenation of events, it produced a political and economic system so powerful that it came to be widely copied around the world. The doctrine of universal recognition on which liberal democracy is based points backward to earlier stages of political development in which societies were more equal and open to broad participation. I noted that hunter-gatherer and tribal societies were far more egalitarian and participatory than the state-level societies that replaced them. Once the principle of equal respect or dignity is articulated, it is hard to prevent human beings from demanding it for themselves. This perhaps helps to explain the seemingly inexorable spread of the notion of human equality in the modern world that was noted by Tocqueville in *Democracy in America*.

ACCOUNTABILITY TODAY

As noted in the first chapter, the failure of democracy to consolidate itself in many parts of the world may be due less to the appeal of the idea itself than to the absence of those material and social conditions that make it possible for accountable government to emerge in the first place. That is, successful liberal democracy requires both a state that is strong, unified, and able to enforce laws on its own territory, and a society that is strong and cohesive and able to impose accountability on the state. It is the balance between a strong state and a strong society that makes democracy work, not just in seventeenth-century England but in contemporary developed democracies as well.

There are many parallels between these early modern European cases and the situation at the beginning of the twenty-first century. Since the beginning of the third wave, there have been numerous struggles between would-be authoritarian leaders who have wanted to consolidate their own power and groups in the society who have wanted a democratic system. This was true in many successor states to the Soviet Union, where rulers

in the post-Communist world—often coming out of the old party apparatus—began to rebuild the state and centralize power in their own persons. But it was also true in Venezuela, Iran, Rwanda, and Ethiopia. In
some places, like Russia under Vladimir Putin after 2000, or Iran after the
presidential election of 2009, this project was successful, and political opposition groups failed to coalesce to block the authoritarian state-building
project. But in Georgia and Ukraine, the mobilization of political opposition succeeded, at least momentarily, in resisting state authority. And in
the former Yugoslavia, the state broke down completely.

The conditions of early modern Europe were obviously very different
from those of the early twenty-first century, but the same scenario of centralization and resistance played itself out. Instead of a nobility, gentry,
Third Estate, and peasants, today there are trade unions, business groups,
students, nongovernmental organizations, religious organizations, and a
host of other social actors (see Figure 12). A much broader and more diverse range of social actors tends to get mobilized in contemporary societies compared to the agrarian ones we have been studying. Any political
analysis of the struggle must begin by understanding the nature of the different actors, both outside the state and within it, and their degree of cohesion. Will civil society show a strong degree of solidarity, or are there
cracks in the coalition? Will the army and intelligence services remain
loyal to the regime, or are there soft-liners willing to negotiate with the

FIGURE 12. POLITICAL POWER TODAY

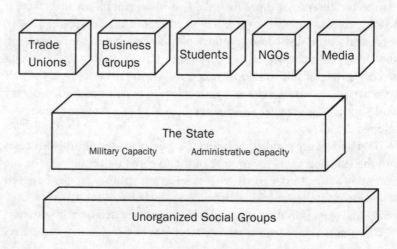

opposition? What is the social base of the regime, and what kind of legitimacy does it command?

The international system impinges on these struggles to a much higher degree today than in the early modern cases we have studied. Opposition groups can get funding, training, and occasionally weapons from outside the country, while the regime can call on like-minded ones for assistance. In addition, the global economy provides alternative sources of fiscal support, such as natural resource rents or foreign aid, that permit governments to bypass their own citizens. The struggle between the king and parliament over taxation could not play out in an oil-rich country, which is perhaps why so few of them are democratic.

WHAT COMES NEXT

Prospectively, we can pose two questions about future political development that are not answerable at this juncture. The first concerns China. I have asserted from the beginning that a modern political system consists of a strong state, a rule of law, and accountability. Western societies possessing all three developed vigorous capitalist economies and became globally dominant under them. But China is today growing rapidly with only a strong state in place. Is this situation sustainable in the long run? Can China continue to grow economically and maintain political stability without either rule of law or accountability? Will the social mobilization triggered by growth be contained by a forceful authoritarian state, or will it lead to unstoppable demands for democratic accountability? Can democracy come to a society in which the state-society balance has been tilted toward the former for such a long time? Can China push back the frontiers of science and technology without Western-style property rights or personal freedom? Or will the Chinese continue to use political power to promote development in ways not available to democratic, rule-of-law societies?

The second question concerns the future of liberal democracies. A society that is successful at one historical moment will not necessarily always remain successful, given the phenomenon of political decay. While liberal democracy may be regarded today as the most legitimate form of government, its legitimacy is conditioned on performance. That performance depends in turn on its being able to maintain an adequate balance between strong state action when necessary and the kinds of individual freedoms that are the basis of its democratic legitimacy and that foster private-sector growth. The failings of modern democracies come in many flavors, but the dominant one in the early twenty-first century is probably state weakness: contemporary democracies become too easily gridlocked and rigid, and thus unable to make difficult decisions to ensure their long-term economic and political survival. Democratic India finds it extremely difficult to fix its crumbling public infrastructure—roads, airports, water and sewage systems, and the like—because existing stakeholders are able to use the legal and electoral systems to block action. Important parts of the European Union find it impossible to cut back on a welfare state that has become clearly unaffordable. Japan has built up one of the highest levels of public debt among developed countries and has not taken measures to eliminate rigidities in its economy that are obstacles to future growth.

And then there is the United States, which has been unable to seriously address long-term fiscal issues related to health, social security, energy, and the like. The United States seems increasingly caught in a dysfunctional political equilibrium, wherein everyone agrees on the necessity of addressing long-term fiscal issues, but powerful interest groups can block the spending cuts or tax increases necessary to close the gap. The design of the country's institutions, with strong checks and balances, makes a solution harder. To this might be added an ideological rigidity that locks Americans into a certain range of solutions to their problems. In the face of these challenges, the United States is not likely to overtly repatrimonialize public office the way ancien régime France did, but it does run the risk of coming up with short-term expedients that will delay but not avoid the final crisis, just as the French government did.

Institutions initially appear for what in retrospect were historically contingent reasons. But certain ones survive and spread because they meet needs that are in some sense universal. This is why there has been institutional convergence over time, and why it is possible to give a general account of political development. But the survival of institutions involves a lot of contingency as well: a political system that works well for a rapidly growing country whose population's median age is in the twenties may not work so well for a stagnant society where a third of the citizenry is at retirement age. If the institution fails to adapt, the society will face crisis or collapse, and may be forced to adopt another one. This is no less true of a liberal democracy than of a nondemocratic political system.

There is, however, an important reason to think that societies with political accountability will prevail over ones without it. Political accountability provides a peaceful path toward institutional adaptation. The one problem that the Chinese political system was never able to solve in dynastic times was that of the "bad emperor," like the empress Wu or the Wanli emperor. An authoritarian system can periodically run rings around a liberal democratic one under good leadership, since it is able to make quick decisions unencumbered by legal challenges or legislative second-guessing. On the other hand, such a system depends on a constant supply of good leaders; under a bad emperor, the unchecked powers vested in the government can lead to disaster. This problem remains key in contemporary China, where accountability flows only upward and not downward.

I noted at the beginning of this volume that the historical account of institutional development given here must be read in anticipation of the different conditions that have prevailed since the Industrial Revolution. I have in a certain sense cleared the decks so that I can more directly address and update the issues raised in *Political Order in Changing Societies*. With the onset of industrialization, economic growth and social mobilization progress at a vastly more rapid rate and change dramatically the prospects for the development of the three components of political order. This is the framework in which I will resume the account of political development in Volume 2.

NOTES

PREFACE

1. Samuel P. Huntington, *Political Order in Changing Societies*. With a New Foreword by Francis Fukuyama (New Haven: Yale University Press, 2006).
2. Francis Fukuyama, *State-Building: Governance and World Order in the 21st Century* (Ithaca: Cornell University Press, 2004).
3. On redistributive economic systems in general, see Karl Polanyi, "The Economy as an Instituted Process," in Polanyi and C. W. Arensberg, eds., *Trade and Market in the Early Empires* (New York: Free Press, 1957).
4. R. J. May, *Disorderly Democracy: Political Turbulence and Institutional Reform in Papua New Guinea* (Canberra: Australian National University State Society and Governance in Melanesia discussion paper 2003/3, 2003); Hank Nelson, *Papua New Guinea: When the Extravagant Exception Is No Longer the Exception* (Canberra: Australian National University, 2003); Benjamin Reilly, "Political Engineering and Party Politics in Papua New Guinea," *Party Politics* 8, no. 6 (2002): 701–18.
5. For a discussion of the pros and cons of traditional land tenure, see Tim Curtin, Hartmut Holzknecht, and Peter Larmour, *Land Registration in Papua New Guinea: Competing Perspectives* (Canberra: State Society and Governance in Melanesia discussion paper 2003/1, 2003).
6. For a detailed account of the difficulties of negotiating property rights in Papua New Guinea, see Kathy Whimp, "Indigenous Land Owners and Representation in PNG and Australia," unpublished paper, March 5, 1998.

1: THE NECESSITY OF POLITICS

1. See the "Country Status and Ratings Overview" in the "Freedom in the World" section of Freedom House's website (freedomhouse.org). Larry Diamond puts the number at around 40, which then increased to 117 by the time the third wave crested. See *The Spirit of Democracy: The Struggle to Build Free Societies Throughout the World* (New York: Times Books, 2008), pp. 41, 50.

2. Larry Diamond, "The Democratic Recession: Before and After the Financial Crisis," in Nancy Birdsall and Francis Fukuyama, eds., *New Ideas in Development After the Financial Crisis* (Baltimore: Johns Hopkins University Press, 2011).

3. Samuel P. Huntington, *The Third Wave: Democratization in the Late Twentieth Century* (Oklahoma City: University of Oklahoma Press, 1991).

4. Diamond, "The Democratic Recession," pp. 240–59.

5. Freedom House, *Freedom in the World 2010: Erosion of Freedom Intensifies* (Washington, D.C.: Freedom House, 2010).

6. Thomas Carothers, "The End of the Transition Paradigm," *Journal of Democracy* 13, no. 1 (2002): 5–21.

7. In constant 2008 dollars, the world economy went from $15.93 trillion to $61.1 trillion from 1970 to 2008. Sources: World Bank Development Indicators and Global Development Finance; U.S. Bureau of Labor Statistics.

8. Francis Fukuyama and Seth Colby, "What Were They Thinking? The Role of Economists in the Financial Debacle," *American Interest* 5, no. 1 (2009): 18–25.

9. Fareed Zakaria, *The Post-American World* (New York: Norton, 2008); for a critique, see Aaron L. Friedberg, "Same Old Songs: What the Declinists (and Triumphalists) Miss," *American Interest* 5, no. 2 (2009).

10. William A. Galston, *Can a Polarized American Party System Be "Healthy"?* (Washington, D.C.: Brookings Institution Issues in Governance Studies No. 34, April 2010).

11. See the chapters by Thomas E. Mann and Gary Jacobson in Pietro S. Nivola and David W. Brady, eds., *Red and Blue Nation?* Vol. 1 (Washington, D.C.: Brookings Institution Press, 2006); also James A. Thomson, *A House Divided: Polarization and Its Effect on RAND* (Santa Monica, CA: RAND Corporation, 2010). There is some debate on exactly how polarized the American public is; on many cultural issues, like abortion and guns, there is a broad centrist group without strong convictions, with far more committed minorities at either end of the spectrum. See Morris P. Fiorina et al., eds., *Culture War? The Myth of a Polarized America*, 3rd ed. (Boston: Longman, 2010).

12. The phenomenon of broader communications bandwidth leading to the increasing compartmentalization of political discourse was predicted some years ago by Ithiel de Sola Pool, *Technologies of Freedom* (Cambridge, MA: Belknap Press, 1983).

13. See, for example, Isabel V. Sawhill and Ron Haskins, *Getting Ahead or Losing Ground: Economic Mobility in America* (Washington, D.C.: Brookings Institution Press, 2008).

14. Organization for Economic Cooperation and Development, "A Family Affair: Intergenerational Social Mobility Across OECD Countries," in *Going for Growth* (Paris: OECD, 2010); Emily Beller and Michael Hout, "Intergeneration Social Mobility: The United States in Comparative Perspective," *Future of Children* 16, no. 2 (2006): 19–36;

Chul-In Lee and Gary Solon, "Trends in Intergenerational Income Mobility," *Review of Economics and Statistics* 91, no. 4 (2009): 766–72.

15. Simon Johnson, "The Quiet Coup," *Atlantic*, May 2009.

16. Amartya K. Sen, "Democracy as a Universal Value," *Journal of Democracy* 10 (1999): 3–17.

17. Michael Hardt and Antonio Negri, *Multitude: War and Democracy in the Age of Empire* (New York: Penguin, 2004). Part of the maturing of an important part of the Left that occurred in the second half of the twentieth century was the acceptance of the Italian socialist Antonio Gramsci's observation that achievement of a progressive agenda required a "long march through institutions," a slogan adopted by the German Greens as they sought to participate in Germany's democratic political process.

18. See Bronislaw Geremek, "Civil Society, Then and Now," in Larry Diamond and Marc F. Plattner, eds., *The Global Resurgence of Democracy*, 2d ed. (Baltimore: Johns Hopkins University Press, 1996).

19. See Charles Gati, "Faded Romance," *American Interest* 4, no. 2 (2008): 35–43.

20. Walter B. Wriston, *The Twilight of Sovereignty* (New York: Scribner, 1992).

21. This can be read, among other places, at http://w2.eff.org/Censorship/Internet_censorship_bills/barlow_0296.declaration.

22. See the chapter "The Golden Straitjacket" in Thomas L. Friedman, *The Lexus and the Olive Tree* (New York: Farrar, Straus and Giroux, 1999), pp. 99–108.

23. See, for example, Ron Paul, *End the Fed* (New York: Grand Central Publishing, 2009); Charles Murray, *What It Means to Be a Libertarian: A Personal Interpretation* (New York: Broadway Books, 1997).

24. See Francis Fukuyama, ed., *Nation-Building: Beyond Afghanistan and Iraq* (Baltimore: Johns Hopkins University Press, 2006).

25. "Getting to Denmark" was actually the original title of Lant Pritchett and Michael Woolcock's "Solutions When the Solution Is the Problem: Arraying the Disarray in Development" (Washington, D.C.: Center for Global Development Working Paper 10, 2002)

26. Economic growth theories under titles like Harrod-Domar, Solow, and endogenous growth theory, are severely reductionist and are of questionable value in explaining how growth actually happens in developing countries.

27. A number of observers have made this argument, beginning with Herbert Spencer in the nineteenth century, continuing through Werner Sombart, John Nef, and Charles Tilly. See Herbert Spencer, *The Principles of Sociology* (New York: D. Appleton, 1896); John Ulric Nef, *War and Human Progress: An Essay on the Rise of Industrial Civilization* (Chicago: University of Chicago Press, 1942); Charles Tilly, *Coercion, Capital, and European States, AD 990–1990* (Cambridge, MA: Blackwell, 1990); and Bruce D. Porter, *War and the Rise of the State: The Military Foundations of Modern Politics* (New York: Free Press, 1994).

2: THE STATE OF NATURE

1. These arguments are made by Thomas Hobbes. His second law of nature states, "That a man be willing, when others are so too, as farre-forth, as for Peace, and defence of him-

selfe he shall think it necessary, to lay down this right to all things; and be contented with so much liberty against other men, as he would allow other men against himselfe." *Leviathan Parts I and II* (Indianapolis: Bobbs-Merrill, 1958), chaps. 13 and 14.

2. John Locke, *Second Treatise on Government* (Indianapolis: Bobbs-Merrill, 1952), chap. 2, sec. 6.

3. Jean-Jacques Rousseau, *Discourse on the Origin and the Foundation of Inequality Among Mankind* (New York: St. Martin's Press, 2010), part 1.

4. Henry Maine, *Ancient Law: Its Connection with the Early History of Society and Its Relation to Modern Ideas* (Boston: Beacon Press, 1963), chap. 5. A similar point is made in Karl Polanyi, *The Great Transformation* (New York: Rinehart, 1944), p. 48.

5. William D. Hamilton, "The Genetic Evolution of Social Behavior," *Journal of Theoretical Biology* 7 (1964): 17–52. This point was elaborated by Richard Dawkins in *The Selfish Gene* (New York: Oxford University Press, 1989).

6. P. W. Sherman, "Nepotism and the Evolution of Alarm Calls," *Science* 197 (1977): 1246–53.

7. For a more detailed account of the game theoretic grounds of social cooperation, see Francis Fukuyama, *The Great Disruption: Human Nature and the Reconstitution of Social Order* (New York: Free Press, 1999), chap. 10; and Matt Ridley, *The Origins of Virtue: Human Instincts and the Evolution of Cooperation* (New York: Viking, 1987).

8. Robert Axelrod, *The Evolution of Cooperation* (New York: Basic Books, 1984).

9. Robert Trivers, "The Evolution of Reciprocal Altruism," *Quarterly Review of Biology* 46 (1971): 35–56.

10. Jerome H. Barkow, Leda Cosmides, and John Tooby, eds., *The Adapted Mind: Evolutionary Psychology and the Generation of Culture* (New York: Oxford University Press, 1992), pp. 167–69.

11. This is described in Trivers, "Reciprocal Altruism," pp. 47–48.

12. Nicholas Wade, *Before the Dawn: Recovering the Lost History of Our Ancestors* (New York: Penguin, 2006), pp. 7, 13–21.

13. Richard Wrangham and Dale Peterson, *Demonic Males: Apes and the Origins of Human Violence* (Boston: Houghton Mifflin, 1996), p. 24. The term "male bonding" was originally coined by the anthropologist Lionel Tiger; see *Men in Groups* (New York: Random House, 1969).

14. Steven A. LeBlanc and Katherine E. Register, *Constant Battles: The Myth of the Noble Savage* (New York: St. Martin's Press, 2003), p. 83.

15. Frans de Waal, *Chimpanzee Politics: Power and Sex Among Apes* (Baltimore: Johns Hopkins University Press, 1989), chap. 2. See also his book *Good Natured: The Origins of Right and Wrong in Humans and Other Animals* (Cambridge, MA: Harvard University Press, 1997).

16. de Waal, *Chimpanzee Politics*, p. 87.

17. Ibid., p. 56.

18. Ibid., p. 66.

19. Ibid., p. 42.

20. N. K. Humphrey, "The Social Function of Intellect," in P.P.G. Bateson and R. A. Hinde, *Growing Points in Ethology* (New York: Cambridge University Press, 1976), pp. 303–17;

Richard Alexander, *How Did Humans Evolve?: Reflections on the Uniquely Unique Species* (Ann Arbor: University of Michigan Press, 1990), pp. 4–7; Richard D. Alexander, "The Evolution of Social Behavior," *Annual Review of Ecology and Systematics* 5 (1974): 325–85.

21. Geoffrey Miller, *The Mating Mind: How Sexual Choice Shaped the Evolution of Human Nature* (New York: Doubleday, 2000); Geoffrey Miller and Glenn Geher, *Mating Intelligence: Sex, Relationships, and the Mind's Reproductive System* (New York: Lawrence Erlbaum, 2008).

22. Steven Pinker and Paul Bloom, "Natural Language and Natural Selection," *Behavioral and Brain Sciences* 13 (1990): 707–84.

23. George E. Pugh, *The Biological Origin of Human Values* (New York: Basic Books, 1977), pp. 140–43.

24. For a compilation of evidence on the universality of religion, see Nicholas Wade, *The Faith Instinct: How Religion Evolved and Why It Endures* (New York: Penguin, 2009), pp. 18–37.

25. See, for example, Christopher Hitchens, *God Is Not Great: How Religion Poisons Everything* (New York: Twelve, 2007); and Richard Dawkins, *The God Delusion* (Boston: Houghton Mifflin, 2006).

26. Mancur Olson, *The Logic of Collective Action: Public Goods and the Theory of Groups* (Cambridge, MA: Harvard University Press, 1965).

27. See Wade, *Faith Instinct*, chap. 5.

28. This view is especially associated with Émile Durkheim. See *The Elementary Forms of Religious Life* (New York: Free Press, 1965). For a critique, see the chapter on Durkheim in E. E. Evans-Pritchard, *A History of Anthropological Thought* (New York: Basic Books, 1981).

29. See, for example, Steven Pinker, *How the Mind Works* (New York: Norton, 1997), pp. 554–58.

30. According to Douglass North, "While we observe people disobeying the rules of a society when the benefits exceed the costs, we also observe them obeying the rules when an individualistic calculus would have them do otherwise. Why do people not litter the countryside? Why don't they cheat or steal when the likelihood of punishment is negligible compared to the benefits? . . . Without an explicit theory of ideology or, more generally, of the sociology of knowledge there are immense gaps in our ability to account for either current allocation of resources or historical change. In addition to being unable to resolve the fundamental dilemma of the free rider problem we cannot explain the enormous investment that every society makes in legitimacy." *Structure and Change in Economic History* (New York: Norton, 1981), pp. 46–47.

31. Trivers, "Reciprocal Altruism."

32. On this general topic, see Francis Fukuyama, *The End of History and the Last Man* (New York: Free Press, 1992), chap. 13–17.

33. Robert H. Frank, *Choosing the Right Pond: Human Behavior and the Quest for Status* (New York: Oxford University Press, 1985).

34. Ibid., pp. 21–25. Conversely, low-status human beings often suffer from chronic depression and have been successfully treated with Prozac, Zoloft, and other so-called selective serotonin reuptake inhibitors, which increase levels of brain serotonin. See

Roger D. Masters and Michael T. McGuire, *The Neurotransmitter Revolution: Serotonin, Social Behavior, and the Law* (Carbondale: Southern Illinois University Press, 1994), p. 10.

35. On this issue, see Francis Fukuyama, "Identity, Immigration, and Liberal Democracy," *Journal of Democracy* 17, no. 2 (2006): 5–20.

36. See Charles Taylor, *Sources of the Self: The Making of the Modern Identity* (Cambridge, MA: Harvard University Press, 1989).

37. Wade, *Before the Dawn*, pp. 16–17.

38. See R. Spencer Wells et al., "The Eurasian Heartland: A Continental Perspective on Y-Chromosome Diversity," *Proceedings of the National Academy of Sciences* 98, no. 18 (2001): 10244–49.

3: THE TYRANNY OF COUSINS

1. Lewis Henry Morgan, *Ancient Society; or, Researches in the Lines of Human Progress from Savagery, through Barbarism to Civilization* (New York: Henry Holt, 1877); Edward B. Tylor, *Primitive Culture: Researches into the Development of Mythology, Philosophy, Religion, Language, Art, and Custom* (New York: G. P. Putnam, 1920).

2. Friedrich Engels, *The Origin of the Family, Private Property, and the State, in Light of the Researches of Lewis H. Morgan* (New York: International Publishers, 1942).

3. Herbert Spencer, *The Principles of Biology* (New York: D. Appleton, 1898); *The Principles of Sociology*.

4. See, for example, Madison Grant, *The Passing of the Great Race; or, the Racial Basis of European History*, 4th rev. ed. (New York: Scribner's, 1921).

5. The classic statement of this is given in Clifford Geertz, *The Interpretation of Cultures* (New York: Basic Books, 1973).

6. Leslie A. White, *The Evolution of Culture: The Development of Civilization to the Fall of Rome* (New York: McGraw-Hill, 1959).

7. Julian H. Steward, *Theory of Culture Change: The Methodology of Multilinear Evolution* (Urbana: University of Illinois Press, 1963).

8. Elman R. Service, *Primitive Social Organization: An Evolutionary Perspective*. 2d ed. (New York: Random House, 1971). One early attempt to revive evolutionary thinking was V. Gordon Childe, *Man Makes Himself* (London: Watts and Co., 1936).

9. Morton H. Fried, *The Evolution of Political Society: An Essay in Political Anthropology* (New York: Random House, 1967).

10. Marshall D. Sahlins and Elman R. Service, *Evolution and Culture* (Ann Arbor: University of Michigan Press, 1960).

11. For background on evolutionary theories, see Henri J. M. Claessen and Pieter van de Velde, "Social Evolution in General," in Claessen, van de Velde, and M. Estelle Smith, eds., *Development and Decline: The Evolution of Sociopolitical Organization* (South Hadley, MA: Bergin and Garvey, 1985).

12. Sahlins and Service, *Evolution and Culture*, chap. 1.

13. Jonathan Haas, *From Leaders to Rulers* (New York: Kluwer Academic/Plenum Publishers, 2001).

14. Service, *Primitive Social Organization*.
15. Numa Denis Fustel de Coulanges, *The Ancient City* (Garden City, NY: Doubleday, 1965); Henry Summer Maine, *Ancient Law* (Boston: Beacon Press, 1963).
16. Fried, *Evolution of Political Society*, pp. 47–54. Much of what is known of this type of society is based on studies of indigenous American groups like the Algonkian or Shoshone Indians, which have since disappeared.
17. Ibid., pp. 94–98.
18. See Ernest Gellner, "Nationalism and the Two Forms of Cohesion in Complex Societies," in Gellner, *Culture, Identity, and Politics* (New York: Cambridge University Press, 1987), pp. 6–28.
19. Adam Kuper, *The Chosen Primate: Human Nature and Cultural Diversity* (Cambridge, MA: Harvard University Press, 1994), pp. 227–28.
20. Fried, *Evolution of Political Society*, p. 83.
21. See the discussion ibid., pp. 90–94.
22. Fried, *Evolution of Political Society*, p. 69.
23. C. D. Forde, quoted in Service, *Primitive Social Organization*, p. 61.
24. Ester Boserup, *Population and Technological Change* (Chicago: University of Chicago Press, 1981), pp. 40–42.
25. Massimo Livi-Bacci, *A Concise History of World Population* (Oxford: Blackwell, 1997), p. 27.
26. Émile Durkheim, *The Division of Labor in Society* (New York: Macmillan, 1933), esp. chap. 6. Durkheim used the term "segmentary" much more broadly than I do here; indeed, probably too broadly to be more generally useful. He applied it to state-level societies at much higher levels of political development. For a critique, see Gellner, "Nationalism and the Two Forms of Cohesion in Complex Societies."
27. In such societies, brother-sister and mother-daughter ties tend to be stronger than husband-wife and father-son relationships. Service, *Primitive Social Organization*, p. 115.
28. In Papua New Guinea, the highlanders are patrilineal, while many of the coastal groups are matrilineal; both systems produce equally strong tribal identities. Ibid., pp. 110–11.
29. E. E. Evans-Pritchard, *The Nuer: A Description of the Modes of Livelihood and Political Institutions of a Nilotic People* (Oxford: Clarendon Press, 1940); and *Kinship and Marriage Among the Nuer* (Oxford: Clarendon Press, 1951).
30. Evans-Pritchard, *The Nuer*, p. 139.
31. Ibid., pp. 142–43.
32. Ibid., p. 173.
33. For an example of how loose tribal identification can be, see Fried, *Evolution of Political Society*, p. 157. Some agnatic tribes admit members under cognatic rules, particularly when it is politically advantageous to do so. Something similar often happened in Europe after the breakdown of the Roman Empire when circumstances dictated. The Salian law that governed much of Europe required strict agnatic inheritance, but when a monarch found himself with no male heirs and a strong-minded daughter, he could contrive to bend the rules to have succession go to her.
34. Fustel de Coulanges, *The Ancient City*, p. 17.

35. Henry Maine, *Early Law and Custom: Chiefly Selected From Lectures Delivered at Oxford* (Delhi: B. R. Pub. Corp., 1985), p. 56.
36. Kwang-chih Chang et al., *The Formation of Chinese Civilization: An Archaeological Perspective* (New Haven: Yale University Press, 2005), p. 165.
37. Fustel de Coulanges, *The Ancient City*, p. 29.
38. Maine, *Early Law and Custom*, pp. 53–54.
39. Hugh Baker, *Chinese Family and Kinship* (New York: Columbia University Press, 1979), p. 26.
40. Tribal societies like the Nuer pose a challenge to rational-choice political science because so much behavior in such groups seems grounded not in individual choice but in complex social norms. It is very difficult to see how one arrives at Nuer social organization based on the individual maximizing choices of the members of the society, as opposed to a sociological explanation that would ground social organization in religious beliefs like ancestor worship.

    The political scientist Robert Bates has taken up this challenge. According to him, the sociological tradition, whether Durkheimian, Marxist, or Weberian, sees order arising from norms that are either moral, coercive, or authoritative. He goes on to review Evans-Pritchard's *The Nuer* through the lens of rational-choice theory, a model that grounds behavior in radical individualism. He argues that many of the choices made by Nuer families or segments in dealing with one another reflect rational calculations of self-interest, usually related to the maximization of cattle resources. He cites the ways dispute resolution among family groups can be modeled using individualistic premises; Nuer institutions can be seen as efficient ways of solving coordination problems and modeled through game theory. He concludes: "It is damning, but true: the problem with political sociology is that it is too sociological. In affirming the primacy of society, it gives little reason to ask if it is possible for organized behavior to be orchestrated out of the decisions of individuals. Further signaling its inability to deal with the problem is the vigorous assertion of such methodological postulates as the 'independent validity of social facts' or the rigorous separation of 'levels of analysis.' An intellectual posture characterized by a conviction that social life is not problematic simply offers little encouragement to those who wish to examine the nexus between private choice and collective behavior. And yet the problem of social order requires precisely such an examination" (Robert H. Bates, "The Preservation of Order in Stateless Societies: A Reinterpretation of Evans-Pritchard's *The Nuer*," in Bates, *Essays on the Political Economy of Rural Africa* [New York: Cambridge University Press, 1983]), p. 19.

    Bates is, however, setting up a false dichotomy between economics and sociology. From a sociological or anthropological perspective, there is no requirement that *all* behavior be understood as normatively based, or any assertion that individual rational choice plays *no* role in final outcomes. There is always some level of social interaction—usually at the level of the most highly aggregated social units—in which rational choice works best as an explanation of behavior of a social unit. Thus, for all their cultural differences from their European counterparts, the Ottomans behaved according to very familiar rules in their foreign policy, following not religious but realpolitik choices to advance their interests. What cannot be so readily explained from a rational-choice perspective is the nature of the lower-level social units themselves. Why do the Nuer organize themselves into descent groups, rather than forming religious fraternities, or organizing themselves into voluntary associations like young Americans? Rational choice provides no theory of social mobilization since it deliberately ignores the role of ideas and norms. The latter may reflect a deeper evolutionary, as opposed to individual, rationality related to the interests of groups. There is a large discussion among evolutionary biologists whether genes can encode behaviors that promote group rather than individual fitness (understood in terms of inclusive fitness). There is no particular reason, however, why social norms cannot facilitate such behavior. The simple existence of phenomena like suicide bombing suggests that this is not unheard of. See David Sloan Wilson and Elliott Sober, *Unto Others: The Evolution and Psychology of Unselfish Behavior* (Cambridge, MA: Harvard University Press, 1998); and David Sloan Wilson, "The Group Selection Controversy: History and Current Status," *Annual Review of Ecological Systems* 14 (1983): 159–87.

4: TRIBAL SOCIETIES: PROPERTY, JUSTICE, WAR

1. "The diversity in the faculties of men, from which the rights of property originate, is not less an insuperable obstacle to a uniformity of interests. The protection of these faculties is the first object of government." Madison, Federalist No. 10.
2. Douglass C. North and Robert P. Thomas, *The Rise of the Western World: A New Economic History* (New York: Cambridge University Press, 1973), pp. 1–2.
3. Garrett Hardin, "The Tragedy of the Commons," *Science* 162 (1968): 1243–48. See also Richard Pipes, *Property and Freedom* (New York: Knopf, 1999), p. 89.
4. See, for example, Yoram Barzel, *Economic Analysis of Property Rights* (New York: Cambridge University Press, 1989).
5. Such rights were said to have spontaneously emerged during the California gold rush of 1849–1850, when miners peacefully negotiated among themselves an allocation of the claims they had staked out. See Pipes, *Property and Freedom*, p. 91. This account ignores two important contextual factors: first, the miners were all products of an Anglo-American culture where respect for individual property rights was deeply embedded; second, these rights came at the expense of the customary rights to these territories on the part of the various indigenous peoples living there, which were not respected by the miners.
6. Charles K. Meek, *Land Law and Custom in the Colonies*, 2d ed. (London: Frank Cass, 1968), p. 26.
7. Quoted in Elizabeth Colson, "The Impact of the Colonial Period on the Definition of Land Rights," in Victor Turner, ed., *Colonialism in Africa 1870–1960*. Vol. 3: *Profiles in Change: African Society and Colonial Rule* (New York: Cambridge University Press, 1971), p. 203.
8. Meek, *Land Law and Custom*, p. 6.
9. Colson, "Impact of the Colonial Period," p. 200.
10. Paul Vinogradoff, *Historical Jurisprudence* (London: Oxford University Press, 1923), p. 327.

11. Meek, *Land Law and Custom*, p. 17.
12. Vinogradoff, *Historical Jurisprudence*, p. 322.
13. For a discussion of the pros and cons of traditional land tenure, see Curtin, Holzknecht, and Larmour, *Land Registration in Papua New Guinea*.
14. For a detailed account of the difficulties of negotiating property rights in Papua New Guinea, see Whimp, "Indigenous Land Owners and Representation in PNG and Australia."
15. The modern economic theory of property rights does not specify the social unit over which individual property rights extend for the system to be efficient. The unit is often presumed to be the individual, but families and firms are often posited as holders of property rights, whose constituent members are assumed to have common interests in the efficient exploitation of the resources they together own. See Jennifer Roback, "Exchange, Sovereignty, and Indian-Anglo Relations," in Terry L. Anderson, ed., *Property Rights and Indian Economies* (Lanham, MD: Rowman and Littlefield, 1991).
16. Vinogradoff, *Historical Jurisprudence*, p. 343.
17. Gregory Clark, "Commons Sense: Common Property Rights, Efficiency, and Institutional Change," *Journal of Economic History* 58, no. 1 (1998): 73–102. See also Jerome Blum, "Review: English Parliamentary Enclosure," *Journal of Modern History* 53, no. 3 (1981): 477–504.
18. Elinor Ostrom cites numerous cases of common pool resources (that is, nonexcludable but rival goods) that have been sustainably managed by communities despite the absence of private property rights. See Ostrom, *Governing the Commons: The Evolution of Institutions for Collective Action* (New York: Cambridge University Press, 1990).
19. Meek, *Land Law and Custom*, pp. 13–14.
20. Colson, "Impact of the Colonial Period," p. 202.
21. Thomas J. Bassett and Donald E. Crummey, *Land in African Agrarian Systems* (Madison: University of Wisconsin Press, 1993), pp. 9–10.
22. Colson, "Impact of the Colonial Period," pp. 196–97; Meek, *Land Law and Custom*, p. 12.
23. During the scramble for Africa that began in the 1870s, European powers sought to build administrative systems on the cheap by using networks of local leaders to enforce rules, conscript corvée labor, and collect capitation taxes. See Mahmood Mamdani, *Citizen and Subject: Contemporary Africa and the Legacy of Late Colonialism* (Princeton: Princeton University Press, 1996).
24. Vinogradoff, *Historical Jurisprudence*, p. 351.
25. Evans-Pritchard, *The Nuer*, pp. 150–51.
26. These examples are ibid., pp. 150–69.
27. Bruce L. Benson, "Customary Indian Law: Two Case Studies," in Anderson, *Property Rights and Indian Economies*, pp. 29–30.
28. Ibid., p. 31.
29. Vinogradoff, *Historical Jurisprudence*, pp. 353–55.
30. Maine, *Early Law and Custom*, pp. 170–71.
31. Vinogradoff, *Historical Jurisprudence*, p. 345.
32. Marshall D. Sahlins, "The Segmentary Lineage: An Organization of Predatory Expansion," *American Anthropologist* 63, no. 2 (1961): 322–45.

33. Lawrence H. Keeley, *War Before Civilization* (New York: Oxford University Press, 1996); LeBlanc and Register, *Constant Battles.*

34. Keeley, *War Before Civilization*, pp. 30–31.

35. Ibid., p. 29.

36. For Tiger, *Men in Groups*, this was the origin of "male bonding." See LeBlanc and Register, *Constant Battles*, p. 90.

37. Jerome Blum, *Lord and Peasant in Russia, from the Ninth to the Nineteenth Century* (Princeton: Princeton University Press, 1961), pp. 38–39.

38. Political scientists like Robert Bates who see politics through the eyes of economics sometimes label warriors as "specialists in violence," as if their occupation were simply another economic category like making shoes or selling real estate. In doing so they mask the noneconomic sources of social solidarity that bind warriors to each other and to their leader. See Robert Bates, *Prosperity and Violence* (Cambridge, MA: Harvard University Press, 2001).

39. Tacitus, *Agricola Germania Dialogus I*, trans. M. Hutton (Cambridge, MA: Harvard University Press, 1970), 13.3–4, 14.1.

40. Ibid., 14.2–3.

41. The intellectual history of this transformation is given in Albert O. Hirschman, *The Passions and the Interests: Political Arguments for Capitalism Before Its Triumph* (Princeton: Princeton University Press, 1977).

42. James Chambers, *The Devil's Horsemen: The Mongol Invasion of Europe* (New York: Atheneum, 1979), p. 6.

43. Tatiana Zerjal et al., "The Genetic Legacy of the Mongols," *American Journal of Human Genetics* 72 (2003): 717–21.

44. Tacitus, *Agricola Germania Dialogus I*, 7.1.

45. Benson, "Customary Indian Law," p. 33.

46. Ibid., p. 36.

47. S. E. Finer, *The History of Government*, Vol. I: *Ancient Monarchies and Empires* (New York: Oxford University Press, 1997), pp. 440–41.

5: THE COMING OF THE LEVIATHAN

1. Some anthropologists, such as Elman Service and Robert Carneiro, distinguish an intermediate level of society between tribes and states, which is the chiefdom. Chiefdoms look very much like states insofar as they are stratified, have a central source of authority, and are legitimated through institutionalized religion. They differ from a state, however, insofar as they don't usually maintain strong standing armies and do not have the power to prevent their own breakdown through fissioning of subordinate tribes or regions. Service, *Primitive Social Organization*, chap. 5; Robert Carneiro, "The Chiefdom: Precursor of the State," in Grant D. Jones and Robert R. Kautz, eds., *The Transition to Statehood in the New World* (New York: Cambridge University Press, 1981).

2. Meyer Fortes and E. E. Evans-Pritchard, eds. *African Political Systems* (New York: Oxford University Press, 1940), pp. 5–6.

3. Karl A. Wittfogel, *Oriental Despotism: A Comparative Study of Total Power* (New Haven: Yale University Press, 1957). See Claessen and van de Velde, "The Evolution of Sociopolitical Organization," in Claessen, van de Velde, and Smith, *Development and Decline*, pp. 130–31; Henri J. M. Claessen and Peter Skalnik, eds., *The Early State* (The Hague: Mouton, 1978), p. 11.

4. See the discussion in Michael Mann, *The Sources of Social Power*, Vol. I: *A History of Power from the Beginning to A.D. 1760* (New York: Cambridge University Press, 1986), pp. 94–98. See also Kwang-chih Chang, *Art, Myth, and Ritual: The Path to Political Authority in Ancient China* (Cambridge, MA: Harvard University Press, 1983), pp. 127–29.

5. See the discussion in Kent V. Flannery, "The Cultural Evolution of Civilizations," *Annual Review of Ecology and Systematics* 3 (1972): 399–426.

6. This point was suggested by Steven LeBlanc, private conversation.

7. See Winifred Creamer, "The Origins of Centralization: Changing Features of Local and Regional Control During the Rio Grande Classic Period, A.D. 1325–1540," in Haas, *From Leaders to Rulers.*

8. Robert L. Carneiro, "A Theory of the Origin of the State," *Science* 169 (1970): 733–38. See also Carneiro, "On the Relationship Between Size of Population and Complexity of Social Organization," *Journal of Anthropological Research* 42, no. 3 (1986): 355–64.

9. This point is made in Flannery, "Cultural Evolution of Civilizations."

10. The three types of authority are defined in Max Weber, *Economy and Society*, Vol. I (Berkeley: University of California Press, 1978), pp. 212–54.

11. For background, see Fred M. Donner, *The Early Islamic Conquests* (Princeton: Princeton University Press, 1981), chap. 2.

12. Ibid., chap. 1; Joseph Schacht, ed., *The Legacy of Islam*, 2d ed. (Oxford: Oxford University Press, 1979), p. 187.

13. Quoted in F. Max Müller, ed., *The Sacred Books of the East*, Vol. III (Oxford: Clarendon Press, 1879), p. 202.

14. Robert C. Allen, "Agriculture and the Origins of the State in Ancient Egypt," *Explorations in Economic History* 34 (1997): 135–54.

15. Jeffrey Herbst, *States and Power in Africa* (Princeton: Princeton University Press, 2000), p. 11.

16. Jack Goody, *Technology, Tradition, and the State in Africa* (Oxford: Oxford University Press, 1971), p. 37.

17. Jeffrey Herbst, "War and the State in Africa," *International Security* 14, no. 4 (1990): 117–39.

18. Herbst, *States and Power in Africa*, chap. 2.

6: CHINESE TRIBALISM

1. Kwang-chih Chang et al., *The Formation of Chinese Civilization*, pp. 2–130.

2. Michael Loewe and Edward L. Shaughnessy, eds. *The Cambridge History of Ancient China: From the Origins of Civilization to 221 B.C.* (New York: Cambridge University Press, 1999), pp. 909–11.

3. For more on the periodization of early China, see Li Xueqin, *Eastern Zhou and Qin Civilizations* (New Haven: Yale University Press, 1985), pp. 3–5.

4. On this period, see Herrlee G. Creel, *The Birth of China: A Study of the Formative Period of Chinese Civilization* (New York: Ungar, 1954), pp. 21–37; and Edward L. Shaughnessy, *Sources of Western Zhou History: Inscribed Bronze Vessels* (Berkeley: University of California Press, 1991).

5. Chang, *Art, Myth, and Ritual*, pp. 26–27.

6. Ibid., p. 35.

7. Ibid., p. 41.

8. Chang et al., *Formation of Chinese Civilization*, p. 85.

9. Chang, *Art, Myth, and Ritual*, p. 124.

10. Chang et al., *Formation of Chinese Civilization*, p. 170.

11. Ibid., pp. 164–65.

12. On the survival of familism in China, see Francis Fukuyama, *Trust: The Social Virtues and the Creation of Prosperity* (New York: Free Press, 1996), pp. 69–95.

13. See Olga Lang, *Chinese Family and Society* (New Haven: Yale University Press, 1946); Maurice Freedman, *Lineage Organization in Southeastern China* (London: Athlone Press, 1958); Freedman, *Chinese Lineage and Society: Fujian and Guangdong* (London: Athlone, 1966); Freedman, *Family and Kinship in Chinese Society* (Stanford, CA: Stanford University Press, 1970); Myron L. Cohen, *House United, House Divided: The Chinese Family in Taiwan* (New York: Columbia University Press, 1976); Arthur P. Wolf and Chieh-shan Huang, *Marriage and Adoption in China, 1845–1945* (Stanford, CA: Stanford University Press, 1980).

14. For a discussion of how contemporary anthropology relates to historical research, see James L. Watson, "Chinese Kinship Reconsidered: Anthropological Perspectives on Historical Research," *China Quarterly* 92 (1982): 589–627.

15. Ibid., p. 594.

16. Paul Chao, *Chinese Kinship* (Boston: Routledge, 1983), pp. 19–26.

17. Michael Loewe, *The Government of the Qin and Han Empires: 221 BCE–220 CE* (Indianapolis: Hackett, 2006), p. 6.

18. Donald Keene, *Emperor of Japan: Meiji and His World, 1852–1912* (New York: Columbia University Press, 2002), p. 2.

19. Loewe, *Government of the Qin and Han*, p. 6.

20. Ke Changji, "Ancient Chinese Society and the Asiatic Mode of Production," in Timothy Brook, ed., *The Asiatic Mode of Production in China* (Armonk, NY: M. E. Sharpe, 1989).

21. Franz Schurmann, "Traditional Property Concepts in China," *Far Eastern Quarterly* 15, no. 4 (1956): 507–16.

22. Chao, *Chinese Kinship*, p. 25.

23. Baker, *Chinese Family and Kinship*, pp. 55–59.

24. Chao, *Chinese Kinship*, p. 19; Fukuyama, *Trust*, pp. 172–73.

25. For background, see John A. Harrison, *The Chinese Empire* (New York: Harcourt, 1972), pp. 36–37. On the origin of the Zhou and their conquest of the Shang Dynasty, see Creel, *The Birth of China*, pp. 219–36.

26. For one effort to make such a comparison, see Victoria Tin-bor Hui, *War and State Formation in Ancient China and Early Modern Europe* (New York: Cambridge University Press, 2005).

27. For a major critique of the uses of the concept of feudalism, see Elizabeth A. R. Brown, "The Tyranny of a Construct: Feudalism and Historians of Medieval Europe," *American Historical Review* 79, no. 4 (1974): 1063–88. See also Jørgen Møller, "Bringing Feudalism Back In: The Historian's Craft and the Need for Conceptual Tools and Generalization," unpublished paper.

28. See the discussion in Joseph R. Levenson and Franz Schurmann, *China: An Interpretive History. From the Beginnings to the Fall of Han* (Berkeley: University of California Press, 1969), pp. 34–40.

29. Marc Bloch, *Feudal Society* (Chicago: University of Chicago Press, 1968), p. 161.

30. Joseph R. Strayer, "Feudalism in Western Europe," in Fredric L. Cheyette, ed., *Lordship and Community in Medieval Europe: Selected Readings* (New York: Holt, 1968), p. 13.

31. Bloch, *Feudal Society*, pp. 190ff.

32. For a fuller discussion of the relationship between Zhou and European feudalism, see Feng Li, "'Feudalism' and Western Zhou China: A Criticism," *Harvard Journal of Asiatic Studies* 63, no. 1 (2003): 115–44. Li suggests that the Western Zhou started out as far more politically centralized than the term "feudalism" suggests.

33. Harrison, *The Chinese Empire*, pp. 37–41; Hsu, *Ancient China in Transition*, p. 53; Levenson and Schurmann, *China*, pp. 30–32.

34. Hsu, *Ancient China in Transition*, p. 79.

35. Mark E. Lewis, *Sanctioned Violence in Early China* (Albany: State University of New York Press, 1990), p. 33.

36. Ibid., p. 35.

37. Ibid., p. 17.

38. Ibid., p. 28.

39. Ibid., pp. 22, 37–38.

7: WAR AND THE RISE OF THE CHINESE STATE

1. Tilly, *Coercion, Capital, and European States*; Tilly, "War Making and State Making as Organized Crime," in Peter B. Evans, Dietrich Rueschemeyer, and Theda Skocpol, eds., *Bringing the State Back In* (Cambridge, MA: Cambridge University Press, 1985). See also Porter, *War and the Rise of the State*.

2. See Cameron G. Thies, "War, Rivalry, and State Building in Latin America," *American Journal of Political Science* 49, no. 3 (2005): 451–65.

3. Hsu, *Ancient China in Transition*, pp. 56–58.

4. Edgar Kiser and Yong Cai, "War and Bureaucratization in Qin China: Exploring an Anomalous Case," *American Sociological Review* 68, no. 4 (2003): 511–39.

5. Hsu, *Ancient China in Transition*, p. 67; Kiser and Cai, "War and Bureaucratization," (2003), p. 520; Hui, *War and State Formation*, p. 87.

6. For an overview, see Joseph Needham, *Science and Civilisation in China*, Vol. 5, pt. 7: *Military Technology* (Cambridge: Cambridge University Press, 1954).

7. Lewis, *Sanctioned Violence in Early China*, pp. 55–58.

8. Ibid., p. 60; Hsu, *Ancient China in Transition*, p. 71.

9. Hsu, *Ancient China in Transition*, pp. 73–75.

10. Lewis, *Sanctioned Violence in Early China*, pp. 58–59.

11. Hsu, *Ancient China in Transition*, pp. 82–87.

12. Kiser and Cai, "War and Bureaucratization," pp. 516–17.

13. Jacques Gernet, *A History of Chinese Civilization* (Cambridge: Cambridge University Press, 1996), pp. 64–65.

14. Ibid., pp. 67–73.

15. Ibid., pp. 82–100.

16. Yu-ning Li, *Shang Yang's Reforms and State Control in China* (White Plains, NY: M. E. Sharpe, 1977), pp. 32–38.

17. Ibid., pp. 38–39.

18. Peasant families are usually too poor to maintain lineages; the well-field system might be thought of as a poor family's alternative to an extended kinship group.

19. James C. Scott, *Seeing Like a State: How Certain Schemes to Improve the Human Condition Have Failed* (New Haven: Yale University Press, 1998).

20. Lewis, *Sanctioned Violence in Early China*, p. 63.

21. Li, *Shang Yang's Reforms*, p. 66.

22. For background, see Burton Watson, trans., *Han Fei Tzu: Basic Writings* (New York: Columbia University Press, 1964), pp. 1–15.

23. Chao, *Chinese Kinship*, pp. 133–34.

24. Baker, *Chinese Family and Kinship*, pp. 152–61.

25. See the discussion in Fukuyama, *Trust*, pp. 93–94.

26. Quoted in Li, *Shang Yang's Reforms*, p. 127.

27. Kung-chuan Hsiao, "Legalism and Autocracy in Traditional China," ibid., p. 16.

28. Loewe and Shaughnessy, *Cambridge History of Ancient China*, p. 1003.

29. Ibid., p. 1009.

30. Hui, *War and State Formation*, pp. 65–66.

31. Consistent with his efforts to undermine the traditional kinship-based order at home, Shang Yang engaged in a Machiavellian foreign policy that overturned the aristocratic rules of engagement and norms that limited conflict. For example, he duped the ruler of his former home state, Wei, into declaring himself king in place of the Zhou monarch, a move that embroiled Wei with its neighbors Han and Qi and led to its defeat by the latter. When Qin invaded Wei in 340 B.C., Shang Yang invited the commander of Wei's forces, Prince Ang, to a peace conference in his camp and promptly took him prisoner. Like the draconian punishments being meted out at home, all of this was justified in terms of pure power politics. See ibid., pp. 70–71.

32. Weber wrote about China in many places; see in particular *The Religion of China* (New York: Free Press, 1951); and *Economy and Society*, Vol. 2, pp. 1047–51.

33. Levenson and Schurmann, *China*, pp. 99–100.

34. Harrison, *The Chinese Empire*, p. 88.
35. Levenson and Schurmann, *China*, pp. 69–70.

8: THE GREAT HAN SYSTEM

1. Harrison, *The Chinese Empire*, pp. 85–86.
2. Quoted in Levenson and Schurmann, *China*, p. 87.
3. Kwang-chih Chang et al., *The Formation of Chinese Civilization*, p. 271.
4. Kiser and Cai, "War and Bureaucratization."
5. Levenson and Schurmann, *China*, pp. 80–81; Harrison, *The Chinese Empire*, pp. 95–96.
6. Loewe, *The Government of the Qin and Han Empires*, p. 43.
7. Chang et al., *The Formation of Chinese Civilization*, p. 276.
8. Levenson and Schurmann, *China*, p. 83.
9. Loewe, *The Government of the Qin and Han Empires*, pp. 95–97.
10. Levenson and Schurmann, *China*, pp. 88–91.
11. The full list of characteristics:

   a. Bureaucrats are personally free and subject to authority only within a defined area.
   b. They are organized into a clearly defined hierarchy of offices.
   c. Each office has a defined sphere of competence.
   d. Offices are filled by free contractual relationship.
   e. Candidates are selected on the basis of technical qualifications.
   f. Bureaucrats are remunerated by fixed salaries.
   g. The office is treated as the sole occupation of the incumbent.
   h. The office constitutes a career.
   i. There is a separation between ownership and management.
   j. Officials are subject to strict discipline and control.

   Weber, *Economy and Society*, Vol. I, pp. 220–21. Many observers have noted that Weber's definition applies best to the Prussian-German bureaucracy with which he was most familiar, but that it does not accurately describe many effective modern public- or private-sector bureaucracies today. For example, many instances of flat management involve delegating high degrees of autonomy to subordinates, relaxing the strict command-and-control hierarchy of classic bureaucracy, and blurring the boundaries between different offices. It seems to me that the most essential characteristics of modern bureaucracy, such as the specificity of office, the subordination of office to higher political authority, and the separation of public and private spheres, are all still characteristic of modern public administration systems. Allen Schick argues that more recent innovations in public management need to be built on a foundation of traditional bureaucracy. See his article "Why Most Developing Countries Should Not Try New Zealand Reforms," *World Bank Research Observer* 13, no. 8 (1998): 1123–31.
12. This point is made in Creel, "The Beginning of Bureaucracy in China."
13. Loewe, *The Government of the Qin and Han Empires*, pp. 74–76.

14. Patrimonialism survived chiefly in the kingdoms and dependent states that had been part of the original Han political settlement. The Qin Dynasty's two-level commandery/prefecture system was replaced by a more complex multilevel one. Commanderies and dependent kingdoms were divided into prefectures or counties, nobilities, estates, and marches. By A.D. 2, there were 1,577 of these units across China. Nobilities were patrimonial offices that could be used to buy off or park the kinsmen of kings or powerful surviving aristocratic families, and could be held on a hereditary basis. In some cases they were used to reward imperial kinsmen. They were not, however, the bastion of an independent hereditary aristocracy as were the feudal domains of Europe. Rather, nobilities appear to have been offices relatively easily created or removed by the central government as means of placating or punishing different political actors. Ibid., pp. 46, 50.

15. Ibid., pp. 24–30.

16. Ibid., pp. 24–25.

17. Ibid., pp. 56–62.

9: POLITICAL DECAY AND THE RETURN OF PATRIMONIAL GOVERNMENT

1. Harrison, *The Chinese Empire*, pp. 174–77.

2. Ibid., pp. 179–81.

3. Ibid., p. 182. There is a great deal of controversy over historical measurement of population in China. Kent Deng, using adjusted official population data, shows China's population dropping from 56.5 million in A.D. 157 to 18.5 million in 280, a decline of 67 percent. Kent G. Deng, "Unveiling China's True Population Statistics for the Pre-Modern Era with Official Census Data," *Population Review* 43, no. 2 (2004): 32–69.

4. See Patricia B. Ebrey, "Patron-Client Relations in the Later Han," *Journal of the American Oriental Society* 103, no. 3 (1983): 533–42.

5. For a contemporary example of this process unfolding in Mexico, see Flannery, "The Cultural Evolution of Civilizations."

6. Thomas R. Malthus, *An Essay on the Principle of Population* (New York: Penguin, 1982).

7. See Angus Maddison, *Growth and Interaction in the World Economy: The Roots of Modernity* (Washington, D.C.: AEI Press, 2001), pp. 21–27.

8. This situation was characterized in China's case as a "high-level equilibrium trap." Mark Elvin, *The Pattern of the Chinese Past: A Social and Economic Interpretation* (Stanford, CA: Stanford University Press, 1973).

9. Étienne Balazs, *Chinese Civilization and Bureaucracy: Variations on a Theme* (New Haven: Yale University Press, 1964), pp. 102–103.

10. Scott Pearce, Audrey Spiro, and Patricia Ebrey, eds., *Culture and Power in the Reconstitution of the Chinese Realm, 200–600* (Cambridge, MA: Harvard University Press, 2001), pp. 8–9.

11. Harrison, *The Chinese Empire*, p. 181.

12. Moss Roberts, "Afterword: About *Three Kingdoms*," in Luo Guanzhong, *Three Kingdoms: A Historical Novel* (Berkeley: University of California Press, 2004), pp. 938–40.

13. J.A.G. Roberts, *A Concise History of China* (Cambridge, MA: Harvard University Press, 1999), pp. 40-44; Patricia B. Ebrey, *The Aristocratic Families of Early Imperial China: A Case Study of the Po-ling Ts'ui Family* (New York: Cambridge University Press, 1978), p. 21.

14. Ebrey, *Aristocratic Families*, pp. 17-18.

15. Ibid., p. 21.

16. Ibid., p. 22.

17. Balazs, *Chinese Civilization and Bureaucracy*, pp. 104-106.

18. Ebrey, *Aristocratic Families*, pp. 25-26.

19. Balazs, *Chinese Civilization and Bureaucracy*, pp. 108-109.

10: THE INDIAN DETOUR

1. Romila Thapar, *From Lineage to State: Social Formations in the Mid-First Millennium B.C. in the Ganga Valley* (Bombay: Oxford University Press, 1984), p. 157.

2. Harold A. Gould, *The Hindu Caste System* (Delhi: Chanakya Publications, 1987), p. 12.

3. See Stanley Wolpert, *A New History of India* (New York: Oxford University Press, 1977), pp. 14-23.

4. Romila Thapar, *Early India: From the Origins to AD 1300* (Berkeley: University of California Press, 2003), pp. 110-11.

5. Ibid., pp. 112-13.

6. Ibid., pp. 114-16.

7. Ibid., p. 120.

8. Ibid., p. 127.

9. Maine, *Ancient Law*; Maine, *Village-Communities in the East and West* (New York: Arno Press, 1974); Patricia Uberoi, *Family, Kinship and Marriage in India* (Delhi: Oxford University Press, 1993), pp. 8-12. Lewis Henry Morgan's work on comparative kinship structures also pointed to similarities in kinship terminology between Dravidian tribes in India and the North American indigenous groups like the Iroquois. Uberoi, pp. 14-15.

10. Irawati Karve, "The Kinship Map of India," in Uberoi, *Family, Kinship and Marriage*, p. 50.

11. Ibid., p. 67.

12. Ibid., p. 53.

13. Ibid., pp. 67-68.

14. Eastern India is inhabited by groups speaking Austro-Asiatic languages such as Mundari and Mon-Khmer, which are also spoken throughout Southeast Asia. This group represents populations that inhabited the subcontinent before the arrival of conquerors like the Indo-Aryans. They survive today in little pockets in forested or otherwise inaccessible parts of the country, and some are still tribally organized. Their kinship rules are quite varied and represent a complex mixture of ancient patterns and more recent influences from the surrounding society. Ibid., p. 72.

15. Arthur L. Basham, *The Wonder That Was India: A Survey of the Culture of the Indian Sub-Continent Before the Coming of the Muslims* (London: Sidgwick and Jackson, 1954), p. 81.

16. Ibid., p. 82.
17. Thapar, *Early India*, p. 112.
18. Thapar, *From Lineage to State*, p. 155.
19. Thapar, *Early India*, p. 117.
20. Thapar, *From Lineage to State*, p. 158.
21. Thapar, *Early India*, p. 144.
22. Ibid., pp. 121–22.
23. Ibid., pp. 137–38.
24. Ram S. Sharma, *Aspects of Political Ideas and Institutions in Ancient India* (Delhi: Motilal Banarsidass, 1968), p. 159.
25. One of those turtles resting on turtles of prior historical causality is why the early Indian tribes, chiefdoms, and states fought fewer wars than their Chinese counterparts. One explanation could be environmental, if indeed the population of northern India was less dense and less circumscribed than the population of China during the Eastern Zhou. But it is possible that religion played a role here as well, by somehow inhibiting the Indian states' ability and motivation to wage war.

11: VARNAS AND JATIS

1. Gary S. Becker, "Nobel Lecture: The Economic Way of Looking at Behavior," *Journal of Political Economy* 101, no. 3 (1993): 385–409.
2. Basham, *The Wonder That Was India*, p. 241.
3. Max Weber, *The Religion of India: The Sociology of Hinduism and Buddhism* (Glencoe, IL: Free Press, 1958), p. 131.
4. Gould, *The Hindu Caste System*, p. 15.
5. Ibid., pp. 15–16; Martin Doornbos and Sudipta Kaviraj, *Dynamics of State Formation: India and Europe Compared* (Thousand Oaks, CA: Sage Publications, 1997), p. 37.
6. Louis Dumont, *Homo Hierarchicus: The Caste System and Its Implications* (Chicago: University of Chicago Press, 1980), p. 150. Other sects, most notably the Jains, carry the principle of ahimsa, or nonviolence, and the noneating of meat much further than orthodox Hindus, avoiding even the possibility of killing insects. Dumont attributes this to the emergence of something like an arms race between sects of renouncers like the Jains and the Brahmins, who sought to outdo each other with regard to ritual purity.
7. Thapar, *Early India*, p. 124.
8. Thapar, *From Lineage to State*, pp. 169–70.
9. Dumont, *Homo Hierarchicus*, p. 176.
10. This assertion is often associated with Louis Dumont, who argued that caste arises out of religion based on a hierarchical ranking of grades of purity, which is separate from a secular realm of power. This view has been heavily criticized from a number of perspectives, particularly by Ronald Inden, who argued that Dumont was importing Western dichotomies and imposing them on a society for which they were not appropriate. Others have argued against the view that the Brahmins ranked higher than the Kshatriyas; they were, rather, two sides of an integrated religious-political system. Others have gone so far as to suggest that caste itself was not that important in Indian

history but was deliberately constructed by British colonial authorities for their own political purposes.

The separation of political and religious realms may be a normative preference in modern Western societies, but the idea that political and religious authority can be separated as analytical categories does not reflect a Western prejudice or bias. These forms of authority can be either separated or melded in a variety of ways in different societies, but without the existence of the categories themselves, it would be impossible to compare India to China or to the Middle East. The critique of Dumont seems rather to reflect a parochial bias of Indologists who are not in the habit of comparing India to other societies. See Ronald B. Inden, *Imagining India* (Bloomington: Indiana University Press, 2000); Gloria Goodwin Raheja, "India: Caste, Kingship, and Dominance Revisited," *Annual Review of Anthropology* 17 (1988): 497–522; V. Kondos, "A Piece on Justice: Some Reactions to Dumont's *Homo Hierarchicus*," *South Asia* 21, no. 1 (1998): 33–47; William S. Sax, "Conquering Quarters: Religion and Politics in Hinduism," *International Journal of Hindu Studies* 4, no. 1 (2000): 39–60; Rohan Bastin, "Death of the Indian Social," *Social Analysis* 48, no. 3 (2004): 205–13; Mary Searle-Chatterjee and Ursula Sharma, eds., *Contextualising Caste: Post-Dumontian Approaches* (Cambridge, MA: Blackwell, 1994); and Nicholas B. Dirks, *The Invention of Caste: Civil Society in Colonial India* (Ann Arbor: University of Michigan, CSST Working Paper 11, 1988).

11. Gould, *The Hindu Caste System*, p. 19.
12. Sharma, *Aspects of Political Ideas and Institutions in Ancient India*, pp. 161–62.
13. Basham, *The Wonder That Was India*, p. 128.
14. Ibid., p. 129.
15. Ibid., pp. 129–30.
16. Joel Migdal, *Strong Societies and Weak States: State-Society Relations and State Capabilities in the Third World* (Princeton: Princeton University Press, 1988).
17. Dumont, *Homo Hierarchicus*, pp. 158–59.
18. As Louis Dumont points out, it was neither democratic nor secular but reflected the relationships of power and dominance that are inherent in the system of jatis. Ibid., pp. 158–63; see also Thapar, *From Lineage to State*, pp. 164–65.
19. Satish Saberwal, *Wages of Segmentation: Comparative Historical Studies on Europe and India* (New Delhi: Orient Longman, 1995), pp. 27–29.
20. Ibid., p. 26.
21. Ibid., p. 25.
22. V. S. Naipaul, *India: A Wounded Civilization* (New York: Vintage, 1978).
23. In 2004, more than 34 percent of India's population lived on less than $1 a day. Shaohua Chen and Martin Ravallion, "Absolute Poverty Measures for the Developing World, 1981–2004" (Washington, D.C.: World Bank Policy Research Working Paper WPS4211, 2007), p. 26.
24. Saberwal, *Wages of Segmentation*, p. 113.
25. Ibid., pp. 114–16.
26. Frank Perlin, "State Formation Reconsidered Part Two," *Modern Asian Studies* 19, no. 3 (1985): 434.

27. Sharma, *Aspects of Political Ideas*, pp. 159–60.
28. Quoted in Sudipta Kaviraj, "On the Enchantment of the State: Indian Thought on the Role of the State in the Narrative of Modernity," *European Journal of Sociology* 46, no. 2 (2005): 263–96.
29. Basham, *The Wonder That Was India*, p. 87.

12: WEAKNESSES OF INDIAN POLITIES

1. Thapar, *Early India*, p. 152.
2. Ibid., p. 156; Basham, *The Wonder That Was India*, p. 131.
3. Thapar, *Early India*, pp. 178–79.
4. Wolpert, *A New History of India*, pp. 55–69. The present-day Republic of India includes the far south and states in the east such as Assam that weren't included in the Mauryan empire, but does not include Pakistan and Bangladesh, the larger parts of which were.
5. For an overview, see Hermann Kulke, "Introduction: The Study of the State in Pre-modern India," in Kulke, ed., *The State in India 1000–1700* (Delhi: Oxford University Press, 1995).
6. Sharma, *Aspects of Political Ideas and Institutions*, pp. 286–87. Sharma argues that while the Mauryan state "may not be regarded rational in the modern sense of the term . . . it is not patrimonial either for it was not a part of the royal household." This is true under only the narrowest of definitions of patrimonialism. See also Thapar, *Early India*, who calculates the ratio of wages to be only 1:96 (p. 195).
7. Sharma, *Aspects of Political Ideas*, pp. 165–66.
8. Perlin, "State Formation Reconsidered."
9. Basham, *The Wonder That Was India*, pp. 93–94.
10. Thapar, *Early India*, p. 206.
11. Some of these tribal groups, such as the Vrjjis, were defeated and incorporated into the Magadhan Empire, while in the west more survived, where they were encountered by Alexander the Great. In the mountainous areas of the northwest fringes of the empire—now eastern Afghanistan—these tribes still exist in the early twenty-first century, where they have battled NATO forces. Basham, *The Wonder That Was India*, pp. 96–97; Sharma, *Aspects of Political Ideas*, pp. 281–82; Thapar, *Early India*, p. 204.
12. Thapar, *Early India*, pp. 185–87; Sharma, *Aspects of Political Ideas*, pp. 288–89.
13. Thapar, *Early India*, p. 189.
14. Doornbos and Kaviraj, *Dynamics of State Formation*, p. 93.
15. Thapar, *Early India*, p. 178.
16. Quoted in Hemchandra Raychaudhuri, *Political History of Ancient India: From the Accession of Parikshit to the Extinction of the Gupta Dynasty* (New Delhi: Oxford University Press, 1996), pp. 288–90. See also Thapar, *Early India*, p. 181.
17. Thapar, *Early India*, p. 219.
18. Burton Stein, "State Formation and Economy Reconsidered," *Modern Asian Studies* 19, no. 3 (1985): 387–413.
19. The weak level of integration of the Chola state led one historian to describe it as "segmentary," built around a small, centrally administered nucleus, but claiming nominal

dominion over a much larger number of self-governing, autonomous settlements around its periphery. See Burton Stein, "Integration of the Agrarian System of South India," in Robert E. Frykenberg, ed., *Land Control and Social Structure in Indian History* (Madison: University of Wisconsin Press, 1969). Stein compared the south Indian state to the pre-state, segmentary tribal society of the Alurs in Africa.

20. Wolpert, *A New History of India*, pp. 88–94.

21. Kaviraj, "On the Enchantment of the State," p. 270.

22. Ibid., p. 273.

23. Sunil Khilnani, *The Idea of India* (New York: Farrar, Straus and Giroux, 1998).

24. See, for example, Bill Emmott, *Rivals: How the Power Struggle Between China, India, and Japan Will Shape Our Next Decade* (New York: Harcourt, 2008); Edward Friedman and Bruce Gilley, eds., *Asia's Giants: Comparing China and India* (New York: Palgrave Macmillan, 2005); Tarun Khanna, *Billions of Entrepreneurs: How China and India Are Reshaping Their Futures—and Yours* (Boston: Harvard Business School Press, 2008).

25. Somini Sengupta, "Often Parched, India Struggles to Tap the Monsoon," *New York Times*, October 1, 2006.

26. Amartya K. Sen, *Development as Freedom* (New York: Knopf, 1999), pp. 234–40.

27. Kaviraj, "On the Enchantment of the State," pp. 227, 230.

28. Ibid., p. 230.

13: SLAVERY AND THE MUSLIM EXIT FROM TRIBALISM

1. I use phonetic Roman rather than modern Turkish spelling; hence *devshirme* rather than *devşirme*, and *sanjak* rather than *sancak*.

2. Albert H. Lybyer, *The Government of the Ottoman Empire in the Time of Suleiman the Magnificent* (New York: AMS Press, 1978), pp. 49–53; Norman Itzkowitz, *Ottoman Empire and Islamic Tradition* (New York: Knopf, 1972), pp. 49–50.

3. Itzkowitz, *Ottoman Empire*, pp. 51–52.

4. This was particularly true after 1574, when the Ottoman Empire conquered Tunis and put North Africa under Muslim rule. See William H. McNeill, *Europe's Steppe Frontier, 1500–1800* (Chicago: University of Chicago Press, 1964), p. 29; Halil Inalcik, *The Ottoman Empire: The Classical Age, 1300–1600* (New Rochelle, NY: Orpheus Publishing Co., 1989), pp. 86–87.

5. Patrick B. Kinross, *The Ottoman Centuries: The Rise and Fall of the Turkish Empire* (New York: William Morrow, 1977), pp. 453–71.

6. Daniel Pipes, *Slave-Soldiers and Islam: The Genesis of a Military System* (New Haven: Yale University Press, 1981), pp. 93–98.

7. Ibn Khaldun, *The Muqaddimah: An Introduction to History*, as quoted in Bernard Lewis, ed. and trans., *Islam from the Prophet Muhammad to the Capture of Constantinople. I: Politics and War* (New York: Oxford University Press, 1987), pp. 97ff.

8. Donner, *The Early Islamic Conquests*, pp. 82–85; Marshall G. S. Hodgson, *The Venture of Islam: Conscience and History in a World Civilization* (Chicago: University of Chicago Press, 1961), pp. 197–98.

9. For a detailed account of these conquests, see Hugh N. Kennedy, *The Great Arab Conquests: How the Spread of Islam Changed the World We Live In* (Philadelphia: Da Capo, 2007).

10. Donner, *The Early Islamic Conquests*, pp. 239–42; Peter M. Holt, Ann K. S. Lambton, and Bernard Lewis, eds., *The Cambridge History of Islam*. Vol. I: *The Central Islamic Lands* (New York: Cambridge University Press, 1970), pp. 64–65.

11. Fred M. Donner, "The Formation of the Islamic State," *Journal of the American Oriental Society* 106, no. 2 (1986): 283–96.

12. See, for example, Douglass C. North, Barry R. Weingast, and John Wallis, *Violence and Social Orders: A Conceptual Framework for Interpreting Recorded Human History* (New York: Cambridge University Press, 2009), who tend to see the state as a collective action problem among a group of relatively equal oligarchs.

13. One of the practical consequences of this was that monarchs often intervened to *lower* the predatory taxes imposed by local elites on their dependent populations. Hodgson, *The Venture of Islam*, pp. 281–82; Donner, "The Formation of the Islamic State," pp. 290–91.

14. See Bernard Lewis, "Politics and War," in Schacht, *The Legacy of Islam*, pp. 164–65.

15. Holt, *Cambridge History of Islam*, p. 72.

16. Donner, *The Early Islamic Conquests*, p. 258.

17. Ibid., p. 263.

18. For general background, see David Ayalon, *Islam and the Abode of War: Military Slaves and Islamic Adversaries* (Brookfield, VT: Variorum, 1994).

19. On the rise of the Abbasids, see Hugh N. Kennedy, *When Baghdad Ruled the Muslim World: The Rise and Fall of Islam's Greatest Dynasty* (Cambridge, MA: Da Capo Press, 2006); also Hodgson, *The Venture of Islam*, p. 284.

20. Hodgson, *The Venture of Islam*, p. 286.

21. Quoted in Ayalon, *Islam and the Abode of War*, p. 2.

22. David Ayalon, *Outsiders in the Lands of Islam: Mamluks, Mongols, and Eunuchs* (London: Variorum, 1988), p. 325.

23. Holt, *Cambridge History of Islam*, p. 125.

24. Quoted in Ayalon, *Islam and the Abode of War*, p. 25.

25. Ibid., p. 29; Holt, *Cambridge History of Islam*, pp. 125–26.

26. Plato, *Republic*, trans. Allan Bloom (New York: Basic Books, 1968), 464c–d.

14: THE MAMLUKS SAVE ISLAM

1. Quoted in Lewis, *Islam from the Prophet Muhammad to the Capture of Constantinople*, pp. 97–98. The *Muqadimmah* is technically only the prolegomenon to a larger work that today is much less read.

2. Ayalon, *Outsiders in the Lands of Islam*, p. 328.

3. Reuven Amitai-Preiss, *Mongols and Mamluks: The Mamluk-Ilkhanid War: 1260–1281* (New York: Cambridge University Press, 1995), pp. 215–16.

4. Ibid., p. 228.

5. See Linda S. Northrup, "The Bahri Mamluk Sultanate, 1250–1390," in Carl F. Petry, ed.,

The Cambridge History of Egypt, Vol. 1: *Islamic Egypt, 640–1517* (New York: Cambridge University Press, 1998).

6. R. Stephen Humphreys, "The Emergence of the Mamluk Army," *Studia Islamica* 45 (1977): 67–99.

7. Peter M. Holt, "The Position and Power of the Mamluk Sultan," *Bulletin of the School of Oriental and African Studies* 38, no. 2 (1975): 237–49; Northrup, "Bahri Mamluk Sultanate," p. 263.

8. Ayalon, *Outsiders in the Land of Islam*, p. 328.

9. Ibid., p. 69.

10. Ibid., p. 72.

11. Ibid., p. 328; Northrup, "Bahri Mamluk Sultanate," pp. 256–57, says that the one-generation principle was never explicitly stated anywhere.

12. Amalia Levanoni, "The Mamluk Conception of the Sultanate," *International Journal of Middle East Studies* 26, no. 3 (1994): 373–92.

13. See Fukuyama, *State-Building*, chap. 2.

14. Jean-Claude Garcin, "The Regime of the Circassian Mamluks," in Petry, *Cambridge History of Egypt*, p. 292.

15. In a contemporary version of this problem, the World Bank advises developing countries to separate the policy maker from the service provider. The latter becomes a pure agent and can be disciplined by the former for nonperformance. See World Bank, *World Development Report 2004: Making Services Work for Poor People* (Washington, D.C.: World Bank, 2004), pp. 46–61.

16. Northrup, "Bahri Mamluk Sultanate," p. 257.

17. Ibid., pp. 258–59.

18. Ibid., pp. 261–62.

19. Garcin, "The Regime of the Circassian Mamluks," p. 290.

20. Carl F. Petry, "The Military Institution and Innovation in the Late Mamluk Period," in Petry, *Cambridge History of Egypt*, p. 468.

21. Ibid., pp. 470–73.

22. Tilly, "War Making and State Making as Organized Crime," in Evans et al., eds.

23. Peter B. Evans, "Predatory, Developmental, and Other Apparatuses: A Comparative Analysis of the Third World State," *Sociological Forum* 4, no. 4 (1989): 561–82.

24. See Petry, "The Military Institution and Innovation," p. 478.

25. David Ayalon, *Gunpowder and Firearms in the Mamluk Kingdom: A Challenge to a Mediaeval Society* (London: Vallentine Mitchell, 1956), p. 98.

26. Petry, "The Military Institution and Innovation," pp. 479–80; Ayalon, *Gunpowder and Firearms*, pp. 101–105.

15: THE FUNCTIONING AND DECLINE OF THE OTTOMAN STATE

1. Niccolò Machiavelli, *The Prince*, trans. Harvey C. Mansfield (Chicago: University of Chicago Press, 1985), pp. 17–18.

2. On early Ottoman history, see Inalcik, *The Ottoman Empire*, pp. 5–8.

3. Ibid., p. 107; I. Metin Kunt, *The Sultan's Servants: The Transformation of Ottoman Provincial Government, 1550–1650* (New York: Columbia University Press, 1983), pp. 9–13. A parallel institution was the Russian *kormlenie*, or feeding.

4. Kunt, *Sultan's Servants*, pp. 14–15.

5. Karen Barkey, *Bandits and Bureaucrats: The Ottoman Route to State Centralization* (Ithaca: Cornell University Press, 1994), p. 36.

6. Kunt, *Sultan's Servants*, p. 24.

7. Barkey, *Bandits and Bureaucrats*, p. 36.

8. Inalcik, *The Ottoman Empire*, p. 109.

9. Ibid., pp. 114–15.

10. McNeill, *Europe's Steppe Frontier*, pp. 38–40.

11. Lybyer, *The Government of the Ottoman Empire*, pp. 66–70.

12. Kunt, *Sultan's Servants*, pp. 31–32.

13. Itzkowitz, *Ottoman Empire and Islamic Tradition*, pp. 58–59.

14. Inalcik, *The Ottoman Empire*, p. 65.

15. Barkey, *Bandits and Bureaucrats*, p. 28.

16. For example, the Kutadgu Bilig, written for the Turkish ruler of the Karakhanids in 1069, which said, "To control the state requires a large army. To support the troops requires great wealth. To obtain this wealth the people must be prosperous. For the people to be prosperous the laws must be just. If any one of these is neglected the state will collapse." Quoted in Inalcik, *The Ottoman Empire*, p. 66.

17. Itzkowitz, *Ottoman Empire*, p. 88.

18. The historian William McNeill suggests another reason why Ottoman peasants were relatively lightly taxed in the empire's early days. The ruling elite were themselves recruited, through the devshirme system, from impoverished rural communities in the Balkans and elsewhere; the soldier-administrators understood the rigors of peasant life and had sympathy for the reaya. He points out, however, that the relatively light burden on the peasantry in the core areas of the empire could be sustained only through continuing predation on the empire's frontiers. The sipahi cavalrymen who constituted the bulk of the army were self-sustaining through their timars; there was a very limited tax base to support any expansion of the army, so larger forces required the conquest of new territories to create new timars. As we will see, the system began to break down when the empire reached the limits of its foreign expansion and was forced to increase tax rates in its core territories. See McNeill, *Europe's Steppe Frontier*, p. 32.

19. Inalcik, *The Ottoman Empire*, p. 59.

20. Ibid., p. 60.

21. Max Weber characterized the Ottoman system as patrimonial; indeed, contemporary political scientists use Weber's term "sultanism" to describe a poorly institutionalized system. The reason for this was that the Ottoman system at the highest levels was indeed only weakly rule bound and therefore still patrimonial. The succession system, which invited a free-for-all among the system's participants, was only one example. As in Persia, Rome, China, and other empires, members of the ruler's family and courtiers in the palace were often far more vulnerable to arbitrary rule, since they were potential

participants in a zero-sum struggle for power. Sultans could and did appoint their sons and other kin to high posts as governors or military commanders. The rise of particular individuals to position of vizier or grand vizier was a matter of patronage networks and personal influence. Political power and private fortunes were dependent on one's personal ties to the court and to the sultan. See Weber, *Economy and Society*, Vol. 2, pp. 1025–26; also Barkey, *Bandits and Bureaucrats*, pp. 30–32.

22. Itzkowitz, *Ottoman Empire*, p. 59.
23. McNeill, *Europe's Steppe Frontier*, p. 42.
24. Jack A. Goldstone, *Revolution and Rebellion in the Early Modern World* (Berkeley: University of California Press, 1991), pp. 355–62; Barkey, *Bandits and Bureaucrats*, pp. 51–52. See also Omer Lutfi Barkan and Justin McCarthy, "The Price Revolution of the Sixteenth Century: A Turning Point in the Economic History of the Middle East," *International Journal of Middle East Studies* 6, no. 1 (1975): 3–28.
25. Itzkowitz, *Ottoman Empire*, pp. 89–90; Goldstone, *Revolution and Rebellion*, pp. 363–64.
26. Itzkowitz, *Ottoman Empire*, pp. 92–93.
27. Goldstone, *Revolution and Rebellion*, pp. 365–66.
28. McNeill, *Europe's Steppe Frontier*, pp. 60–61; Itzkowitz, *Ottoman Empire*, p. 91.
29. There were many symptoms of the breakdown of the Ottoman system. At the turn of the seventeenth century, the countryside experienced a series of revolts by bandit armies, many of them composed of demobilized sekban forces, former peasants who had been taught military skills but who could find no employment when they returned to their villages. Some of the bandit armies grew to be as large as twenty thousand men, and the central government lost control of its own territory in central Anatolia in the first decade of the seventeenth century. This phenomenon is the subject of Barkey, *Bandits and Bureaucrats*. See also Itzkowitz, *Ottoman Empire*, pp. 92–93.
30. Itzkowitz, *Ottoman Empire*, pp. 91–92.
31. McNeill, *Europe's Steppe Frontier*, pp. 133–34.

16: CHRISTIANITY UNDERMINES THE FAMILY

1. John Hajnal, "European Marriage Patterns in Perspective," in David V. Glass and D.E.C. Eversley, eds., *Population in History: Essays in Historical Demography* (Chicago: Aldine, 1965).
2. Henry Maine, *Lectures on the Early History of Institutions* (London: John Murray, 1875); and *Early Law and Custom*.
3. Frederick Pollock and Frederic W. Maitland, *The History of English Law Before the Time of Edward I* (Cambridge: Cambridge University Press, 1923).
4. For an overview of this literature, see the introduction by Lawrence Krader to Krader and Paul Vinogradoff, *Anthropology and Early Law: Selected from the Writings of Paul Vinogradoff* (New York: Basic Books, 1966).
5. Maine, *Ancient Law*, chap. 5.
6. See, for example, Peter Laslett, ed., *Household and Family in Past Time* (Cambridge: Cambridge University Press, 1972); and Richard Wall, ed., *Family Forms in Historic Europe* (New York: Cambridge University Press, 1983).

7. Alan MacFarlane, *The Origins of English Individualism* (Oxford: Blackwell, 1978), p. 83.
8. Ibid., p. 95.
9. Ibid., p. 125.
10. Ibid., pp. 131–33.
11. Ibid., p. 142.
12. Ibid.
13. Bloch, *Feudal Society*, pp. 125–27, 131–32.
14. Ibid., pp. 138–39.
15. On the effects of the ending of trade, see Henri Pirenne, *Medieval Cities: Their Origins and the Revival of Trade* (Princeton: Princeton University Press, 1969), pp. 3–25.
16. Bloch, *Feudal Society*, p. 142.
17. Ibid., p. 148.
18. MacFarlane does not purport to explain why individualism developed so early in England. Bloch suggests that the decline of kinship was related to the increases in trade that began in the eleventh century. It is not clear why the latter should be the case, since rising and falling levels of trade were not clearly correlated to the stability of lineages in other parts of the world like China or the Middle East.
19. Jack Goody, *The Development of the Family and Marriage in Europe* (New York: Cambridge University Press, 1983). See also Goody, *The European Family: An Historico-Anthropological Essay* (Malden, MA: Blackwell, 2000).
20. Goody, *The Development of the Family*, p. 39.
21. Ibid., p. 95.
22. Ibid., p. 43.
23. Ibid., p. 105.
24. Jenö Szücs, "Three Historical Regions of Europe: An Outline," in John Keane, ed., *Civil Society and the State: New European Perspectives* (New York: Verso, 1988), p. 302. I am grateful to Gordon Bajnai for this reference.

17: THE ORIGINS OF THE RULE OF LAW

1. For a discussion of meanings of the rule of law, see Judith N. Shklar, "Political Theory and the Rule of Law," in Stanley Hoffmann, ed., *Political Thought and Political Thinkers* (Chicago: University of Chicago Press, 1988).
2. William Blackstone argues that there is a single law of nature, discoverable through reason, which "is binding over all the globe in all countries, and at all times; no human laws are of any validity, if contrary to this." He goes on to argue that religious laws are simply a different version of the universal law of nature, and that "the revealed law is of infinitely more authenticity than that moral system, which is framed by ethical writers, and denominated the natural law." See Blackstone, *Commentaries on the Laws of England* (Philadelphia: Birch and Small, 1803), pp. 41–42.
3. See, for example, Krishna Kumar, ed., *Postconflict Elections, Democratization, and International Assistance* (Boulder, CO: Lynne Rienner, 1998).
4. For an overview of this literature, see Stephan Haggard, Andrew MacIntyre, and Lydia Tiede, "The Rule of Law and Economic Development," *Annual Review of Political Sci-*

ence 11 (2008): 205–34. See also Stephen Knack and Philip Keefer, "Institutions and Economic Performance: Cross-Country Tests Using Alternative Measures," *Economics and Politics* 7 (1995): 207–27; Philip Keefer, *A Review of the Political Economy of Governance: From Property Rights to Voice* (Washington, D.C.: World Bank Institute Working Paper 3315, 2004); Daniel Kaufmann, Aart Kraay, and Massimo Mastruzzi, *Governance Matters IV: Governance Indicators for 1996–2004* (Washington, D.C.: World Bank Institute, 2005).

5. Barzel, *Economic Analysis of Property Rights*.
6. Barry Weingast, "The Economic Role of Political Institutions: Market-Preserving Federalism and Economic Development," *Journal of Law, Economics, and Organization* 11 (1995): 1–31.
7. "Good enough" property rights is suggested by Merilee S. Grindle, "Good Enough Governance: Poverty Reduction and Reform in Developing Countries," *Governance* 17, no. 4 (2004): 525–48.
8. Schurmann, "Traditional Property Concepts in China."
9. Douglass North argues that technological innovation will not happen without property rights that permit private returns from innovation that are close to the social returns. See, for example, North, *Structure and Change in Economic History*, pp. 159–60. While this may be true of technology that embeds scientific knowledge in specific products, a great deal of scientific research that produces technological advance has a public goods character that needs to be supported by public institutions. It may also be that property rights in land and chattels may have rather different effects from intellectual property rights (patents, copyright, etc.).
10. Quoted in Alexis de Tocqueville, *Democracy in America*, trans. Harvey C. Mansfield and Delba Winthrop (Chicago: University of Chicago Press, 2000), Vol. II, part 3, chap. 1, p. 537.
11. For a review of current programs to promote the rule of law, see Thomas Carothers, *Promoting the Rule of Law Abroad: In Search of Knowledge* (Washington, D.C.: Carnegie Endowment, 2006).
12. Friedrich A. Hayek, *Law, Legislation and Liberty* (Chicago: University of Chicago Press, 1976), 1:72.
13. This argument was the basis for the attack made by Hayek and the economist Ludwig von Mises on socialist central planning in the 1930s and '40s. See Friedrich A. Hayek, "The Use of Knowledge in Society," *American Economic Review* 35, no. 4 (1945): 519–30. See also *Fatal Conceit: The Errors of Socialism* (Chicago: University of Chicago Press, 1988).
14. Hayek, *Law, Legislation and Liberty*, pp. 72–74.
15. Ibid., p. 85.
16. See, for example, Rafael La Porta, Florencio Lopez-de-Silanes, Andrei Shleifer, and Robert W. Vishny, "Legal Determinants of External Finance," *Journal of Political Economy* 52 (1997): 1131–50; and "Law and Finance," *Journal of Political Economy* 106 (1998): 1113–55. This literature has sparked a large debate. It is not clear that common law systems provide clear advantages over civil law ones with regard to economic growth. Hayek himself, though preferring common law, noted that the Justinian Code on

which civil law systems were based was itself the product of incremental accumulation of decisions by Roman jurists. It is easy in the end to overstate the differences between these systems. See Hayek (1976), p. 83.

17. J.G.A. Pocock, "Burke and the Ancient Constitution—A Problem in the History of Ideas," *Historical Journal* 3, no. 2 (1960): 125–43.

18. Robert C. Ellickson, *Order Without Law: How Neighbors Settle Disputes* (Cambridge, MA: Harvard University Press, 1991).

19. For a critique of Hayek, see Shklar, "Political Theory and the Rule of Law."

20. For background, see Richard E. Messick, "The Origins and Development of Courts," *Judicature* 85, no. 4 (2002): 175–81. Some people define law as rules enforceable by third parties, in which case law as such does not exist in a tribal society. I will nonetheless continue to refer to tribal law.

21. Harold J. Berman, *Law and Revolution: The Formation of the Western Legal Tradition* (Cambridge, MA: Harvard University Press, 1983), p. 54.

22. Ibid., p. 56.

23. Quoted in Bloch, *Feudal Society*, p. 113.

24. Pollock and Maitland, *The History of English Law*, p. 184.

25. Joseph R. Strayer, *On the Medieval Origins of the Modern State* (Princeton: Princeton University Press, 1970), pp. 29–30; Martin M. Shapiro, *Courts: A Comparative and Political Analysis* (Chicago: University of Chicago Press, 1981), p. 74.

26. Paul Brand, "The Formation of the English Legal System, 1150–1400," in Antonio Padoa-Schioppa, ed., *Legislation and Justice* (New York: Clarendon Press, 1997), p. 107.

27. Ibid., p. 108.

28. On this point, see Arthur T. von Mehren, *The Civil Law System: Cases and Materials for the Comparative Study of Law* (Boston: Little, Brown, 1957), pp. 7–11.

29. Strayer, *Medieval Origins of the Modern State*, pp. 26–31.

30. Brand, "Formation of the English Legal System," p. 104.

31. Maine, *Early Law and Custom*, pp. 296–328. In fact, the French state during the eighteenth century had increasingly supported peasant legal claims against the local seigneurs, eroding even this aristocratic privilege. As Tocqueville suggests, this led to a corresponding rise of peasant expectations that fed the anger they felt at remaining inequalities. See Hilton Root, *Peasants and King in Burgundy: Agrarian Foundations of French Absolutism* (Berkeley: University of California Press, 1987), pp. 20–21.

32. See Tom R. Tyler, *Why People Obey the Law* (New Haven: Yale University Press, 1990).

33. Pollock and Maitland, *The History of English Law*, p. 182.

34. Martin Shapiro argues that English judicial independence has always been exaggerated, and that the English have always had a countervailing belief in the unified sovereignty of the king in Parliament. See Shapiro, *Courts*, pp. 65–67.

18: THE CHURCH BECOMES A STATE

1. Norman F. Cantor, *The Civilization of the Middle Ages*, rev. ed. (New York: Harper, 1993), pp. 86–87.

2. Berman, *Law and Revolution*, p. 91.

3. Ibid., p. 88.

4. Already in the late ninth century, Frankish ecclesiastics had begun to argue that Christian kingship was based on a delegation of the right to rule as a "vicar of God." They sought to divest kingship of the religious authority it enjoyed under rulers like Charlemagne and to locate religious legitimacy in the church alone. The involvement of priests and bishops in politics was highly corrupting and provoked a series of reform movements in the tenth and eleventh centuries. The first of these was the Clunaic movement, named after the Abbey of Cluny in southern France, which for the first time united like-minded monasteries across Europe into a single, hierarchical order. The Clunaic movement promoted the idea of the Peace of God, under which Christians were enjoined from committing acts of violence or warfare against clerics, pilgrims, merchants, Jews, women, or peasants. Wilfred L. Warren, *The Governance of Norman and Angevin England, 1086–1272* (Stanford: Stanford University Press, 1987), pp. 15–16.

5. For background, see Cantor, *Civilization of the Middle Ages*, pp. 249–65.

6. This case was laid out not just by the Clunaic movement but also in works such as Humbert of Moyenmoutier's *Three Books Against the Simoniacs*, published in 1058 before Gregory's papacy, that denounced the buying and selling of offices. James R. Sweeney, "Review of Harold Berman, *Law and Revolution*," *Journal of Law and Religion* 2, no. 1 (1984): 201.

7. Berman, *Law and Revolution*, pp. 89–90.

8. There was a precedent for this in Pope Gelasius's excommunication of the patriarch of Constantinople for being too subservient to the emperor. See Cantor, *Civilization of the Middle Ages*, p. 86.

9. Strayer, *Medieval Origins of the Modern State*, pp. 21–22.

10. Harold J. Berman, *Faith and Order: The Reconciliation of Law and Religion* (Atlanta: Scholars Press, 1993), p. 40.

11. The Roman law had been developed since the time of the late Republic by a class of men known as jurisconsults, who were professional legal specialists and the precursors of modern judges. While the Code was used in the Byzantine Empire, an authoritative text had been lost in most parts of Western Europe for many centuries. Cantor, *Civilization of the Middle Ages*, pp. 125–26.

12. Mary Ann Glendon, Michael W. Gordon, and Paolo G. Carozza, *Comparative Legal Traditions* (St. Paul, MN: West Publishing, 1999), p. 19. The achievement of the Code was to slim down and make consistent the massive body of earlier Roman law. See Shapiro, *Courts*, pp. 128–30.

13. The university constituted a new model of teaching where relatively wealthy students supported their professors through fees. Their control over teaching methods and subject matter should be a matter of envy for later generations of students unhappy with their professors. Berman, *Law and Revolution*, pp. 123–27.

14. Strayer, *Medieval Origins of the Modern State*, pp. 25–26; Glendon, Gordon, and Carozza, *Comparative Legal Traditions*, p. 25.

15. Shapiro, *Courts*, p. 131.

16. Glendon, Gordon, and Carozza, *Comparative Legal Traditions*, p. 24.

17. Ibid., pp. 22–23.

18. Harold J. Berman, "Religious Foundations of Law in the West: An Historical Perspective," *Journal of Law and Religion* 1, no. 1 (1983): 9.

19. Udo Wolter, "The *officium* in Medieval Ecclesiastical Law as a Prototype of Modern Administration," in Padoa-Schioppa, *Legislation and Justice*, p. 31.

20. Strayer, *Medieval Origins of the Modern State*, p. 34.

21. See Harold J. Berman, "Some False Premises of Max Weber's Sociology of Law," in Berman, *Faith and Order*, pp. 244–50.

22. Thomas Ertman, *Birth of the Leviathan: Building States and Regimes in Medieval and Early Modern Europe* (New York: Cambridge University Press, 1997), pp. 53–54.

23. Strayer, *Medieval Origins of the Modern State*, pp. 42–43.

24. David Harris Sacks, "The Paradox of Taxation," in Philip T. Hoffman and Kathryn Norberg, eds., *Fiscal Crises, Liberty, and Representative Government* (Stanford: Stanford University Press, 1994), p. 15.

25. Strayer, *Medieval Origins of the Modern State*, p. 46.

26. Lincoln in his debates with Stephen Douglas argued that the Constitution was based on the principle of equality enunciated in the Declaration of Independence, which limited the ability of even properly constituted democratic majorities to make some men slaves of others. Douglas by contrast argued that there was no principle higher than democracy that could decide such issues. See Harry V. Jaffa, *Crisis of the House Divided: An Interpretation of the Lincoln-Douglas Debates* (Seattle: University of Washington Press, 1959).

27. Modern constitutions refer to universal principles like natural or human rights, but they also require democratic ratification and don't fully confront the issue of how the two are to be reconciled in cases when they conflict.

28. See Tom Ginsburg, "Introduction: The Decline and Fall of Parliamentary Sovereignty," in Ginsburg, ed., *Judicial Review in New Democracies: Constitutional Courts in Asian Cases* (New York: Cambridge University Press, 2003).

29. For example, Christianity was imposed on the indigenous populations of the western hemisphere by conquest and violence. Contemporary Catholicism in countries with large indigenous populations, such as Mexico and Peru, is a syncretic mixture of Christian and pagan practices, like the celebration of the Day of the Dead. It nonetheless still makes sense to think of them as historically Catholic countries.

19: THE STATE BECOMES A CHURCH

1. John W. Head, "Codes, Cultures, Chaos, and Champions: Common Features of Legal Codification Experiences in China, Europe, and North America," *Duke Journal of Comparative and International Law* 13, no. 1 (2003): 1–38. See also Shapiro, *Courts*, pp. 169–81.

2. For background, see J. Duncan M. Derrett, *Religion, Law, and the State in India* (London: Faber, 1968), chaps. 3–4.

3. See Richard W. Lariviere, "Justices and Panditas: Some Ironies in Contemporary Readings of the Hindu Legal Past," *Journal of Asian Studies* 48, no. 4 (1989): 757–69.

4. J. Duncan M. Derrett, *History of Indian Law (Dharmasastra)* (Leiden: E. J. Brill, 1973).

5. Lariviere, "Justices and Panditas," pp. 763–64.

6. Alfred Stepan and Graeme Robertson note that the real deficit in liberal democracy lies more in the Arab world than in the Muslim world more generally. See Alfred C. Stepan and Graeme B. Robertson, "An 'Arab' More Than a 'Muslim' Democracy Gap," *Journal of Democracy* 14, no. 3 (2003): 30–44.

7. Bernard Lewis, "Politics and War," pp. 165–66.

8. Ibid., p. 168.

9. Noah Feldman, *The Fall and Rise of the Islamic State* (Princeton: Princeton University Press, 2008), pp. 37–38.

10. The limits of the caliph's authority were made evident whenever one tried to intervene too far into politics. The Bahri Mamluk sultanate had transferred the Abbasid caliph from Baghdad to Cairo, where he played a relatively minor role in legitimating Mamluk sultans. Toward the end of the sultanate, the caliph al-Mutawakkil III got involved in anti-Circassian intrigues, for which he was deposed and then later reinstated. His son al-Mustain was used by the emirs for their own purposes, but then he was deposed as caliph, as was another successor, al-Qaim, who participated in an attempted coup. Jean-Claude Garcin, "The Regime of the Circassian Mamluks," in Petry, ed.

11. Inalcik, *The Ottoman Empire*, p. 70.

12. Wael B. Hallaq, *The Origins and Evolution of Islamic Law* (New York: Cambridge University Press, 2005), pp. 75–80. Max Weber asserted that the kadi sat in the marketplace and rendered decisions on a completely subjective basis, without any reference to formal rules or norms. They were for Weber the archetype of substantive irrationality in his taxonomy of legal systems. In fact, the kadis operated on the basis of case law and precedent in a manner similar to European judges. The problem was that Muslim law had not undergone the kind of synthesis and systematization that happened to both canon and secular law in Europe after the Gregorian reform. The imprecision of the underlying law added significantly to the discretionary powers of the individual judge. See Inalcik, *The Ottoman Empire*, p. 75; and Max Rheinstein, "Introduction," in Max Weber, *Max Weber on Law in Economy and Society* (Cambridge, MA: Harvard University Press, 1954), p. xlviii.

13. Lybyer, *The Government of the Ottoman Empire*, pp. 36–37.

14. Feldman, *The Fall and Rise of the Islamic State*, pp. 50–52. To this day, the government of the Turkish Republic tightly controls the Muslim religious establishment.

15. "Binding constraint" is taken from Dani Rodrik, Ricardo Hausmann, and Andres Velasco, "Growth Diagnostics," in Narcís Serra and Joseph E. Stiglitz, eds., *The Washington Consensus Reconsidered* (New York: Oxford University Press, 2008). There were many other constraints on the emergence of sustained economic growth in the Muslim world beyond poor property rights. Perhaps the most important was a growing intellectual unwillingness to engage in public debate over the social system itself as it was being overtaken by the West, particularly after the conflict with the Safavids at the end of the seventeenth century. For an overview of theories of how Islam relates to economic backwardness, see Timur Kuran, *Islam and Mammon: The Economic Predicaments of Islamism* (Princeton: Princeton University Press, 2004), pp. 128–47.

16. Inalcik, *The Ottoman Empire*, p. 75.

17. Timur Kuran, "The Provision of Public Goods Under Islamic Law: Origins, Impact and Limitations of the Waqf System," *Law and Society* 35 (2001): 841–97.
18. Derrett, *History of Indian Law*, pp. 2–3.
19. Head, "Codes, Cultures, Chaos," pp. 758–60.
20. Muhammad Qasim Zaman, *The Ulama in Contemporary Islam: Custodians of Change* (Princeton: Princeton University Press, 2002), pp. 21–31.
21. Feldman, *The Fall and Rise of the Islamic State*, pp. 62–68.
22. See ibid., pp. 111–17.
23. Shaul Bakhash, *Reign of the Ayatollahs: Iran and the Islamic Revolution* (New York: Basic Books, 1984).

20: ORIENTAL DESPOTISM

1. Denis Twitchett, ed., *The Cambridge History of China*, Vol. 3: *Sui and T'ang China, 589–906, Part I* (New York: Cambridge University Press, 1979), pp. 57–58, 150–51.
2. Ibid., pp. 86–87.
3. For intellectual developments during the Song Dynasty, see James T. C. Liu, *China Turning Inward: Intellectual-Political Changes in the Early Twelfth Century* (Cambridge, MA: Harvard Council on East Asian Studies, 1988).
4. For an overview, see Anatoly M. Khazanov, *Nomads and the Outside World*, 2d ed. (Madison: University of Wisconsin Press, 1994).
5. Frederick W. Mote, *Imperial China 900–1800* (Cambridge, MA: Harvard University Press, 1999), chaps. 2–12, 17–19.
6. Richard L. Davis, *Wind Against the Mountain: The Crisis of Politics and Culture in Thirteenth-Century China* (Cambridge, MA: Harvard Council on East Asian Studies, 1996), p. 4.
7. Angus Maddison, *Chinese Economic Performance in the Long Run*. 2nd. ed., revised and updated: *960–2030 AD* (Paris: OECD Development Centre, 2007), p. 24. Kent Deng puts the figures at forty-three million in 1006 and seventy-seven million in 1330. Deng, "Unveiling China's True Population Statistics."
8. Naito Torajiro, "Gaikatsuteki To-So jidai kan," *Rekishi to chiri* 9, no. 5 (1922): 1–12. Joshua A. Fogel, *Politics and Sinology: The Case of Naito Konan (1866–1934)* (Cambridge, MA: Harvard Council on East Asian Studies, 1984). I am grateful to Professor Demin Tao of Kansai University for background information on Naito.
9. Hisayuki Miyakawa, "An Outline of the Naito Hypothesis and Its Effects on Japanese Studies of China," *Far Eastern Quarterly* 14, no. 4 (1955): 533–52.
10. See, for example, Robert M. Hartwell, "Demographic, Political, and Social Transformations of China, 750–1550," *Harvard Journal of Asiatic Studies* 42, no. 2 (1982): 365–442; and Patricia B. Ebrey and James L. Watson, *Kinship Organization in Late Imperial China 1000–1940* (Berkeley: University of California Press, 1986). Naito is a controversial figure in Chinese historiography due to his association with the Japanese occupation of China. See Fogel, *Politics and Sinology*, pp. xvii–iii.
11. The account of the empress Wu presented here is taken from Twitchett, *Cambridge History of China*, Vol. 3, chaps. 5 and 6.

12. Denis C. Twitchett and Frederick W. Mote, eds., *The Cambridge History of China*, Vol. 8: *The Ming Dynasty, 1368-1644, Part 2* (New York: Cambridge University Press, 1978), p. 18.

13. There were, of course, soothsayers, astrologers, and oracle readers who looked for signs of favor or disfavor in the stars or other natural phenomena. The major dynastic struggles always involved favorable or unfavorable omens, such as a prophecy during the Sui that a new dynasty would be founded by someone with the surname Li. The oracles could themselves be manipulated by political contenders, such as the white stone found in a river that was said to portend the rise of the empress Wu (see Twitchett, *Cambridge History of China*, Vol. 3, p. 302). During the Sui and Tang dynasties, powerful Buddhist and Daoist religious establishments were created, but they never played a role comparable to the religious establishments in other parts of the world.

14. See Twitchett and Michael Loewe, *The Cambridge History of China*, Vol. 1, pp. 726-37.

15. Mote, *Imperial China*, p. 97.

16. Ibid., p. 562.

21: STATIONARY BANDITS

1. Mancur Olson, "Dictatorship, Democracy, and Development," *American Political Science Review* 87, no. 9 (1993): 567-76.

2. See, for example, Bates, *Prosperity and Violence*; Robert Bates, Avner Greif, and Smita Singh, "Organizing Violence," *Journal of Conflict Resolution* 46, no. 5 (2002): 599-628; and North, Weingast, and Wallis, *Violence and Social Orders*.

3. The other part of Olson's theory, that democratic societies tax at lower rates than autocratic ones, is wrong as well. As we will see in chapter 27, the advent of parliamentary accountability in England led to a massive *increase* in the rate of taxation.

4. Quoted in William Theodore de Bary and Irene Bloom, eds., *Sources of Chinese Tradition*, 2d ed. (New York: Columbia University Press, 1999), 1:39.

5. Twitchett and Mote, *Cambridge History of China*, Vol. 8, p. 110; Ray Huang, "Fiscal Administration During the Ming Dynasty," in Charles O. Hucker and Tilemann Grimm, eds., *Chinese Government in Ming Times: Seven Studies* (New York: Columbia University Press, 1969), p. 105.

6. Maddison, *Chinese Economic Performance in the Long Run*, p. 24.

7. Twitchett and Mote, *Cambridge History of China*, p. 131.

8. Huang, "Fiscal Administration During the Ming," p. 82.

9. Twitchett and Mote, *Cambridge History of China*, pp. 128-29.

10. Ibid., pp. 107-109.

11. Ray Huang, *Taxation and Government Finance in Sixteenth-Century Ming China* (New York: Cambridge University Press, 1974), p. 85.

12. Herbert Simon, "Theories of Decision-Making in Economics and Behavioral Science," *American Economic Review* 49 (1959): 253-83; Simon, "A Behavioral Model of Rational Choice," *Quarterly Journal of Economics* 59 (1955): 98-118.

13. The idea that Chinese rulers were "revenue maximizers" projects backward in time modern behavioral assumptions that have no basis in historical fact. Maximization

would require a much higher level of effort on their part, and it was likely to increase their costs substantially in the form of political opposition, peasant uprisings, protests from the bureaucracy, and the like. In the later years of the dynasty, there was strong tax resistance from the wealthy gentry of the rich lower Yangtze region, which led to astounding levels of tax arrearages. The government simply did not exert itself to correct this problem, and in fact announced a reduction in tax rates. Huang, "Fiscal Administration During the Ming," pp. 107–109.

14. Herbert Simon, *Administrative Behavior: A Study of Decision-Making Processes in Administrative Organization* (New York: Free Press, 1957), pp. 180–85.

15. Twitchett and Mote, *Cambridge History of China*, pp. 52–53.

16. Lien-Sheng Yang, "Local Administration," in Hucker and Grimm, *Chinese Government in Ming Times*, p. 4.

17. Twitchett and Mote, *Cambridge History of China*, p. 21.

18. Charles O. Hucker, "Governmental Organization of the Ming Dynasty," *Harvard Journal of Asiatic Studies* 21 (1958): 25.

19. Twitchett and Mote, *Cambridge History of China*, p. 21.

20. Ibid., pp. 32–33.

21. Ibid., p. 38.

22. Ibid., pp. 41–53.

23. Hucker, "Governmental Organization of the Ming Dynasty," p. 28; Twitchett and Mote, *Cambridge History of China*, pp. 104–105.

24. For a more intimate picture of the reign of the Wanli emperor, see Ray Huang, *1587, a Year of No Significance: The Ming Dynasty in Decline* (New Haven: Yale University Press, 1981).

25. Huang, "Fiscal Administration During the Ming," pp. 112–16; Mote, *Imperial China*, pp. 734–35.

26. See Koenraad W. Swart, *Sale of Offices in the Seventeenth Century* (The Hague: Nijhoff, 1949), chapter on China.

27. North, Weingast, and Wallis posit three "doorstep conditions" that facilitate the transition from what they label a "natural" order to an "open access" one: civilian control over the military, rule of law for elites, and "permanently lived" organizations (what other social scientists call institutions). China met all three of these conditions at least as well as many early modern European states that went on to become "open access" orders, if one accepts my contention that China had "good enough" property rights. See *Violence and Social Orders*.

28. David S. Landes, *Revolution in Time: Clocks and the Making of the Modern World*, rev. ed. (Cambridge, MA: Belknap Press, 2000), pp. 15–16, drawing on Joseph Needham, Ling Wang, and Derek de Solla Price, *Heavenly Clockwork: The Great Astronomical Clocks of Medieval China* (Cambridge: Cambridge University Press, 1960).

22: THE RISE OF POLITICAL ACCOUNTABILITY

1. For a discussion, see Francis Fukuyama, "The March of Equality," *Journal of Democracy* 11, no. 1 (2000): 11–17.

2. Tocqueville discusses at length the impact of the changing intellectual climate in France in the late eighteenth century in Alexis de Tocqueville, *The Old Regime and the Revolution*, Vol. One (Chicago: University of Chicago Press, 1998), book III, chap. 1.

3. Herbert Butterfield, *The Whig Interpretation of History* (London: G. Bell, 1931).

4. Otto Hintze, *The Historical Essays of Otto Hintze* (New York: Oxford University Press, 1975); Tilly, *Coercion, Capital, and European States*. The more fully developed form of Tilly's thesis involves the interplay between war and capital as drivers of European state formation.

5. Ertman, *Birth of the Leviathan*.

6. Winfried Schulze, "The Emergence and Consolidation of the 'Tax State,'" in Richard Bonney, ed., *Economic Systems and State Finance* (New York: Oxford University Press, 1995), p. 267.

7. Maddison, *Growth and Interaction in the World Economy*, p. 21.

8. Schulze, "Emergence and Consolidation of the 'Tax State,'" pp. 269–70.

9. Ibid., p. 268.

10. Marjolein 't Hart, "The Emergence and Consolidation of the 'Tax State,'" in Bonney, *Economic Systems and State Finance*, p. 282.

11. Philip T. Hoffman, "Early Modern France, 1450–1700," in Hoffman and Norberg, *Fiscal Crises, Liberty, and Representative Government*, p. 282.

12. For an overview of the organization of the Spanish army, see Geoffrey Parker, *The Army of Flanders and the Spanish Road, 1567–1598: The Logistics of Spanish Victory and Defeat in the Low Countries' Wars* (London: Cambridge University Press, 1972), pp. 21–41.

13. In one of the few explicit scholarly comparisons of European and Chinese state building, Victoria Hui points to this difference as a key weakness in the European approach (Hui, *War and State Formation in Ancient China and Early Modern Europe*, pp. 32, 36). She refers repeatedly to the European failure to engage in state "self-strengthening" as Chinese states did, without explaining why European rulers were constrained from doing so.

14. While this general correlation exists, it is not a perfect predictor of state building. Many European states in this period felt the need for mobilization, in ways that did not correlate well with the objective degree of threat they faced. The Spanish king faced a dynastic rather than an existential threat from his upstart Dutch provinces during the sixteenth century, but this didn't prevent him from bankrupting his kingdom in an ultimately futile effort to keep the Dutch in line. Poland and Hungary, by contrast, did face existential threats from their powerful neighbors and yet failed to spend proportionately as much on military preparations.

23: RENTE SEEKERS

1. Hoffman, "Early Modern France," p. 276.

2. For an overview, see Swart, *Sale of Offices in the Seventeenth Century*.

3. Ertman, *Birth of the Leviathan*, pp. 98–99.

4. Hoffman, "Early Modern France," p. 230; Richard Bonney, *The King's Debts: Finance and Politics in France 1589–1661* (New York: Oxford University Press, 1981), pp. 15–16.

5. A large census, "L'état des paroisses et des feux de 1328" (The State of Parishes and Hearths in 1328), was taken in the fourteenth century.

6. Richard Bonney, "Revenue," in Hoffman and Norberg, *Fiscal Crises, Liberty, and Representative Government*, p. 434. This problem is very common in contemporary developing countries. See the account of the Colombian government's efforts to perform a cadastral survey and property assessment in Albert O. Hirschman, *Journeys Toward Progress: Studies of Economic Policy-Making in Latin America* (New York: Twentieth Century Fund, 1963), pp. 95–158.

7. Hoffman, "Early Modern France," pp. 231–32.

8. Ertman, *Birth of the Leviathan*, pp. 72–73.

9. Hoffman, "Early Modern France," p. 229.

10. Bonney, *The King's Debts*, p. 55.

11. Technically, the old law had required that offices revert to the Crown if the officeholder died within forty days of transferring it to another person; the law introduced by Charles Paulet exempted them from this in return for payment of a small annual fee that came to be known as the paulette. Hoffman, "Early Modern France," pp. 243–44.

12. Swart, *Sale of Offices in the Seventeenth Century*, p. 15.

13. Bonney, *The King's Debts*, pp. 7, 12.

14. See Richard Bonney, "Revenues," in Bonney, *Economic Systems and State Finance*, pp. 424–25; Bonney, *The King's Debts*, p. 14.

15. Bonney, *The King's Debts*, pp. 14–15.

16. Richard Bonney, *Political Change in France Under Richelieu and Mazarin, 1624–1661* (New York: Oxford University Press, 1978), p. 434.

17. Bonney, "Revenue," p. 436n.

18. Tocqueville, *The Old Regime and the Revolution*, pp. 120–21.

19. Bonney, *Political Change in France*, pp. 32–33.

20. Hoffman, "Early Modern France," pp. 228, 280; Bonney, *Political Change in France*, pp. 239–40.

21. Bonney, *Political Change in France*, pp. 52–56.

22. François Furet, *Revolutionary France, 1770–1880* (Malden, MA: Blackwell, 1992), p. 6.

23. Bonney, *Political Change in France*, pp. 71–74; Tocqueville, *The Old Regime*, pp. 122–24.

24. Root, *Peasants and King in Burgundy*, p. 49.

25. Tocqueville, *The Old Regime*, pp. 124–25.

26. Ibid., p. 129.

27. Bonney, *Political Change in France*, pp. 441–42.

28. Kathryn Norberg, "The French Fiscal Crisis of 1788 and the Financial Origins of the Revolution of 1789," in Hoffman and Norberg, *Fiscal Crises, Liberty, and Representative Government*, p. 277.

29. Ibid., pp. 277–79.

30. Furet, *Revolutionary France*, pp. 17–18.

31. Ertman, *Birth of the Leviathan*, pp. 143–44.
32. Furet, *Revolutionary France*, pp. 25–26.
33. Ertman, *Birth of the Leviathan*, pp. 224, 237–38.
34. Tocqueville, *The Old Regime*, pp. 154–55.
35. Ibid., pp. 157, 164.
36. Ibid., pp. 158–63.

24: PATRIMONIALISM CROSSES THE ATLANTIC

1. For 2009, upper middle income status is a GNI per capita of $3,856–$11,905. Latin American and Caribbean countries in this category include Argentina, Brazil, Chile, Colombia, Costa Rica, the Dominican Republic, Grenada, Jamaica, Mexico, Panama, Peru, Uruguay, and Venezuela. Source: World Bank website.
2. See the chapters by James Robinson, Adam Przeworski, and Jorge Dominguez in Francis Fukuyama, ed., *Falling Behind: Explaining the Development Gap Between the United States and Latin America* (New York: Oxford University Press, 2008).
3. Latin America has been notably more democratic than East Asia, both before and after the onset of the third wave. See Francis Fukuyama and Sanjay Marwah, "Comparing East Asia and Latin America: Dimensions of Development," *Journal of Democracy* 11, no. 4 (2000): 80–94.
4. On the decline in inequality in the 2000s in Latin America, see Luis Felipe Lopez-Calva and Nora Lustig, eds., *Declining Inequality in Latin America: A Decade of Progress?* (Washington, D.C.: Brookings Institution Press, 2010).
5. On the general problem of informality, see Hernando De Soto, *The Other Path: The Invisible Revolution in the Third World* (New York: Harper, 1989); and Santiago Levy, *Good Intentions, Bad Outcomes: Social Policy, Informality, and Economic Growth in Mexico* (Washington, D.C.: Brookings Institution Press, 2008).
6. See, for example, the chapter on Chile in Hirschman, *Journeys Toward Progress*, pp. 161–223.
7. An "electoral authoritarian" regime validates itself through elections, but in a highly manipulated process that does not permit a true level playing field for democratic contestation. See Andreas Schedler, "The Menu of Manipulation," *Journal of Democracy* 13, no. 2 (2002): 36–50.
8. Quoted in Henry Kamen, *Spain's Road to Empire: The Making of a World Power 1493–1763* (London: Penguin, 2003), p. 124.
9. Parker, *The Army of Flanders and the Spanish Road*, pp. 118–31.
10. Ibid., pp. 4–9.
11. I.A.A. Thompson, "Castile: Polity, Fiscality, and Fiscal Crisis," in Hoffman and Norberg, *Fiscal Crises, Liberty, and Representative Government*, p. 141.
12. Ertman, *Birth of the Leviathan*, p. 117.
13. Ibid., p. 116.
14. Thompson, "Castile," p. 160.
15. Ibid., p. 161.

16. Alec R. Myers, *Parliaments and Estates in Europe to 1789* (New York: Harcourt, 1975), pp. 59–65.

17. Thompson, "Castile," pp. 145–46. This was not true for the Aragonese Cortes, which had stronger powers and was anchored in free cities and towns. However, Spain never developed a national Cortes for the peninsula as a whole.

18. Ibid., pp. 183–84.

19. Ertman, *Birth of the Leviathan*, pp. 114–15.

20. Swart, *Sale of Offices in the Seventeenth Century*, p. 23.

21. As one observer remarked, "Why should anybody be willing . . . to buy for several thousands of ducats an office of regidor (councilor) to which only a salary of 2000 to 3000 maravedis was attached?" Ibid., p. 26.

22. Ertman, *Birth of the Leviathan*, pp. 118–19.

23. Kamen, *Spain's Road to Empire*, p. 28.

24. Parker, *The Army of Flanders*, chap. 3.

25. Ertman, *Birth of the Leviathan*, p. 120.

26. Thompson, "Castile," pp. 148–49.

27. J. H. Elliott, *Empires of the Atlantic World: Britain and Spain in America, 1492–1830* (New Haven: Yale University Press, 2006), p. 20.

28. Ibid., p. 40.

29. Ibid., p. 127.

30. See Jared Diamond, *Guns, Germs, and Steel: The Fates of Human Societies* (New York: Norton, 1997), pp. 210–12.

31. Kamen, *Spain's Road to Empire*, p. 273. For a detailed description of the conflict between indigenous landowners and ladino settlers in Central America, and the Spanish government's attempts to protect the former, see David Browning, *El Salvador: Landscape and Society* (Oxford: Clarendon Press, 1971), pp. 78–125.

32. Elliott, *Empires of the Atlantic World*, p. 169.

33. Ibid., p. 170.

34. Ibid., p. 175.

35. It also convinced the philosopher Georg F. W. Hegel that the historical process had come to an end.

36. See Hans Rosenberg, *Bureaucracy, Aristocracy, and Autocracy: The Prussian Experience, 1660–1815* (Cambridge, MA: Harvard University Press, 1958); and Hans-Eberhard Mueller, *Bureaucracy, Education, and Monopoly: Civil Service Reforms in Prussia and England* (Berkeley: University of California Press, 1984).

25: EAST OF THE ELBE

1. Jerome Blum, "The Rise of Serfdom in Eastern Europe," *American Historical Review* 62 (1957).

2. Jerome Blum, *The European Peasantry from the Fifteenth to the Nineteenth Century* (Washington, D.C.: Service Center for Teachers of History, 1960), pp. 12–13.

3. Ibid., pp. 15–16.

4. Tocqueville, *The Old Regime and the Revolution*, book II, chaps. 8, 12.
5. Richard Hellie, *Enserfment and Military Change in Muscovy* (Chicago: University of Chicago Press, 1971), pp. 77–92.
6. Blum, *Lord and Peasant in Russia*, p. 370.
7. Pirenne, *Medieval Cities*, pp. 77–105.
8. See Max Weber, *The City* (Glencoe, IL: Free Press, 1958).
9. Szücs, "Three Historical Regions of Europe," in Keane, ed., pp. 310, 313.
10. See László Makkai, "The Hungarians' Prehistory, Their Conquest of Hungary and Their Raids to the West to 955," and "The Foundation of the Hungarian Christian State, 950–1196," in Peter F. Sugar, ed., *A History of Hungary* (Bloomington: Indiana University Press, 1990).
11. László Makkai, "Transformation into a Western-type State, 1196–1301," in Sugar, *A History of Hungary*; Ertman, *Birth of the Leviathan*, p. 271.
12. Denis Sinor, *History of Hungary* (New York: Praeger, 1959), pp. 62–63.
13. János M. Bak, "Politics, Society and Defense in Medieval and Early Modern Hungary," in Bak and Béla K. Király, eds., *From Hunyadi to Rakoczi: War and Society in Late Medieval and Early Modern Hungary* (Brooklyn, NY: Brooklyn College Program on Society and Change, 1982).
14. Unlike the Russian state, where power rested on a firm alliance between the king and the lower gentry, the Hungarian king found himself opposed by this class, as well as by the barons and the church. And unlike the English king, he had no powerful court or incipient royal bureaucracy on which to base his power. Ertman, *Birth of the Leviathan*, pp. 272–73; Makkai, "Transformation to a Western-type State," pp. 24–25.
15. Sinor, *History of Hungary*, pp. 70–71.
16. Thomas Ertman argues that Hungary faced no serious geopolitical pressure until the rise of the Ottomans in the fifteenth century, but it is not certain that this was the case in light of the wars fought by Louis and later kings. Ertman, *Birth of the Leviathan*, pp. 273–76.
17. Pal Engel, "The Age of the Angevins, 1301–1382," in Sugar, *A History of Hungary*, pp. 43–44.
18. C. A. Macartney, *Hungary: A Short History* (Chicago: Aldine, 1962), pp. 46–47.
19. János Bak, "The Late Medieval Period, 1382–1526," in Sugar, *A History of Hungary*, pp. 54–55.
20. On the institutionalization of the Hungarian Diet, see György Bonis, "The Hungarian Federal Diet (13th–18th Centuries)," *Recueils de la société Jean Bodin* 25 (1965): 283–96.
21. Martyn Rady, *Nobility, Land and Service in Medieval Hungary* (New York: Palgrave, 2001), p. 159.
22. Pal Engel, *The Realm of St. Stephen: A History of Medieval Hungary, 895–1526* (London: I. B. Tauris Publishers, 2001), p. 278.
23. Bak, "The Late Medieval Period," p. 65.
24. On the rise of Hunyadi, see Engel, *The Realm of St. Stephen*, pp. 288–305.
25. Ertman, *Birth of the Leviathan*, p. 288.
26. Bak, "The Late Medieval Period," pp. 71–74.
27. Makkai, "Transformation to a Western-type State," pp. 32–33.

28. Blum, "The Rise of Serfdom."
29. Bak, "The Late Medieval Period," pp. 78–79.
30. McNeill, *Europe's Steppe Frontier*, p. 34.

26: TOWARD A MORE PERFECT ABSOLUTISM

1. See Andreas Schedler, *Electoral Authoritarianism: The Dynamics of Unfree Competition* (Boulder, CO: Lynne Rienner, 2006).
2. These rankings come from the 2008 Corruption Perception Index, http://transparency.org/policy_research/surveys_indices/cpi.
3. Nicholas V. Riasanovsky, *A History of Russia* (New York: Oxford University Press, 1963), p. 79.
4. Marquis de Custine, *La Russie en 1839* (Paris: Amyot, 1843).
5. In Mongolia itself, Genghis Khan is today revered as a national hero. But even in Russia there has been a search for the nation's authentic roots that has cast the Mongol period in a better light. See, for example, Jack Weatherford, *Genghis Khan and the Making of the Modern World* (New York: Crown, 2004).
6. For a summary judgment, see Riasanovsky, *A History of Russia*, pp. 70–83.
7. Ibid., p. 116; Sergei Fedorovich Platonov, *History of Russia* (Bloomington: University of Indiana Prints and Reprints, 1964), pp. 101–24.
8. See Hellie, *Enserfment and Military Change in Muscovy*, chap. 2; John P. LeDonne, *Absolutism and Ruling Class: The Formation of the Russian Political Order 1700–1825* (New York: Oxford University Press, 1991), p. 6; Blum, *Lord and Peasant in Russia*, pp. 170–71.
9. As usual, many Soviet historians used a very broad economic definition of feudalism and argued that it existed from Kievan times up to the late nineteenth century. Using a Blochian definition of feudalism, it is clear that there were similarities but also definite differences, and that "Russian social forms often appear to be rudimentary, or at least simpler and cruder, versions of Western models." Riasanovsky, *A History of Russia*, pp. 127–28.
10. Ibid., p. 164.
11. Ibid., p. 257.
12. Blum, *Lord and Peasant in Russia*, pp. 144–46.
13. Riasanovsky, *A History of Russia*, pp. 164–70. According to the English traveler Giles Fletcher, who visited Moscow after Ivan's death, this "pollicy and tyrannous practice (though now it be ceased) hath so troubled that countrey, and filled it so full of grudge and mortall hatred ever since, that it will not be quenched (as it seemeth now) till it burne againe into a civill flame." Quoted in Sergei Fedorovich Platonov, *The Time of Troubles: A Historical Study of the Internal Crises and Social Struggle in 16th- and 17th-Century Muscovy* (Lawrence: University Press of Kansas, 1970), p. 25.
14. This connection was made by Sergei Eisenstein in his movie *Ivan the Terrible*, and by Stalin himself. I am grateful to Donna Orwin for making this point.
15. Riasanovsky, *A History of Russia*, pp. 88–93; Platonov, *History of Russia*, pp. 62–63.
16. Riasanovsky, *A History of Russia*, pp. 209–10.

17. Platonov, *History of Russia*, pp. 100–101.
18. Ibid., p. 132.
19. LeDonne, *Absolutism and Ruling Class*, p. 64.
20. Riasanovsky, *A History of Russia*, pp. 212–13.
21. "A survey of several provinces in 1822 reveals that the internal structure of the army had been transplanted into the provincial administration, with marshals, judges, captains, and sheriffs representing the 'line' (*stroi*), the civilian treasurers and accountants, the noncombatants (*nestroevoi*)." LeDonne, *Absolutism and Ruling Class*, p. 19.
22. Blum, *The End of the Old Order in Rural Europe*, pp. 202–203.
23. Riasanovsky, *A History of Russia*, pp. 205–206.
24. Blum, *The End of the Old Order in Rural Europe*, pp. 247–68.
25. LeDonne, *Absolutism and Ruling Class*, p. 6.
26. Riasanovsky, *A History of Russia*, pp. 256–58.
27. Blum, *The End of the Old Order in Rural Europe*, p. 203.
28. LeDonne, *Absolutism and Ruling Class*, p. 20.

27: TAXATION AND REPRESENTATION

1. See MacFarlane, *The Origins of English Individualism*; Warren, *The Governance of Norman and Angevin England*, pp. 1–9; Richard Hodges, *The Anglo-Saxon Achievement: Archaeology and the Beginnings of English Society* (Ithaca, NY: Cornell University Press, 1989), pp. 186–202.
2. I am grateful to Jørgen Møller for pointing this out.
3. Frederic W. Maitland, *The Constitutional History of England* (Cambridge: Cambridge University Press, 1961), p. 40.
4. Ibid., p. 42.
5. Ertman, *Birth of the Leviathan*, p. 43.
6. Maitland, *The Constitutional History of England*, p. 43.
7. Ibid., p. 46.
8. Ibid., pp. 49–50.
9. Yoram Barzel posits a different origin of English property rights. He suggests that the English monarch started out as an absolute dictator who came to understand over time that he could maximize his own revenues if he established the state's credibility through an independent third-party enforcer. This is an example of rational-choice economists projecting modern assumptions about behavior backward in time in total disregard of actual historical facts. Yoram Barzel, "Property Rights and the Evolution of the State," *Economics of Governance* 1 (2000): 25–51.
10. Sacks, "The Paradox of Taxation," in Hoffman and Norberg, eds., p. 16.
11. Maitland, *The Constitutional History of England*, pp. 262–63.
12. Ibid., p. 269.
13. See, for example, Christopher Hill, *Puritanism and Revolution: Studies in Interpretation of the English Revolution of the Seventeenth Century* (New York: Schocken, 1958); Lawrence Stone, *The Causes of the English Revolution, 1529–1642* (New York: Harper, 1972).

14. G. E. Aylmer, *Rebellion or Revolution? England, 1640–1660* (New York: Oxford University Press, 1986), pp. 28–32.

15. Weber, *The City*; Pirenne, *Medieval Cities*.

16. In the *Communist Manifesto*, Marx says, "Each step in the development of the bourgeoisie was accompanied by a corresponding political advance of that class. An oppressed class under the sway of the feudal nobility, an armed and self-governing association in the mediaeval commune; here independent urban republic (as in Italy and Germany), there taxable 'third estate' of the monarchy (as in France), afterwards, in the period of manufacture proper, serving either the semi-feudal or the absolute monarchy as a counterpoise against the nobility, and, in fact, corner-stone of the great monarchies in general, the bourgeoisie has at last, since the establishment of Modern Industry and of the world-market, conquered for itself, in the modern representative State, exclusive political sway. The executive of the modern State is but a committee for managing the common affairs of the whole bourgeoisie." Political power is thus for him the consequence and not the cause of this class's economic power.

17. Adam Smith, *An Inquiry into the Nature and Causes of the Wealth of Nations* (Indianapolis: Liberty Classics, 1981), book III, chap. 1.

18. Ibid., part III, chap. 2.

19. Ibid., part III, chap. 3.

20. Ibid., part III, chap. 5.

21. Ertman, *Birth of the Leviathan*, pp. 176–77.

22. Aylmer, *Rebellion or Revolution?*, pp. 5–6.

23. Joel Hurstfield, *Freedom, Corruption and Government in Elizabethan England* (Cambridge, MA: Harvard University Press, 1973), pp. 137–62.

24. Ertman, *Birth of the Leviathan*, p. 184.

25. As in all wars, the back-and-forth fortunes of the two sides was subject to considerable contingency, based on individual acts of heroism, misjudgment, cowardice, or incompetence. The war invites comparison to the Fronde uprising that took place in France more or less contemporaneously, which similarly pitted supporters of the French parlementaires against the forces of Louis XIV. The French monarchy won its struggle while the English one lost; given the role of chance in determining military outcomes, it is easy to imagine the results having been reversed. Would the French state then have gone on to adopt parliamentary government, while the English monarchy consolidated an absolutist state?

Although it is useful to be reminded of the contingency of events that seem inevitable in hindsight, there are nonetheless a number of reasons for thinking that even a parliamentary defeat in the Civil War would not have spelled the end of representative government in England. The parliamentary side in the Civil War was far more cohesive and represented a much broader section of English society than the Frondeurs. Indeed, the Fronde itself was divided into two phases, a Fronde of the parlementaires and the Fronde of the nobles, who from the beginning failed to work together effectively. The French parlementaires were squabbling individuals seeking to protect their families' privileges and had none of the corporate consciousness or internal discipline of the English parliamentarians. Moreover, the parliamentary side was in effect finally defeated after Oliver Cromwell's death and the collapse of the Protectorate in 1660, yet the restored monarchy lasted only another eighteen years until it was in turn over-thrown in the Glorious Revolution. This suggests that the evolution of English politi-cal institutions was not simply subject to the chance fortunes of war.

26. G. E. Aylmer, *The Crown's Servants: Government and Civil Service Under Charles II, 1660–1685* (New York: Oxford University Press, 2002), pp. 213–19.

27. Ertman, *Birth of the Leviathan*, pp. 196–97.

28. Huntington, *The Third Wave*, p. 65.

29. The religious dimensions of the crisis were very complex. The fundamental divide in England in this period was not between Protestants and Catholics but between High Church Anglicans—represented before the Civil War by Archbishop Laud—and dis-senting Protestants including the Congregationalists and Quakers. The former were often suspected by the latter of being sympathetic to Catholic practices and interests; the Dissenters' rights were restricted after the Restoration. The balance between the two groups was altered with the accession of the Calvinist William, weakening the High Churchmen and strengthening the position of the Dissenters. One of William's motives for seeking the English throne was to end any possibility of an English-French alliance against the Netherlands.

30. See John Miller, *The Glorious Revolution*, 2d ed. (New York: Longman, 1997); Eveline Cruickshanks, *The Glorious Revolution* (New York: St. Martin's Press, 2000).

31. Locke was living in exile in the Netherlands after 1683 and returned to England with William of Orange's wife in 1689. The two *Treatises* were published in late 1689, though they may have been written considerably earlier.

32. Sacks, "Paradox of Taxation," p. 33.

33. Ibid., pp. 34–35.

34. Douglass North and Barry Weingast have argued that the Glorious Revolution solved the problem of governments credibly committing to secure property rights by setting up an institutional system from which none of the parties could profitably defect. Doug-lass C. North and Barry R. Weingast, "Constitutions and Commitment: The Evolution of Institutions Governing Public Choice in Seventeenth-Century England," *Journal of Economic History* 49, no. 4 (1989): 803–32. Most of the statistics North and Weingast cite to bolster their case that the Glorious Revolution had a positive effect on growth are actu-ally about growth of public borrowing; their empirical evidence for positive increases in economic growth rates traceable to the constitutional settlement is much sketchier.

35. I have already noted Mancur Olson's theory of "stationary bandits" in traditional soci-eties who seek to extract as much as they can in tax revenues, up to a point where further taxes become self-defeating. Olson went on to argue that after the Glorious Revolution and the advent of democracy, tax rates should have fallen, since rulers who were held accountable to the population as a whole would be prevented from extract-ing such high levels of taxes. Olson, "Dictatorship, Democracy, and Development."

36. Figures taken from Ertman, *Birth of the Leviathan*, p. 220. See also John Brewer, *The Sinews of Power: War, Money, and the English State, 1688–1783* (Cambridge, MA: Har-vard University Press, 1990).

37. North and Weingast argue that the constitutional settlement of 1688–1689 locked in

secure property rights because it created an equilibrium from which neither of the parties—king or Parliament—could deviate without seriously harming their own interests. It is not the form of the settlement so much as the relative power and coherence of the contracting parties that underpinned its durability. Any number of countries have adopted English-style constitutions that vest tax and legislative authority in a parliament that shares power with an executive, yet this has not prevented ambitious rulers from subsequently violating the agreement and violating citizens' property rights. What made the English settlement durable was solidarity of the Commons and the fact that it was balanced by a strong state. That solidarity was due, as argued earlier in the chapter, on much earlier precedents like local government, social structure, and law.

38. Alexandre Kojève, *Introduction to the Reading of Hegel*, trans. James H. Nichols Jr. (New York: Basic Books, 1969).

39. See Walter Russell Mead, *God and Gold: Britain, America, and the Making of the Modern World* (New York: Knopf, 2007); and Michael Mandelbaum, *The Ideas That Conquered the World: Peace, Democracy, and Free Markets in the Twenty-First Century* (New York: Public Affairs, 2002).

28: WHY ACCOUNTABILITY? WHY ABSOLUTISM?

1. The greater sense of national community fostered by broad-ranging political participation is reflected in the contrast between the Magna Carta and the Golden Bull. The Golden Bull was driven not by barons but by the class of royal soldiers and castle guardians who wanted protection from the barons. The English barons claimed to speak on behalf of the whole national community, including the church and ordinary Englishmen, and demanded constitutional protections for their rights. The Hungarian gentry promoting the Golden Bull, by contrast, were primarily interested in protecting their own sectional interests. They, like the French and Russian aristocracy, understood liberty to be a privilege rather than a general condition of citizenship, and when they took care of themselves, they had little interest in defending the rights of anyone else. Sacks, "Paradox of Taxation," p. 15.

2. For an account of this period, see Ronald Hutton, *The Restoration: A Political and Religious History of England and Wales, 1658–1667* (New York: Oxford University Press, 1985).

3. See Gert and Gunnar Svendsen, "Social Capital and the Welfare State," in Michael Böss, ed., *The Nation-State in Transformation* (Aarhus, Denmark: Aarhus University Press, 2010).

4. Kenneth E. Miller, *Government and Politics in Denmark* (Boston: Houghton Mifflin, 1968), p. 23.

5. For a description of the medieval peasant economy in neighboring Sweden, see Eli F. Heckscher, *An Economic History of Sweden* (Cambridge, MA: Harvard University Press, 1954), pp. 25–29.

6. Thomas K. Derry, *A History of Scandinavia: Norway, Sweden, Denmark, Finland and Iceland* (Minneapolis: University of Minnesota Press, 1979), pp. 90–91.

7. See Bonney, "Revenues," p. 452.

8. Ove Korsgaard, *The Struggle for the People: Five Hundred Years of Danish History in Short* (Copenhagen: Danish School of Education Press, 2008), pp. 21–26.

9. Miller, *Government and Politics in Denmark*, p. 26; Nils Andren, *Government and Politics in the Nordic Countries* (Stockholm: Almqvist and Wiksell, 1964), p. 29.

10. Uffe Østergård, "Denmark: A Big Small State: The Peasant Roots of Danish Modernity," in John Campbell, John A. Hall, and Ove K. Pedersen, eds., *National Identity and the Varieties of Capitalism: The Danish Experience* (Kingston, Ontario: McGill-Queen's University Press, 2006).

11. Harald Westergaard, *Economic Development in Denmark: Before and During the World War* (Oxford: Clarendon Press, 1922), pp. 5–6.

12. Østergård, "Denmark," pp. 76–81; Korsgaard, *The Struggle for the People*, pp. 61–65.

29: POLITICAL DEVELOPMENT AND POLITICAL DECAY

1. On this point, see the critique of rational choice in John J. DiIulio, Jr., "Principled Agents: The Cultural Bases of Behavior in a Federal Government Bureaucracy," *Journal of Public Administration Research and Theory* 4, no. 3 (1994): 277–320.

2. Frank, *Choosing the Right Pond*; and *Luxury Fever* (New York: Free Press, 1999).

3. North, *Structure and Change in Economic History*, pp. 45–58; see also North and Arthur Denzau, "Shared Mental Models: Ideologies and Institutions," *Kyklos* 47, no. 1 (1994): 3–31.

4. Friedrich Hayek understood perhaps better than any other social scientist that it was complexity that distinguished the natural from the social sciences and made it impossible to achieve a positive social science that could approach physics or chemistry in predictive ability. See Bruce Caldwell, *Hayek's Challenge: An Intellectual Biography of F. A. Hayek* (Chicago: University of Chicago Press, 2004).

5. For example, Dawkins, *The God Delusion*, and Hitchens, *God Is Not Great*.

6. Wade, *The Faith Instinct*, pp. 43–45.

7. The classic analysis of the development of religion in social anthropology is James G. Frazer, *The Golden Bough: A Study in Magic and Religion* (New York: Oxford University Press, 1998).

8. See, for example, North, *Structure and Change*, p. 44.

9. Hayek, *Law, Legislation and Liberty*, 1:9–11.

10. Hayek, "The Use of Knowledge in Society."

11. This point is also made in Armen A. Alchian, "Uncertainty, Evolution, and Economic Theory," *Journal of Political Economy* 58 (1950): 211–21.

12. Huntington, *Political Order in Changing Societies*, p. 123.

13. Stephen Jay Gould and R. C. Lewontin, "The Spandrels of San Marco and the Panglossian Program: A Critique of the Adaptationist Programme," *Proceedings of the Royal Society of London* 205 (1979): 581–98.

14. Oscar Handlin and Mary Handlin, "Origins of the American Business Corporation," *Journal of Economic History* 5, no. 1 (1945): 1–23.

15. Huntington, *Political Order in Changing Societies*, p. 12. Douglass North, founder of the New Institutional Economics, defines an institution as "humanly devised constraints

that shape human interaction," meaning that it includes both formal and informal rules. He distinguishes an institution from an organization, which is the embodiment of rules among a specific group of people. The problem with North's definition of an institution is that it is too broad, encompassing everything from the U.S. Constitution to my habits in selecting ripe oranges. Most important, it elides a critical distinction traditionally made between formal institutions like constitutions and legal systems, and informal norms that fall into the realm of culture. Many critical controversies have arisen in social theory as to the relative importance of formal versus informal institutions, but for North and his followers, they are all simply "institutions." Moreover, he does not provide criteria like complexity, adaptability, autonomy, and coherence to measure the degree of institutionalization. Douglass C. North, *Institutions, Institutional Change, and Economic Performance* (New York: Cambridge University Press, 1990), p. 3.

16. Huntington, *Political Order in Changing Societies*, pp. 12–24.

17. Among modern organizations, the Japanese Ministry of Finance is an elite body that recruits classes of new bureaucrats from Japan's most prestigious universities. The ministry has its own vision of how to manage the Japanese economy and at times has manipulated its political bosses rather than being subordinated by them. It is therefore often seen as a paradigmatic case of an autonomous institution. See Peter B. Evans, *Embedded Autonomy: States and Industrial Transformation* (Princeton: Princeton University Press, 1995).

18. Leon Festinger, *A Theory of Cognitive Dissonance* (Stanford, CA: Stanford University Press, 1962). See also Carol Tavris, *Mistakes Were Made (But Not by Me): Why We Justify Foolish Beliefs, Bad Decisions, and Hurtful Acts* (New York: Mariner Books, 2008).

19. This is the argument made about twentieth-century Britain in Mancur Olson, *The Rise and Decline of Nations* (New Haven: Yale University Press, 1982). This book is based on the more general theory of collective action he outlined in *The Logic of Collective Action*.

20. Steven LeBlanc, private conversation.

21. See, for example, Bates, *Prosperity and Violence*; Bates, Greif, and Singh, "Organizing Violence"; North, Weingast, and Wallis, *Violence and Social Orders*.

30: POLITICAL DEVELOPMENT, THEN AND NOW

1. For background, see Nils Gilman, *Mandarins of the Future: Modernization Theory in Cold War America* (Baltimore: Johns Hopkins University Press, 2003), chap. 1. See also Vernon Ruttan, "What Happened to Political Development?" *Economic Development and Cultural Change* 39, no. 2 (1991): 265–92.

2. See, for example, David C. McClelland, *The Achieving Society* (Princeton: Van Nostrand, 1961); Talcott Parsons and Edward A. Shils, eds., *Toward a General Theory of Action* (Cambridge, MA: Harvard University Press, 1951).

3. A more up-to-date version of this argument was made by Huntington's student Fareed Zakaria, who emphasized rule of law in addition to state building as a component of political order. See *The Future of Freedom: Illiberal Democracy at Home and Abroad* (New York: Norton, 2003).

4. See Maddison, *Growth and Interaction in the World Economy*, pp. 12–30. The assertion

of Gregory Clark that there were no increases in productivity from hunter-gatherer times to 1800 is highly implausible. Clark, *A Farewell to Alms*.

5. Livi-Bacci, *A Concise History of World Population*.

6. Maddison, *Growth and Interaction in the World Economy*, p. 9.

7. See, for example, David S. Landes, *The Unbound Prometheus: Technological Change and Industrial Development* (New York: Cambridge University Press, 1969); and Landes, *The Wealth and Poverty of Nations: Why Some Are So Rich and Some So Poor* (New York: Norton, 1998); Nathan Rosenberg and L. E. Birdzell, *How the West Grew Rich* (New York: Basic Books, 1986); North and Thomas, *The Growth of the Western World*; Philippe Aghion and Steven N. Durlauf, eds., *Handbook of Economic Growth*, Vol. 1 (Amsterdam: Elsevier/North Holland, 2005), particularly the chapter by Oded Galor, "From Stagnation to Growth: Unified Growth Theory"; Oded Galor and David N. Weil, "Population, Technology, and Growth: From Malthusian Stagnation to the Demographic Transition and Beyond," *American Economic Review* 90 (2000): 806–28.

8. Massimo Livi-Bacci, *Population and Nutrition: An Essay on European Demographic History* (New York: Cambridge University Press, 1991), p. 12.

9. Livi-Bacci, *Concise History of World Population*, p. 28.

10. See Alan Macfarlane, "The Malthusian Trap," in William A. Darrity Jr., ed., *International Encyclopedia of the Social Sciences*, 2d ed. (New York: Macmillan, 2007).

11. Boserup, *Population and Technological Change*, pp. 63–65. See also Boserup, *Economic and Demographic Relationships in Development* (Baltimore: Johns Hopkins University Press, 1990).

12. Livi-Bacci, *Population and Nutrition*, p. 119.

13. Livi-Bacci, *Concise History of World Population*, p. 36.

14. See Marcus Noland and Stephan Haggard, *Famine in North Korea: Markets, Aid, and Reform* (New York: Columbia University Press, 2007).

15. This is the subject of Jared Diamond, *Collapse: How Societies Choose to Fail or Succeed* (New York: Viking, 2005).

16. Livi-Bacci, *Concise History of World Population*, p. 31; Maddison, *Growth and Interaction in the World Economy*, p. 7.

17. Livi-Bacci, *Concise History of World Population*, p. 31.

18. Livi-Bacci, *Population and Nutrition*, p. 20; Diamond, *Guns, Germs, and Steel*; Boserup, *Population and Technological Change*, pp. 35–36.

19. LeBlanc and Register, *Constant Battles*, pp. 68–71.

20. See Paul Collier, *The Bottom Billion: Why the Poorest Countries Are Failing and What Can Be Done About It* (New York: Oxford University Press, 2007).

21. Knack and Keefer, "Institutions and Economic Performance"; Dani Rodrik and Arvind Subramanian, "The Primacy of Institutions (and what this does and does not mean)," *Finance and Development* 40, no. 2 (2003): 31–34; Kaufmann, Kraay, and Mastruzzi, *Governance Matters IV*.

22. Jeffrey Sachs, *The End of Poverty: Economic Possibilities for Our Time* (New York: Penguin, 2005).

23. See Melissa Thomas, "Great Expectations: Rich Donors and Poor Country Governments," Social Science Research Network working paper, January 27, 2009.

24. Stephen Haber, Noel Maurer, and Armando Razo, *The Politics of Property Rights* (New York: Cambridge University Press, 2003); and Mushtaq H. Khan and Jomo Kwame Sundaram, eds., *Rents, Rent-Seeking and Economic Development: Theory and Evidence in Asia* (New York: Cambridge University Press, 2000).

25. Seymour Martin Lipset, "Some Social Requisites of Democracy: Economic Development and Political Legitimacy," *American Political Science Review* 53 (1959): 69–105; for a review of the literature, see Larry Diamond, "Economic Development and Democracy Reconsidered," *American Behavioral Scientist* 15, nos. 4–5 (1992): 450–99.

26. Robert J. Barro, *Determinants of Economic Growth: A Cross-Country Survey* (Cambridge, MA: MIT Press, 1997).

27. Adam Przeworski et al., *Democracy and Development: Political Institutions and Material Well-Being in the World, 1950–1990* (Cambridge: Cambridge University Press, 2000).

28. Ernest Gellner, *Conditions of Liberty: Civil Society and Its Rivals* (New York: Penguin, 1994).

29. Ibid.

30. For an example, see Sheri Berman, "Civil Society and the Collapse of the Weimar Republic," *World Politics* 49, no. 3 (1997): 401–29.

31. George Gray Molina, "The Offspring of 1952: Poverty, Exclusion and the Promise of Popular Participation," and H. Klein, "Social Change in Bolivia since 1952," in Merilee S. Grindle, ed., *Proclaiming Revolution: Bolivia in Comparative Perspective* (London: Institute of Latin American Studies, 2003).

32. This point is made by Thomas Carothers, "The 'Sequencing' Fallacy," *Journal of Democracy* 18, no. 1 (2007): 12–27; and Marc F. Plattner, "Liberalism and Democracy," *Foreign Affairs* 77, no. 2 (1998): 171–80.

33. Juan J. Linz and Alfred Stepan, eds., *The Breakdown of Democratic Regimes: Europe* (Baltimore: Johns Hopkins University Press, 1978).

34. On the general problem of inequality in Latin America and its relationship to democratic stability, see Fukuyama, *Falling Behind*.

35. See Jung-En Woo, *Race to the Swift: State and Finance in Korean Industrialization* (New York: Columbia University Press, 1991).

36. See Alexander Gerschenkron, *Economic Backwardness in Historical Perspective* (Cambridge, MA: Harvard University Press, 1962).

37. Wriston, *The Twilight of Sovereignty*.

38. See Moses Naim, *Illicit: How Smugglers, Traffickers, and Copycats Are Hijacking the Global Economy* (New York: Doubleday, 2005).

BIBLIOGRAPHY

Aghion, Philippe, and Steven N. Durlauf, eds. 2005. *Handbook of Economic Growth*, Vol. 1. Amsterdam: Elsevier/North Holland.

Alchian, Armen A. 1950. "Uncertainty, Evolution, and Economic Theory." *Journal of Political Economy* 58:211–21.

Alexander, Richard D. 1974. "The Evolution of Social Behavior." *Annual Review of Ecology and Systematics* 5:325–85.

———. 1990. *How Did Humans Evolve?: Reflections on the Uniquely Unique Species.* Ann Arbor: University of Michigan Press.

Allen, Robert C. 1997. "Agriculture and the Origins of the State in Ancient Egypt." *Explorations in Economic History* 34:135–54.

Amitai-Preiss, Reuven. 1995. *Mongols and Mamluks: The Mamluk-Ilkhanid War: 1260–1281.* New York: Cambridge University Press.

Anderson, Terry L., ed. 1991. *Property Rights and Indian Economies.* Lanham, MD: Rowman and Littlefield.

Andren, Nils. 1964. *Government and Politics in the Nordic Countries.* Stockholm: Almqvist and Wiksell.

Axelrod, Robert. 1984. *The Evolution of Cooperation.* New York: Basic Books.

Ayalon, David. 1956. *Gunpowder and Firearms in the Mamluk Kingdom: A Challenge to a Mediaeval Society.* London: Vallentine, Mitchell.

———. 1988. *Outsiders in the Lands of Islam: Mamluks, Mongols, and Eunuchs.* London: Variorum.

———. 1994. *Islam and the Abode of War: Military Slaves and Islamic Adversaries.* Brookfield, VT: Variorum.

Aylmer, G. E. 1986. *Rebellion or Revolution? England, 1640–1660.* New York: Oxford University Press.

———. 2002. *The Crown's Servants: Government and Civil Service Under Charles II, 1660–1685*. New York: Oxford University Press.

Bak, János M., and Béla K. Király, eds. 1982. *From Hunyadi to Rakoczi: War and Society in Late Medieval and Early Modern Hungary*. Brooklyn, NY: Brooklyn College Program on Society and Change.

Baker, Hugh. 1979. *Chinese Family and Kinship*. New York: Columbia University Press.

Bakhash, Shaul. 1984. *Reign of the Ayatollahs: Iran and the Islamic Revolution*. New York: Basic Books.

Balazs, Étienne. 1964. *Chinese Civilization and Bureaucracy: Variations on a Theme*. New Haven: Yale University Press.

Barkan, Omer Lutfi, and Justin McCarthy. 1975. "The Price Revolution of the Sixteenth Century: A Turning Point in the Economic History of the Middle East." *International Journal of Middle East Studies* 6(1):3–28.

Barkey, Karen. 1994. *Bandits and Bureaucrats: The Ottoman Route to State Centralization*. Ithaca: Cornell University Press.

Barkow, Jerome H., Leda Cosmides, and John Tooby, eds. 1992. *The Adapted Mind: Evolutionary Psychology and the Generation of Culture*. New York: Oxford University Press.

Barro, Robert J. 1997. *Determinants of Economic Growth: A Cross-Country Survey*. Cambridge, MA: MIT Press.

Barzel, Yoram. 1989. *Economic Analysis of Property Rights*. New York: Cambridge University Press.

———. 2000. "Property Rights and the Evolution of the State." *Economics of Governance* 1:25–51.

Basham, Arthur L. 1954. *The Wonder That Was India: A Survey of the Culture of the Indian Sub-Continent Before the Coming of the Muslims*. London: Sidgwick and Jackson.

Bassett, Thomas J., and Donald E. Crummey. 1993. *Land in African Agrarian Systems*. Madison: University of Wisconsin Press.

Bastin, Rohan. 2004. "Death of the Indian Social." *Social Analysis* 48(3):205–13.

Bates, Robert H. 1983. *Essays on the Political Economy of Rural Africa*. New York: Cambridge University Press.

———. 2001. *Prosperity and Violence*. Cambridge, MA: Harvard University Press.

Bates, Robert, Avner Greif, and Smita Singh. 2002. "Organizing Violence." *Journal of Conflict Resolution* 46(5):599–628.

Bateson, P.P.G., and R. A. Hinde, eds. 1976. *Growing Points in Ethology*. New York: Cambridge University Press.

Becker, Gary S. 1993. "Nobel Lecture: The Economic Way of Looking at Behavior." *Journal of Political Economy* 101(3):385–409.

Beller, Emily, and Michael Hout. 2006. "Intergeneration Social Mobility: The United States in Comparative Perspective." *Future of Children* 16(2):19–36.

Berend, Nora. 2001. *At the Gate of Christendom: Jews, Muslims and "Pagans" in Medieval Hungary, c. 1000–c. 1300*. New York: Cambridge University Press.

Berman, Harold J. 1983. *Law and Revolution: The Formation of the Western Legal Tradition*. Cambridge, MA: Harvard University Press.

———. 1983. "Religious Foundations of Law in the West: An Historical Perspective." *Journal of Law and Religion* 1(1):3–43.

———. 1993. *Faith and Order: The Reconciliation of Law and Religion*. Atlanta: Scholars Press.

Berman, Sheri. 1997. "Civil Society and the Collapse of the Weimar Republic." *World Politics* 49(3):401–29.

Birdsall, Nancy, and Francis Fukuyama, eds. 2011. *New Ideas in Development After the Financial Crisis*. Baltimore: Johns Hopkins University Press.

Blackstone, William. 1803. *Commentaries on the Laws of England*. Philadelphia: Birch and Small.

Bloch, Marc. 1968. *Feudal Society*. Chicago: University of Chicago Press.

Blum, Jerome. 1957. "The Rise of Serfdom in Eastern Europe." *American Historical Review* 62:807–36.

———. 1960. *The European Peasantry from the Fifteenth to the Nineteenth Century*. Washington, D.C.: Service Center for Teachers of History.

———. 1961. *Lord and Peasant in Russia, from the Ninth to the Nineteenth Century*. Princeton: Princeton University Press.

———. 1978. *The End of the Old Order in Rural Europe*. Princeton: Princeton University Press.

———. 1981. "Review: English Parliamentary Enclosure." *Journal of Modern History* 53(3): 477–504.

Bonis, György. 1965. "The Hungarian Feudal Diet (13th–18th Centuries)." *Recueils de la Société Jean Bodin* 25:287–307.

Bonney, Richard. 1978. *Political Change in France Under Richelieu and Mazarin, 1624–1661*. New York: Oxford University Press.

———. 1981. *The King's Debts: Finance and Politics in France 1589–1661*. New York: Oxford University Press.

———, ed. 1995. *Economic Systems and State Finance*. New York: Oxford University Press.

Boserup, Ester. 1981. *Population and Technological Change*. Chicago: University of Chicago Press.

———. 1990. *Economic and Demographic Relationships in Development*. Baltimore: Johns Hopkins University Press.

Böss, Michael, ed. 2010. *The Nation-State in Transformation: Economic Globalization, Institutional Mediation and Political Values*. Aarhus, Denmark: Aarhus University Press.

Brewer, John. 1990. *The Sinews of Power: War, Money, and the English State, 1688–1783*. Cambridge, MA: Harvard University Press.

Brook, Timothy, ed. 1989. *The Asiatic Mode of Production in China*. Armonk, NY: M. E. Sharpe.

Brown, Elizabeth A. R. 1974. "The Tyranny of a Construct: Feudalism and Historians of Medieval Europe." *American Historical Review* 79(4):1063–88.

Browning, David. 1971. *El Salvador: Landscape and Society*. Oxford: Clarendon Press.

Butterfield, Herbert. 1931. *The Whig Interpretation of History*. London: G. Bell.

Caldwell, Bruce. 2004. *Hayek's Challenge: An Intellectual Biography of F. A. Hayek*. Chicago: University of Chicago Press.

Campbell, John, John A. Hall, and Ove K. Pedersen, eds. 2006. *National Identity and the Varieties of Capitalism: The Danish Experience*. Kingston, Ontario: McGill–Queen's University Press.

Cantor, Norman F. 1993. *The Civilization of the Middle Ages*. Rev. ed. New York: Harper.

Carneiro, Robert L. 1970. "A Theory of the Origin of the State." *Science* 169:733–38.

———. 1986. "On the Relationship Between Size of Population and Complexity of Social Organization." *Journal of Anthropological Research* 42(3):355–64.

Carothers, Thomas. 2002. "The End of the Transition Paradigm." *Journal of Democracy* 13(1):5–21.

———. 2006. *Promoting the Rule of Law Abroad: In Search of Knowledge*. Washington, D.C.: Carnegie Endowment.

———. 2007. "The 'Sequencing' Fallacy." *Journal of Democracy* 18(1):12–27.

Chambers, James. 1979. *The Devil's Horsemen: The Mongol Invasion of Europe*. New York: Atheneum.

Chang, Kwang-chih. 1983. *Art, Myth, and Ritual: The Path to Political Authority in Ancient China*. Cambridge, MA: Harvard University Press.

——— et al. 2005. *The Formation of Chinese Civilization: An Archaeological Perspective*. New Haven: Yale University Press.

Chao, Paul. 1983. *Chinese Kinship*. Boston: Routledge.

Chen, Shaohua, and Martin Ravallion. 2007. "Absolute Poverty Measures for the Developing World, 1981–2004." Washington, D.C.: World Bank Policy Research Working Paper WPS4211.

Chesterman, Simon, Michael Ignatieff, and Ramesh Thakur, eds. 2005. *Making States Work: State Failure and the Crisis of Governance*. New York: United Nations University Press.

Cheyette, Fredric L., ed. 1968. *Lordship and Community in Medieval Europe: Selected Readings*. New York: Holt.

Childe, V. Gordon. 1936. *Man Makes Himself*. London: Watts and Co.

Claessen, Henri J. M., and Peter Skalnik, eds. 1978. *The Early State*. The Hague: Mouton.

———, Pieter van de Velde, and M. Estelle Smith, eds. 1985. *Development and Decline: The Evolution of Sociopolitical Organization*. South Hadley, MA: Bergin and Garvey.

Clark, Gregory. 1998. "Commons Sense: Common Property Rights, Efficiency, and Institutional Change." *Journal of Economic History* 58(1):73–102.

———. 2007. *A Farewell to Alms: A Brief Economic History of the World*. Princeton: Princeton University Press.

Cohen, Myron L. 1976. *House United, House Divided: The Chinese Family in Taiwan*. New York: Columbia University Press.

Cohen, Ronald, and Elman R. Service, eds. 1978. *Origins of the State: The Anthropology of Political Evolution*. Philadelphia: Institute for the Study of Human Issues.

Collier, Paul. 2007. *The Bottom Billion: Why the Poorest Countries Are Failing and What Can Be Done About It*. New York: Oxford University Press.

Connolly, Bob. 1988. *First Contact: New Guinea's Highlanders Encounter the Outside World*. New York: Penguin.

Creel, Herrlee G. 1954. *The Birth of China: A Study of the Formative Period of Chinese Civilization*. New York: Ungar.

———. 1964. "The Beginning of Bureaucracy in China: The Origin of the Hsien." *Journal of Asian Studies* 23(2):155–84.

Cruickshanks, Eveline. 2000. *The Glorious Revolution*. New York: St. Martin's Press.

Curtin, Tim, Hartmut Holzknecht, and Peter Larmour. 2003. *Land Registration in Papua New Guinea: Competing Perspectives*. Canberra: SSGM discussion paper 2003/1.

Custine, Marquis de. 1843. *La Russie en 1839*. Paris: Amyot.

Darrity, William A., Jr., ed. 2007. *International Encyclopedia of the Social Sciences*. 2d ed. New York: Macmillan.

Davis, Richard L. 1996. *Wind Against the Mountain: The Crisis of Politics and Culture in Thirteenth-Century China*. Cambridge, MA: Harvard Council on East Asian Studies.

Dawkins, Richard. 1989. *The Selfish Gene*. New York: Oxford University Press.

———. 2006. *The God Delusion*. Boston: Houghton Mifflin.

de Bary, William Theodore, and Irene Bloom, eds. 1999. *Sources of Chinese Tradition*. 2d ed. New York: Columbia University Press.

De Soto, Hernando. 1989. *The Other Path: The Invisible Revolution in the Third World*. New York: Harper.

de Waal, Frans. 1989. *Chimpanzee Politics: Power and Sex Among Apes*. Baltimore: Johns Hopkins University Press.

———. 1997. *Good Natured: The Origins of Right and Wrong in Humans and Other Animals*. Cambridge, MA: Harvard University Press.

Deng, Kent G. 2004. "Unveiling China's True Population Statistics for the Pre-Modern Era with Official Census Data." *Population Review* 43(2):32–69.

Derrett, J. Duncan M. 1968. *Religion, Law, and the State in India*. London: Faber.

———. 1973. *History of Indian Law (Dharmasastra)*. Leiden: E. J. Brill.

Derry, Thomas K. 1979. *A History of Scandinavia: Norway, Sweden, Denmark, Finland and Iceland*. Minneapolis: University of Minnesota Press.

Diamond, Jared. 1997. *Guns, Germs, and Steel: The Fates of Human Societies*. New York: Norton.

———. 2005. *Collapse: How Societies Choose to Fail or Succeed*. New York: Viking.

Diamond, Larry. 1992. "Economic Development and Democracy Reconsidered." *American Behavioral Scientist* 15(4–5):450–99.

———. 2008. *The Spirit of Democracy: The Struggle to Build Free Societies Throughout the World*. New York: Times Books.

———, and Marc F. Plattner, eds. 1996. *The Global Resurgence of Democracy*. 2d ed. Baltimore: Johns Hopkins University Press.

DiIulio, John J., Jr. 1994. "Principled Agents: The Cultural Bases of Behavior in a Federal Government Bureaucracy." *Journal of Public Administration Research and Theory* 4(3): 277–320.

Dirks, Nicholas B. 1988. *The Invention of Caste: Civil Society in Colonial India*. Ann Arbor, MI: University of Michigan, CSST Working Paper 11.

Donner, Fred M. 1981. *The Early Islamic Conquests*. Princeton: Princeton University Press.

————. 1986. "The Formation of the Islamic State." *Journal of the American Oriental Society* 106(2):283–96.

Doornbos, Martin, and Sudipta Kaviraj. 1997. *Dynamics of State Formation: India and Europe Compared.* Thousand Oaks, CA: Sage Publications.

Dumont, Louis. 1980. *Homo Hierarchicus: The Caste System and Its Implications.* Chicago: University of Chicago Press.

Durkheim, Émile. 1933. *The Division of Labor in Society.* New York: Macmillan.

————. 1965. *The Elementary Forms of Religious Life.* New York: Free Press.

Ebrey, Patricia B. 1978. *The Aristocratic Families of Early Imperial China: A Case Study of the Po-ling Ts'ui Family.* New York: Cambridge University Press.

————. 1984. "Patron-Client Relations in the Later Han." *Journal of the American Oriental Society* 103(3):533–42.

————, and James L. Watson. 1986. *Kinship Organization in Late Imperial China 1000–1940.* Berkeley: University of California Press.

Ellickson, Robert C. 1991. *Order Without Law: How Neighbors Settle Disputes.* Cambridge, MA: Harvard University Press.

Elliott, J. H. 2006. *Empires of the Atlantic World: Britain and Spain in America, 1492–1830.* New Haven: Yale University Press.

Elvin, Mark. 1973. *The Pattern of the Chinese Past: A Social and Economic Interpretation.* Stanford, CA: Stanford University Press.

Emmott, Bill. 2008. *Rivals: How the Power Struggle Between China, India, and Japan Will Shape Our Next Decade.* New York: Harcourt.

Engel, Pal. 2001. *The Realm of St. Stephen: A History of Medieval Hungary, 895–1526.* London: I. B. Tauris.

Engels, Friedrich. 1942. *The Origin of the Family, Private Property, and the State, in Light of the Researches of Lewis H. Morgan.* New York: International Publishers.

Ertman, Thomas. 1997. *Birth of the Leviathan: Building States and Regimes in Medieval and Early Modern Europe.* New York: Cambridge University Press.

Evans, Peter B. 1989. "Predatory, Developmental, and Other Apparatuses: A Comparative Analysis of the Third World State." *Sociological Forum* 4(4):561–82.

————. 1995. *Embedded Autonomy: States and Industrial Transformation.* Princeton: Princeton University Press.

————, Dietrich Rueschemeyer, and Theda Skocpol, eds. 1985. *Bringing the State Back In.* New York: Cambridge University Press.

Evans-Pritchard, E. E. 1940. *The Nuer: A Description of the Modes of Livelihood and Political Institutions of a Nilotic People.* Oxford: Clarendon Press.

————. 1951. *Kinship and Marriage Among the Nuer.* Oxford: Clarendon Press.

————. 1981. *A History of Anthropological Thought.* New York: Basic Books.

Feldman, Noah. 2008. *The Fall and Rise of the Islamic State.* Princeton: Princeton University Press.

Festinger, Leon. 1962. *A Theory of Cognitive Dissonance.* Stanford, CA: Stanford University Press.

Finer, S. E. 1997. *The History of Government,* Vol. 1: *Ancient Monarchies and Empires.* New York: Oxford University Press.

Fiorina, Morris P., et al., eds. 2010. *Culture War? The Myth of a Polarized America*. 3rd ed. Boston: Longman.

Flannery, Kent V. 1972. "The Cultural Evolution of Civilizations." *Annual Review of Ecology and Systematics* 3:399–426.

Fogel, Joshua A. 1984. *Politics and Sinology: The Case of Naito Konan (1866–1934)*. Cambridge, MA: Harvard Council on East Asian Studies.

Fortes, Meyer, and E. E. Evans-Pritchard, eds. 1940. *African Political Systems*. New York: Oxford University Press.

Frank, Robert H. 1985. *Choosing the Right Pond: Human Behavior and the Quest for Status*. New York: Oxford University Press.

———. 1999. *Luxury Fever*. New York: Free Press.

Frazer, James G. 1998. *The Golden Bough: A Study in Magic and Religion*. New York: Oxford University Press.

Freedman, Maurice. 1958. *Lineage Organization in Southeastern China*. London: Athlone.

———. 1966. *Chinese Lineage and Society: Fujian and Guangdong*. London: Athlone.

———. 1970. *Family and Kinship in Chinese Society*. Stanford, CA: Stanford University Press.

Freedom House. 2010. *Freedom in the World 2010: Erosion of Freedom Intensifies*. Washington, D.C.: Freedom House.

Fried, Morton H. 1967. *The Evolution of Political Society: An Essay in Political Anthropology*. New York: Random House.

Friedberg, Aaron L. 2009. "Same Old Songs: What the Declinists (and Triumphalists) Miss." *American Interest* 5(2).

Friedman, Edward, and Bruce Gilley, eds. 2005. *Asia's Giants: Comparing China and India* New York: Palgrave Macmillan.

Friedman, Thomas L. 1999. *The Lexus and the Olive Tree*. New York: Farrar, Straus and Giroux.

Frykenberg, Robert E., ed. 1969. *Land Control and Social Structure in Indian History*. Madison: University of Wisconsin Press.

Fukuyama, Francis. 1992. *The End of History and the Last Man*. New York: Free Press.

———. 1996. *Trust: The Social Virtues and the Creation of Prosperity*. New York: Free Press.

———. 1999. *The Great Disruption: Human Nature and the Reconstitution of Social Order*. New York: Free Press.

———. 2000. "The March of Equality." *Journal of Democracy* 11(1):11–17.

———, and Sanjay Marwah. 2000. "Comparing East Asia and Latin America: Dimensions of Development." *Journal of Democracy* 11(4):80–94.

———. 2004. *State-Building: Governance and World Order in the 21st Century*. Ithaca: Cornell University Press.

———. 2006. "Identity, Immigration, and Liberal Democracy." *Journal of Democracy* 17(2): 5–20.

———, ed. 2006. *Nation-Building: Beyond Afghanistan and Iraq*. Baltimore: Johns Hopkins University Press.

———, ed. 2008. *Falling Behind: Explaining the Development Gap Between Latin America and the United States*. New York: Oxford University Press.

————. 2008. "State-Building in the Solomon Islands." *Pacific Economic Bulletin* 23(3):18–34.

————, and Seth Colby. 2009. "What Were They Thinking? The Role of Economists in the Financial Debacle." *American Interest* 5(1):18–25.

Furet, François. 1992. *Revolutionary France, 1770–1880*. Malden, MA: Blackwell.

Fustel de Coulanges, Numa Denis. 1965. *The Ancient City*. Garden City, NY: Doubleday.

Galor, Oded, and David N. Weil. 2000. "Population, Technology, and Growth: From Malthusian Stagnation to the Demographic Transition and Beyond." *American Economic Review* 90:806–28.

Galston, William A. 2010. *Can a Polarized American Party System Be "Healthy"?* Washington, D.C.: Brookings Institution Issues in Governance.

Gati, Charles. 2008. "Faded Romance." *American Interest* 4(2):35–43.

Geertz, Clifford. 1973. *The Interpretation of Cultures*. New York: Basic Books.

Gellner, Ernest. 1987. *Culture, Identity, and Politics*. New York: Cambridge University Press.

————. 1994. *Conditions of Liberty: Civil Society and Its Rivals*. New York: Penguin.

Gernet, Jacques. 1996. *A History of Chinese Civilization*. Cambridge: Cambridge University Press.

Gerschenkron, Alexander. 1962. *Economic Backwardness in Historical Perspective*. Cambridge, MA: Harvard University Press.

Gilman, Nils. 2003. *Mandarins of the Future: Modernization Theory in Cold War America*. Baltimore: Johns Hopkins University Press.

Ginsburg, Tom, ed. 2003. *Judicial Review in New Democracies: Constitutional Courts in Asian Cases*. New York: Cambridge University Press.

Glass, David V., and D.E.C. Eversley. 1965. *Population in History: Essays in Historical Demography*. Chicago: Aldine.

Glendon, Mary Ann, Michael W. Gordon, and Paolo G. Carozza. 1999. *Comparative Legal Traditions*. St. Paul, MN: West Publishing.

Goldstone, Jack A. 1991. *Revolution and Rebellion in the Early Modern World*. Berkeley: University of California Press.

Goody, Jack. 1971. *Technology, Tradition, and the State in Africa*. Oxford: Oxford University Press.

————. 1983. *The Development of the Family and Marriage in Europe*. New York: Cambridge University Press.

————. 2000. *The European Family: An Historico-Anthropological Essay*. Malden, MA: Blackwell.

Gould, Harold A. 1987. *The Hindu Caste System*. Delhi: Chanakya Publications.

Gould, Stephen Jay, and R. C. Lewontin. 1979. "The Spandrels of San Marco and the Panglossian Program: A Critique of the Adaptionist Programme." *Proceedings of the Royal Society of London* 205:581–89.

Grant, Madison. 1921. *The Passing of the Great Race; or, the Racial Basis of European History*. 4th rev. ed. New York: Scribner's.

Grindle, Merilee S. 2003. *Proclaiming Revolution: Bolivia in Comparative Perspective*. London: Institute of Latin American Studies.

————. 2004. "Good Enough Governance: Poverty Reduction and Reform in Developing Countries." *Governance* 17(4):525–48.

Guanzhong, Luo. 2004. *Three Kingdoms: A Historical Novel*. Berkeley: University of California Press.

Haas, Jonathan. 2001. *From Leaders to Rulers*. New York: Kluwer Academic/Plenum Publishers.

Haber, Stephen, Noel Maurer, and Armando Razo. 2003. *The Politics of Property Rights*. New York: Cambridge University Press.

Haggard, Stephan, Andrew MacIntyre, and Lydia Tiede. 2008. "The Rule of Law and Economic Development." *Annual Review of Political Science* 11:205–34.

Hall, John A. 1986. *Powers and Liberties: The Causes and Consequences of the Rise of the West*. Berkeley: University of California Press.

Hallaq, Wael B. 2005. *The Origins and Evolution of Islamic Law*. New York: Cambridge University Press.

Hamilton, Peter. 1991. *Max Weber: Critical Assessment 1*. New York: Routledge.

Hamilton, William D. 1964. "The Genetic Evolution of Social Behavior." *Journal of Theoretical Biology* 7:7–52.

Handlin, Oscar, and Mary Handlin. 1945. "Origins of the American Business Corporation." *Journal of Economic History* 5(1):1–23.

Hardin, Garrett. 1968. "The Tragedy of the Commons." *Science* 162:1243–48.

Hardt, Michael, and Antonio Negri. 2001. *Multitude: War and Democracy in the Age of Empire*. New York: Penguin.

Harrison, John A. 1972. *The Chinese Empire*. New York: Harcourt.

Hartwell, Robert M. 1982. "Demographic, Political, and Social Transformations of China, 750–1550." *Harvard Journal of Asiatic Studies* 42(2):365–442.

Hayek, Friedrich A. 1945. "The Use of Knowledge in Society." *American Economic Review* 35(4):519–30.

———. 1976. *Law, Legislation and Liberty*. Chicago: University of Chicago Press.

———. 1988. *Fatal Conceit: The Errors of Socialism*. Chicago: University of Chicago Press.

Head, John W. 2003. "Codes, Cultures, Chaos, and Champions: Common Features of Legal Codification Experiences in China." *Duke Journal of Comparative and International Law* 13(1):1–38.

Heckscher, Eli F. 1954. *An Economic History of Sweden*. Cambridge, MA: Harvard University Press.

Hegarty, David, et al. 2004. *Rebuilding State and Nation in the Solomon Islands: Policy Options for the Regional Assistance Mission*. Canberra: SSGM Discussion Paper 2004/2.

Hellie, Richard. 1971. *Enserfment and Military Change in Muscovy*. Chicago: University of Chicago Press.

Herbst, Jeffrey. 1990. "War and the State in Africa." *International Security* 14(4):117–39.

———. 2000. *States and Power in Africa*. Princeton: Princeton University Press.

Hill, Christopher. 1958. *Puritanism and Revolution: Studies in Interpretation of the English Revolution of the Seventeenth Century*. New York: Schocken.

Hintze, Otto. 1975. *The Historical Essays of Otto Hintze*. New York: Oxford University Press.

Hirschman, Albert O. 1963. *Journeys Toward Progress: Studies of Economic Policy-Making in Latin America*. New York: Twentieth Century Fund.

———. 1977. *The Passions and the Interests: Political Arguments for Capitalism Before Its Triumph*. Princeton: Princeton University Press.

Hitchens, Christopher. 2007. *God Is Not Great: How Religion Poisons Everything*. New York: Twelve.

Hobbes, Thomas. 1958. *Leviathan Parts I and II*. Indianapolis: Bobbs-Merrill.

Hodges, Richard. 1989. *The Anglo-Saxon Achievement: Archaeology and the Beginnings of English Society*. Ithaca, NY: Cornell University Press.

Hodgson, Marshall G. S. 1961. *The Venture of Islam: Conscience and History in a World Civilization*. Chicago: University of Chicago Press.

Hoffman, Philip T., and Kathryn Norberg, eds. 1994. *Fiscal Crises, Liberty, and Representative Government*. Stanford: Stanford University Press.

Hoffmann, Stanley, ed. 1988. *Political Thought and Political Thinkers*. Chicago: University of Chicago Press.

Holt, Peter M., Ann K. S. Lambton, and Bernard Lewis, eds. 1970. *The Cambridge History of Islam*, Vol. I: *The Central Islamic Lands*. New York: Cambridge University Press.

———. 1975. "The Position and Power of the Mamluk Sultan." *Bulletin of the School of Oriental and African Studies* 38(2):237–49.

Hsu, Cho-yun. 1965. *Ancient China in Transition*. Stanford, CA: Stanford University Press.

Huang, Ray. 1974. *Taxation and Government Finance in Sixteenth-Century Ming China*. New York: Cambridge University Press.

———. 1981. *1587, a Year of No Significance: The Ming Dynasty in Decline*. New Haven: Yale University Press.

Hucker, Charles O. 1958. "Governmental Organization of the Ming Dynasty." *Harvard Journal of Asiatic Studies* 21:1–66.

———, and Tilemann Grimm, eds. 1969. *Chinese Government in Ming Times: Seven Studies*. New York: Columbia University Press.

Hui, Victoria Tin-bor. 2005. *War and State Formation in Ancient China and Early Modern Europe*. New York: Cambridge University Press.

Humphreys, R. Stephen. 1977. "The Emergence of the Mamluk Army." *Studia Islamica* 45: 67–99.

Huntington, Samuel P. 1965. "Political Development and Political Decay." *World Politics* 17(3).

———. 1991. *The Third Wave: Democratization in the Late Twentieth Century*. Oklahoma City: University of Oklahoma Press.

———. 2006. *Political Order in Changing Societies*. With a New Foreword by Francis Fukuyama. New Haven: Yale University Press.

Hurstfield, Joel. 1973. *Freedom, Corruption and Government in Elizabethan England*. Cambridge, MA: Harvard University Press.

Hutton, Ronald. 1985. *The Restoration: A Political and Religious History of England and Wales, 1658–1667*. New York: Oxford University Press.

Inalcik, Halil. 1989. *The Ottoman Empire: The Classical Age, 1300–1600*. New Rochelle, NY: Orpheus Publishing Co.

Inden, Ronald B. 2000. *Imagining India*. Bloomington: Indiana University Press.

Itzkowitz, Norman. 1972. *Ottoman Empire and Islamic Tradition*. New York: Knopf.

Jaffa, Harry V. 1959. *Crisis of the House Divided: An Interpretation of the Lincoln-Douglas Debates*. Seattle: University of Washington Press.

Johnson, Simon. May 2009. "The Quiet Coup." *Atlantic*.

Johnston, Richard F., Peter W. Frank, and Charles D. Michener, eds. 1974. *Annual Review of Ecology and Systematics*, Vol. 5. Palo Alto, CA: Annual Reviews.

Jones, Grant D., and Robert R. Kautz. 1981. *The Transition to Statehood in the New World*. New York: Cambridge University Press.

Kamen, Henry. 2003. *Spain's Road to Empire: The Making of a World Power 1493–1763*. London: Penguin.

Karve, Irawati. 1965. *Kinship Organization in India*. New York: Asia Publishing House.

Kaufmann, Daniel, Aart Kraay, and Massimo Mastruzzi. 2005. *Governance Matters IV: Governance Indicators for 1996–2004*. Washington, D.C.: World Bank Institute.

Kaviraj, Sudipta. 2005. "On the Enchantment of the State: Indian Thought on the Role of the State in the Narrative of Modernization." *European Journal of Sociology* 46(2): 263–96.

Keane, John, ed. 1988. *Civil Society and the State: New European Perspectives*. New York: Verso.

Keefer, Philip. 2004. *A Review of the Political Economy of Governance: From Property Rights to Voice*. Washington, D.C.: World Bank Institute Working Paper 3315.

Keeley, Lawrence H. 1996. *War Before Civilization*. New York: Oxford University Press.

Keene, Donald. 2002. *Emperor of Japan: Meiji and His World, 1852–1912*. New York: Columbia University Press.

Kennedy, Hugh N. 2006. *When Baghdad Ruled the Muslim World: The Rise and Fall of Islam's Greatest Dynasty*. Cambridge, MA: Da Capo Press.

———. 2007. *The Great Arab Conquests: How the Spread of Islam Changed the World We Live In*. Philadelphia: Da Capo.

Khan, Mushtaq H., and Jomo Kwame Sundaram, eds. 2000. *Rents, Rent-Seeking and Economic Development: Theory and Evidence in Asia*. New York: Cambridge University Press.

Khanna, Tarun. 2008. *Billions of Entrepreneurs: How China and India Are Reshaping Their Futures—and Yours*. Boston: Harvard Business School Press.

Khazanov, Anatoly M. 1994. *Nomads and the Outside World*. 2d ed. Madison: University of Wisconsin Press.

Khilnani, Sunil. 1998. *The Idea of India*. New York: Farrar, Straus and Giroux.

Kinross, Patrick B. 1977. *The Ottoman Centuries: The Rise and Fall of the Turkish Empire*. New York: William Morrow.

———. 1978. *Ataturk: A Biography of Mustafa Kemal*. New York: William Morrow.

Kiser, Edgar, and Yong Cai. 2003. "War and Bureaucratization in Qin China: Exploring an Anomalous Case." *American Sociological Review* 68(4):511–39.

Knack, Stephen, and Philip Keefer. 1995. "Institutions and Economic Performance: Cross-Country Tests Using Alternative Measures." *Economics and Politics* 7:207–27.

Kojève, Alexandre. 1969. *Introduction to the Reading of Hegel*. Trans. James H. Nichols Jr. New York: Basic Books.

Kondos, V. 1998. "A Piece on Justice: Some Reactions to Dumont's *Homo Hierarchicus*." *South Asia* 21(1):33–47.

Korsgaard, Ove. 2008. *The Struggle for the People: Five Hundred Years of Danish History in Short.* Copenhagen: Danish School of Education Press.

Krader, Lawrence, and Paul Vinogradoff. 1966. *Anthropology and Early Law: Selected from the Writings of Paul Vinogradoff.* New York: Basic Books.

Kulke, Hermann. 1995. *The State in India 1000–1700.* Delhi: Oxford University Press.

Kumar, Krishna, ed. 1998. *Postconflict Elections, Democratization, and International Assistance.* Boulder, CO: Lynne Rienner.

Kunt, I. Metin. 1983. *The Sultan's Servants: The Transformation of Ottoman Provincial Government, 1550–1650.* New York: Columbia University Press.

Kuper, Adam. 1993. *The Chosen Primate: Human Nature and Cultural Diversity.* Cambridge, MA: Harvard University Press.

Kuran, Timur. 2001. "The Provision of Public Goods Under Islamic Law: Origins, Impact and Limitations of the Waqf System." *Law and Society* 35:841–97.

———. 2004. *Islam and Mammon: The Economic Predicaments of Islamism.* Princeton: Princeton University Press.

Landes, David S. 1969. *The Unbound Prometheus: Technological Change and Industrial Development.* New York: Cambridge University Press.

———. 1998. *The Wealth and Poverty of Nations: Why Some Are So Rich and Some So Poor.* New York: Norton.

———. 2000. *Revolution in Time: Clocks and the Making of the Modern World.* Rev. ed. Cambridge, MA: Belknap Press.

Lang, Olga. 1946. *Chinese Family and Society.* New Haven: Yale University Press.

Lariviere, Richard W. 1989. "Justices and Panditas: Some Ironies in Contemporary Readings of the Hindu Legal Past." *Journal of Asian Studies* 48(4):757–69.

Larmour, Peter. 1997. *Governance and Reform in the South Pacific.* Canberra: ANU National Centre for Development Studies.

La Porta, Rafael, Florencio Lopez-de-Silanes, Andrei Shleifer, and Robert W. Vishny. 1997. "Legal Determinants of External Finance." *Journal of Political Economy* 52:1131–50.

———. 1998. "Law and Finance." *Journal of Political Economy* 106:1113–55.

Laslett, Peter, ed. 1972. *Household and Family in Past Time.* Cambridge: Cambridge University Press.

LeBlanc, Steven A., and Katherine E. Register. 2003. *Constant Battles: The Myth of the Noble Savage.* New York: St. Martin's Press.

LeDonne, John P. 1991. *Absolutism and Ruling Class: The Formation of the Russian Political Order 1700–1825.* New York: Oxford University Press.

Lee, Chul-In, and Gary Solon. 2009. "Trends in Intergenerational Income Mobility." *Review of Economics and Statistics* 91(4):766–72.

Levanoni, Amalia. 1994. "The Mamluk Conception of the Sultanate." *International Journal of Middle East Studies* 26(3):373–92.

Levenson, Joseph R., and Franz Schurmann. 1969. *China: An Interpretive History. From the Beginnings to the Fall of Han.* Berkeley: University of California Press.

Levy, Santiago. 2008. *Good Intentions, Bad Outcomes: Social Policy, Informality, and Economic Growth in Mexico.* Washington, D.C.: Brookings Institution Press.

Lewis, Bernard, ed. and trans. 1987. *Islam from the Prophet Muhammad to the Capture of Constantinople. I: Politics and War.* New York: Oxford University Press.

Lewis, Mark E. 1990. *Sanctioned Violence in Early China.* Albany: State University of New York Press.

Li Feng. 2003. "'Feudalism' and Western Zhou China: A Criticism." *Harvard Journal of Asiatic Studies* 63(1):115–44.

Li Xueqin. 1985. *Eastern Zhou and Qin Civilizations.* New Haven: Yale University Press.

Li Yu-ning. 1977. *Shang Yang's Reforms and State Control in China.* White Plains, NY: M. E. Sharpe.

Linz, Juan J., and Alfred Stepan, eds. 1978. *The Breakdown of Democratic Regimes: Europe.* Baltimore: Johns Hopkins University Press.

Lipset, Seymour Martin. 1959. "Some Social Requisites of Democracy: Economic Development and Political Legitimacy." *American Political Science Review* 53:69–105.

Liu, James T. C. 1988. *China Turning Inward: Intellectual-Political Changes in the Early Twelfth Century.* Cambridge, MA: Harvard Council on East Asian Studies.

Livi-Bacci, Massimo. 1990. *Population and Nutrition: An Essay on European Demographic History.* New York: Cambridge University Press.

———. 1997. *A Concise History of World Population.* Oxford: Blackwell.

Locke, John. 1952. *The Second Treatise of Government.* Indianapolis: Bobbs-Merrill.

Loewe, Michael. 2006. *The Government of the Qin and Han Empires: 221 BCE–220 CE.* Indianapolis: Hackett.

———, and Edward L. Shaughnessy, eds. 1999. *The Cambridge History of Ancient China: From the Origins of Civilization to 221 B.C.* New York: Cambridge University Press.

Lopez-Calva, Luis Felipe, and Nora Lustig, eds. 2010. *Declining Inequality in Latin America: A Decade of Progress?* Washington: Brookings Institution Press.

Lybyer, Albert H. 1978. *The Government of the Ottoman Empire in the Time of Suleiman the Magnificent.* New York: AMS Press.

Macartney, C. A. 1962. *Hungary: A Short History.* Chicago: Aldine.

Macfarlane, Alan. 1978. *The Origins of English Individualism.* Oxford: Blackwell.

Machiavelli, Niccolò. 1985. *The Prince.* Trans. Harvey C. Mansfield. Chicago: University of Chicago Press.

Maddison, Angus. 2001. *Growth and Interaction in the World Economy: The Roots of Modernity.* Washington, D.C.: AEI Press.

———. 2007. *Chinese Economic Performance in the Long Run.* 2nd. ed., revised and updated: *960–2030 AD.* Paris: OECD Development Centre.

Maine, Henry. 1875. *Lectures on the Early History of Institutions.* London: John Murray.

———. 1963. *Ancient Law: Its Connection with the Early History of Society and Its Relation to Modern Ideas.* Boston: Beacon Press.

———. 1974. *Village-Communities in the East and West.* New York: Arno Press.

———. 1985. *Early Law and Custom: Chiefly Selected from Lectures Delivered at Oxford.* Delhi: B. R. Pub. Corp.

Maitland, Frederic W. 1961. *The Constitutional History of England.* Cambridge: Cambridge University Press.

Malthus, Thomas R. 1982. *An Essay on the Principle of Population*. New York: Penguin.

Mamdani, Mahmood. 1996. *Citizen and Subject: Contemporary Africa and the Legacy of Late Colonialism*. Princeton: Princeton University Press.

Mandelbaum, Michael. 2002. *The Ideas That Conquered the World: Peace, Democracy, and Free Markets in the Twenty-First Century*. New York: Public Affairs.

Mann, Michael. 1986. *The Sources of Social Power*, Vol. I: *A History of Power from the Beginning to A.D. 1760*. New York: Cambridge University Press.

Masters, Roger D., and Michael T. McGuire. 1994. *The Neurotransmitter Revolution: Serotonin, Social Behavior, and the Law*. Carbondale: Southern Illinois University Press.

May, R. J. 2003. *Disorderly Democracy: Political Turbulence and Institutional Reform in Papua New Guinea*. Canberra: Australian National University.

McClelland, David C. 1961. *The Achieving Society*. Princeton: Van Nostrand.

McNeill, William H. 1964. *Europe's Steppe Frontier, 1500–1800*. Chicago: University of Chicago Press.

Mead, Walter Russell. 2007. *God and Gold: Britain, America, and the Making of the Modern World*. New York: Knopf.

Meek, Charles K. 1968. *Land Law and Custom in the Colonies*. 2d ed. London: Frank Cass.

Messick, Richard E. 2002. "The Origins and Development of Courts." *Judicature* 85(4): 175–81.

Migdal, Joel. 1988. *Strong Societies and Weak States: State-Society Relations and State Capabilities in the Third World*. Princeton: Princeton University Press.

Miller, Geoffrey. 2000. *The Mating Mind: How Sexual Choice Shaped the Evolution of Human Nature*. New York: Doubleday.

———, and Glenn Geher. 2008. *Mating Intelligence: Sex, Relationships, and the Mind's Reproductive System*. New York: Lawrence Erlbaum.

Miller, John. 1997. *The Glorious Revolution*. 2d ed. New York: Longman.

Miller, Kenneth E. 1968. *Government and Politics in Denmark*. Boston: Houghton Mifflin.

Miyakawa, Hisayuki. 1955. "An Outline of the Naito Hypothesis and Its Effects on Japanese Studies of China." *Far Eastern Quarterly* 14(4):533–52.

Møller, Jørgen. 2010. "Bringing Feudalism Back In: The Historian's Craft and the Need for Conceptual Tools and Generalizations." Paper presented at the annual meeting of the Danish Society of Political Science, Vejle Fjord, Denmark.

Morgan, Lewis Henry. 1877. *Ancient Society; or, Researches in the Lines of Human Progress from Savagery, Through Barbarism to Civilization*. New York: Henry Holt.

Mote, Frederick W. 1999. *Imperial China 900–1800*. Cambridge, MA: Harvard University Press.

Mueller, Hans-Eberhard. 1984. *Bureaucracy, Education, and Monopoly: Civil Service Reforms in Prussia and England*. Berkeley: University of California Press.

Müller, F. Max, ed. 1879. *The Sacred Books of the East*, Vol. III. Oxford: Clarendon Press.

Murray, Charles, 1997. *What It Means to Be a Libertarian: A Personal Interpretation*. New York: Broadway Books.

Myers, Alec R. 1975. *Parliaments and Estates in Europe to 1789*. New York: Harcourt.

Naim, Moses. 2005. *Illicit: How Smugglers, Traffickers, and Copycats Are Hijacking the Global Economy*. New York: Doubleday.

Naipaul, V. S. 1978. *India: A Wounded Civilization*. New York: Vintage.

Naito Torajiro. 1922. "Gaikatsuteki To-So jidai kan." *Rekishi to chiri* 9(5): 1–12.

Needham, Joseph. 1954. *Science and Civilisation in China*, Vol. 5, pt. 7: *Military Technology*. Cambridge: Cambridge University Press.

———, Wang Ling, and Derek de Solla Price. 1960. *Heavenly Clockwork: The Great Astronomical Clocks of Medieval China*. Cambridge: Cambridge University Press.

Nef, John Ulric. 1942. *War and Human Progress: An Essay on the Rise of Industrial Civilization*. Chicago: University of Chicago Press.

Nelson, Hank. 2003. *Papua New Guinea: When the Extravagant Exception Is No Longer the Exception*. Canberra. Australian National University.

Nivola, Pietro S., and David W. Brady, eds. 2006. *Red and Blue Nation?* Vol. 1. Washington, D.C.: Brookings Institution Press.

Noland, Marcus, and Stephan Haggard. 2007. *Famine in North Korea: Markets, Aid, and Reform*. New York: Columbia University Press.

North, Douglass C. 1981. *Structure and Change in Economic History*. New York: Norton.

———. 1989. "Institutions and Economic Growth: An Historical Introduction." *World Development* 17(9):1319–32.

———. 1990. *Institutions, Institutional Change, and Economic Performance*. New York: Cambridge University Press.

———, and Arthur Denzau. 1994. "Shared Mental Models: Ideologies and Institutions." *Kyklos* 47(1):3–31.

———, and Robert P. Thomas. 1973. *The Growth of the Western World*. New York: Cambridge University Press.

———. 1973. *The Rise of the Western World: A New Economic History*. New York: Cambridge University Press.

———, and Barry R. Weingast. 1989. "Constitutions and Commitment: The Evolution of Institutions Governing Public Choice in Seventeenth-Century England." *Journal of Economic History* 49(4):803–32.

———, Barry R. Weingast, and John Wallis. 2009. *Violence and Social Orders: A Conceptual Framework for Interpreting Recorded Human History*. New York: Cambridge University Press.

Olson, Mancur. 1965. *The Logic of Collective Action: Public Goods and the Theory of Groups*. Cambridge, MA: Harvard University Press.

———. 1982. *The Rise and Decline of Nations*. New Haven: Yale University Press.

———. 1993. "Dictatorship, Democracy, and Development." *American Political Science Review* 87(9):567–76.

Organization for Economic Cooperation and Development. 2010. *Going for Growth*. Paris: OECD.

Ostrom, Elinor. 1990. *Governing the Commons: The Evolution of Institutions for Collective Action*. New York: Cambridge University Press.

Padoa-Schioppa, Antonio, ed. 1997. *Legislation and Justice*. New York: Clarendon Press.

Parker, Geoffrey. 1972. *The Army of Flanders and the Spanish Road, 1567–1598: The Logistics of Spanish Victory and Defeat in the Low Countries' Wars*. London: Cambridge University Press.

Parsons, Talcott, and Edward A. Shils, eds. 1951. *Toward a General Theory of Action*. Cambridge, MA: Harvard University Press.

Paul, Ron. 2009. *End the Fed*. New York: Grand Central Publishing.

Pearce, Scott, Audrey Spiro, and Patricia Ebrey, eds. 2001. *Culture and Power in the Reconstitution of the Chinese Realm, 200–600*. Cambridge, MA: Harvard University Press.

Perlin, Frank. 1985. "State Formation Reconsidered Part Two." *Modern Asian Studies* 19(3): 415–80.

Petry, Carl F., ed. 1998. *The Cambridge History of Egypt*, Vol. 1: *Islamic Egypt, 640–1517*. New York: Cambridge University Press.

Pinker, Steven. 1997. *How the Mind Works*. New York: Norton.

———, and Paul Bloom. 1990. "Natural Language and Natural Selection." *Behavioral and Brain Sciences* 13:707–84.

Pipes, Daniel. 1981. *Slave-Soldiers and Islam: The Genesis of a Military System*. New Haven: Yale University Press.

Pipes, Richard. 1999. *Property and Freedom*. New York: Knopf.

Pirenne, Henri. 1969. *Medieval Cities: Their Origins and the Revival of Trade*. Princeton: Princeton University Press.

Plato. 1968. *The Republic of Plato*. Trans. Allan Bloom. New York: Basic Books.

Platonov, Sergei Fedorovich. 1964. *History of Russia*. Bloomington: University of Indiana Prints and Reprints.

———. 1970. *The Time of Troubles: A Historical Study of the Internal Crises and Social Struggle in 16th- and 17th-Century Muscovy*. Lawrence: University Press of Kansas.

Plattner, Marc F. 1998. "Liberalism and Democracy." *Foreign Affairs* 77(2):171–80.

Pocock, J.G.A. 1960. "Burke and the Ancient Constitution—A Problem in the History of Ideas." *Historical Journal* 3(2):125–43.

Polanyi, Karl. 1944. *The Great Transformation*. New York: Rinehart.

———, and C. W. Arensberg, eds. 1957. *Trade and Market in the Early Empires*. New York: Free Press.

Pollock, Frederick, and Frederic W. Maitland. 1923. *The History of English Law Before the Time of Edward I*. Cambridge: Cambridge University Press.

Pool, Ithiel de Sola. 1983. *Technologies of Freedom*. Cambridge, MA: Belknap Press.

Porter, Bruce D. 1994. *War and the Rise of the State: The Military Foundations of Modern Politics*. New York: Free Press.

Pritchett, Lant, and Michael Woolcock. 2002. *Solutions When the Solution Is the Problem: Arraying the Disarray in Development*. Washington, D.C.: Center for Global Development Working Paper 10.

Przeworski, Adam, et al. 2000. *Democracy and Development: Political Institutions and Material Well-Being in the World, 1950–1990*. Cambridge: Cambridge University Press.

Pugh, George E. 1977. *The Biological Origin of Human Values*. New York: Basic Books.

Rady, Martyn. 2001. *Nobility, Land and Service in Medieval Hungary*. New York: Palgrave.

———. 2003. "The Medieval Hungarian and Other Frontiers." *Slavonic and East European Review* 81(4):698–709.

Raheja, Gloria Goodwin. 1988. "India: Caste, Kingship, and Dominance Revisited." *Annual Review of Anthropology* 17:497–522.

Raychaudhuri, Hemchandra. 1996. *Political History of Ancient India: From the Accession of Parikshit to the Extinction of the Gupta Dynasty.* New Delhi: Oxford University Press.

Reilly, Benjamin. 2002. "Political Engineering and Party Politics in Papua New Guinea." *Party Politics* 8(6):701–18.

Riasanovsky, Nicholas V. 1963. *A History of Russia.* New York: Oxford University Press.

Ridley, Matt. 1987. *The Origins of Virtue: Human Instincts and the Evolution of Cooperation.* New York: Viking.

Roberts, J.A.G. 1999. *A Concise History of China.* Cambridge, MA: Harvard University Press.

Rodrik, Dani, and Arvind Subramanian. 2003. "The Primacy of Institutions (and what this does and does not mean)." *Finance and Development* 40(2):31–34.

Root, Hilton. 1987. *Peasants and King in Burgundy: Agrarian Foundations of French Absolutism.* Berkeley: University of California Press.

Rosenberg, Nathan, and L. E. Birdzell. 1986. *How the West Grew Rich.* New York: Basic Books.

Rosenberg, Hans. 1958. *Bureaucracy, Aristocracy, and Autocracy: The Prussian Experience, 1660–1815.* Cambridge, MA: Harvard University Press.

Rousseau, Jean-Jacques. 2010. *Discourse on the Origin and the Foundation of Inequality Among Mankind.* New York: St. Martin's Press.

Ruttan, Vernon. 1991. "What Happened to Political Development?" *Economic Development and Cultural Change* 39(2):265–92.

Rystad, Göran, ed. 1983. *Europe and Scandinavia: Aspects of the Process of Integration in the 17th Century.* Stockholm: Esselte Studium.

Saberwal, Satish. 1995. *Wages of Segmentation: Comparative Historical Studies on Europe and India.* New Delhi: Orient Longman.

Sachs, Jeffrey. 2005. *The End of Poverty: Economic Possibilities for Our Time.* New York: Penguin.

Sahlins, Marshall D. 1961. "The Segmentary Lineage: An Organization of Predatory Expansion." *American Anthropologist* 63(2):322–345.

———, and Elman R. Service. 1960. *Evolution and Culture.* Ann Arbor: University of Michigan Press.

Sawhill, Isabel V., and Ron Haskins. 2008. *Getting Ahead or Losing Ground: Economic Mobility in America.* Washington, D.C.: Brookings Institution Press.

Sax, William S. 2000. "Conquering Quarters: Religion and Politics in Hinduism." *International Journal of Hindu Studies* 4(1):39–60.

Schacht, Joseph, ed. 1979. *The Legacy of Islam.* 2d ed. Oxford: Oxford University Press.

Schedler, Andreas. 2002. "The Menu of Manipulation." *Journal of Democracy* 13(2):36–50.

———. 2006. *Electoral Authoritarianism: The Dynamics of Unfree Competition.* Boulder, CO: Lynne Rienner.

Schick, Allen. 1998. "Why Most Developing Countries Should Not Try New Zealand Reforms." *World Bank Research Observer* 13(8):1123–31.

Schurmann, Franz. 1956. "Traditional Property Concepts in China." *Far Eastern Quarterly* 15(4):507–16.

Scott, Ben. 2005. *Re-Imagining PNG: Culture, Democracy and Australia's Role.* Double Bay, NSW: Lowy Institute Paper 09.

Scott, James C. 1998. *Seeing Like a State: How Certain Schemes to Improve the Human Condition Have Failed*. New Haven: Yale University Press.

Searle-Chatterjee, Mary, and Ursula Sharma, eds. 1994. *Contextualising Caste: Post-Dumontian Approaches*. Cambridge, MA: Blackwell.

———. 1999. *Development as Freedom*. New York: Knopf.

Sen, Amartya K. 1999. "Democracy as a Universal Value." *Journal of Democracy* 10:3–17.

Sengupta, Somini. 2006. "Often Parched, India Struggles to Tap the Monsoon." *New York Times*, October 1.

Serra, Narcis, and Joseph E. Stiglitz, eds. 2008. *The Washington Consensus Reconsidered*. New York: Oxford University Press.

Service, Elman R. 1971. *Primitive Social Organization: An Evolutionary Perspective*. 2d ed. New York: Random House.

Shapiro, Martin M. 1981. *Courts: A Comparative and Political Analysis*. Chicago: University of Chicago Press.

Sharma, Ram S. 1968. *Aspects of Political Ideas and Institutions in Ancient India*. Delhi: Motilal Banarsidass.

Shaughnessy, Edward L. 1991. *Sources of Western Zhou History: Inscribed Bronze Vessels*. Berkeley: University of California Press.

Sherman, P. W. 1977. "Nepotism and the Evolution of Alarm Calls." *Science* 197:1246–53.

Simon, Herbert. 1955. "A Behavioral Model of Rational Choice." *Quarterly Journal of Economics* 59:98–118.

———. 1957. *Administrative Behavior: A Study of Decision-Making Processes in Administrative Organization*. New York: Free Press.

———. 1959. "Theories of Decision-Making in Economics and Behavioral Science." *American Economic Review* 49:253–83.

Sinor, Denis. 1959. *History of Hungary*. New York: Praeger.

Smith, Adam. 1981. *An Inquiry into the Nature and Causes of the Wealth of Nations*. Indianapolis: Liberty Classics.

Spencer, Herbert. 1896. *The Principles of Sociology*. New York: D. Appleton.

———. 1898. *The Principles of Biology*. New York: D. Appleton.

Stein, Burton. 1985. "State Formation and Economy Reconsidered." *Modern Asian Studies* 19(3):387–413.

Stepan, Alfred C., and Graeme B. Robertson. 2003. "An 'Arab' More Than a 'Muslim' Democracy Gap." *Journal of Democracy* 14(3):30–44.

Steward, Julian H. 1963. *Theory of Culture Change: The Methodology of Multilinear Evolution*. Urbana: University of Illinois Press.

Stone, Lawrence. 1972. *The Causes of the English Revolution, 1529–1642*. New York: Harper.

Strayer, Joseph R. 1970. *On the Medieval Origins of the Modern State*. Princeton: Princeton University Press.

Sugar, Peter F., ed. 1990. *A History of Hungary*. Bloomington: Indiana University Press.

Swart, Koenraad W. 1949. *Sale of Offices in the Seventeenth Century*. The Hague: Nijhoff.

Sweeney, James R. 1984. "Review of Harold Berman, *Law and Revolution*." *Journal of Law and Religion* 2(1):197–205.

Tacitus. 1970. *Agricola Germania Dialogus*. Cambridge, MA: Harvard University Press.

Tavris, Carol. 2008. *Mistakes Were Made (But Not by Me): Why We Justify Foolish Beliefs, Bad Decisions, and Hurtful Acts*. New York: Mariner Books.

Taylor, Charles. 1989. *Sources of the Self: The Making of the Modern Identity*. Cambridge, MA: Harvard University Press.

Thapar, Romila. 1984. *From Lineage to State: Social Formations in the Mid-First Millennium B.C. in the Ganga Valley*. Bombay: Oxford University Press.

———. 2003. *Early India: From the Origins to AD 1300*. Berkeley: University of California Press.

Thies, Cameron G. 2005. "War, Rivalry, and State Building in Latin America." *American Journal of Political Science* 49(3):451–65.

Thomas, Melissa. 2009. "Great Expectations: Rich Donors and Poor Country Governments." Social Science Research Network Working Paper.

Thomson, James A. 2010. *A House Divided: Polarization and Its Effect on RAND*. Santa Monica, CA: RAND Corporation.

Tiger, Lionel. 1969. *Men in Groups*. New York: Random House.

Tilly, Charles. 1990. *Coercion, Capital, and European States, AD 990–1990*. Cambridge, MA: Blackwell.

Tocqueville, Alexis de. 1998. *The Old Regime and the Revolution*, Vol. One. Chicago: University of Chicago Press.

———. 2000. *Democracy in America*. Trans. Harvey C. Mansfield and Delba Winthrop. Chicago: University of Chicago Press.

Trivers, Robert. 1971. "The Evolution of Reciprocal Altruism." *Quarterly Review of Biology* 46:35–56.

Turner, Victor, ed. 1971. *Colonialism in Africa 1870–1960*, Vol. 3: *Profiles in Change: African Society and Colonial Rule*. New York: Cambridge University Press.

Twitchett, Denis, ed. 1979. *The Cambridge History of China*, Vol. 3: *Sui and T'ang China, 589–906, Part I*. New York: Cambridge University Press.

———, and Michael Loewe, eds. 1986. *The Cambridge History of China*, Vol. 1: *The Ch'in and Han Empires, 221 B.C.–A.D. 220*. New York: Cambridge University Press.

———, and Frederick W. Mote, eds. 1978. *The Cambridge History of China*, Vol. 8: *The Ming Dynasty, 1368–1644, Part 2*. New York: Cambridge University Press.

Tyler, Tom R. 1990. *Why People Obey the Law*. New Haven: Yale University Press.

Tylor, Edward B. 1920. *Primitive Culture: Researches into the Development of Mythology, Philosophy, Religion, Language, Art, and Custom*. New York: G. P. Putnam.

Uberoi, Patricia. 1993. *Family, Kinship and Marriage in India*. Delhi: Oxford University Press.

Vinogradoff, Paul. 1920. *Outlines of Historical Jurisprudence*. New York: Oxford University Press.

———. 1923. *Historical Jurisprudence*. London: Oxford University Press.

von Mehren, Arthur T. 1957. *The Civil Law System: Cases and Materials for the Comparative Study of Law*. Boston: Little, Brown.

Wade, Nicholas. 2006. *Before the Dawn: Recovering the Lost History of Our Ancestors*. New York: Penguin.

———. 2009. *The Faith Instinct: How Religion Evolved and Why It Endures*. New York: Penguin.

Wall, Richard, ed. 1983. *Family Forms in Historic Europe*. New York: Cambridge University Press.

Warren, Wilfred L. 1987. *The Governance of Norman and Angevin England, 1086–1272*. Stanford: Stanford University Press.

Watson, Burton, trans. 1964. *Han Fei Tzu: Basic Writings*. New York: Columbia University Press.

Watson, James L. 1982. "Chinese Kinship Reconsidered: Anthropological Perspectives on Historical Research." *China Quarterly* 92:589–627.

Weatherford, Jack. 2004. *Genghis Khan and the Making of the Modern World*. New York: Crown.

Weber, Max. 1930. *The Protestant Ethic and the Spirit of Capitalism*. New York: Scribner.

———. 1951. *The Religion of China*. New York: Free Press.

———. 1954. *Max Weber on Law in Economy and Society*. Cambridge, MA: Harvard University Press.

———. 1958. *The City*. Glencoe, IL: Free Press.

———. 1958. *The Religion of India: The Sociology of Hinduism and Buddhism*. Glencoe, IL: Free Press.

———. 1978. *Economy and Society*. Berkeley: University of California Press.

Weingast, Barry. 1995. "The Economic Role of Political Institutions: Market-Preserving Federalism and Economic Development." *Journal of Law, Economics, and Organization* 11:1–31.

Wells, R. Spencer, et al. 2001. "The Eurasian Heartland: A Continental Perspective on Y-Chromosome Diversity." *Proceedings of the National Academy of Sciences* 98(18): 10244–49.

Westergaard, Harald. 1922. *Economic Development in Denmark: Before and During the World War*. Oxford: Clarendon Press.

Whimp, Kathy. 1998. "Indigenous Land Owners and Representation in PNG and Australia." Port Moresby: unpublished paper.

White, Leslie A. 1959. *The Evolution of Culture: The Development of Civilization to the Fall of Rome*. New York: McGraw-Hill.

Wilson, David Sloan. 1983. "The Group Selection Controversy: History and Current Status." *Annual Review of Ecological Systems* 14:159–87.

———, and Elliott Sober. 1998. *Unto Others: The Evolution and Psychology of Unselfish Behavior*. Cambridge, MA: Harvard University Press.

Wittfogel, Karl A. 1957. *Oriental Despotism: A Comparative Study of Total Power*. New Haven: Yale University Press.

Wolf, Arthur P., and Chieh-shan Huang. 1980. *Marriage and Adoption in China, 1845–1945*. Stanford, CA: Stanford University Press.

Wolpert, Stanley. 1977. *A New History of India*. New York: Oxford University Press.

Woo, Jung-En. 1991. *Race to the Swift: State and Finance in Korean Industrialization*. New York: Columbia University Press.

World Bank. 2004. *World Development Report 2004: Making Services Work for Poor People.* Washington, D.C.: World Bank.

Wrangham, Richard, and Dale Peterson. 1996. *Demonic Males: Apes and the Origins of Human Violence.* Boston: Houghton Mifflin.

Wright, Robert. 2009. *The Evolution of God.* New York: Little, Brown.

Wriston, Walter B. 1992. *The Twilight of Sovereignty.* New York: Scribner.

Zakaria, Fareed. 2003. *The Future of Freedom: Illiberal Democracy at Home and Abroad.* New York: Norton.

———. 2008. *The Post-American World.* New York: Norton.

Zaman, Muhammad Qasim. 2002. *The Ulama in Contemporary Islam: Custodians of Change.* Princeton: Princeton University Press.

Zerjal, Tatiana, et al. 2003. "The Genetic Legacy of the Mongols." *American Journal of Human Genetics* 72:717–21.

ACKNOWLEDGMENTS

This book could not have been written without a great deal of help from a wide variety of people and institutions. It was conceived and drafted while I was a professor at the Johns Hopkins School of Advanced International Studies (SAIS) and director of its International Development Program. SAIS provided a congenial environment for writing and thinking about the topic, and I am very grateful to the school and its dean, Jessica Einhorn, for the support I was given. I lectured on the topic of the book while it was being written at SAIS, at the University of Aarhus in Denmark, at Michigan State University, and at Stanford, where I received numerous helpful comments.

I am very grateful to my publisher at Farrar, Straus and Giroux, Jonathan Galassi, for supporting this project, and to my editor at FSG, Eric Chinski, for his help. Eric was an extremely thoughtful and sympathetic reader who helped me think through many important issues in the text. As always, I am very appreciative of my literary agents, Esther Newberg at International Creative Management and Betsy Robbins at Curtis Brown, who did an enormous amount to make this and other of my writings possible.

I would like to thank the following people who helped me in writing this book: Seth Colby, Mark Cordover, Charles Davidson, Larry Diamond, Nicolas Eberstadt, Adam Garfinkle, Saurabh Garg, Charles Gati, Mary Ann Glendon, Francisco Gonzalez, George Holmgren, Steve Kautz, Sunil Khilnani, Pravin Krishna, Ove Korsgaard, Steven LeBlanc, Brian Levy, Peter Lewis, Arthur Melzer, Rick Messick, Jørgen Møller, Mitchell Orenstein, Donna Orwin, Uffe Østergård, Bruce Parrott, Steven Phillips, Marc Plattner, Jeremy Rabkin, Hilton Root, Nadav Samin, Abe Shulsky, Georg Sørensen, Melissa Thomas, Avi Tuschman, Justin Vaisse, Jerry Weinberger, Jason Wu, and Dick Zinman. The following served as research assistants: Khalid Nadiri, Kevin Croke, Michael Leung, Matt Scharf, Bryan Prior, Purun Cheong, and Kamil Dada. Mark Nugent did a great job preparing the book's maps. I would also like to thank my assistant at SAIS, Robin Washington, for all the help she has given me on this and other endeavors. Finally, my wife, Laura Holmgren, and my children, Julia, David, and John Fukuyama, read parts of the book as it was being written and were always supportive.

PALO ALTO, CALIFORNIA

INDEX

Abbasid dynasty, 189, 192, 196, 198, 200, 218, 278, 516n10
Abd al-Malik, 194
Abd Manaf, 195
Abkhaz, 208
Aborigines, Australian, 53
absolutism, 271, 295, 325, 327, 331–35, 351, 434; in China, 121, 125, 337, 400, 422, 426; in Denmark, 433, 434; English resistance to, 408–409, 417, 419, 428, 527n25; in France, 305, 327, 334, 337–38, 344, 348–53, 373, 399, 419, 422, 425–26, 527n25; in Hungary, 373, 382; patrimonial, 338–43, 349, 355, 400; in Prussia, 327; in Russia, 18, 21–22, 327, 334, 386–87, 393, 396, 397, 399–400, 403, 422, 426–28; in Spain, 305, 327, 334, 355, 357–58, 361–62, 373, 399, 422, 425–26; weak, 332, 334, 338, 362, 373, 399, 422, 424–26
Abu Bakr, Caliph, 193
accountability, 10, 11, 15–17, 21–22, 45, 240, 271, 315, 321–27, 335, 422, 424 437, 457, 479–81, 518n3; in China, 6, 19, 121, 133–34, 150, 309, 312–15, 321, 400, 481, 483; corruption and lack of, 386, 416; in Denmark, 334, 434; in England, 322, 326, 334, 402–403, 406–407, 418, 420, 421, 426, 429–31, 434, 445, 472, 475, 479, 518n3; in France, 337, 349, 373, 422; in Hungary, 373–74, 422; in Latin America, 355; procedural, 321–22; rule of law and, 286–88; in Russia, 386–87, 400; in Spain, 373, 422; in United States, 475
Afghanistan, x, 14, 154, 184, 303, 477; elections in, 16; Ghaznavid empire in, 200; Kushana dynasty in, 182; in Mauryan empire, 176; per capita spending on government services in, 469–70; tribalism in, 18, 86, 90, 92; U.S. war in, 13
Africa, 3, 13, 18, 90–91, 93, 313, 355, 439, 494n23; Chinese fleet in, 307; democracy in, 325; human evolution in, 46, 47, 97, 448; Indian trade with, 170; kinship structures in, 66; lineage systems in, 56, 57; patrimonialism in, 134; poverty in, 6; religion in, 66; sub-Saharan, 13, 81, 457; tribalism in, 69, 240; see also North Africa; specific nations